CONSTITUTIONAL AND ADMINISTRATIVE LAW

AUSTRALIA
Law Book Co.
Sydney

CANADA AND USA
Carswell
Toronto

HONG KONG
Sweet & Maxwell Asia

NEW ZEALAND
Brookers
Wellington

SINGAPORE and MALAYSIA
Sweet & Maxwell Asia
Singapore and Kuala Lumpur

CONSTITUTIONAL AND ADMINISTRATIVE LAW

Other Titles in the Textbook Series

Employment Law

Equity & Trust

Environmental Law

Criminal Law

Land Law

Public Law

Tort

Contract

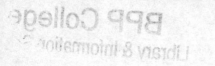

CONSTITUTIONAL AND ADMINISTRATIVE LAW

Textbook Series

By Elizabeth Giussani

First Edition

LONDON
SWEET & MAXWELL
2008

First edition 2008

Published in 2008 by
Sweet & Maxwell Limited of 100 Avenue Road,
http://www.sweetandmaxwell.co.uk
Typeset by YHT Ltd, London
Printed and bound in Great Britain by
Ashford Colour Press

No natural forests were destroyed to make this product;
only farmed timber was used and re-planted.

British Library Cataloguing in Publication Data

A CIP catalogue record for this book
is available from the British Library

ISBN 978-1-84703-219-5

PREFACE

The study of constitutional law in the 21st century is the study of one of the most exciting areas of English law. Since Tony Blair and the Labour Government came to power in 1997, there have been unprecedented reforms in this area, with 1998 alone seeing the introduction of the Human Rights Act and devolution of power from Westminster to a parliament in Scotland and assemblies in Northern Ireland and Wales. This process of change continues to this day with the creation of a new Supreme Court proposed to operate from 2009 and open dialogue regarding a British Bill of Rights, and even a "written" or codified constitution for the United Kingdom.

The purpose of this book is to introduce students to the fundamental principles of the United Kingdom constitution through its constitutional principles, administrative law and human rights law. It has been written for students undertaking legal studies at undergraduate level and those studying the Graduate Diploma in Law.

One of the aims of this book is to provide a clear and accessible textbook which will guide students through the core components of a constitutional law course. The book does not aim to be exhaustive of all material that could fall within the subject, but concentrates on the key topics falling within many law syllabi. In the first and second parts of the book, we look at the fundamental principles and structures of the United Kingdom Constitution. Many of the legal and political principles included in this book are explained by reference to judicial decisions to give the book a real and practical focus. However, constitutional and administrative law cannot be fully understood without some awareness of the historical, political and social development of the United Kingdom. The book does not aim to give a full account of such areas, but to put them into a modern context and focus on those which are necessary to an understanding of the key principles which form the core of early study.

Parts three and four of the book give a stronger emphasis to the place of administrative law and human rights than commonly found in some textbooks. The place and role of judicial review in particular is emphasised as it represents one of the practical ways of ensuring the constitution remains democratic and that government remains accountable. The book sets out the process of judicial review and considers the main grounds of review that can lead to a successful challenge. Likewise, since the Human Rights Act 1998 came into force, the role of human rights has become an important aspect of most of our lives. While there are many courses available which enable a student to study human rights in detail, this book aims to introduce the student to the key principles of the Act's operation. It also illustrates the role human rights plays within the Constitution by the examination of some key rights including liberty, due process, privacy and expression. Contrary to many textbooks, this book takes a Human Rights Act focus as opposed to a civil liberties focus.

I have endeavoured to state the law as at March 1, 2008. However, given the pace with which the law in this area moves, the reader is advised to supplement their knowledge by keeping an eye on the written press, legal journals and various government and institutional websites.

I would like to acknowledge the help I have received in the preparation of this book. Thanks go my colleagues with whom I have been able to talk about my work, and friends who have supported me all the way. Particular thanks go to Christopher who has provided much valued advice and support and without whom this book would never have been written. I would also like to thank all those at Sweet & Maxwell who have demonstrated an outstanding tolerance as I endeavoured to put the book together and who have now pushed the book to production. Mistakes made are mine.

This edition is dedicated to my mother, Susan, who has provided much support and encouragement throughout my academic career.

Elizabeth Giussani
April 2008

CONTENTS

7 PARLIAMENTARY SOVEREIGNTY

9 THE HOUSE OF COMMONS

10 THE HOUSE OF LORDS

11 PARLIAMENTARY PRIVILEGE

12 THE EXECUTIVE: CROWN, PRIME MINISTER AND CABINET

20 THE EUROPEAN CONVENTION ON HUMAN RIGHTS

23 RIGHT TO RESPECT FOR PRIVATE LIFE

24 FREEDOM OF EXPRESSION

ACKNOWLEDGEMENTS

Grateful acknowledgement is made to the following authors and publishers for their permission to quote from their works:

BLAKE, R.: *The Office of the Prime Minister* (OUP, 1975). By permission of Oxford University Press.

CHURCHILL, W.; KING-HALL, S.: "Duties of a Member of Parliament" *Parliamentary Affairs*, Vol.8 (1954-55).

COMMONWEALTH SECRETARIAT: *The Declaration of the Commonwealth*, Singapore (1971).

CRAIG, P.: "Formal and Substantial Conceptions of the Rule of Law" (1997) P.L. 467.

DE SMITH, S.A.; WOOLF; JOWELL, A.: *Judicial Review of Administrative Action*, 5th edn (London: Sweet & Maxwell, 1995). By permission of Sweet & Maxwell.

DICEY, A.V.: *An Introduction to the Study of the Law of the Constitution* Wade, E.C.S (ed.) 10th edition (London: Macmillan, 1959):

EUROPEAN COURT OF HUMAN RIGHTS: Case Processing Flowchart at *http://www.echr.coe.int/NR/rdonlyres/BA3F06A3-133C-4699-A25D-35E3C6A3D6F5/0/PROGRESS_OF_A_CASE.pdf*

FORSYTH, C.F.; HARE, I.: *The Golden Metwand and the Crooked Cord* (Oxford: OUP, 1998). By permission of Oxford University Press.

HEFFERNAN, R.; WEBB, P.: "The British Prime Minister: Much More than First Among Equals" in Webb, P. and Poguntke, T. (eds) *The Presidentialization of Politics: A Comparative Study of Modern Democracies* (Oxford: OUP, 2005). By permission of Oxford University Press.

LEXISNEXIS: All English Law Reports.

MAY, E.: *Parliamentary Practice*, 22nd edn (1997). By permission of LexisNexis.

OLIVER, D.: "The Power of Privileges of Parliament" in Feldman, D. (ed.) *English Public Law* (2004). By permission of Oxford University Press.

OFFICE FOR OFFICIAL PUBLICATIONS OF THE EUROPEAN COMMUNITIES: Foster v British Gas plc (Case C-188/89) [1990] ECR 1-3133.

—: *Costa v ENEL* [1964] ECR 585. Only European Community Legislation printed in the paper edition of the *Official Journal of the European Union* is deemed authentic.

OFFICE OF PUBLIC SECTOR INFORMATION: Shifting the Balance, 2000-01,

Liaison Committee; Report of the House of Commons Select Committee on the Official Secrets Act (1939).

—: "A Debt of Honour", First Report of Session 2005-06, HC 735, House of Commons Public Administration Select Committee.

—: "Tribunals: Their organisation and Independence" (1997), Command Paper CM 3744.

—: *Hansard*, March 20, 2007, Col.1151. Reprinted with the permission of the Office of Public Sector Information.

—: House of Lords.

RAZ, J.: "The Rule of Law and its Virtue" (1977) 93 L.Q.R. 195. By permission of Sweet & Maxwell.

SCOTTISH COUNCIL OF LAW REPORTING: *MacCormack v Lord Advocate* (1953) S.C. 296.

SWEET & MAXWELL: *Sunday Times v UK* (1979-80) 2 E.H.R.R. 245.

THE INCORPORATED COUNCIL OF LAW REPORTING FOR ENGLAND AND WALES: Weekly Law Reports; Appeal Cases; Kings Bench Law Reports; Queen's Bench Division.

England and Wales High Court and Court of Appeal (Civil Division)

WOOLF: "Droit Public—English Style" (1995) P.L. 57. By permission of Sweet & Maxwell.

While every care has been taken to establish and acknowledge copyright, and contact the copyright owners, the publishers tender their apologies for any accidental infringement. They would be pleased to come to a suitable arrangement with the rightful owners in each case.

TABLE OF CASES

(References are to paragraph number)

TABLE OF STATUTES

(References are to paragraph number)

TABLE OF STATUTORY INSTRUMENTS

(References are to paragraph number)

Chapter 1

CONSTITUTIONS—WHAT, WHY & CHARACTERISTICS

INTRODUCTION

Constitutional law is concerned with the role and powers of state institutions and with the relationship between citizens and the state. It requires study of how the United Kingdom is structured, the way the state organs interact with each other, what rights individual citizens have and what redress there is against the government who misuse their power. It is a dynamic and exciting area of law and none more so since the Labour government began a raft of reforms in 1998.

    The study of the United Kingdom constitution however requires slightly more imaginative methods than traditionally encountered in other jurisdictions. The reason is simple: there is no document entitled, "The Constitution of the United Kingdom and Northern Ireland". The United Kingdom constitution has evolved and is not a product of developed thought. Unique to the United Kingdom and two other countries, the constitution is found in a myriad of sources, both legal and non-legal, and requires study of our history to understand its contribution and how it impacts on constitutional issues today. It requires us to study political theories which have shaped and continue to inform our constitutional development and it requires consideration of the political factors that shape the day. For many coming to constitutional law without a historical, philosophical or political background this might appear a daunting task. Yet it is this that makes constitutional law different and exciting from other legal areas and involves far more than the study of mere legal rules.

    It seems logical at the start of a textbook on constitutional law to define what the study of the subject is about by considering what a constitution is and why we have them. To assist in identifying the nature of the United Kingdom constitution, this chapter then considers characteristics typically found in constitutions so that an assessment can then be made of the United Kingdom.

1–001

WHAT IS A CONSTITUTION?

1–002   Every social or sports club, residents association and country has a constitution which set out their goals or objectives and/or defines their organisational structures. For some it may be an informal relationship; such as an agreement between friends to run a monthly book club. Such a constitution would be relatively easy to formulate and would not require much organisation structure. A residents association on the other hand might formalise their constitution perhaps in a written document. They would probably set out their aims and objectives, establish a chairman and provide for his appointment. They would consider what other committee roles might be required such as a secretary, and might also set out how they collect membership fees and what they do with the money.

These two brief examples give an idea of what a constitution is and why organisations have them. Now imagine being the leader of a new country; there is no doubt that you would probably want some sort of arrangement to assist you in establishing your country. You would also probably start to ask yourself similar questions to the residents association but of course on a much bigger scale. After all you may need to build and for that you need finance; what about defence and security? Do you need to pass laws or at least give guidance to people in your country about what they can expect from you and you can expect from them? If so, how are you going to do this? As your country grows and become prosperous, you might start to think about future development and your people might expect certain minimum standards from you which you need to provide for.

1.   Definition

1–003   Given the discussion above, providing a definition of a constitution would appear to be easy. The *Concise Oxford English Dictionary* (10th edn (OUP, 2001)) (COED) defines one as "a body of fundamental principles or established precedents according to which a state or organisation is governed". Even with definitions helpfully provided by dictionaries like the COED, it is perhaps somewhat surprising that when the House of Lords Select Committee on the Constitution (First Report: Reviewing the Constitution: Terms of Reference and Method of Working (HL 11, 2001)) asked for a definition of a constitution they got a wide variety of answers. The exercise they embarked on shows that defining a constitution is not as simple as it might at first appear and is in fact quite difficult to formulate an exact definition. Does it, for example, include an organisation whose structure is not formulated on paper or is a constitution purely a formal document? Does it merely include "laws" or is it also non-legal rules, theories and principles?

There are two consistent approaches to defining what a constitution is: the narrow and the broad approach. The narrow or formal approach suggests that a constitution is a single document promulgated at a particular point in time, antecedent to government and, adopted by an authorisation procedure under the title "constitution" or equivalent rubric. A. Bradley and K. Ewing, *Constitutional and Administrative Law* (14th edn (Essex: Pearson, 2007), p.4) define such a document as "having a special legal sanctity which sets out the framework and principal functions of the organs of government and decides the principles by which those organs must operate". Such constitutions can said to be codified. However, to limit a country's constitution to that one document is too narrow. A codified (written) constitution may be short and tell you very little about the structures, organisation and principles of the state. The constitution of the United States, for example, is only twelve pages long. Such a short constitution cannot provide the detail necessary to ensure the smooth working of the government and explain how the rules should operate. The lack of detail within the constitutional text makes it necessary to study the constitutions other sources, these may be statutes or judicial decisions which interpret the constitution, or they may be customary rules which evolve to allow the formal rules to operate with fluidity. The narrow definition then does not provide the whole picture of what is the constitution of that particular state.

The alternative view is broader and defines a constitution as a body of rules, legal and non-legal, which regulate the structure of the state, allocates power and governs relationships. It establishes bodies which define the parameters of the relationships between citizen and state, and between various organs of a state. H. Bolingbroke, writing in 1733 in *A Dissertation Upon Parties*, sums up the alternative approach:

> "By constitution we mean, whenever we speak with propriety and exactness, that assemblage of laws, institutions and customs, derived from certain fixed principles of reason, directed to certain fixed objects of pubic good, that compose the general system, according to which the community hath agree to be governed."

The distinction is also important for another reason, as the narrow approach suggests a constitution must be set out in a document and would preclude those countries that do not have such a formal document. In this sense, the United Kingdom does not have a constitution. The broader approach to definition is more helpful for the study of the United Kingdom constitution as, quite clearly, the UK has an established set of rules which regulate the structure of power and governs relationships. The broader approach can also incorporate the narrow approach.

What consensus can be gleaned from the two approaches is the fact a constitution regulates power and provides a framework by which the organisation or state can operate. It will most likely be composed of a combination of legal and non-legal rules. The House of Lords Select Committee on the Constitution (above) came up with the following working definition of a constitution which is useful as a starting point:

> "it is the set of laws, rules and practices that create the basic institutions of the state and its component and related parts, and stipulate the powers of those institutions and the relationship between the different institutions and between those institutions and the individual."

WHY

1.   Why and how do constitutions come about?

1–004   Narrow constitutions or those written down primarily come about through a defining constitutional moment such as revolution (France and the United States), devolution or grant of power from a former legislative body such as India or some other similar upheaval (war, for example, Iraq and Afghanistan). One feature which characterises all constitutions of this type is the break with the former regime or state function and the desire to start anew. This desire manifests itself into a document setting out the proposed system of government and asserts their values and objectives. Thomas Paine, in his work *The Rights of Man* (Collins (ed.), p.93) said that "[a] constitution is not the act of a government, but of a people constituting a government, and a government without a constitution is power without right ... A constitution is a thing antecedent to a government; and a government is only a creature of a constitution".

2.   Purpose of constitutions and the principle of constitutionalism

1–005   Constitutions serve many purposes; they exist to ensure the state has stability and order and confers legitimacy on the state both domestically and internationally. A constitution may affirm particular goals and values such as democracy and ensure that the country operates with the consent of its people. One main purpose of a constitution is to establish the organisational structures of the state and define the manner in which rules operate. In modern western thinking a constitution exists to delimit and control power and ensure the state follows the principles of constitutionalism. These principles govern the legitimacy of government action and control the use of power, amongst them they include the requirement that:

(1)   power be dispersed amongst the institutions of the states to avoid the abuse of power. This is known as the separation of powers, see Ch.6;

(2)   there must be an independent judiciary and court system, an essential requirement of both the rule of law and separation of powers, see Chs 5 and 6;

(3)   the exercise of power be within the legal limits conferred by Parliament and those who exercise it are accountable in law, see Ch.5 and Chs 14–17 on judicial review;

(4)   the exercise of power respects the basic rights of individuals, see Ch.5 on the rule of law and Chs 20–24;

(5)   the government and legislature are accountable to the people on whose trust power is held, known as the doctrine of responsible government, see Chs 9 and 12 in particular.

CHARACTERISTICS

While there may be similarities between constitutions, no constitution is exactly the same as each typically reflects the values, beliefs and structure of the time or those the drafter aspired towards. Professor K.C. Wheare in his book *Modern Constitutions* (2nd edn (New York: OUP, 1966)) famously identified a number of characteristics which he suggested could be used to identify the nature of a constitution. These were: **1–006**

  (1)   written and unwritten;

  (2)   rigid and flexible;

  (3)   supreme and subordinate;

  (4)   federal and unitary;

  (5)   separated and fused;

  (6)   republican and monarchical.

These classifications are discussed below, however it should be borne in mind that they are somewhat artificial and say very little about the substance of any constitution.

1.   Written and unwritten

A constitution which is written would typically be found in one document or a series of documents and is usually associated with constitutions in the narrow sense. Historically, this was one of the main ways to classify constitutions and the classic and oft cited example of a "written" constitution is the Constitution of the United States of America. By contrast under this classification an "unwritten" constitution would be one where the framework of government, its rules and structure were not written down in any document.   **1–007**

  One problem that is immediately apparent with this classification is the term "unwritten" as it suggests an "unwritten" constitution has no written sources that provide a framework of government. Of the three alleged unwritten constitutions, New Zealand, Israel and the United Kingdom, all of them have a combination of written and unwritten sources that could be said to form their constitution. The constitution of New Zealand, like the UK, is a constitutional monarchy with the Queen as Head of State but represented by the Governor General. The New Zealand constitution is made up of a variety of sources including the prerogative powers of the Queen, various statutes with constitutional significance (e.g. the Constitution Act, the Electoral Act, the New Zealand Bill of Rights Act), relevant English and United Kingdom statutes that have been incorporated into New Zealand law (such as the Magna Carta), the decisions of the courts and arguably the Treaty of Waitangi. In no sense can it be said that New Zealand has an unwritten constitution, instead it is better to characterise the constitution as uncodified, in the sense it is not found in one document. Such a characterisation works for both Israel and the United Kingdom constitutions. By contrast, the Constitution of the United States is a codified constitution with its major rules being found in one document and subsequent amendments to that document.

Another problem with the written/unwritten classification is the idea that the whole constitution is found in the written source. As indicated in para.1–003, this is not necessarily the case especially if the constitution is a short one. However, even where the written text is over one hundred pages, as is the German Constitution, the written rules of the constitution still require to be interpreted or be supplemented by unwritten political practices and conventions.

2.   Rigid and flexible

1–008   Rigid constitutions are those where amendments to the constitution are difficult to make as they require a special procedure for change. This requirement for a special procedure to amend provisions amounts to entrenching them and is often found in constitutions that are written or codified. Using the US constitution as an example, under art.v only Congress can make amendments to the constitution and then only if two-thirds of both Houses agree to the change. Other forms of entrenchment provisions include the requirement for a referendum, a direct vote in which the electorate are required to agree or disagree with a proposal. For example, under the Constitution of Ireland a public referendum is required to ratify the Lisbon Treaty which makes amendments to the European Union. Constitutions are entrenched to provide a degree of protection for the provisions as it ensures that no changes are made unless there is consensus. In many situations the provisions setting down this requirement are themselves entrenched, as to do otherwise would enable them to be easily repealed and the constitution could then also be amended easily.

In contrast, a flexible constitution requires no special procedure to be followed for change to be effected. Amendments to such constitutions are normally by the ordinary legislative process, for example, the Constitution of Israel can be changed by an Act of its legislature. The benefit of such constitutions is of course the flexibility that comes with being able to amend easily. Under the United States constitution, only three amendments were accepted between 1813 and 1913 and six amendments between 1913 and 1933. By contrast, the UK constitution represents the height of flexibility as constitutional amendments can be passed with a simply majority in Parliament, for example, the Constitutional Reform Act 2005 which made fundamental changes to the judicial system. However, the issue of flexibility obviously has its negatives as important constitutional law can be easily repealed.

3.   Supreme and subordinate

1–009   This classification overlaps to some degree with federal and unitary states. A supreme constitution is one where legislative powers of the state are unlimited. By contrast a subordinate constitution is one where the legislature has limited power, for example,

New South Wales, Australia is a subordinate constitution, see *Att-Gen for New South Wales v Trethowan* (1931) 44 C.L.R. 394, discussed further in Ch.7.

4. Federal and unitary

A federal constitution divides power between the national and local level (regions, **1–010** states, provinces) with each having its own legislature, powers and functions. The individual states or provinces may possess their own constitutions outlining the allocation of their power, however, in the event of conflict, the federal constitution usually takes precedence. For example, in the German constitution power is split between the Federal (national) administration and the 16 counties called "Laender". Federal states differ in their structure, for example, the United States Constitution provides that all powers not specifically granted to the federal government in the constitution is retained by the states. Conversely, the Canadian constitution states that all power not explicitly granted to the provincial governments are retained by the federal government.

A unitary state is one with a single, centralised, national tier of government. However, unitary states may include one or more self-governing regions which are created through devolution. This differs from a federation because the autonomous status of the self-governing regions exists by permission of the central government, and may be unilaterally revoked or have their powers varied. France for example, is a unitary state.

5. Separated and fused

The separation of powers is a fundamental constitutional concept and a key component **1–011** of constitutionalism. The doctrine is discussed more fully in Ch.6 but for now it is simply the requirement that the three functions of a state, the law making, executing policy and judicial functions, be vested in different bodies so as to avoid a concentration of power. A separated constitution refers to the degree to which a constitution adopts and conforms to the doctrine. Many constitutions conform in some way to the doctrine, the United States constitution being a clear example with power dispersed between Congress (law making), Supreme Court (judicial) and President (executing policy). Each body has its own functions and exercises some control or check over the other two.

At the other extreme, a constitution which is fused will concentrate all power in one body, typically characteristic of a totalitarian regime or pure monarchical system such as the Tsarist system in Russia before the Revolution in 1917. Brunei, Oman and Saudi Arabia today maintain a style of absolute monarchy and are effectively fused systems.

6. Republican and monarchical

1–012 A republican constitution provides for a democratically elected president who is usually Head of State. In some states, the president is Head of State and Head of government as in the United States. In others, the president has no real political power and is a figurehead, such as the Presidents of France and Germany. A monarchy has as its head a monarch, usually a single person. Monarchs hold their position by birth right for life and usually pass the position onto their children or other family members when they die. The actual extent of powers that a monarch has varies from state to state, though most now have a limited form of power and are known as constitutional monarchs. In constitutional monarchies, sovereignty formally rests with the Crown but politically with the people and the monarch practically has little real power.

7. Parliamentary and presidential

1–013 Not specifically identified by Wheare but linked to the discussion above is the classi-fication of parliamentary or presidential. The UK has a parliamentary system by which the head of the Executive branch, normally the Prime Minister and other members of the Executive are drawn from the Parliament (Legislature). The Prime Minister remains accountable and responsible to Parliament for his/her actions (discussed more fully in Chs 9 and 12). This is also allied to the concept of separated and fused. By contrast, in a presidential system, the president is Head of State and Head of the Executive and does not come from the legislature (Parliament) but is completely separated. The US is oft cited as a good example of a presidential system.

THE CONSTITUTION OF THE UNITED KINGDOM

1–014 In the majority of countries, the constitution is set down in a single codified document. In such situations the constitution exists in tangible form, copies of which can be purchased. Contrary to this, in asking the question whether the UK has a constitution the first thing to notice is there is an absence of any formal or codified document that can be called the constitution of the United Kingdom. In referring to the definition in para.1–003 it then becomes clear that according to the narrow approach the UK does not have a constitution. For those countries that do have codified constitutions it is normal to be able to pin-point a particular event and time that led to the formation of their constitution. The UK has never experienced such an event, the exception possibly being 1649–1659 when England was a republic under the protectorate of Oliver Cromwell, following the execution of the monarch, Charles I, in 1649. The "Institute of Government" which established the Cromwell system was in form a type of constitution but, the restoration of the monarchy in 1660 simply meant a return to the original monarchical system. Since 1660, the UK has not experienced any event that has necessitated a need to codify a constitution and its unbroken history has allowed the constitution to develop over a period of time. It is interesting to note that the oldest written constitution is the United States written in 1789, over a hundred years after the UK's last event when a written constitution could have been written. Since 1660 and in light of developments in constitutional theories that came about in the 18th century and continued since then, there have often been calls to codify the UK constitution. However, few constitutions are conceived because of perceived shortcomings with their existing system.

To say that the UK does not have a constitution because of the lack of a codified document is to forget its history and dismiss the substance of the UK's system in which there are established institutions of government and defined relationships between the organs and the state and individual. Sir Ivor Jennings, *The Law and the Constitution* ((London: University of London Press, 1959), p.36), arguing on a functional basis that the United Kingdom does have a constitution, said "If a constitution means a written document, then obviously Great Britain has no constitution ... But the document itself merely sets out the rules determining the creation and operation of governmental institutions, and obviously Great Britain has such institutions and such rules. The phrase "British constitution" is used to describe those rules". So, for Jennings the existence of the institutions and rules to regulate their behaviour was sufficient evidence that a constitution existed.

Ridley would disagree with Jenning's analysis and believes that the UK does not have a constitution but has instead a system of government (F. Ridley, "There is no British Constitution: A Dangerous Case of the Emperor's New Clothes" (1988) 41 *Parliamentary Affairs* 340). Ridley identifies a number of characteristics which for him establish the existence of a constitution and goes on to refute them in relation to the UK. He is particularly critical of the fact that the UK constitution was not prior or antecedent to the system of government and has not been formally ratified by the people. He further notes that the constitution is not superior to any other law nor is it entrenched in any form and, as a result, key constitutional provisions can be repealed as easily as any other Act. He points out that if constitutions exist to limit and control power then lack of entrenchment means the constitution is unprotected against a parliamentary majority. Ridley concludes the "term British constitution is near meaningless even as used by British writers. It is impossible to isolate parts of the system of government to which the label may authoritatively be attached".

Fenwick and Phillipson (*Text, Cases and Materials on Public Law and Human Rights* (London: Cavendish, 2001), p.23) note two criticisms of Ridley's analysis which are certainly valid. Firstly, Ridley's insistence that any worthwhile constitution must be entrenched excludes those codified/written constitutions like Singapore which are fully written but entirely flexible. Secondly, they feel he goes too far in alleging that there are no parts of the UK constitutional order to which any special legal sanctity attaches. The traditional theory of the sovereignty of Parliament, which purports that Parliament can pass any law it wants, has in recent years come under attack from membership of the European Community (European Communities Act 1972) and the Human Rights Act 1998, suggesting that these two Acts cannot be as easily repealed (see Ch.7 for further discussion).

1.   Characteristics

1–015   Using Wheare's classification as a starting point, before considering aspects of the constitution in detail it is worthwhile setting out the key features of the UK constitution.

(a)   *Uncodified*

1–016   The constitution of the United Kingdom is uncodified and is comprised of a mixture of written and unwritten sources (discussed more in Ch.3).

(b)   *Flexible*

1–017   The UK is said to be flexible as there are no special requirements to change any constitutional measures. Change can be effected using the normal procedure required for passing a statute. Supporters of the UK constitution will emphasise its flexibility and ability to adapt to new needs. Indeed the longevity of the constitution can be attributed to its flexible nature. On the negative side, there is as Ridley pointed out, no protection against abuse by those in power who can change key aspects of the constitution easily. However, this orthodoxy was challenged by Lord Justice Laws in *Thoburn v Sunderland* [2002] EWHC 195 (Admin) who classified some statutes as "constitutional" (see Chs 3 and 7 for more discussion on the impact of this decision), the suggestion being that they could not be repealed as easily as other statutes.

(c)   *Unitary*

1–018   Legal and political power in the UK is centred in Westminster which makes the UK a unitary system. As noted above at para.1–010, devolution does not affect the unitary status of the UK as Parliament in Westminster has the legal power to legislate for all of the UK regardless of the devolved status of Scotland, Northern Ireland and Wales. It can also revoke the devolution legislation should it so wish. In addition to devolution to the three countries above, there is a strong system of local government in the UK (see Ch.2). However, this is purely an administrative system and though local government has the power to make secondary legislation it only does so through the authority of Westminster.

(d)   *Constitutional monarchy*

1–019   The UK operates a constitutional monarchical system, with the monarch being Head of State. Her role is largely ceremonial and although much power is still vested in the

Crown, this power is exercised by the Executive on the monarch's behalf. In a sense monarchial powers are constitutionally limited.

(e) *Representative liberal democracy*

The UK has a parliamentary democracy where the composition of the legislature **1–020** (House of Commons) is determined by the people through periodic and free national elections. The UK is also a liberal democracy as it protects the liberties of its people. From as early as 1215, Magna Carta, the idea of liberty became a common characteristic of the constitution. Liberty is respected in the UK through the rule of law and the Human Rights Act 1998.

(f) *Bi-cameral sovereign parliament*

The legislature (principal law maker) in the UK is Parliament which is a bi-cameral **1–021** system. Parliament consists of two chambers, the House of Commons (Lower House) and House of Lords (Upper House). The House of Lords is unelected and despite its name as the upper house is the subordinate of the two. The House of Commons is elected with membership being determined on a first past the post system. The benefit of two chambers allows for a system of check and balance; each chamber has different expertise (see Chs 9 and 10) which can be used effectively to ensure government is responsible to them and hence the electorate and also to pass effective laws.

In contrast to many constitutions, Parliament is the sovereign body and in traditional theory is not prohibited by higher law from passing any law it wants. Parliamentary sovereignty is a complex area of the constitution and unique to the UK and New Zealand (and to a degree Finland). It will be covered in detail in Ch.7.

(g) *Parliamentary Executive*

The UK constitution is a parliamentary Executive which means its Executive arm, or **1–022** part of it, is drawn from Parliament. This is in contrast to countries like the US where the Executive and Parliament are completely independent of it. The system of parliamentary Executive has consequences for the application of the doctrine of separation of powers.

(h) *Separation of powers*

One of the key requirements of a constitution is to prevent tyranny by dispersing power **1–023** so that no one body has a monopoly. In many codified constitutions this is often clearly laid out. The UK Constitution, partly as a result of its incremental development and partly because of the parliamentary system, does not adhere to a pure formulation of the doctrine of separation of powers. However, to dismiss the relevance of the doctrine is not appropriate as, in particular, the UK has a strong independent judiciary. It can therefore be said that the UK does have a separation of powers, which some commentators call partial (see further Ch.6).

2.   Should the United Kingdom have a written constitution?

1–024   There is no doubt that the UK constitution is difficult for the average person to identify. A codified constitution would go some way to dealing with this problem and provide a clear, accessible and coherent account of the rules and principles which govern the state and the citizen's rights and obligations under it. However, does that make it necessary? Codifying the constitution would be an incredibly difficult task; would, for example, the exercise simply be a statement of the constitution as it is or would it be used to start debate about changes to the constitutional system. There is no doubt that attempting to codify the constitution would open up all sorts of debates and not necessarily achieve any consensus.

In July 2007, The Prime Minster Gordon Brown delivered a speech which for the first time hinted that a current government might consider codifying the constitution or at least some aspects of it (*http://www.number10.gov.uk/output/Page12274.asp*). The speech was followed by a release of a Green Paper, "The Governance of Britain" (Cm 7170) which continued the theme. The Green Paper suggested a number of areas in which the government wished to consult, one of which cautiously aired was whether there was a need for codification of the constitution.

> "Today, we have to ensure that our country remains a cohesive, confident society in dealing with the challenges of the 21st century. Previous sections of this document have discussed the need to provide a clearer articulation of British values, and greater clarity about the nature of British citizenship. But there is now a growing recognition of the need to clarify not just what it means to be British, but what it means to be the United Kingdom. This might in time lead to a concordat between the Executive and Parliament or a written constitution."

Since the summer 2007 there has been movement on some aspects of the Green paper, but nothing on the "written" constitution. In February 2008, Jack Straw in a lecture, "Modernising the Magna Carta" (delivered to George Washington University (USA)) sent out a strong signal that the government was ready to draw up a written constitution. However, in an interview to the BBC he highlighted one of the problems with codification; this was the process could take up to 20 years. The BBC further reported that Professor Robert Hazell, of the University College London Constitution Unit, thought it unlikely that Britain would ever have a written constitution. Professor Hazell is said to have stated, "Constitutions don't get written in cold blood ... Written constitutions typically follow defeat in war, a revolution, independence or the collapse of the previous system of government ... None of those fates is likely to befall the UK. So however desirable it may be, a written constitution isn't going to happen". (*http://news.bbc.co.uk/1/hi/uk_politics/7241942.stm*).

At present then, it seems that though there may be some movement towards considering the process of codifying the constitution, any movement is going to be slow and drafting will at best take many years.

FURTHER READING

Barnett, H. *Britain Unwrapped, Government and Constitution Explained* (London: **1–025** Penguin, 2002)

Bogdanor, V., Khaitan, T. and Vogenauer S. "Should Britain Have a Written Constitution?" (2007) *The Political Quarterly* 78(4)

Finer, S.E. (ed) *Comparing Constitutions* (New York: OUP, 1995)

Le Sueur, A. "Gordon Brown's new constitutional settlement" (2008) P.L. 21–27

Marshall, G. "The Constitution: Its Theory and Interpretation" in V. Bogdanor (ed.) *The British Constitution in the Twentieth Century* (Oxford: OUP, 2004)

Ridley, F. "There is no British Constitution: A Dangerous Case of the Emperor's New Clothes" (1988) 41 *Parliamentary Affairs* 340

Chapter 2

STRUCTURE OF UNITED KINGDOM GOVERNANCE

INTRODUCTION

The United Kingdom of Great Britain and Northern Ireland is a complex historical **2–001** amalgam of a number of nations whose political relations and governance have changed considerably since the Labour election victory of 1997. As governance of the United Kingdom is discussed elsewhere in this book, this chapter explores the governance of some of the citizens of the United Kingdom through its devolved assemblies and local administration. In addition, it highlights the international relations which the United Kingdom enjoys with the Commonwealth and the European Union.

DEFINING THE NATION

1. The parts of the United Kingdom

The United Kingdom is made up of England, Wales, Scotland and Northern Ireland. **2–002** As a nation, England was formed around the tenth century, having previously been a collection of smaller kingdoms. The Principality of Wales joined a union with England towards the end of the thirteenth century, thereby effectively becoming part of England. Following a rebellion by the Welsh which was quashed in the fifteenth century, the union was formalised by Act of Parliament in 1536. The Act of Union 1707 effected a political union between England and Scotland (though the Crowns had been joined since James VI of Scotland became King of England on the death of his cousin, Elizabeth I). Scotland's joining with England and Wales created Great Britain. Ireland, whose history with England, then Britain, was one of toil, officially joined a Union with Great Britain in 1800 with the passing of the Act of Union creating the United Kingdom of Great Britain and Ireland. Through partition of the island of Ireland and the creation of the Irish Free State, then the declaration of the Republic, it became a United Kingdom of Great Britain and Northern Ireland, remaining as such today. The new nation was ruled by the Parliament at Westminster.

Since the countries joined to become the United Kingdom of Great Britain and Northern Ireland, it is right to speak of the United Kingdom Constitution. However, there is no one legal system through this constitutionally defined area and it would not be right to speak of a United Kingdom law; each country having its own distinct legal system. The countries that make up the United Kingdom are all headed by the monarch and largely legislated by the Westminster Parliament, except those issues that have been devolved. Though change was brought about following the Labour election this was achieved by legislation from Westminster and the United Kingdom remains. The object of devolution was to provide greater representation for regional areas and to strengthen rather then undermine the Unions with England.

2.   Devolution

2–003   The Labour Party was elected in the 1997 general election on a manifesto commitment to hold referenda to determine the devolution of power from Westminster to Scotland and Wales. Though there was no similar commitment to the same for Northern Ireland, the Party was committed to the peace process which had already started between the British and Irish governments. However, this was the basis for the devolved assembly which now exercises powers in Northern Ireland. Shortly after their election, referenda were held in Wales and Scotland with the consequence that the National Assembly for Wales was established on the waterfront at Cardiff, and a Parliament established in Scotland, at Holyrood in Edinburgh. The peace process in Northern Ireland led to the Good Friday agreement and the establishment of a devolved assembly at Stormont in Belfast.

3.   National Assembly for Wales

2–004   The National Assembly for Wales is based in Cardiff and was created by the Government of Wales Act 1998 and amended by the Government of Wales Act 2006. The Assembly has 60 members who take the style "AM" after their name; "Assembly Member", comprised of 40 constituency members and 20 regional members. Wales also has its own Executive, "Cabinet", led by the First Minister, and containing up to 12 Welsh Ministers and Deputy Ministers appointed by him or her. The Government of Wales Act 2006 effected a true separation of powers between the Assembly and the government. At March 31, 2008, there are eight Ministers, and four Deputy Ministers, not including the First Minister and the Assembly's Law Officer who make up a Cabinet of 14.

The Assembly has limited law-making powers in that it cannot draft and pass primary legislation, nor does it have fiscal powers (i.e. the power to vary taxation).

However, it does have power to make subordinate legislation over matters such as health and education. Because the Assembly does not have tax-varying powers, it draws its funding from HM Treasury, though the funding is diverted through the Assembly to meet the needs of the Welsh people. In other words, the Assembly determines how the money should be spent.

4. Scottish Parliament

Section 1 of the Scotland Act 1998 established a Parliament for Scotland. In contrast to **2–005** the National Assembly for Wales, the Parliament has powers to make primary legislation and a limited power to vary income tax.

  The Parliament is arranged in the following way. It comprises some 129 MSPs and elections take place every four years with the consequence that Parliaments are set for a certain period. The electoral system is a modified version of the Westminster system of "first-past-the-post". The electorate get two votes. The first vote is used to elect a constituency MSP. This is done on the traditional "first-past-the-post" system and the candidate with the most votes is elected as the constituency MSP. There are 73 constituencies, therefore 73 MSPs are elected by this method. The second vote is for a political party and this is designated by region. The MSPs under this method are elected on the basis of being drawn from a party list in the eight electoral regions in Scotland which, for convenience, are the same as those used for election to the European Parliament. The regions elect seven MSPs each through the "Additional Member System" which is a form of proportional representation. In total, 56 MSPs are elected in this way. Under the electoral system to the Scottish Parliament, each constituent is represented by eight MSPs; one which is directly elected using "first-past-the-post", and seven elected as a regional MSP.

  The powers enjoyed by the Parliament include both the power to draft and implement primary legislation (Acts of the Scottish Parliament) and the power to vary taxes. However, the matters over which the Scottish Parliament has legislative competence are limited to such as education and training, the environment, health of the nation, local government, social services, and so on. Therefore, though the Parliament has considerable legislative competence, it has no competence in respect of the following matters (reserved matters):

- the Scottish Parliament cannot pass legislation to limit the powers of the United Kingdom Parliament to make laws for Scotland;

- as is the position with the Parliament of the United Kingdom, the Scottish Parliament cannot legislate inconsistently with European Union Law, nor incompatibly with the European Convention on Human Rights as incorporated into United Kingdom law by the Human Rights Act 1998;

- the Scottish Parliament may not legislate on matters concerned with foreign or defence policy, or on matters within the exclusive domain of the United Kingdom Parliament;

- certain other "reserved matters", Schs 4 and 5 to the Scotland Act 1998, are not within the legislative competence of the Scottish Parliament, including, therefore, any changes to the constitutional arrangement between Scotland and the Union.

As mentioned, the Scottish Parliament has powers to vary tax. In the referendum held in 1997, of the 74 per who voted in favour of a Scottish Parliament, only 64 per cent voted for the Parliament to have tax-varying powers. Under s.73 of the Scotland Act 1998, the Scottish Parliament has power to vary the basic rate of income tax for that year within a three percentage point range. The power has, to date, not been exercised.

One final point relates to the residue of power in the hands of the Westminster Parliament. Section 28(7) of the Scotland Act 1998 states that nothing in that Act shall limit the powers of the United Kingdom Parliament to legislate for Scotland; this makes it clear that despite its devolved status the Westminster Parliament remains supreme. See Ch.7 for discussion of the implications of this.

5.   Northern Ireland Assembly

2–006   The current Northern Ireland Assembly is a product of the post-1997 era and the "Good Friday Agreement". The "Good Friday Agreement" was a cross-party and inter-governmental agreement on the future formula for the governance of Northern Ireland. 71.2 per cent supported the agreement in a referendum held in Northern Ireland in May 1998. Section 1 of the Northern Ireland Act 1998 restates that Northern Ireland is part of the United Kingdom and provides that its status shall not be altered without the consent of the majority of the people of Northern Ireland voting so. The Act creates a Northern Irish Assembly which has 108 elected members, each being elected under the single transferable vote method of election. Once the respective members are settled, Ministerial posts are allocated in direct proportion to the number of members each party has in the Assembly; a pro rata allocation.

The Assembly has reasonably wide powers to legislate in areas such as education, health, agriculture, employment and so on. However, certain matters are retained within the legislative competence of the United Kingdom Parliament. The matters retained are divided into "reserved" and "excepted" matters. The former are reserved in the sense that they might, in the future, be transferred to the Assembly and include matters such as the criminal law, policing and finance. "Excepted" matters, on the other hand, are those which are retained by the United Kingdom Parliament. These matters include foreign and defence policy, and the conferment of honours.

The Northern Irish Executive is headed by a First Minister and deputy who are elected jointly with the support of the majority of all the Assembly and composed of ten other Ministers determined jointly by the First Minister and Deputy and approved by the Assembly with cross community support. The Executive has no power to make subordinate legislation or take any action incompatible with European Union Law or the Human Rights Act 1998.

As a devolved assembly, power remains with Westminster which reserves the right to suspend the Assembly, as happened in the case of the Northern Ireland Assembly in

2004, before it was reformed in 2007. Indeed, this makes an important point. All these devolved bodies, namely the Welsh Assembly, Scottish Parliament and Northern Ireland Assembly, are just that, devolved. Power remains with Westminster to withdraw devolved status from those bodies and re-establishing that power in the hands of the relevant Secretary of State.

COMMONWEALTH AND EUROPE

The United Kingdom has had a recognised role on the international stage not only from the days of Empire, but because of its role in the Second World War, particularly in the post-War period of rebuilding Europe and in the drafting of, for example, the European Convention on Human Rights and Fundamental Freedoms. However, to some degree the UK's role as an international powerhouse has been challenged not only by its membership of the European Union, but by the economic strength of emerging nations such as China and India.   2–007

1.   Commonwealth

The Commonwealth is an international collective of independent nation states bound together *in the common interests of their citizens for development, democracy and peace.* Presently, there are 53 members of the Commonwealth and all (save for Mozambique), at some point in their history, were part of the British Empire. The Commonwealth is administered by the Commonwealth Secretariat based in London, but does not have a written constitution to govern its activities. Instead, the Commonwealth Heads of government meet regularly, publishing Declarations, sets of Principles, and so on, all of which guide the Commonwealth in its actions.   2–008

After the Commonwealth Heads of Government Meeting in Singapore in 1971, *The Declaration of Commonwealth Principles* gave a definition for the Commonwealth:

> "The Commonwealth of Nations is a voluntary association of independent sovereign states, each responsible for its own policies, consulting and co-operating in the common interests of their peoples and in the promotion of international understanding and world peace." (p.1)

Agreeing to certain principles:

- we believe that international peace and order, global economic development and the rule of international law are essential to the security and prosperity of mankind;

- we believe in the liberty of the individual under the law, in equal rights for all citizens regardless of gender, race, colour, creed or political belief, and in the individual's inalienable right to participate by means of free and democratic political processes in framing the society in which he or she lives;

- we recognise racial prejudice and intolerance as a dangerous sickness and a threat to healthy development, and racial discrimination as an unmitigated evil;

- we oppose all forms of racial oppression, and we are committed to the principles of human dignity and equality;

- we recognise the importance and urgency of economic and social development to satisfy the basic needs and aspirations of the vast majority of the peoples of the world, and seek the progressive removal of the wide disparities in living standards amongst our members.

(*The Declaration of Commonwealth Principles*, Singapore, 1971)

These principles were affirmed at Harare, Zimbabwe, in 1991, but with an explicit commitment to the promotion of democracy, human rights, and the rule of law. Ironically, Zimbabwe withdrew from the Commonwealth after it had been suspended by the Commonwealth for alleged human rights abuses and electoral fraud. A further commitment to implement the Harare Declaration by means of an action plan was agreed in the 1995 Declaration at Millbrook, New Zealand.

In addition to the co-operation on the lines outlined above, certain Commonwealth nations continue to regard the United Kingdom as the supreme authority on legal matters and regard the Judicial Committee of the Privy Council as the final appellate court. However, a diminishing number of countries continue to appeal to the Privy Council, the last significant nation to discontinue appeals being New Zealand in 2003.

2.   Europe

2–009   The United Kingdom has been a member of the European Union since January 1, 1973 when the European Communities Act 1972 became law. Membership of the European Union has touched virtually every aspect of British life and continues to do so. In the modern world, nations exist as constituent parts of larger bodies where greater influence might be brought to bear over trade and other matters. Obviously, the United Kingdom's membership of a Union which has superior law-making powers has consequences for the rule of law, but importantly for parliamentary sovereignty. See Chs 4 and 7 for a detailed discussion of these areas.

GOVERNMENT

1. National Government

Most of the United Kingdom constitutional framework is concerned with the structure   **2–010**
of government at the national level. The National Government amongst many things
takes responsibility for matters that affect the nation as a whole such as defence, foreign
policy and taxation. It is also the main legislative body for all the countries that make
up the Union.

  The governance of the United Kingdom is discussed fully at Chs 9, 10, 11 and 12.

2. Local Government

Although there has been recent activity in the devolution of power from the central   **2–011**
government to regional assemblies and parliaments, the concept of devolving power to
a local level is nothing new as powers have been devolved to local government for
centuries. Central government is ill equipped to deal with many local matters such as
education, housing, recreational facilities and so power is devolved to local government
to take over this responsibility.

(a) *Structure and functions of Local Government*

In England, Wales and Scotland, local government is arranged along one of two lines.   **2–012**
First, there are unitary, also known as single-tier authorities. These are often restricted
to large urban (metropolitan) areas such as Merseyside, Greater Manchester and Tyne
& Wear. Secondly, there is a two-tier system in which two councils share responsibility
for the functions of local government between county councils and district councils. For
example, Hertfordshire County Council has responsibility for schools, highways and
public libraries in Hertfordshire, while St Albans District Council, for example, in
common with other district councils in the county of Hertfordshire has responsibility
for planning applications, waste collection and revenue collection.

  Local government have no powers other then those given by Parliament. In respect of
matters within their competence, local authorities are able to create delegated legislation known as bye-laws. As a consequence, local authorities create something of a
technical conundrum for purists of the separation of powers (see Ch.6) for though part
of the Executive (see Ch.12) because of their power to create delegated legislation they
also perform the functions of a legislature.

(b)   *Funding Local Government*

2–013   Local authorities have the power to raise local taxation in the form of the council tax which is a tax levied on home ownership within a council's catchment area. However, the council tax accounts for only one-quarter of local authority funding, with the majority coming from central government grants.

(c)   *Local Government Association*

2–014   The Local Government Association (LGA) is a voluntary lobby group which was established to promote better local government. Its membership is drawn from the county councils, metropolitan district councils, English unitary authorities, London boroughs, shire district councils and Welsh unitary authorities. Additionally, the LGA represents the fire and police authorities, among others.

(d)   *Local Government ombudsman*

2–015   In line with the general scheme of ombudsmen in the United Kingdom constitutional framework, there is also an ombudsman for Local Government. The function of the ombudsman is to investigate complaints of injustice arising from maladministration by local authorities. For a detailed discussion of ombudsmen, see Ch.19.

Chapter 3

SOURCES OF THE UNITED KINGDOM CONSTITUTION

INTRODUCTION

In codified constitutions such as Germany, the United States and France, the primary   **3–001**
source is the written text of the constitution itself and any examination of such a
constitution must necessarily start with that text. That is not to say it is the extent of
their constitution, as study must include any amending legislation, judicial decisions
concerning interpretation of the constitution and political rules that guide the constitution. In the United Kingdom, its uncodified nature means that there is no document entitled the "United Kingdom Constitution" from which studies can begin. Yet,
the United Kingdom does have a constitution comprising legislation, judicial decision
and political rules amongst other written and unwritten sources and it is the study of
these that form the basis of this chapter.

1. Difficulties with the United Kingdom constitution

As a result of its incremental and pragmatic development the UK constitution is made up   **3–002**
of multiple sources. Lord Scarman, in a Charter 88 Sovereignty lecture, "Why Britain
Needs a Written Constitution" (July 20, 1992), stated the constitution was "hidden and
difficult to find". This obviously makes the study of the constitution that bit more
difficult than other countries. One of the main difficulties lies in identifying exactly what
is a constitutional source. Essentially, there are two main types of source which form the
UK constitution: legal sources and non-legal sources. Legal sources consisting of statutes, judicial decisions and prerogative power are the principal sources of the constitution and constitutional law. Other important legal sources include international
treaties and European Community legislation. Non-legal sources are primarily political
rules of behaviour termed conventions but also include authoritative academic works.

LEGAL SOURCES

1. Statute

3–003 Whilst recognising that the main source of our constitution is to be found in statute, the First Report of Session 2001–02 of the House of Lords Select Committee on the Constitution (HL Paper 11 2001: 8) noted: "The constitution is uncodified and although it is in part written there is no single, accepted and agreed list of statutes which form that part of the constitution which is indeed written down".

Seaton and Winetrobe provide some assistance in "The passage of constitutional Bills in Parliament" (1998) 4 *Journal of Legislative Studies* 33, when they attempted to summarise what counts as a constitutional Bill which in turn would lead to it being a constitutional statute. They suggested that:

> "Any proposed legislation relating to the basic existence of the United Kingdom as a political and geographical entity (such as Northern Ireland or devolution legislation); the structure, operation and powers of Parliament and the Crown (in its political, official and monarchical contexts; elections and the franchise; emergency powers; innovations such as referendums or Bills of rights), and major issues of foreign affairs (for example EU treaties) would generally be regarded as prima facie constitutional matters."

Whilst a workable definition, it is at the same time quite wide. Under this definition in the period between 1997 and 2005, 55 Bills were published which would count as constitutional (R. Hazell, "Time for a new convention: parliamentary scrutiny of constitutional bills 1997–2005" (2006) P.L. 247–298).

The difficulty in identifying constitutional statutes is exacerbated by the fact that under the doctrine of parliamentary sovereignty all statutes have the same legal status and there is no formal recognition of constitutional statutes. For example, the Wildlife and Countryside Act 1981 which raises no constitutional issue according to the definition above, has the same legal status as the Constitutional Reform Act 2005 which creates a new Supreme Court and removes appellate jurisdiction from the House of Lords. Dicey in the *Law of the Constitution* (10th edn (London: Macmillan, 1959)) highlights this:

> "There is under the English constitution no marked or clear distinction between laws which are not fundamental or constitutional and laws which are fundamental or constitutional." (at p.89)

In addition to the above argument all statutes in the UK are passed in the same manner, proceeding through both chambers and receiving Royal Assent. Hazell ("Time for a new convention: parliamentary scrutiny of constitutional bills 1997–2005" (2006) P.L. 247–298) notes some assistance is provided by the existence of a constitutional convention whereby Bills of "first class" constitutional importance are considered in a Committee of the Whole House rather then in a smaller general (formerly standing) committee. However, little practical assistance is forthcoming here unless one wants to study in detail the passage each Bill makes through Parliament. Generally, constitutional statutes cannot be simply identified by looking at how they were enacted in Parliament.

The traditional orthodoxy that there is no hierarchy of statutes has been questioned; Lord Justice Laws in an obiter comment in *Thoburn v Sunderland* [2002] EWHC 195 (Admin) recognised the idea of constitutional statutes existing. Such statutes according to him could not be impliedly repealed (see Ch.7).

"We should recognise a hierarchy of Acts of Parliament: as it were 'ordinary' statutes and 'constitutional' statutes. The two categories must be distinguished on a principled basis. In my opinion a constitutional statute is one which (a) conditions the legal relationship between citizen and state in some general, overarching manner, or (b) enlarges or diminishes the scope of what we would now regard as fundamental constitutional rights. (a) and (b) are of necessity closely related: it is difficult to think of an instance of (a) that is not also an instance of (b). The special status of constitutional statutes follows the special status of constitutional rights." (at para.60)

He further goes on to give examples of his "constitutional" statutes:

- Magna Carta 1215;
- the Bill of Rights 1688;
- the Union with Scotland Act 1706;
- the Reform Acts which distributed and enlarged the franchise (Representation of the People Acts 1832, 1867 and 1884);
- the Human Rights Act 1998;
- the Scotland Act 1998;
- the Government of Wales Act 1998;
- the European Communities Act 1972.

Lord Justice Law's statement is not without controversy and is contradictory to the established norms above. However, it provides a useful starting point from which to begin an analysis of constitutional legal sources.

(a) *Statutes relating to the structure of the United Kingdom*

(i) Union with Scotland Act 1706

This Act provided for the union of Scotland and England and created the Parliament of Great Britain. Of particular interest is art.XVIII which says that "no alteration can be **3–004** made in laws which concern private rights except for the evident utility of the subjects within Scotland". This particular article was the subject of judicial consideration in *Gibson v Lord Advocate* [1975] S.L.T. 134 which concerned a challenge to a European Community common fisheries policy measure because it gave access to Scottish waters. Gibson argued that this was a change in private law which was not for the "evident utility" of Scots as required by the Act of Union. The court held that access to fisheries was not "private law" and therefore the measure could not be challenged.

(ii)   Union with Ireland Act 1800

3–005   This Act merged Great Britain with Ireland effective from January 1, 1801 and created the United Kingdom of Great Britain and Ireland. Its corresponding Act in Ireland was the Act of Union (Ireland) Act 1800.

(iii)   European Communities Act 1972

3–006   This statute provides the legal framework for incorporation of the UK's membership of the European Community. Constitutionally this statute has much significance. It has raised issues regarding the sovereignty of the UK Parliament (see further Ch.7), given judges more power where there is a conflict between domestic law and EC obligations and created certain rights for individuals.

(iv)   Scotland Act 1998

3–007   The Scotland Act 1998 devolves powers to Scotland and creates the Scottish Parliament.

(v)   The Government of Wales Acts 1998 and 2006

3–008   Like the Scotland Act 1998, these Acts devolve powers to Wales by establishing a National Assembly for Wales. The 2006 Act gives further power to Wales regarding legislation and aims to more clearly demarcate between Executive and Legislative functions (see further Ch.2).

(b) *Statutes regulating the three organs of the State*

(i) Magna Carta 1215

The Magna Carta, latin for Great Charter, is often seen as the corner-stone of liberty   **3–009**
and against arbitrary and unjust rule. It contains few statements of principle but is in
fact a series of concessions granted by King John to his barons. The barons, unhappy at
high taxation, harsh rule and the unfair administration of justice by King John, had
rebelled and succeeded in capturing London in May 1215. They demanded a charter of
liberties and in June 1215, a document called the "Articles of the Barons" was signed at
Runnymede, a meadow by the Thames. This document granted a number of concessions such as the right of "freeman" not to be imprisoned or his land taken away
without "lawful judgment of his peers" (Ch.29), in other words without a fair trial. This
document was then put into a formal royal grant drafted by the royal chancery which
became the Magna Carta.

The importance of the Magna Carta as a constitutional statute is that for the first
time it showed that the power of the King could be limited and is the first recognition of
the writ of habeas corpus (the right to challenge detention). Four copies of the original
charter still survive (two at the British Library and one each in the Cathedral Archives
at Lincoln and Salisbury).

(ii) Bill of Rights 1688

The name "Bill of Rights" is slightly misleading as it is not in fact a list of human rights   **3–010**
but rather a document which sets out the condition on which William of Orange (later
William III) ascended the throne. The Bill altered the constitutional relationship
between Parliament and the Crown and is often seen as a clear statement of Parliament's supremacy. Of particular note is art.2 which prohibits the Crown from suspending laws without Parliament's consent, art.6 which prohibits the keeping of a
standing army without Parliament's consent and art.9 which protects the freedom of
speech in Parliament and gives them legal immunity (see Ch.11).

(iii) Act of Settlement 1700

This Act settled the Crown on James I's granddaughter, Princess Sophia, Dowager   **3–011**
Duchess of Hanover and provided that the Crown could only pass to those of the
Protestant faith.

(iv)   Parliament Acts 1911 and 1949

3–012   The Parliament Act 1911 asserts the supremacy of the House of Commons in the legislature and removed the power of the House of Lords to veto legislation. The Act came about as a direct result of the House of Lords' refusal to pass Lloyd George's "people's budget" which would have introduced, amongst other things, a land tax on the wealthy. The Act removed the power to veto and provided that the House of Lords could only delay Money Bills for one month and other Public Bills, except a Bill to extend the life of Parliament, for two years. The Act also set the maximum duration of a Parliament at five years. The 1949 Act passed using the Parliament Act 1911 procedure, further limiting the power of delay to one year (see Ch.10 on the House of Lords for further detail).

(v)   House of Commons Disqualification Act 1975

3–013   This Act was a consolidating Act bringing together provisions on who was disqualified from being a Member of Parliament. The Act disqualifies members of the Judiciary, Civil Service, Police and Armed Forces from eligibility (s.1). It also limits to 95 the number of MPs that can be Ministers in government (s.2).

(vi)   House of Lords Act 1999

3–014   This Act removed the vast majority of hereditary peers from the right to sit in the House of Lords. Following the Act's passing only 92 Peers retained the right to sit. This was intended to be temporary pending completion of the House of Lords reform (see Ch.10).

(vii)   Constitutional Reform Act 2005

3–015   The Constitutional Reform Act provided for the creation of a Supreme Court to replace the Appellate Committee of the House of Lords. It also reformed the role of the Lord Chancellor and provided for a new "open" system of judicial appointments. The Act represents further the importance of the separation of powers in the UK as it sought to clearly delineate the separation of the judicial function from the other two organs (see Ch.6).

(c)   *Statutes regulating the relationship between the State and her citizens*

(i)   The Reform Acts (Representation of the People Acts 1832, 1867, 1884 and 1983)

These Acts distributed and enlarged the franchise. Constitutionally, they are of great   **3–016** importance as they relate directly to the idea of democracy and the constitutional relationship between the state and the individual (see Ch.8).

(ii)   Police and Criminal Evidence Act 1984

PACE, as this statute is colloquially known, sets out the powers of the police and the   **3–017** rights of an individual in respect of stop, search, seizure and detention.

(iii)   Prevention of Terrorism Acts 1975, 1989 and 2005, Terrorism Acts 2000 and 2006

These Acts restrict the freedom of individuals in a variety of ways. They give power to   **3–018** the Executive in respect of terrorist issues and provide for amongst many things the right of the Executive to proscribe certain organisations, to detain suspected terrorist suspects for up to 28 days and to impose control orders.

(iv)   Human Rights Act 1998

The Human Rights Act gives legal effect to the European Convention on Human   **3–019** Rights and provides a procedural framework for asserting Convention rights in domestic courts (see Ch.21).

(v)   Freedom of Information Act 2000

The Act came fully into force January 1, 2005 and provides individuals with the right to   **3–020** access certain types of information held by public authorities. It came into being as a result of Labour's 1997 election manifesto and aims to make government more transparent. It also aims for government to maintain adequate public information schemes to ensure the public is more fully informed.

   In 2007, the Freedom of Information (Amendment) Bill was introduced as a private members Bill. The Bill, if passed into law, will exempt MPs and Peers from the provisions of the Act.

3–021   **Delegated legislation:** Although primary legislation is the main constitutional source in the UK, delegated legislation can also have constitutional significance. Delegated legislation is described by the Joint Committee on Delegated Legislation, (HL 184, HC 475, 1971–72, para.6) as "every exercise of power to legislate conferred by or under an Act of Parliament". Delegated legislation can take many forms but the most common are statutory instruments (SI). There are two types of statutory instrument: an enabling act will confer legislative power either on a government Minister to be exercised by statutory instrument (specific to a government department) or on the Queen in Council to be exercisable by Order in Council (cross departments). A second type of delegated legislation is Orders in Council which are made under prerogative and distinct from Orders in Council made under a parent statute. A third type of delegated legislation is bye-laws which are primarily made by bodies such as local authorities, public utilities, operators of public transport. Their application is limited to a particular local area.

2.   European Community law

3–022   As noted above, the European Communities Act 1972 (ECA) provides for the incorporation of European law into the UK's domestic legal system. The law of the European Union represents a significant source of constitutional law in the UK and will be discussed more fully in Ch.4. For the purposes here, it is necessary to be aware of the legislation that comes from Europe and which forms part of the UK's constitution.

Broadly speaking, there are two types of European Legislation:

(a)   *Primary sources*

3–023   The primary source of the European Union is its treaties. These include the founding treaties: the Treaties of Rome 1957, the Treaty of European Union 1992 (Maastricht), the Treaty of Amsterdam 1997, the Treaty of Nice 2001 and the Lisbon Treaty 2007 (European Reform Treaty). The Lisbon Treaty was signed by Member States on the December 13, 2007 but has yet to be formally ratified by individual Member States. The European Union (Amendment) Bill (at the time of writing the Bill was in the Committee stage of the House of Commons) will give effect to the Treaty in the UK. It is intended that the Treaty will come into effect for all Member States in early 2009.

(b)   *Secondary sources*

3–024   These are laws made by the institutions of the EU and include regulations, directives, decisions and recommendations. Regulations, directives and decisions have binding effect albeit they take different forms. Recommendations do not have binding form.

(i) Regulations

These are of general application and are used whenever there is a need for uniformity. **3–025**
One hallmark of regulations is that they are directly applicable and binding in their
entirety. This means they enter into force either 20 days after publication in the Official
Journal or on the date specified in the regulation. From this date they are immediately
incorporated into domestic law and require no further implementation.

(ii) Directives

These are binding as to the result to be achieved on those states to which they are **3–026**
addressed; in practice this is usually them all. Distinct from regulations, directives set
out a desired result but leave it to the Member States to decide how to implement them.
In the UK, this is usually in the form of either statute or delegated legislation. Directives tend to give a deadline by which Member States must transpose its obligations into
national law and a failure to meet the deadlines can lead to legal consequences. An
example of a directive is Directive 95/46/EC on the protection of individuals with
regard to the processing of personal data and on the free movement of such data which
was given effect in the UK by the Data Protection Act 1998.

(iii) Decisions

These are addressed to particular parties such as a company or to Member States and **3–027**
are binding upon those to whom they are addressed.

(iv) Recommendations and opinions

These measures do not have legally binding effect. **3–028**

3. Case law

Courts play an important part in all constitutional systems. In countries with a codified **3–029**
constitution the courts are charged with interpreting the constitution and those laws
made under it. An oft quoted example is the United States Supreme Court's decision in
Marbury v Madison (1803) 5 US Cranch 137 where the Supreme Court interpreted
art.III of the constitution to confer the power of judicial review on the Court regarding
the constitutionality of a statute. As a result of this decision, the Supreme Court has the
right to strike down legislation. In the absence of a codified constitution, the UK courts
still play an important role. The UK is a common law jurisdiction meaning law is made
by judges and applied on the basis of precedent (stare decisis). Judge made law takes
two forms: law that arises from the common law with no express statutory authority
and law that arises from the interpretation of statutes and other written laws.

(a)   *Common law*

3–030   The UK constitution has evolved over a long period of time and much of the constitution has been developed by the courts through declaration of the common law.
When there is no authoritative statement of the law, judges have the authority and duty
to declare what the law is by creating precedent. Many judicial decisions have declared
important constitutional principles and provide the legal foundation of constitutionalism. An early case illustrating such a principle is *Entick v Carrington* (1765)
19 St. Tr. 1029. Here the court ruled that a general warrant issued by the Home
Secretary to enter and search Entick's premises amounted to trespass and hence illegal.
The court found there to be no law authorising the Home Secretary's action and so the
warrant was issued without lawful authority, i.e. the court's decision established the
constitutional principle that government had to act in accordance with law which is a
principle of the rule of law.

As with statutes, not every case will have constitutional significance. Also it is
important to note that court decisions can be overruled by Parliament passing a statute
and, in limited circumstances (see, for example, the *House of Lords Practice Statement*
[1966] 1 W.L.R. 1234) the courts can overrule themselves.

(b)   *Interpretation of law*

3–031   Much of the UK's law is now brought about through statute and the court's role here is
to interpret and apply the law. Courts cannot rule on the validity of an Act of Parliament but have instead the task of interpreting the statutes in cases before them. In
aiding their interpretation, courts employ rules of interpretation (literal, golden, mis-
chief and purposive rules). Courts generally seek to give effect to the literal meaning of a
statute unless such an interpretation would produce an absurdity or is not possible
because of uncertainty or ambiguity. In such situations the courts could look to the
purpose of the statutory provision and interpret with that in mind (purposive
approach). The European Communities Act 1972 and the Human Rights Act 1998 have
given the courts new and stronger powers of interpretation for cases within their
respective jurisdictions; see for example, *R. v A (Complainant's Sexual History) (No.2)*
[2001] UKHL 25 a case concerning the interpretation of the Youth Justice and Criminal
Evidence Act 1999 to ensure its compatibility with human rights (art.6(1), right to fair
trial), discussed in detail in Ch.21.

The courts also employ certain presumptions to aid them. These include the presumption that Parliament does not intend to legislate retrospectively, inconsistently
with international law, to restrict a person's access to court or to exclude the power of
judicial review. For example, in *Waddington v Miah* [1974] 1 W.L.R. 683, the House of
Lords interpreted the Immigration Act 1971 so it did not have retrospective effect and
in *R. v Lord Chancellor Ex p. Witham* [1998] Q.B. 575, the Queen's Bench Division held
that without clear and express words, s.130 of the Supreme Court Act 1981 did not
empower the Lord Chancellor to prescribe fees so as to deny the poor access to the
courts.

4. Prerogative power

Prerogative power derives from the common law and is the discretionary power   **3–032**
belonging to the monarch. Prior to the existence of a Parliament, the monarch ruled by
this power alone. Originally, this power was vested in the monarch alone but is now
exercised by the Executive on her behalf. Much prerogative power has also been cur-
tailed or lost by the imposition of statute and since 1611 the courts have ruled that the
monarch "hath no prerogative but what the law of the land allows him" (*Case of
Proclamations* (1611) 12 Co. Rep. 74). Prerogative power remains an important source
of constitutional law as it is used, for example, to commit the armed forces to war.

5. International law

International Treaties such as the Universal Declaration of Human Rights 1948 and the   **3–033**
International Covenant of Civil and Political Rights 1966 are also important as an
influence on the UK's constitution. While they do not form a direct part of the constitution they are significant in helping to shape its development and are often used in
aiding the courts interpretation.

6. Law and custom of Parliament

Each House of Parliament has certain rights and immunities which offers protection   **3–034**
from external interference and enables Parliament to discharge its functions. Known as
parliamentary privilege it includes the right of free speech and to regulate its own
affairs. Such privileges are respected by the courts. Much of the law and custom of
Parliament is found in the standing orders of the Houses and is summarised in Erskine
May, *Parliamentary Practice* (22nd edn (London: Butterworths, 1997)). While it does
not have the force of statute nor confer rights on individual citizens it remains an
important source of constitutional law as it regulates and governs Parliament.

NON-LEGAL SOURCES

1. Constitutional conventions

All constitutions have a mixture of legal and non-legal sources. Legal sources such as   **3–035**
statutes or a constitutional text cannot cover every eventuality and constitutions need
to be able to develop and be flexible to some degree of change. Constitutional conventions are some of the constitution's most important non-legal rules which supplement the legal rules of the constitution. W. Jennings, *The Law and the Constitution* (5th

edn (London: University of London Press, 1959)) famously said that conventions "provide the flesh which clothes the dry bones of the law" (pp.81–81).

(a)   *Definition of constitutional conventions*

3–036   There is a debate over what in fact constitutes a constitutional convention. Dicey in *An Introduction to the Study of the Law of the Constitution* (1959, p.24) identified a source of constitutional law which he terms "Conventions, understandings, habits or practices, which, though they may regulate the conduct of officials are not in reality laws at all since". He used the term inclusively and does not distinguish between conventions and habits, practice or understandings. Hilaire Barnett in *Constitutional and Administrative Law* (6th edn (London: Cavendish, 2006)) offers a good analysis of the distinction between them all. Barnett's key distinction is that conventions are binding because there is a sanction for breach.

The binding nature of conventions is a common characteristic in definitions since Dicey. Sir Kenneth Wheare in *Modern Constitutions* ((New York: OUP, 1951), p.179) said "by convention is meant a binding rule, a rule of behaviour accepted as obligatory by those concerned in the working of the constitution". Similarly, O'Hood, Phillips and Jackson, *Constitutional and Administrative Law* (8th edn (London: Sweet & Maxwell, 2001)) described conventions as "rules of political practice which are regarded as binding by those to whom they apply, but which are not laws as they are not enforced by the courts or by the Houses of Parliament". G. Marshall, *Constitutional Conventions: The Rules and Forms of Political Accountability* (Oxford: Clarendon, 1986) also takes this view and defines conventions as "certain rules of constitutional behaviours which are considered to be binding by and upon those who operate the constitution, but which are not enforced by the law courts, nor by the Presiding officers in the House of Parliament". Whether conventions are descriptive rules or prescriptive rules of behaviour (binding) is a common debate in this area and we will return to it below.

It is important to be aware that constitutional conventions are different from conventions in international law. In international law, a convention is another name for an international Treaty, for example, the European Convention of Human Rights. The use of the term convention is used to set a standard for behaviour in respect of a particular area and impose a degree of obligation to follow that standard. International conventions are not binding domestically unless specifically incorporated, but can be binding in international law.

(b)   *Identifying a convention*

3–037   Identifying the origins of statute or case law is relatively easy; identifying a convention is a much harder process. Conventions develop over time, in essence they evolve and identifying when a course of conduct or habit becomes a convention is not clear cut. In addition, unlike laws and cases, they are generally unwritten and it may be difficult to identify the parameters of the convention. Jennings in *The Law and the Constitution* set out three tests which should be asked to establish whether a course of conduct is a convention:

(1)   What are the precedents for the convention?

(2)   Do those connected with this rule believe they bound by it?

(3)   Is there a constitutional reason for the rule?

The Jennings test received positive judicial recognition by the Canadian Supreme Court in *Reference re Questions Concerning Amendment of Constitution of Canada* [1981] 1 S.C.R. 753 and is a useful tool for establishing a convention.

(c)   *Conventions distinguished from laws*

It is important at this juncture to drawn a distinction between laws and conventions.   **3–038** There are many similarities between laws and conventions for example, if we take as the consensus that conventions are binding, then both conventions and laws can be regarded as rules which impose an obligation to follow (see below).

   Dicey would disagree with the above description and was quite clear in his distinction between the two; conventions are descriptive, laws are prescriptive; laws are enforceable by the courts and conventions are not. Of the latter, there is not doubt; a fact confirmed by the courts on a number of occasions (see *Att-Gen v Jonathan Cape* [1976] Q.B. 752; *Madzimbamuto v Lardner-Burke* [1967] 1 A.C. 645). It is this fact that is the real distinction between conventions and laws.

   Of the former, it is fair to say that Dicey's analysis is too simplistic as laws and conventions both prescribe a course of behaviour because of the consequences of a failure to follow. Jennings, *The Law and the Constitution* (1959, p.117) certainly took this view and also believed there was "no distinction of substance or nature" between the two. He pointed to certain kinds of similarity and stated "conventions are like most fundamental rules of any constitution in that they rest essentially upon general acquiescence, the same can be said for a written constitution whose legal force depends on its provisions being accepted and obeyed". Munro, *Studies in Constitutional Law* (2nd edn (New York: OUP, 1999)) feels this distinction is "quite misleading" (p.70) as though conventions rest upon acquiescence, laws do not. Laws may be unpopular or even widely disobeyed but they are still laws and enforceable as such. Conventions on the other hand depend for their existence on the parties' acquiescence. The existence of a convention presupposes that there is a necessity for it, that the parties believe in the reason for the convention and consider it binding. If the convention is no longer regarded as binding then there becomes no need to follow it and hence the convention ceases to exist.

(d)   *Examples of constitutional conventions*

3–039   There is no definitive list of what constitutional conventions exist. There are conventions in virtually all aspects of the constitution and there are many examples. A few will be considered below.

(i)   Conventions relating to Parliament

3–040   The rules governing parliamentary practice and procedure are regarded as the law and custom of Parliament and as such are not classified as conventions. There are however, a number of conventions relating to Parliament. Two of the most important conventions relating to the relationship between the House of Commons and House of Lords are the convention that the House of Lords will pass Bills based on the government's manifesto and the convention that government business in the House of Lords should be considered in reasonable time.

3–041   **The Salisbury-Addison convention:** This is described in a report of the Royal Commission on the Reform of the House of Lords (Cm 4534, 2000) as "an understanding that a 'manifesto' Bill, foreshadowed in the governing party's most recent election manifesto and passed by the House of Commons, should not be opposed by the second chamber on Second or Third Reading" (para.4.21). The convention is also suggested to include the principle that the Lords will not pass wrecking amendments to such a Bill. The origins of the Salisbury Convention lie in the 19th century and the development of the primacy of the House of Commons over the Lords. It was further developed by the Marquis of Salisbury, a Conservative Peer, in the wake of a Labour landslide in the General Election in July 1945. The Marquis of Salisbury (Viscount Cranborne) believed that because the Labour government, and so the House of Commons, had such a clear mandate to deliver their manifesto proposals it would be wrong for the House of Lords to oppose them. It would be constitutionally wrong for an un-elected Chamber to oppose proposals that have been put to the electorate. The Joint Committee on Conventions ("Conventions of the UK Parliament" Report of Session 2005–06 HL Paper 265–I, HC 1212–I) noted that the Convention has changed since 1945; it applies to a manifesto Bill introduced in the House of Lords and is recognised by the whole House, not just the Labour and Conservative frontbenches who originally formulated it. They suggested that in view of this it should be renamed to the Government Bill Convention.

3–042   **Reasonable time convention:** The Joint Committee on Conventions ("Conventions of the UK Parliament" Report of Session 2005–06 HL Paper 265–I, HC 1212–I) recognised the existence of the convention that government business in the Lords should be considered in reasonable time. How long is reasonable varies and depends on the context whether for example the Bill had pre-legislative scrutiny or whether it was fully scrutinised in the Commons.

(ii)   Conventions relating to the monarch

Many of the prerogative powers of the Crown are regulated by Convention, for **3–043** example, the law requires that before a Bill becomes an Act of Parliament it must be passed by both Houses and receive the assent of the monarch. By convention where a Bill has passed both Houses of Parliament, the royal assent is given as a matter of course. Under the Royal Assent Act 1967, the monarch's assent can be granted in writing. The monarch's legal right to refuse assent was last used by Queen Anne in 1708 in relation to the Scottish Militia Bill, though this was apparently done with the approval of her Ministers and with no objection from Parliament. Two other occasions merit consideration. In 1913 King George V considered whether to give royal assent to the Government of Ireland Bill. This Bill was being put through Parliament under the newly passed Parliament Act 1911 procedure which removed the House of Lord's veto over legislation. The Bill was opposed by Conservative and Unionists who had the majority in the House of Lords. In the end the King did not refuse assent but according to Jennings, *Cabinet Government* (3rd edn (Cambridge University Press, 1959), p.400) his actions signalled that the King believed he had the right to refuse assent. In 1999, Queen Elizabeth II, acting on the advice of government, refused to signify consent to a Private Members Bill, the Military Action Against Iraq (Parliamentary Approval) Bill. This Bill proposed to transfer power to authorise military action from the Crown (government) to Parliament. As this proposed modification of the Queen's prerogatives, the monarch's consent was required before the Bill received its second reading in the House. Her refusal meant the Bill never received its second reading.

   (*http://news.bbc.co.uk/1/hi/uk_politics/320514.stm*).

   The offices of Prime Minister and the Cabinet are conventional. By convention, the monarch invites the Leader of the majority party in the House of Commons to become Prime Minister and form a government. It is also a convention that the Prime Minister will be a Member of the House of Commons as the principle of democracy requires the Prime Minister to be accountable to the elected chamber. The last Prime Minister to be chosen from the House of Lords was Sir Alec Douglas-Home, Prime Minister from October 1963 to October 1964. When Harold MacMillan resigned as Prime Minister in 1963, Lord Home, as he then was, was invited to become Prime Minister. Lord Home relinquished his title under the Peerages Act 1963 and contested a by-election so that he could take a seat in the House of Commons.

(iii)   Conventions relating to the Executive

The twin conventions of ministerial responsibility, individual ministerial responsibility **3–044** and collective ministerial responsibility, form part of the conventions relating to the Crown. These conventions are important in regulating the relationship between Ministers and between Ministers and Parliament. The convention of individual ministerial responsibility at its simplest requires that Ministers are responsible to Parliament for their departments. In its classic form, a Minister was responsible for both personal acts and the conduct of officials in his or her department. In its modified form, a Minister is responsible only for his own conduct. The convention of collective ministerial responsibility requires the Cabinet to speak as one voice, to act collectively. If a Minister is unable to agree with the direction of government or a particular policy choice, then he or she should resign. A recent example of such a resignation was Robin Cook, Leader of the House of Commons who resigned in March 2003 over the government's decision to go to war in Iraq. Both these conventions are considered in more detail in Ch.12.

Though the conduct of an election is governed by statutory rules there is no legal rule that's regulates the behaviour of the Prime Minister once an election result is known. By convention, the government must have a majority in the House of Commons. If the existing government loses the election, by convention, the Prime Minister should resign.

(iv)   Conventions relating to the Judiciary

3–045   Once appointed as a judge all political affiliations and ties should be severed as it is a convention that judges are apolitical. This is particularly important for the Law Lords (Lords of Appeal in Ordinary) who form the Appellate Committee of the House of Lords. While they may take part in the legislative work of the House of Lords, by convention they do not belong to a political party and do not participate in debates of political controversy. Under the Constitutional Reform Act 2005 Pt 3, this will change when the new Supreme Court is established and takes over the appellate functions of the House of Lords.

(e)   *Function of conventions*

3–046   A simple way to characterise the functions of conventions is that they fill in the gaps in the law. Jennings' analogy in *The Law and the Constitution* (1959) is that conventions "provide the flesh which clothes the dry bones of the law" (p.81–81). Loveland, *Constitutional Law, Administrative Law and Human Rights* (4th edn (New York: OUP, 2006)) says they "provide a moral framework within which government Ministers or the monarch should exercise non-justiciable legal powers" (p.304). This is clearly seen if we look at the convention relating to royal assent. The monarch has the legal right to consent or refuse legislation however as a non-elected person it would be undemocratic for a monarch to refuse legislation and so the convention regulates the use of her legal power.

A broader function of conventions is they regulate the relationship between the organs of the state and allow the constitution to change without formal recourse to legislation. In effect they imbue the constitution with flexibility, an idea reflected by Jennings who noted they "keep the constitution in touch with the growth of ideas". In *Re Amendment of the Constitution of Canada* [1982] 125 D.L.R. 1, the Supreme Court of Canada stated "the main purpose of constitutional conventions is to ensure that the legal framework of the constitution will be operated in accordance with the prevailing constitutional values or principles of the period".

(f)   *Are conventions binding?*

One clear characteristic found in the definition of constitutional conventions is they are   **3–047**
not legally enforceable and so not legally binding. This has also been confirmed by the
courts in a number of cases; in *Att-Gen v Jonathan Cape Ltd* [1976] Q.B. 752 for
example, Lord Widgery noted that the convention of collective ministerial responsibility was an obligation in morals only and not binding in law. Though they may not be
legally binding, it is commonly accepted that they are binding constitutionally. Conventions prescribe a course of conduct or pattern of behaviour and are binding because
they impose an obligation to follow them. As Jennings, *Cabinet Government* (3rd edn,
Cambridge University Press, 1959, p.2) wrote, conventions "not only are followed but
have to be followed".

(i)   Why are they obeyed?

Looking at why conventions are obeyed necessarily leads to a discussion of what   **3–048**
happens if they are breached. There is no definite rule or sanction for breach of a
convention and as stated it is clear the court will not enforce a convention. Dicey
however argued that breaches of some conventions could bring the offender into
conflict with the law and that is why they are followed:

> "The sanction which constrains the boldest political adventurer to obey the fun-
> damental principles of the constitution and the conventions in which these prin-
> ciples are expressed, is the fact that the breach of these principles and of these
> conventions will almost immediately bring the offender into conflict with the courts
> and the law of the land." (pp.445–446)

Dicey illustrated his argument by reference to the convention that Parliament must
meet annually. If this convention were broken Dicey argued the Army Annual Act
would expire, the consequences of which would mean either the Army being disbanded
or, if kept, it would be illegal as art.6 of the Bill of Rights 1688 states, "raising and
keeping an army during peacetime without Parliament's consent" to be unlawful. In
modern Britain, Dicey's evidence for his argument is weak as Parliament meets or is in
session for about 34 weeks a year and would have plenty of opportunity to authorise
the keeping of the army.

   While it may be difficult to imagine a breach of convention leading to a direct breach
of law, it is less difficult to imagine a breach of convention having an indirect effect on
the law. *Att-Gen v Jonathan Cape Ltd* [1976] Q.B. 752 concerned the publication of the
diaries of a former Cabinet Minister, Richard Crossman. The diaries included records
of Cabinet discussions which, under the convention of collective ministerial responsibility were confidential, and could not be revealed without the authority of the Cabinet
Secretary. Proposed publication was therefore in breach of the convention and so the
Attorney-General sought an injunction to prohibit such a course of action. Lord
Widgery clearly stated that the convention could not be directly enforced by the court.

He did however develop a potential parallel means which would indirectly have the effect of upholding the convention or, to put it another way, used the convention to develop the law. Lord Widgery accepted the argument that Ministers owed each other a legally enforceable duty of confidentiality. This duty was created by an extension of the equitable doctrine of confidentiality which had previously only applied in private law. Lord Widgery found that cabinet discussions fulfilled the test of confidentiality and the maintenance of joint cabinet responsibility was generally in the public interest, hence restraint of publication would also be in the public interest. However, there was a time limit after which the confidential character of the information would lapse and the duty of the court to restrain publication would then also lapse. On the facts he concluded this to be the case as the time span was over 10 years.

The above discussion relates to the idea of legal consequences and cases like *Jonathan Cape* are rare. A more satisfactory reason for the binding nature of conventions lies in the political arena. Jennings preferred the view that "conventions are obeyed because of the political difficulties that follow if they are not". This view stems from the nature of conventions being rules of behaviour accepted as obligatory by those concerned and has much merit. With reference to the convention of royal assent discussed earlier, it is not impossible to imagine the consequences that would follow a monarch who refused assent of their own volition. A good example of Jennings's argument is found in *Reference re Questions Concerning Amendment of Constitution of Canada* [1981] 1 S.C.R. 753.

The British North America Act had created the self-governing dominion of Canada. To effect any changes to their constitution an Act of the Westminster Parliament was required. As a federal country, a convention developed that the Canadian Government would not send a Bill to the UK Parliament unless it enjoyed the support of all Provinces particularly, where it might affect the federal-provincial relationship or alter the powers, rights or privileges granted or secured by the constitution to the provinces. In the 1980s, the Canadian Government under President Trudeau wanted to patriate the Canadian Constitution (a play on the word repatriation meaning to bring home). This could only be achieved by Canada asking Westminster to enact amending legislation. Eight out of the ten provinces opposed the scheme including Quebec. Three provinces, Newfoundland, Manitoba and Quebec, made a reference to the Supreme Court of Canada asking whether the constitutional convention existed and if it did, whether it had "crystallised" into constitutional law. The Supreme Court embarked on a detailed analysis of the convention considering the reason for its existence and whether it had been followed in the past. They concluded that while a convention could not crystallise into law, the agreement of the provinces was constitutionally required. In other words, to act without the provinces consent would be unconstitutional in the conventional sense. The strength of their comments and the approach taken had the desired effect and the government took their proposals back to the provinces for further negotiation.

Finally, it is worth noting that breach of a convention may lead to it being given (at least partial) statutory force. In 1908 the House of Lords rejected a Finance Bill in contravention of the convention that the Lords would give way to the Commons (especially in relation to Money Bills). This led to the government passing the Parliament Act 1911 which removed the House of Lord's power of veto.

While it appears clear that conventions are binding, is it fair to say they are all binding to the same degree? Munro argues that conventions exist on a continuum or scale; some conventions are more binding then others. This echoes an earlier comment by F.W. Maitland, *The Constitutional History of England* (Cambridge: Cambridge University Press, 1908, p.398) who said "we find them of every degree of stringency and of definiteness". Some conventions are easy to define and because of the reason for the existence of that convention, a failure to follow would lead to severe consequences. The convention of royal assent provides a good example of this. The convention is clear and requires the monarch to always give assent to legislation. The rationale for the convention is also clear; the monarch is not democratically elected and should not frustrate legislation proposed by the democratic body. In short the convention upholds democratic principles. Any failure to follow the convention would probably lead to accusations of undemocratic conduct and consequences may include the downfall of the monarchy. It would require "near-revolutionary" circumstances to justify any refusal of assent and legitimise the monarch's action. Assent was last officially refused in 1708 and in modern times, it is hard to imagine a situation when assent would be refused of the monarch's own choosing, though such examples might be:

- a Bill to extend the life of the House of Commons; this could be for a long period, indefinitely or in circumstances where the House of Lords has been abolished (see Bogdanor, *The Monarchy and the Constitution* (Oxford: Clarendon Press, 1995), p.126; Loveland, *Constitutional Law, Administrative Law and Human Rights* (4th edn, New York: OUP, 2006), p.316);

- a Bill limiting or removing the franchise so subverting the idea of democratic representative government;

- a Bill to remove the requirement for Royal Assent particularly if the grant of Royal Assent were regarded as a constitutional safeguard.

Even in such circumstances as these, though the monarch's action may be legitimised, the consequence of breach would still be severe. Any attempt to pass legislation that may not have a democratic mandate and a refusal by the monarch to assent to it would certainly cast question marks over the competence and democratic nature of the government. An easily imagined consequence of the breach of convention in this circumstance could be the downfall of the government. It is fair to say then that because of the reason for its existence and the consequences of breach, this convention has a high degree of obligation to follow and so is strongly binding or, in Munro's words, toward the top end of the continuum.

A similar argument can be made in respect of selection of Prime Minister. It is hard to imagine the monarch choosing a Prime Minister that is not from either the democratically elected House of Commons or at the very least the House of Lords.

Lower down the scale is the convention of collective ministerial responsibility which Lord Widgery in *Att-Gen v Jonathan Cape* (p.770) noted "I find overwhelming evidence that the doctrine of joint responsibility is generally understood and practised and equally strong evidence that it is on occasion ignored". Briefly, the rationale for the convention is to allow free and informed debate within cabinet and presenting a united front in public once a decision has been made enforces the idea of strong government. Breach of the convention would not create such a constitutional crisis as the royal assent example and so can be considered less binding. A similar argument can be made for the convention of individual ministerial responsibility. Here the scope of the convention is not "definite" and evidence shows that the convention as originally formulated is occasionally followed (Sir Thomas Dugdale following the Crichel Down Affair) and equally broken. The binding nature of this convention depends wholly on the particular situation, whether for example, the political situation has made it such that the Minister has lost the support of the Prime Minister and/or Party (for a fuller discussion on these conventions see Ch.12).

One thing that is apparent from the above discussion is the parties feel bound to follow the convention because of the reason for its existence. The other factor that contributes to the binding nature of the convention are the sanctions that arise for breaching the convention.

(g) *The courts and conventions*

3–049 Dicey and Jennings both agree that conventions are not legally enforceable. Such has been made clear in a number of cases. Following a declaration of independence by Rhodesia, the Westminster Parliament enacted the South Rhodesia Act 1965 which invalidated all legislation put forward by the illegal regime. The 1965 Act was passed in contravention of the convention that it would not legislate for a dominion unless requested by the dominion themselves. In *Madzimbamuto v Lardner-Burke* [1967] 1 A.C. 645, a subsequent challenge to the legality of detention under a Southern Rhodesian emergency regulation was successful. An argument put forward that the 1965 Act should not be applied because it was in contravention of the convention was not successful. A similar argument and conclusion was reached in *Manuel v Att-Gen*; *Noltcho v Att-Gen* [1983] Ch. 77 concerning a challenge to the Canada Act 1982 by a group of Indians.

Though the courts will not legally enforce a convention it does not mean that the courts do not have a role to play regarding conventions. The Courts have recognised conventions and used them to inform their decision making (see *Att-Gen v Jonathan Cape Ltd*). In *Carltona v Commissioner of Works* [1943] 2 All E.R. 560, the Court of Appeal in determining the powers of a government Minister to delegate his decision making power drew on the convention of individual ministerial responsibility. The Court of Appeal felt it would not be practicable for Ministers to personally make all decisions and the existence of the convention meant the Minister would still be constitutionally and politically accountable to Parliament, despite not having personally made the decision. Similarly, in *Liversidge v Anderson* [1942] 1 A.C. 206, the House of Lords was influenced by the convention of ministerial responsibility when considering the powers of the Home Secretary to detain individuals during the Second World War.

(h) *Codification*

If conventions are important rules of the constitution it is a fair question to ask why **3–050**
they are not codified. Certainly some conventions in the UK have been codified and
become laws. Section 4 of the Statute of Westminster 1931 codified the convention that
the UK would not legislate for a Dominion without the Dominions' consent. Similarly,
the Parliament Act 1911 codified the convention that the House of Lords give way to
the House of Commons following its breach by the former.

However, once codified the convention becomes law and loses the benefits of flexibility and change. Conventions would also develop to fill in the gaps of the new laws.
In addition, many conventions regulate the political arena and to codify them would
draw the judiciary into political debates.

In 2006, the Joint Committee on Conventions (First Report of Session 2005–06 of the
Joint Committee on Conventions, Conventions of the UK Parliament, HL 265, HC
1212 (2006) was appointed to consider the practicality of codifying the key conventions
on the relationship between the two Houses of Parliament which affect the consideration of legislation. The Committee concluded that codification would:

> "Raise issues of definition, reduce flexibility, and inhibit the capacity to evolve. It
> might create a need for adjudication, and the presence of an adjudicator, whether
> the court or some new body, is incompatible with parliamentary sovereignty." (at
> para.279)

They also thought that it could damage the relationship between the two Houses,
making it more confrontational which would not benefit either government or Parliament. They recommended instead that the convention the government should have its
business considered in a reasonable time be adopted by way of House of Lords resolution. In December 2006, the government, in its formal reply, accepted the Committee
recommendations (Government Response to the Joint Committee on Conventions
Report of Session 2005–06: Conventions of the UK Parliament, Cm 6997).

2.   Academic Authors

The opinions of academic authors may be of great value to the courts when considering **3–051**
a statute that has not yet been judicially interpreted or where the common law is
unclear. In a similar vein, some writings can assist the courts with the development of
the law. Dicey's *Law of the Constitution* has heavily influenced judicial reasoning and in
particular the development of administrative law. Similarly, Jennings is often referred
to, as in the Canada case discussed earlier. Other more recent writers include the works
of Jeffrey Jowell and Dawn Oliver, and Wade and Forsyth's *Administrative Law* to
name but a few.

In the area of parliamentary practice, Erskine May's work on *Parliamentary Practice*
is considered the authoritative text. It was first published in 1844 and is regularly
updated by the Clerk to the House.

FURTHER READING

3–052 Hazell, R. "Time for a new convention: parliamentary scrutiny of constitutional bills 1997–2005" (2006) P.L. 247–298

Jaconelli, J. "Do Constitutional Conventions Bind?" (2005) 64(1) C.L.J. 149

Maley, W. "Laws & Conventions revisited" (1985) 48 M.L.R. 121–139.

Munro, C. "Laws & Conventions distinguished" (1975) 91 L.Q.R. 218.

Munro, C. "Dicey on Constitutional Conventions" (1985) P.L. 637

Munro, C. *Studies in Constitutional Law*, 2nd edn, (New York: OUP, 1999), Ch.3.

Chapter 4

MEMBERSHIP OF THE EUROPEAN UNION

INTRODUCTION

The European Union, as it now is, arguably forms the most significant source of law in   **4–001**
the United Kingdom's constitutional framework. When the United Kingdom acceded
to what was then the European Economic Community with the Republic of Ireland and
Denmark in 1973, it was a body with a membership of nine, including the newly
acceded nations. However, over time the Union has grown to membership of some 27
nations with the two newest members, Bulgaria and Romania, acceding to the Union in
2007. Membership of the Union brings with it certain freedoms, for example, the
freedom to trade with European neighbours without barriers. But the Union is more
than the largest economic area in the world, for through its reforms political institutions
have been created making it an economic, political and social community of nations.

1.   Evolution of the Union—Treaties

The operation, basis and legitimacy of the European Union is drawn from Treaties. At   **4–002**
its foundation in 1952, a European Coal and Steel Community was created with six
members (Treaty of Paris). Two further Treaties were signed at Rome in 1957, one
creating the European Atomic Energy Community and a second, the more famous one,
creating the European Economic Community. It is common to refer to the latter as the
"Treaty of Rome", even though two Treaties were signed at Rome that year. Since
those Treaties, a number of further Treaties have been signed further developing links
between the nations of the Community.

2.   Treaty of Rome 1957

4–003   The Treaty of Rome was a framework document which set down the objectives for the Economic Community, but with the detail to be completed by European legislation (regulations, directives and decisions of the Court of Justice of the European Communities). Articles 2 and 3 were the significant provisions:
Article 2:

> "The Community shall have as its task, by establishing a common market and progressively approximating the economic policies of Member States, to promote throughout the community a harmonious development of economic activities, a continuous and balanced expansion, an increase in stability, an accelerated raising of the standard of living and closer relations between the states belonging to it."

Article 3 built on the general statement in art.2 by providing a list of objectives for the fulfilment of the commitment in art.2. These included the elimination of customs duties and quantity restrictions on the trade of goods between Member States; the agreement to establish a common customs tariff towards countries outside the Community; the removal of barriers preventing the freedom of movement for persons, services and capital within the Community; and the approximation of the laws of Member States to the extent required for the proper functioning of the common market. These represent a sample of the most important of the founding objectives of the Economic Community.

By way of conclusion, the Preamble to the Treaty of Rome provided that the Community was, "determined to lay the foundations of an ever closer union among the peoples of Europe", and this was something which was worked on as the years progressed.

In the period following the Treaty of Rome, a number of Treaties were agreed between the Member States, but these were not significant in the development of the Union.

3.   Single European Act 1986

4–004   The Single European Act (SEA) of 1986 represented a major reform of the Treaties which had been agreed to that point. Though named an Act, it was, in fact, a Treaty and its function was to establish a deadline for the implementation of the single European market, something which had been originally envisaged in the Treaty of Rome, as December 31, 1992. However, completing the market was a significant logistical undertaking for a Community which required unanimity for its decisions. Consequently, the SEA sought to streamline the process of legislative implementation by introducing the principle of qualified majority voting with the consequence that unanimity was no longer a necessary requirement for decisions designed to establish the single market. The single market was established by the deadline, largely as a result of the reformed voting method.

4.   Treaty of European Union 1992 (Maastricht Treaty)

The Treaty of Maastricht was negotiated and signed in a new Europe, that is, one   **4–005**
without Communist rule for the first time in approximately half a century. This had
particular consequences for Germany, one of the Union's original Member States.
Because of these dramatic changes on the continent of Europe, the Treaty had two
aims: an outward-looking aim which sought to affirm the international position of the
Union in the new world order, and an inward-looking aim which sought to build on
the work started by the SEA.

The Treaty sought to increase the powers of the European Union in certain areas by
increasing the powers of the European Parliament (see para.4–013, below), and
by creating a single currency for use in Member States of the EU as a replacement for
the different national currencies. In its outward-looking aspect, the Treaty committed
the EU to a common foreign and community policy as the broader aim of achieving a
common defence policy, something which failed in the 1950s. However, the United
Kingdom obtained important opt-outs during the negotiations, including the opt-out
from the single currency which continues to this day. The Treaty came into force on
November 1, 1993.

5.   Treaty of Amsterdam 1997

The Treaty of Amsterdam of 1997 increased the Union's powers by, for example,   **4–006**
creating a common employment policy. However, an important provision was that it
renumbered the articles of the Treaties. Where the Treaty provision is renumbered, the
new number is given first, with the old number following in parentheses, e.g. art.234 EC
(ex 177).

The Treaty came into force on May 1, 1999.

6.   Treaty of Nice 2001

The Treaty of Nice prepared the European Union for enlargement. The Treaty of Nice   **4–007**
was the culmination of work started by the Intergovernmental Conference (IGC) with
the following remit:

- size and composition of the Commission;

- weighting of votes in the Council;

- extension of qualified-majority voting;

- enhanced co-operation.

Broadly, the Treaty made changes to the voting in the Council and to the size of the
Commissions, changes which were thought necessary to the efficient running of the

Union which was about to become much enlarged. Indeed, between the Treaty of Nice and 2007, 12 new members joined the European Union.

However, arguably the most significant proposal under the Treaty was the creation of a European Constitution, discussions on which stalled after it was rejected by the Irish, French and Dutch in referenda. This rejection led to a reformulation of the constitution part of the document and the most recent Treaty.

7.   Treaty of Lisbon 2007

4–008   Such was the discord among a number of EU Member States over the constitution proposed in the Treaty of Nice, the Treaty of Lisbon sought to achieve a compromise by producing a reform Treaty for the operation of the European Union, steering clear of labelling it a constitution. The Preamble to the Treaty states that its aim is, "*to complete the process started by the Treaty of Amsterdam and by the Treaty of Nice with a view to enhancing the efficiency and democratic legitimacy of the Union and to improving the coherence of its action*". To this end, the Treaty seeks to create a more democratic and transparent Union; a more efficient Europe; a Europe of rights and values, freedom, solidarity and security; and a Europe with an enhanced role on the International stage.

These values are achieved by giving greatly enhanced legislative powers to the directly elected European Parliament; by extending the principle of qualified majority voting to a greater number of EU areas; by the introduction of a Charter of Fundamental Rights into EU law, guaranteeing the rights of its citizens; and by creating new roles within the Union to give Europe a coherent voice in foreign affairs.

Though arguably still as politically-sensitive in the Member States as the Treaty of Nice, the Treaty was signed on December 13, 2007 and its implementation brings forward new challenges for the governments of the Union.

(a)   *Other forms of EU Law*

4–009   The other sources of EU law are Regulations, Directives, Decisions, Recommendations and opinions. See further Ch.3.

INSTITUTIONS

4–010   The institutions which govern the European Union have undergone considerable change since the inception of the Community in the 1950s. Indeed, their powers have increased significantly over the years and by the mechanisms developed in subsequent Treaties.

The institutions of the European Union are: the European Commission; the Council of the EU; the European Parliament; the Court of Justice of the European Communities and the Court of Auditors.

1.   European Commission

The Commission effectively acts as the European Union's Cabinet. It is comprised of a   **4–011**
representative from each of the Member States of the EU, therefore, it has some 27
Commissioners. The Commissioners holds office for a fixed term of five years and is
headed by a Commission President, a position held since 2004 by José Manuel Barroso.
   Membership of the Commission operates in the following way. First, a Commissioner is recommended by the Council. The matter is then put to the European Parliament which approves the appointment. However, the Parliament has the power to veto appointments as it did in 2004 causing a rethink on the formation of the present Commission. Once appointed, a Commissioner is required to eschew the self-interest of the nation from which he is drawn and act in the interests of the EU; they are representative of the latter, not representatives of their national government.
   The Commission has power to investigate breaches of EU law, even referring matters to the Court of Justice of the European Communities should it be required. Additionally, the Commission has the power to impose sanctions for breach of Competition laws. For example, in 2005, the Commission fined Peugeot-Citroen nearly 50 million euros for blocking cross-border sales of new cars from the Netherlands. However, companies fined by the Commission have the ability to appeal the decision to the Court as ICI did in 1999, causing the fine to be reduced.

2.   Council

The Council comprises representatives from the government of each of the Member   **4–012**
States of the EU. It meets approximately four times a year, being chaired by the
member from the Member State holding the Presidency of the Council, a role which, in
itself, is rotated every six months. Unlike the Commission which represents the Union,
the Council represents the Member States.
   The Minister required to attend the meeting will depend on the subject under discussion. There are nine separate groupings:

- General Affairs and External Relations;

- Economic and Financial Affairs (ECOFIN);

- Justice and Home Affairs (JHA);

- Employment, Social Policy, Health and Consumer Affairs;

- Competitiveness;

- Transport, Telecommunications and Energy;

- Agriculture and Fisheries;

- Environment; and

- Education, Youth and Culture

The Council enjoys a number of responsibilities and these are as follows: passing European Laws (in conjunction with the European Parliament); the co-ordination of broad economic policies of the Member States; conclusion of international agreements between the EU and other countries or international organisations; approval of the EU's budget (in conjunction with the European Parliament); the development of the EU's Common Foreign and Security Policy; the coordination of cooperation between the national courts and police forces in criminal matters. This final role is especially important in the fight against money laundering and the funding of international terrorism.

Decisions are taken using the system of qualified majority voting used widely throughout the EU. This gives a greater vote weighting to countries with large populations.

The Council should not be confused with the European Council, which is the regular meetings (or summits) of the EU Member States' Heads of State or government.

3.   European Parliament

4–013   The European Parliament has been directly elected by the citizens of the European Union since 1979, which occur every five years. The size of each country's Parliamentary representation varies according to the size of the country; the larger the country, the greater the number of Members of the European Parliament (MEP) that country elects. Germany, as the largest country in the EU by population, elects 99, while France, Italy and the United Kingdom elect 72, and so on down a sliding scale of representation.

Functionally, the European Parliament has three main roles. First, it passes law in conjunction with the Council (see para.4–012, above). This is something of an increased role for the Parliament and one which has gradually been passed to it since it received a legitimate democratic mandate for the first time in elections in 1979. Prior to that, the Parliament had a nominated representation. Second, the Parliament exercises democratic supervision over the EU institutions, and especially over the European Commission. As already stated, the European Parliament has the power to veto nominations to the Commission, something which it did in 2004. Third, the Parliament has power, again in conjunction with the Council, over the EU budget.

Something more should be said of the Parliament's power to pass laws. As stated, it does this in conjunction with the Council, and the procedure governing what is known as "codecision" is set down in art.251 of the EC Treaty. Simply, the procedure requires that where a proposal for legislation is put forward, it must have the agreement of the Council acting under its qualified majority voting powers, and the consent of the Parliament. Thus, the Parliament is given equal legislative power under the codecision procedure. Where the bodies are unable to agree to the legislation, it is passed to a

Conciliation Committee. In theory, where the Parliament and the Council are unable to agree, the Conciliation Committee is the legislation's last chance to become law.

Under art.251(4) the Committee, "shall be composed of the Members of the Council or their representatives and an equal number of representatives of the European Parliament". They then have the task of reaching agreement on a joint text. By art.251(5), if the Conciliation Committee is able to agree a joint text, the Parliament and the Council then have a period of six weeks from that approval in which to adopt the legislation in question. "If either of the two institutions fails to approve the proposed act within that period, it shall be deemed not to have been adopted".

The Parliament's role in passing legislation is, however, limited to its areas of competency. In those areas where it has no legislative competency, for example, in economic policy matters, and on issues relating to immigration and visas, though it has no power to vote on any proposed legislation, it nevertheless enjoys the right to be consulted.

4. European Court of Justice

The Court of Justice of the European Communities, or the European Court, was established under Title II, Chapter IV of the European Coal and Steel Community 1952 as one of the four institutions of the nascent community established by the Treaty. Under art.31, the court was given the function of ensuring, "the rule of law in the interpretation and application of the ... Treaty and of its implementing regulations". Since then, the court has developed into one of the central institutions of the European Union, in some ways forging a way for the development along the lines originally envisaged in the Treaty of Rome.

4–014

In terms of its jurisdiction and power, the court has the jurisdiction to hear matter brought before it in disputes between Member States of the European Union, disputes between the institutions of the European Union, and disputes between businesses and individuals arising against a Member State, or against each other. Further, national courts can make a reference to the European Court of Justice for adjudication on a point of EU law, which is what happened in the *Factortame* litigation (see Ch.7). By being the superior court for the adjudication of matters concerning EU law, it ensures that a common interpretation of EU law is formed across the 27 Member States of the European Union. The court has the power to ensure compliance with a European law which it finds a Member State has breached, and does have the power to fine a state which has breached a law.

The court consists of 27 judges, one for each of the Member States of the European Union. Obviously, therefore, it does not sit as a court of 27 judges as this would be unworkable, producing a bewildering series of judgments. Generally, it sits as a "Grand Chamber" of 13, or in chambers of five or three judges. To maintain the court's integrity as a functioning institution, only one judgment is delivered—the judgment of the court—with no dissenting judgment. This is in sharp contrast to the system of senior appellate courts in the United Kingdom where dissenting judgments are set down separately and decisions are based on majority. The court is assisted by "advocates-general" whose role is to present opinions on matters brought before the court.

The court is called upon in the discharge of its work to make: (a) preliminary rulings (where a national court asks for the court's interpretation of a matter of EU law—art.234); (b) proceedings for failure to fulfil an obligation (these may be instituted by the Commission against a Member State); (c) actions for annulment (annulling an unlawful article of EU law); (d) actions for failure to act (requiring the institutions to take action in accordance with their obligations where they have failed to do so).

A case is brought before the court in a number of stages:

(a) Submission of the case to the registry in Luxembourg where it is allocated a judge and advocate-general.

(b) The parties must submit written statements enabling the judge to summarise the case and set the legal background to it.

(c) Public hearing. The complexity/general importance of the case determines the judges committed to it: 3, 5, 13, or a full court. At this stage the parties can be questioned.

(d) Advocate-general gives their opinion.

(e) Judges give a reserved judgment at a later date.

By 1989, the European Union had an increasing influence over many aspects of the lives of its citizens through its adoption of further areas of competency by the various treaties. One consequence of this was the increasing workload of the Court, such that the court of first instance was established which the task of ruling in relation to actions brought by private individuals, companies and in relation to matters of competition law.

5. Court of Auditors

4–015 Through its history, and especially as the European Union has moved up the political agendas of Members States, there has been considerable controversy over its budget. To counter these criticisms, and to improve the EU's financial management, the Court of Auditors was established in 1975 to check that EU funds were being collected and distributed lawfully and in pursuit of their intended purpose. The court is comprised of membership from each of the Member States of the EU. During the 1990s, the Court performed an invaluable role in the pursuit of fraud at the heart of the European Union.

PRINCIPLES OF EU LAW

4–016 The Treaties and the other legislation can only go so far. As is so often the case, gaps are left to be completed and the spirit of the legislation to be filled by the judiciary. In this sense, one might almost argue that the European ideal set down in the Treaty of

Rome and subsequent treaties and also in legislation has been saved by the judicial activism of the Court of Justice of the European Communities. The court has developed the principles of direct and indirect effect bringing international law into private law.

1. Direct effect

Rights and obligations which are generated by EU law may be capable of direct effect.   **4–017** The principle of direct effect is not one which can be found in the Treaties, Regulations or Directives of the European Union, but is one which has been developed by the courts as a means of promoting the European ideals. At this point it is worth mentioning the principle of direct *applicability*, with which it is often confused. Direct applicability is the rule that laws from the EU take effect in all Member States as soon as they are passed without the need for intervention from the state. Consequently, regulations are directly applicable, though directives are not directly applicable.

The principle of direct effect comes from the case of *Van Gend en Loos* [1963] E.C.R. 1. In the case, the applicant imported a product into the Netherlands from Germany. The importation was made the subject of Dutch import taxes which the applicant did not consider he should pay. The validity of the levy was challenged under art.25 (ex 12) EC Treaty, as being contrary to law. In a reference to the Court of Justice of the European Communities, it was determined that the levy was contrary to EU law.

The decision is interesting because it made clear that the Treaty right was directly effective against the national court; this is direct effect. Any individual who is a citizen of a Member State of the European Union is able to use any provision of EU law as a directly effective piece of legislation so long as it satisfies the following criteria:

- it must be clear and unambiguous;

- it must be unconditional; and

- it must require no further action by the Member State for its implementation.

Thus, the effect of the *Van Gend en Loos* case was to render legislation which fell within the criteria as directly effective and capable of application in national courts. *Van Gend en Loos* was a dramatic case in which the court adopted a purposive interpretation, looking at the objective of the Treaty of Rome and its design to establish a European Economic Community by the removal of barriers to trade, etc. Therefore, using that as its influence, the decision turned as it did. The ECJ has continued in the spirit of *Van Gend* and held many Treaty articles to be directly effective.

However, *Van Gend en Loos* was a case against the State, so thereby limited to vertical direct effect, i.e. the idea that the right can be enforced against the State. Could there be horizontal direct effect—the idea that such rights could be enforceable as between individuals in actions in the national court? The question was answered in the case of *Defrenne v Sabena (No.2)* [1976] E.C.R. 455.

In *Defrenne*, the applicant was an air hostess with the Belgian airline, SABENA. She discovered, during the course of her employment, that she was being paid less than her male colleagues doing the same job. She brought an action against the defendant in the airline in the Belgian courts alleging breach of art.141 (ex 119) EC, which provides for equal pay for men and women engaged in the same work. Under the reference procedure, the Belgian court referred certain questions to the ECJ under art.234 (ex 177), the main question being whether the applicant could rely upon the article against her employer. The ECJ held that she was able to do so. The article was not only applicable to employment by the State, but also employment by individuals.

As a consequence of *Defrenne*, an individual is able to plead an article under a Treaty when enforcing rights against another individual in national courts. This principle is of general application and not restricted in its operation to the article in the case. This was as significant a decision as *Van Gend* for though the obligations under a Treaty are addressed to the State, the court allowed their application to operate horizontally. To summarise, the articles of a Treaty have both vertical and horizontal direct effect. But what of other EU law: Regulations and Directives.

(a)   *Regulations*

4–018   Article 249 (ex 189) EC, provides: "A regulation shall have general application. It shall be binding in its entirety and directly applicable in all Member States". Regulations take immediate effect without further implementation; often described as legally perfect instruments. Consequently, one might have thought there would be no issue in there being directly effective both vertically and horizontally, and so the ECJ has found. The former was decided in the case of *Leonesio v Italian Minister of Agriculture* (Case 93/71) [1972] E.C.R. 287, while the latter though assumed to follow from the judgment of the court in *Leonesio*, was conclusively decided in the case of *Antonio Munoz Cia SA v Frumar Ltd* (Case C-253/00) [2002] E.C.R. I-7289.

(b)   *Directives*

4–019   Article 249 (ex 189) EC, provides: "A directive shall be binding, as to the result to be achieved, upon each Member State to which it is addressed, *but shall leave to the national authorities the choice of form and methods*" (my emphasis). Directives create problems for the principle of direct effect as set down in *Van Gend en Loos*. The third requirement for the case to operate is that the law must require no further action by the state for its implementation, but the directive can be implemented at the choice of the Member State. This would have obvious consequences for the principle in European Union law because so much of the legislation which comes from the EU is in the form of directive, and it with this problem that the Court in *Van Duyn v Home Office* (Case 41/74) [1974] E.C.R. 1337 was faced.

However, unbound by difficulties, the ECJ held that a directive can be directly effective provided certain conditions are satisfied:

- terms of the Directive must be clear, precise and unconditional (the *Van Gend en Loos* criteria);

- the date for implementation of the Directive must have passed; and

- the person against whom the Directive is being pleaded must be the State, or an emanation of the State.

The third criterion, namely that the principle of direct effect might only be used against the State, or an emanation thereof, places a restriction on the applicability of Directives which does not operate in respect of Treaty articles, or Regulations. This would seem, in a sense, an artificial distinction. However, the power to implement a directive rests in the hands of the State. Consequently, it would be somewhat unjust to allow an action against a private individual (giving it horizontal effect) when it was not their responsibility to implement the Directive. The fact that direct effect only operates vertically in respect of Directives was confirmed by the ECJ in the case of *Marshall v Southampton & SW Hampshire Area Health Authority* (Case 152/84) [1986] E.C.R. 723.

As strict as the criteria may seem, some room for manoeuvre has been provided by the "emanation of the State" element of the third criterion. The courts have given a very broad definition of what amounts to an emanation of the State. In *Foster v British Gas plc* (Case C-188/89) [1990] E.C.R. I-3133, the ECJ stated:

"a Directive could be relied on against organisations or bodies which were subject to the authority or control of the State, or had special powers beyond those which result from the normal rules applicable to relations between individuals." (para.18)

"a body, whatever its legal form, which has been made responsible, pursuant to a measure adopted by the State, for providing a public service under the control of the State and has for that purpose special powers beyond those which result from the normal rules applicable in relations between individuals." (para.22)

(c) *"Incidental" horizontal direct effect*

No discussion of horizontal effect would be complete without a discussion on "inci-   **4–020** dental" horizontal direct effect. The concept is a tricky one and has at its core an unimplemented piece of EU legislation. It works in the following manner:

(1) a Member State of the European Union has failed to implement a piece of EU legislation;

(2) that Member State has a piece of national legislation which appears to conflict with the unimplemented EU legislation;

(3) the unimplemented piece of EU law is used to disapply the piece of national legislation, rendering it void;

(4) the problem comes because the law which was thought to govern the relationship can no longer apply;

(5) therefore, something else replaces the law which was disapplied by the unimplemented EU legislation;

(6)   parties relationship is affected because the legislation is now disapplied.

The decision looks like one of horizontal effect because the relationship which has been affected by the decision is a private one, however, the fact that it affects their private relationship is merely incidental, hence, "incidental" horizontal direct effect. A good example might be drawn from the case of *Unilever Italia SpA v Central Foods SpA* (C-443/98) [2000] E.C.R. I-7535. The parties had a contract for the supply of olive oil; under an EU Directive which the Italian government had failed to implement, olive oil had to be labelled in a particular way. Instead, there was an Italian national law which conflicted with the EU Directive. The delivery of olive oil was refused on the basis that it failed to comply with Italian law, but the supplier contended that they should take it as it conformed with EU law. The ECJ held, somewhat unsurprisingly, that the EU Directive prevailed with the consequence that the national law was disapplied. However, the Directive did not directly replace the national law, so the court held that the Italian law of contract applied to the delivery and that the olive oil should be accepted by the buyer. The national law was disapplied, but its effect was incidental to the horizontal relationship between the parties.

2.   Indirect effect

4–021   The concept of indirect effect places an obligation on national courts to read national legislation in order to meet the demands of the unimplemented European Union legislation and comes from the case of *Von Colson and Kamann v Land Nordrhein-Westfalen* (Case 14/83) [1984] E.C.R. 1891. In *Von Colson*, two women applied for posts in a German prison, but were unsuccessful. Being suspicious that their rejection was far from on meritorious grounds, and rather based on their gender, they sued under Directive 76/207/EEC—the equal treatment directive. The German state had implemented the Directive, but failed to do so fully. Under the German law so implemented any action for breach of the obligations under the Directive was met by a very limited remedial response which amounted to nothing more than the injured party's expenses. The ECJ held that there was an obligation on the national court to interpret the legislation so as to read in accord with the Directive.

The source for the creation of indirect effect is art.10 (ex 5), EEC which provides that Member States should take all appropriate measures to ensure fulfilment of the obligations arising out of the Treaty or resulting from action taken by the institutions of the Community (paraphrased). In a sense, the *Von Colson* case was an easy one for the courts in that the body was the state, but did indirect effect apply horizontally? In the case of *Marleasing SA* (Case-106/89) [1990] E.C.R. I-4135, the ECJ held that it did.

(a)   *Limitations on the indirect effect interpretation*

4–022   Obviously it is not open to the courts to interpret as freely as they might, and limitations are placed on interpretation so as to give indirect effect to the legislation:

- Legislation can only be interpreted so far as possible compatibly with the unimplemented legislation (*Wagner Miret v Fondo de Garantia Salarial* (Case C-334/92) [1993] E.C.R. I-6911).

- Where it would be contrary to the principles of legal certainty or non-retrospective application of legislation (*Officier van Justitie v. Kolpinghuis Nijmegen* (Case 80/86) [1987] E.C.R. 3969).

- Where interpretation would impose an obligation on an individual under the Directive which had not been transposed (*Luciano Arcaro* (Case C-168/95 [1996] E.C.R. I-4705)). *Cf. Litster v Forth Dry Dock & Engineering Co Ltd* [1990] 1 A.C. 546.

Though indirect effect has had checks placed on its development by the ECJ, it remains an important interpretive tool to ensure protection of private individuals through national courts.

3. State liability

Though these various forms of effect, i.e. direct and indirect effect, and "incidental" **4–023** horizontal direct effect do provide some protection, there are those individuals who continue to fall outside the protection even these attempts have made at guiding EU legislation in a particular direction. As a consequence, and because such individuals have often incurred substantial financial losses, the concept of state liability has been developed.

The concept comes from the case of *Francovich v Italy* (Cases C-6 & 9/90 [1991] E.C.R. I-5357) and operates as a separate principle, not dependent on direct or indirect effect. Again, as with indirect effect, the authority for state liability is drawn from art.10 of the Treaty with the consequence that Member States are under an express obligation to implement Directives correctly, to apply Regulations and to ensure adherence to Treaty obligations. The conditions for recovery are:

- the Directive must involve the conferment of rights on individuals;

- the content of the rights must be identified on the basis of the provisions of the Directive;

- breach must be sufficiently serious; and

- there must be a causal link between the State's failure and the damage suffered.

The principle of state liability is applicable to total failure to implement a Directive, as in *Francovich*, or partial failure as in the case of *Brasserie du Pêcheur* and *Factortame* (Cases C-46 & 48/93 [1996] E.C.R. I-1029).

Once the liability of the state has been established, the amount of compensation is determined by national courts.

CONCLUSION

4-024   European Union law is a central part of the United Kingdom's constitutional framework. Through its institutions and its attempts to forge ever greater ties—Community—it enters more of the United Kingdom's everyday activities. It is important therefore to understand its framework and the effect it can have on the lives of all those who are citizens of its Union.

FURTHER READING

4-025   Johnston, A. "Judicial reform and the Treaty of Nice" (2001) 38 C.M.L.R. 499.
Munro, C. *Studies in Constitutional Law*, 2nd edn (New York: OUP, 1999), Ch.6.
Shaw, J. "The Treaty of Nice: Legal and constitutional implications" (2001) 7 E.P.L. 195.

Chapter 5

THE RULE OF LAW

INTRODUCTION

A. V. Dicey, *Introduction to the Study of the Law of the Constitution* (10th edn (London: **5–001** Macmillan, 1959)) believed the British Constitution (as he called it) rested upon two fundamental principles, the sovereignty of Parliament and the rule of law. Of the two, it was the sovereignty of Parliament which was the dominant force. The rule of law is largely a political principle and in its most basic form means government must act according to the law. It is an important aspect of constitutionalism and in the absence of a codified constitution, the rule of law has become especially important as a way of constraining governmental action. As a result it plays an especially important role in the United Kingdom constitution. The courts play an important part in upholding the rule of law and frequently invoke it as a means to assess whether Executive power has been abused. In recent years, the principal has heavily influenced case law and most radically some judges have suggested the hierarchy with the sovereignty of Parliament has changed and the rule of law is the "ultimate controlling force on which our constitution is based" (Lord Hope in *R. (on the application of Jackson) v Att-Gen* [2005] UKHL 56). The principle has also for the first time found itself specifically mentioned in statute, section 1 of the Constitutional Reform Act 2005 insisting that the Act "does not adversely affect the existing constitutional principle of the rule of law". The first part of this chapter will provide a brief analysis of the definitions of the doctrine including an analysis of Dicey's theory. The second half of the chapter will focus on the practical application of the doctrine in the United Kingdom in the 21st century.

DEFINITION

1.   Meaning of the rule of law

5–002   The meaning of the rule of law is a concept that constitutional scholars and parliamentarians have found notoriously difficult to define. In essence it means that government must act under the law and its rationale is to control the exercise of public
power and ensure that it is exercised according to the law and within legal limits. In this
sense the rule of law is part of the principle of constitutionalism. There are two main
camps in interpretation of the rule of law: procedural and substantive.

2.   Procedural or formal conceptions of the rule of law

5–003   Definitions of the rule of law in this camp see the principle as a procedural mechanism
and emphasise the need for rules and procedures to control and limit power. Formal
conceptions of the rule of law do not say anything about the content of laws but are
merely concerned that law has been passed in the correct manner. Joseph Raz writing in
1977 is a strong advocate of the formal approach ("The rule of law and its virtue"
(1977) 93 L.Q.R. 195) and believes that the rule of law is a political ideal that individuals should be ruled by the law and the law must be able to guide individuals so that
they can plan their life accordingly.
　　Raz's theory contains eight principles:

(1)　the law should be general, prospective, open and clear;

(2)　law should be relatively stable and not subject to frequent and unnecessary
alterations;

(3)　open, stable, clear and general rules should govern Executive law making.
This means that delegated legislation should be enacted in the context of more
detailed ground rules laid down in general laws;

(4)　independence of the judiciary must be guaranteed;

(5)　application of law should accord with the rules of natural justice. This
includes the right to a fair hearing and the right to have a decision made free
from bias. Jowell (below) has argued that this is one of the central features of
the rule of law;

(6)　courts should have power of review over law making and administrative
action to ensure compliance;

(7)　courts should be easily accessible (no delays and unnecessary expense). In *R. v
Lord Chancellor Ex p. Witham* [1997] 2 All E.R. 779, Mr Witham complained
that increased court fees denied him access to justice as he could not afford to
pay them. He was unable to obtain legal aid as it was unavailable for his

course of action (defamation). Justice Laws stated "access to the courts is a constitutional right. It can only be denied by the government if it persuades Parliament". This principle of Raz's is also enshrined within art.6 of the European Convention of Human Rights which guarantees the right to a fair trial and access to the Courts;

(8)   discretion of the police, prosecuting authorities and courts should not be allowed to pervert the law.

The application of Raz's idea can be seen in a number of cases. In *Phillips v Eye* (1870) L.R. 6 QB1, Willes J. noted:

"Retrospective laws are, no doubt, prima facie of questionable policy, and contrary to the general principle that legislation by which the conduct of mankind is to be regulated ought, when introduced for the first time, to deal with future acts ... Accordingly, the courts will not ascribe retrospective force to new laws affecting rights, unless by express words or necessary implication it appears that such was the intention of the legislature."

Here the rule of law acts as a principle of statutory interpretation and gives the courts discretion to interpret in accordance with the rule of law unless Parliament's intention is clear. One problem in the United Kingdom constitution is the position of the common law. As the common law is declared by the courts, by its nature it is necessarily retrospective. In *R. v R.* [1992] 1 A.C. 599, the appellant was convicted of attempted rape of his wife who had left the matrimonial home a few days earlier. The husband had argued his conviction was based on an act which was not an offence when it was committed; at the time there was a common law exception to marital rape. The House of Lords removed the common law exception and dismissed his appeal. The defendant took his case to the European Court of Human Rights on the grounds that this amounted to a retrospective offence contrary to ECHR art.7, *SW and CW v UK* (1996) 21 E.H.R.R. 363. The ECtHR disagreed, recognising the House of Lord's decision as reasonably foreseeable and a natural development of the law (see also discussion of this case in relation to separation of powers, Ch.6).

The principles espoused by Raz are also key principles of the European Convention of Human Rights which, by virtue of the Human Rights Act 1998, is now applicable domestically. For any interference under the European Convention to be legitimate it must be "in accordance with (or prescribed by) a law". In *Sunday Times v UK* (1979–80) 2 E.H.R.R. 245 the European Court of Human Rights gave consideration to the meaning of the phrase and found that it must meet the following requirements:

(1)   there must a legal basis for the restriction, i.e. there must a law. This can be either statute or common law (known as the principle of legality);

(2)   the law must be adequately accessible. This means that an individual must be able to have an indication of the legal rules applicable in any given case. This must be what is adequate in the circumstances;

(3)   the law must be formulated with sufficient precision to enable the citizen to regulate his conduct. By this, an individual must be able to foresee, to a degree that is reasonable in the circumstances, the consequences of his action. This does not equate to absolute certainty as excessive rigidity should be avoided. Laws are often couched in vague terms requiring judicial interpretation.

One key point is that the rule of law as articulated by Raz is concerned with whether or not a system is a legal system, not whether we approve of the outcomes it produces. The rule of law is not concerned with the content of the law. This of course means that a government could pass laws that are open, clear, prospective but morally wrong or interfere with individual rights. The decision in *Inland Revenue Commissioners (Appellants) v Rossminster Ltd (Respondents)* [1980] A.C. 952 plays this out well. The case concerned the validity of a warrant issued under s.20c of the Taxes Management Act 1970 (as amended). The Act prescribed that if a judge was satisfied that there was "reasonable grounds for suspecting that an offence involving any form of fraud in connection with, or in relation to, tax" had been committed, and that evidence of the fraud could be found within an address specified by the IRC, the judge could issue a warrant authorising search of the premises and removal of anything they had reasonable cause to believe was evidence of such a fraud. A warrant issued under this section did not need to specify the suspected offence or give particulars of the persons suspected of them. A warrant under s.20 was issued against Rossminster Ltd and others, under which the IRC entered homes and took papers including personal letters belonging to other members of the family and children's school reports. As Lord Denning pointed out in the Court of Appeal, this was a "military style operation". Rossminster Ltd brought an action alleging the warrants were invalid as they should have given some indication of what was being searched for. Overruling the Court of Appeal, the House of Lords found the warrants to be lawful. Section 20 did not require the warrant to state what criminal offence or offences are suspected. The majority of the House of Lords were prepared to question the vagueness and uncertainty of the Act but accepted that as the requirements of the statute had been met, then the action was in accordance with law. What this case shows us is that as long as the law has been followed then action under even a "bad" law is legitimate and in accordance with the rule of law.

While adherence to the idea of the rule of law above provides no guarantees as to the outcomes a legal system may produce, it works to ensure internal consistency. If the above premises are observed an individual will be guided by the law and certain of their position within a society in given circumstances. This is the value of Raz's analysis.

3.   Substantive conceptions of the rule of law

5–004   The second camp sees the rule of law as having a substantive element to it. In essence, laws passed should conform to the procedural requirements and encapsulate certain fundamental values such as human rights. Under this camp, s.20 of the Taxes Management Act (above) which permitted interference with individual property rights would fall foul of the rule of law. Paul Craig, "Formal and Substantial Conceptions of the Rule of Law: an Analytical Framework" (1997) P.L. 467 summarises the two camps:

"Formal concepts of the rule of law address the manner in which the law was promulgated. Formal conceptions of the rule of law do not however seek to pass judgment upon the actual content of the law itself. They are concerned with whether the law was a good or bad law. Those who espouse substantive conceptions of the rule of law seek to go beyond this. They accept that the rule of law has the formal attributes but wish to take the doctrine further. Certain substantive rights are said to be based on or derived from the rule of law."

Proponents of the substantive camp include Ronald Dworkin, *A Matter of Principle* (Harvard University Press, 1985, pp.11–12) who terms this second conception the rights conception. He sees the rule of law as requiring substantive justice, "it requires, as part of the ideal of law, that the rules in the book capture and enforce moral rights". Other theorists in this camp include Sir John Laws (see "Law and Democracy" (1995) P.L. 72; "The Constitution: Morals and Rights" (1996) P.L. 622), Trevor Allan and Lon Fuller (*The Morality of Law* (New Haven: Yale University Press, 1964)). Fuller's focus was on the morality of law. He believed that for a system to be a legal system it must have an "inner morality". A government must seek to provide the environment in which each citizen can reach his maximum potential, society must be free and directed to the good of each of its members. Failure to achieve this would mean the system had failed to meet the standards of a legal system. Jeffrey Jowell, "The Rule of Law and its underlying values" in *The Changing Constitution* (6th edn, OUP, 2007, p.5) also believes the rule of law to have a substantive element to it. He feels that the rule of law is a principle of institutional morality which he argues is manifest in courts willingness to strike down Executive action if unreasonable, arbitrary or capricious.

Until recently, the application of the substantive conception of the rule of law was thin. In *Rossminster* (above), Lord Denning in the Court of Appeal applied a substantive interpretation to his reasoning. In assessing the validity of the warrant he concluded that in pursuance of the traditional role of the court to protect the liberty of the individual he should interpret the statute, and therefore the warrant, to require particularisation of the specific offence. His interpretation was of course subsequently overturned by the House of Lords. More recently, in two cases before the House of Lords, *R. (on the application of A) v Secretary of State for Home Department* [2004] UKHL 56 (detention of foreign nationals suspected of terrorism) and [2005] UKHL 71 (use of evidence obtained under torture), the House of Lords appeared to apply substantive conceptions to their reasoning. In the first *A* case, Lord Hoffman for example, drew attention to the fact that laws such as the Anti-Terrorism Crime and Security Act 2001 which authorised indefinite detention of foreign nationals suspected of terrorism were incompatible with our constitution (at para.98) and were the "real threat to the life of the nation".

4.   Legal concept: the principle of legality

The rule of law can be seen as a principle of legality which operates as a procedural **5–005** mechanism controlling and limiting the exercise of governmental power. In many constitutions this principle is given direct expression for example, art.20 of the German

Constitution states, "the Executive and judiciary are bound by the law". In the UK constitution, the principle of legality operates as an important constraint ensuring that officials act in accordance with the law (see *Entick v Carrington* (1765) 19 St. Tr. 1029). In *R. v Secretary of State for the Home Department Ex p. Simms* [1999] 3 All E.R. 400, the court invoked the principle of legality to preclude statutory interference with rights unless expressly provided for in statute. Simms and another had been convicted of murder and claimed to be victims of miscarriages of justice. Under the Prison Rules they were refused permission to give interviews with journalists unless the journalists gave an undertaking not to publish any part of the interviews. The House of Lords held the blanket ban on interviews with prisoners was unlawful. Lord Hoffman gave expression to the principle of legality, stating:

> "But the principle of legality means that Parliament must squarely confront what it is doing and accept the political cost. Fundamental rights cannot be overridden by general or ambiguous words. This is because there is too great a risk that the full implications of their unqualified meaning may have passed unnoticed in the democratic process. In the absence of express language or necessary implication to the contrary, the courts therefore presume that even the most general words were intended to be subject to the basic rights of the individual. In this way the courts in the United Kingdom, though acknowledging the sovereignty of Parliament, apply principles, of constitutionality little different from those which exist in countries where the power of the legislature is expressly limited by a constitutional document."

5.   The rule of law in international law

5–006   The rule of law is often used in an international context and as we have seen it finds expression in the European Convention on Human Rights. The European Union make reference to it in the 1997 Treaty of Amsterdam when it states that the European Union is founded on respect for democratic principles, human rights and the rule of law. The Preamble to the Universal Declaration of Human Rights (1948) adopted by the General Assembly of the United Nations also confirms respect for human rights and the rule of law:

> "Whereas it is essential, if man is not to be compelled to have recourse, as a last resort, to rebellion against tyranny and oppression, that human rights should be protected by the rule of law."

What is clear from this expression is the link between human rights and the rule of law; this gives their interpretation of the principle a substantive element.

See also the Declaration of Delhi, issued by the International Commission of Jurists in 1959.

THE RULE OF LAW IN THE BRITISH CONSTITUTION

In the UK, the rule of law has been closely associated with the work of A.V. Dicey, **5–007**
Introduction to the Study of the Law of the Constitution (1959). Dicey's rule of law had
three meanings: firstly, an individual would only be punished for a distinct breach of the
law and the predominance of regular law over arbitrary power; secondly, equality
before the law and, thirdly, the principles of the constitution are the result of the
ordinary law decided by the courts. Dicey's ideas have been heavily criticised but they
have had an influence over the development of administrative law in the UK and so
they still provides a useful starting point when assessing the significance of the principle
in the UK.

DICEY AND THE RULE OF LAW

1.   Dicey's first strand

According to Dicey the rule of law means: **5–008**

> " ... no man is punishable or can be lawfully made to suffer in body or goods
> except for a distinct breach of law established in the ordinary legal manner before
> the ordinary courts of the land ... It means, in the first place, the absolute
> supremacy or predominance of regular law as opposed to the influence of arbitrary
> power, and excludes the existence of arbitrariness, of prerogative, or even of wide
> discretionary authority on the part of the government." (pp.188 and 202)

This principle can be broken down into two further strands: firstly, an individual is only
punishable for a distinct breach of the law and secondly, the absence of arbitrary power
and supremacy of regular law. The first strand encapsulates the general idea of the rule
of law that action must have a legal basis. This principle has been a key requirement in
the UK constitution since the decision in *Entick v Carrington* (1765) 19 St. Tr. 1029. In
this case, agents of the King acting under authority of a general warrant issued by the
Secretary of State, entered Entick's property and seized papers. Entick successfully sued
for trespass, the court holding that the Secretary of State had no specific legal foundation for the issue of the warrant.

In the second strand, Dicey argued the predominance of regular law and the absence
of wide discretionary power which he equated with arbitrary action. He believed that
wide discretionary power lacked clear legal parameters which made it difficult for an
individual to challenge if abused by an official. Dicey appeared to underestimate the
degree of discretionary power that government had at the time through the Crown, for
example, prerogative power. Importantly Dicey also ignored the fact that discretionary
power is a necessary consequence of the growth of governmental power. Jennings, *The
Law and the Constitution* (1933) delivered a particularly strong attack on Dicey here and

felt it implicitly promoted Dicey's political views. Dicey was of the laissez faire school
and had resisted the increasing regulatory role of the state.

Far from being a negative, it is clear that in a modern state discretion is necessary. It
enables a government to perform its functions efficiently and justly and mitigates the
harshness of law. For example, the welfare state system requires the use of discretion to
be effective. Certainly, discretion if left unchecked has the ability to interfere with the
rule of law. As we saw in *Rossminster* (discussed above), the wide powers given to the
Inland Revenue Commissioners enabled them to enter a person's property and take
whatever they deemed necessary without any effective control from the courts. However, rather then attack its existence, it is better to ensure there is a good system of
control. In the UK, the growth of delegated legislation has brought about a corresponding growth in the legal mechanisms of control, judicial review.

2.   Dicey's second strand

5–009   Dicey's second strand referred to equality before the law. He stated:

> " . . . not only that with us no man is above the law, but (what is a different thing)
> that here every man, whatever be his rank or condition, is subject to the ordinary
> law of the realm and amenable to the jurisdiction of the ordinary tribunals . . .
> equality before the law, or the equal subjugation of all classes to the ordinary law
> of the law administered by the ordinary courts." (pp.193 and 202)

Dicey's formulation is essentially concerned with formal equality. His strand does not
prohibit unequal laws but simply requires that all individuals are treated equally under
the ordinary laws of the land. So for example, if a state official breached the law they
would be treated in any litigation the same as ordinary citizens; *Entick v Carrington*
nicely illustrates this principle. In *Entick*, the officials of the state who had entered
Entick's property and taken papers were sued in exactly the same way a private individual would have been.

The idea of all being subject to the same law was at play in *M v Home Office* [1994] 1
A.C. 377. M, a citizen of Zaire, was unsuccessful in seeking political asylum in the UK.
On the day he was scheduled to be deported from the UK he made a renewed application for judicial review. Garland J. stayed M's departure so he could consider the new
evidence and believed he had received an undertaking from a Home Office official to
this effect. Due to a breakdown in communication M was placed on a plane by
immigration officials. Garland then issued a "without notice" order, a mandatory
injunction, requiring the Home Secretary to procure M's return. The Home Secretary
determined that his underlying asylum decision had been correct and that the mandatory injunction against a Minister of the Crown had been made without jurisdiction.
As a result, arrangements for M's return were cancelled. Proceedings were then brought
against the Home Office and the Home Secretary alleging contempt of court. The
House of Lords held that the construct of the Crown had two personalities: the
monarch and the government. While a finding of contempt could not lie against the
monarch, it could lie against a Minister acting in his/her official capacity, but not in a

personal capacity. Lord Templeman stated: " ... the argument that there is no power to enforce the law by injunction or contempt proceedings against a minister in his official capacity would, if upheld, establish the proposition that the Executive obey the law as a matter of grace and not as a matter of necessity, a proposition which would reverse the result of the Civil War" (p.395). The Home Secretary was thus guilty of contempt of court.

One criticism of Dicey's formulation of equality is at the time he was writing there were, as William Robson, *Justice and Administrative Law* (2nd edn (London: Macmillan, 1928), p.342) pointed out, "colossal distinctions" between the rights and duties of private individuals and government officials. Many of these distinctions still exist today for example, the Crown and Members of Parliament enjoy special immunities; s.20 of the State Immunity Act 1978 and art.9 of the Bill of Rights 1688 respectively; judges have immunity provided they act within their jurisdiction and diplomats enjoy legal immunity under the Diplomatic Privileges Act 1964.

Another equally forceful criticism was Dicey's dismissal of the French administrative system, "*droit administratif*". Dicey felt that a separate system of administrative law would be automatically biased towards the Executive. William Robson, *Justice and Administrative Law* (2nd edn, 1928, p.342) heavily criticised Dicey, arguing that Dicey laboured under a misapprehension as to the role of the French administrative system. As the French system was staffed by experts far from being automatically biased towards government, it enabled them to better work out the extent of official liability. One clear negative that arose from Dicey's view here was the delay in the growth of an administrative law system in the UK. The UK now has a separate administrative court, staffed by experts who apply special rules of procedure and principles in matters against the Executive (judicial review). The court is however, still part of the existing court system and does not sit outside it.

3.   Dicey's third strand

Dicey in his third strand stated: **5–010**

> "We may say that the constitution is pervaded by the rule of law on the ground that the general principles of the constitution (as for example the right to personal liberty, or the right of public meeting) are with us the result of judicial decisions determining the rights of private persons in particular cases brought before the courts ... with us the law of the constitution, the rules which in foreign countries naturally form part of a constitutional code, are not the source but the consequence of the rights of individuals, as defined and enforced by the courts." (pp.195 and 203)

Firstly, Dicey is recognising the principles of the constitution arise from the judges declaring the common law. He also draws a comparison with foreign constitutions; in particular he argued that civil liberties were better protected through the common law than through a constitutional code, i.e. written constitution. In *Entick v Carrington* for example, Entick sued the state official in the ordinary law of trespass and did not have to rely on any constitutional code. Dicey was of the view that this practical approach provided a better remedy and protection of rights than those on the continent. He considered Bills of Rights to be ineffective as a mechanism for protection of rights since they could be easily dismissed by government, whereas rights developed under the common law would be harder to get rid of as they have been built up as a result of numerous court decisions.

Dicey's ideal that the common law is the better way to protect individual rights is not always borne out by the cases. When Dicey was writing the UK had a system of residual or negative rights which meant you were free to do anything not prohibited by law. This of course meant that such rights could be easily eroded by statute, as was done when Parliament passed the War Damages Act 1965 to nullify the effect of a judicial decision granting compensation for damage caused by the government. At the time Dicey was writing there was minimal statutory interference in individual lives; now it is common place. The principle of parliamentary sovereignty also means that once enacted a statute cannot be challenged on grounds of procedure or substance. However, note needs to be taken here of *R. (on the application of Jackson) v Att-Gen* [2005] UKHL 56 (for facts see Ch.7). Lords Steyn and Hope made obiter comments to the effect that Parliament's unlimited legislative ability may in future have to give way to rights and/or the rule of law.

However, the courts can only protect an individual if a particular right had been recognised by the common law or statute. Such a situation arose in *Malone v MPC* [1979] Ch. 344 involving the tapping of Malone's telephone. Malone argued this interfered with his right to privacy but was unsuccessful because, as Lord Justice Glidewell said, "it is well known that in English law there is no right to privacy".

The enactment of the Human Rights Act 1998 would appear to be at odds with Dicey's third strand as it provides a positive enactment of rights in the UK. However, the decisions of the courts are central to the operation of this Act and in a sense, can buttress Dicey's position, giving greater protection in the face of statutory interference. While the courts do not have the power to strike down legislation, they have been given wide powers of interpretation under s.3 which can be used effectively. In addition, any law that cannot be interpreted but is deemed incompatible with human rights can be declared so under s.4. While this does not mean the law has to be changed, invariably that has been the end result. See for example, *R. (on the application of A) v Secretary of State for Home Department* [2004] UKHL 56.

THE RULE OF LAW IN THE UNITED KINGDOM—ITS MODERN APPLICATION

5–011 The significance of the rule of law in the UK should not be underemphasised and as shown, the courts have often used the principle to underpin their decisions. In *Entick v Carrington* (as discussed above), for example, the principle played an important role in ensuring the Secretary of State had legal justification for his action. Similarly in *R. v Horseferry Road Magistrates' Court Ex p. Bennett* [1994] 1 A.C. 42 the court used the principle to justify controlling Executive behaviour after the government had illegally kidnapped Bennett, a New Zealand citizen. Bennett was kidnapped from South Africa and brought to England to face criminal charges without regard to his rights and the extradition Treaty. The issue was whether the unlawful abduction of Bennett was an abuse of power. The House of Lords, by majority, held it was and as a result, his prosecution was stayed. Lord Griffiths stated at pp.61-61:

"... In the present case there is no suggestion that the appellant cannot have a fair trial, nor could it be suggested that it would have been unfair to try him if he had been returned to this country through extradition procedures. If the court is to have the power to interfere with the prosecution in the present circumstances it must be because the judiciary accept a responsibility for the maintenance of the rule of law that embraces a willingness to oversee Executive action and to refuse to countenance behaviour that threatens either basic human rights or the rule of law."

In a more recent case, *R. (on the application of Anufrijeva) v Secretary of State for the Home Department* [2003] 3 W.L.R. 252, the rule of law was again brought in as a principle underpinning the courts decision. In this case a decision concerning termination of income support following refusal of asylum was not communicated to the individual. Lord Steyn in the House of Lords held this violated the "constitutional principle requiring the rule of law to be observed" (para.28).

1.   Judicial deference and the rule of law

One particular area of concern has been the area of national security and discretionary power. Historically, in such cases, the courts have been very deferential to the actions of the Executive. In doing so they allow discretionary power to be potentially abused by not providing an effective check on its use. In failing to do this they are also compromising the rule of law. One case that illustrates this approach well is *Liversidge v Anderson* [1942] A.C. 206. This case concerned the interpretation of reg.18B of the Defence (General) Regulations 1939 which allowed the Secretary of State to detain any person if he had "reasonable cause to believe" that person was of hostile origin or association. Mr Liversidge was detained under the power and brought an action for unlawful detention. The issue for the House of Lords was the interpretation of "reasonable" and whether the power given to the Secretary of State was subjective or objective. The majority held that the court could not inquire as to whether in fact the Minister had reasonable grounds. In the minority, Lord Atkin believed the condition for detention under reg.18B was objective rather than subjective and claimed the authority for detention given to the Secretary of State was conditional upon reasonableness. He concluded that if Parliament had wished to give the Home Secretary unlimited discretion it would not have qualified the grant of power with the word "reasonable". The use of the word reasonable suggested there needed to be in existence facts that led to the conclusion to detain; mere belief was not sufficient.

In this case Lord Atkin saw judges as standing between the citizen and the State and any attempted encroachment on their liberty by the Executive should be justified with reference to law. In a strongly worded dissent, Lord Atkin accused the majority of

5–012

being "more executive minded than the executive". He believed the function of the court was to give words their natural meaning. While he recognised the existence of the state of war, he concluded that legislation during such time speak the same language as at any other time and should not be strained because of the situation. While much criticised at the time, Lord Atkin's approach is closer now to judicial orthodoxy.

In a similar deferential approach, the Court of Appeal considered where a case raised a conflict between the freedom of the individual on one hand and the interests of national security on the other, the balance between the two was not a matter for the courts. Such was the conclusion in *R. v Secretary of State for Home Department Ex p. Hosenball* [1977] 1 W.L.R. 700. Here an American journalist was issued with a deportation notice under the auspices of national security pursuant to s.3 of the Immigration Act 1971. It was alleged that Hosenball has obtained information harmful to security. Hosenball was informed he could make representations but could not appeal the decision; the Secretary of State declined to provide further information as to the particulars. Hosenball's judicial review was denied, the Court of Appeal holding that the principles of natural justice were modified when national security was involved and public policy necessitated the withholding of information.

By contrast to the above, in *R. (on the application of A) v Secretary of State for Home Department* [2005] UKHL 51, the House of Lords in a surprising and strong 8–1 majority decision declared the government's practice of detaining foreign nationals suspected of terrorism to be incompatible with art.5, right to liberty, in the European Convention on Human Rights. The case concerned a number of foreign nationals who were detained in Belmarsh maximum security prison without trial. Detention was authorised under s.23 of the Anti-Terrorism and Crime and Security Act 2001, passed in the aftermath of September 11, 2001. The individuals could not be deported because of allegations of serious risk to their lives if they were returned to their home countries (prohibited under ECHR art.3) and as the government did not want to release them, they were indefinitely detained. Such detention was clearly incompatible with art.5(1) of the ECHR, right to liberty and security of persons, so the government obtained a derogation from the article under art.15 of the ECHR which then lawfully permitted the interference. The question for the House of Lords was whether the critieria for the derogation under art.15 was met; two questions were considered:

(1)   Whether there was an public emergency threatening the life of the nation.

(2)   Whether the measures taken under the emergency was strictly required by the exigencies of the situation (proportionate).

(a)   *Emergency threatening the life of the nation*

5–013   The majority of the House of Lords did not disturb the Court of Appeal's decision and considered themselves ill-equipped to deal with the question; the exception to this was Lord Hoffman. Lord Bingham placed considerable emphasis on *Lawless v Ireland (No.3)* (1961) 1 E.H.R.R. 15, a case concerned with very low level IRA terrorist activity in Ireland and Northern Ireland between 1954 and 1957 and on decisions such as *Ireland v UK* (A/25) (1979–80) 2 E.H.R.R. 25, ECHR and *Brannigan v UK* (1993) 17

E.H.R.R. 539. In these cases, the European Court of Human Rights accorded a wide "margin of appreciation" to the nation state. This meant that the ECtHR felt the state was best placed to know what the national security situation was and so they accorded them a lot of discretion (deference) in making their decisions. Lord Bingham concluded that the court should equally give much discretion to the Executive because it was essentially a political judgment (see para.29). Lord Bingham drew a clear distinction between the first and second question though, interestingly, he observed that if the government were to decide there was a public emergency when clearly there was not, then it would be the duty of the court to intervene. So even though Lord Bingham (and the others) were being deferential they were not prepared to abdicate all responsibility in the future, arguably a change from the majority position in *Liversidge*.

Lord Hoffman took a different approach and started from the position that detention without trial was antithetical to instincts and traditions of the people of the UK (see para.86). He thought the margin of appreciation relied on by Lord Bingham to be irrelevant. At para.96, Lord Hoffman stated, "terrorist violence, serious as it is, does not threaten our institutions of government or our existence as a civil community". He went on to say, "The real threat to the life of the nation, in the sense of a people living in accordance with its traditional laws and political values, comes not from terrorism but from laws such as these. That is the real measure of what terrorism may achieve". Lord Hoffman's reasoning is certainly robust and places the emphasis firmly on the state to convincingly justify that the relevant threat exists. There is some attraction to his argument that when considering the suspension of fundamental rights there must be a threat to the values, institutions and way of life of a nation rather than the threat of large scale loss of life. Such argument places the protection of fundamental rights firmly at the forefront of judicial consideration. However Lord Hoffman's test for when there may be a threat to the life of the nation can be criticised as being unrealistically high; he mentions the threat of Hitler as possibly justifying it.

(b) *"Strictly required by the exigencies of the situation" (proportionate)*

Their Lordships approached the second question quite differently. Although they recognised deference was important, the Law Lords did not accept that because it was national security they should accord a high degree of deference or that judicial decision making in this area was undemocratic. Lord Rodgers at (para.176) stated "due deference does not mean abasement before [the] views [of government and Parliament]". Seven Law Lords concluded that the measures (i.e. the indefinite detention) was not strictly required, a number of reasons were given. Firstly, s.23 only applied to foreign nationals. There was no logical reason for such a distinction unless there was no UK national that posed a threat. The House of Lords were disinclined to believe that was the case so concluded that the government had found an alternative way of dealing with them. Secondly, the government was happy for the foreign nationals to voluntarily leave the UK and for example go to France. The Law Lords found this hard to reconcile as they could surely pursue their criminal intentions as easily from abroad and so would still pose a threat to the UK. Thirdly, the government had not shown whether monitoring arrangements or restrictions of movements could work. As a result of this

5–014

conclusion the House of Lords found the derogation to be unlawful and quashed the derogation order. This in turn led to a declaration of incompatibility regarding s.23.

Previously, as seen above in *Liversidge v Anderson*, the courts had been willing to defer to the Executive in times of emergency. The decision in *A* represents an important development in the relationship between government and the courts and shows the courts taking a much more robust approach. The incorporation of direct protection of human rights through the Human Rights Act 1998 has given the courts vast power which they can use to control Executive excesses. The decision in *A* suggests that the courts are taking a more substantive approach to their analysis and application of the principle relying on the HRA to give them legitimacy. Commentary of the case has noted the significance of the decision in these terms. Dame Marden ((2005) L.Q.R. 604) has stated the decision "is a powerful statement by the highest court in the land of what it means to live in a society where the Executive is subject to the rule of law". Elliot in *Beatson, Matthews and Elliott's Administrative Law: Text and Materials* (OUP, 2005) notes that this break with tradition is an important milestone in the development of human rights and the doctrine of deference.

SUMMARY

5–015 The rule of law is an important principle in the UK constitution and an essential element of constitutionalism. In recent years there appears to have been a movement towards employing the rule of law in both its procedural and substantive conceptions as justification for judicial interference in controlling the Executive. In *R. (on the application of Jackson) v Att-Gen* [2005] UKHL 56, obiter comments by some of the Law Lords seemed to suggest that in the future this will continue. Lord Hope for example, took the view that "the rule of law enforced by the courts is the ultimate controlling factor on which our constitution is based" (at para.107). A similar view was taken by Baroness Hale who noted that "the courts will treat with particular suspicion (and might even reject) any attempt to subvert the rule of law by removing governmental action affecting the rights of the individual from all judicial powers" (at para.159). What will be interesting is to see how far the courts can employ the principle in forthcoming cases dealing with the terrorist threat and other threats to national security.

FURTHER READING

5–016   Allen, T.R.S. *Constitutional Justice: A Liberal Theory of the Rule of Law* (OUP, 2001)
Arden (2005) 121 L.Q.R. 604
Bingham, T. "Dicey Revisited" (2002) P.L. 39
Bradley, A. and Ewing, K. *Constitutional and Administrative Law*, 14th edn (Pearson, 2006), Ch.6

Craig, P. "Formal and Substantial Conceptions of the Rule of Law: an Analytical Framework" (1997) P.L. 467

Dicey, A.V. *Introduction to the Study of the Law of the Constitution*, 10th edn by E.C.S. Wade (London: Macmillan, 1959), Ch.4

Elliott, M.C. *Beatson, Matthews and Elliott's Administrative Law: Text and Materials* (OUP, 2005), in particular the appendix

Jennings, I. *The Law and the Constitution*, 5th edn (London: University of London Press, 1959)

Jowell, J. "The Rule of Law Today". In J. Jowell and D. Oliver (eds) *The Changing Constitution*, 6th edn (OUP, 2007)

Laws, J. "Law and Democracy" (1995) P.L. 72

Laws, J. "The Constitution: Morals and Rights" (1996) P.L. 622

Raz, J. "The Rule of Law and Its virtue" (1977) 93 L.Q.R. 195

Woolf, "The Rule of law and a change in the constitution" (2004) C.L.J. 317

Chapter 6

SEPARATION OF POWERS

INTRODUCTION

In 1887 Lord Acton famously stated, "Power tends to corrupt, and absolute power **6–001** corrupts absolutely. Great men are almost always bad men" (April 3, 1887 in a letter to the Bishop of London, Mandell Creighton). The principle of constitutionalism requires that powers of the state be sufficiently dispersed so as to avoid concentration of powers which might damage liberty and democracy. Separation of powers is a political doctrine and, like the rule of law, is a key element of constitutionalism. It prescribes that the functions of a state, executive, legislative and judicial, be separate in order that none should have excessive power. If you asked an observer whether the United Kingdom constitution has a separation of powers between its three organs of state, for many the answer would be a clear no. Yet to say that is to see only half the picture and to focus on the abstract rather than its exercise in practice. It is fair to say that the United Kingdom does not conform to any absolute form of the separation of powers common in many constitutions. Its version is unique and will always be so considering the UK's historical development over hundreds of years and its unbroken past. Any study of the separation of powers in the United Kingdom cannot be undertaken without an awareness of this historical development. The doctrine has certainly been influential in the development of constitutional structures notably the independence of the judiciary and none more so than in recent years with the passage of the Constitutional Reform Act 2005. This chapter will consider the evolution and definition of the doctrine and the constitutional significance of the doctrine in the United Kingdom in the 21st century.

THE DOCTRINE OF SEPARATION OF POWERS

1. Historical development

6–002 The doctrine of separation of powers can be traced back to Greece and Aristotle, *Politics* (Bk iv, xiv 1297b35) who identified three elements of a constitution; "the deliberative, which discusses everything of common importance; ... the officials, and ... the judicial element". Aristotle stated that if the three elements were "well arranged, the constitution is bound to be well arranged, and the differences in constitution are bound to correspond to the differences between each of these elements".

F.W. Maitland, *The Constitutional History of England* (Cambridge University Press, 1920) traces evidence of the doctrine within the UK constitution to the reign of Edward I (1272–1307) when the functions of the state became more separate. Much constitutional writing in the eighteenth century concentrated on the respective allocation of functions between the organs of state and of the importance of independence of the judiciary. The views of Locke and Montesquieu became especially influential during this period. Locke in his *Second Treatise of Civil Government* 1689 (Laslett (ed.), 1960) believed that the legislative and Executive functions should be placed in separate hands and insisted upon the supremacy of the legislative function. Bolingbroke writing in 1748 (*Remarks on the History of England*) recognised the protection of liberty within the state depended upon maintaining equilibrium between the Crown, Parliament and its people. In relation to the English constitution (as it then was) he noted, "In a constitution like ours, the safety of the whole depends on the balance of the parts".

2. Montesquieu

6–003 Though there is early evidence of the doctrine existing both in theory and in practice, it is the writing of Montesquieu who is credited with the modern expression. Charles Louis de Secondat, Baron Montesquieu was a French aristocrat and judge who having toured England from 1729 to 1731 was a confirmed admirer of English liberty and the political arrangements that gave rise to it. In his book on government, *De L'Esprit des Lois* (Bk xi, Ch. 6, 1748), Montesquieu gave an account of the English constitution and it was during this chapter that he outlined the doctrine of separation of powers.

There are three aspects to Montesquieu's theory. Firstly, he recognised that government had three main functions "that of making laws, that of executing public affairs, and that of adjudicating on crimes or individual cases". Secondly, he stipulated that there should be three corresponding organs of government; the legislature, the Executive and the judiciary. Finally, he stated that these three functions should be held by three separate branches in order to uphold and protect liberty:

"When the legislative and Executive powers are united in the same person, or in the same body of magistrates, there can be no liberty ... Again, there is no liberty if the power of judging is not separated from the legislative and Executive. If it were joined with the legislative, the life and liberty of the subject would be exposed to arbitrary control; for the judge would then be the legislator. If it were joined to the Executive power, the judge might behave with violence and oppression. There would be an end to everything, if the same man, or the same body, whether of the nobles or the people, were to exercise those three powers, that of enacting laws, that of executing public affairs, and that of trying crimes or individual causes."

It is possible to interpret the final sentence above as Montesquieu advocating a complete or strict separation of powers. Munro (*Studies in Constitutional Law*, (2nd edn (London: Butterworths, 2001), p.301) states though this is a possible interpretation, it is not clear which of the several forms of separation Montesquieu is describing. Subsequent interpretations of Montesquieu (for example Jennings), have argued that Montesquieu was not advocating a strict or complete separation of powers. For Montesquieu, the genius of the British system of government lay in combining separation with supervision. Although, Montesquieu stated neither the legislature nor the Executive should exercise the power of the other, he did not mean that they should have no influence over the other. In other words, Montesquieu recognised that there should be some overlapping or checks between the three organs, "constant experience shews us, that every man invested with power is apt to abuse it, and to carry his authority as far as it will go. Is it not strange, though true, to say, that virtue itself has need of limits". However, the independence of the judiciary must not to be compromised in any way.

3. Checks and balances?

Whether or not a state accords to the doctrine depends entirely on the interpretation **6–004** given to it. Geoffrey Marshall (*Constitutional Theory* ((Oxford: Clarendon Press, 1971), p.124) believed that the phrase separation of powers was one of the most confusing in the vocabulary of political and constitutional thought. He thought it to be "infected with so much imprecision and inconsistency that it may be counted little more than a jumbled portmanteau of arguments for policies".

For some proponents, the separation of powers necessitates a strict operation with no organ encroaching on the area of the others; in terms of both personnel and/or functions. For those proponents, a system of checks and balances would interfere with the doctrine. Those who disagree with this view argue that such a formulation of the doctrine is extreme and doctrinaire. Bradley and Ewing (*Constitutional and Administrative Law*, 14th edn (Pearson, 2006), p.87) argue that a strict separation of powers is "possible neither in theory nor in practice". In a similar vein, Barnett (*Constitutional and Administrative Law*, 6th edn (Cavendish, 2006), p.94) recognises that a complete separation of powers would be unworkable. A lack of co-operation and conciliation between the three organs could easily result in legal and constitutional deadlock.

The strict reading of the doctrine is not always taken and many proponents advocate a system of checks and balances. This is certainly a justifiable position considering that the doctrine's desired end, the avoidance of tyranny, could be compromised by a strict application as above. Indeed the avoidance of tyranny may well be better achieved through efficient checks and balances and could represent the doctrine in its highest form.

4.   Separation of powers in the United States and other constitutions

6–005   The constitution of the United States (1787) was heavily influenced by the writing of Locke and Montesquieu and the framers drew a clear distinction between the three organs of state and their respective roles. Article 1 vests legislative power in Congress which consists of a Senate and House of Representatives; by virtue of art.2, Executive power is vested in the President; and art.3 vests judicial power in the Supreme Court and other federal courts that might be established. The constitution compounds this separation by ensuring other protections are built in, for example, different terms of office for the Executive and legislature and even between the two chambers of the legislature can mean different political parties dominate the various positions. However, the United States constitution also exhibits a strong system of checks and balances and the system requires co-operation between the organs. For example, the President may recommend legislation but cannot initiate it, this can only be done by Congress. Congress, as the legislature, has the power to pass legislation and the President then has a power of veto over it. However, to ensure the Presidential veto does not allow the position to become too powerful, the veto may be overridden by a two-third majority in both Houses of Congress. Another example showing the interplay between all three organs is the appointment of a Supreme Court Justice. The President nominates, the Senate must approve and, once appointed, Justices are independent and have security of tenure meaning they cannot be easily removed.

Many other constitutions around the world offer some degree of separation of powers; it is particularly prevalent in codified constitutions that have been designed specifically with the doctrine in mind. The Australian Constitution exhibits a division of the institutions of government; Parliament (the House of Representatives and the Senate), the Executive and the Judiciary. However unlike the US model, the separation between Parliament and the Executive is less distinct and there is some overlap in personnel and functions. The Ministry which forms part of the Executive government is drawn from and responsible to Parliament. In addition, while Parliament can pass laws, these laws often confer legislative functions onto the Executive.

Separation of Powers in the United Kingdom

1.   Historical analysis

6–006   It is important to remember that the doctrine of separation of powers is a political theory put forward as a prescription of what ought to be done in order to accord liberty. In evaluating the significance of the theory in the UK constitution it is also important to remember that the UK constitution with its unbroken history cannot conform to any strict theoretical model. In contrast to the United States where the doctrine is more readily apparent, the UK does not have a single constitutional document which sets out the foundational rules of government and so there is no clear demarcation between key parts of government, personnel and function. It is therefore more difficult to discern whether the theory holds any weight within the UK Constitution and actually best describes the current governmental situation.

Although the doctrine of separation of powers has not been deliberately incorporated into the UK constitution there is clear evidence that limits on the exercise of power have existed for many years. Historical analysis shows that the principle behind the doctrine was evident as far back as 1215 with Magna Carta, which was an attempt to place formal limits on Royal power. From the 14th century onwards a clear distinction between the monarch and Parliament began to arise. The conflict between the King and Parliament in the 17th century further concentrated people's minds on the respective functions of the state and two pieces of legislation clearly show the general principles of control and dispersal of power at force; the Bill of Rights 1688 which established the ascendancy of the legislature over the Crown and the Act of Settlement 1700 which established, amongst other things, the independence of the judiciary. Munro (*Studies in Constitutional Law* p.303) argues that in the early 18th century the UK did possess some semblance of separation particularly relative to other countries; in France for example the monarch was both law maker and Executive.

2.   Contemporary significance in the United Kingdom

It has already been mentioned that the UK constitution has evolved and so cannot   **6–007** conform to any strict theoretical model. Study of the constitution clearly shows there are significant functional and institutional departures from the doctrine. As a result, academics have often reputed the existence of the theory in the UK constitution. S.A. De Smith and R. Brazier, *Constitutional and Administrative Law* (8th edn (Penguin, 1998), p.18) claimed in 1998 "no writer or repute would claim that it [the separation of powers] is a central feature of the modern constitution". A similar view was expressed by Marshall, *Constitutional Theory* (1971). However, leading judges have had a tendency to disagree. Three years before De Smith wrote, Lord Mustill in *R. v Secretary of State for Home Department Ex p. Fire Brigades Union* [1995] 2 A.C. 513 at p.567 stated:

> "it is a feature of the peculiarly British conception of the separation of powers that Parliament, the Executive and the courts have each their distinct and largely exclusive domains. Parliament has the legal unchallengeable right to make whatever law it thinks fit. The Executive carries on the administration of the country in accordance with the powers conferred on it by law. The courts interpret the laws, and see that they are obeyed."

Lord Diplock in a case in 1980, *Duport Steels Ltd v Sirs* [1980] 1 W.L.R. 142 took the view that "it cannot be too strongly emphasised that the British constitution, though largely unwritten, is firmly based on the separation of powers".

Some academics do concur with the judicial view and are more sympathetic to the application of the doctrine within the UK, T.R.S. Allan, *Law, Liberty and Justice* (1993), E. Barendt, "Separation of powers and constitutional government" (1995) P.L. 599 and Colin Munro, *Studies in Constitutional Law* (1999) for example. Munro, following his examination of the application of the docrine, concluded "the separation in the British constitution, although absolute, ought not to be lightly dismissed".

This divergence of opinion could simply be down to different definitional usage or it could be down to a difference between theoretical considerations and practical application. What the divergence does highlight is the particular problem with the UK constitution and necessitates a study of the functional and institutional overlaps and the system of checks and balances. This is best undertaken by examining the relationships between the three organs, evaluate to what degree there are overlaps in their personnel and functions and assess to what degree there is a system of checks and balances in place.

3.   Overlaps and checks and balances

6–008   Two roles, the monarch and the Lord Chancellor, occupy a unique position in the United Kingdom constitution in that they sit (or used to) in all three organs of the state. But can such a clear overlap be said to fundamentally undermine any idea of separation of powers?

(a)   *The monarch*

6–009   The monarch has a place within each of the three organs as the head of the legislature (assent required for legislation), the Executive and the judiciary. However, the monarch's role is purely formal and poses little substantive problems for separation of powers. By convention, the monarch always give her assent to legislation, she plays no formal role in the judicial process, her prerogative power is largely exercised by Ministers on her behalf and what power she does use is always on the advice of her Ministers.

(b)   *The Lord Chancellor*

6–010   It was the role of the Lord Chancellor whose position so dramatically demonstrated the overlapping of personnel which was used to justify the view that there was little or no separation of powers. Until recently (Constitutional Reform Act 2005), the Lord Chancellor performed a substantive role in all branches of government. As a member of the legislature, the Lord Chancellor was Speaker of the House of Lords. In his judicial role, the Lord Chancellor was head of the Judiciary with responsibility for appointments, dismissal, discipline, as well as the right to sit as a member of the Appellate Committee and on other courts. Lastly, as part of the Executive, he was a senior Cabinet member responsible for the Lord Chancellor's department and judicial affairs.

Since the earliest development of the role, it was not without criticism. The role was described by Bagehot, in *The English Constitution* ((Crossman, 1963), p.117) as a "heap of anomalies" and Lord Steyn writing in 1996 ("The Weakest and least Dangerous Department of Government" (1997) P.L. 84 at 90) criticised the office as "inconsistent with the constitutional principle of separation of Executive and judicial function". Though the role clearly seemed to undermine the separation of powers, many senior judges defended the position which was seen as "constitutional buffer" (Lord Hailsham) and a necessary "safety valve". Lord Woolf (P.L. 1998) summarised these views:

> " ... the Lord Chancellor of the day can act as a safety valve avoiding undue tension between the judiciary and the government and possibly between the judiciary and Parliament as well. As a member of the Cabinet, he can act as an advocate on behalf of the courts and the justice system. He can explain to his colleagues in the Cabinet the proper significance of a decision which they regard as being distasteful in consequence of an application for judicial review. He can, as a member of the government, ensure that the courts are properly resourced. On the other hand, on behalf of the government he can explain to the judiciary the realities of the political situation and the constraints on resources which they must inevitably accept."

See also Lord Hailsham, "The Office of Lord Chancellor and the Separation of Powers" (1989) Civil Justice Quarterly 308 at 311; Lord Mackay "The Lord Chancellor in the 1990s", p.251 and Lord Irvine H.L. Deb., November 25, 1997, col. 945).

Recognition of the potential conflict between the Lord Chancellor's role as an independent and impartial judge and his role as a Cabinet Minister collectively responsible for government policy grew in the 1990s. The judicial function of the Lord Chancellor gradually diminished and from October 1990 to October 2000, the Lord Chancellor sat 84 times in the House of Lords and Privy Council. The constitutional anomaly was somewhat compounded by the European Court of Human Rights decision in *McGonnell v UK* (2000) 30 E.H.R.R. 289 in a case concerning the Bailiff of Guernsey. The Bailiff was a position similar to that of the Lord Chancellor, overlapping each of the organs of state. The court concluded that the position compromised the art.6(1) right to fair trial because it could not be said to be impartial and independent. Following the decision, Lord Irvine (the then Lord Chancellor) stated an intention never to sit in any case concerning legislation in which he had been directly involved, nor in any case where the interests of the Executive were directly engaged (HL Debs February 23, 2000, Col. 31). By 2003, the Lord Chancellor's judicial role had become a mere fiction and it became clear that an argument for maintaining the role as Head of Judiciary had gone.

The Constitutional Reform Act 2005 formally brought about the removal of judicial office from the role. Section 7(1) provides that the Lord Chief Justice shall be the President of the Courts of England and Wales and Head of the Judiciary of England and Wales. The Lord President of the Court of Session and Lord Chief Justice of Northern Ireland are representative of their own respective jurisdictions (s.5). A number of the functions of the Lord Chancellor have been reallocated; these include judicial deployment, complaints and discipline. These responsibilities are now shared between the Lord Chief Justice and the Lord Chancellor, a result of the Concordat.

Although, the Lord Chancellor still has a role in appointments, this is now largely governed by the creation of a judicial appointment commission.

4.   Executive and legislature

6–011   The United Kingdom is a parliamentary Executive, as by convention the personnel of government are drawn from the legislature. Walter Bagehot's, *The English Constitution* ((1963), p.65) described this as a "nearly complete fusion, of the executive and legislative powers". He characterised this aspect of the constitution as "the efficient secret of the English Constitution".

The idea of complete fusion is not entirely correct. While there is some overlap in personnel, this is limited by statute (House of Commons Disqualification Act 1975 s.2(1)) to not more than 95 persons. Moreover, except for those Ministers, the remainder of the Executive are disqualified from the House of Commons (House of Commons Disqualification Act 1975 s.1). These include the civil service, police and armed forces. Yet the significance of the overlap between the government and the legislature of those 95 persons should not be downplayed. Since the advent of mass political parties, Barendt, "Separation of powers and constitutional government" (1995) P.L. 599 argues that even when there is a significant party split, the government effectively controls the legislature. This view appears to reiterate that taken by Lord Hailsham, Lord Chancellor 1979–87, who coined the phrase "elective dictatorship" to describe the relationship between the two. Members of Parliament are chosen by party members and any hope of progression up the governmental ladder ensures Member co-operation with government's legislative agenda. The overlap also compromises the effectiveness of the Chamber in holding government to account.

This would seem to suggest a potential for abuse of power as identified by Montesquieu. The constitutional principle of responsible government requires that government is responsible and accountable to Parliament. This is achieved through parliamentary mechanisms such as debates and Select Committees and through the conventions of collective and individual ministerial responsibility (see further, discussions in Ch.9 and Ch.12). Parliamentary procedures exist to scrutinise legislation and government cannot always expect to get their legislative proposals through Parliament, even with a strong majority. Of particular note is the role of the House of Lords in this regard. The House of Lords, as the second Chamber, have to assent to all Bills before they become Acts of Parliament. Since 1911, they have only had the power to delay but have often used their existing power to gain concessions for example, the Immigration and Asylum (Treatment of Claimants) Bill where the House of Lord's objections led to the removal of a clause ousting judicial supervision.

In a sense, Parliament does ultimately control the government since they can oust them in a vote of no confidence. This was seen in 1979 when the Labour government under James Callaghan lost a vote of no confidence which led to the calling of a general election. The threat of such a vote can be equally effective.

Despite these overlaps, there is still a clear distinction between the primary functions of the two organs; government may control the legislature but it still has to legislate through Parliament. Amery, *Thoughts on the Constitution* (p.28) notes:

"Government and Parliament, however, closely intertwined and harmonized, are still separate and independent entities, fulfilling the distinct functions of leadership, direction and command on the one hand, and of critical discussion and examination on the other."

Since the *Case of Proclamation* (1611) 12 Co. Rep. 74, the Crown has no power to change the law without parliamentary consent, it cannot raises taxes without parliamentary authority nor keep an army. In *R. v Secretary of State for Home Department Ex p. Fire Brigades Union* [1992] 2 A.C. 513, the House of Lords held that the Home Secretary could not use his prerogative power to introduce a criminal injuries compensation scheme significantly at variance with a statutory scheme not yet implemented. For the Home Secretary to be allowed to do so would have the impact of going against the intention of Parliament and amount to a form of legislating. However, the existence of delegated or secondary legislation raises questions about the Executive legislating. The principal justification for the use of delegated legislation is efficiency and the inability of statute to go into technical detail. In recent years, the volume of delegated legislation has increased, on average around 3000 statutory instruments are passed each year in comparison to 31 Acts (2007) and 55 Acts (2006). Though the power to make delegated legislation would appear to undermine the separation of powers, its use is authorised by the legislature through a parent act. In addition, the use of delegated legislation is controlled; by the judiciary who ensure that Ministers act within their power, by Parliament through Select Committees and the Statutory Instruments Act 1946 which requires such legislation to be laid before Parliament, and, finally, through a constitutional convention that delegated legislation may not be used for important matters. Aside from delegated legislation arising from statutory provision, the Executive also have residual powers under prerogative which allows them to legislate under orders in council.

5.   Judiciary and legislature

While all full time judicial appointees are disqualified from the House of Commons under the House of Commons Disqualification Act 1975, one major overlap between the judiciary and the legislature remain the Lords of Appeal in Ordinary, the Law Lords who at present still form part of the House of Lords. While the 12 members of the serving House of Lords Appellate Committee technically sit within the legislative body, it is accepted that they do not involve themselves in the political aspect of the House such as debates. Part 3 of the Constitutional Reform Act 2005 formally brings to an end this overlap. The Act makes provision for the creation of a new Supreme Court for the United Kingdom completely separate from the legislature. The 12 Law Lords in office at the date of the move will become the first Justices of the Supreme Court, and remain members of the House of Lords. On their retirement, ss.25–31 of the Act sets down the provisions relating to the appointment of new Justices of the Supreme Court. Such new Justices of the Supreme Court will not be members of the House of Lords, thus the link between the Lords and judicial office will end, strengthening the separation of powers. The court is scheduled to open for business in October 2009.

6–012

Judges in the exercise of their judicial functions should be free from criticism and influence from either of the other organs of state. Parliamentary practice prohibits the criticism of judges unless a specific motion has been passed expressing criticism or under an address by the Crown seeking removal of a judge. However, conventional rules can be broken and it is not unknown for judicial decisions to be criticised in the chamber, particularly in the field of sentencing. Margaret Thatcher for example criticised the imposition of a light sentence on a child molester (HC Deb Vol. 34 Cols 123–25, 285–86). In addition to this rule, debates on a particular court case can be barred where the Speaker feels it might prejudice the trial and in criminal matters no reference should be made to the proceedings at all once a charge has been made; this is known as the *sub judice* rule.

In the relationship between the two organs, it would appear that Parliament has the upper hand. The traditional doctrine of parliamentary sovereignty requires that the courts cannot question the validity of an Act of Parliament in terms of procedure and substance. Courts are required to simply interpret and give effect to legislation. In *Dupont Steels Ltd v Sirs* [1980] 1 W.L.R. 142, the Iron and Steel Trade Confederation called a strike of its members employed by the British Steel Corporation (nationalised industry) in a dispute over wages. The Confederation sought to put pressure on the government and purported to extend its strike to the private steel industry. Dupont Steel and other private steel companies sought injunctions against the Confederation to stop them inducing their workers to break their terms of employment. The House of Lords overturned the Court of Appeal decision and refused the injunction. They found that under s.13 of the Trade Union and Labour Relations Act 1974 (as amended 1976) the Confederation had immunity in tort in respect of acts done in contemplation or furtherance of a trade dispute. Lord Diplock in a glowing indictment of the doctrine of separation of power's applicability in the UK constitution stated "It cannot be too strongly emphasised that the British Constitution, though largely unwritten, is firmly based upon the separation of powers; Parliament makes the laws, the judiciary interprets the law". He then affirmed the role of the courts:

" . . . the role of the judiciary is confined to ascertaining from the words that Parliaments has approved as expressing its intention what that intention was, and to give effect to it. Where the meaning of the statutory words is plain and unambiguous it is not for the judges to invent fancied ambiguities as an excuse for failing to give effect to its plain meaning because they themselves consider that the consequence of doing so would be inexpedient, or even unjust or immoral."

In the UK constitution the line between development of the common law and legislating is hard to draw. To a large degree the nature of a common law system means that judges are "formulating and developing law" (Lord Scarman, *Dupont Steel v Sirs*). Much of Lord Denning's judicial career can be said to fall into this bracket and on many occasions he was accused of usurping the legislative function and was overruled by the House of Lords (see *R. v Inland Revenue Commissioner Ex p. Rossminster Ltd*; *sub nom. Inland Revenue Commissioners v Rossminster Ltd; Rossminster and Tucker, Re* [1980] A.C. 952 and *Magor and St Mellons Rural District Council v Newport Corporation* [1965] A.C. 189). A case that illustrates the inherent problem with a common law system in this regard is *R. v R* [1992] 1 A.C. 599. Here the appellant had been convicted of attempted rape of his wife who had left the matrimonial home a few days earlier with the intention to divorce. He appealed against his conviction arguing that it was well known that a man could not rape his wife. The House of Lords dismissed his appeal. The statutory law on rape did not include an exception for marital rape which had appeared to develop from the common law, originating in the 18th century at a time when a wife was considered a "subservient chattel" of her husband. It was argued that use of the word "unlawful" in the Sexual Offences (Amendment) Act 1976 meant it was only rape if outside marriage. Lord Keith (who gave the opinion of the court) did not agree and concluded that the proposition should be departed from on grounds of principle. He concurred with the Court of Appeal's view that this was "not the creation of a new offence, it is a removal of a common law fiction which has become anachronistic and offensive". The defendant took his case to the European Court of Human Rights on the grounds that at the time he committed the act it was not an offence, so contrary to ECHR art.7, *SW and CW v UK* (1996) 21 E.H.R.R. 363. At para.39, the ECtHR reiterated that the House of Lords had not created a new offence, though they did note that the offence of rape had been extended to include conduct which until then was not covered by the common law. However, they noted that they did not adapt the law to a new type of conduct but rather to a change of social attitudes. They concluded that the British courts had done no more than "continue a perceptible line of case-law development dismantling the immunity ... ". As a result, judicial recognition of the absence of immunity was a reasonably foreseeable development of the law.

While morally the decision is completely understandable, from a legal standpoint it is easy to appreciate the view that the House of Lords created a new law. At the time Mr R committed the act, the marital rape exception was the existing principle, a fact affirmed by the Law Commission in 1990, and so in effect there was no crime.

R. v R shows the difficulties inherent in a common law system; on the one hand the approach taken was simply a development of the law and on the other, judicial law making in contravention of the separation of powers.

In cases such as the above where accusations of judicial law making can be made, it must not be forgotten that if the courts stray too far into the domain of the legislature then Parliament can themselves rectify the position. Such was the case following the decision of the House of Lords in *Burmah Oil Co v Lord Advocate* [1965] A.C. 75 which was nullified by the War Damages Act 1965 (see Ch.7).

It might appear from this discussion that Parliament controls the judiciary, in which case, it is important to ask who controls Parliament to ensure that they do not abuse their power. The court's power of interpretation should never be underestimated. In *Anisminic Ltd v Foreign Compensation Commission* [1969] 2 A.C. 147; [1969] 2 W.L.R. 163; [1969] 1 All E.R. 208, HL, the House of Lords embarked on an interesting interpretation of a clause ousting judicial review, holding it only applied to a determination of a decision, a decision in their interpretation was one made legally. The clause was held not to apply to purported decisions, i.e. those decisions tainted with illegality, unreasonableness or procedural impropriety. In effect, the courts interpretation rendered the clause ineffective. The court's powers of interpretation have also been enhanced with the passing of the European Community Act 1972 and the Human Rights Act 1998, which have given them wider powers of interpretation. Unless Parliament uses clear and express words, the courts are able to interpret legislation even to the point of linguistically straining the meaning, to achieve compatibility with both the UK's European and human rights obligations, for example *Garland v British Rail Engineering Lt*d [1983] 1 A.C. 751 in relation to EU and, *R. v A (Complainant's Sexual History) (No.2)* [2001] UKHL 25 in relation to human rights (discussed in more detail in Ch.7). Though the courts have wider powers of interpretation, the Human Rights Act was drafted with the intention of preserving both parliamentary sovereignty and separation of powers. The courts may interpret but unlike other jurisdictions cannot strike down legislation. Section 4 of the Human Rights Act gives them power to declare the legislation incompatible, so putting Parliament on notice to that effect, however, the law remains valid until the legislation is formally amended.

6.   Executive and judiciary

6–013   There are some overlaps in personnel between the executive and judicial functions though most (except the Attorney-General) are of little concern since the removal of the Lord Chancellor's role as Head of the Judiciary.

The courts are the Queen's courts but judicial functions are exercised by the judges. The Privy Council is an Executive body and is also a court, the Judicial Committee of the Privy Council. The Committee was set up by statute in 1833 and hears appeals from some Commonwealth jurisdictions, the Isle of Man and the Channel Islands. At present the Council also hears appeals on devolution matters but this function has been removed by the Constitutional Reform Act 2005 which transfers it to the Supreme Court.

The law officers of the Crown: the Attorney-General, Solicitor General and Lord Advocate in Scotland, have some overlapping functions with the judiciary. The Attorney-General is a Minister of the Crown (Chief Legal Advisor of the Crown), with responsibility for the Crown Prosecution Service, Serious Fraud Other and Revenue and Customs Prosecutions amongst others. He is also Guardian of the Public Interest having supervisory powers over prosecutions. Some prosecutions cannot be commenced without his consent, he also has the power to halt prosecutions (*nolle prosequi*), and to appoint "special advocates" in national security cases. The role has existed since 1461 but in recent years the nature of the Attorney-General's responsibilities has given rise to debate over the potential tension between the executive side and the judicial side. These tensions have led a number of commentators (including the Constitutional Affairs Select Committee who reported in July 2007 (Constitutional Role of the Attorney-General, HC 306 2006–07) to suggest the role needs reforming. In July 2007 the Prime Minister as part of his Governance of Britain proposals, announced a review of the office of Attorney-General. In a statement made on July 3, 2007, the Prime Minster, Gordon Brown MP stated:

> "The role of Attorney General, which combines legal and ministerial functions, needs to change. While we consult on reform, the Attorney General has herself decided, except if the law or national security requires it, not to make key prosecution decisions in individual criminal cases."

The review concluded that the Attorney-General should remain a government

Minister. The government's draft plans were published in the Draft Constitutional Renewal Bill. Amongst the proposals for reform of the office is the abolition of *nolle prosequi* and the ending of certain functions regarding consent in prosecutions (as of February 2008).

One area that remains important and independent is the separation of functions between the two organs. Historically, the Home Secretary (Executive), had some judicial functions notably in relation to sentencing which involved the setting of the tariff period for discretionary and mandatory prisoners sentenced to life imprisonment. However in a number of cases this power was challenged as being incompatible with arts 5 and 6 of the European Convention on Human Rights. In *T & V v UK* (2000) E.H.R.R. 121 (concerning child prisoners) and *Stafford v UK* (2002) 35 E.H.R.R. 32 (adult prisoners) the European Court of Human Rights held that art.5(4) had been violated and felt that the role of the Home Secretary in setting such tariff was "increasingly difficult to reconcile with the notion of separation of powers between the executive and the judiciary". Likewise, in *Wilson v UK* (2002) 35 E.H.R.R. 20 the court held that the Home Secretary's role was "objectionable" and at para.35, observed, "This is not a matter of form but impinges on the fundamental principle of separation of powers and detracts from a necessary guarantee against the possibility of abuse ... ". These decisions were followed by a similar ruling in the House of Lords in *R. (on the application of Anderson) v Secretary of State for Home Department* [2002] UKHL 46. Subsequent to these decisions, Parliament enacted the Criminal Justice and Courts Service Act 2000 s.60 in relation to juveniles and the Criminal Justice Act 2003 for adult offenders which passed the power to the judiciary.

(a) *Judicial independence*

It is of paramount importance that the judiciary are independent both from the **6–014** Executive and the legislature. This is necessary from a rule of law point of view as well as separation of powers and is formally recognised in s.3 of the Constitutional Reform Act 2005 which imposes a duty on the Lord Chancellor to uphold continued independence.

One important requirement of judicial independence is the ability of either organ of state to remove judges at whim. Since the Act of Settlement 1700, the judiciary have security of tenure (given modern expression in the Senior Courts Act 1981), hold their office during good behaviour, are paid from the consolidated fund free from political control and can only be removed by a joint address of both Houses of Parliament. Of equal importance is how the judiciary are appointed. Prior to the Constitutional Reform Act 2005, judicial appointments were at the behest of the Lord Chancellor and Prime Minister and as such raised questions over independence. Appointment of judges is now by a Judicial Appointments Commission which was brought about under Constitutional Reform Act 2005 and formally launched in April 2006. The Commission is appointed by the Queen on the recommendation of the Lord Chancellor and consists of a lay chairman and 14 other members. For appointment of the Lord Chief Justice, Master of the Rolls, President of the Queen Bench, Family and Chancery Divisions, the selection panel must include the Lord Chief Justice. Appointment of Supreme Court

Justices is done by an ad-hoc Supreme Court Selection Commission which is convened when required by a vacancy. The Prime Minister nominates the person who is selected by the Commission. Throughout the appointment procedure there is consultation with the Lord Chancellor and senior judges. A recommendation is put to the Lord Chancellor who has the power to veto but only on the grounds that the person is not suitable for the office concerned. While there is still executive involvement in the judicial appointments process, it is much more transparent and controlled and the Lord Chancellor has limited grounds for refusing the recommendation put to him.

A constitutional convention exists which dictates there should be no criticism of the judiciary from members of the Executive (an equal rule applies to Parliament, see above). This convention though is often broken and frequently the Executive criticises the leniency of judicial sentencing. For example, following the decision in *R. (Q) v Secretary of State for Home Department* [2003] EWHC 191, David Blunkett, Home Secretary reacted angrily which led to criticism of the judge in the press.

(b)   *Control of the Executive*

6–014A   Judicial independence is particularly important in ensuring that they are free from political interference and can be effective in controlling the Executive. Control of the Executive is achieved primarily through the mechanism of judicial review of administrative action and is an important check and balance, especially considering the overlap between the legislature and Executive. If a Minister or Crown Officer acts beyond the power conferred on them by Parliament then the courts, through judicial review, can quash the decision and remit it back to the government. Since the decision in *Council for Civil Service Unions (CCSU) v Minister for the Civil Service* [1985] A.C. 374 the courts also have the power to review the exercise of prerogative power. This case was an important step forward in ensuring the accountability of the Executive and the misuse of vast power to the detriment of the people (see Ch.13 for more discussion on the courts expansion of judicial review over prerogative power). Given the power of judicial review in controlling the Executive it is important that the courts do not involve themselves in essentially political matters. The courts are conscious of not overstepping the constitutional boundary and questioning decisions which are outside their competence. For example, the courts rarely involve themselves in questions regarding the allocation of resources and accord what is known as deference to the Executive (see, for example, *Nottinghamshire CC v Secretary of State for the Environment* [1986] A.C. 240). A good illustration of these points comes from the *R. (on the application of A) v Secretary of State for the Home Department* [2004] UKHL 56 (see Ch.5 for facts). The majority of the House of Lords in *A* did not wish to question the decision of the government that the United Kingdom was in an "emergency threatening the life of the nation" as required by art.15 of the European Convention of Human Rights. Lord Bingham at para.29 stated:

> " ... I would accept that great weight should be given to the judgment of the Home Secretary, his colleagues and Parliament on this question, because they were called on to exercise a pre-eminently political judgment. It involved making a

factual prediction of what various people around the world might or might not do, and when (if at all) they might do it, and what the consequences might be if they did."

In contrast to the majority was the approach advocated by Lord Hoffman. He took a less deferential view, concluding that the UK was not in a state of emergency. In a strongly worded conclusion, Lord Hoffman stated (at para.97):

"The real threat to the life of the nation, in the sense of a people living in accordance with its traditional laws and political values, comes not from terrorism but from laws such as these. That is the true measure of what terrorism may achieve. It is for Parliament to decide whether to give the terrorists such a victory."

Taking these two approaches, it could be said that the majority achieved the right balance in being unwilling to overturn the government's political decision but then questioning the government's reaction on proportionality grounds. If this view is preferred then Lord Hoffman's approach amounts to interference with the Executive arm of the state and so compromises separation of powers. Two points can be made in defence of Lord Hoffman's approach; firstly, he does not just disagree with the factual conclusion reached by the government but analyses the decision on legal grounds by reference to establishing principles from the European Court of Human Rights. In effect he is doing the role he was employed to do and is ensuring the government acts legally. Secondly, if the Executive are able to easily pass laws that amount to a draconian and discriminatory use of power then surely it is the appropriate place of the courts to question that power. After all, that is what the doctrine of separation of powers is about.

The *A* case is unusual and the reasoning is reflective of this fact. However, it does show the competing factors at stake in accessing the interplay between the various organs. Rather worryingly, if one advocated a pure separation of powers then the ability of government to put forward, and of Parliament to pass, such laws would go unchecked and tyranny and abuse of power could begin to set in.

Summary

If it is taken that a state only demonstrates separation of powers if it separates out its   **6–015** functions and personnel, as in the United States, then clearly the United Kingdom does not have a separation of powers. However, to say and do this is to focus too much on the form and not on how it operates in practice. Granted there exists in the United Kingdom significant overlaps in both functions and personnel but there equally exists a strong system of checks and balances, which although not perfect, has enabled the United Kingdom constitution to exist for over 300 years. Changes in recent years have sought only to increase the significance of the doctrine in the UK constitution. The Constitutional Reform Act 2005 had at its core the doctrine of separation of powers and the changes it has made, and will continue to make, serves only to make the doctrine more evident in the constitution.

FURTHER READING

6–016   Allan, T.R.S. *Law, Liberty and Justice: The Legal Foundations of British Constitutionalism* (Clarendon Press, 1993)

Barendt, E. "Separation of powers and constitutional government" (1995) P.L. 599

Hale, B. "A Supreme Court for the United Kingdom" (2004) 24 *Legal Studies* 36

Hailsham, "The Office of Lord Chancellor and the Separation of Powers" (1989) *Civil Justice Quarterly* 308

Hope "A phoenix from the ashes? Accommodating a new Supreme Court" (2005) 121 L.Q.R. 253

Munro, C. *Studies in Constitutional Law*, 2nd edn (OUP, 1999), Ch.9.

Munro, C. "The separation of powers: not such a myth" (1981) P.L. 19

Steyn, "The weakest and least dangerous department of government" (1997) P.L. 84

Steyn, "The Case for a Supreme Court" (2002) 118 L.Q.R. 382

Tomkins, A. *Public Law* (OUP, 2003) for a contextual analysis of the doctrine

Windlesham "The Constitutional Reform Act 2005: members, judges and constitutional change: Part 1" (2005) P.L. 806

Chapter 7

PARLIAMENTARY SOVEREIGNTY

INTRODUCTION

In *R. (on the application of Jackson) v Att-Gen* [2005] UKHL 56, Lord Bingham stated **7–001**
that the "bedrock of the British Constitution is ... the supremacy of the Crown in
Parliament" thus re-asserting what Professor Albert V. Dicey had stated in his
authoritative text, *An Introduction to the Study of the Law of the Constitution* (10th edn
(London: Macmillan, 1959)), in 1885, some 130 years earlier. Broadly speaking, the
theory means that the Queen in Parliament (a theoretical entity composed of the
monarch, House of Lords and House of Commons), is the sovereign body in the UK
and can legally make any law that it wants without fear that the courts will overturn it
as incompatible with the constitution. This defining feature of the British constitution
lies in direct contrast to many codified constitutions where the constitution is supreme
and the legislature is subordinate to that constitution. In such constitutions, the courts
can challenge and overturn legislation on the grounds that it is incompatible with their
constitution.

Despite the clear assertion from Lord Bingham in the above case, other Law Lords in
the same case, whilst recognising the dominance of the principle in the British Constitution, equally indicated that it is "no longer, if it ever was, absolute" (Lord Hope at
[104]). This chapter examines what is mean by the sovereignty of Parliament (or
supremacy of Parliament) and considers whether there are limits on the legislative
authority of Parliament in the 21st century.

DEFINITION

Dicey's theory, although not the first, (Coke and Blackstone had commented on the **7–002**
theory), remains the most authoritative definition of the continuing theory of the

sovereignty of Parliament. He said that the Queen, House of Lords and House of Commons acting together as the "Queen in Parliament" had the right to make or unmake any law whatsoever and further that no person or body was recognised by the law of England as having the right to override or set aside legislation (A. V. Dicey, *An Introduction to the Study of the Law of the Constitution* ((1959) at p.40)). Dicey's parliamentary sovereignty can be viewed as having both a positive and negative side: positive in that Parliament can pass any law it wants and negative, that no body can question an Act of Parliament.

1. Origins of sovereignty: historical analysis

7–003   Given the importance of sovereignty in the UK constitution it is perhaps surprising that the exact origin of parliamentary sovereignty is unclear. It is not laid down by statute; as Salmond states, "No statute can confer this power upon Parliament, for this would be to assume and act on the very power that is to be conferred". Similarly, Wade in his introduction to Dicey's *An Introduction to the Study of the Law of the Constitution* (1959) states "there is no statute which says that the Courts must enforce without question Acts of Parliament". He also concludes that the source must be the common law (see also H.R.W. Wade, "The basis of Legal Sovereignty" (1955) C.L.J. 172–197). Lord Steyn in *R. (on the application of Jackson) v Att-Gen* [2005] UKHL 56 similarly said that "parliamentary sovereignty is a construct of the common law. The judge created this principle".

(a)   *Why did judges create the principle?*

7–004   To fully understand this question, it is necessary to consider the historical development of the modern UK constitution, especially those of the 17th century.

(i)   Pre-1688

7–005   The early 17th century was a period typified by conflict between the monarchy and Parliament over their respective powers and who had supremacy.

Charles I (1625–1649) believed in the divine right of kings which placed the king as God's lieutenant on earth; answerable only to him. In 1628 Charles claimed that the House of Commons was attempting to "break through all respects and ligaments of government, and to erect a universal overswaying power to themselves, which belongs only to us and not to them" (Royal Proclamation (1628) quoted in J. Goldsworthy, *The Sovereignty of Parliament: History and Philosophy* (OUP at p.124). Squabbles over their respective powers were often waged in the courts and legislation had no automatic precedence over the actions of the King. In *Bonham's Case* (1610) 8 Co. Rep. 113, KB for example, Chief Justice Cooke cited various medieval precedents to support his contention that "when an Act of Parliament is against common right and reason, or repugnant, or impossible to be performed, the common law will control it, and adjudge such an Act to be void" (at p.118).

The conflict between the two produced the Civil War (1642–1651) which was largely an argument about who possessed this universal overswaying power. The Royalists believed it belonged to the king, the parliamentarians to Parliament. The Parliamentarians won the Civil War, executed Charles I and England became a republic, first as a Commonwealth and secondly a protectorate under the control of Oliver Cromwell. The protectorate collapsed in 1659 and the monarchy was restored with Charles II becoming king (1660–1685). Squabbles continued, though to a slightly lesser extent then earlier. Following Charles II's death he was succeeded by his Catholic brother James, who became James II.

James II (1685–1688) reign saw the conflict between the monarchy and Parliament gain momentum again. Some historians have James II as a Catholic despot who attempted to impose an absolute monarchy on a largely Protestant Britain. Parliament was prorogued in 1685 and not recalled during the four years of James' reign. James largely bypassed Parliament and governed the country using his common law powers (prerogative powers). Of particular note, James ignored the fundamental principles in Magna Carta of levying taxes with consent and had a penchant for keeping a standing army in peacetime contrary to English tradition.

(ii)   1688 political settlement

The sovereignty of Parliament really began to evolve following the Glorious Revolution in 1688. The reign of James II had caused much disquiet amongst the English ruling classes and in June 1688 a group of Protestant nobles invited the Protestant William III of Orange to come to England. James II fled to France and William and his wife Mary (James' sister) were invited to take the "vacant" throne. The result was the 1688–89 settlement culminating in The Bill of Rights 1689.   **7–006**

The Declaration of Rights (which later formed the basis of the Bill of Rights) took the form of condemning the previous "unconstitutional" and "illegal" actions of James II and instigated a number of changes which made the Crown subordinate to Parliament and prevented any future monarch from abusing their throne. These included the guarantee that Parliament could not be simply dismissed or suspended, that the Crown could not raise revenue without Parliamentary consent nor could they keep a standing army; freedom of speech in Parliament was also guaranteed. In short the Bill laid the foundations for the ultimate sovereignty of Parliament.

The courts recognised the political fact of this shift in the seat of sovereignty from the King to Parliament. Legal consequences flowed from this recognition resulting in judicial obedience to statute. Wade, illustrating this point in his article "The Legal Basis of Sovereignty" (1955) C.L.J. 172, states: "the role of judicial obedience is in one sense a rule of common law, but in another sense, which applies to no other rule of common law, it is the ultimate political fact upon which the whole system of legislation hangs".

2.   Legal and political sovereignty distinguished

7–007   Sovereignty is a legal theory concerned with what Parliament can legally do. It should be contrasted with political sovereignty which rests with the people (electorate) and is therefore associated with representative government and the doctrine of mandate. Dicey emphasised this and acknowledged that there may be political limits on what Parliament can do, "the electors can always enforce their will" in other words, revoke their authority to Parliament in the next general election. An extreme example, but one that is often used, is Sir Leslie Stephens (*The Science of Ethics* (Smith Elder, 1882)), who stated that Parliament could if it wanted "pass a law that all blue eyes babies should be killed". In legal theory as Parliament can pass any law it wishes, it can pass such a heinous law. It would of course be politically unthinkable for a modern Parliament to pass such a law and so the example highlights well the distinction between legal theory and political reality.

SOVEREIGNTY ILLUSTRATED: ANALYSIS OF DICEY

7–008   Dicey's theory can be split up into three principles.

(1)   Parliament is the supreme law making body and can make any law whatsoever regardless of subject, time and geographical limits. Linked with this is the idea that Parliament can unmake any law it wants.

(2)   No body, notably the British courts, can question an Act of Parliament.

(3)   A third premise, which has arisen from the conflict between the first two premises, is that as Parliament is supreme it cannot be bound by a predecessor or successor. This means that Parliament can unmake any law it wants regardless of any special procedures incorporated into a statute. Where there is a conflict between an earlier and later statute, the courts will apply the later statute.

1.   Principle 1: Parliament can make or unmake any law it chooses

7–009   Dicey's first premise is quite simple. Parliament can "legally" make any law that it desires, this law will be obeyed and adopted by the courts. For example, Parliament can alter the constitution, change its constituent parts, and legislate contrary to international principles. There is no hierarchy of statutes in the UK constitution and regardless of the subject matter, no statute is protected; all have the same status. As a result there is no law that Parliament cannot change (unmake).

(a) Law affecting constitutional matters

Parliament has passed many statutes which amend or alter the constitution. Dicey, in **7–010** purporting to show Parliament could legislate on anything, highlighted that Parliament has regulated succession to the throne in measures such as The Act of Settlement 1700 which settled succession on the heirs of Sophia of Hanover (granddaughter of James I) and her protestant descendants. Any alteration to the succession also requires parliamentary consent, for example, His Majesty's Declaration of Abdication Act 1936 made possible Edward VIII's abdication and the subsequent assumption of the Crown by his brother George VI.

Parliament has also passed statutes affecting its own composition and redefining how legislation is enacted. In 1911 Parliament enacted legislation that a Bill could become law only when passed by the House of Commons and the Queen (Parliament Act 1911). Similarly with the House of Lords Act 1999, Parliament changed the composition of the House of Lords by, amongst other things, abolishing the right of hereditary peers to a seat in the House as a right.

(b) Retrospective legislation

Perhaps the clearest example of Parliament's power to make any law is its power to **7–011** legislate prospectively and retrospectively. Retrospective legislation is where Parliament passes a law which nullifies a decision or makes something unlawful which at the time was legal. This is directly contrary to the rule of law and the principle of legal certainty (see Ch.5). A famous example of Parliament doing this was *Burmah Oil v Lord Advocate* [1965] A.C. 75. Burmah Oil was a company whose property had been pre-emptedly destroyed by British forces during the Second World War to stop them falling into Japanese hands. The company successfully sued for compensation in the courts. The House of Lords held that the exercise of royal prerogative that resulted in damaged or destroyed property could not be exercised without making payment for it. The decision would have resulted in a massive drain on the UK's financial resources and so Parliament passed the War Damage Act 1965 s.1 of which abolished the right to claim for compensation at common law. Section 2 gave the Act retrospective effect:

> "Where any proceedings to recover at common law compensation in respect of such damage or destruction have been instituted before the passing of this Act, the court shall, on the application of any party, forthwith set aside or dismiss the proceedings, subject only to the determination of any question arising as to costs or expenses."

(Note this section was repealed by the Statute Law (Repeals) Act 1995).

(i)   Retrospective legislation and human rights

7–012   The passing of retrospective criminal legislation is contrary to principles enshrined in the European Convention of Human Rights art.7. The European Convention of Human Rights (ECHR) has been incorporated into UK domestic law by the Human Rights Act 1998 (HRA). Section 3 of the HRA imposes an obligation on the courts to interpret domestic legislation compatibly with the ECHR. Where an interpretation is not possible, the court can issue a statement that the legislation is incompatible with human rights under s.4 (a declaration of incompatibility). This does not affect the validity of the statute. Therefore, Parliament can still pass legislation that imposes retrospective criminal liability and such legislation will be enforceable in the courts.

The impact of the HRA on parliamentary sovereignty will be considered in more detail below.

(c)   *Domestic law and international law*

7–013   Parliament is not bound by international law and can pass legislation which is in direct conflict with international laws. There is a presumption that where possible the courts will interpret domestic legislation and international law so that there is no conflict. However, where the domestic law is clear and unequivocal, then domestic law will always take precedence. Two cases illustrate this point clearly. In the first, *Mortensen v Peters* (1906) 14 S.L.T. 227, the Master of a Norwegian trawler was convicted of using an illegal fishing method contrary to the Sea Fisheries (Scotland) Amendment Act 1985 and Herring Fishery (Scotland) Acts 1889, 1895. Mortensen was fishing five miles from shore in the Moray Firth. He argued that the bye-law did not cover him as he was not a British national and was fishing in international waters. The domestic boundary recognised in international law lay at three miles, contrary to the five mile territorial limit imposed by the British statute. The Court of Justiciary (Scotland) stated that they were duly bound to apply the terms of the British statute as it was not their place to question the validity of the statue vis a vis international law. "For us an Act of Parliament duly passed by Lords and Commons and assented to by the King, is supreme, and we are bound to give effects to its terms".

The second case, *Cheney v Conn* [1968] 1 W.L.R. 242, concerned a challenge to the validity of the Finance Act 1964. Cheney, a taxpayer, argued that the assessment of his taxes was illegal as a substantial part of it would be used to finance construction of nuclear weapons which was contrary to the Geneva Convention. In dismissing the case, Ungoed-Thomas J. said "what the statute itself enacts cannot be unlawful, because what the statute says and provides is itself the law, and the highest form of law that is known to this country. It is the law which prevails over every other form of law" (at p.247).

(i)   Extra-territorial limits

7–014   Parliament can legislate outside of its own territory for example, Jennings in *The Law of the Constitution* said that Parliament could legislate to ban smoking in the streets of

Paris. This law would be legally binding domestically but would of course have no effect in France itself. Further, it would be difficult in reality to enforce such a law although theoretically possible against British subjects. Such an example highlights the distinction between legal theory and practical/political reality.

A practical example of Parliament legislating outside its own territory is the War Crimes Act 1991. Even making the Act was controversial and it only became law after use of the Parliament Act procedure to avoid the opposition in the House of Lords which refused to consent to it. Section 1 of the Act confers jurisdiction on the UK courts to prosecute any murders, manslaughters or homicides alleged to have been committed by any person, irrespective of nationality, in German occupied territory during the Second World War. Only one person, Anthony Sawoniuk, has ever been convicted under this Act.

2. Restraints on Parliament's ability to make or unmake any law

Although in legal theory Parliament can legislate on whatever it so wishes, there are **7–015** restraints on this exercise. Colin Munro (*Studies in Constitutional Law* ((London: Butterworths, 1999), p.135) noted sovereignty "denotes only the absence of legal limitations, not the absence of all limitations or . . . . inhibitions, on Parliament's actions". Lord Woolf M.R. in "Droit Public" (1995) P.L. 57 also asserted "there are even limits on the supremacy of Parliament which it is the courts' inalienable responsibility to identify and uphold" (at p.69). Some areas of restraint are considered below; even though they are dealt with under separate headings, all interlink.

(a) *Political restraints*

Although there may be an absence of legal limitations on what Parliament may legis- **7–016** late, there are of course political limitations. Dicey says "the external limits to the real power of a sovereign consists in the possibility or certainty that his subjects or a large number of them, will disobey or resist his laws" (*An Introduction to the Study of the Law of the Constitution*, pp.76–77). In this sense legal sovereignty cannot truly be separated from political sovereignty, as Parliament is unlikely to pass any law which a substantial section of the population violently disliked (a point made clear by Jennings, *The Law and the Constitution* (5th edn (London: University of London Press, 1959), p.148)).

(b) *Practical restraints*

The Statute of Westminster 1931 s.4 states that no Act of Westminster shall extend to **7–017** the Dominion unless the Dominions so requests. In strict legal theory Parliament could repeal this Statute and legislate without the dominions consent though such a course would be unlikely due to both practical and political problems. Lord Sankey L.C. in *British Coal Corporation v The King* [1935] A.C. 500 makes this point clearly:

"It is doubtless true that the power of the Imperial Parliament to pass on its own initiative any legislation that it thought fit extending to Canada remains in theory unimpaired; indeed, the Imperial Parliament could, as a matter of abstract law, repeal or disregard s.4 of the Statute. But that is theory and has no relations to realities." (at p.520)

Similarly, repeal by Parliament of the various Grants of Independence revoking the countries independent status would have a similarly limited effect. Lord Denning in *Blackburn v Att-Gen* [1971] 1 W.L.R. 1037 at p.1040 famously stated "freedom once given cannot be take away. Legal theory must give way to practical politics".

(c)   *International restraints*

7–018   Notwithstanding the above, Parliament is constrained by the international treaties that it ratifies. Although in legal theory Parliament can pass legislation that directly conflicts with the UK's international obligations it tries to avoid doing so. Legislation that directly conflicted with an international Treaty would render the UK open to international criticism and condemnation and would in practice render the Treaty obligation meaningless. Where a conflict appears to arise, the courts presume Parliament did not intend this to be the case and interpret domestic legislation so that it complies with the international obligation. If they cannot interpret without fundamentally changing the meaning and purpose of the domestic legislation, then domestic law is applied irrespective of the Treaty obligations.

(d)   *Political entrenchment*

7–019   According to legal theory Parliament cannot be bound and can unmake any law it wishes (see below for more discussion). However, it may be the situation that certain Acts are politically entrenched and to repeal them without a popular consensus could be politically disastrous. One such example could be the Human Rights Act 1998. Parliament could in legal theory expressly repeal this statute with a simple majority; however, it might be difficult to get the political support for such a repeal. Repealing without such support could lead to the downfall of that government. In the same way, repeal of the European Communities Act 1972 and removal from Europe would be a difficult affair, needing at the least a political consensus.

(e)   *Constitutional limitations*

7–020   In spite of the lack of a codified constitution outlining constitutional rights and providing limits on legislative power, it would be wrong to say there are no constitutional limitations on what Parliament can do. Sir John Laws in a number of articles ("Law and Democracy" (1995) P.L. 87 and "The Constitution, Morals and Rights" (1996)

P.L. 635) has argued that true sovereignty belongs not to Parliament but to the constitution. Lord Woolf writing extra-judicially in "Droit Public-English Style" (1995) P.L. 57 stated:

> "If Parliament did the unthinkable, then I would say that the courts would also be required to act in a manner which would be without precedent. Some judges might chose to do so by saying that it was an unrebuttable presumption that Parliament could never intend such a result. I myself would consider there were advantages in making it clear that ultimately there are even limits on the supremacy of Parliament which it is the courts' inalienable responsibility to identify and uphold ... they are no more than are necessary to enable the rule of law to be preserved." (at p.69)

The emphasis in academic writing such as the above and recently in some dicta of their Lordships in *R. (on the application of Jackson) v Att-Gen* [2005] UKHL 56 is that Parliament cannot legislate contrary to the rule of law. The *Jackson* case (discussed in more detail at paras 7–032 and 7–041) concerned a challenge to the legality of the Hunting Act 2004 passed by the House of Commons without the House of Lords' consent under the Parliament Acts 1911 and 1949 procedure. The applicants argued that the Parliament Act 1949 was invalid. In concluding that both the Parliament Act 1949 and any legislation passed under it was validly enacted legislation, three of their Lordships went into a wider discussion of the constitutional limits on parliamentary sovereignty. Lord Steyn gave some examples of what might be considered unacceptable:

> "It is not unthinkable that circumstance could arise where the courts may have to qualify a principle established on a different hypothesis of constitutionalism. In exceptional circumstances involving an attempt to abolish judicial review or the ordinary role of the courts, the Appellate Committee of the House of Lords or a new Supreme Court may have to consider whether this is a constitutional fundamental which even a sovereign Parliament acting at the behest of a complaisant House of Commons cannot abolish." (at para.102)

Action such as the abolition of free elections, judicial review or other fundamental principals of the constitution could result in action by the court to invalidate or simply disapply the statutory provision. As a product of the common law the court may be prepared to change or suspend the rules relating to sovereignty if Parliament were to pass a law that undermined aspects of the UK constitution. However, whilst it seems that the courts can contemplate situations where they would have to act in the last resort to limit what Parliament can do, these situations are theoretical and the courts have made it clear that such actions would not be taken lightly. If judges were to repudiate the doctrine because they were finding and exercising unwritten rights, they could be seen as claiming in fact the ultimate authority for themselves. This would amount to a transfer of power to the judges, which would be a transfer initiated by the judges to protect rights chosen by them, rather than one brought about democratically by parliamentary enactment.

3.   Principle 2: courts cannot challenge an Act of Parliament

7–021   Dicey's second principle represents the negative limb of sovereignty: that no body, particularly the courts, can challenge the validity of an Act of Parliament. This is a corollary of the first principle and sets out the relationship between the courts and Parliament. The courts are subordinate and their role is to interpret and apply legislation passed by Parliament, whatever that may be.

(a)   *What is an Act of Parliament?*

7–022   The principle states that the courts cannot challenge an Act of Parliament so it becomes necessary to consider what a valid Act of Parliament is. In the absence of a codified constitution the definition of an Act of Parliament is a matter of common law (called the rule of recognition). In Britain for a Bill to become law it must have been passed by the House of Commons and House of Lords and given Royal Assent by the monarch. In *Stockdale v Hansard* (1839) 9 AD & E 2 the court ruled that a resolution of the House of Commons was not an Act of Parliament. In this case the House of Commons sought to include Hansard publications within parliamentary privilege. Stockdale sought to rely on Hansard in court and argued that the resolution did not amount to a validly enacted Act of Parliament.

   The courts are not concerned with the internal processes of Parliament such as whether a Bill has had two or three readings or went before a Public Bill committee. They are simply concerned that the three constituent components (whatever their composition) have agreed to the legislation.

(b)   *No challenge on grounds of substance*

7–023   Parliament can pass any law it wishes and so the courts cannot invalidate or allow a challenge on the grounds of its substance. In *R. v Jordan* [1967] Crim. L.R. 483 the High Court held that the courts did not have the power to question the validity of primary legislation. Jordan had argued that the Race Relations Act 1965 under which he was convicted of offences was invalid as it infringed the constitutional right of freedom of expression. The Court was clear that no challenge lay against primary legislation and Jordan's challenge failed.

(c)   *No challenge on grounds of procedure*

7–024   When Acts of Parliament have been challenged on grounds of procedure, the courts have followed what is called "the enrolled bill rule" as stated by Lord Campbell in *Edinburgh & Dalkeith Railway Co v Wauchope* (1842) 8 Cl. & F. 710:

"All that a court of justice can look to is the parliamentary roll; they see that an Act has passed both Houses of Parliament, and that it has received the royal assent, and no court of justice can inquire into the manner in which it was introduced into Parliament, what was done previously to its being introduced, or what passed in Parliament during the various stages of its progress through both Houses of Parliament." (at p.725)

In this case, Wauchope argued that provisions of a private Act should not be applied because during its passage it had not complied with the standing orders of the House of Commons requiring consultation of those likely to be affected by the legislation.

This principle was re-affirmed by the House of Lords in *Pickin v British Railways Board* [1974] A.C. 765 and is clearly stated in Halsburys Laws of England. Lord Morris in *Pickin* stated (at p.789) "When an enactment is passed there is finality unless and until it is amended or repealed by Parliament. In the courts there may be argument as to the correct interpretation of the enactment: there must be none as to whether it should be on the Statute Book at all". A similar point was made by Lord Simon (at p.798) who stated the position that "the courts in this country have no power to declare enacted law to be invalid".

(i) Constitutional justification for the rule

In addition to the general principle of sovereignty there is further justification for the court's reluctance to question the validity of a statute on grounds of procedure. Parliament has the right to regulate its own proceedings (parliamentary privilege) and any interference by the court would contravene the privileges of Parliament and also potentially bring the courts into conflict with art.9 of the Bill of Rights (see Ch.11). For example, if Parliament decides that in future all Bills will have only two readings and be scrutinised by a specially convened committee, a failure to follow this procedure would not form a ground to challenge the validity of any subsequent enactment if both chambers and the monarch had consented to it.   7–025

However, as noted above, the courts can rule whether an Act is indeed an Act and this would not be infringing the rule in *Pickin* (see Lord Campbell's comments in *Edinburgh & Dalkeith Railway Co* above). In *R. (Jackson) v Att-Gen* [2005] UKHL 56, the first obstacle Mr Jackson had to overcome regarding the validity of the Parliament Act 1949 and the Hunting Act 2004 was the jurisdiction of the Court to hear the case. The validity of the Acts was held to be a justiciable issue. The House of Lords made it clear that the issue before them involved no question of parliamentary procedure (as in *Pickin*) but was rather a question of the proper interpretation of the provisions of the 1911 Act, therefore judicial inquiry was permissible (see Lord Bingham, para.27). However, although this was a unanimous decision and no argument was put forward on behalf of the Attorney-General that jurisdiction should be declined, Lord Hope noted "the fact that your Lordships have been willing to hear this appeal and to give judgement upon it is another indication that the courts have a part to play in defining the limits of Parliament's legislative power" (para.107).

4.   Principle 3: no Parliament can bind or be bound

7–026   In order for a legal system or constitution to reflect the principles and ideals of the time, the legislature must be able to change the laws. In many codified constitutions certain "important" principles or sections have a special legal status and cannot easily be changed. In short, they require certain procedures to be satisfied before that provision can be changed. This is known as entrenchment. The UK is different, not simply because it does not have a codified constitution where certain provisions are entrenched but also because of the continuing theory of sovereignty. The continuing theory states that Parliament is created anew every time it meets. The "new" Parliament has the same legislative power as the previous Parliament, irrespective of what previous Parliaments have enacted.

Arising from the operation of the first two principles of sovereignty is the third, that Parliament cannot be bound by a predecessor. Let us presuppose that the Human Rights Act 1998 contains a clause that it could not be repealed unless there was a referendum of the people and a two-thirds majority in both Houses of Parliament. According to the continuing theory of sovereignty, the 2018 Parliament would be able to repeal the HRA in the normal way with a majority in Parliament. It could arguably even do this without the consent of the House of Lords by using the Parliament Acts 1911 and 1949. The rationale for the third premise is simple: if a future Parliament could be bound by a particular statute or previous Parliament, then that future Parliament would no longer be sovereign. Indeed the sovereign Parliament would be the now defunct Parliament which enacted that entrenched statute.

There are two mechanisms of repeal; express and implied.

(a)   *Express repeal*

7–027   This is relatively simple and is the easiest and clearest example of the third principle in operation. Express repeal is when Parliament passes an Act with an express clause amending or repealing earlier legislation, for example, s.122(1) of the Land Registration Act 2002 states:

"The Land Registry Act 1862 (c.53) shall cease to have effect."

(b)   *Implied repeal*

7–028   Parliament does not always clearly indicate its intentions and expressly repeal earlier statutes. Situations arise where provisions of a later statute conflict with an earlier statute. If, for example, s.122 of the Land Registration Act 2002 had not been passed there would be a conflict between the Land Registry Act and the provisions in the Land Registration Act. The courts have developed a general rule that if a statute is wholly or partially inconsistent with a previous statute than the previous statute is impliedly repealed to the extent of the inconsistency. This is known as the doctrine of implied repeal and is illustrated in the following two cases arising out of similar facts.

In *Vauxhall Estates v Liverpool Corporation* [1932] 1 K.B. 733, the plaintiff claimed compensation for land which had been compulsorily purchased from the plaintiff by Liverpool Corporation. The plaintiff claimed that compensation should be assessed under the terms of the earlier and more generous Acquisition of Land (Assessment of Compensation) Act 1919 and relied on ss.1 and 7 of the Act in support. The defendants argued that the later Housing Act 1925 applied. Section 1 of the Acquisition of Land (Assessment of Compensation) Act 1919 provided that claims for compensation where land was compulsorily acquired whether under this statute or a future statute should be dealt with under the terms of the 1919 statute. Further, s.7 stated that:

> "The provisions of the Act or order by which the land is authorised to be acquired
> ... shall, in relation to the matters dealt with in this Act, have effect subject to this
> Act, and so far as inconsistent with this Act those provisions shall cease to have or
> shall not have effect: ... "

In other words s.7 of the 1919 Act rendered the Housing Act 1925 ineffective by attempting to bind future Parliaments. Avory J. stated that no Act of Parliament could provide that no future Act could interfere with its provisions and so applied the later 1925 Act. The fact that the 1925 Act made no express mention or repeal of the 1919 Act was irrelevant, the repeal was implied. In relation to any inconsistency, the 1919 Act had been impliedly repealed.

The doctrine was explained more clearly in a case concerning the same Act; *Ellen Street Estates v Minister of Health* [1934] 1 K.B. 590. Maugham L.J., in a much quoted dictum, said:

> "The Legislature cannot, according to our constitution, bind itself as to the form of
> subsequent legislation, and it is impossible for Parliament to enact that in a sub-
> sequent statute dealing with the same subject-matter there can be no implied
> repeal. If in a subsequent Act Parliament chooses to make it plain that the earlier
> statute is being to some extent repealed, effect must be given to that intention just
> because it is the will of the Legislature." (at p.597)

(i)   Implied repeal and constitutional statutes

It is clear from Maugham L.J.'s dictum that the doctrine as understood in 1934 per-   **7–029**
mitted no exceptions. As Dicey had articulated in the 19th century, all statutes coming from Parliament have the same status, with the most recent statute prevailing as it represents the current Parliament's intentions.

However, recent developments have suggested that the doctrine of implied repeal is a general rule to which there are exceptions. These exceptions may exist for what are termed "constitutional statutes"; statutes which are considered of fundamental importance in shaping the constitution and/or governing relations between the state and its citizens. One such statute is the European Communities Act 1972 (ECA) which put into domestic effect the UK's membership of the European Union. It was recognised by Lord Denning in *Macarthys Ltd v Smith* [1979] I.C.R. 785 that s.2(4) of the ECA had abolished the doctrine of implied repeal in so far as community law was concerned. It is also considered not to apply to the Human Rights Act 1998 (see discussion at para.7–034).

In *Thoburn v Sunderland City Council*; *Hunt v Hackney London Borough Council*; *Harman v Cornwall County Council*; *Collins v Sutton Borough Council* [2002] EWHC 195 (Admin), Lord Justice Laws gave a clear articulation of these exceptions. The case concerned domestic legislation which gave effect to European Union Directives which made it compulsory for Member States to adopt a metric system of weights and measures. Domestic legislation was brought in by virtue of s.2 of the ECA. The defendants in the first three cases and Collins in the fourth case were all food traders who relied on the Weights and Measures Act 1985 which expressly permitted the use of both imperial and metric weights. It was claimed that this Act impliedly repealed the ECA.

Laws L.J. found no inconsistency but nonetheless went on to discuss the doctrine of implied repeal. At para.60 he stated:

> "In the present state of its maturity the common law has come to recognise that there exist rights which should properly be classified as constitutional or fundamental ... We should recognise a hierarchy of Acts of Parliament: as it were 'ordinary' statutes and 'constitutional' statutes. The two categories must be distinguished on a principled basis. In my opinion a constitutional statute is one which (a) conditions the legal relationship between citizen and state in some general, overarching manner, or (b) enlarges or diminishes the scope of what we would now regard as fundamental constitutional rights. ... The special status of constitutional statutes follows the special status of constitutional rights. Examples are Magna Carta 1297, the Bill of Rights 1689, the Union with Scotland Act 1706, the Reform Acts which distributed and enlarged the franchise (Representation of the People Acts 1832, 1867 and 1884, the Human Rights Act 1998, the Scotland Act 1998 and the Government of Wales Act 1998. The 1972 Act clearly belongs in this family. It incorporated the whole corpus of substantive Community rights and obligations, and gave overriding domestic effect to the judicial and administrative machinery of Community law. It may be there has never been a statute having such profound effects on so many dimensions of our daily lives. The 1972 Act is, by force of the common law, a constitutional statute ... Ordinary statutes may be impliedly repealed. Constitutional statutes may not. For the repeal of a constitutional Act or the abrogation of a fundamental right to be effected by statute, the court would apply this test: is it shown that the legislature's actual—not imputed, constructive or presumed—intention was to effect the repeal or abrogation? I think the test could only be met by express words in the later statute, or by words so specific that the inference of an actual determination to effect the result contended for was irresistible. The ordinary rule of implied repeal does not satisfy this test. Accordingly, it has no application to constitutional statutes."

Whilst perhaps recognising the practical reality, Laws L.J.'s statement is not without controversy. Laws is suggesting that a hierarchy of statutes exist, with those operating at a constitutional level having a higher status than other statutes. This is not consistent with Dicey's approach. While these statutes cannot be impliedly repealed they can be expressly repealed with a simple majority and in the same way as any other statute, in this sense they do not have a higher status. It should also be noted that whilst Laws was recognising the practical situation in so far as implied repeal is concerned, his obiter has not been affirmed in the higher courts.

(ii)   Legal entrenchment of the substance of legislation

The nature of the UK constitution is that all laws have equal status. This is not so in   **7–030** any other country with a codified constitution where substantive parts are entrenched or protected against easy repeal or alteration. The obvious advantage of entrenchment is that it protects the values and content of a constitution against the actions of a single government and acts as a check against abuse or misuse of power. In the UK it is commonly accepted that the power of Parliament to repeal the European Communities Act 1972 and the Human Rights Act 1998 remains, though there may well be political and practical restraints on the exercise of this theoretical power. The Act of Union between England and Scotland in 1706 is one measure which is said by some to have the special status of a constituent or parental act giving birth to the Parliament of Great Britain. Some provisions within the Act of Union are also said to be fundamental and to govern "forever" (for example provisions relating to the Protestant church).

However, this assertion has little merit or practical evidence. Dicey for example argued that the Act had no greater status than the Dentists Act 1878. He stated that the old Parliaments of England and Scotland "abolished" themselves and simply re-constituted in a new equally supreme Parliament of the UK which retained all the characteristics of the old English Parliament but with an expanded territory. He argued that if the intention of the two countries at the time was that the Acts of Union would be supreme then they would have left alive the Parliaments of England and Scotland and/or conferred power on the UK Parliament to pass law that did not infringe or repeal the Act of Union.

However, the Scottish Courts have given some credence to the argument. In *Mac-Cormick v Lord Advocate* [1953] S.C. 396, Scottish Nationalists raised an objection to the designation of Queen Elizabeth as the Second. They argued that as a matter of fact the first Queen Elizabeth had been Queen of England not Scotland. The application was dismissed but the Lord President, Lord Cooper, in obiter stated that he could not find in the Union legislation any provision which made the legislature of Great Britain "absolutely sovereign":

> "The principle of the unlimited sovereignty of Parliament is a distinctively English principle which has no counterpart in Scottish Constitutional law . . . . Considering that the Union legislation extinguished the parliaments of Scotland and England and replaced them by a new Parliament, I have difficulty in seeing why it should have been supposed that the new Parliament of Great Britain must inherit all the peculiar characteristics of the English Parliament, as if all that happened in 1707 was that Scottish representatives were admitted to the Parliament of England. That is not what was done." (at p.411)

However, the Lord President's statements are obiter and there is little practical evidence to suggest that the Act of Union has a special status. In particular, core components of the Union legislation have been amended by ordinary Acts of Parliament. For example, art.II on the succession of the monarchy was amended by ordinary Act of Parliament in His Majesty's Declaration of Abdication Act 1936 and the requirement that university professors subscribe to the Protestant religion was partly repealed by the Universities (Scotland) Act 1853.

A similar argument has been made regarding the Act of Union with Ireland 1800 (which unified the UK with Ireland). Article 5 of the Union (regarding the United Church of England and Ireland) was supposed to "remain in full force for ever". In 1869 the Irish Church was de-established and in 1949 the Ireland Act recognised the republican status and independence of the South, so effectively terminating the union.

At times, the ability of the United Kingdom Parliament to legislate for former colonies has been questioned suggesting that Parliament has bound itself (see *Blackburn v Att-Gen* [1971] 1 W.L.R. 1037; *Manuel v Att-Gen* [1983] Ch. 77), however, the rulings in these cases clearly show the distinction which must be drawn between the idea of legal supremacy and political supremacy. Lord Denning M.R. in *Blackburn* stating "legal theory does not always march alongside political reality". However, a clear illustration that Parliament can still legislate for former colonies is *Madzimbamuto v Larder-Burke* [1969] 1 A.C. 645. Here Parliament legislated for Rhodesia without its consent and contrary to the Statute of Westminster s.4, and the courts did not hold the Act invalid.

7–031 **The self-embracing theory of sovereignty and the doctrine of manner and form:** Hart, in *The Concept of Law* (2nd edn (Clarendon Press, 1994)), distinguished between two types of sovereignty: continuing and self-embracing. The continuing theory, of which Dicey is the main advocate, regards each "new" Parliament as having the same legislative power as the previous, irrespective of any and all legislation the previous Parliament may have passed. Under the traditional continuing theory of sovereignty any entrenchment clause would not be binding and the doctrine of implied or express repeal would operate.

The self-embracing theory holds that Parliament's sovereignty does include the power to bind itself and its successors as to the manner and form in which legislation is passed (procedural entrenchment). All the Parliaments taken together are still sovereign and so Parliament remains sovereign, but over time. Thus, if a statute were to prescribe a particular manner or form for its amendment or repeal this would be binding and any attempt to achieve alteration by an alternative method would be ineffective.

The manner and form argument, which is an off-shoot of the self-embracing theory, stems largely from Jennings, *Law and the Constitution* (1959). According to Jennings the common law has developed a rule for determining what a valid statute is. This is known as the rule of recognition and is satisfied when the House of Commons, House of Lords and monarch assent to legislation. As statute is legally superior to common law it follows that Parliament can redefine the rule of recognition by enacting legislation, for example, requiring that to amend a statute, a two-third's majority in both Houses is required. The courts would then be bound to apply this new rule. Jennings formulated the argument in the following terms:

"Legal sovereignty is merely a name indicating that the established legislature has for the time being power to make laws of any kind in the manner required by law. That is, a rule expressed to be made by the Queen [the House of Commons and the House of Lords] will be recognised by the courts including a rule which alters this law itself. If this be so, the legal sovereign may impose legal limitations upon itself, because its power to change the law includes the power to change the law affecting itself ... "

Jennings arguments found support with Heuston, *Essays in Constitutional Law* (2nd edn (London: Stevens & Sons Ltd, 1964)) who termed it the "new view" of sovereignty; Geoffrey Marshall, *Constitutional Theory* (1971)) and S.A. De Smith, *Constitutional and Administrative Law* (2nd edn (1973)). The distinction between the two views of sovereignty appears relatively straightforward. The old traditional view holds that Parliament cannot be bound whilst the new view supports the idea that Parliament can redefine itself and bind its successors as to the procedure (manner and form) required to amend the legislation.

The logic of the manner and form argument rests on the assumption that the rule of recognition is a common law principle. Wade "The Basis of Legal Sovereignty" (1955) C.L.J. disagrees with this assumption and believes the rule of recognition is something prior to and superior to the common law. In essence its basis is political fact stemming from the 1688 Revolution and not legal theory. As a result, something equally significant would be necessary to break this settlement and allow Parliament to redefine itself.

Academic theory aside, what practical evidence exists to support the argument put forward by the "new" theorists? Three cases from the Commonwealth are often used as support for the manner and form argument. These are *Att-Gen for New South Wales v Trethowan* [1932] A.C. 536, PC; *Harris v Minister of the Interior* (1952) (2) S.A. 428 and *The Bribery Commissioner v Pedrick Ranasinghe* [1965] A.C. 172.

Att-Gen for New South Wales v Trethowan was a decision of the Privy Council. The Colonial Laws Validity Act 1865 s.5 (passed by the UK Parliament) provided that the New South Wales legislature would have full power to make law "provided that such laws shall have been passed in such manner and form provisions in force at the time". The Constitution Amendment Act 1929 (amending the New South Wales Constitution Act 1902) provided that no Bill abolishing the Upper House of the legislature (Legislative Council) shall be presented for Royal Assent unless approved by a referendum. It further held that this clause could not be repealed except by the same process. Effectively, the provisions were doubly entrenched. In 1930, two Bills passed through both House removing the referendum requirement and abolishing the Upper House. Two members of the threatened Upper House sought an injunction to restrain submission of the Bills for Royal Assent.

The Privy Council said the case was one of interpretation and depended entirely on a consideration of the meaning and effect of s.5 of the Colonial Laws Validity Act. The New South Wales legislature was a subordinate body which derived its power from the sovereign UK and was therefore bound to follow the provisions in s.5. As a result, the Privy Council held that the requirement of a referendum was binding on the legislature until it had been abolished by a law passed in the manner and form required. The specific manner and form were those laid down in the 1929 Act.

Harris v Minister of the Interior (1952) (2) S.A. 428 concerned a similar issue. The UK passed the South Africa Act 1909 uniting the four South African colonies under a single legislature and creating a constitution. The South African legislature mirrored the UK version with a bi-cameral system; a requirement for a simple majority in both houses and Royal Assent to pass legislation. However, there were some exceptions to the majority principle. In particular, s.35 provided that the rights of coloured citizens to be registered on the same electoral role as whites could not be removed unless such legislation had a two-thirds majority in both Houses sitting in a joint session. Section 152 further provided that s.35 could not be repealed unless agreed to by a two-thirds majority of members in a joint session of both Houses.

The Statute of Westminster 1931 recognised South Africa as a sovereign state though no changes were made to the 1909 Constitution Act. In 1951, the Separate Representation of Voters Act was passed by a simple majority. The Act created separate electoral registers and voting systems for white and coloured citizens. The constitutionality of the Act was challenged by several coloured voters on the basis that the procedure in s.35 of the South Africa Act had not been complied with.

The government argued that after 1931 South Africa had become a sovereign state, with a sovereign legislature and was therefore not bound by the 1909 constitution, enacted whilst a colony. The Supreme Court of South Africa agreed that South Africa was a sovereign state with a sovereign legislature but concluded that the Representation of Voters Act was unconstitutional. The court held that South Africa had adopted s.35 of the 1909 as part of its constitutional settlement when it gained independence. Until such time as two-thirds of both House repealed the section, they remained bound by it.

In *The Bribery Commissioner v Pedrick Ranasinghe* [1965] A.C. 172, s.29(4) of Ceylon's Constitution Order 1946 (now Sri Lanka) provided that Parliament could amend or repeal any of the provisions of the Order provided that any Bill presented for Royal Assent had been approved by the Speaker who had certified that two-thirds of the Members of the House of the Representatives had voted in favour of the Bill. Section 55 of the Constitution Order provided for the appointment of junior members of the judiciary by a Judicial Service Commission.

The Bribery Amendment Act 1958 created Bribery Tribunals for the trial of persons prosecuted for bribery. Section 41 provided for the appointment of tribunal members by the Governor-General on the advice of the Minister of Justice. It did not have a Speaker's certificate nor was it passed by the necessary majority. Ranasingh was prosecuted for a bribery offence before the tribunal and was convicted and sentenced to a term of imprisonment and a fine. The question before the Privy Council was whether the statutory provisions for the appointment of members of the panel of the Bribery Tribunal otherwise than by the Judicial Service Commission conflicted with s.55 of the constitution, and, if so, whether those provisions were valid. The Privy Council affirmed the decision of the Supreme Court that in the case of amendment and repeal of the constitution the Speaker's certificate was a necessary part of the legislative process. As the Bribery Amendment Act did not conform to the manner and form requirements, it was invalid and ultra vires. Mr Ranasingh's conviction was also null and void.

Munro, *Studies in Constitutional Law* (2nd edn (London: Butterworths, 1999), p.158) indicates that two views are possible of these cases. Firstly that there is a general rule that legislation may only be enacted in the manner and form required by law and that the UK Parliament is as bound by this requirement as was the New South Wales

Legislature. Secondly, that the decisions have little relevance to the UK. Whilst in each of these cases the manner and form requirements were held to be binding on the legislatures concerned, each legislature concerned was subordinate.

Heusten, *Essays in Constitutional Law*, would seem to prefer the first view. He argues the cases demonstrate manner and form requirements must be obeyed unless changed in accordance with the procedures. He feels it irrelevant whether the rule which identifies the sovereign body comes entirely from the common law or from statute. Geoffrey Marshall, *Constitutional Theory*, takes a similar view and makes much of one of Lord Pearce's remarks in *Bribery Commissioner*:

> "But the proposition which is not acceptable is that a legislature, once established, has some inherent power derived from the mere fact of its establishment to make a valid law by the resolution of a bare majority which its own constituent instrument has said shall not be a valid law unless made by a different type of majority or by a different legislative process and this is the proposition which is in reality involved in the argument." (at p.198)

Marshall feels this remark implies "that both non-sovereign and sovereign legislatures may be subject to procedural rules entrenching parts of the law from simple majority repeal" (at p.55). Munro, dealing with these arguments, says "it is hard to see how this can tell us anything about the United Kingdom Parliament, whose powers are not defined or derived from any statute" (at p.158). To take Lord Pearce's words, the UK legislature is not subject to any constituent instrument. Wade, "The Basis of Legal Sovereignty", would appear to agree and argues that if you transpose these decisions to the British context they are simply instances of statutory bodies created by Parliament acting beyond the confines of the authority bestowed on them by Parliament. The legislatures in *Trethowan & Bribery Commissioner* were subordinate and in *Harris* the Supreme Court's decision was determined by political issues not legal ones.

Overall, Munro feels that the cases cited by the:

> "manner and form school do not, in the end, seem very helpful. The powers and forms of law-making by the United Kingdom Parliament, as Lord Pearce observed, are not prescribed by any higher law. As to whether Parliament may alter these so as to restrict future parliaments, the suggestion has not been supported in British cases, and was denied in *Vauxhall Estates Ltd*." (at p.160)

The Parliament Acts: The arguments surrounding whether Parliament can be bound by manner and form requirements has come to prominence more recently with some obiter comments made in the *R. (Jackson) v Att-Gen* [2005] UKHL 56 (*Jackson*) case. **7–032**

It can be argued (for example, De Smith and Brazier, *Constitutional & Administrative Law* (5th edn (Penguin, 1985) at p.93) that Parliament has the legal capacity to regulate its own component parts and redefine itself. Parliament as a body is supreme, and the Commons, Lords and the monarch as part of Parliament are legally inferior to Parliament itself. It follows from this that Parliament may enact legislation placing specific limits on the legal competence of either House and the courts will adhere to Parliament's will by ensuring those limits are observed. Heutson, *Essays in Constitutional Law*

(1964) advanced a similar idea but supports his argument by reference to the Commonwealth cases. A similar but slightly different approach is that taken by Jennings and concerns the rule of recognition. The rule of recognition is a common law concept and can either be redefined by Parliament or by the courts without parliamentary initiative. With the Parliament Acts, Parliament altered the rule of recognition and the courts recognised this as such. Loveland notes that Jennings' thesis, taken to its logical conclusion, suggests that the common law is legally superior to Act of Parliament. Importantly he argues that this suggests that the "courts and not the legislature are the ultimate source of legal authority", and resulting from this we might find "that at any moment the courts had exercised a power explicitly to refuse to apply statutes of which they disapproved" (p.789).

Whatever theoretical basis is argued the point is similar, Parliament can stipulate a certain manner and form requirement and this will be observed by the courts. With the obiter comments in *Jackson*, it seems possible that this may be the case. The Parliament Act 1911 provides that in certain circumstances a Bill can become an Act without the approval of the House of Lords. The key part of the *Jackson* case relevant for discussion here is the express exception mentioned in s.2(1) of the Parliament Act 1911. Section 2(1) expressly prohibits the procedure being used to extend the life of Parliament or for private or local Bills. Of particular note are the comments by their Lordships relating to whether s.2(1) was binding on future parliaments.

All of their Lordships concluded that s.2(1) was binding in the sense that Parliament composed of the Queen and Commons could not act contrary to it. Lord Steyn and Baroness Hale argued by passing the Parliament Act 1911, Parliament had redefined its composition to just be the Queen and Commons. This re-definition binds the courts and so Parliament when composed of the Queen and Commons cannot pass legislation extending the life of Parliament. Lord Hope stated:

" ... But, apart from the traditional method of law making, Parliament acting as ordinarily constituted may functionally redistribute legislative power in different ways. For example, Parliament could for specific purpose provide for a two-thirds majority in the House of Commons and the House of Lords. This would involve a redefinition of Parliament for a specific purpose. Such redefinition could not be disregarded."

Baroness Hale took the argument one step forward:

"If the sovereign Parliament can redefine itself downwards, to remove or modify the requirement for the consent of the Upper House, it may very well be that it can also redefine itself upwards, to require a particular Parliamentary majority or a popular referendum for particular types of measure. In each case, the courts would be respecting the will of the sovereign Parliament as constituted when that will had been expressed." (at para.163)

Their Lordships went further than this and also considered whether Parliament could achieve by two steps what they would not allow by one. In other words, could they use the Parliament Act procedure to remove the exception in s.2(1) and then use the "new" Parliament Act procedure to extend the life of Parliament; Lord Bingham thought this to be permissible as there is nothing in the 1911 Act that says it cannot be amended (see para.32). However, the majority of their Lordship's suggested that the two step process would not be permissible. Baroness Hale (at para.164) believed "Parliament was disabled from using the procedure to remove the exception". Lord Hope was more expressive:

" ... But I believe, in agreement with a majority of your Lordships, that such an obvious device to get round the express prohibition would be as vulnerable to a declaration of invalidity as a direct breach of it. In other words, there is an implied prohibition against the use of the section 2(1) procedure in such circumstances." (at para.122)

So where does this leave the manner and form debate? Loveland (p.785) feels "it is now rather less difficult to construct a legal argument supporting the idea of entrenched legislation than it was in the 1950s, when *Harris* and *McCormack* triggered a rash of interest ... ". If the dicta in *Jackson* is taken to represent the views of the majority then it seems possible that certain entrenchment provisions could be binding. As to what ones, well this would largely depend on the substance of the legislation and the political situation that led to the passage of the Act. A point that comes across from the *Jackson* decision as a whole is the importance of the history behind the passage of the Parliament Act 1911 and recognition of this fact led many of their Lordships to come to the conclusions they did.

5. Parliamentary sovereignty and devolution

In 1998 Parliament devolved power to Scotland (Scotland Act 1998), Northern Ireland   **7–033** (Northern Ireland Act 1998) and Wales (Government of Wales Act 1998). Each country has a different form of devolution, with Scotland being the most independent (see Ch.2 for further detail). Whilst devolution on its face might suggest Parliament has bound itself in terms of subject matter, each country remains subordinate to Westminster. Section 28(7) of the Scotland Act 1998 illustrates this clearly as it provides that Westminster can still legislate for Scotland; "this section does not affect the power of the United Kingdom to make laws for Scotland". Practically, there is also evidence; from October 2000 to May 2007 the Northern Ireland Assembly was suspended and its powers reverted to the Northern Ireland Office in Westminster.

That Parliament retains legal sovereignty is thus clear, but the distinction between legal and political reality must be kept in mind. As legal theory must give way to practical reality and while Parliament legislating for Ireland is not impossible to envisage, a similar course of action in relation to Scotland would be less likely. In relation to Scotland, a constitutional convention has recently been established, the Sewel Convention, which regulates the relationship between the two Houses. The Convention provides that Westminster will not legislate for Scotland on a devolved matter without first obtaining the consent of the Scottish Parliament. So whilst Westminster could pass legislation on devolved matters without the Scottish Parliament's consent, to do so would be unconstitutional and therefore unlikely.

6.   Parliamentary sovereignty and human rights

7–034   The Human Rights Act 1998 (HRA) incorporates the European Convention on Human Rights into domestic law and aims to provide a domestic remedy for violations of the ECHR by a public authority. The HRA seems to preserve sovereignty. Lord Steyn in *R. v DPP Ex p. Kebilene* [1999] 3 W.L.R. 972 noted "it is crystal clear that the carefully and subtly drafted Human Rights Act 1998 preserves the principles of Parliamentary sovereignty". The HRA does not give power to the courts to invalidate Acts of Parliament that are inconsistent with ECHR rights; instead under s.4 of the HRA the higher courts can issue a declaration of incompatibility. Such a declaration does not affect the continuing validity of the statute (s.4(6)(a), though the government through Parliament may if it wishes, amend the offending legislation. A clear example of this is the declaration of incompatibility issued against s.23 of the Anti-Terrorism Crime and Security Act 2001 (ATCSA). The ATCSA permitted indefinite detention of foreign nationals suspected of terrorism and was found to be inconsistent with art.5(1) (liberty and security of person). Despite "winning" their case, those detained under s.23 remained so until the section was repealed by the Prevention of Terrorism Act 2005 s.16(2)(a).

A second point to note is the HRA does not attempt to bind future Parliaments from legislating in breach of human rights. Instead s.3(1) of the HRA imposes a new interpretative obligation on the courts. It provides that:

"[s]o far as possible to do so, primary and subordinate legislation must be read and given effect in a way which is compatible with Convention rights."

Lord Steyn in *R. v A (Complainant's Sexual History) (No.2)* [2001] UKHL 25 stated:

" . . . [T]he interpretative obligation under section 3 of the 1998 Act is a strong one. It applies even if there is no ambiguity in the language in the sense of the language being capable of two different meanings." (at para.44)

While the interpretative duty under s.3 is certainly a strong one and can result in the HRA prevailing over a subsequently enacted statute, it does not violate Parliamentary sovereignty. It is only permissible to construe legislation in accordance with convention rights "so far as it is possible to do so" and it seems that as a general rule the judiciary are unwilling to use s.3 in a manner that involves radical statutory reform (see *Re S (Children) and Re W (Care Orders)* [2002] UKHL 10; *Bellinger v Bellinger* [2003] UKHL 21; *Ghaidan v Godin-Mendoza* [2004] UKHL 30 discussed in Ch.21).

Consistent with the principle that Parliament cannot bind or be bound, the HRA does not have a special legal status and is not protected. In direct contrast to a Bill of Rights found in many codified constitutions, the HRA can be expressly repealed with a simple majority. However, to dismiss the HRA as an ordinary statute is too simplistic. It can be argued that the HRA is at least politically entrenched and it cannot be impliedly repealed by legislation passed after 1998 (see comment by Laws L.J. in *Thoburn v Sunderland City Council* [2002] EWHC 195 (Admin)).

EU and Parliamentary Sovereignty

The UK has a dualist constitutional system with domestic and international law sitting **7-035** separately and side by side. Any international Treaty signed by the Executive does not create directly enforceable legal obligations in domestic law until brought into effect by an Act of Parliament. Following the signing of the Treaty of Accession, Parliament passed the European Communities Act 1972 to take the UK into the European Community (as it then was).

The sovereignty of Parliament, in particular the principle that Parliament can make or unmake any law, seems at odds with the idea of european union. The primacy of European law, well known at the time of the UK's ascension, would appear to fundamentally qualify the operation of parliamentary sovereignty in the UK. Inevitably, membership of the EC raised the question of how the courts should deal with incompatibility between EC law and an inconsistent Act of Parliament.

1. The primacy of European Law

The primacy of European Law is not expressly set out in the EC Treaty but was made **7-036** clear by the European Court of Justice in the early 1960s. According to the ECJ, by joining the EC Member States transferred some of their legislative competence to the EC institutions. In *Van Gend & Loos v Nederlandse administratie der belastingen* [1963] E.C.R. 1 the court stated as much:

> " ... the Community constitutes a new legal order of international law for the benefit of which the states have limited their sovereign rights, albeit within limited fields, and the subjects of which comprise not only Member States but also their nationals."

This principle was re-affirmed in *Costa v ENEL* [1964] E.C.R. 585, where on a reference to the ECJ, the Italian government argued later Italian law superseded EC law. The ECJ stated:

> "by creating a community of unlimited duration, having its own institutions, its own personality, its own legal capacity and capacity of representation on the international plane and, more particularly, real powers stemming from a limitation of sovereignty or a transfer of powers from the states to the community, the Member States have limited their sovereign rights and have thus created a body of law which binds both their nationals and themselves ... however framed, without being deprived of its character as community law and without the legal basis of the community itself being called into question."

2.   European Communities Act 1972

7–037   The European Communities Act 1972 came into effect January 1, 1973. Section 2(1) of the Act gives direct effect to community law and provides:

> "All such rights, powers, liabilities, obligations and restrictions from time to time arising by or under the treaties ... are without further enactment to be given legal effect ... in the United Kingdom."

Section 2(2) provides for the making of secondary legislation for the purpose of implementing EC legislation which is not directly applicable (for example, directives). Section 2(4) is the most controversial section of the Act, providing that any domestic legislation:

> "passed or to be passed, other than one contained in this part of the this Act, shall be construed and have effect subject to the foregoing provisions of this section [s2(1) and 2(2)]."

The key part of s.2(4) is it applies to legislation that has been passed as well as to legislation that is to be passed. The doctrine of implied repeal would operate for inconsistent legislation passed before 1973, the provisions in s.2(4) clearly signalling the 1972 Parliament's intent that this should be so. However, the provision applies to future legislation and literally appears to bind future Parliaments as to the legislation they can make.

3.   European Communities Act 1972 section 2(4): a rule of construction?

7–038   The courts have taken s.2(4) as an obligation to interpret domestic legislation in a way that ensures domestic law conforms to EC law. In *Macarthys Ltd v Smith* [1979] 1 W.L.R. 1189 the Court of Appeal was asked to consider whether the literal wording of the Equal Pay Act 1970 as amended by the Sex Discrimination Act 1975 was consistent with art.119. Following a four month vacancy Macarthys Ltd employed Mrs Smith to manage their stockroom. Her duties were slightly different and she was paid less than the previous employee in the position, who was male. Mrs Smith brought proceedings before an industrial tribunal alleging discrimination. In the first Court of Appeal case ([1979] 1 W.L.R. 1189), Lord Denning considered the scope of s.2(4) stating:

> "In construing our statute, we are entitled to look to the Treaty as an aid to its construction; but not only as an aid but as an overriding force. If on close investigation it should appear that our legislation is deficient or is inconsistent with Community law by some oversight of our draftsmen then it is our bounden duty to give priority to Community law. Such is the result of s 2(1) and (4) of the European Communities Act 1972." (at p.329)

Lord Denning considered that he was obliged to construe the statute purposively because of ECA s.2(4). He took the view that the Sex Discrimination Act 1975 and the Treaty should be read as a "harmonious whole" (at p.330). As the purpose of the domestic statutes was to eliminate discrimination against women, the Equal Pay Act should be interpreted so as to apply to cases where a woman is employed at the same job doing the same work "in succession" to a man. However, the majority of the Court of Appeal did not feel the same way and because of the perceived uncertainty in art.119, they referred the question to the ECJ for a preliminary ruling on the true meaning of art.119. The ECJ held that the majority view was wrong and post-accession legislation by a Member State must comply with EC legislation and must also be applied purposively. This was subsequently applied by the Court of Appeal in [1981] 1 Q.B. 180.

In *Garland v British Rail Engineering Ltd* [1983] 1 A.C. 751, Lord Diplock echoed the approach of Lord Denning. He considered that:

> "anything short of an express positive statement in an Act of Parliament passed after 1 January 1973, that a particular provision is intended to be made in breach of an obligation assumed by the United Kingdom under a Community Treaty, would justify an English court in construing that provision in a manner inconsistent with a Community Treaty obligation of the United Kingdom, however wide a departure from the prima facie meaning of the language of the provision might be needed in order to achieve consistency." (at p.771)

The cases above concerned the impact of directly effective Community law. However, the principles from the cases have been extended to cover indirect effect Community law. Where there appears to be an inconsistency between a directive and the Act of Parliament giving effect to the directive, the House of Lords in *Pickstone v Freeman* [1989] A.C. 66 thought the Act should be interpreted in a way which gives effect to the Community provision. This is even though it may mean some distortion of the literal interpretation. However, where there is inconsistency between a directive and Act of Parliament that is not specifically intended to give effect to the directive, then the courts only seek consistency in so far as permitted by the words used in the legislation (*Webb v EMO Cargo (UK) Ltd* [1992] 4 All E.R. 929).

It is clear from the preceding discussion that unless Parliament's intention is clear through the use of express words, the courts will construe the later statute in conformity with European law; a point made clearly by both Lord Diplock in *Garland v British Rail Engineering Ltd* [1983] 1 A.C. 751 (above) and Lord Denning in *Macarthys Ltd v Smith* [1979] 1 W.L.R. 1189 when he said:

> "If the time should come when our Parliament deliberately passes an Act with the intention of repudiating the Treaty or any provision in it or intentionally of acting inconsistently with it and says so in express terms then I should have thought that it would be the duty of our courts to follow the statute of our Parliament ... Unless there is such an intentional and express repudiation of the Treaty, it is our duty to give priority to the Treaty." (at p.329)

Whilst it is clear from this approach that the doctrine of implied repeal does not operate for the ECA, this interpretative approach does not erode parliamentary supremacy.

While there can be recognition that the 1972 Parliament has bound future parliaments as to the substance of future legislation regarding EC issues, it is at best a weak manner and form argument. The courts do no more than "give effect" to Parliament's intention as laid down in the ECA. The courts do not recognise Community law as part of a superior constitutional and legal order but merely interpret legislation "purposively" in order to give effect to the UK's Treaty obligations. If Parliament were to make its intentions expressly clear, then according to the dicta above the courts would respect that intention.

4. The Factortame Litigation

7–039 None of the cases above concerned a direct challenge between legislation and European Community law. This challenge was not long in coming however, with a dispute over fishing rights which led to the *Factortame* series of cases.

The Merchant Shipping Act 1894 allowed foreign owned vessels to register as "British" and thereby gain fishing rights. As a result of the Common Fisheries Policy which limited the weight of fish which could be landed by the "British" fishing fleet, concerns were raised over these foreign owned vessels. The British government introduced the Merchant Shipping Act 1988 and the Merchant Shipping (Registration of Fishing Vessels) Regulations 1988 which altered the registration rules for ships whose catch would form part of the UK's fishing quota. For a vessel to be registered as British, individual owners either had to be British citizens or residents or the company had to be incorporated in Britain with 75 per cent of their shares owned by British citizens or residents. 95 Spanish companies who had previously been registered could not meet the new nationality requirements and had to cease fishing once the Act was in force. The Spanish applicants contended that the Act breached their rights under art.52 (rights of establishment) and sought an injunction suspending the operation of the Act.

The High Court referred the substantive question of the Act's compatibility to the ECJ (the first reference) and pending their ruling (estimates were given that it would take two years) granted an interim injunction against the Minister for Transport ordering that the Act should be "disapplied" and not enforced against the applicants. The Court of Appeal set aside the injunction on the basis that the High Court had no power to issue it. The House of Lords agreed.

The House of Lords accepted the applicants would suffer irreparable damage if the interim relief which they sought was not granted and they were successful in the main proceedings. However, they found that they did not have jurisdiction to grant interim relief for the following reasons:

- there was no authority for a British court to suspend or disapply an Act of Parliament because of the possibility it might prove incompatible. If the applicants failed to establish the rights they claimed before the ECJ the effect of the injunction would be to confer upon them rights directly contrary to what Parliament intended and equally to deprive British fishing vessels of their rights as determined by Parliament under the Act;

- the House of Lords could not grant an injunction against the Crown. Section 21 of the Crown Proceedings Act 1947 expressly precluded the granting of injunctions against the Crown in its official capacity;

- there was no overriding principle of EC law requiring the House of Lords to issue interim relief for rights which had not been pronounced by the ECJ.

The House of Lords referred the question of whether it was required to provide interim relief as a general principle of European Community Law (the second reference) to the ECJ. The ECJ in response to the second reference (*R. v Secretary of State for Transport Ex p. Factortame (No.2)* [1990] E.C.R. I-2433) affirmed that national courts should grant interim relief for the purpose of suspending national legislation where it appeared to be in conflict with directly effective provisions of community law. Any rule of law which sought to inhibit the granting of such relief (for example, the Crown Proceeding Act) was inconsistent with Community law. The case was remitted back to the House of Lords to apply the principles.

The House of Lords found in Factortame's favour and reinstated the injunction, thus disapplying the MSA. They announced they would give reasons at a later date. During the period between decision and reasons, Prime Minister Margaret Thatcher denounced the decision and the loss of sovereignty. Lord Bridge in *R. v Secretary of State for Transport Ex p. Factortame (No.2)* [1991] A.C. 603 took the opportunity to comment on the claims that the decision was a "novel and dangerous invasion by a Community institution of the sovereignty of the United Kingdom Parliament".

"But such comments are based on a misconception. If the supremacy within the European Community of Community law over the national law of Member States was not always inherent in the EEC Treaty ... it was certainly well established in the jurisprudence of the European Court of Justice long before the United Kingdom joined the Community. Thus, whatever limitation of its sovereignty Parliament accepted when it enacted the European Communities Act 1972 was entirely voluntary. Under the terms of the Act of 1972 it has always been clear that it was the duty of a United Kingdom court, when delivering final judgment, to override any rule of national law found to be in conflict with any directly enforceable rule of Community law ... Thus there is nothing in any way novel in according supremacy to rules of Community law in those areas to which they apply and to insist that, in the protection of rights under Community law, national courts must not be inhibited by rules of national law from granting interim relief in appropriate cases is no more than a logical recognition of that supremacy." (at p.659)

In *R. v Secretary of State for Transport Ex p. Factortame (No.3)* [1992] 1 Q.B. 680, the Divisional Court applied the ruling of the ECJ in respect of the first reference which had been issued in July 1991. They issued a declaration that the Merchant Shipping Act breached Community Law. Parliament subsequently passed the Merchant Shipping (Registration) Act 1993 amending the rules on registration.

In a case just a few year later, the House of Lords in *R. v Secretary of State for Employment Ex p. Equal Opportunities Commission* [1994] 2 W.L.R. 409 disapplied a provision of the Employment Protection (Consolidation) Act 1978 without a reference to the ECJ so establishing that the power to disapply lay with any court irrespective of whether a reference had been made.

5. Evaluation

7–040   The *Factortame* litigation not only re-emphasised the supremacy of Community law where a ruling had been given that there was an inconsistency but gave power to national courts to disapply Act of Parliaments where they appeared to conflict with EC law. Although Parliament did not expressly signal their intention to prevent EC nationals from registering their vessels as British, the purpose behind the Merchant Shipping Act was clear. On the one view, the decision of the House of Lords and the disapplication of the MSA challenges the sovereignty of Parliament to make any laws it wants. On the other hand if Parliament chose, it could expressly repeal the European Communities Act 1972. Given the early dicta of the British courts it is likely that the court would give legal effect to such a statute. However, as the UK becomes more involved in the European Community it is unlikely that such a course of action would result. For all practical purpose where the European Union has competence, sovereignty rests with them.

It has been argued that in *Factortame* the courts did something which Dicey suggested was impossible: they challenged an Act of Parliament. Whilst this may be the case, it is worth remembering the courts did not void an Act of Parliament or strike it down as unconstitutional, they simply denied its effects to the extent that it was inconsistent with EC law. In so far as the MSA was concerned, the Act remained in force and applied to non-EC nationals.

The constitutional significance of *Factortame* is not universally agreed. Some view the approach taken by Lord Bridge as simply one of construction. This view takes the basis that Parliament is presumed not to intend statutes to override EC law and any inconsistencies between the UK and EC statutes should be resolved in favour of the latter. This is unless Parliament has expressly indicated the contrary. Craig believes that this view is more likely to be favourable to judges because it is based on the will of Parliament and does not require them to deal with the idea of a limitation of sovereignty. Another view is that the *Factortame* decision is "revolutionary". An interesting consideration arising out of the litigation is not to what extent sovereignty has transferred to Europe but how, in Lord Bridge's words, the UK Parliament managed to "voluntarily limit its sovereignty". Loveland, *Constitutional, Administrative Law and Human Rights* (4th edn (OUP, 2006) at p.483) notes that the House of Lords did not grapple with how exactly the UK Parliament had managed to do this. H.R. Wade, "Sovereignty—revolution or evolution?" (1996) L.Q.R. 568 points out that Lord Bridge's reasoning makes very little sense. Lord Bridge does not rely on statutory construction and appears to take it for granted that Parliament can accept a limitation of its sovereignty which is effective both for the present and for the future. Wade believes the decision amounts to a "judicial revolution". The House of Lords altered the rule of recognition in order to given Community law the primacy that it required, with the result that the 1972 Parliament bound its successors. As Wade has often stated, the rule of recognition is a political fact which the courts can change when confronted with a new situation which so demands.

Whether it be Parliament and/or the courts who have bound successor Parliaments, Loveland notes that *Factortame* entrenchment is an "extremely weak procedural kind ... it merely requires that Parliament express itself in unusually blunt language". However, the obvious issue arising from this discussion is that if Parliament managed in 1972 to entrench the ECA, on what basis can it now be said that Parliament cannot entrench other legislation as well.

PARLIAMENTARY SOVEREIGNTY AND CONSTITUTIONAL DEVELOPMENT

In the last 40 years developments in the UK constitution have raised questions over the continued place of parliamentary sovereignty as the keystone of the UK constitution. Membership of the European Union, devolution and the Human Rights Act form part of the changing constitutional landscape which is causing, as Mark Elliott, "Parliamentary Sunder Pressure" (2004) International Journal of Constitutional Law 2(3), 545 notes, "the net around parliamentary sovereignty to tighten". He further notes, "the category of legislation that it is politically impossible for Parliament to enact is expanding substantially".

In addition, there are signs that some judges are also beginning to consider that the theory should be recast in light of the constitutional landscape. Throughout this chapter mention has been made of the House of Lords decision in *R. (Jackson) v Att-Gen* [2005] UKHL 56 (*Jackson*); this case is seminal in considering the change in some judicial attitudes and so the case will be fully replayed here.

7–041

1. The Jackson decision

The Hunting Act 2004 made the hunting of wild animals with dogs illegal. The passing of the Act was controversial and was eventually passed using the Parliament Acts 1911 and 1949 procedure. The Parliament Acts 1911 and 1949 provides that a Bill may become an Act without having been approved by the House of Lords in any two successive terms. Jackson, Chairman of the Countryside Alliance, argued that the Parliament Act 1949 was an invalid piece of legislation as it had been passed by the House of Commons under the Parliament Act 1911. As a consequence, the Hunting Act and any other statutes passed under the Parliament Act 1911 had no legal effect.

The applicants had two main arguments: firstly, that the Parliament Act 1911 created a subordinate body (House of Commons and the monarch) and as a subordinate body it could not pass legislation amending itself, in particular it could not expand its own power in that way. Secondly, the Parliament Act 1911 procedure could not be used for major constitutional changes. The case depended on the interpretation of s.2(1) of the Parliament Act 1911 which states:

7–042

"If *any* [my italics] Public Bill (other than a Money Bill or a Bill containing any provision to extend the maximum duration of Parliament beyond five years) is passed by the House of Commons in three successive sessions (whether of the same Parliament or not), and, having been sent up to the House of Lords at least one month before the end of the session, is rejected by the House of Lords in each of those sessions, that Bill shall, on its rejection for the third time by the House of Lords, unless the House of Commons direct to the contrary, be presented to His Majesty and *become an Act of Parliament* [my italics] on the Royal Assent being signified thereto, notwithstanding that the House of Lords have not consented to the Bill."

(a) *Subordinate body*

7–043 The argument put forward was that the Parliament Act 1949 was subordinate legislation because it had been made under the 1911 Act. The 1949 Acts existence and validity depended wholly on a prior statute. As a matter of statutory interpretation the House of Lords dismissed this argument. Section 2 of the Parliament Act 1911 referred to legislation complying with its provisions as becoming "an Act of Parliament". On a literal interpretation this clearly suggested that any legislation was to be viewed as primary legislation and not delegated legislation. Moreover, the House of Lords looked at the purpose behind the 1911 Act and concluded that the purpose was not to delegate power to the House of Commons, nor enlarge its power, but to restrict the power of the House of Lords (see in particular Lord Bingham at para.25). In effect, Parliament had simply created an alternative route for passing legislation.

(b) *Limitations*

7–044 This argument was that Parliament in 1911 did not intend for the Parliament Act procedure to be used to amend the Act itself. Parliament could not use the 1911 procedure requiring delay over three successive terms to change the procedure to delay over two successive terms. It was argued that by actually doing this and creating the Parliament Act 1949, the House of Commons had increased its own power. Jowell, "Parliamentary Sovereignty under the New Constitutional Hypothesis" (2006) P.L. 562 calls this the "bootstraps argument":

"It could not pull itself up by its own bootstraps or, to change the metaphor, the 1949 Act could not cut the bough on which it sits. It could not remove two of the conditions upon which its law-making powers were predicated." (at p.568)

The Court of Appeal had doubted whether the 1911 Act could be used to make "changes of a fundamental nature in the relationship between the House of Commons and House of Lords" but could be used for modest changes, of which they believed the 1949 Act was.

The House of Lords however dismissed all arguments on this point. As a matter of interpretation they held that the provisions in s.2 of the 1911 Act provided that the procedure could be used for "any Public Bill" except those contrary to the express exceptions. The *expressio unis est exlusio alteris* rule of interpretation can also apply. The express mention in s.2(1) of the 1911 Act of exceptions to when the procedure could be used specifically excludes the inclusion of other exceptions being implied into the Act. Lord Bingham also pointed out that during the passage of the Bill attempts had been made to exclude constitutional Bills from the ambit of the Act.

(c)   *Wider obiter*

Although Jackson emphatically lost the case in the House of Lords, the case poses some   **7–045** interesting issues for the theory of sovereignty. A number of their Lordships in obiter raised wider issues about the place of the theory in the modern United Kingdom. The issues can be narrowed down to two broad categories: (1) whether Parliament could bind itself and (2) limits on what legislation Parliament can pass.

(1)   Can Parliament bind itself? The House of Lords concluded that s.2(1) of the 1911 Act was binding on Parliament when constituted as the House of Commons and the monarch. Moreover, a number of their Lordships suggested that the House of Commons and the monarch could not use the Parliament Act procedure to remove the express exceptions. Only Parliament fully constituted could do this. (These arguments have been discussed more fully above).

(2)   Limits on what legislation Parliament can pass: it is clear following the above that there are some limits to what the House of Commons and monarch acting together can pass. Although the House of Lords expressly refused to recognise the Parliament Act procedure could not be used to effect changes of fundamental nature, they did state that it could not be used to extend the life of Parliament.

Of particular significance are the comments of Lord Steyn, Lord Hope and Baroness Hale who suggested there were constitutional limits to what Parliament (fully constituted) could pass. Lord Steyn noted that because sovereignty was a construct of the common law and created by judges it could be qualified by judges. He stated:

"If that is so, it is not unthinkable that circumstances could arise where the courts may have to qualify a principle established on a different hypothesis of constitutionalism. In exceptional circumstances involving an attempt to abolish judicial review or the ordinary role of the courts, the Appellate Committee of the House of Lords or a new Supreme Court may have to consider whether this is a constitutional fundamental which even a sovereign Parliament acting at the behest of a complaisant House of Commons cannot abolish." (at para.102)

Lord Hope took the view that "the rule of law enforced by the courts is the ultimate controlling factor on which our constitution is based" (at para.107). He further believed that "Parliamentary sovereignty is an empty principle if legislation is passed which is so absurd or so unacceptable that the populace at large refuses to recognise it as law" (at para.120). A similar view was taken by Baroness Hale who noted that "the courts will treat with particular suspicion (and might even reject) any attempt to subvert the rule of law by removing governmental action affecting the rights of the individual from all judicial powers" (at para.159).

If, as some of their Lordships indicated, parliamentary sovereignty is no longer absolute, where does the authority of the courts to question legislation come from?

Jowell, "Parliamentary Sovereignty under the New Constitutional Hypothesis" (2006) P.L. 562 identifies two justifications for judicial intervention: firstly legitimacy and secondly, constitutionalism. Jowell notes that the legitimacy of parliamentary sovereignty rests upon Parliament's representative and accountable features. A point also made by Lord Hope who stated "the principle of parliamentary sovereignty which in the absence of higher authority has been created by the common law is based on the assumption that Parliament represents the people whom it exists to serve". If legislation was passed that undermined Parliament's representative feature such as restricting elections then this would justify judicial interference (at p.573). Jowell's second point is based on a "different hypothesis of constitutionalism". Democracy is not just linked to the idea of majority rule but has a wider ambit including protection of human rights and the rule of law. He notes the growth of judicial review in recent years as well as a changing perception of what the rule of law actually is. In addition, the Constitutional Reform Act 2005 which will enhance the independence of the judiciary by creating a new and separate Supreme Court will increase the status of the rule of law as a constitutional principle. Ultimately these will enhance the authority of the judiciary to be "guardians of constitutional propriety" (pp.573–574).

2.   Summary

7–045A   Dicey noted that the twin pillars of the constitution were parliamentary sovereignty and the rule of law. He further noted that of the two, parliamentary sovereignty was the most important. It is without doubt that the constitution has changed since the time of Dicey's writing. Membership of Europe and the Human Rights Act have brought additional rights and responsibilities; the UK's conception of the rule of law has changed with the focus more readily on substance as opposed to procedure (see Ch.5). The comments in *Jackson* suggest movement towards the rule of law as the defining and guiding feature of our constitution. If Parliament were to try to subvert the rule of law or abolish judicial review then, under the new constitutional settlement the UK finds itself in, the courts would be justified in stepping in and controlling Parliaments legal power. Should the court's ever find themselves in this situation then there would clearly be a radical alteration in the relationship between the organs of state and particularly between the judiciary and Parliament.

However, what is stated in *Jackson* and elsewhere is very much a pragmatic view of sovereignty. It has always been recognised that there are political and practical limits to what Parliament may do. Their lordships in *Jackson* were giving expression to this fact, a point Lord Hope makes when he says "I do not think it is open to a court of law to ignore reality". However, to take Lord Carswell's final remarks in his opinion in *Jackson*, "I would at once express the hope and belief that such possibilities are so unlikely to occur as to be purely theoretical. Our constitution has for the last 200 years developed by evolution rather than revolution. Successive governments, even those with massive majorities, have wisely recognised this in exercising the degree of moderation with which they have approached radical changes which some of their supporters ardently wished to put into effect, observing the principle expressed by Gladstone, that the constitution depends on the good sense and good faith of those who work it" (see para.176).

FURTHER READING

Bingham, T. "Dicey Revisited" (2002) P.L. 39   **7–046**
Bradley, A. "The Sovereignty of Parliament—Form or Substance?" in J.L. Jowell and
    D. Oliver (eds), *The Changing Constitution*, 6th edn (OUP, 2007)
Burns, S. "When is an Act of Parliament not an Act of Parliament?" (2006) 156 N.L.J.
    191
Elliott, M. "Parliamentary sovereignty under pressure" (2004) *International Journal of
    Constitutional Law* 2(3), 545
Goldsworthy, J. The Sovereignty of Parliament: History and Philosophy (OUP, 2001)
Gravells, N. "Effective protection of Community law rights: temporary disapplication
    of an Act of Parliament" (1999) P.L. 180–191
Jowell, J. "Parliamentary Sovereignty under the New Constitutional Hypothesis"
    (2006) P.L. 562
Lyon, A. *Constitutional History of the United Kingdom* (London: Cavendish, 2003)
McLean, I. and McMillan, A. "Professor Dicey's contradictions" (2007) P.L. 435
Wade, H.R. "The Basis of Legal Sovereignty" (1955) C.L.J. 172
Woolf "Droit Public" (1995) P.L. 69
Young, A. "Hunting Sovereignty: Jackson v Her Majesty's Attorney-General" (2006)
    P.L. 187

Chapter 8

ENFRANCHISEMENT AND ELECTIONS

INTRODUCTION

The United Kingdom has a bicameral legislature, composed of the House of Commons **8–001** and House of Lords. The House of Lords is an unelected Chamber which, since the House of Lords Act 1999, has been predominantly composed of life peers. The composition of the House of Commons is determined by the electorate voting in general elections for the candidate chosen by a party to stand in their constituency.

The constitutional significance of elections cannot be underplayed. The Electoral Commission in a report on voter turnout published following the 2005 general election, (*Election 2005: Turnout: How Many, Who and Why?* (2005)), made the following statement:

> "Elections underpin our democracy, ensuring that our representative institutions are both accountable to public opinion and legitimised by it. They provide an opportunity for politicians and political parties to outline their ideas and to defend their performance. Elections can interest, inform and empower people and, by doing so, can help to build political engagement." (at p.53)

The importance of elections within a democracy is also emphasised by the guarantee in art.3 of Protocol No.1 of the European Convention on Human Rights which provides that signatories to the Convention, " . . . undertake to hold free elections at reasonable intervals by secret ballot, under conditions which will ensure the free expression of the opinion of the people in the choice of the legislature".

Given the importance of elections, who can vote and who can stand for election becomes a necessary consideration. This chapter considers entitlement to vote in Parliamentary elections, the nature of general elections, and the role of a Member of Parliament in the House of Commons. In the next three chapters, we examine the structure of both Houses within Parliament and their privileges.

THE FRANCHISE—WHO CAN VOTE

1. Background

8–002 The Reform Acts in the 19th century (Representation of the People Acts 1832, 1867 and 1884) increased the electorate (franchise) substantially. Yet even with the Reform Act 1884, which established the vote for all male property owners in both towns and countryside and increased the franchise to around eight million, the UK was still a long way short of universal suffrage. Since 1884 the franchise in the United Kingdom has continued to increase. Some key developments include the Representation of the People Act 1918 which gave women over the age of 30 the right to vote. This was increased to full equality with men in the Representation of the People Act 1928. The Representation of the People Act 1949 abolished plural voting and gave those on the register the right to vote only once. The age of eligibility was lowered for all from 21 to 18 with the Representation of the People Act 1960. There was a period of relative quiet from the mid-20th century until the Representation of the People Act 2000 which introduced a number of reforms and amended the 1983 Act. Importantly, it allowed the creation of a rolling register (see below) and extended the right to vote by post. Essentially the 2000 Act gave the right to vote based on citizenship rather than residence in a particular area.

2. Eligibility to vote

8–003 The UK now has a system of universal suffrage for all those over the age of 18. Those eligible to vote in an election include:

   (i) British citizens;

   (ii) Overseas British citizens. Overseas British citizens gained the right to vote under the Representation of the People Act 1985 (RPA 1985). If a British citizen had previously been registered to vote, the RPA 1985 gave the right for them to vote up to five years after they left the country. The Representation of the People Act 2000 extended this to 20 years;

  (iii) Commonwealth citizens. The Representation of the People Act 1918 provided that only British subjects could register as electors. However, the term "British subject" included any person who, at that time owed allegiance to the Crown, regardless of the Crown territory in which they were born, i.e. citizens of the British Empire. Following the British Nationality Act 1948 this right was retained when the Empire gradually became the Commonwealth;

  (iv) Citizens of the Irish Republic. Following Ireland's partition in 1922, Irish citizens were given the right to vote as part of the Commonwealth. This right was retained when Ireland left the Commonwealth in 1949 by virtue of the Ireland Act 1949.

The following categories of people are excluded:

(i)   anyone under the age of 18. However, an individual can register if they are to reach the age of 18 during the following year;

(ii) members of the House of Lords. Under the House of Lords Reform Act 1999, the disqualification for hereditary peers was removed save for the 92 "excepted" peers who retain the right to sit in the House of Lords;

(iii) EU Citizens. Although EU citizens are entitled to vote in local elections;

(iv) citizens of any other country (RPA 2000 s.1);

(v)   convicted persons serving a sentence in prison (Representation of the People Act 1983 (RPA 1983) s.3). This does not apply to prisoners on remand. The RPA 2000 s.5 inserts a new s.7A into the RPA 1983 and provides that remand prisoners may be registered in the constituency where the prison is situated if they can be regarded as resident. See discussion below;

(vi) anyone found guilty within the last five years of corrupt or illegal practices in connection with elections.

The disenfranchisement of prisoners has come under particular scrutiny in light of the provision in art.3 of Protocol No.1 of the European Convention on Human Rights which provides that signatories to the Convention " . . . undertake to hold free elections at reasonable intervals by secret ballot, under conditions which will ensure the free expression of the opinion of the people in the choice of the legislature". In *Hirst v UK* (2006) 42 E.H.R.R. 41, the Grand Chamber of the European Court of Human Rights considered the compatibility of prisoner disenfranchisement with this article. Hirst had been convicted of manslaughter and was serving life imprisonment so was disenfranchised under the RPA 1983 s.3.

Only eight countries in Europe including the UK did not give convicted prisoners the right to vote. Twenty did not disenfranchise at all and eight provided some restrictions. The Chamber held that the right to vote was not a privilege and the presumption was in favour of universal suffrage. However, the right was not absolute and the Chamber assessed whether the interference pursued a legitimate aim and was proportionate. The Chamber recognised the reason the UK gave for disenfranchising prisoners was to enhance civic responsibility and respect for the rule of law. However, whether or not an offender was deprived of the right to vote depended entirely on whether the judge imposed a custodial sentence or not. There was no direct link between the facts of any individual case and the removal of the right to vote. As the ban applied automatically to all convicted prisoners whilst in prison, irrespective of the length of their sentence and nature or gravity of their offence, it amounted to an indiscriminate and disproportionate restriction.

As a result of this decision an amendment to s.3 of the RPA 1983 is pending.

3.   The electoral register

8–004   Only individuals whose names appear on the electoral register can vote in parliamentary elections. Even if a person satisfies all the requirements for eligibility, he/she cannot vote until their name appears on the register. The RPA 2000 Sch.1 amends the 1983 Act requirements for the maintenance and drawing up of the register. Registration Officers are required to canvass annually who is resident in their constituency on October 15 in that year. A fine can be imposed for a failure to complete the form or giving misleading or false information. The register is published on December 1 each year. The 1948 Act had provided for annual updates of the electoral register. However, this meant that individuals who moved constituencies had to wait until the next canvass for the ability to register and importantly could miss out on their right to vote. The 2000 Act amended this to a system of rolling registration, whereby a person moving into a constituency can make an application to join the register for that area. The register can be updated monthly between January and September following such applications.

4.   Residence

8–005   Prior to 1948 it was necessary to prove residence in the constituency for three months prior to the qualifying date. The RPA 2000 removed this and the position now is that as long as the person is not suffering from any legal incapacity and satisfies the age and nationality requirements he/she is entitled to register in the constituency where he/she is resident at the time he/she makes the application (RPA 1983, as amended by RPA 2000 s.1). Section 3 of the RPA 2000 substitutes a new s.5 into the 1983 Act. It sets out the matters to be taken into account when determining whether someone is resident in a particular constituency. A key factor to be taken into account is the person's reason for presence at the address. Temporary absence due to the "performance of any duty arising from or incidental to any office, service or employment held or undertaken by him" (s.3) or by reason of attendance at an academic institution (s.5) does not disqualify a person as long as he intends to resume residence within six months and it would normally be his permanent residence where he would be resident, save for the performance of the duty. By virtue of subs.2, temporary residence is acceptable as long as the person has no other home. Subsection 6 excludes those persons detained at an institution as being resident there.

5.   Declarations of local connection

8–006   The RPA 2000 s.6 extended the franchise to persons who may not be able to satisfy the conditions of residence such as the homeless and persons detained in mental hospitals and on remand in prison. This represents a substantial step towards ensuring full participation in the democratic process. In situations such as these the person has to make a declaration of local connection. Such declarations must include:

(i)   the person's name;

(ii) an address for correspondence or an undertaking to collect such correspondence from the electoral registration office;

(iii) a statement that the person falls with one of the categories: (a) persons in mental hospitals or on remand and (b) homeless persons;

(iv) in the case of category (a), the name of the institution where the person is detained and where the person would be living if not detained:

(v)   in the case of (b), an address where, or near to, the person spends most of the time.

Elections

1.   Constituencies and boundaries

At the last general election (May 2005), the UK was divided into 646 constituencies; **8–007** (529 constituencies in England, 59 in Scotland, 40 in Wales and 18 in Northern Ireland). Each constituency elects one Member of Parliament (MP) who represents that constituency in Parliament (a single member constituency). The size of constituencies varies according to a number of factors but there is a principle that each MP should carry equal weight of representation in Parliament. The Parliamentary Constituencies Act 1986 (as amended by the Boundary Commissions Act 1992) created four Boundary Commissions, one for each of the countries of the UK. The Commissions are required to undertake a general review every 8–12 years in order to ensure electoral equality. Under s.14 of the Political Parties, Elections and Referendums Act 2000, the four Boundary Commissions were scheduled to be subsumed under the Electoral Commission. Section 14 has been brought into force by the Political Parties, Elections and Referendums Act 2000 (Commencement No.2) Order 2001 (SI 2001/3526) but only in relation to the Boundary Commission for England.

Review can either be general or localised. General reviews may result in large scale changes to the boundaries, the creation of new constituencies and the merger or disappearance of others. Localised reviews tend to be "tweaks" to reflect localised shifts in population. The fifth general review for England was completed in 2007 (The Boundary Commission for England's Fifth Report Cm 7032). The proposal was to increase the number of constituencies to 533 (approximately 69,935 voters for each constituency). The Parliamentary Constituencies (England) Order 2007 brought these proposals into effect (June 2007) and will be used at the next general election.

The redrawing of constituencies can have a major impact on the political parties with the loss or gain of potential seats. The redrawing of boundaries can be controversial and lead to a legal challenge in judicial review proceedings. In *R. v Boundary Commission for England Ex p. Foot* [1983] 1 Q.B. 600, the labour party challenged a redraw of constituencies. Michael Foot, the leader of the Labour Party, was unsuccessful in his challenge to prohibit the boundary commission from submitting to the Home Secretary revised constituencies. Foot had argued that in respect of a large number of constituencies the commission had failed to give effect to the principle of equal representation for electors. The Court of Appeal held that he had failed to show that the decision was unreasonable.

2.   General elections

8–008   General elections are usually held 17 working days after the dissolution of Parliament. By convention, elections are held on a Thursday; the last one to be held on a day other than a Thursday was Tuesday October 7, 1931 (Source: *Parliament.gov.uk*). Typically, they are held in spring or autumn; if the weather is bad then people are less inclined to vote and in summer many people are on holiday.

(a)   *When are they called?*

8–009   There is no statutory requirement as to when a general election should be called and Parliament dissolved. The Parliament Act 1911 establishes the maximum life of a Parliament as five years. An election can be called at any time during that period. Parliament has been extended beyond five years twice during the two world wars. The 1911 Parliament was extended to eight years by the Parliament and Registration Act 1916 and the Parliament and Local Elections Acts 1916 and 1918. The 1935 Parliament was extended to 10 years by the Prolongation of Parliament Acts 1940, 1941, 1942, 1943 and 1944. The Prime Minister determines the length of Parliament and when a general election should be called. A Parliament is dissolved either by the passage of time or by proclamation issued by the Crown (monarch) under royal prerogative. By constitutional convention, the exercise of this prerogative is on the advice of the Prime Minister.

(b)   *System of voting*

8–010   The British electoral system is a first past the post system (FPTP). Simply put it means the person with the largest number of votes wins the constituency. The UK is divided into 646 parliamentary constituencies (though this is set to change in the next general election) with each constituency sending one MP to Parliament (single member constituency). The system is relatively easy to use; each voter puts a cross on the ballot paper next to their chosen candidate. Once polling closes, the votes are all counted and the candidate who has secured the most votes is declared to be elected the MP for that constituency. The way the system operates means that often the winning candidate does not have the majority of votes. For example, the following table shows the result for the St Albans seat in the 2005 election:

Candidate	Party	Number of Votes	% of votes
Main, A	Conservative	16953	37.3
Pollard, KP	Labour	15592	34.3
Green, MA	Liberal Democrat	11561	25.4
Evans, RM	UK Independence Party	707	1.6
Girsman, JR	St Albans Party	430	0.9
Reynolds, MJ	Independent	219	0.5

Anne Main, Conservative, who was elected MP for St Albans had a majority of 1361 over the Labour Party candidate. Labour and Liberal Democrat Candidates together polled 59.7 per cent of the vote overall.

By convention the leader of the party with the majority of seats will be invited by the Queen to form Her Majesty's government. As with individual constituencies, the party with the majority of the seats will typically not have the majority of votes but have simply passed the post first. The following table shows the political breakdown of the 2005 election (source: Electoral Commission, Vote 2005 A review of social and academic research into voting at UK Parliamentary general elections Research report—April 2005).

Party	Votes cast	% of votes
Labour	9,552,436	35.2
Conservative	8,784,915	32.4
Liberal Democrat	5,985,454	22

The Labour party had a majority of 2.8 per cent of votes over the Conservative party. When this is translated into seats it gave them 157 more seats then the Conservatives.

Party	Seats
Labour	355
Conservative	198
Liberal Democrat	62
Democratic Unionist Party	9
Scottish National Party	6
Sinn Fein	5
Plaid Cymru	3
Social Democratic & Labour Party	3
Others	4
Speaker	1
Total	**646 MPs**

Since 1945, the FPTP electoral system has produced strong majority governments and what former Lord Chancellor, Lord Hailsham, *Dilemma of Democracy* (London: Collins, 1978) has termed "an elective dictatorship". Such a system affects the constitutional balance between the Executive and the House of Commons and their effective control over the Executive (see Ch.9). Rather than the House of Commons being separate and exercising control over the government, with a strong majority the government can effectively control the House of Commons. It is unlikely for a government to be defeated on its legislative proposals and also unlikely that the government would suffer a vote of no confidence, so one of the theoretical checks on government becomes in effect meaningless (the last time a vote of no confidence was successful was in 1979). In addition to these, the composition of Select Committees reflects party composition and so the government will always have a majority in committees.

3.   Supervision and conduct of elections

8–011   The Political Parties, Elections and Referendums Act 2000 created the Electoral Commission. The Commission is an independent body that oversees the conduct of elections. It regulates donations to the political parties and campaign spending. It also has a remit to review electoral law and practice and to promote public awareness in the electoral process. Part I also provides for the transfer to the Electoral Commission of the functions of the four Parliamentary Boundary Commissions and of the Local Government Commission for England and the Local Government Boundary Commissions for Scotland and Wales.

4.   Election turnout

8–012   In the 2005 general election, the Electoral Commission (source: *Electoral Commission: Election 2005: turnout. How many, who and why?* (2005)) identified 17 million people who did not vote, but who were registered to vote. Turnout for the election stood at 61.4 per cent, a slight improvement on the 2001 turnout which was 59.4 per cent. The 2001 turnout was the worst since 1918 (57.2 per cent when many voters were still abroad following the war) and a significant drop from the 71.6 per cent in the 1999 election. The general decline shows that voters are disconnected from the electoral and parliamentary process and casts questions over the legitimacy of the government of the day and whether it is truly representing the people.

In its report, one of the factors identified by the Electoral Commission as contributing to the low turnout is the perception that voting makes little difference, either because the result was a foregone conclusion or because nothing would change. Whilst every seat is contested at a general election, only a few actually change hands. A number of seats are "safe" seats where the majority is so big it would take a large swing to the other side for that party to lose the seat. For example in the 2001 general election, the MP for Bishop Auckland had a 13,926 majority and so this was considered a safe Labour seat. At the 2005 general election, the Labour party comfortably won, though the overall majority dropped slightly to 10,047. The turnout for these "safe" seats tends to be lower as voters feel their vote makes little difference. In the 2005 general election, voter turnout for Bishop Auckland was below the national average at 56.1 per cent. This pattern tends to be repeated across the country; Liverpool Riverside, had a 13,950 majority following the 2001 election, and the lowest turnout at 41.4 per cent in the 2005 election. At the 1997 general election, where there was a large swing nationally to Labour, a total of 180 seats (about a quarter of those contested), changed hands. In 2001, the number changing hands fell to 28, the lowest number since 1955.

Other factors which played a part in the 2005 election included a difficulty in deciding which political party to vote for because of the perceived similarities between the main parties. The election campaign was also seen as lacklustre and there was a perceived general disillusionment with politics.

In order to address voter apathy attempts have been made to engage with voters using different forms of voting. In the 2005 election there was an increase in the number of postal votes used and early voting in supermarkets has been tried. Other suggestions include voting over the internet or by phone, polling over several days, moving polling day to the weekend and changing the voting form (for example by providing a "none of the above option" on the form). The Electoral Administration Act 2006 makes changes to electoral registration easier and it also provides a framework for local authorities to review their polling stations. It is a start towards achieving the highest possible turnout at elections.

Suggestions that voting should be compulsory in the UK as they are in other constitutions, for example Australia, have not been examined by the Electoral Commission and at present do not seem a preferred option.

5. Advantages and disadvantages of First Past the Post (FPTP)

(a) *Advantages of FPTP*

The FPTP system is simple. It is easy for voters to understand as they only have to place one cross on the ballot paper next to the candidate they wish to elect. In theory such simplicity should encourage greater participation. It is also straightforward to administer; the counting of ballot papers is fast so results can be released quickly, and it is relatively inexpensive. FPTP systems have single member constituencies with close geographical links between voters and their MP. It also allows voters to more easily identify their representative at Parliament and to build links between them. Overall, the FPTP produces strong government and hence a stable system dominated by two parties. This allows the government to be decisive and get its election promises into law more easily. Defenders of the system argue that majority governments by one party are more accountable to the electorate for their actions. Voters have a clear alternative between party systems and governments can be easily held accountable at the next election. Some countries which use proportional representation systems find the formation of a stable government very difficult. In both Italy and Israel, for example, minority governments are more likely and these can prove to be unstable, short termed

8–013

and weak. The winner-takes-all aspect of the system also encourages the major parties to maintain a broad appeal, thus discouraging extremism. It is also difficult for extremist parties to establish a strong enough base to win seats at Westminster.

(b)   *Arguments against FPTP*

8–014   The main criticism of FPTP is that it does not represent the true proportion of votes as the numbers of votes do not transfer to the actual number of seats gained in Parliament. More people can vote against an MP and a party than for them, for example at the 2005 General Election, Labour received 35.2 per cent of the vote, the Conservatives and Liberal Democrats together received 54.4 per cent. In this sense, the Labour government cannot really claim they have the support of the majority of their people. In 2005, only three MPs elected secured more than 40 per cent of the vote of their constituents. This method of voting favours the larger and majority parties and tends to discriminate against minority parties. The Liberal Democrats received 22 per cent of the vote in the 2005 general election but only gained 62 seats. It might also put people off voting in an election for a minority party as they know that their vote will be wasted or makes no difference.

It has been argued that FPTP wastes huge numbers of votes as votes cast for a losing candidate or those for the winning candidate once he has reached the post count for nothing. This can contribute towards low voter turnout particularly in seats where it would make little difference. The Electoral Reform Society, a campaign group for changing the way politicians are chosen, calculated that 70 per cent of votes were wasted in this way (*www.electoral-reform.org.uk*)

FPTP does not allow the voter to exercise a free choice in both the selection of a constituency representative and the determination of the government of the country. It forces the voter to give priority to one or the other. The Jenkins Commission (see para.8–020) found in the great majority of cases voters were more concerned with who the Prime Minister would be, rather than the member for their constituency. As a result, voters tend to vote for the political party they want to be in government rather than the person who might be better for their constituency. Although, sometimes independent candidates are elected, for example, Martin Bell, a former BBC correspondent, was elected MP for Tatton in Cheshire. Tatton was one of the Conservative Party's safest seats but its sitting MP, Neil Hamilton, was embroiled in sleaze allegations at the time.

6.   Other systems of voting and reform

8–015   Following devolution in 1998 a number of other systems of voting were employed in the UK to the devolved Parliaments and Assemblies. These include the single transferable vote, additional member system and supplementary vote.

(a) Single transferable vote (STV)

This system of voting uses multi-member constituencies. A candidate does not require a **8–016** majority to be elected but has to reach a certain quota of votes. Each voter has one vote and numbers candidates in order of preference. Bottom candidates are eliminated and the preferences redistributed until all seats are filled. Surplus votes for elected candidates are also reallocated to their supporter's second preference. The benefit of STV is that it ensures no votes are wasted. This style of voting is popular in the Republic of Ireland and will be used for local elections in Scotland. It is also used in the Northern Ireland Assembly.

(b) Additional member system (AMS)

This is a hybrid voting system which is part FPTP and past closed party list. Each voter **8–017** gets two votes, onc for a candidate in a constituency and one for a party. Each constituency returns candidates in the traditional FPTP style. With the second vote, electors vote for a political party not directly for an individual. The particular individuals selected come from lists drawn up by the political parties before the election, at a national or regional level. This voting system is used for the National Assembly for Wales, the Scottish Parliament and the Greater London Assembly.

(c) Supplementary vote (SV)

Voters choose a first and second choice of candidate only. If no candidate receives an **8–018** absolute majority of first choice votes on the first count, all but the two leading candidates are eliminated and their votes redistributed to help determine a winner in a second and final round. The supplementary vote is used in elections for directly elected mayors such as the Mayor of London.

(d) Alternative vote (AV)

Under this system, voters indicate their preference among candidates in a single **8–019** member constituency. A candidate requires an overall majority of votes to be elected. If no candidate obtains a majority with the first preference, the lowest placed candidate is eliminated and his voters second place preferences are transferred to the remaining candidates. This continues until there is a candidate with an overall majority. The advantage of this system in the UK is that it would not require boundaries to be changed and can eliminate tactical voting. However, the use of the alternative vote does not necessarily result in proportionate representation.

7.   Reform

8–020   Reform of the electoral process has on occasion found itself onto the political agenda. Concern over Conservative dominance led to Labour and the Liberal Democrats agreeing a package of reforms whilst in opposition. Following the 1997 election, the Labour government set up an independent commission to consider the voting systems under the former Labour Deputy Leader, Roy Jenkins. The Jenkins Commission was asked to recommend a voting system that fulfilled (or best fulfilled) four criteria:

(1)   the maintenance of a geographical link between MP and their constituency;

(2)   the need for stable government;

(3)   the desire for broad proportionality;

(4)   an extension of voter choice.

The Jenkins Commission (The Report of the Independent Commission on the Voting System (1998, Cm 4090-I) Ch.9) recommended a form of the alternative vote known as AV+ to replace the FPTP system. The Commission suggested that each voter would have two votes; the first vote would be for electing the MP for the constituency based on the alternative vote system; approximately 85 per cent of MP would be elected this way. The second vote would be for the remaining 15 per cent of MPs who would represent large regional seats. Voters would choose from either their favourite party or candidate from a party list of MPs. These votes would be used to decide how many additional seats each party should get within the region and are allocated to the party or parties most disadvantages by the share of constituency seats. The individual appointed would be the person from the winning party list who gets the most individual votes. The idea behind the + is to address the lack of proportionality in the AV system. The government did not formally respond to the Commission's report but it was debated in 1998.

In January 2008, the government published a review of voting systems that have been used in the UK in the last ten years for the devolved administrations and the London Mayor and Assembly (additional member system, single transferable vote system and supplementary vote). The review does not make any recommendations for reform but described the strengths and weakness of the different voting systems. Overall it found that the new voting systems led to a more proportional allocation of seats in devolved administration which resulted in more parties being represented and gave rise to more coalition government. The review concluded that in the UK experience voter participation had not risen, though evidence on the continent showed that it could increase voter participation.

THE MEMBER OF PARLIAMENT

1. Who can stand for election?

Any person who is a British, Commonwealth or Irish Republic citizen over the age of   **8–021**
18 can stand for parliamentary election. Historically the age for standing for election
was 21 years. However, this was lowered to 18 years by the Electoral Administration
Act 2006.

A number of people are disqualified from sitting in the House of Commons. These
include:

(a) minors: under s.17(1) of the Electoral Administration Act 2006 any person
under the age of 18 years cannot stand for election;

(b) aliens: non British citizens may not stand as an MP subject to the exclusion
for Commonwealth or Irish Republic citizens (the British Nationality Act
1981). The British Nationality Act makes it clear that European Union
nationals do not have the right to stand for election to the Westminster
Parliament;

(c) Members of the House of Lords: those who are members of the House of
Lords cannot also sit in the House of Commons. Under the House of Lords
Reform Act 1999, those hereditary peers who no longer sit in the House are
entitled to stand for election as an MP;

(d) un-discharged bankrupts: under s.266 of the Enterprise Act 2002, an individual who has a current bankruptcy order (in England and Wales) is disqualified. This also applies if an individual is declared bankrupt (Northern
Ireland) or had their estate sequestered (Scotland) (s.427 of the Insolvency
Act 1986);

(e) offenders detained and sentenced to more than one year in prison: under the
Representation of the People Act 1981 those convicted and serving a term of
imprisonment of more than one year are disqualified. If a sitting member is
imprisoned his or her seat is vacated and a by-election called. The Representation of the People Act 1981 was introduced following the election of
Bobby Sands, a member of the Provisional IRA who was imprisoned and on
hunger strike at the time of his election. Sands was a Member of Parliament
for only twenty-five days before he died from his hunger strike; he never took
his seat or oath;

(f) persons convicted of illegal or corrupt practice at elections: under the
Representation of the People Act 1983 s.159, a person convicted of an illegal
electoral practice (excessive expenditure) is disqualified from sitting or
standing for election for the constituency concerned for seven years. A person
convicted of a corrupt practice (bribery) is disqualified from sitting or
standing for election in the constituency in which the offence was committed
for ten years;

(g)   archbishops and bishops who sit in the House of Lords: the House of Commons (Removal of Clergy Disqualification) Act 2001 abolished the restriction on other members of the clergy (Church of England and Roman Catholic) from standing for election. Now all religious denominations can stand except those in the House of Lords;

(h)   those disqualified under the House of Commons Disqualification Act 1975 which disqualifies civil servants, judges, ambassadors, members of the armed forces, police force, paid members of boards of nationalised industries and directors of the Bank of England.

2.   Role and functions of an MP

8–022   A MP is elected by his or her constituency to represent their interests and concerns in the House of Commons. He is also a member of the national Parliament and so an MP's role also includes working for the House of Commons and ensuring that its functions are carried out (see Ch.9).

Sir Winston Churchill in "Duties of a Member of Parliament", *Parliamentary Affairs*, Vol.8, (1954–55) famously stated:

> "The first duty of a member of Parliament is to do what he thinks in his faithful and disinterested judgement is right and necessary for the honour and safety of Great Britain. His second duty is to his constituents, of whom he is the representative but not the delegate. Burke's famous declaration on this subject is well known. It is only in the third place that his duty to party organisation or programme takes rank. All these three loyalties should be observed, but there in no doubt of the order in which they stand under any healthy manifestation of democracy." (at p.302)

The Jenkins Commision (The Report of the Independent Commission on the Voting System (Cm 4090-I) para.10) outlined four key functions of the role of an MP; to represent their constituencies, to provide a pool from which the holders of ministerial officer are chosen, to shape and enact legislation and to hold the government to account. An MP splits his or her time between working for their constituency, working in Parliament and working for their political party.

(a)   *Working for their constituency*

8–023   In their constituency MPs often hold a "surgery" where local people can attend and discuss matters that concern them. As a representative of their constituency and a direct link to the national Parliament and government, MPs can raise questions on their constituent's behalf to government concerning the quality of services, schools or decisions affecting the area. MPs may also get involved in specific campaigns affecting their area such as major planning proposals. MPs receive written correspondence from constituent members and can assist in resolving grievances or refer an issue to the Parliamentary ombudsman.

Although MPs are elected representatives of the people they are not simply delegates. This point was clearly made by Edmund Burke's, an Anglo-Irish politician (1729–1797) in a Speech to the Electors of Bristol, November 3, 1774.

> "Your representative owes you, not his industry only, but his judgment; and he betrays, instead of serving you, if he sacrifices it to your opinion ... Parliament is not a congress of ambassadors from different and hostile interests, which interests each must maintain, as an agent and advocate, against other agents and advocates; but Parliament is a deliberative assembly of one nation, with one interest, that of the whole; where, not local purposes, not local prejudices ought to guide, but the general good, resulting from the general reason of the whole. You choose a member indeed; but when you have chosen him, he is not member of Bristol, but he is a member of Parliament."

In many matters MPs exercise their own judgement as to the best course. For example, some issues that come before Parliament are defined as free vote issues which mean an MP is free to vote how they wish without concerns about the party line. Typically, such issues concern morals or controversial issues, for example, votes on reform of the House of Lords were free votes and the abolition of the death penalty.

(b) *Parliamentary work*

When Parliament is sitting, MPs either spend their time on the floor of the House of Commons attending debates, votes and raising issues on behalf of their constituents or participating in one of the Committees. As a Parliamentarian, one of the MP's main jobs is to hold the government to account through debates and their involvement in committees. **8–024**

MPs have to strike a balance between their constituency and parliamentary work. The Hansard Society conducted a survey of new members in 2005 to find the division of time between the various aspects of the job. The table below shows that a large amount of time is spent in constituency work.

Constituency	49%
Chamber	14%
Committees	14%
Other	22%

(c)   *Working for their political party*

8–025   Though they may win their seat on the basis of a manifesto pledge, once elected there is no formal mechanism to compel an MP to do what was promised. On the other hand, the political party is in a stronger position to exert positive pressure and encourage compliance with party policy. This is done through the whip system (named after the whippers-in who controlled the pack of foxhounds in a hunt) which compels MPs to act or vote for the party line. If an MP does not follow the party line their prospects within the party can be harmed, as well as future selection for candidacy in an election.

Backbench MP or those without party affiliation can be more effective as they are not as easily swayed by the whips. For example, division in the Conservative party over the EU led to a backbench rebellion for John Majors' government and a vote of no confidence over the issue which the government narrowly won.

FURTHER READING

8–026   Curtice, J. "The Electoral System" in Bogdanor, V. (ed.) *The British Constitution in the Twentieth Century* in (OUP, 2004)
Kavannagh, D. *British Politics: Continuity and Change* (OUP, 2000)

Chapter 9

THE HOUSE OF COMMONS

INTRODUCTION

The Legislature or Parliament of the United Kingdom is bicameral, composed of two **9–001** Chambers, the House of Commons and the House of Lords. The monarch also forms part of Parliament and so its full name is the Queen in Parliament. The principal functions of Parliament are to make law and subject the government to scrutiny. This chapter concentrates on the structure and functions of the House of Commons, though there is necessarily some overlap with the functions of the House of Lords discussed in Ch.10.

1.   Origins

The origins of Parliament go back to the 12th century when Kings Councils were held **9–002** which discussed finance and advised the king. These gradually took on a more formal role with knights representing distinct geographical areas. By the 14th century Parliament's two Houses had become distinct. The lower House, the Commons was composed of representative from the counties, towns and cities, whereas the Lords, the Upper House, was composed of the aristocracy and clergy. In the 17th century, battle between the monarch and Parliament culminated in the Bill of Rights 1688 and the establishment of Parliament's superior authority over the Crown (see Ch.7). A further battle between the Lords and Commons in the early 20th century saw the Lords lose their power of veto over legislation and established conclusively the dominant position of the House of Commons.

2.   Life of Parliament

9–003   Parliament sits for a term which is the period between general elections. Each parliamentary term is divided into a number of sessions, each session lasting approximately one year. Each session typically begins in November with the State Opening of Parliament and the Queen's Speech and ends the following October. There is no statutory requirement as to the length of a session and following a general election may be longer than one year. Following the 2005 general election, the first session ran from June 2005 to October 2006. At the end of each session, Parliament is suspended (prorogued). Once suspended all business, except judicial, ceases.

COMPOSITION

1.   Size and composition

9–004   Composition of the House of Commons is determined by electoral voting at least every five years (see Ch.8). The size of the House of Commons is set out in statute. At the last general election in 2005, the House of Commons had 646 seats composed of 529 constituencies in England, 59 in Scotland, 40 in Wales and 18 in Northern Ireland. In the next general election, the number of English seats will increase by 4 to 533. If there are no changes in the Scottish, Welsh and Northern Irish seats then the House of Commons will have 650 MPs following the next general election in 2010 at the latest.
   As of March 13, 2008, the current state of the parties represented in the House of Commons was: Labour 352 seats, Conservative 193, Liberal Democrat 63 and others 38. The Labour government has a working majority of 67.

2.   The Speaker

9–005   The role of Speaker can be traced to 1377 and the appointment of Sir Thomas Hungerford. The Speaker is a senior member appointed by common agreement of all members and is politically independent. The Speaker regulates the proceedings of the House and is the presiding officer responsible for ensuring that rules of conduct are observed. The Speaker is also the representative of the Commons to the monarch and it is through the Speaker that the privilege of access to the Crown is achieved (see Ch.11).

3.   The party whips

9–006   Party political control of Members of Parliament is the responsibility of party whips. A whip is a member of one of the political parties and their responsibility is to ensure that

Members turn up for certain debates and question times and vote according to government wishes. The degree of coercion depends entirely on the importance of the issue. When attendance is absolutely required, a "three line whip" is announced where attendance is necessary but not essential a "two-line whip" is applied. Failure to attend on a two-line whip does not lead to sanctions.

FUNCTIONS

Many writers have attempted to list the principal functions of the House of Commons. **9–007** Walter Bagehot, *The English Constitution* stated the functions of the House of Commons to be the expressive function (expressing the opinion of the people), the teaching function and the informing function as well as legislating and finance. More recently, the Select Committee on Procedure (First Report HC 588–I (1977–1978)) concluded that the main functions of the Commons fell into four categories:

(1) legislation;

(2) scrutiny of the activities of the Executive;

(3) control of finance; and

(4) redress of grievances.

These categories overlap and according to Bradley (*Constitutional and Administrative Law* (14th edn (Pearson Publishing, 2006), p.193) the list does not include the broader political functions of the House. It is important that categorisation does not obscure the central theme of these which is the ability of the House of Commons to identify Executive inadequacies. The four functions will be considered below with greater emphasis on the first two.

LEGISLATIVE

One of Parliament's and hence the House of Common's main roles is the passage of **9–008** legislation. The process by which government policies are turned into law has three broad stages: before publication of the Bill, the passage of the Bill through Parliament and after the Bill has received Royal Assent.

1. Primary Legislation

Government policies require legislation for them to become law in the UK. Parliament **9–009** legislates directly through primary legislation of which there are four types: Public Bills, Private Members Bills, Private Bills and hybrid Bills.

(a)   *Public Bills*

9–010   These Bills are the most common type of Bill to pass through Parliament. They apply to the general population and so have general application. The majority of Public Bills are formulated by government pursuant to government policy.

(b)   *Private Members Bills*

9–011   Private members Bills are introduced into Parliament by an MP or Lord who is not part of government. They are a type of Public Bill whose purpose is to change the law for the general population. They are serious attempts at legislation in a well defined field and sometimes cover controversial subjects. Less time is dedicated to debate of these Bills and as a result they are less likely to proceed through all stages and pass into law. However, the publicity surrounding a Private Member's Bill can affect changes in the law indirectly. In the 2006–07 session, four Private Member's Bills received Royal Assent; the Sustainable Communities Act 2007, Building Societies (Funding) and Mutual Societies Act 2007, Vehicle Registration Marks Act 2007 and Forced Marriage (Civil Protection) Act (source: The Success of Private Members' Bills, House of Commons Information Office Factsheet L3, December 2007).

The procedure for introducing into and passing a private members Bill can be different from Public Bills and so they are treated as separate type of Bills. They can be introduced into either House and go through the same stages. In the House of Commons, a member introduces a Bill by providing its short title and its long title describing briefly what the Bill intends to do. There are three ways of introducing PMB: these include the ballot, ten minute rule and presentation.

At the beginning of each parliamentary session the names of members who wish to introduce a Private Members Bill are drawn in a ballot. Normally over 400 Members enter the ballot and 20 are successful. The majority of the 400 have no particular subject for a Bill in mind but if they are drawn high in the ballot will be besieged by pressure groups or other members who suggest draft Bills. The 20 Members who are successful stand at the front of the Private Members legislative queue. Debates of these Bills are set down for Fridays and as there are only seven Fridays available typically only the first seven ballot Bills get a debate. These have the best chance of becoming law because they get priority on the limited time available for debate of Private Members Bills. Members placed lower than seventh have to put their Bill down for a Friday when they will not be first. A Bill can be given a second reading without debate at 2.30pm (end of the day's business). The clerk reads out the title and if no-one objects the Bill is passed. If any one member objects, and typically the whips will, the Bill is adjourned. This option is the only option for Private Members Bills under the Ten Minute Rule.

Ten minute rule Bills are an opportunity for Members to voice an opinion on a subject or aspect of legislation and are not considered serious attempts to get a Bill passed. They are a good way of raising the profile of an issue such as a problem with an aspect of law and can be used to gauge whether such a Bill would have support amongst other Members. Introduced under Standing Order 23, members make speeches of no more than ten minutes outlining their position: another member may oppose in a similar short speech. The speeches are made in the House after question time when the benches are likely to be filled and press coverage may be significant. The Member asks the House for permission to introduce the Bill and if the House agrees the Bill will get its first reading.

The final way to introduce a Private Member's Bill is through normal presentation. A Member must give notice of their intention to introduce a Bill. The Bill is formally presented by introducing the title of the Bill and the Member does not speak in support of it. Bills cannot be presented in this way until all ballot Bills have been presented and put down for second reading. As a result they are not high up the Private Member's Bill list and rarely become law.

Private Member's Bills introduced into the Lords have to go through the same stages for passage. As they take second place to any House of Commons Bill they rarely become law.

(c)   *Private Bills*

Private Bills were particularly common in the 19th century and have a narrower remit **9–012** then Public Bills, seeking to change a particular area or activity such as local government or railways. Where local government promotes a Private Bill they are often referred to as local Bills and are used where existing legislation is not sufficient for something it wishes to do. Private Bills can be promoted by a private company and this will usually be where the company proposes to do something which affects private or public rights; these are sometimes referred to as Personal Bills.

Notice of the intention to promote a Private Bill should be given in advertisement in newspapers and the London Gazette and in writing to all persons whose interests may be affected. When this has been done, a petition signed by the promoters and a copy of the Bill must be presented at the Private Bill Office of the House of Commons by November 27 each year.

Private Bills go through the same stages for passage into legislation though different rules apply, particularly at committee stage.

(d)   *Hybrid*

Hybrid Bills have characteristics of both Public and Private Bills. A Hybrid Bill is one **9–013** of general application (public) which will also have a significant impact for a specific group or individual (private). The Bills passed concerning the Channel Tunnel was a hybrid Bill as it also affected the private rights of landowners who property was compulsorily purchased. The current Crossrail Bills are also Hybrid Bills.

2.   Pre-legislative stages

9–014   In preparation for legislation the relevant government department may issue a Green Paper which enables consultation with interested parties or White Papers which represent a statement of policy. Public Bills are drafted by lawyers in the Parliamentary Counsel Office on the instructions of the government department concerned. Draft Bills may then go through a process of pre-legislative scrutiny which enables specialist individuals and groups to contribute to the Bill. The Select Committee on Modernisation concluded (The Legislative Process, 7 (HC 1079 2005–06)) this "can play an important role in improving the law, even where there has already been lengthy and extensive external consultation by government. Whatever its impact on the passage of legislation, the purpose of pre-legislative scrutiny is not to secure an easy ride for the government's legislative programme, it is to make better laws by improving the scrutiny of Bills and drawing the wider public more effectively into the Parliamentary process".

In addition to these stages, the Joint Committee on Human Rights examines every Bill which is presented to Parliament to assess its compatibility with human rights. The Committee can also examine draft Bills which have been published for consultation before presentation to Parliament.

3.   Legislative stages

9–015   A Bill must be agreed by both the House of Commons and House of Lords unless the Parliament Act procedure is used (see Ch.10). Bills can start in either House, though finance Bills start in the House of Commons and Bills of constitutional significance (i.e. Reform Bills) tend to start in the House of Lords. Both Chambers have to consent to the Bill before it can be presented for Royal Assent. The formal stages are essentially the same for all Bills though there are some differences in procedure, notably for Private Bills at Committee stage.

(a)   *First reading*

9–016   The first reading of a Bill is a formality and takes place without any debate. On the day scheduled for the first reading a dummy copy (title only) is laid on the table of the House. In the House of Commons, the clerk reads out the title of the Bill which constitutes its first reading. In the House of Lords, the title is read by the Member in charge of the Bill. Once formally presented, the Bill is printed and published and a date is set for its second reading.

(b) *Second reading*

The second reading is the first opportunity for in-depth scrutiny of the Bill which takes   **9–017**
place on the floor of the House in the form of a debate. The second reading of a
government Bill is introduced by a Minister in the relevant department (for a Private
Member's Bill, the Member responsible speaks instead) who outlines the overall purpose of the Bill, highlights the parts considered most important and speaks in favour of
the Bill. The Official Opposition spokesperson then probes and questions the Bill,
followed by a general debate of the whole House. Detailed amendments may be suggested but are not formally proposed at this stage. In exceptional circumstances the
second reading debate may be referred to a committee for consideration. This procedure is reserved for non-controversial matters and a vote on the Bill is still taken in the
whole House. At the end of the debate, the House decides whether the Bill should be
given its second reading, meaning it can proceed to the next stage. A failure of the
second reading means the Bill can progress no further and must either be re-introduced
or abandoned.
   In the House of Lords the procedure is essentially the same.

(c) *Committee stage*

At committee stage individual clauses of the Bill receive detailed scrutiny and con-   **9–018**
sideration. In the House of Commons, Bills go to one of two types of committees; a
Public Bill committee or a Committee of the entire House. In the House of Lords, Bills
go to a Committee of the Whole House and exceptionally to a Committee of the Grand
Chamber.

(i) Public Bill Committees

Formerly known as Standing Committees, this part of the legislative process was often   **9–019**
criticised. The Hansard Society in evidence to the House of Commons Select Committee on Modernisation (The Legislative Process, First Report of Session 2005–06, HC
1097) noted, for example, that Standing Committees:

   "fail to deliver genuine and analytical scrutiny of [Bills], their political functions
   are neutered, dominated almost exclusively by government . . . , they fail to engage
   with the public and the media (in contrast to Select Committees) and they do not
   adequately utilise the evidence of experts or interested parties."

Following the recommendations of the Select Committee, Standing Committee were
renamed Public Bill Committees (effective November 15, 2006). A majority of Bills are
dealt with in these committees. Each committee has between 16 and 50 members
reflecting party composition in the House. At least one Minister from the government
Department in charge of the Bill will be on the committee, as well as front-bench

spokesmen from each of the opposition parties. A new Public Bill committee is appointed for each Bill and the membership of each committee is discharged when it has reported its Bill to the House. There may be several Public Bill committees appointed at any one time and they are named after the Bill that they examine, for example, the Pensions Bill Committee.

Public Bill Committees now resemble Select Committees with both an initial evidence-taking role which then moves into a deliberative role. Committees now have the power to "send for persons, papers and records" and to hear oral evidence which will be given in public. The Committee does not repeat the pre-legislative scrutiny but can take evidence from Ministers in the relevant department, specialists or other interested parties to answer questions and aid their scrutiny of the Bill. The Criminal Justice and Immigration Bill Committee for example received written memoranda from over 100 individuals and heard oral evidence from 24 witnesses. The Child Maintenance and Other Payments Bill received written memoranda from six individuals or groups such as "Families Need Fathers" and heard oral evidence from an additional six witnesses. The evidence-taking process ensures that Members are fully informed about the Bill and its content and allows the wider public to become more engaged. It also leads to a more collaborative and informed deliberative role. At the deliberative stage the Bill is examined clause by clause. Amendments may be proposed by Members giving notice to the Public Bill Office of the House of Commons. These amendments might be minor such as deleting or adding a word or of major substance.

(ii)   Committee of the whole House

9–020   Few Bills are considered by the whole House, those that are include: Bills affecting the constitution, for example, the Human Rights Bill; Bills that are not controversial; and Bills which the government needs to pass quickly. The Prevention of Terrorism Bill 2005 for example completed all of its stages within one month of being presented.

(iii)   Private Bills

9–021   Private Bills go to one of two committees:

(1)   Opposed Bill Committee: a Private Bill goes to this Committee if it has been opposed (petition against it). The Committee consists of four impartial (no personal or constituency interest) Members nominated by the Committee of Selection.

(2)   Unopposed Bill Committee: If there is no opposition to the Bill it proceeds to this Committee. The Unopposed Bill Committee consists of five Members. The main issue of this Committee is for the Promoter to prove the need for the Bill and answer questions put by the Committee.

Both Committees sit semi-judicially and the parties may have counsel representing them. Unlike other Parliamentary Committees, Members attached to either of these two Committees must attend meetings. There are two possible outcomes at the completion of Committee stages: case proved or case not proved. If the case is proved, the Committee have declared that the purpose of the Bill has been established as proper and desirable. After Committee stage, the Bill if amended is reprinted and then proceeds through the remaining stages (usually a formality).

(d) Report stage

Once the committee stage has finished the Bill moves into report stage. If any amendments were made by the Public Bill Committee, the Bill is printed again. The Committee reports to the House its conclusions and any amendments made. Members then debate the Bill further, though at this stage the Bill is considered whole and not clause by clause. Further amendments may be introduced at this stage, but the Speaker will be careful to ensure that arguments dealt with in committee are not repeated. As there is a delay between Committee and Report the government have time to consider and so may bring forward their own amendments in lieu of amendments rejected or withdrawn at Committee. The House can also remove amendments made by the Committee. Report stage can take a number of hours and be spread over a period of days depending on the nature of the Bill. Unamended Bills from the Committee of the whole House go straight to third reading. **9–022**

(e) Third reading

The third reading is the final stage of the Bill in the Chambers and is usually taken directly after the conclusion of report. This enables the House to take an overview of the Bill, as amended in Committee or on report. In the Commons no amendments can be made at this stage; the House of Lords may make amendments provided the issue has not already been voted on. Amendments in the House of Lords are often used to clarify specific parts of the Bill and to allow the government to make good any promises of changes to the Bill made at earlier stages. Debates on third reading are usually very short. After a successful third reading, the Bill moves to first reading in the other House. **9–023**

(f) House of Lords

Proceedings in the House of Lords are similar to those of the House of Commons, there are two major differences: after second reading the Bill is sent to a Committee of the whole House and amendments can be made at third reading. If the House of Lords amend a Bill the amendments must be agreed to by the House of Commons (and vice versa if the Bill started in the Lords). The House of Commons may agree with those amendments, agree to them with some amendments of their own or disagree with them. If they make amendments, they ask the House of Lords to agree to those amendments. **9–024**

If they disagree a message is sent to the House of Lords giving reasons for their disagreement and the Lords consider the matter further. As consensus is required before a Bill can be put forward for Royal Assent, a Bill can bounce back and forth between the two Houses for some time. On occasions, deadlock is reached where neither side proposes any more amendments or agrees. In this situation, the Bill can be passed under the Parliament Acts 1911 and 1949, if the following conditions are satisfied:

- the Bill went to the House of Lords at least one month before the end of the session;

- one year must have elapsed between the Second Reading of the Bill in the House of Commons in the first session and the Bill being passed by the House of Commons in the second session;

- the Bill in the second session is identical to the Bill in the first session, containing only amendments which are necessary to take account of the passage of time.

(g) *Royal Assent*

9–025 Once the Bill is agreed by both Houses, the Bill is submitted to the monarch for Royal Assent. Royal Assent is an exercise of prerogative power and is usually a formality (see Chs 3 and 13).

(h) *"Carrying Over"*

9–026 Normally, a Public Bill must complete all its stages in one session of Parliament and should a Bill fail to complete all its stages it would have to start again at the beginning of the legislative procedure the following year. While the above rule acted as important discipline on parliamentary procedure, the Select Committee on Modernisation (Third Report of 1997–98, Carry-over of Public Bills (HC 543 1997–98) felt it should be applied more flexibility. The Committee recommended that "in defined circumstances and subject of certain safeguards" government Bills should be able to be carried over from one session to the next. This ensures that important legislation is not rushed through the last few stages and also that debate and discussion on a Bill is not completely wasted. The first Bill to be treated in this way was the Financial Services and Markets Bill 1998–99, which the House agreed to carry over into the 1999–2000 session after a debate on October 25, 1999. The Criminal Justice and Immigration Bill was carried over from the 2006–07 session to 2007–08.

4.   Delegated legislation

Delegated legislation is a body of legislation made by a subordinate authority (usually   **9–027**
the Executive) which is given power by primary legislation to enact legislation. The
Joint Committee on Delegated Legislation (Report of the Joint Committee on Delegated Legislation, HL 184, HC 475, 1971–72, para.6) described delegated legislation as
covering "every exercise of power to legislate conferred by or under an Act of Parliament". Such Acts of Parliament known as a "parent" or "enabling act" may delegate
legislative powers to government departments, Ministers, local authorities or other
bodies to be exercised for the purposes stated in the Act.

The use of delegated legislation has increased tremendously in recent years and has
become the most prolific source of law in the United Kingdom. The increase is primarily due to the lack of parliamentary time necessary to pass all the laws the United
Kingdom needs to function. In addition, delegated legislation has certain advantages
over primary legislation; it can deal with more complicated and technical points that are
often not suitable for inclusion into a general statute; can give the law flexibility and can
be passed relatively quickly, a necessity in times of emergency.

While delegated legislation is an essential part of any legislature it has many critics,
amongst them Dicey who thought its use was contrary to the rule of law. It is therefore
important that there are clear mechanisms for control of delegated legislation. In the
United Kingdom, control of delegated legislation happens in both the judicial and
political arena. Delegated legislation in the form of statutory instruments (Orders in
Council also take the form of SIs) are subject to scrutiny by a variety of methods in
both Houses.

Some statutory instruments (SIs) do not receive any parliamentary scrutiny; typically
these will be commencement orders which are used to bring part of or a whole statute
into force. The Statutory Instruments Act 1946 provides for two procedures by which
Parliament confirms the suitability of (SIs). The SIs enabling acts will state which
procedure should be followed.

(a)   *Negative resolution procedure*

This is the most common procedure and requires that the statutory instrument be laid   **9–028**
before Parliament for a period of 40 days. If either House passes a negative resolution
during that period the statutory instrument ceases to have effect. This procedure has the
advantage of preserving parliamentary control without wasting time.

(b)   *Affirmative resolution procedure*

This is used for statutory instruments which are more controversial. The SI must be laid   **9–029**
before Parliament (one or both Houses) for a certain period of time set down in its
enabling act. Parliament must then pass an affirmative resolution within the period
agreeing with the SI.

All statutory instruments are subject to scrutiny by a number of Select Committees: House of Commons Select Committee on statutory instruments; House of Lords Delegated Powers and Regulatory Reform Committee; the Merits of Statutory Instruments Committee and the Joint Select Committee on Statutory Instruments.

The Joint Committee on Statutory Instruments is responsible for scrutinising all statutory instruments made in exercise of powers granted by Act of Parliament. SIs not laid before Parliament are included within the Committee's remit but local instruments and instruments made by devolved administrations are not unless they are required to be laid before Parliament. SIs which are laid before the House of Commons only are considered by the Select Committee on Statutory Instruments, which is comprised of the Commons members of the Joint Committee.

The two Committees are empowered to draw the attention of the House to an SI if it fits into one of the following grounds (found in House of Commons Standing Order 151):

(i)   that it imposes a charge on the public revenues or contains provisions requiring payments to be made to the Exchequer or any government department or to any local or public authority in consideration of any licence or consent or of any services to be rendered, or prescribes the amount of any such charge or payment;

(ii)   that it is made in pursuance of any enactment containing specific provisions excluding it from challenge in the courts, either at all times or after the expiration of a specific period;

(iii)   that it purports to have retrospective effect where the parent statute confers no express authority so to provide;

(iv)   that there appears to have been unjustifiable delay in the publication or in the laying of it before Parliament;

(v)   that there appears to have been unjustifiable delay in sending a notification under the proviso to s.4(1) of the Statutory Instruments Act 1946, where an instrument has come into operation before it has been laid before Parliament;

(vi)   that there appears to be a doubt whether it is intra vires or that it appears to make some unusual or unexpected use of the powers conferred by the statute under which it is made;

(vii)   that for any special reason its form or purport calls for elucidation;

(viii)   that its drafting appears to be defective.

SCRUTINY OF THE EXECUTIVE

9–030   In addition to the passage of legislation, one of Parliament's important functions is ensuring the accountability of government to the electorate. Consistent with the doctrine of responsible government Parliament ensures that the government of the day acts in accordance with the principles of constitutionalism and democracy (the structure of central government and the concept of ministerial responsibility are considered in Ch.11). Parliament, principally through the House of Commons, ensures compliance through three main procedural mechanisms: parliamentary questions, debates and Select Committees.

1.   Parliamentary questions

The first recorded question was put by the House of Lords in 1721 (see Patrick   **9–031** Howarth, *Questions in the House: The History of a Unique British Institution* (London: Bodley Head, 1956), pp.11–14) and in the House of Commons in about 1835. According to Erskine May (pp.344–45), "the purpose of a question is to obtain information or press for action" and "should relate to the public affairs with which they [Ministers] are officially connected, to proceeding pending in Parliament or to matters of administration for which they are responsible".

Parliamentary questions are used by Members of Parliament to seek information or press for action. They oblige Ministers to explain and defend their work, policy decisions and actions of their departments. There are four main types of question and approximately 80,000 parliamentary questions are asked each year:

(1)   questions for oral answers;

(2)   urgent questions;

(3)   cross cutting questions; and

(4)   questions for written answer.

(a)   *Questions for oral answer*

Question time of Departmental Ministers takes place Monday to Thursday for one   **9–032** hour and is one of the most publicised aspects of the House of Commons' work. It remains the principle way in which information from Ministers is obtained. Each government department answers questions according to a rota called the Order of Oral Questions. Questions for oral answer must be "tabled" (notice is given of a question by handing it or sending it to the Clerks in the Table Office) at least three days before so they can be circulated to the relevant Minister and department. Since 1972, a Member cannot table more that two questions on any one day and both of these must be to different Ministers. Questions asked must relate to the responsibilities of the government department concerned, have a factual basis and must seek information or press for action. They must also be a single question not requiring a lengthy answer. Questions must not offer or seek expression of opinion nor can they refer to issues dealt with during debate or pending in committee or involve discussion of the monarch. Such questions that attempt to do any of these or are not within the Minister's remit are deemed "out of order" questions and are not asked.

The order in which the questions are asked in the House is randomly determined by computer, known as the "shuffle". Following the House of Commons Select Committee on Procedure's review of question time (Third Report, Parliamentary Questions, HC 622, 2001–02), Parliament reduced the number of questions that could be asked relative to the time the Minister spends in the dispatch box. The following table shows the number of questions that can be asked, correct as of December 2007:

Time in Dispatch Box	Number of Questions
55 minutes	25
50 minutes	20
45 minutes	20
30 minutes	15
15 minutes	10
10 minutes	8

This reduction in number is significant for departments who previously had to prepare answers to all questions that went into the shuffle even in the knowledge that a majority would not be asked on the floor of the House. In the House, the Speaker calls the first Member on the list who reads out the number of their question. When the Minister has answered the question, the Member concerned can ask a supplementary question which must be on the same subject as the original question. The Speaker may allow other Members to put supplementaries, usually alternating between the government and Opposition. This process continues for the duration of question time. The last 10–15 minutes of question time is reserved for "topical matters" which allows Members to ask supplementary questions on anything relating to the department's responsibilities. The effect of a supplementary is it allows Members to ask questions for which no notice has been given. A Minister can refuse to answer a question if, for example, an answer was contrary to the public interest or the cost of finding information would be excessive. Erskine May states (p.352), "An answer to a question cannot be insisted upon, if the answer be refused by a Minister".

(i)   Prime Minister Question Time (PMQs)

9–033   The Prime Minister answer questions for 30 minutes every Wednesday. The session usually starts with a routine question from an MP about the Prime Minister's engagements. This then allows the MP to ask a supplementary question on any subject, typically one of current political significance. The Leader of the Opposition and the Liberal Democrat Leader can follow up or ask another topic. Those MPs who tabled the same question are called to ask their supplementary question. The strength of PMQs is in theory the Prime Minister does not know what questions he could be asked and requires him to demonstrate competence across the full range of government policy. However, in practice, the Prime Minister will be extensively briefed about subjects that could arise.

(ii)   Advantages and disadvantages of question time

Oral questions have some clear advantages over the written format. As they are **9–034** answered on the floor of the House they can attract greater publicity and allow the wider public to become more involved in parliamentary business. The use of supplementary questions which are not tabled means that an answer is not so obviously prepared. Importantly, question time is the only regular occasion upon which the government is formally required to account to Parliament for its decisions and the state of the nation's affairs. As such it represents an important aspect of accountability and responsible government. For backbench Members, question time allows them to become involved and question Ministers on issues of their own choosing.

An obvious criticism of question time is the lack of time allocated to it and, due to the number of questions put forward, it is impossible for in depth questioning to take place. This is mitigated slightly by the use of written questions which can be more detailed and receive a similarly detailed answer. In addition to the short allocated time, time can be effectively wasted by a known practice of government Backbenchers to "feed" questions to Ministers. This is done in order to reduce the time for Opposition questions, enable a Minister to make an announcement, explain a policy choice or provide information that flatters the government. One important criticism often levied at question time is the lack of spontaneity as questions must be tabled in advance and the Civil Service can prepare extensive answers. Hilaire Barnett (*Constitutional and Administrative Law*, 6th edn, (Routledge Cavendish, 2006), p.406) believes that question time is not supposed to be a spontaneous affair and should not be criticised for not being so. The purpose of questions is, as Erskine May stated above, to allow Members to get information about Executive activity. If questions were spontaneous then less information would be gleaned from the exercise and it would become one of politicking rather than accountability and information gathering. In addition, the Member has the use of the supplementary question which is not tabled. Other criticism of question time is their use by the Opposition to point score by selecting issues which may embarrass and discredit the government. This is particularly apparent in Prime Minister Question Time which often becomes a battle of personalities. This point is brought out by Lord Norton in evidence to the House of Commons Select Committee on Procedure (Third Report, Parliamentary Questions, HC 622, 2001–02). He commented:

> "Question Time used to be an opportunity for backbenchers to seek information from Ministers. It has in recent decades become more an opportunity for front-benchers to intervene and for Opposition Members to try to catch out Ministers, as well as for government backbenchers to support Ministers and put questions about Opposition policy. This change in nature has been a feature especially of Prime Minister's Question Time."

(b)   *Urgent questions*

Prior to the 2002–03 session of Parliament urgent questions were known as a Private **9–035** Notice Questions. Urgent questions arise when a matter requires an immediate ministerial response. Urgent questions are subject to the same rules about content as ordinary oral questions but also have two additional requirements; the matter must be urgent and it must be of public importance. In order to ask an urgent question application must be made to the Speaker on the day in which the answer is required (before noon on Monday or Tuesday, 10.30am on Wednesday, 9.30am on Thursday or 10am on a sitting Friday). The department concerned is immediately informed. It is the Speaker's discretion whether to allow an urgent question which is taken immediately after question time; the procedure is the same as for oral questions.

(c)   *Cross cutting questions*

9–036   These were introduced in January 2003 and are asked in Westminster Hall. They enable Members to ask questions on topics that crosses the responsibilities of a number of government departments.

(d)   *Questions for written answer*

9–037   Questions for written answer are used to extract more detailed information from Ministers and government departments. Questions can be more exacting and can be transferred between departments. There are three types of written question:

(1)   Questions for oral answer which were successful in the shuffle and were not dealt with in the Chamber due to time. These questions must receive a written answer on the day of the oral session.

(2)   Ordinary written questions. These are requested to be answered two days after they are tabled. By constitutional convention, they must be answered at the latest within seven days.

(3)   Named day questions. When tabled these questions name a specific date by which they must receive an answer. A minimum of two days notice is required and no more than five questions can be tabled for one day. However, the answer provided by a Minister can be a holding reply to the effect that the Minister will reply with a substantive answer as soon as possible.

Questions are tabled in the same way as oral questions and are answered directly to the Members who asked the question. The texts of answers are reported in Hansard. Written questions have the advantage of being able to elicit more detailed information from the Minister or department and can be very effective in calling the government to account and/or starting a line of investigation. However, it must be remembered that government can still refuse to answer a written question for the same reasons they can an oral one.

2.   Debates

The main business of the House takes place in debates which may include full-day   **9–038**
debates on topics chosen by the government including second reading of its Bills as well
as debates on motions and Opposition days. Debates represent an important platform
by which the government can be called to account, though according to Adam Tomkins, *Public Law* ((OUP, 2003), p.160) they are the "least penetrating method of
accountability". Debates can force Ministers to explain and justify their policy choices
and provide an opportunity for the Opposition to expose flaws and present counter-
arguments and suggestions. They can also provide the opportunity for dissatisfied
Members to display dissent and give Members the opportunity to represent their
constituent's interests in matters of policy. There are a number of debates relevant to
scrutiny of the Executive.

(a)   *Substantive Debates*

A number of debates on substantive issues take place in the House. Such debates tend   **9–039**
to be more lengthy and detailed than adjournment debates (below). They may be
moved by the government when they seek approval for some aspect of government
policy or they may be moved by the Opposition. The Opposition are allocated 20 days
in each session for such debates; 17 for the main Opposition and three for the other
opposition parties (Opposition Days). These debates are party political and can be used
by the Opposition to criticise some aspect of government policy or expose flaws, for
example, the 8th Opposition day (2007–08 session) was used to debate the call for a
public inquiry into the war in Iraq. Other substantive debates are those immediately
following the Queen's speech when the government's legislative agenda is set out. The
topics for debate are chosen by the Opposition and such debates can run for five or six
days.

(b)   *Adjournment debates*

At the end of the day's public business (normally 10pm on Mondays and Tuesdays,   **9–040**
7pm on Wednesdays, 6pm on Thursdays and 2.30pm on Fridays) a half hour is made
available for Members to raise particular issues relating to his constituency or matters
of public concern. The Speaker is notified in advance and a ballot is held once a week
for the four Members who can speak the following week. The Speaker chooses the
Member to speak on Thursdays. The Member who tabled the adjournment debate is
called to speak and a Minister replies. The Member has no right of response unless the
Minister allows it. These debates do not lead to a formal vote and instead are used as a
way of raising issues.

(i)   Emergency adjournment debates

9–041   In place of the "daily" adjournment debates, an emergency adjournment debates can be called. This is a more substantial debate to discuss a specific and important matter that should have urgent consideration for example, a motion was passed on March 19, 2002 for an emergency debate on the war in Afghanistan. The Speaker must be satisfied that the matter is urgent and that it comes within the competence of the Minister of the day. The request for an emergency adjournment must be supported by at least 40 Members.

(ii)   Westminster Hall adjournment debates

9–042   Prior to 2000, there was little opportunity for Backbenchers to bring constituency problems or other topics to the personal attention of Ministers. In November 2000, a parallel chamber was created, Westminster Hall, to sit alongside the main Chamber and help meet Backbench demand. Westminster Hall is aimed at fostering a new style of debate which is constructive rather then confrontational and according to the government it has "greatly widened the opportunities for members to raise matters of concern to them" (HC 440 (2001–02)). Sessions are open to all Members who sit in a elongated horseshoe arrangement. Adjournment debates are also held in Westminster Hall. On Tuesdays and Wednesday mornings debates are for Backbench and other Members to raise issues. On Thursday afternoons, there is a single adjournment debate on either a topic chosen by the government or on a select report chosen by the Liaison Committee. These consist of two one and half hour debates, which are intended to be more general and involve a number of Members, and three half hour debates.

(c)   *Early day motions*

9–043   These are formal motions submitted for debate but for which no date has been fixed. Motions cover anything from congratulating a sports team (for example, EDM 1162, 2003–04) to criticism of legislation or government approach (EDM 75, Reform of the Mental Health Act 1983, 2006–07). Early day motions exist to allow Members to put on record their opinion on a particular subject and to canvass support from other Members. These motions very rarely progress to debate but do attract much publicity and media attention for example, a number of early day motions were submitted in relation to the war in Iraq (see for example, EDM and EDM 1088, 2006–07 session).

Early day motions must have a short title and a brief paragraph that describes what the motion is about, for example, early day motion 1162, Adrian Flook MP, 2003–04 session stated:

> "That this House congratulates the England Cricket team who have won 10 out of 11 test matches this year including seven in a row over the summer, the best performance for 75 years, with series wins against the West Indies and New Zealand; and calls on the government to recognise fully the contribution made by

cricket and the England and Wales Cricket Board during the year and to this summer of sporting endeavour and achievement."

While a majority of early day motions do not progress to debate, some do so, a good example was that tabled by Margaret Thatcher MP as leader of the opposition on March 22, 1979. Her motion was that "this House has no confidence in her Majesty's government". The motion was debated on March 28 and agreed to, leading to the calling of a general election at which the then Labour government, under James Callaghan, lost.

(d)   *Estimate days*

During each parliamentary session, three days are given over for debate on government **9–044** expenditure (supply estimates). These are spread through the year, one may be taken as two half days and the two full days may be divided into two separate debates. The choice of subject lies with the Liaison Committee which recommends particular Select Committee reports which can be attached to an individual estimate. After the estimates for discussion have been voted on, all other estimates are voted on formally without debate.

(e)   *Disadvantages*

While debates are good for providing the opportunity to scrutinise government policy **9–045** and raise general issues, there are some key disadvantages with them as a forum for accountability. Perhaps one of the principle problems is the lack of time available for debating. Debates are dominated by Frontbenchers and Backbench Members often lack opportunity to speak which means that scrutiny is not as effective as it could be; it is rare to find a Frontbench Member willing to criticise the government. In recent years, attempts to increase the time available and opportunity for Backbench Members to participate by the opening of a parallel chamber in Westminster Hall have been successful but opportunities are still limited. Debates very rarely influence government and the nature of the whip system means that they do not influence the way Members vote. However, if the purpose of debates is to provide the opportunity to raise issues and highlight inadequacies then this "flaw" does not prove fatal to that purpose. While some debates are poorly attended and do not receive much media coverage, full details of debates are always available in Hansard.

3.   Select Committees

Select committees are permanent parliamentary committees appointed by the House. **9–046** They are arguably the most effective mechanism for holding government to account.

(a)   History and development

9–047   Select Committees have been in existence since the 17th century when the Committee of Privileges was first appointed. The system developed on an ad-hoc basis either in response to needs to relieve the pressure on the House or because of new obligations. After 1945 little use was made of committees for scrutinising the administration of the government and in 1965 the Select Committee on Procedure was of the view that the House needed to possess a more efficient system of scrutiny of administration and more information should be available to Members on the way government departments carried out their responsibilities. The view at this time was a perceived failure of Parliament to keep pace with the increase in the scope of governmental activity. In the later 1960s some reforms were attempted by Richard Crossman, the then Leader of the House, with the appointment of more specialist committees and a growth in overall use.

In 1977 the Select Committee on Procedure (First Report HC 588 (1977–78)) reviewed the Select Committee system. They took the view (at para.5.14) that despite the growth of the system since 1964, the development remained piecemeal and resulted in "decidedly patchy coverage of the activities of governmental departments and agencies, and of the major areas of public policy and administration". They concluded (at para.5.15) that the House should not be content with an incomplete and unsystematic scrutiny of the Executive and favoured a reorganisation of existing Select Committees to produce a more effective means for the regular scrutiny of the Executive and areas of public policy. They recommended the creation of a departmental committee structure. These committees would have the power to summon Ministers and civil servants and their reports should be debated on the floor of the House. The existing Select Committees were all abolished save for the Public Accounts Committee and the Committees for Statutory Instruments and European Legislation.

During the 1979 general election, the Conservative party pledged that they would debate the report and vote for its implementation if elected. Following their election, the Conservative government adopted the Committee recommendations.

(b)   Types of Select Committees

9–048   Select Committees take many different forms and include:

- Committees dealing with important issues of general concern such as the Committee on the Armed Forces Bill, the Committees on Arms Export Controls (formerly the Quadripartite Committee), Public Accounts Committee, Public Administration Select Committee European Scrutiny Committee, Regulatory Reform Committee and Select Committee on Statutory Instruments;

- Committees dealing with matters internal to the House, these include: Administration Committee (created in 2005 to replace the five domestic committee), Finance and Services Committee, Liaison Committee (the chairmen of all Select Committees form the Liaison Committee which looks at the work of all the committees), Modernisation of the House of Commons, Procedure

Committee and Standards & Privileges Committee; Committee on Standards in Public Life;

- departmental committees.

(c)   The Departmental Committee structure

Each government department is shadowed by a departmental Select Committee. As of February 2008, the current list of departmental committees was: **9–049**

Business and Enterprise Committee;

Children, Schools and Families Committee;

Communities and Local Government Committee;

Culture, Media & Sport Committee;

Defence Committee;

Environmental Audit Committee;

Environment, Food and Rural Affairs Committee;

Foreign Affairs Committee;

Health Committee;

Home Affairs Committee;

Innovation, Universities, Science and Skills Committee;

International Development Committee;

Justice Committee;

Northern Ireland Affairs Committee;

Scottish Affairs Committee;

Transport Committee;

Treasury Committee;

Welsh Affairs Committee;

Work and Pensions Committee.

(d)   Powers and functions

Select committee's role is to examine "the expenditure, administration and policy" of the relevant department and its "associated public bodies" (for example, regulators and quangos). Select committees have the power to determine their own agenda and so,   **9–050** within their remit, decide what matters they will discuss. This is incredibly important as on the floor of the House it is the government, through the Leader of the House, who sets the agenda and so the government can prevent an issue from coming onto the floor. Government cannot, however, prevent a Select Committee from investigating sensitive or controversial issues. Select Committees can also appoint specialist advisors to supply information or elucidate matters of complexity. They also have the power to "send for persons and papers", which means that they have the power to secure the attendance of witnesses and production of written evidence. One oft cited criticism is the lack of enforcement powers in this area as they cannot compel a Member of Parliament or Minister to attend. For example, in 1988 following her resignation over comments that "most eggs produced in the country were infected with salmonella", the Select Committee on Agriculture invited Edwina Currie to give evidence but she declined. An exchange of letters between the Chairman and Edwina Currie eventually led to her attendance. Normally however, Ministers do attend willingly. A similar issue arises with regards to civil servants. Following the Westland Helicopter Affair (concerning a dispute over the allocation of defence contracts), three Select Committees started investigations. The government refused to allow witnesses from the Department of Trade and Industry to attend and give evidence. As a result, the Committees were severely hampered in their scrutiny of the Westland episode. Similarly a Trade and Industry Select Committee inquiry into the Iraqi supergun affair was obstructed by the government's refusal to contact two retired civil servants whose evidence was required by the Committee.

Where a committee requests to take evidence from a civil servant there is a presumption that the Minister will agree to meet the request. However, the final decision on who should best represent the Minister rests with the Minister and it is within his right to suggest an alternative or appear instead. If the committee is adamant they want a particular person, a request can be made to Parliament to order attendance. When civil servants do attend it is on behalf of their Minister and under their direction. Rules known as the Osmotherly Rules give detailed guidance for Civil Servants appearing before a Select Committee.

Since 1997 anyone giving evidence before a Select Committee is required to take a formal oath. Anyone found to have lied to the committee faces criminal prosecution. If the person is a Member of Parliament then the committee will ask the House of Commons to remove the Member's immunity from prosecution.

When the system was established in 1979 it was felt that the appointment of members to committees should be free from government interference. As a result, appointment was given to the Committee of Selection. The number of members varies between eleven (nine committees) and sixteen members (Environment Audit Committee). Members are appointed on a cross parliamentary basis and the Committee follows three general principles when appointing members: the government should have a majority on any committee; overall membership should reflect the party strengths of the House; and no Ministers, whips, private parliamentary secretaries or principal opposition spokesman should be nominated. By constitutional convention membership is limited to backbenchers who, because they are separate from the Executive, can't in theory make them less likely to be influenced by the government. Each committee has a chairman chosen from among the members at the first meeting. The Chairman plays a key role in leading the committee's work and has a casting vote in the event of a tie. Select committees last the life of a Parliament which provides stability of membership, security of tenure and an opportunity for members to gain expertise in the subject matter so making them more effective at scrutinising government.

However, the objective behind the 1979 decision for independence from government interference does not seem to have been fully achieved. The Committee of Selection is heavily influenced by the whips who put names forward for appointment to the various Select Committees. The Committee of Selection can then either reject or accept the recommendations. In considering the role of the Committee of Selection, the Liaison Committee noted that there was no doubt that Members had been kept off lists or removed from committees because of their views. They criticised this practice of the Committee of Selection and proposed a new system. The government rejected any changes and a motion to establish a Committee of Nominations independent from party whips in 2002 was also rejected.

Despite this obvious link with government, the Committees recommendations must still be voted on by the whole House and on occasion are overturned. This was the case following the general election in 2001 when the Chairs of the Transport Committee (Gwyneth Dunwoody) and the Foreign Affairs Committee (Donald Anderson) were effectively removed from their posts by not being included on the nomination lists. Both Chairs were considered to be too independent minded for the Labour government. However the government was forced to do a U-turn after allowing a free vote on the issue. Labour MPs voted overwhelmingly to reject the government's favoured line up for the two Select Committees. As a result a new list was put forward which included Anderson and Dunwoody who were duly appointed.

(e)   Reports

Following an investigation the Select Committee produces a report which reflects the **9–051** majority view of the committee. Reports are published and the government are expected to reply within 60 days unless a longer period has been agreed with the committee. Few reports are actually debated however; from May 1997–November 2000 only 29 reports were debated in the Chamber. This fact is one which undermines the effectiveness of Select Committees. The Liaison Committee (Shifting the Balance, 2000–01) recommended an increase in debating of reports on the floor of the House on substantive motions. The government did not agree with the proposal but since then the creation of the parallel chamber in Westminster Hall has assisted in more reports being debated as Thursday afternoons are set aside for such debates. In addition, the Liaison Committee can choose an additional six reports to be debated.

Another criticism often levied at Select Committees is the fact their proposals are not binding and they cannot impose sanctions for non co-operation with its recommendations. However in the event of non-co-operation, the committee can make a special report to the House and table a debate on the Minister's conduct. Yet, despite the absence of power to impose formal sanctions, the Committees' biggest weapon is publicity. As Select Committees operate in public and their reports are freely available, they can easily gain publicity when controversial issues are discussed. For example, the report of the House of Commons Foreign Affairs Committee, The Decision to go to

War in Iraq (Ninth Report of Session 2002–03, Volume I, HC 813–I) was eagerly awaited and was open to more scrutiny then many other reports, principally because of the controversial nature of the issue. In addition, the Opposition would most readily use government's failure to respond or accept the recommendation of a committee as a way of criticising the government in the Chamber.

(f) Review

9–052 In 2000 the Liaison Committee (Shifting the Balance, 2000–01) underwrote a review of the Select Committee system. Its report concluded that the 1979 system was a success.

> "It has enabled the questioning of Ministers and civil servants, and has forced them to explain policies. On occasion, it has exposed mistaken and short-sighted policies and, from time to time, wrong-doing both in high places and low. It has been a source of unbiased information, rational debate, and constructive ideas. It has made the political process less remote, and more accessible to the citizen who is affected by that process ... Its very existence has been a constant reminder to Ministers and officials, and many others in positions of powers and influence, of the spotlight that may swing their way when least welcome."

Despite this apparent glowing report on the success of Select Committee, the Liaison committee also commented that the performance of committees has not been consistent and on occasion the government has been able to thwart the committee's purpose. This final point is perhaps borne out by House of Commons Foreign Affairs Committee, The Decision to go to War in Iraq (Ninth Report of Session 2002–03, Vol.I, HC 813–I) who stated at para.168.

> "We conclude that continued refusal by Ministers to allow this committee access to intelligence papers and personnel, on this inquiry and more generally, is hampering it in the work which Parliament has asked it to carry out."

It is fair to accept that the system is patchy and spasmodic, while some committees are assiduous (Foreign Affairs committee for example) in questioning Ministers others are less interested. Time to debate reports in the House is not always available and governments can withhold information and the attendance of people. However the Select Committee system has had a big impact in ensuring that Ministers and civil servants explain their actions in public which is a positive contribution to accountability in a modern democracy. This has been strengthened by the decision in April 2002 for the Prime Minister to appear before the Liaison Committee twice a year to discuss international and domestic affairs. This represents a strong movement forward in accountability and allows for in-depth questioning of the Prime Minister about his government which is simply not available in other formats like Prime Minister Questions.

CONTROL OF FINANCE

One of the main responsibilities of the House of Commons is to hold the government to   **9–053** account for the way it spends its money. Parliamentary authority over national finance was asserted in the 17th century through art.4 of the Bill of Rights 1688, which made "levying money for or to the use of the Crowne … without grant of Parlyament … illegal". Government accountability to Parliament through the requirement that taxation and expenditure be enshrined in legislation remains a cornerstone of the governmental system in the United Kingdom.

The financial affairs of government are debated in the House on Estimate days, following the budget, debates on the Finance and Consolidated Fund Bills and when financial resolutions are passed authorising expenditure. Members are not given the opportunity to consider taxing or expenditure proposals in any depth and cannot amend the substance of financial proposals. Members can only debate the general policy proposals. Also since the Parliament Act 1911, the House of Lords cannot veto or delay Money Bills (note the Finance Act is rarely certified as a Moncy Bill).

Revenue in the United Kingdom principally comes from three sources: taxation, borrowing and revenue from Crown lands, and is deposited in the Bank of England. All withdrawals of money require statutory approval. Some expenditure is immune from political scrutiny as it is considered inappropriate. This is authorised by the Consolidated Fund Act and is used for payments of judicial salaries, the Speaker of the House of Commons, Comptroller, Auditor General, Parliamentary Commissioner for Administration for example.

The bulk of annual expenditure comes under supply services which require annual approval. Departments in consultation with the Chancellor request the monies needed for year (known as supply estimates). Parliament scrutinises the supply estimates on the three estimates days (see above). The House of Commons must then approve these requests in Appropriation Acts. To support each request the government provides detailed information on what the money is for. After the expenditure, the department is audited by the national Audit Office who are supported by the Public Accounts Committee.

There are six types of estimates:

(1) Votes on account: these are requests for interim funds pending passage of the Appropriation Act.

(2) Main estimates: these set out the budgets for each department.

(3) Supplementary estimates: requests for additional funds.

(4) Excess votes: covers department expenditure which has exceeded its budget. A department which has exceeded its budget is audited who report to the House. The Public Accounts Committee approves or rejects the proposed additional expenditure which is put to Parliament without debate.

(5) Votes of credit.

(6) Exceptional grants.

1.   Budget

9–054   The Budget is the annual financial statement and review of the levels of taxation presented to the House of Commons. The Budget is held in the Spring, though a pre-budget report is issued in November. The Budget is presented to Parliament by the Chancellor in his Budget speech. The speech generally has two parts; a resume of the current economic situation and a summary of the measures required to meet the situation (ways and means). The Budget resolutions are tabled as soon as the Chancellor has finished the Budget speech and are voted on at the end of the debate. By constitutional convention, following the speech the Leader of the Opposition makes a general speech on the state of the economy. The Shadow Chancellor responds to the government's proposals in detail the following day. The debate on the government's proposals continue and can last anywhere from three to five days. Following the budget debate, the government introduce the Finance Bill for the year which has its second reading within a number of weeks.

Income tax can only lawfully be collected pursuant to a Finance Act which expires on April 5 each year. Any attempt to collect tax without statutory authority will be ruled unlawful. While in most cases the Finance Act can be passed before the expiration of this period, there have been occasions where debate has lengthened its passage. In 1909 for example, the Finance Bill took a year to pass. In *Bowles v Bank of England* [1913] 1 Ch. 57, the court stated that a resolution of the House of Commons did not authorise the collection of income tax and so the deduction of income tax by the Bank of England on Mr Bowles share purchase was illegal. As a consequence of this decision, the Provisional Collection of Taxes Act 1913 was passed. This was amended by the Provisional Collection of Taxes Act 1968. The Act allows the tax proposals in the Chancellor's speech to come into effect immediately. Only tax changes and tax continuations can come into effect this way, proposals for new taxes must wait until the Finance Bill is approved and comes into effect. The Act provides that the resolutions passed be confirmed by a second reading of the Bill relating to the tax within 30 days of the House approving the resolution. The Act also provides that the resolutions statutory effect continues only until August 5 for a March or April Budget or May 5 for an Autumn budget; this is effectively the timetable for the Finance Bill to receive Royal Assent (see also *Att-Gen v Wilts United Dairies* (1921) 37 T.L.R. 884.

2.   Public Accounts Committee

9–055   Control over national finance by Parliament does not end with voting on taxation and expenditure measures. One of the most effective Select Committees established in the Commons is the Public Accounts Committee. In existence since 1861, the Public Accounts Committee, with the assistance of the Comptroller and Auditor-General, performs an important role in exposing inefficient or wasteful expenditure of public money by government. The Committee consists of 15 Members and its principal functions include monitoring and scrutinising government expenditure to check that money is being used for the purpose granted and to highlight wastage and over expenditure.

REDRESS OF GRIEVANCES

Parliament also has a role to play in dealing with the redress of grievances of citizens. **9–056**
Grievances which individuals or interest/pressure groups may have with respect to any
aspect of public administration may be addressed directly to their MP as their representative. Many can be dealt with through the mechanisms of debate and questions or
Select Committees. Additionally, a Parliamentary Ombudsman's Office was created in
1967, through which complaints by individuals about central government may be
investigated; this is dealt with more fully in Ch.19.

FURTHER READING

Tomkins, A. "Government information and Parliament" (1996) P.L. 472

Chapter 10

THE HOUSE OF LORDS

INTRODUCTION

The House of Lords occupies a unique position in British democratic life, for not only is   **10–001**
it the second chamber, or Upper House, in our bicameral system of democracy, but it
exercises appellate jurisdiction as the final court of appeal in civil matters, even in this
post-devolution world, from England, Scotland, Wales and Northern Ireland, and
criminal appellate jurisdiction from all but the Scottish courts. This is, in truth, an
accident of history, but it has the effect of moulding the second chamber into the body it
is today. This chapter concentrates on the legislative and judicial functions of the
chamber, and the proposals for its reform to meet the challenges of a modern
democracy.

1.   Origins

The House of Lords, in the form it takes today, came into being in the 14th century,   **10–002**
with the separation of Parliament into two houses: Commons (Ch.9) and Lords. The
Lords, as a reflection of society of the time, consisted of the Lords Spiritual, principally
religious men, later restricted to those with a bishopric, and Lords Temporal, being
largely drawn from the aristocracy. It was the superior chamber.

COMPOSITION

1.   Hereditary peers

10–003   The House of Lords has always been composed of some peers who enjoyed their position as part of the legislature by reason of birth; an hereditary peerage. As the 20th century developed, the hereditary principle became increasingly difficult to justify, especially given the social and economic changes the United Kingdom was undergoing. However, no success in removing hereditary peers from their seat in the legislature was achieved until after the Labour Party won their landslide election victory in 1997 on a manifesto promise to reform the House of Lords. The first stage of the reform was the House of Lords Act 1999, which reduced the number of hereditary peerages from approximately 700 to 92 (s.2). Originally, the government's intention had been to abolish the right to sit on an hereditary basis, but during Bill stage, an amendment to retain 92 was inserted, and eventually accepted, by the government—"the Weatherill amendment".

The consequence of the section is that those 92 hereditary peers are retained in the following manner. First, two hold the Great Offices of State by Royal Appointment, and they are the Earl Marshall and Lord Great Chamberlain (s.2(2)); secondly, 15 are elected by the whole of the membership of the House of Lords as office holders, i.e. Deputy Speakers and Committee Chairs; thirdly, the remaining 75 are elected from their respective political party or grouping in the Lords. In the election to the House of Lords held in November 1999, 42 peers were elected for the Conservatives, three for the Liberal Democrats, two for Labour, and 28 cross-bench peers (i.e. those without party affiliation). The proportions reflected the pro rata status of the parties prior to the Act coming into force with the consequence that the Conservatives were always going to "elect" the majority of hereditary peers. It is, perhaps, a final irony of the reforms that the hereditary peers became "elected" and able to face their unelected peers, i.e. the Life Peers, with a greater confidence of their right to be there.

The hereditary peer will become extinct as the progress towards a fully-reformed House of Lords reaches its conclusion. However, for the moment, the (elected) hereditary peers remain part of the legislature.

As part of an earlier reform to the House of Lords, hereditary peers were given the right to disclaim their peerage under the Peerage Act 1963. The Act originated because Labour MP, Tony Benn, succeeded his father to the hereditary title Viscount Stansgate on the latter's death in 1960. As a peer, Benn was prevented from taking his seat in the Commons and, therefore, disqualified from his seat. At the bye-election which followed, Benn won the seat, but was refused the chance to take it because of his peerage, and the seat was given to the runner-up. As a consequence, Benn sought a change in the law which was duly implemented by the government as the Peerage Act 1963, under which Benn became the first peer to disclaim his title. When a title is disclaimed, it is disclaimed for the life of the person so disclaiming. Additionally, the Act also allowed hereditary peeresses to take their seat in the House of Lords for the first time, having previously been barred from doing so.

2.   Life peers

Life peers represent the majority of peers in the modern House of Lords. Though there   **10–004**
were instances through history where life peerages were created, indeed, Law Lords are
life peers, the modern law is derived from the Life Peerages Act 1958. The power to
appoint a life peer is Her Majesty's, acting on the advice of the Prime Minister, and
gives the recipient the right to "attend the House of Lords and sit and vote therein", but
"shall expire on ... death" (s.1(2)). For the first time, the Act conferred the right to sit
and vote in the Lords on women (s.1(3)), whereas hereditary peeresses had to wait until
the Peerage Act 1963 s.6.

Life peers might be appointed either as political or non-political appointees. The
Prime Minister enjoys considerable patronage in the appointment of party political
peers, though in 2005 issued a statement that he would limit himself to the appointment
of not more than ten non-party political life peers in any one Parliament. The main
responsibility for the appointment of non-party political peers rests with the House of
Lords Appointments Commission.

The Commission, established in 2000 as part of the process of reform of the House,
assesses self and peer-nominated applications for a life peerage. Those nominations
which satisfy the criteria are then recommended to Her Majesty. The process of
nomination is open to a British, Irish or Commonwealth citizen, at least 21 years of age,
domiciled in the United Kingdom. However, in addition, the Commission assesses each
application in accordance with the following criteria:

- a record of significant achievement within their chosen way of life that
  demonstrates a range of experience, skills and competencies;

- an individual able to make an effective and significant contribution to the work
  of the House of Lords, not only in their areas of particular interest and special
  expertise but the wide range of other issues coming before the House;

- an individual with understanding of the constitutional framework, including
  the place of the House of Lords, and the skills and qualities needed to be an
  effective member of the House;

- an individual with the time available to ensure they can make an effective
  contribution within the procedures and working practices of the House of
  Lords. At first blush this appears to place an undue burden on applicants,
  especially where they demonstrate the required skills, but have to continue in
  their work. However, the Commission recognises that such peers will continue
  in their work and attend where they're able to do so;

- demonstrate outstanding personal qualities, in particular integrity and
  independence;

- a strong personal commitment to the principles and highest standards of public
  life;

- party political independence.

(*Adapted from the House of Lords Appointments Commission website*)

At February 1, 2008, there were some 609 life peers in the House of Lords.

3. Spiritual peers

10–005   The Church has always enjoyed a close association with the state by the establishment of the Church of England, and so this continues in the modern House of Lords. At present, there are 26 spiritual peers made up of the Archbishops of Canterbury and York, the bishops of Durham, London and Winchester, and 21 senior Diocesan bishops. Unlike the Law Lords, see below, where a bishop retires, their right to sit in the House is lost, unless they are later appointed a life peer. This happened when the Archbishop of Canterbury, George Carey, resigned in 2002, but returned to the House later the same year as Lord Carey of Clifton, a life peer.

By constitutional convention, though Lords Spiritual might speak in the Lords where it exercises its legislative function, they do not vote on matters.

4. Law Lords

10–006   The peers who discharge the House's judicial functions as the Appellate Committee of the House of Lords also enjoy the right to sit. Although the House of Lords' function as a judicial body has historical origins (Hart, *Justice upon petition: The House of Lords and the Reformation of Justice*, 1991), the appellate functions are now governed by the Appellate Jurisdiction Act (AJA) 1876, which will eventually be repealed by the Constitutional Reform Act 2005.

Lords of Appeal in Ordinary, to give their formal title, or more colloquially, "Law Lords", are peers in their own right, enjoying the right to sit in the Lords after their retirement from judicial office. They are appointed by the Queen on the advice of the Prime Minister (though the Prime Minister's role will be transferred to the Judicial Appointment Commission) and enjoy office "during good behaviour" (AJA 1876 s.6). There are 12 Law Lords, and a minimum of three might hear appeals (AJA 1876 s.5), though the number is usually five. However, on occasion, and where the appeal is significant, the Committee sits with a panel of nine, as it did in the recent case of *A v Secretary of State for the Home Department* [2004] UKHL 56. Though judicial appointments, because they are peers in their own right, Law Lords have the right to sit in the Lords when it sits in its legislative capacity. However, they limit their contributions from the cross-benches, and, by convention, do not vote.

The Appellate functions of the House of Lords will be transferred to a Supreme Court in October 2009 following the implementation of that part of the Constitutional Reform Act 2005.

5. Party political composition

10–007   One of the consequences of reform of the House of Lords has been to even out the political composition of the Chamber. At February 1, 2008, the Conservatives had 202

Lords taking the whip, while Labour had 215. The Liberal Democrats had 78, while the number of cross-benchers not affiliated to any political party stood at 200. In total, including those Lords Spiritual and those Lords not affiliated to any political party or grouping, there were 734 noble Lords. (Source: *www.parliament.uk*)

These statistics bear comparison with the composition of the House of Lords prior to the House of Lords Act 1999 when there were approximately 1,300 Lords: 640 were eligible hereditary peers, approximately 300 of whom took the Conservative Party whip. Consequently, there was a political bias in favour of the Conservative Party among the hereditary peers, which gave the Conservatives an in-built majority. The reforms have, to a degree, altered the political composition of the Chamber equalising the main political parties.

6. Disqualification from membership of the House of Lords

In July 2001, Lord Archer, novelist and Conservative Peer, was found guilty on four **10–008** counts, two each of perverting the course of justice and of perjury, in relation to a successful libel action he brought in the 1980s against tabloid newspaper allegations that he had slept with a prostitute in a London hotel. It transpired that during that libel trial, he had arranged a false alibi from a friend and it was on that basis that he was later tried and convicted. Lord Archer was sentenced to four years' imprisonment and, inevitably, questions of his suitability to serve as a peer were raised.

At present, a Member of Parliament is not permitted to sit in the Commons where they have been convicted of a criminal offence and sentenced to more than 12 months' imprisonment. In such circumstances, they would be disqualified from the Commons and their seat declared vacant. Should they wish to return to the Commons, they should seek re-election in the normal way. Additionally, they would be disqualified where declared bankrupt (as happened to Archer when he was an MP in the 1960s and became bankrupt!), or detained under the Mental Health Act 1983. While the former applies to Lords, the latter does not.

However, and especially in relation to imprisonment, there is no such provision restricting Lords. Following release from prison, a peer is entitled, without more, to resume their seat in the Lords and vote on matters of criminal legislation and penal reform, etc. In 2003, the government sought to address this ironic anomaly and stated in a Department of Constitutional Affairs (now Department of Justice) Consultation Paper, *Constitutional Reform: Next steps for the House of Lords*, that the rules should be assimilated and that, further, a peer would lose their seat and title: "[The govern-ment] does not believe that it is right that those who have broken the law in a manner sufficiently serious to warrant a significant custodial sentence should be able to resume their role as a legislator, or continue to lay claim to a title which was given as a personal dignity, without any period of rehabilitation" (para.62). It concluded, grimly for the likes of Lord Archer, that the provision would be retrospective.

There were 108 responses to the consultation document and these were published in April 2004, some 91 per cent of respondents agreeing the same rules should apply to disqualification as between the Commons and the Lords. The view of the Bar Council Law Reform Committee appeared to summarise the view of the majority: "There can be no doubt in the Committee's view that the same rules on disqualification that apply to the Commons should apply equally to the Lords. It is anomalous that the position should be otherwise and it is entirely inconsistent with the proper role and function of a second chamber that the position should be otherwise". However, a significant number of respondents felt that the retrospective effect of any provision would be unwise, possibly even vindictive.

The reform process stalled until publication in February 2007 of a government White Paper entitled, *The House of Lords: Reform* (Cm 7027) which, at para.9.40, restates the government's intention to assimilate the rules on disqualification between the Lords and the Commons. However, there is no mention either of the retrospective application of any such legislation, nor that any noble Lord so convicted would lose their title. It remains to be seen whether these will appear in a subsequent Bill.

POWERS

1. Pre-Parliament Acts

10–009   Despite being the unelected chamber, whose body was drawn from the largely hereditary classes, the House of Lords enjoyed considerable power within the Legislature, equal to that of the Commons. Prior to the reforms effected by the Parliament Acts, the House of Commons and the House of Lords had equal status and power. Where the Lords rejected a Bill which had passed through the Commons, short of a compromise, or getting the monarch to flood the Lords which new peers, the Bill fell. Matters came to a head at the beginning of the 20th century when the Liberal government of David Lloyd George attempted to pass its "People's budget" in order to fund a series of social reforms. However, the Conservative majority in the Lords blocked the Bill out of self-interest as it sought to impose a land tax. As a consequence, Lloyd George sought to trim the powers of the Lords to veto legislation passed in the Commons by introducing a Parliament Bill. On a promise from the monarch that he would create a number of Liberal peers to out-number the Conservative majority in the Lords, the Lords backed the Bill to trim its powers rather than lose its powers completely through having the upper chamber flooded with Liberal peers.

2. Parliament Acts 1911 and 1949

10–010   The Parliament Act 1911 introduced what is known as the suspensory veto, which limited the power of the Lords to delaying a Bill which had been passed in the Commons. However, in respect of Money Bills, the Act had a more dramatic effect. By s.1(1) of the Act, "if a Money Bill, ... is not passed by the House of Lords without amendment within one month after it is so sent up to that House, the Bill shall, ... be presented to His Majesty and become an Act of Parliament on the Royal Assent being signified, notwithstanding that the House of Lords have not consented to the Bill". The reason for such a dramatic legislative curtailment of the Lords' powers stems from the fact that it was the defeat of a Money Bill which prompted the initial dispute with the Lords.

A Money Bill is defined in s.1(2) of the Act as one which relates only to taxation; the imposition of charges on the Consolidated Fund, the National Loans Fund, or on money provided by Parliament; supply; the appropriation of money, or loans. A Bill which includes other matters will not be a Money Bill.

Section 2 of the Act makes provision in relation to other (non-money) Bills. This provision allows the Lords to delay a Bill, but ensures that the will of Parliament ultimately prevails where the Commons passes a Public Bill in two successive sessions and the House of Lords rejects it. A period of one year must elapse between the date of the Commons second reading of the Bill in the first session and the date on which it passes the Commons in the second session (s.2(1) as amended by the Parliament Act 1949). The Bill must be presented to the House of Lords at least one month before the end of the session and then on the second rejection the Bill shall be presented for Royal Assent. That delay is designed to give the government and Commons time to think again about the measure, but also to provide for a maximum period of enforced delay. Consequently, the House of Lords has a delaying power of thirteen months. Finally, any rejected Bill, when presented for Royal Assent, must be identical to the Bill sent to the Lords in the first session subject to amendments made necessary due to passage of time. The Parliament Acts have been used on seven occasions since passage of the first Act in 1911. The first three were passed under the Parliament Act 1911 and the last four under the amended provisions of the 1949 Act:

(1)   Government of Ireland Act 1914;

(2)   Welsh Church Act 1914;

(3)   Parliament Act 1949;

(4)   War Crimes Act 1991;

(5)   European Parliamentary Elections Act 1999;

(6)   Sexual Offences (Amendment) Act 2000;

(7)   Hunting Act 2004.

In a number of situations threat of usage has secured the Lord's agreement in the second session for example, the Trade Union and Labour Relations (Amendment) Bill 1975–76 was rejected by the House of Lords in the first session, certified by the Speaker as suitable for the Parliament Acts and agreed to by the House of Lords after a compromise in the second life. Equally in many situations, both Houses in an attempt to avoid conflict have reached a compromise over legislation. A future use of the Parliament Acts could arise with the Fraud (Trials without a Jury) Bill 2006–07. The following statement by Lord Goldsmith (*Hansard* March 20, 2007: Column 1151) highlights the attempts at compromise between the two Houses that is common and also a direct threat by the government to use the Parliament Acts in an attempt to pressurise the House of Lords into agreement.

> "We said in our manifesto that we would overhaul laws on fraud and the way that fraud trials are conducted to update them for the 21st century and make them quicker and more effective. We have listened to the views of this House on more than one occasion. We have debated, consulted and twice taken back this issue for further discussion and to consider amendments. We have held many meetings with Opposition Members to see if there is a way forward. The government, having listened and made those attempts, are committed to this Bill. It will be no surprise to anybody, therefore, for me to make plain that this Bill, if rejected today, will be reintroduced next Session, with a view to using the Parliament Acts."

Regardless of this threat, the House of Lords agreed an amendment which had the effect of rejecting the Bill. By February 2008, the Bill had not been reintroduced.

Despite the removal of the veto in the above situations, there remain instances where the House of Lords retains its veto. The two most prominent being where a Bill is introduced into Parliament by the Lords. The reason for this first exception is a matter of statutory interpretation. The Bill, in order to come within the Act, must first be passed by the House of Commons in order for the Lords to refuse and thereby engage the section. Secondly, any Bill which proposes to extend the life of Parliament beyond the usual five years. The second exception was the subject of obiter commentary in *R. (on the application of Jackson) v Att-Gen* [2005] UKHL 56 (see Ch.7).

The Parliament Act 1949 amended the 1911 Act by reducing the effective period of delay the House of Lords enjoyed over non-Money Bills from two years to one year. The Parliament Act 1949 was passed using the 1911 procedure. As a result of this, the validity of the Parliament Act 1949 and any legislation made under it was challenged in *R. (on the application of Jackson) v Att-Gen*. The House of Lords (Appellate Committee) unanimously concluded that the 1949 Act was a valid piece of primary legislation (see further Ch.7).

FUNCTIONS

10–011 In her book, *Reform of Parliament*, Dawn Oliver comments that the "House of Lords has in principle the same powers as the House of Common ... " (p.191), and notwithstanding what has been written in relation to the proposals for reform of the Lords, there were no proposals to reform its powers. In the 2007 White Paper (Cm 7027), the government's position is that the Lords should broadly retain the powers which it currently enjoys in relation to the making and scrutiny of legislation. However, it was accepted not only by the Royal Commission, but also by the Joint Committee on Conventions, which was established to analyse the conventions governing the relationship between both Houses of Parliament, that a reformed House of Lords might acquire greater legitimacy and consequently cause a strain in relations between both Houses. Consequently, the government accepted proposals that if a reformed House were to retain much of its current powers, then it would require a codification of the conventions governing the relationship between both Houses.

The functions of the House of Lords were summarised in a government paper, Reform of the House of Lords (Cmnd 3799: 1968) as:

- the provision of a forum for full and free debate on matters of public interest;

- the revision of Public Bills brought from the House of Commons;

- the initiation of public legislation, including in particular those government Bills which are less controversial in party political terms and private members' Bills;

- the consideration of subordinate legislation;

- the scrutiny of the activities of the Executive; and

- the scrutiny of private legislation.

(*Reform of the House of Lords* (Cmnd 3799: para.8).

However, in the interests of streamlining, this list has been reduced to four (though the fourth will transfer to the Supreme Court) core functions, in the recently published annual review, *The Work of the House of Lords*, 2006–07. They are now:

- make laws;

- keep a check on government activities;

- act as a forum of independent expertise; and

- carry out judicial work—it is the highest court in the UK.

The document is worth further consideration for its deconstruction of the work of the Lords. The Lords spends almost two-thirds of its time on legislation (60 per cent), where the rest of its parliamentary time is devoted to scrutiny, broken down as follows: debates 29 per cent; questions 7 per cent; statements 4 per cent, amounting to 40 per cent. However, important work in the Lords is undertaken in the scrutiny of delegated legislation, something which is little done in the Commons.

1. Scrutiny of primary and secondary (delegated) legislation

The consent of the House of Lords is required before a Bill can become an Act of Parliament (subject to use of the Parliament Acts discussed above). A Bill proceeds through exactly the same stages as the House of Commons (see Ch.9), the main difference being the Committee stage which in the Lords is of the whole House. Such a role allows the Lords to question legislation in debates and suggest amendments to it as it passes through the House. The Lords is known for making useful amendments to legislation, for example, the Corporate Manslaughter and Corporate Homicide Bill. The Lords agreed with the Bill in principle but wished the provisions to apply to deaths in custody. The Commons had continually rejected the amendment and the Lords had re-instated it four times. Eventually, the government conceded and agreed to extend the

10–012

provisions to deaths in custody within three to five years. Vernon Bogdanor, Professor of Government, Oxford University writing in the *Sunday Telegraph* ("Why the Lords doesn't need more politicians", February 11, 2007) has stated that the House of Lords "small but significant powers over legislation can be used to make a government think again and draw public attention to issues across party divisions, especially civil liberties, on which the Lords has become a powerful and much needed pressure group" (see also discussion on the Mental Health Bill, the Immigration and Asylum Bill and various terrorist Bills).

While the Lords plays a valuable role in scrutinising primary legislation, it is in its work on delegated legislation, and especially through Committees of the House of Lords, that the Chamber has received not only praise, but prominence and an acknowledged level of expertise.

Delegated legislation (statutory instruments) amounts to the most significant volume of statute produced by Parliament. Drafted by government officials and given the seal of approval by the nominated Secretary of State, it presents little opportunity for scrutiny and examination. However, that would tend to be the case without the Lords' Committees for the scrutiny of such legislation: the Delegated Powers and Regulatory Reform Committee and the Merits of Statutory Instruments Committee, the latter of which won the Select Committee of the Year award in the House Magazine Parliamentary Awards 2007 in recognition of the work it does in scrutinising delegated legislation.

The Merits of Statutory Instruments Committee, as its name suggests, examines the merits of any statutory or other legislative instrument which is subject to parliamentary procedure. The Committee draws to the "special attention of the House" any instrument laid in the previous week which it considers may be interesting, flawed or inadequately explained by the government. Of special interest is the fact that the Committee, in March 2006, published a Report on the Management of Secondary Legislation. This report has recently been followed-up with a supplementary report entitled "The Management of Secondary Legislation: follow-up". The purpose of the Report was to highlight how the legislative process could be better managed across Whitehall, making recommendations as to how the quality and planning of SIs might be improved. The new report assesses progress which has been made since March 2006, making the following recommendations:

- departments should take a more active approach to ensure senior policy officials systematically check the material they intend to lay before Parliament for efficacy, accuracy and completeness;

- non-compliance with the 12–week consultation requirement should be exceptional and always explained fully. The analysis of a consultation exercise is not an afterthought but should drive policy. The full analysis should always be available when the SI is laid, as should any other supporting documents;

- departments should routinely produce and publish plans for the secondary legislation to be made in consequence of a new Act: this could lead to less and better focused legislation;

- more resources should be devoted to consolidation and simplification, at the very least to the publication of on-line consolidations; and

- the Minister for Better Regulation could do more to publicise and encourage the setting of (measurable) policy objectives and success criteria in impact assessments, and the regular adoption of post-implementation review.

Clearly, the Committee recognises the reality of delegated legislation and that the same is necessary to the effective and efficient running of government. However, in its role as scrutiniser of legislation, it has developed an invaluable and unparalleled expertise such as to be in the position to produce a document from which government departments might draw guidance on good practice.

2.   Provision of the highest court of appeal

It has already been seen that the constitution of the United Kingdom has never quite achieved a pure separation of powers, and nowhere is this more acutely demonstrated than by the House of Lords and its exercise of judicial functions. It is the case that since the Middle Ages, the House of Lords has sat as the High Court of Parliament, such judicial functions remaining, for the time being, to this day.   **10–013**

The House of Lords exercises appellate jurisdiction on civil matters from all courts in England and Wales, and from the Court of Session in Scotland, and also from Northern Ireland. In addition, it exercises appellate jurisdiction in criminal appeals from all but Scotland.

The Appellate Committee of the House of Lords, to give its full title, sits during the normal legal terms and hears appeals in a Committee room in the House. It used to hear its cases in the Chamber of the Lords but this practice stopped due to the bombing of Parliament during the Second World War, with the consequence that the Commons had to sit in the Lords, and the Lords moved out to Committee rooms where the judicial functions of the Lords remain to this day. The judges in the Lords sit in lounge suits, abandoning the traditional robes of the other superior courts. At the essence of the Lords' judicial function is the idea that each case heard is a debate. Consequently, their Lordships do not deliver judgments, rather they deliver opinions as speeches in the Lords. However, the practice of reading the full opinion in the Chamber of the Lords has been abandoned for sake of expedience to be replaced with the formality of each judge indicating whether they would allow or dismiss the appeal, with full transcripts of the opinions being made available in print form and (since 1996) later that same day on the internet (*http://www.publications.parliament.uk/pa/ld/ldjudgmt.htm*).

The judicial functions which the House of Lords enjoys will be removed to a new Supreme Court at the Middlesex Guildhall, off Parliament Square, opposite its present location, when Pt 3 of the Constitutional Reform Act 2005 comes into force. The 12 Law Lords in office at the date of the move will become the first Justices of the Supreme Court, and remain members of the House of Lords. On their retirement, ss.25–31 of the Act set down the provisions relating to the appointment of new Justices of the Supreme

Court. Such new Justices of the Supreme Court will not be members of the House of Lords, thus the link between the Lords and judicial office will end, strengthening the separation of powers. The court is scheduled to open for business in October 2009.

3.   Scrutiny of the Executive

10–014   Across the range of government institutions, holding the Executive to account is seen as one of the crucial factors in the administration of an effective democracy. In the United Kingdom constitutional framework, scrutiny is undertaken by the various Committees of Parliament, and, of course, by the Legislature; Commons and Lords.

As many government Ministers are drawn from the ranks of the House of Lords, as well as from the MPs in the Commons, the Lords is able to scrutinise the government and hold it to account on the floor of the House by asking questions of government Ministers. Such questions might be raised orally or in written form. The procedure followed is slightly different from that in the House of Commons particularly in relation to oral questions. Four oral questions are asked for half an hour at the beginning of business. Unlike the Commons, questions are directed at the government as a whole (see Ch.9 for discussion on the House of Commons procedure and written questions).

As discussed in Ch.9, robust scrutiny of the Executive by the Commons tends to occur in the Committees which, though with a ruling party majority, tend to act with greater equanimity than they do on the floor of the House. They might act more vigorously loyal in the Commons for a number of reasons. First, the party machines rule the Commons through the Whips Office. Political agitation against the Executive might lead to expulsion from the party or loss of political patronage. Secondly, and linked to the first, is the idea that many MPs will ruin their political career by acting in a manner inconsistent with their party. Consequently, the result is that many MPs tend to "toe-the-line".

A separate point relates to the electoral system used to elect to the Commons which can lead, as Lord Hailsham memorably termed it in the 1976 Dimbleby Lecture, to "elective dictatorship". This is the idea that such is the government's control in the Commons, where they have a large majority, legislation passes through it without much more than a simple vote. A good example of this was the Labour-dominated Commons after the 1997 and 2001 general elections where the Labour government of the day had an elective dictatorship because of its majority, 179 and 167 respectively. Because of such commanding majorities, the opposition is significantly smaller, less dominant and, indeed, effective, especially where it is more concerned with the election of its own leader and in-party divisions.

Taken together, these reasons lead to the conclusion that the Lords, particularly post-reform, is a robust scrutiniser of the Executive and this should not be downplayed. It could legitimately be claimed that the Lords, pre-reform, was a less legitimate body because of its significant hereditary core. However, post-reform, the parties have been, to a large degree, equalised and the hereditary peers removed, save for those from their number who have been "elected" under the limited scheme of retention devised under the House of Lords Act 1999. Further, it may be argued that it lies in the gift of the government of the day to reform the House of Lords if it does not approve of its voting and scrutiny and one might question whether the government should criticise as illegitimate something which is a creature of its own devising.

The House of Lords Select Committees compliment those of the Commons. However, in many respects because of the expertise of their members they can be more effective in scrutiny of government action. In addition the Lords lacks the political problems associated with Commons debates and Committees and as a result can take a more deliberative approach. There are five permanent Committees in the House of Lords: European Union Committee, Science and Technology Committee, Constitution Committee, Economic Affairs Committee and Communications Committee. Of particular note are the European Union and Constitution Committees. The Constitution Committee has been instructive in bringing to the attention of the House the constitutional implications of Bills such as the Freedom of Information (Amendment) Bill and the Serious Crime Bill. In addition, members of the House of Lords sit on Joint Select Committees with the House of Commons.

Therefore, the House of Lords does have an important role in the scrutiny of the Executive. The Lords, post-reform, is a more equal chamber in the sense that its political composition is more balanced than the Commons, and much less harangued by the whips system so dominant in the Commons. Further, there is a significant number of cross-benchers able to balance debates and, ultimately, to defeat a government Bill. This is not such a bad thing, as it gives the Lords, as a Chamber, greater freedom to test the currency of a Bill and challenge the government where it may have erred or, possibly, acted out of kilter with the wishes of the public. Michael Rush, Professor of Politics at the University of Exeter makes the point that: "If strong party discipline and cohesion were the norm in the second chamber, it would be less effective in fulfilling its legislative and non-legislative scrutiny functions". As Rush concludes, a reformed Lords combines legitimacy with functional effectiveness. (Rush, *Reform of the House of Lords: The Second Stage*, (*www.dca.gov.uk/constitution/holref/holrefresp/ex/ rush_michael_prof.pdf*))

REFORM

Reform of the House of Lords has been on, then off, then back on the political agenda   **10–015** as the politics of the governments of the day change. The most active period of reform for the Lords has happened under the current Labour government since its landslide election victory in 1997. That is not to say, however, that this is the only period of reform activity.

1.   Bryce Conference

The Conference on the Reform of the Second Chamber (Cmnd 9038), chaired by   **10–016** Viscount Bryce, hence the "Bryce Conference", was established by the Prime Minister in August of 1917 with the following terms of reference:

To inquire and report:

(i)   as to the nature and limitations of the legislative powers to be exercised by a reformed Second Chamber;

(ii)   as to the best mode of adjusting differences between the two Houses of Parliament;

(iii)   as to the changes which are desirable in order that the Second Chamber may in future be so constituted as to exercise fairly the functions appropriate to a Second Chamber.

Under the heading, "Elements that ought to find a place in the Second Chamber", the Conference felt that a reformed Chamber ought to consist of, "persons of experience in various forms of public work … ; [and] persons possessing special knowledge of important departments of the national life" (para.7(1)). Further, at para.7(3), the Chamber should have a proportion who are not, "extreme partisans, but of a cast of mind which enables them to judge political questions with calmness and comparative freedom from prejudice or bias. No assembly can be expected to escape party spirit, but the excesses of that spirit usually can be moderated by a good many who do not yield to it".

Interestingly, given the make-up of the Conference, containing as it did a number of hereditary peers, it was felt that the hereditary principle alone was not an appropriate basis for membership of the Lords. However, that was the limit of agreement on the matter since there was no consensus on how it should be replaced, something which does present proposals for reform. In all, five alternatives were suggested: (i) Nomination: this was something which did not find favour with the Conference. It is important to note that the Conference was arranged some 50 years before the Life Peerages Act came onto the statute book, and the only real life peers at the time were the Law Lords appointed to hear judicial appeals to the Lords. (ii) Direct Election: this would be by the persons who elected the MPs to the Commons, and there were, "strong arguments advanced for this plan" (para.13), the Conference further stating:

> "It would produce a Chamber both homogenous and directly responsible to the people, and with the weight of their will behind it. Coming straight from the people it would enjoy their confidence and mirror their views and ideas. If the elections took place frequently, there would be a constant ascertainment and renewal of the most recent public opinion, refreshing and strengthening the Second Chamber." (para.14)

However, the counter was that a Chamber elected in a manner similar to the House of Commons might become a rival to it, undermining democracy. An alternative was that there might be (iii) Election by Local Authorities: where the members would be chosen by council officials and elected representatives. This did not have widespread support. A further method of selection was by (iv) Joint Standing Committee of Both Houses: though this had support, it was suggested that the Second Chamber needed more than merely nomination by Committee. The final suggestion was (v) Election by the House of Commons, which found favour with the Conference.

Though the Bryce Conference represented a radical gesture in the reform agenda, its proposals were not implemented because of the pressing matter of the First World War which was ongoing, and the (limited) social reform agenda which overtook it in the post-War years.

2.   Parliament Bill 1968

As indicated, the reform agenda in the Lords changed as the government of the day   **10–017** changed. The driver for change on most occasions was the Labour Party, when in government, and so it was with a further attempt at reform which started with the Labour Party's victory in the 1966 general election. They were elected on a manifesto promise to safeguard Bills passed in the Commons from being defeated in the Lords. As a means of achieving consensus, the Prime Minister opened cross-party talks, but these fell when the Conservative majority in the House of Lords rejected a piece of secondary legislation with the consequence that the government went ahead and issued its own recommendations, though they were based on the conclusions of the cross-party talks.

The proposals were that hereditary and infrequently attending life peers should have their rights to vote removed and that there should be a slight majority of peers in the ruling party so as to reflect the political make-up of the Commons, and, therefore, the will of the people. There was also a recommendation to limit the Lords' power to delay Bills, reducing this power to six months, with its power to veto secondary legislation abolished. However, the Bill never became law because it was talked down by MPs on all sides of the House of Commons.

3.   House of Lords Act 1999

The Labour Party was swept to power in the landslide election victory of 1997 with a   **10–018** commitment that the House of Lords, "must be reformed" with the aim of creating a *modern House of Lords*. The first stage of the reform process, which continues to this day, was the House of Lords Act 1999.

Section 1 of the Act removed the hereditary principle as a qualification for sitting in the Legislature by providing that, "no-one shall be a member of the House of Lords by virtue of a hereditary peerage". However, as already identified during the Bill stage the "Weatherill amendment" retained 92 hereditary peers by allowing for a limited election process. The Act represented the first modern stage in the reform of the House of Lords.

4.   Royal Commission on Reform of the House of Lords

In 1999, the government established a Royal Commission under the chairmanship of   **10–019** Lord Wakeham "to consider and make recommendations on the role and functions of the second chamber" and "to make recommendations on the method or combination of methods of composition required to constitute a second chamber fit for that role and those functions". After consultation, it reported in January 2000, *Royal Commission on* *the Reform of the House of Lords: A House for the Future* (Cmnd 4534), recommending changes both to the composition and functions of the House.

The Commission, echoing the Bryce Conference some 80 years earlier, asserted that the Commons should be the superior Chamber, whilst recommending that the House of Lords should retain its suspensory veto as set down in the Parliament Acts (see above). It made a number of recommendations, stating that a reformed House of Lords should have four main roles:

(a)   it should bring a range of different perspectives to bear on the development of public policy;

(b)   it should be broadly representative of British society;

(c)   it should play a vital role as one of the main "checks and balances" within the partly codified, party uncodified UK constitution, and that its role should be a complement to the House of Commons in identifying points of concern and requiring the government to reconsider or justify its policy intentions. If necessary, it should cause the House of Commons to think again. The second chamber should engender second thoughts. Thus, it was imagined that the reformed House would have a key role in the scrutiny of legislation;

(d)   it should provide a voice for the nations and regions of the United Kingdom at the centre of public affairs.

Insofar as the composition of the Lords was concerned, the Commission was careful not to recommend a wholly or largely directly elected second chamber, or one derived from indirect election from the devolved institutions, nor on grounds of random selection or co-option. Instead, it recommended that the reformed House should have around 550 peers serving a fixed term. These peers should be made-up of:

(a)   a significant minority should be "regional members" chosen on a basis which reflects the balance of political opinion within each of the nations and regions of the United Kingdom;

(b)   other members should be appointed on the nomination of a genuinely independent Appointments Commission with a remit to create a second chamber which was broadly representative of British society;

(c)   the Appointments Commission should be responsible for maintaining the proportion of independents in the new second chamber at around 20 per cent of the total membership;

(d)   among the politically-affiliated members, the Appointments Commission would be required to secure an overall political balance matching the political opinion of the country as a whole, as expressed in votes cast at the most recent general election.

In order to ensure the Chamber was not given a strong political bias, it was proposed to remove the Prime Minister's powers of patronage over appointment as a peer.

5.   Government White Paper—House of Lords: Completing the Reform

Following re-election in 2001, the Labour government published a White Paper, *The*   **10–020**
House of Lords: Completing the Reform (Cm 5291). The White Paper broadly endorsed
the recommendations of the Royal Commission stating that the remaining 92 hereditary peers left after the first phase of reform will lose their seats. It further proposed that
the government's control over the Lords should be ended and a statutory Appointments Commission should choose not only the independent members, but also determine the political composition of the Lords, thereby consolidating the removal of the
Prime Minister's powers of patronage. The majority of the members of the new
chamber will be nominees of the major political parties, but around one fifth of the
House will be independent of party politics, being elected to represent the nations and
the regions, with a continuing role for the Church of England bishops.

6.   Joint Committee on House of Lords Reform

The Joint Committee was appointed in 2002 to consider the continuing issue of House   **10–021**
of Lords reform. In its first report published in December 2002 (HL Paper 17; HC
Paper 171), the Committee recommended that the conventions governing the relationship between the Commons and the Lords ought to be retained, namely, that the
House of Commons shall finally have its way, and that the government is entitled to
have its business considered without undue delay. Further, the Committee endorsed the
conclusions of the Royal Commission that increased representation will confer a
legitimacy on the House of Lords and that representation from all members of the
United Kingdom would be appropriate.

It further stated that the reformed House must maintain the principle that no one
political party should be able to be dominant in it, and that independent non-party
affiliation is not jeopardised or diminished. "We consider this independence an
important element in any reconstituted House" (para.40). This is a common theme not
only of the Bryce Conference, but also the Royal Commission Report and the Joint
Committee's First Report.

In its Second Report (HL Paper 97; HC Paper 668), published in April 2003, the
Joint Committee noted a lack of progress (not least from the government) and consensus, yet was "unanimous in its view that simply to maintain the status quo is
undesirable" (para.3). It reported on votes taken in the Commons and Lords and that
in the former there was no endorsement of any one option, but that in the Lords, the
preferred option was 100 per cent appointment as opposed to election. In its Third
Report (HL Paper 155; HC Paper 1027), the Committee reported on the government
response to the Committee's Second Report. The Committee's Report was largely
endorsed by the government.

7.   Government's White Paper—The House of Lords: Reform

10–022   As a means of consolidating much of the work which had been undertaken since 1997, in February 2007, the government produced a White Paper (Cmnd 7027) with the aim, "to set the stage for ... free votes on the composition of a future House of Lords" (para.1.1). In it the government proposed that the House of Commons should remain the principle law-making body within Parliament, but that the reformed House of Lords should effect appropriate scrutiny of the government and legislation, not rubber-stamping it. In ensuring this, its membership should be different from that of the Commons. The government further asserted the idea that the reformed House should be an independent body, where no political party should have a majority and that at least 20 per cent should be drawn from non-party political applicants.

However, the paper goes on to state that in a modern democracy, it is difficult to justify a legislative body without democratic mandate, and that any reformed House should be a hybrid, with a partly elected element of 50 per cent, amounting to some 270 members of the 540 members of the reformed House. Elections to the House would be made at the same time as the European Parliamentary elections, using the same constituencies, though with a different electoral system. Members would serve long, non-renewable terms. The remaining 50 per cent would be drawn from appointment by independent Commission, 20 per cent being non-party-political appointments, with the remaining 30 per cent being appointed party political members. There would be no Prime Ministerial appointments to the reformed House, thus ending the Prime Minister's historic powers of patronage. Vernon Bogdanor however is highly critical of the idea of any more politicians in the House of Lords and raises concerns about low election turnout, and the fear that regionalisation would be artificial and unsuccessful. He feels that few people would want to stand for elections and so places would be given to the "old party faithful". Of course, these concerns lead to issues about the effectiveness of the Lords in their role in the legislative chamber.

In March of 2007, the Commons and Lords voted on the options for reform of the Lords contained in the White Paper. The Commons voted, somewhat surprisingly, for a 100 per cent elected House of Lords, while a week later the Lords voted for a 100 percent appointed House of Lords.

8.   Next steps

10–023   The one thing that can be said for certain about the House of Lords is that it will lose its judicial function. However, the composition of this part of the legislature remains to be settled. The process of reform started by the Labour government in 1997 has effectively stalled as both Houses struggle to reach consensus on composition. The importance of achieving the right composition for the House cannot be under-emphasised. The dominance of the Commons by the government ensures the Commons weakness in holding the government to account. This is somewhat mitigated by the House of Lords who are less partisan than there counterparts, do not have constituency concerns and have a body of expertise that could be difficult to replicate. If the United Kingdom is to maintain some sort of effective separation of powers and ensure adherence to the rule of law, then the House of Lords must maintain its ability to challenge the government and to criticise its legislative proposals.

FURTHER READING

Bogdanor, V. "Why the Lords doesn't need more politicians" *Sunday Telegraph,*   **10–024**
    February 11, 2007
Hart, J.S. *Justice Upon Petition: The House of Lords and the Reformation of Justice,*
    1621–1675 (Routledge, 1991)

Chapter 11

PARLIAMENTARY PRIVILEGE

INTRODUCTION

Parliamentary privilege consists of the rights and immunities which both Houses of **11–001** Parliament possess which offers protection from external interference and enables Parliament to discharge its functions. It can be compared to Royal Prerogative (see Ch.13) in that it represents a unique aspect of law reserved for a special class of persons. Constitutionally, parliamentary privilege is significant particularly, in the relationship between Parliament and the courts. The privileges of Parliament form part of the law and custom of Parliament (*lex et consuetude parliament*) and as such it is for Parliament to adjudicate on such matters and not the courts. The courts can decide whether a privilege exists or if an action falls under privilege but, are cautious before accepting jurisdiction to intervene mindful of separation of powers. This chapter considers the nature of privilege, the court's role in relation to privilege and finally a brief consideration of member's interests.

1. Definition

Erskine May in *Parliamentary Practice* (22nd edn (London: Butterworths, 1997), p.69) **11–002** defines privilege as:

> "the sum of the peculiar rights enjoyed by each House collectively as a constituent part of the High Court of Parliament, and by Members of each House individually, without which they could not discharge their functions, and which exceed those possessed by other bodies or individuals. Thus privilege, though part of the law of the land, is to a certain extent an exemption from the general law."

Privilege falls into two groups; the first group include those claimed by the Speaker of the House of Commons at the beginning of each new Parliament. The Speaker, informs the House she has " ... in your name and on your behalf made claim by humble petition to Her Majesty, to all your ancient and undoubted rights and privileges, particularly to freedom of speech in debate, freedom from arrest, and freedom of access to Her Majesty wherever occasion may require, and that a most favourable construction may be placed upon all your proceedings". The Lord Chancellor replies to the Speaker's petition that "Her Majesty most readily confirms all the rights and privileges which have ever been granted to or conferred upon the Commons, by Her Majesty or any of Her Royal Predecessors". The four petitions as they are known include:

- freedom of speech;

- freedom from civil arrest;

- freedom of access to the Crown;

- the most favourable construction be placed upon proceedings in the House.

The latter two are in modern terms less significant. Both Houses have access to the Sovereign and according to Erskine May the request for favourable construction be placed upon proceedings in the House is today a formal courtesy.

The second group of privileges are those not claimed expressly but accepted as part of the law and custom of Parliament. These include:

- the right of the House to regulate its own internal composition;

- the right of the House to regulate its own internal proceedings;

- the right to punish for breach of privilege and contempt of Parliament.

The privileges of the two Houses are substantially the same though the House of Lords having enjoyed its privileges from early times do not demand the confirmation of them by the Crown at the beginning of each Parliament. In addition, the House of Lords lacks the financial privileges of the House of Commons.

2. History

11–003 The source of parliamentary privilege is ancient practice which has been asserted by Parliament over time and accepted by the Crown. This ancient practice is recorded in the rolls of Parliament and the journals of the two Houses. Some of the House of Commons privileges such as freedom from arrest were claimed from the monarch and upheld with their consent. Others were claimed by the House of Commons and frequently asserted thereafter. The privileges of Parliament were fully established during the struggle between Parliament and the Crown in the 17th century.

FREEDOM OF SPEECH

Freedom of speech can be considered the most important privilege. It is guaranteed by art.9 of the Bill of Rights 1688 "freedom of speech and debates or proceedings in Parliament ought not to be impeached or questioned in any court or place out of Parliament". Article 9 affords legal immunity from both civil and criminal liability ("ought not to be questioned") to Members for what they say or do in "proceedings in Parliament". The immunity is absolute and applies in "any court or place out of Parliament" against any civil or criminal proceedings in a court of law in respect of matters it covers. There are two constitutional rationales for freedom of speech in Parliament. Firstly, Members must be able to freely debate and perform their duties without fear of penalty. This is fundamental to the effective working of Parliament as a deliberative chamber. As a consequence of this privilege, no action can be brought against a member of either House of Parliament because of what that Member said as part of any speech, debate or proceeding in Parliament. Secondly, the privilege ensures a separation between the judiciary and legislature as the courts cannot interfere in debates and speeches within Parliament. The underlying principle is that such proceedings cannot be inquired into by any body other than Parliament itself. These two rationales were accepted by the European Court of Human Rights in *A v United Kingdom* (2003) 36 E.H.R.R. 917 where the European Court of Human Rights found that absolute parliamentary privilege did not violate art.6(1), right of access to court, because it pursued the legitimate aim of free speech and was proportionate.

11–004

1.   Proceedings in Parliament

It is not clear how far the privilege of freedom of speech extends. Article 9 covers "speech", "debates" and "proceedings in Parliament". Debates and questions on the floor of the House are clearly covered, as are proceedings on Bills, proceedings within committees and their sub-committees formally appointed by either House. In *Dillon v Balfour* (1887) 20 L.R. 600, Dillon sued Balfour, a government Minister, for defamation in respect of comments made about her during the passage of a Bill in the House of Commons. The action was struck out as the comments were privileged and could not be used as the basis of any legal claim.

11–005

The difficulty lies in what precisely constitutes a proceeding in Parliament as this has never been conclusively defined and remains contentious. A good starting point is Erskine May who describes proceedings in Parliament as "some formal action, usually a decision, taken by the House in its collective capacity" (*Parliamentary Practice* (22nd edn, 1997, p.95). This implies the phrase covers the business of Parliament. A similar definition is provided by Dawn Oliver, "The Powers and Privileges of Parliament", *English Public Law* (D. Feldman (ed.) (Oxford: OUP, 2004)) who explains:

> "This extends to the whole process leading up to a decision, including debates in which members participate. Proceedings in Parliament include the tabling of parliamentary questions, things done and said by a member in the exercise of his

functions in a committee or in the House, or undertaken in the course of parliamentary business." (p.131)

Parliamentary consideration of the meaning of proceeding in Parliament arose in the *Duncan Sandys* case in 1938. Duncan Sandys, Conservative MP for Norwood, sent a draft parliamentary question to the Secretary of State for War which contained confidential information regarding the state and shortage of military equipment. In the view of the Attorney-General such information could only have been obtained in breach of the Official Secrets Acts 1911–20. Sandys was questioned about the information and complained he was being threatened with prosecution which would be a breach of privilege. A House of Commons Select Committee was convened to enquire into the applicability of the Official Secrets Act to Members of Parliament acting in their official capacity (Report of the House of Commons Select Committee on the Official Secrets Act (1939): HC 101 (1938–1939). Concluding that the Official Secrets Act would not apply to Members in their official capacity, the Committee noted that:

"while the term 'proceeding in Parliament' has never been construed by the courts, it covers both the asking of a question and the giving written notice of a question, and includes everything said or done by a member in the exercise of his functions as a member in a committee of either House, as well as everything said or done in either House in the transaction of parliamentary business." (at para.3)

They further observed that:

"words spoken or things done by a Member beyond the walls of Parliament will generally not be protected. Cases may, however, easily be imagined of communications between one member and another, or between a member and a Minister, so closely related to some matter pending in, or expected to be brought before the House, that though they do not take place in the chamber or a committee room they form part of the business of the House, as, for example, where a member sends to a Minister the draft of a question he is thinking of putting down or shows it to another member with a view to obtaining advice as to the propriety of putting it down or as to the manner in which it should be framed." (at para.4)

From the Committees view it is clear that proceedings in Parliament cover communications between Members of Parliament outside the Chambers and Committees as long as they relate to official business. Perhaps more controversially verbatim repetition by a Member of what was said during proceedings has no protection (*Aims of Industry Case*, 1973–74 HC Debs 246).

One further case illustrate the scope of proceedings in Parliament. In *Rost v Edwards* [1990] 2 Q.B. 460, the plaintiff, a Member of Parliament, brought an action for libel arising out of a newspaper article which alleged he was seeking to sell privileged and confidential information. Rost wished to rely on the fact he had been de-selected from membership of a Standing Committee and not appointed as Chairman of a Select Committee as a result of the article. The defendants wished to rely on Rost's failure to register his interest. The court held that the appointment of a chairman and membership of a committee were proceedings in Parliament. However, as the Register of Members' Interest was a public document, there were no reasons for ousting jurisdiction and it was not privileged.

(a) *Letters*

Whether letters written by Members are proceeding in Parliament was considered in the **11–006** *London Electricity Board and George Strauss* case. George Strauss MP wrote a letter to the Paymaster General which described the London Electricity Board's behaviour as "a scandal which should be instantly remedied". The letter was passed onto the Board who threatened to sue Strauss for libel. Mr Strauss alleged that this was a breach of privilege. The Select Committee of Privileges (Fifth Report HC 305 1956–57) considered whether the letter was a proceeding in Parliament and also whether a threat to sue for libel was a breach of privilege. The Committee followed the approach of the Committee in *Sandys* and concluded that the letter was a proceeding in Parliament. The logic was where a Member writes to a Minister concerning a nationalised industry and criticises the administration of that industry it is a reasonable possibility that the MP would seek to debate the matter in the House.

The Committee were undecided as to whether the Parliamentary Privilege Act 1770 (which seemed to suggest that action or threat of action against a Member was not a breach of privilege) applied. The Committee suggested that as the question as to the effect of the 1770 Act was a legal one, the opinion of the Judicial Committee of the Privy Council should be sought.

While the Committee's approach appears consistent with the approach taken in *Sandys* (above), the House of Commons, by a narrow majority (218–213), determined that the letter was not a proceeding in Parliament as it did not relate to anything before the House (1957–58 260; HC Deb 591 cc 207–346). In support of the majority it was argued that Members should not widen the scope of absolute parliamentary privilege and the letter would attract the defence of qualified privilege. Munro, *Studies in Constitutional Law* ((New York: OUP, 1999), p.222) takes the view that it is difficult to infer much from this decision as the vote was narrow and it is perhaps significant that the subject matter of the letter was not within the competence of the Minster to answer and could not have formed the basis of a parliamentary question. It is important to note that the 1957 Commons resolution does not bind the House or the courts.

Both the 1967 and 1977 Committee on Parliamentary Privilege believed the law should be changed and correspondence between Members and Ministers should be absolutely privileged. This was affirmed by the 1989 Joint Select Committee.

The position following the House of Commons decision in *Strauss* is that letters from a Member to a Minister, informal discussions and negotiations taking place between Members all of which do not relate to current or imminent parliamentary businesses are not proceedings in Parliament and so not protected by absolute privilege. However, it is implicit from this and, consistent with *Sandys*, that communication between an MP and a Minister or between MPs on matters relating to current or imminent parliamentary business or following an invitation given by the Minister in Parliament will be proceedings in Parliament. In *Rost v Edwards* [1990] 2 Q.B. 460, it was held that correspondence between Members relating to questions to be raised in the House was a proceeding in Parliament and so privileged.

Alongside the above it is important to note that much of the work of a Member of Parliament would not constitute a proceeding in Parliament (a fact noted by the Joint Committee on Parliamentary Privilege (Parliamentary Privilege First Report, 1989 HL 43–I/HC 214–I). Such is clear from two cases, *R. v Rule* [1937] 2 K.B. 375 and *Beach v Freeson* [1972] 1 Q.B. 14. In *R. v Rule* a letter written by a constituent to his MP complaining about the conduct of a police officer and magistrate did not attract the protection of absolute privilege but the defence of qualified privilege was available. This defence can be rebutted if the person acted with malice. A similar conclusion was reached in *Beach v Freeson* where a Member of Parliament forwarded on a letter written by a constituent to the Lord Chancellor and Law Society. The letter was defamatory and the court held that the Member's action was protected by qualified privilege but not absolute.

While the business of Parliament conducted in the Chambers attracts the protection of art.9, something does not constitute a proceeding in Parliament merely because it happens within the House (Palace of Westminster). In *Rivlin v Bilainkin* [1953] 1 Q.B. 485, the applicant alleged defamation in respect of comments made by her former husband and an interim injunction was granted preventing the defendant's husband from repeating the statements. In alleged breach of the injunction, the defendant repeated the statements in five letters addressed to named MPs. One letter was handed to the Messenger of the House to personally deliver to an MP and the other four were posted in the House of Commons post office; none of the letters ever left the building. In contempt of court proceedings for breach of the injunction the court concluded that the letters did not constitute a proceeding in Parliament and were not protected by privilege simply because they were posted within the Palace of Westminster. A similar argument was raised in relation to the proposed showing of a film within the House. An injunction against the showing of a film made for the BBC about the government secret spy project (Zircon) was obtained on national security grounds. A number of MPs proposed to show the film within the House and another injunction was sought prohibiting this showing until the House could make a decision. The application was refused by the court as being a matter for the House's own competence. Subsequently, the Speaker issued an order stopping the film being shown before the House could consider the matter. This action was referred to the Committee as to whether the order affected the privileges of Parliament. The Committee of Privileges (First Report from the Committee of Privileges 1986–87 HC 365 Speakers Order on January 22, 1987 on a matter of national security) ruled that the showing of a film within the precincts of the House of Parliament is not a proceeding in Parliament and those Members responsible could be subject to judicial sanction for breach of an injunction.

(b) *Parliamentary papers*

11–007   Whether proceedings in Parliament covered publication outside Parliament famously arose in *Stockdale v Hansard* (1839) 112 E.R. 1112. Stockdale sued Hansard, the official printer to the House, for defamation in publishing a report of comments made in the

Chamber. The House of Commons passed a resolution declaring the report to be a proceeding in Parliament and so Hansard pleaded as his sole defence that the report was covered by privilege. The court held the Commons resolution to be ineffective as it did not have the force of law and so the report was not a proceeding in Parliament. Damages for defamation were awarded to Stockdale. The Commons' response was to order Hansard not to pay the damages. On Stockdale's instructions the Sheriff of Middlesex then sought to levy execution on Hansard's property to satisfy the judgment. The result of this action was the arrest and imprisonment of the Sheriff and his officers on the order of the House of Commons for contempt. Habeas corpus proceedings to secure their release failed, the court holding that the Commons was entitled to imprison for contempt. The potentially damaging conflict between the Commons and the courts in this instance was resolved with the passing of the Parliamentary Papers Act 1840, which conferred absolute privilege on official reports published on the authority of either House. If an action was brought against a printer for defamation then he could immediately apply to the court for the action to be struck out. A defence of qualified privilege on bona fide extracts or abstracts of published reports was also provided for in the statute. The defence operates if the defendant acted without malice.

(c)   *Broadcast and other published parliamentary proceedings*

The Parliamentary Papers Act 1840 did not extend to typical newspaper reporting and   **11–008** certainly did not cover publication in the modern mediums seen today. The common law has extended qualified privilege to cover fair comment upon extracts or abstracts of parliamentary material as long as they represented a fair and accurate record of what was said or done and without malice. *Dingle v Associated Newspapers* [1961] 2 Q.B. 162 provides a good example. A Select Committee produced a report in which it charged Mr Dingle with discreditable conduct. This printed report was absolutely privileged. As soon as the report was available a number of newspapers published extracts from the report and made comments on it. These were qualified privileged as they were published bona fide and without malice. Five weeks later the Daily Mail published an article containing facts and figures which filled out the charge against Mr Dingle. These facts and figures turned out to be untrue and even though the Daily Mail acted in good faith and without malice, the article did not attract qualified privilege.

The Parliamentary Papers Act 1840 was amended by the Defamation Act 1952 to cover reports on radio and the Broadcasting Act 1990 in respect of television. Section 15 of the Defamation Act 1996 gave statutory footing to the common law defence and provides the defence of qualified privilege to a fair and accurate report of the proceedings in Parliament. This does not meant that the report must précis what was said but as Lord Denning stated in *Cook v Alexander* [1974] Q.B. 279, the report must be "a fair presentation of what took place so as to convey to the reader the impression which the debate itself would have made on the hearer of it".

2.   Ought not to be impeached or questioned in court

11–009   The second part of art.9 requires that freedom of speech ought not to be impeached. The Joint Select Committee felt that the meaning of "impeach" was not clear but could include hinder, charge with a crime, challenge or censuring Parliament or its Members. Where art.9 would appear more controversial is that proposition that freedom of speech and proceedings in Parliament cannot be questioned in court (see Ch.7 for discussion on how this relates to parliamentary sovereignty). However, since the decision of the House of Lords in *Pepper v Hart* [1993] A.C. 593 the courts can make reference to parliamentary materials as an aid to interpreting legislation. The use of *Pepper v Hart* is limited to situations where the legislation in question is ambiguous, obscure or absurd. The only material that can be relied on is statements made by the Minister or promoter of the Bill and they must be clear. Lord Browne-Wilkinson made it clear that the decision was not about impeaching the privileges of the House but was "motivated by a desire to carry out the intentions of Parliament in enacting legislation". The House of Lords stated they had "no intention or desire to question the processes by which such legislation was enacted or of criticising anything said by anyone in Parliament in the course of enacting it" (at p.646).

One important development of the use of Hansard is that it has enabled the use of Parliamentary statements to be used in judicial review proceedings where challenges have been made to the lawfulness of policy statements announced in Parliament (see for example *R. v Home Secretary Ex p. Hindley* [1998] Q.B. 751). In cases such as these the court have scrutinised the ministerial decision and the explanations given by Minister in Parliament. Without this development the Executive would be able to rely on Parliamentary privilege to protect itself from legitimate legal challenge which would be an unacceptable situation, compromising both the separation of powers and rule of law.

3.   Defamation Act 1996

11–010   One major problem with art.9 was the inability of MPs to rely on statements made in Parliament in actions for defamation and equally newspapers were unable to rely on statements in their defence to such an action. In 1995, Neil Hamilton MP brought an action in defamation against the Guardian over allegation that Mr Hamilton had asked questions in Parliament in return for payment ("cash for questions"). The Guardian wished to assert evidence about Mr Hamilton's conduct and motives in tabling question. The court ruled this was contrary to art.9 and as it would be unfair to allow an action to proceed where the defendant could not use evidence to show justification, the action was stayed. In a similar case in New Zealand, *Prebble v Television New Zealand* [1995] 1 A.C. 321, the Judicial Committee of the Privy Council decided that art.9 and the principle of separation of powers precluded the court from examining the truth or propriety of statements made in Parliament.

In order to remedy the perceived injustices caused by cases such as *Hamilton*, the Defamation Act 1996 was passed, which, under s.13, allows for a waiver of absolute privilege. Section 13 permits a Member of either House to waive his right to absolute privilege in defamation proceedings. Section 13 has been much criticised for being unworkable in some cases, for example, where there are two members involved in a case and only one waives privilege for applying only in defamation proceedings and undermining the basic principle of freedom of speech in Parliament. The Joint Committee on Parliamentary Privilege (Parliamentary Privilege First Report, 1989 HL 43–I/ HC 214–I) were particularly critical that the fundamental flaw of s.13 is it undermines the basis of Parliamentary privilege as privilege is of the House as a whole and not that of an individual. The Committee recommended that s.13 be replaced with a new statutory provision enabling the House, and not any individual, to waive the privilege in court proceedings. In addition, waiver would apply to all court proceedings not just defamation actions.

4.   Abuse of freedom of speech

One issue arising out of art.9 is abuse of the privilege. The absolute immunity conferred   **11–011** on debates and proceedings in Parliament allows for MPs to state things knowing full well there can be no legal redress. The Committee of Privileges (Third Report of the Committee of Privilege, 1986–86 HC 604) recognised there is "no clear dividing line between statements which represent a legitimate exercise of freedom of speech, on the one hand, and those which constitute an abuse, on the other". The Committee noted that "irresponsible or reckless use of privilege can cause great harm to outside individual who enjoy no legal redress ... the strongest safeguard ... is the self-discipline of individual members".

   A number of examples show both that privilege can and is abused and the consequential hardship that can arise from the lack of legal redress; a few are given here. In 1980, Jeff Rooker MP made a number of false allegations against the Director of Rolls Royce. In *A v United Kingdom*, a Member of Parliament, during a speech in Parliament on housing policy had named the applicant on a number of occasions, given her address and labelled her a "neighbour from hell". As a result of his speech the woman was spat at and abused in the street and received numerous hate mail. The woman stated that the MP had never tried to communicate with her or check the veracity of her statements. The European Court of Human Rights agreed with the applicant that the allegations made against her were extremely serious and unnecessary but because of the absolute nature of the privilege, she had no legal recourse. Finally, in October 2006, a woman with a long history of crying rape who had sent an innocent man to jail for two years was publicly named by Lord Campbell-Savours in Parliament. Anonymity laws meant that she could not be named by the courts so the Lord used the protection offered by Parliamentary privilege to expose her identity in the Chamber.

Freedom of Arrest

The privilege of freedom of arrest was according to Erskine May (p.74) first recorded in   **11–012** 1340. The privilege extends to freedom of civil arrest only: in 1404, the House of

Commons claimed that Members were privileged against arrest for "debt, contract, or trespass of any kind according to the custom of the realm". Though the privilege was often ignored by the monarch in the 15th and 16th century, by 1641 the House again declared that arrest of its Members was contrary to the law and privilege of Parliament. The privilege is enjoyed during the session of Parliament and for 40 days before and after. It thus covers long adjournments such as the summer recess.

The constitutional reason behind freedom of arrest is to enable Members to attend the House so they can perform their functions. Justification for its continuance resides in the principles that Parliament should have first claim on the service of its Members even to the detriment of the civil rights of others. Historically, the privilege was of particular importance as arrest for debt was common. Since the Debtors Act 1869, the privilege is now of negligible practical importance. It may still operate to prevent arrest or imprisonment for disobeying a court order (civil contempt) such as in *Stourton v Stourton* [1963] 1 All E.R. 606. Here a peer who had not complied with the provisions of a maintenance order availed himself of the privilege. In 1999 the Joint Committee on Parliamentary Privilege (1999, Joint Committee on Parliamentary Privilege, Report, Vol.1, Report and proceedings of the Committee, HL Paper 43–I, HC 214–I (1999), p.85) recommended that it be abolished.

RIGHT TO REGULATE ITS OWN COMPOSITION

11–013   Historically one important aspect of this privilege was the right of the House of Commons to determine disputed elections. In *Goodwin v Fortescue* (1604) St. Tr. 91, for example, the Crown through the Court of Chancery attempted to deny Sir Francis Goodwin's election on the grounds he was an outlaw. The House of Commons vigorously complained and the Crown backed down. Following the Parliamentary Elections Act 1868 the jurisdiction to determine dispute elections was given to the courts. Though the privilege is preserved in form as the court's finding is certified to the Speaker which allows for the House to take appropriate action. In practice, the House is bound to accept the courts decision.

Despite the practical removal of this aspect of the privilege, the Houses retain the right to decide whether a particular Member is fit to serve, whether a Member is qualified to sit and the right to determine when a writ should be issued for a by-election.

The House of Commons has the privilege to expel members deemed unfit to serve, for example, on conviction of a criminal offence. In modern times this power is used very rarely and only three expulsions occurred in the 20th century. In 1922 Horatio Bottomley was expelled after he was convicted of fraud, in 1947 the House expelled Gary Allighan for gross contempt of the House (see below) and finally in 1954 when Conservative MP Peter Baker was expelled after being convicted of forgery. While the House of Commons has the privilege to expel if it wishes, under the Representation of the Peoples Act 1981, a person sentenced to more than one year's imprisonment for an offence is automatically disqualified from sitting.

The Houses have the right to determine whether someone is qualified to take their place in the House or to disqualify Members. In *Bradlaugh v Gossett* (1884) 12 QBD

271, Bradlaugh was prevented from taking his place in the House of Commons. As an atheist, the House of Commons took the view that Bradlaugh should be prevented from taking the oath sworn by all Members and so be excluded. The House would not accept that the Parliamentary Oaths Act 1866 gave Bradlaugh the right to make a non-religious affirmation. In 1960 Tony Benn succeeded his father as Viscount Stansgate, as a result his seat in the House of Commons was declared vacant and he was barred from the Chamber. The law was changed with the Peerages Act 1963.

In a similar vein, the House of Lords has the right to determine the succession to peerages. In 1997, the Committee of Privileges had to consider who the Barony of Moynihan passed to on the death of the Third Baron. There were three contenders, two purported children of the Baron and the Barons half brother. The Committee of Privilege concluded that the title could not pass to either of the children; one was genetically proven not to be the Baron's son and the other was declared illegitimate, the Baron having never divorced his fourth wife. Instead, the title passed to the half brother.

The final aspect of this privilege is the right to determine when a writ should be issued for the holding of a by-election. When a vacancy arises due to death, expulsion or disqualification, it is for the House to decide when the by-election should be held. It is interesting to note that a Member disqualified from the House is not barred from standing again, such was the case when John Wilkes was expelled from the House on numerous occasions in 1769 only to be re-elected every time.

RIGHT TO REGULATE ITS OWN INTERNAL PROCEEDINGS

This privilege is often called "exclusive cognisance of internal affairs" and is inex-   **11–014** tricably linked with Parliament's freedom of speech (ought not to be impeached) and the right to regulate its own composition. In its modern form, the privilege consists of a collection of related rights and immunities such as the right to decide what it will consider, the right to make rules for its own proceedings and to determine if those proceedings have been followed.

As a result of this privilege the courts have refused to inquire into alleged procedural defects in the passage of a Bill through Parliament (see *Pickin v British Railway Board* [1974] A.C. 765 in Ch.7). Similarly, in *Dingle v Associated Newspapers* [1961] 2 Q.B. 162, the court refused to consider whether a report of a Select Committee of the House was invalid due to procedural defects. In *Bradlaugh v Gossett* (above), Bradlaugh sought to argue that the House of Commons had misconstrued the Parliamentary Oaths Act 1866 and the decision to prevent him taking up his seat should be set aside. The court refused as it could not question parliamentary procedure.

> "It seems to follow that the House of Commons has the exclusive power of interpreting the statute so far as the regulation of its own proceedings within its own walls is concerned; and that, even if that interpretation should be erroneous, this Court has not power to interfere with it directly or indirectly." (at p.280)

However, if a matter happens within Parliament but unconnected with the business of Parliament, the ordinary courts may be entitled to assume jurisdiction to deal with the matter. This point was made clear by Stephen J. in *Bradlaugh v Gossett* who stated (at p.283), "I know of no authority for the proposition that an ordinary crime committed in the House of Commons would be withdrawn from the ordinary course of criminal justice". In 1970, the House voted to allow an offender to be prosecuted when he threw CS gas into the chamber.

Part of the privilege means that unless there is express provision to the contrary, each House is exempt from statute law. In *R. v Graham-Campbell Ex p. Herbert* [1935] 1 K.B. 594, an attempt to convict members for the sale of alcohol within Parliament without a licence failed as it was not an appropriate matter for the courts to consider. Potentially this can have far-reaching consequences; as Colin Munro *Studies in Constitutional Law* ((1999), p.230) states, Parliament could become a "statute free zone" and important legislation such as Health and Safety provisions would not apply. However, while the privilege may mean this, the two Houses voluntarily apply many statutory provisions. The Joint Committee on Privileges (para.251) recommended that it should be made clear in statute that every law applies to Parliament unless statute expressly excludes Parliament.

The right to regulate its own proceedings also includes the right to maintain discipline during speeches and debates. Each House also has the right to institute inquiries and require the attendance of witnesses and the production of documents. Wilful failure to attend committee proceedings or answer questions or produce documents may be punished by the House.

THE COURTS AND PARLIAMENTARY PRIVILEGE

11–015   Erskine May states "In cases affecting parliamentary privilege the tracing of a boundary line between the competence of the courts and the exclusive jurisdiction of the House is a difficult question of constitutional law". Historically, questions of privilege were a source of conflict between the courts and Parliament and have resulted in some interesting cases over competition for jurisdiction. One such line of cases arose out of the publication of an Inspector's report in Hansard which described a book as "of the most disgusting nature". The publisher, Stockdale, sued for libel and in the first decision, *Stockdale v Hansard* (1837) 2 Mood & R. 9, the court denied that privilege extended to the publication (the court found for Hansard on other grounds). Following this decision, the House of Commons passed a resolution purporting to privilege Hansard. They further stated that prosecution of any action which brought the privileges of Parliament into court constituted a breach of privilege and all parties concerned could be punished by the House. Stockdale brought a second action, which the court found in his favour on the ground that a resolution of one House did not alter the law (*Stockdale v Hansard* (1839) 9 Ad. & El. 1. Following the decision the Sherriff of Middlesex (the position was held by two men) took steps to enforce the judgment and was subsequently imprisoned by the House of Commons for breach of privilege. An application for Habeas Corpus was unsuccessful because the court held that it could not go behind the Speaker's warrant which gave no reasons for the arrest save, that a breach of privilege and contempt had been committed. The Sherriff was eventually freed on their undertaking not to execute the court order against Hansard and then, as a result were imprisoned for contempt of court. This battle was solved by the passing of the Parliamentary Papers Act 1840 though the Act did nothing to solve the argument over jurisdiction.

Both Houses claim to be the exclusive judges of their own privileges and the problem is one of reconciling the law of privilege with the general law. The solution adopted by the courts has been to insist on their right in principle to decide all questions of privilege in litigation before them. However, this is subject to exceptions in favour of parliamentary jurisdiction, such as the right of each House to control its own internal proceedings and the right to commit and punish for contempt. Although, it cannot be said that there has been any formal acceptance of this situation by either House, a tacit arrangement may be inferred from the fact that a century has elapsed without conflict between the courts and Parliament. Lord Simon of Glaisdale in *Pickin v British Railway Board* summarised the position:

"It is well known that in the past there have been dangerous strains between the law courts and Parliament – dangerous because each institution has its own particular role to play in our constitution, and because collision between the two institutions is likely to impair their power to vouchsafe those constitutional rights for which citizens depend on them. So for many years Parliament and the courts have been astute to respect the sphere of action and the privileges of the other."

While it would seem there is an agreement between Parliament and the courts at present, there is still scope for disagreement. The court must continue to be respectful of art.9 and their use of proceedings in Parliament in judicial review and other court cases.

RIGHT TO PUNISH FOR BREACH OF PRIVILEGE AND CONTEMPT

Parliament has the right to punish for breach of privilege and contempt of Parliament. **11–016** An interference with one of the known privileges of Parliament amounts to a breach of privilege. Contempt is wider and covers any conduct which undermines the authority of the House or brings it into dispute; all breaches of privilege amounts to contempt. Erskine May defines contempt as:

" . . . any act or omission which obstructs or impedes either House of Parliament in the performance of its functions, or which obstructs or impedes any Member of Officer of the House in the discharge of his duty or which has a tendency, directly or indirectly, to produce such results."

1.   Examples of contempt

11–017   Examples of contempt include dishonesty, misconduct by Members such as deliberately misleading the House or disorderly conduct in the House, obstructing other Members such as assaulting them or preventing them from attending the House. In the *Daily Graphic case* (1956–57 HC 27) a newspaper editor was in contempt when it published the private telephone number of Arthur Lewis MP. The Newspaper invited the public to telephone Mr Lewis and express disapproval about his stance on the Suez crisis. As a result of the publication, Mr Lewis was inundated with calls which hampered his ability to perform his parliamentary duties. Publication of material which is derogatory of the House amounts to a contempt, in *Duffy's Case* (HC 129, 1964–65) an allegation of drunkenness among members amounted to contempt. In *Junor's case* (HC 38, 1956–57), the Sunday Express ran an article criticising MPs over the allocation of petrol allowances during a time of rationing. The article claimed they were giving themselves preferential treatment and its publication was held to be contempt. John Junor, the editor, was required to attend the Bar of the House and be formally admonished by the Speaker.

The 1999 Report of Joint Committee on Parliamentary Privilege recommended that contempt of Parliament be defined in statute as part of its proposals for a new Parliamentary Privileges Act.

2.   Punishment for contempt

11–018   The fact that action amounts to contempt does not mean that Parliament will take action against the offender. The 1967 Committee on Privileges recommended that the House use its penal jurisdiction sparingly. This was agreed in 1978 when the House accepted it would only use its penal jurisdiction:

> " ... when the House is satisfied that to exercise it is essential in order to provide reasonable protection for the House, its members or its officers, from such improper obstruction or attempt at or threat of obstruction as it causing or is likely to cause substantial interference with the performance of their respective functions."

Where the House does choose to invoke its penal jurisdiction, the House has a number of punishments available ranging from imprisonment to reprimand. The two most serious punishments are imprisonment and expulsion; both have not been used in recent times. The House has the power to imprison both Members and non-members, the House of Commons for a maximum of one Parliamentary session and the House of Lords indefinitely. The power to imprison has not been used since 1880 and the Select Committee of Privileges recommended its abolition. Equally, expulsion from the House was last used in 1954 in the case of Peter Baker who was convicted of a crime. Gerry Allighan was the last person expelled for contempt in 1947.

A more common punishment for serious contempt is suspension with loss of pay.

Ron Brown MP was suspended for 20 days in 1988 for damaging the Mace. In 1999, Ernie Ross was suspended for 10 days for unlawfully leaking a report of the Select Committee on Foreign Affairs. More recently, George Galloway, MP for Bethnal Green and Bow, was suspended from the House for eighteen actual sitting days on the recommendation of the Select Committee (House of Commons Select Committee on Standards and Privileges, Conduct of George Galloway, Sixth Report of Session 2006–07 HC 909–I). Allegations were made that George Galloway had been receiving substantial undeclared personal financial benefits from Saddam Hussein's regime by way of an Oil for Food Programme. The Committee concluded Mr Galloway's behaviour in concealing the true source of Iraqi funding, his conduct towards the Committee and others and his calling into question the integrity of the Commissioner for Parliamentary Standard and the Select Committee had damaged the reputation of the House.

A formal admonishment by the Speaker is one of the lesser punishments. Non members, such as newspapers, are brought to the Bar of the House and before the assembled Members are admonished by the Speaker. The last non-member admonished by the Speaker was John Junor in 1957 for publication of an article in the Sunday Express casting doubt on the honour and integrity of Members (see above). The last Member to be admonished was Tam Dalyell in 1968.

Where a member is causing disruption to the House (such as continuously interrupting a speaker) the Speaker will firstly request the Member to order and, if he continues, to resume his seat. Should the disruptive behaviour continue the Speaker can request the Member to leave the chamber. If he does not leave, the Speaker can direct the Member to withdraw immediately and the Member must leave Parliament for the duration of the day (Standing Order No.42). If a member does not comply with an order to withdraw the Speaker can formally "name" the member and put down a motion that he be suspended from the service of the House (see Standing Orders No.43). Such suspension will last for five days (first offence), 20 days (second offence) and to a period which the House decides (third offence).

3. Members interests

It is contempt to bribe an MP or otherwise attempt to influence his conduct in the House by a fee, reward or other inducement. It is also contempt for an MP to accept any such influence. No contempt is committed though if a MP is offered and receives payment to represent the general interests of a particular organisation or group so long as no pressure is put on the MP to vote in a particular way and the contractual arrangement does not seek to limit the MPs freedom of action. In *Browne's Case* (HC 118, 1946–47), a decision by a trade union to terminate its relationship with the MP due to dissatisfaction with his conduct was not contempt. However, a threat that unless an MP votes in a particular way financial support would be terminated does amount to contempt, as in *Scargill's Case* (HC 634, 1974–75).

In 1975, the House of Commons established a Register of Members' Interests requiring all members to note financial issues. A failure to register a relevant interest may be contempt as the case of John Browne MP who in 1990 was suspended from the House and lost his salary for 14 days for such an omission.

11–019

(a) *The Nolan Committee*

11–020 The Committee on Standards in Public Life was established in October 1994, under the Chairmanship of Lord Nolan, in response to concerns about the financial probity of Members of Parliament arising out of issues like the "Cash for Questions" affair.

The Committee's original terms of reference was "to examine current concerns about standards of conduct of all holders of public office, including arrangements relating to financial and commercial activities, and make recommendations as to any changes in present arrangements which might be required to ensure the highest standards of propriety in public life". In 1997, Tony Blair extended the term of reference to cover funding to political parties. The Committee published their first report in 1995 following a six month investigation of standards amongst Members (*Standards in Public Life: First Report of the Committee on Standards in Public Life* (1995) Cm 2850).

The Committee recommended the creation of a Parliamentary Commissioner for Standards to oversee the rules on MP's interests; that ex-Ministers seek clearance for jobs they take on within two years of leaving office; and a new Public Appointments Commissioner to ensure the highest standards of propriety in appointments to Quangos. They recommended a new code of conduct for Members of Parliament and established The Seven Principles of Public Life under the headings:

(1) selflessness;

(2) integrity;

(3) objectivity;

(4) accountability;

(5) openness;

(6) honesty; and

(7) leadership.

The Committee's report also led to the creation of a Select Committee on Standards and Privileges to replace the Committee of Privileges to oversee the role of the Parliamentary Commissioner for Standards.

FURTHER READING

11–021 Joint Committee on Parliamentary Privilege (Parliamentary Privilege First Report, 1989 HL 43–I/HC 214–I
Munro, C. *Studies in Constitutional Law*, 2nd edn (New York: OUP, 1999)
Standards in Public Life: First Report of the Committee on Standards in Public Life (1995) Cm 2850

Chapter 12

THE EXECUTIVE: CROWN, PRIME MINISTER AND CABINET

INTRODUCTION

The Executive is a collective term which encompasses many aspects of modern gov-   **12–001**
ernment. At it centre are three key elements in the administration of government in the
United Kingdom: Crown, the Prime Minister and the Cabinet. Together they represent
HM government. Their development is no product of design, but largely the creature of
evolutionary circumstances, so common to the United Kingdom Constitution.

PERSONNEL

1.   The monarch

As explained in chapter one, the United Kingdom is a constitutional monarchy with a   **12–002**
sovereign at its head; hence, Head of State. As such, the monarch appoints and removes
Ministers of State and civil servants from office, is Commander-in-Chief of the armed
forces, and gives her assent (the Royal Assent) to Bills once they have passed through
the Commons and the Lords. In constitutional theory, therefore, the monarch possesses
significant powers (see Ch.13), though by convention these powers are exercised on her
behalf by the Prime Minister and other Ministers of State duly appointed, i.e. by the
government. Indeed, such is the nature of the modern constitutional framework, that it
would not only be manifestly undemocratic, but also (probably) unconstitutional for
the monarch to use the powers enjoyed (see Ch.3). As a consequence, the monarch's
role is reduced to a core of largely symbolic and ceremonial functions, for example,

where the monarch continues to attend at the House of Lords for the State Opening of Parliament, or meets the Heads of State of other nations, here and abroad.

Consequently, the terminology is somewhat misleading. Though we continue to make reference to Her Majesty's Government, and that the courts are presided over by Her Majesty's judges, the monarch is divorced from the day-to-day policy formulation and law-making of modern democratic government.

This modern constitutional arrangement, i.e. the evolution of constitutional monarchy from it absolutist origins, came about by dint of a curious quirk of Englishness, namely the Act of Settlement 1700 which sought to ensure the Protestant succession after the religious turmoil of the previous decades. Scouting around the monarchies of Western Europe after the death of Queen Anne, though many had a better claim, George, Elector of Hanover, was deemed to be the most appropriate choice given that he did not suffer the problem those with a better claim had. In other words, he was not a catholic. King George I, as he became, was central to the development of the constitutional framework because he did not speak English. Consequently, it was thought necessary to appoint a person to act for him; a Prime Minister. So, from the Hanoverian period, to this, the Ministers of the Crown became directly responsible for the day-to-day running of the government, such that by the reign of Queen Victoria (1838–1901), the monarch, "reigns but does not rule" (Munro, *Studies in Constitutional Law* (2nd edn (New York: OUP, 1999), p.256).

Such a shift in the role of the monarch over three centuries inevitably leads to the question of what remains in the residue of the monarch's power. Bagehot in *The English Constitution* commented that, "she has the right to be consulted, the right to encourage and the right to warn ministers" (p.11). Rodney Brazier, in an essay entitled "The Monarchy" published in Bogdonor (ed.), *The British Constitution* (OUP, 2003), suggests that the right to be informed and to advise should be added to that list, which, in a sense, could happen on a weekly basis given that the Prime Minister, by convention, is given a weekly audience with the monarch.

At this weekly meeting, the monarch is kept fully informed of the affairs of government and has access to all Cabinet papers. The monarch is free to offer her opinion, though it might be that she is regarded as having a duty to so offer her opinion. Recent incumbents of the office of Prime Minister have spoken reflectively and with warmth of the relationship and advice the present Queen was able to offer. In his autobiography, John Major, Prime Minister from 1990–1997, commented as follows: "I hope Tony Blair seeks her advice and heeds her response. I found them invaluable on many occasions" (*John Major: The Autobiography* (London: HarperCollins, 1999, p.508)). His predecessor, Margaret Thatcher in *The Downing Street Years* stated that, "Her Majesty brings to bear a formidable grasp of current issues and breadth of experience" (London: HarperCollins, 1993, p.18). This is notwithstanding the fact that it was widely reported the two did not always see eye-to-eye. Indeed allegations appeared that the monarch did not always agree with Thatcher's policy agenda.

Any advice the monarch might offer the Prime Minister is regarded, as indeed is any other comment, in the strictest confidence. In fact, Tony Blair commented before his resignation as Prime Minister that there were only two people in the world he could trust, namely his wife, and Her Majesty; a reference to the strict confidence which is observed between the two during their weekly meeting. However, the Prime Minister is not bound to take any such advice from the monarch, and may politely decline it.

One final point relates to definitions and the use of the term "Crown". It is a generic term with a use which has two senses (see discussion of *M v Home Office* [1993] 1 W.L.R. 433 in Ch.5). First, it is used to signify the monarch him/herself and, second, to signify the government of the day. It is this second sense in which the term is typically used.

2.   The Prime Minister

Though the monarch is Head of State and of the Executive, the Prime Minister is, in practice, the Head of Government. This might neatly be contrasted with the position in the United States of America where the President is not only Head of State, but also Head of the Government. Unlike the Office of the President of the United States, the office of Prime Minister has no basis in statute, nor in any constitutional document, but has instead developed by convention. By convention, the monarch appoints the leader of the party in the Commons able to command a majority and form a government. The Prime Minister hasn't always been appointed from the Commons, indeed the last Prime Minister from the House of Lords, Marquess of Salisbury, ended his third term in office in 1902. However, since Sir Alec Douglas Home was invited to form a government by Her Majesty in 1963, the position has been held, by convention, by a Member of Parliament. In fact, Home renounced his Earldom under the recently passed Peerage Act 1963 (see Ch.10, House of Lords) and won a by-election in order to become Prime Minister becoming the first peer to leave the Lords in order to enter the Commons.

12–003

The Prime Minister was famously described by Bagehot in *The English Constitution* (1867) as *primus inter pares*, first amongst equals. This label was attached because of the idea that the Prime Minister, though head of the Cabinet, was equal to all other Ministers, as each commanded the same respect and influence; they are equals. However, such has been the manner of recent Prime Ministers, it is doubted whether this remains the case. In *The Presidentialization of Politics: A Comparative Study of Modern Democracies* (Oxford: OUP, 2005), Heffernan and Webb contend there has been a move to a more presidential-style of United Kingdom government since the Thatcher years (1979–1990):

> "Widespread charges of presidentialization were levied against Margaret Thatcher when she was Prime Minister. Where Thatcher blazed a trail, Tony Blair has followed. This is not just a product of two ambitious individuals and their staffs, but indicates a set of cumulative structural changes over time, which have built on the Executive's traditional freedom of manoeuvre within the UK system of parliamentary government. These changes have enhanced the power of the Prime Minister. Furthermore, they have been complemented by he enhancement of leaders' traditional intra-party power, and by the personalizing of electoral processes. This suggests that many of the claims identified by the 'presidentialization' of Britain's parliamentary democracy may be more than mere journalistic hyperbole." (p.27)

At the heart of this critique is the idea that the Prime Minister has considerable individual power in his/her ability to control cabinet meetings, and through the membership and growth of inner cabinets; cabinets within cabinets (see below). Further, the personality of the Prime Minister, the personification and directing hand of the party, rather than the reverse being the case, demonstrates a style which is viewed as more presidential than one where the office-holder is the first among equals. Peter Hennessy in *The Prime Minister: The Office and Its Holders since 1945* (Penguin, 2001) at p.476 quotes a "Senior Whitehall figure" as stating: "The idea that the Prime Minister is primus inter pares is wrong. The Prime Minister is not pares. He's way above that. Like Caesar, he bestrides his world like a Colossus".

However, it might be rather too simplistic to attach the label "Presidential" to the role of Prime Minister. The systems are, after all, significantly different, with Presidents being elected for a fixed term, limited by a fully-codified constitution, with a singular inability to dominate the legislature, all of which cannot be said to be the case in the British constitutional framework. Further, the personality of the incumbent cannot be downplayed. For example, Margaret Thatcher, whether one supported her or not, could not be doubted to have a strong character. During Cabinet meetings, it was known she would set down her views first full in the knowledge that Ministers would find it difficult to dissent thereafter with the consequence that they would be bound to follow. Thatcher was famously quoted as commenting that she was extraordinarily patient, "provided I get my own way in the end". However, high-handed a particular government might be, it can be difficult where dissent builds on the backbenches of Parliament, and the number of damaging resignations increases. By contrast, Thatcher's successor, John Major was a more conciliatory Prime Minister who sought to encourage debate in the Cabinet and, some might argue, was a less strong leader because of it.

With that characterisation of the modern role of Prime Minister in British Constitutional life, what are the powers of the Prime Minister? First, the Prime Minister presides over the Cabinet and determines its agenda with the Cabinet Secretary, the Senior Civil Servant, and attached to the Cabinet Office. Additionally, and as identified at para.12–002, above, the Prime Minister acts as the link between the Cabinet and the administration of government and the monarch. This is performed through the weekly meetings. In addition to these roles, the Prime Minister is Minister for the Home Civil Service and, as such, has statutory and prerogative powers.

Though, technically, Ministers are appointed by the monarch, this task is performed, in reality, by the Prime Minister. As much as the Prime Minister has Ministerial appointments within his gift, he also has the power to remove such Ministers from office. The appointment and removal of a Minister is a fine balancing act between maintaining a coherent Cabinet, whilst retaining the balance of power in the Legislature. During Tony Blair's Premiership, much was made of the balance between "Blairite" and "Brownite" Ministers in Cabinet; the former being staunch supporters of Blair, while the latter were supporters of Gordon Brown who, at the time, was Chancellor of the Exchequer. This balancing of political allegiances was essential to the success of the government because perception of divisions in the Cabinet undermines confidence in the government.

However, Prime Ministers need to be mindful of the problems which might be caused by overuse of the power to remove, as history is littered with instances of former Ministers becoming problems on the backbenches. For example, when John Major reshuffled his Cabinet in the early 1990s, he moved Norman Lamont from Chancellor of the Exchequer, instead offering him the Secretary of State for the Environment, a considerable demotion. Lamont refused the appointment and became a thorn in the Prime Minister's side from the backbenches for the remainder of his time in office.

The Prime Minister has the power to request a dissolution of Parliament. This power is regarded as being solely within the power of the Prime Minister and whilst there may be a discretion to consult with the Cabinet on the point, there is no obligation on him to do so. Indeed, the change from this being a collective decision of Cabinet to being within the exclusive power of the Prime Minister appears to be a somewhat unexplained development at the beginning of the 20th century. In *The Office of the Prime Minister* (OUP, 1975), Robert Blake comments:

> "Until the First World War no one doubted that the decision to advise the Crown to dissolve Parliament was a collective decision of the Cabinet, or at any rate of those members of it who sit in the House of Commons ... For reasons which are not wholly clear, the practice since 1918 has been for the decision to rest with the Prime Minister alone, taking such advice (or none) as he sees fit." (p.58)

Importantly, the Prime Minister is also responsible for the issuance and revision of the Ministerial Code. The Code seeks to establish the standards expected of Ministers of the Crown in the discharge of their ministerial responsibilities. The most recent edition was published in July 2007. The remainder of the Prime Minister's power relates to responsibility for the co-ordination of government policy (the Cabinet, at least in theory, formulates it), along with the power to establish non-statutory bodies, for example, quangos.

Some final mention needs to be made of the Prime Minister's Private Office and Strategy Unit. The former is staffed by civil servants and special advisers, the latter being appointed by the Prime Minister, support the Prime Minister in the functions he undertakes, though principally these are restricted to policy matters. The Strategy Unit has three main roles. First, it provides strategy and policy advice to the Prime Minister; secondly, it supports government departments in developing effective strategies and policies; and, thirdly, it identifies and disseminates emerging issues and policy challenges to the wider administrative bodies and to the community. The Unit works with other departments, e.g. the Home Office on the recent reform of Charities Law, and other "stakeholders" in ensuring policy is appropriately formulated at the domestic level.

3.   The Cabinet

The Cabinet rests at the heart of the British political system. In constitutional theory it is the supreme decision-making body in government with responsibility for all policy decisions (see I. Jennings, *Cabinet Government* (Cambridge: Cambridge University Press, 1969)). Jennings regarded the Cabinet as being at the core of the British constitutional system. The Cabinet and its origins can be traced to the 16th century, though perhaps further back to the Privy Council. The Privy Council was the principal body from which the monarch took advice and good counsel during the period of absolute

12–004

monarchy. It was a small group of advisers, principally drawn from the nobility, who would provide advice to the monarch on matters as diverse as domestic policy, to war. The Privy Council remains to this day, though its influence on the monarch and the government is considerably reduced.

The move to a Cabinet-style government, and the removal of the Privy Council's status as the body with responsibility for providing the monarch with advice can be traced to the reign of George I, as outlined at para.12–002, above. At this point in history, Cabinet began to take its modern characteristics by governing the nation without the monarch's consent and the British system began to be characterised as "Cabinet Government"; a collective form of government with collective decision-making on major policy issues made by a body of senior Ministers. This is even though many commentators use the term "Prime Ministerial Government" because of the dominance of the Prime Minister (J.P. Mackintosh, *The British Cabinet* (Stevens, 1962), p.451). Mackintosh argues that the role of the modern "Cabinet Government" is more one of the co-ordination of administration and ensuring that legislative proposals were acceptable, thus diminishing the importance of the Cabinet as a decision-making body, bound by the collective decision. This style of "Cabinet Government" has arisen because government departments of state have increased in size during the 20th century, particularly with the advent of the welfare state, with the consequences that Ministers commit more time to dealing with decisions made in their own departments than in other forums. As a result, few decisions are actually made in Cabinet.

As the concept of "Cabinet Government" developed, it was somewhat haphazard, with little in the way of formality. However, it acquired an institutional character under Prime Minister David Lloyd George and the Permanent Secretary to the Cabinet, Maurice Hankey, after whom the reforms were named. The reforms introduced a central machinery to the Cabinet Office with decisions being recorded by the taking of minutes. Because it was a time of war a series of sub-Committees were established to consider specialised areas of policy for recommendation to the full Cabinet. By this series of reforms, the post of Cabinet Secretary was created with responsibility for organising Cabinet business. Maurice Hankey, later Baron Sankey, was renowned for his organisational skills and must be said to be the father of the modern Home Civil Service. He remains the longest-serving Cabinet Secretary in British political history.

Membership of the Cabinet is determined, as already stated, by the Prime Minister. Generally, the Cabinet consists of between 20 and 25 individuals, comprising the various Secretaries of State, Leaders of the House of Commons and the House of Lords, and others Ministers handling aspects of the government's political business. The number in the Cabinet is not formally set because there should be a permitted flexibility in the government and setting the body at a certain number would require a statutory amendment, or other such change in order to ensure legitimacy. A good example is the Secretaries of State for Scotland and Wales which, in the post-devolution constitution, were much diminished roles. The remaining functions of those departments have been merged with other Ministerial appointments. For example, at April 1, 2008, the Rt Hon Des Browne, MP, is Secretary of State for Defence and for Scotland. Finally, there is a 95 member limit on the number of Ministerial office holders who might be drawn from the Commons (House of Commons Disqualification Act 1975 s.2(1)). Consequently, Ministers, generally approximately 120 in every Parliament, must be drawn from the Commons and the Lords.

Cabinet meets weekly every Tuesday during Parliament. This is a recent change implemented by Gordon Brown to fit around Ministerial and Parliamentary schedules. Under the Blair premiership, Cabinet meetings tended not to last much more than one hour (Hennessy, *The Prime Minister: The Office and Its Holders since 1945*, p.481). However, the move initiated by Brown suggests that Cabinet meetings may last longer because the move effectively allows for more time.

(a)   *Functions of Cabinet*

The Cabinet system, like much of the United Kingdom constitution, is a creature of circumstance, with the consequence that few hard and fast rules have been set down as to its operation and the functions it performs. However, there is a core of functions which can be said to be identifiable with Cabinet Government, and these are: **12–005**

- implement the government's agenda (law and policy);

- respond to emergencies and crises;

- develop, formulate and enliven the government's domestic and foreign policy; and

- provide collective political leadership.

The first is, arguably, the Cabinet's key role. A political party is elected, at least in some part, on the understanding that it will implement its election promises. Thus, after government is formed, it begins the work of implementing its manifesto commitments. However, a great deal of planning must go into this, along with consideration of other matters such as competing calls on the public purse, whether adequate Parliamentary time can be dedicated to the legislative programme, and so on. This matter is complicated further where the Cabinet convenes because of unforeseen circumstances. For example, following the terrorist attacks of 9/11, combating terrorist activity and the loosely labelled "War on Terror" became of greater concern to the government.

Allied to that later point is the idea that the government tends to convene in Cabinet where there is an emergency or some crisis or other. For example, when Islamic extremists attempted to attack London and Glasgow in the summer of 2007, the Cabinet met to assess its response and the efforts being undertaken to bring the perpetrators to justice. Indeed, the Prime Minister was called back from his holiday in the south-west of England.

Further, a government which has been in power for some considerable time must pay attention to its policies and continue to develop, formulate and enliven its government by the creation of new policies not only to improve the lot of the voters, but as a response to the circumstances of society and the changes which occur.

Finally, the Cabinet is a collective body. Since the Cabinet is responsible for providing governance, it is essential that the Cabinet is seen to be united, holding to the principle of collective responsibility (see below). A disunited Cabinet undermines confidence in the government and its ability to govern effectively.

(b)   *Cabinet Committees*

12–006   Though the Cabinet is the recognised body with the responsibilities detailed, a good deal of work is conducted through Cabinet sub-committees and, so-called, Inner Cabinets. This system, developed by Maurice Hankey, was in recognition of the fact that a Cabinet can become burdened with many pressing matters of state and that for the better administration of government certain specialist Committees can deal with these matters, thereby making the decision-making elements of Central Government more effective.

There are Cabinet Committees, and then sub-Committees of that Committee. So, for example, the Ministerial Committee on Domestic Affairs has seven sub-Committees including the Sub-Committee on Border and Migration and the Sub-Committee on Public Engagement and the Delivery of Services. In all, there are 11 Ministerial Committees and 21 Sub-Committees. The latest list of Cabinet Committees was published by the Cabinet Office in January 2008.

Cabinet Committees ensure that a matter which may never get to Cabinet because of pressure of time, etc. can nevertheless get a full hearing in the relevant Cabinet Committee with responsibility for the issue and with the necessary expertise. Thus, though a matter may not have been heard by the whole Cabinet, it is nevertheless given such an extensive consideration that it can be deemed to have been authoritatively analysed. A complete list of the Cabinet Committees and Sub-Committees is available at the Cabinet Office website (*www.cabinetoffice.gov.uk*).

(c)   *Inner Cabinets*

12–007   Outside the main Cabinet and the Cabinet Committees are more informal Cabinets, known as Inner Cabinets. Inner Cabinets are drawn from a small and select group of trusted Ministers and advisors, able to make decisions quickly, especially in times of crisis. However, the Inner Cabinet has the potential to undermine the government where it is used to by-pass open discussion in the main Cabinet. Arguably, this is precisely what happened when Margaret Thatcher used an Inner Cabinet to make a decision in relation to the Westland Affair in 1986 which caused the resignation of the Secretary of State for Defence, Michael Heseltine, and later the resignation of the Secretary of State for Industry, Leon Britten. The Inner Cabinet can be the cause of dissent and dissatisfaction within the whole Cabinet, ultimately undermining the convention of collective Cabinet responsibility (see below).

4.   **Junior Ministers**

12–008   Within each department of state, under the Secretary of State, is a team of Ministers. Immediately below the Secretary of State in ministerial rank are the Ministers of State, then below them are the Under Secretaries of State, and at the bottom of the ministerial ladder are the Parliamentary Private Secretaries (PPSs).

5.   The Civil Service

The Civil Service, or Home Civil Service as it is sometimes know, is the administrative **12–009** engine behind the government. Each department of state has a dedicated team, often running into thousands, working to ensure the policies and laws of the government are implemented. This is done by drafting legislation, reports and all other documentation necessary for the running of government. The Civil Service is sometimes known as the "government in residence", for though Ministers and their parties might be voted out at general elections, the Civil Servants remain in place, no matter what the political colour of the government. As a consequence of this, the Civil Service must act in accordance with certain principles set down in the Civil Service Code. At para.2 of the most recent version of the Code (published, June 2006), under the heading "Civil Service values" it is stated that a member of the Home Civil Service must act with integrity, honesty, objectivity, and, importantly, with impartiality. As Sir Robert Armstrong, Head of the Civil Service 1979–1988 put it in a Memorandum in 1985 ("the Armstrong Memorandum"):

> "Civil servants are servants of the Crown. For all practical purposes the Crown in this context means and is represented by the government of the day … the Civil Service as such has no constitutional personality or responsibility separate from the duly elected government of the day." (*Civil Servants and Ministers: Duties and Responsibilities* (Cmnd 9841; 1986)

Though Civil Servants are, generally, protected from political scrutiny by the Minister who ultimately must take responsibility for the Department concerned, it is nevertheless the case that a Civil Servant can be required to give evidence before a Select Committee of Parliament. Where required to do so, the position is governed by rules termed the Departmental Evidence and Response to Select Committees, sometimes referred to as the "Osmotherley Rules". These rules are designed to provide guidance to civil servants in giving evidence to Select Committees of both Houses of Parliament. Under the rules, "civil servants who give evidence to Select Committees do so on behalf of their Ministers and under their directions" (para.40). When appearing before a Committee, "it is the duty of officials to be as helpful as possible to Select Committees. Officials should be as forthcoming as they can in providing information, whether in writing or in oral evidence, to a Select Committee. Any withholding of information should be decided in accordance with the law and care should be taken to ensure that no information is withheld which would not be exempted if a parallel request were made under the FOI Act." In other words, civil servants should volunteer information which could be found out by another legitimate means! The latest version was published in 2005 and can be accessed at *www.cabinetoffice.gov.uk/propriety_and_ethics/civil_service/osmotherly_rules.aspx*.

6.   Executive Agencies, "Next Step" and Quangos

(a)   *Executive Agencies (Next Step Agencies)*

12–010   Though most of the work and administration of government is done through the various departments of state, certain functions are undertaken by Executive Agencies. In the late 1980s, the Conservative government initiated a process of reforming the management of the civil service with the effect that some government functions were separated from the Minister, but given autonomy within a department of state and headed by a Chief Executive. At the time, the Prime Minister, Margaret Thatcher, commented in the House of Commons:

> " ... to the greatest extent practicable the Executive functions of government, as distinct from policy advice, should be carried out by units clearly designated within Departments ... [and that] responsibility for the day-to-day operations of each Agency should be delegated to a chief Executive. He would be responsible for management within a framework of policy objectives and resources set by the responsible Minister ... " (*Improving Management in Government–The Next Steps Agencies: Review 1990* (Cmnd 1261; 1989/90))

The net effect of these changes is to create agencies within departments, but with separate leadership. An example is HM Prison Service, an Executive agency under the auspices of the Home Office, with a separate Director-General who, at time of writing, is Phil Wheatley. One of the inevitable impacts of the Next Steps reform is that the traditional role of the civil servant behind the Minister has diminished, with some heads of these Executive Agencies being almost as famous or notorious as the Minister responsible for the department. Indeed, HM Prison Service is a good example since in the 1990s, after a series of high-profile escapes from prisons, a clash developed between the then Home Secretary, Michael Howard, and the Director-General of the Prison Service, Derek Lewis. This led to a memorable exchange on BBC's *Newsnight* (see below, individual ministerial responsibility, at para.12–026).

(b)   *Quangos*

12–011   Quangos is an acronym for quasi-autonomous non-governmental organisation. These are non-governmental bodies which perform government functions with government funding. Examples include the Potato Marketing Board and the Energy Savings Trust.

7.   Other members

Finally, the Executive is also said to include the police and the armed forces.   **12–102**

RELATIONSHIP BETWEEN THE EXECUTIVE AND PARLIAMENT

In modern democratic societies, it is important that the government is held to account   **12–013**
for its laws and policies, taking responsibility for the decisions it has made. In our
system of democracy, this means holding the Executive to account in the Legislature
through the various mechanisms of requiring Ministers to respond to Parliamentary
questions and/or, to appear before a Select Committee (see Ch.9).

Insofar as the relationship between the Executive and the Legislature is concerned,
two constitutional conventions provide that Ministers are accountable to Parliament
for the policies, decisions and actions of government. These are the conventions of
Collective Ministerial Responsibility and Individual Ministerial Responsibility. It will
be noted that as conventions (see Ch.3, Constitutional Conventions), they are not
legally binding, but political consequences may flow from breach.

1.   Collective ministerial responsibility

All Ministers of State (and, usually, private secretaries) must accept Cabinet decisions.   **12–014**
Where they disagree with the decision, they may voice dissent around the Cabinet table,
or privately to ministerial colleagues, but they must support the decision in public if
they wish to remain in the Cabinet. If a Minister feels they will be unable to support, in
public, the decision made in Cabinet, then their only option is to resign. The convention
of collective ministerial responsibility requires that the Cabinet is of one voice. Paragraph 2.1 of the Ministerial Code provides:

> "Collective responsibility requires that Ministers should be able to express their
> view frankly in the expectation that they can argue freely in private while main-
> taining a united front when decisions have been reached. This in turn requires that
> the privacy of opinions expressed in Cabinet and Ministerial Committees including
> in correspondence, should be maintained."

It follows from this that there are two important facets to the convention. First, it
implies a duty, an obligation, of public acquiescence to government policy. Secondly, it
requires that dissent and disagreement be concealed not only from the public but also,
and more controversially, from Parliament.

The rationale for the convention is that it seeks to ensure strong and robust government, which has not only the confidence of the general public, but also the confidence of Parliament. The confidence is sought throughout the whole of government as

the convention applies to Cabinet Committees and Junior Ministers. For convenience, the convention has three aspects: confidence; unanimity; and, confidentiality.

(a) *Confidence*

12–015   The idea of confidence, one which has already been touched upon, relates to the fact that the government should enjoy the confidence of Parliament to remain in office. This does not mean that for every government defeat in Parliament, the Prime Minister should seek a dissolution of Parliament and subsequent election. However, it may mean that where there is a loss of confidence in the government, manifest by a vote of "no confidence" in the Commons, the government should, by convention, resign and an election called. Confidence motions, as they are known, are generally called by the opposition, though they can be used by the Prime Minister as a tactic to ensure that a difficult vote is won, or that a party ends clandestine discussions as to leadership.

An example of the former can be drawn from the tumultuous times in the mid-late 1970s and the government of James Callaghan. The government lost a number of votes, but it wasn't until a specific vote of confidence was lost in Parliament, proposed by the then Leader of the Opposition, Margaret Thatcher, that the government resigned, precipitating a General Election, which the Conservative Party won. An example of a Prime Minister using a motion of "no confidence" comes from John Major's premiership which was beset by arguments and party disagreement over Europe, and the role the United Kingdom should have in the European Union. As Major attempted to push European Treaties through the Commons, he used the tactic of also making the vote one of confidence in his government. This was a tactical use of the confidence motion as it ensured the Conservatives could pass a politically difficult piece of legislation, the alternative being the government's resignation and a possible loss at a general election was the party was politically unpopular.

The justification for there being no basis for government resignation every time it suffers a Parliamentary defeat rests on the idea that a party, hence a government, is elected on a package of reforms, rather than on the basis of one specific reform. Thus, defeat on one policy objective does not express a lack of confidence in the whole of the government or its programme. A motion of no confidence, on the other hand, establishes a lack of confidence in the government's entire programme and in its ability to govern.

(b) *Unanimity*

12–016   This idea is embodied in the Ministerial Code and expressed as a *united front*. Unanimity ensures that the government, hence the party, has a party line along which it might be identified. As Loveland, *Constitutional and Administrative Law* (OUP, 2006) expresses it, there is collective loyalty to collective decisions. The advantage of unanimity is that it enables Parliament to identify exactly what the government's position is on an issue, and though the Code has no legal force, it tends to be followed by Ministers.

However, the idea of unanimity is not without its problems. First, the requirement of unanimity comes up against significant problems given the size of the government. As already stated, the government can have as many as 120 Ministers, of varying rank, of whom some 20 or so take part in Cabinet. Consequently, there is a considerable number of Ministers bound by the Convention who have taken no part in the decisions, nor expressed a view, but yet are expected to follow the party line and vote for something when an ordinary MP would not be expected to do so.

Secondly, the Prime Minister, along with the Cabinet Secretary, determines the agenda for every Cabinet. Even something as simple as a policy's place on the agenda can affect the quality of debate and the amount of time dedicated to it. Blair's Cabinets were known for their brevity, thereby limiting the time for discussion of the issues arising from the agenda. One would have to question that in a Cabinet meeting of 20 or so Ministers whether there would be the time to discuss matters freely and openly, yet at the same time it is expected the Cabinet maintains unanimity.

Thirdly, above, the strengthening of the role of the Prime Minister (as discussed at para.12–004) and how the style is becoming more presidential, especially through the increased use of Inner Cabinets and policy advisors. This might suggest that Cabinet is less a forum for discussion as to the substance of a policy, rather moving to becoming a forum for the presentation of the Prime Minister's pre-determined policies. This was a feature of the Thatcher administration through the 1980s, and one which was continued by Blair in the late 1990s and up to his resignation. Indeed, when Claire Short resigned as Secretary of State for International Development prior to the Iraq war, her resignation speech to the House of Commons made reference to the way Cabinet Government was moving:

> "I am ashamed that the UK government has agreed the resolution tabled in New York and *shocked by the secrecy and lack of consultation with departments with direct responsibility for the issues referred to in the resolution.*" [my italics]

Resignation because of a lack of consultation undermining the unanimity of the convention has occurred on a number of occasions in the recent past.

(i)   Michael Heseltine—"Westland Affair"

A UK helicopter manufacturer, Westland, was in financial difficulty and there was an issue over whether it should be rescued by a US or European company. Heseltine, who was Secretary of State for Defence at the time, preferred a European takeover, with the hope it would produce a competitor to the US. The Prime Minister, on the other hand, preferred a US takeover. A Cabinet meeting which had been scheduled to discuss the matter was cancelled and the decision made to go with the US option without the consultation of relevant Ministers. As a result, Heseltine claimed the unanimity requirement had broken down and that as he had had no input in the decision, he could not support it. He subsequently, resigned.   **12–017**

(ii)   Nigel Lawson—Exchange Rate Mechanism

12–018   In the late 1980s the Chancellor of the Exchequer, Nigel Lawson, favoured the pursuit of a policy which would have seen the United Kingdom enter the European Exchange Rate Mechanism. However, the Prime Minister did not wish to follow the policy, instead taking the advice of Alan Walters, her Economic Advisor, over her appointed Minister. Lawson resigned on the basis that he felt he could not support a decision which had been made on the advice of a non-Cabinet member; a special advisor.

(iii)   Robin Cook—Invasion of Iraq

12–019   Before the decision to invade Iraq in 2003, Robin Cook, who was then Leader of the House of Commons, a Cabinet post, resigned because of a lack of unanimity in the decision to invade. Cook's resignation speech was a powerful polemic and one of the great Parliamentary speeches in recent times. It is available to view on the BBC website.

(c)   *Confidentiality*

12–020   The idea of confidentiality is a sister requirement of unanimity since it would be impossible to maintain the principle of unanimity if Cabinet Ministers were not required to maintain confidentiality of their ministerial colleagues. Further, if there were no obligation to treat Cabinet colleagues' discussions and comment confidential, it might hinder the full and frank discussion which the obligation arguably facilitates. The obligation is a continuing one, and applies even after a Minister has resigned from the Cabinet.

(i)   Exceptions to the requirement of confidentiality

12–021   The confidential nature of material does not have a blanket operation and will not operate in three separate sets of circumstances:

- where documents are deemed to be in the public domain;

- where the matter is known to foreign governments;

- where the written opinions of law officers.

In addition, lapse of time may make the materials less confidential. See, for example, Lord Widgery's comments in *Att-Gen v Jonathan Cape* [1976] Q.B. 752.

(d)   *Avoiding the convention*

The convention can been avoided in the following circumstances. First, where it has   **12–022**
been suspended by the Prime Minister. Second, where information is leaked. Third,
where memoirs have been published.

(i)   Suspension by the Prime Minister

The Prime Minister has the power to suspend the convention in the interests of political   **12–023**
expediency. For example, if the government is discussing a controversial issue over
which not only the Cabinet, but also the public, on the evidence of opinion polls, is
divided, the Prime Minister might find it politically better to suspend the convention to
avoid a political fall-out from ministerial resignations and the political damage which
comes with it.

   However, it is rare for the Prime Minister to suspend the convention because it can be
politically damaging in the eyes of the electorate. One notable occasion on which the
convention was suspended happened in the 1970s during the referendum on whether the
United Kingdom should withdraw from the European Union. The Labour government
led by Harold Wilson was so divided on the issue that the Prime Minister decided that
the politically sensible approach would be to suspend the convention and allow Cabinet
Ministers to campaign for or against membership. However, Wilson paid for his
decision with his job as he was replaced 12 months later by James Callaghan: suspending the convention can show weakness. A prudent Prime Minister should weigh-up
the potential harm to all concerned and determine whether it might be better to have a
Cabinet all of one voice and allow dissenters to resign, so upholding the convention.

(ii)   Leaks

A leak occurs where information which was previously in the private domain of the   **12–024**
Cabinet appears in the public domain, usually the press, from an anonymous source.
This sort of leaking is known as unattributable leaking and is recognised to be one of
the "safety valves" in the convention allowing for the removal of "pressure". Ministers
who disagree with the decision of a Cabinet, but elect to stay in the government rather
than resign are permitted the luxury of being able to leak their dissatisfaction in an
unattributed form to a journalist.

   Though leaking doesn't officially occur, disagreements are widely known in the press
and, indeed, during the Blair premiership, it was widely known that there were disagreements between the Lord Chancellor, Derry Irvine and Jack Straw over constitutional matters. Further, that the Chancellor of the Exchequer, Gordon Brown,
disagreed with Peter Mandelson on economic matters. However it is perhaps interesting
to note that leaking does not tend to be a Prime Ministerial's activity. James Callaghan,
Prime Minister in the late 1970s commented that "I brief, you leak, he, she or it blow
the whistle" (*Frank's Inquiry on Official Secrets*, 1972).

(iii)   *Memoirs*

12–025   As seen from the case of *Att-Gen v Jonathan Cape*, the convention is not legally enforceable and the publication of ministerial memoirs is common place (discussed more fully in Ch.3). However, in the case, the Lord Chief Justice, Lord Widgery, brought the convention within the evolving doctrine of confidence. The Attorney-General had sought an injunction to restrain publication of ministerial diaries which was refused. His Lordship based his decision squarely in the law of confidence stating that only the clearest cases of continuing confidence demand intervention and, in this case, the time lapse permitted publication. Since the decision of *Jonathan Cape*, clear guidelines have been established to which Cabinet Ministers should adhere before publication will be allowed. Indeed, it is now quite common to see ministerial memoirs published, and in many cases not long after leaving office as happened, for example, after Robin Cook resigned as Leader of the House of Commons.

2.   Individual ministerial responsibility

12–026   The convention of individual ministerial responsibility is the most difficult of the conventions to formulate due to its uncertain limits. However, it might be said to consist in the following:

- to inform and explain their actions and policies to Parliament, and to keep Parliament abreast of developments within their portfolio. Consequently, Ministers give statements to Parliament and can be called upon to respond to questions in Parliament;

- to apologise where an error has occurred, whether their own or by their official, i.e. their Civil Servants;

- to take appropriate action in response to problems;

- to resign, which is the ultimate action for a Minister. The circumstances which might cause a Minister to resign are complex and detailed below.

(Adapted from *Individual ministerial responsibility—issues and examples*, House of Commons Research Paper 04/31)

Essentially, therefore, the requirement is that a Minister is in charge of a Department and that they alone are answerable to Parliament for the exercise of powers, whether in their own name or by their officials. The Minister takes sole responsibility for the actions of his department because they are the appointed face of the department with responsibility for it. Civil servants are the administrators of government policies, providing the logistical support; doing the Minister's bidding. It would be unacceptable, therefore, to have the civil servants take the consequences of the Minister's policy failing, provided they had acted in accordance with the wishes of the Minister. Liability is political, not legal. Unless a Minister breaches a law, the Minister suffers a loss of his political position, i.e. by resignation, should the circumstances require it.

However, recent analysis would seem to suggest that resignation is not the only method by which a Minister might be held responsible and that a distinction appears to be developing between responsibility and accountability; between operation and policy.

(a)   *Crichel Down*

This case involved the compulsory acquisition of land during the Second World War, which the owner wished to reclaim thereafter. An inquiry found that the owner had been treated with hostility and the matter had been handled inefficiently, inaccurately and in a muddled, even deceptive manner by the department concerned. The controversy led to the resignation of Sir Thomas Dugdale, Secretary of State for Agriculture. Dugdale took responsibility for the actions of his department by making the ultimate sacrifice of resignation.

12–027

Following the Crichel Down controversy, Sir David Maxwell Fyfe, Home Secretary, distinguished four sets of circumstances in which a Minister would be responsible for the actions of civil servants. A Minister would not be required to resign where (a) a civil servant made a mistake on an unimportant issue or (b) where the action by the civil servant was disapproved of and the Minister had no knowledge of the conduct beforehand. In such circumstances, the Minister would not be required to resign because of a lack of personal knowledge. This is the basis of the modern formulation of the convention. However, the alternative is that a Minister would be required to resign where (c) the civil servant were carrying out the express orders of the Minister or (d) where the civil servant is acting in accordance with a public policy. The underlying rationale is that the Minister must protect the civil servant but even in circumstances (a) and (b), the Minister remains accountable and responsible.

(b)   *Rationale for the shift in the convention*

The convention dates from the 19th century when the State was considerably smaller than it is today. Government did not manage the massive social programmes which are in place today, limiting its concerns to the matters of trade, Empire, and war. Because the extent of government intervention in life was small, so was the number of people needed to administer it. Thus, Ministers could be expected to take responsibility for their civil servant's actions, no matter how trivial, because they could be expected to know their civil servants and have knowledge of the decision taken.

12–028

Further, there have been considerable changes in the mechanics of civil service administration over the last twenty or so years which have placed strain on the doctrine as developed through the 19th century. The increase in Executive Agencies and Next Step Agencies under the control of a Chief Executive distances the Minister further from administrative decisions.

If the problem is one of operation, the administration of the policy in practice, the Minister cannot be expected to have personal knowledge of it, therefore not be responsible, though they will continue to be required to account for the failure.

However, it is often difficult to conclude on such sharp distinctions, especially where the policy, such as the budget, has operational effect.

(c)   Operation versus policy

12–029   Between 1954 (the year of Dugdale's resignation) and 1982, there were no Ministerial resignations under the convention of individual ministerial responsibility due to operation failures being to blame, though that is not to say that calls for resignation did not occur.

(i)   Prison escapes

12–030   During the 1990s, there was a series of high profile prison riots and escapes, some of whom were convicted terrorists. At the time, the Director-General of HM Prison Service, an Executive Agency under the government's civil service reforms, was Derek Lewis. The Prison Service assumed responsibility for the day-to-day running of prisons, under the aegis of the Home Secretary who, at the time, was Michael Howard. Howard was said to have threatened to overrule Lewis if he did not sack the Governor of the prison concerned, something which later memorably caused trouble for Howard in a BBC Newsnight interview with Jeremy Paxman (*www.youtube.com/watch?v= Uwlsd8RAoqI&feature=related*). There were calls for Howard's resignation, but the publication of a report into the problems in the prisons led to Lewis falling on his sword and tendering his resignation, though some say it was a sacking.

This was a tricky case, especially when certain allegations were made during the Conservative leadership election in 1997. Howard put himself forward as a candidate which caused Ann Widdecombe, Prisons Minister at the Home Office under Howard, to allege that Howard had misled the Commons over the resignation of Derek Lewis as head of the Prison Service, which Howard denied. Widdecombe suggested that following the breakout from Parkhurst in 1995, Howard was asked by a Home Affairs Select Committee whether he had delayed the installation of security phones at Parkhurst in order to finance work in other prisons. He said he had not, but then conceded six months later that his answer had been inaccurate. He said that he had not been informed of the decision which was taken by the Prison Service and not by the Home Office.

(ii)   Brixton Prison escapes

12–031   It might be argued that Howard was set a precedent by Kenneth Baker, Home Secretary in 1991 when several IRA prisoners escaped from Brixton Prison. He, like Howard after him, refused to resign.

(iii) Arms to Iraq

During the 1980s, a number of arms manufacturers sold arms to Iraq under govern- **12–032**
ment sanction. A large-scale Inquiry was launched in 1992, headed by the Appeal Court
judge, Sir Richard Scott. Among many points identified as areas of concern in the
report which was published in 1996, Sir Richard highlighted the failure of Ministerial
responsibility in that no-one resigned over the affair.

(iv) Invasion of the Falkland Islands

In 1982, Argentina launched an invasion of the Falkland Islands over which it believed **12–033**
it had a territorial claim. At the time, the Foreign Secretary, Lord Carrington resigned
even though the convention would not have been violated had he chosen to stay in
office. There was no precedent for resignation on the grounds that a threat from a
hostile nation had not been anticipated. He has since made clear his reasons for stepping down:

> "It was not a sense of culpability that led me to resign. But the fact of shock and
> fury were felt throughout Britain, and in those circumstances—with people
> naturally turning on the government and accusing it of mismanagement – it is
> right, in my judgment that there must be a resignation ... I was also very aware
> that my membership of the Lords was at that moment an embarrassment to the
> Prime Minister and a weakness ... when there is a real political crisis it is in the
> House of Commons that the life and death of the government is decided and I
> bitterly regretted that I could not face the House at Margaret Thatcher's side ...
> The more particular reason was my awareness that the government was in for a
> hard time and that my presence would make it not easier but harder ...   my
> departure would put a stop to the search for scapegoats. It would serve the cause of
> unity and help turn the eyes of all from the past to the immediate future."
> [reference for this quote]

(v) Literacy and numeracy standards

However, a more recent example provides an instance of where a Secretary of State may **12–034**
have resigned at least within the spirit of the convention. Estelle Morris, Secretary of
State for Education 2001–2002, stated in her (extremely candid) resignation speech that
she was not up to the job as Secretary of State. Morris gave a commitment to the
Commons that she would resign if literacy and numeracy levels did not improve. When
the results were published showing that results had not improved, her resignation
followed a short time afterwards. Arguably, one might argue that the resignation was
within the spirit of the convention, even if not explicitly so.

(d)   *Responsibility versus accountability*

12–035   Recently a distinction appears to have been drawn between responsibility and accountability. When Sir Robin Butler gave evidence to the Select Committee which was convened to discuss the ramifications of the Scott Inquiry into the sale of armaments to Iraq, he drew a distinction between accountability and responsibility, stating that this was the same as identified in the Crichel Down affair. Ministers are required to account for everything that goes on in their Ministry, but that they are only responsible, in the sense of being required to resign, for serious failures resulting from policy or from personal actions. (See the inquiry into exports of defence equipment to Iraq, HC 115, 1995–96.)

However, Fyfe, discussed above, stated after the Crichel Down affair that there was no distinction between accountability and responsibility, and though it is certainly capable of this interpretation, the Ministerial Code picks up on the distinction by stating that Ministers have a duty to account which, though not legally binding, is considered a clear Parliamentary rule. Additionally, they must take responsibility for deciding how to act. So a Minister is accountable but not personally responsible for every failing of administration.

This would seem to limit the scope for a Minister being required to resign. Indeed, resignations have, in recent political history, been limited to sex, drugs and morality, a number of examples bearing this out. First, John Profumo, Secretary of State for War, had an affair with a call girl, Christine Keeler, then lied about it to Parliament causing him to resign. Cecil Parkinson, Secretary of State for Trade and Industry, resigned after it was revealed that his mistress, Sara Keays, was carrying his child. David Mellor, Secretary of State at the Department for National Heritage, was exposed to have had an affair with Antonio de Sancha, but it was revelations that he had received free holidays from various individuals which eventually led to his resignations. Ron Davies was forced to resign as Secretary of State for Wales after a moment of madness in a public toilet on Clapham Common.

Special mention ought to be made of David Blunkett, holder of a number of Cabinet posts, resigning from both under a cloud. First, Blunkett was Home Secretary from 2001–2004 when he was forced to resign after it emerged that he had tried to use his influence to speed the visa application of Kimberley Quinn's nanny. The problem was complicated because he was having an affair with Quinn at the time. The Prime Minister did not seek his resignation because of the affair, but his position became untenable after the visa revelations appeared in the press. Undaunted, after the 2005 General Election, Blunkett was re-appointed to the Cabinet as Secretary of State for Work and Pensions. However, concern began to grow about a possible conflict of interest he might have in a directorship he held in a company bidding for government contracts. Blunkett failed to take the advice of the Advisory Committee on Business Appointments, despite being told by its Chairman to do so. The problem did not go away and in November that same year Blunkett was forced to resign for a second time.

These resignations, forced under circumstances outside the convention, rather beg the question of why one should be concerned about such issues. So long as the Department for which the Minister is responsible is performing effectively and efficiently why should these issues have an impact? Well, it is argued that such events go to the very heart of decency in public life and cast doubts on the ability of the person to do their job, whether justified or not. However, in the case of Mellor, he was hamstrung by John Major's Back to Basics campaign for a return to morality in private and public life. Barnett, *Constitutional and Administrative Law* ((Cavendish, 2006), p.288) argues that resignations should occur sooner rather than later since it can have consequences for the public's confidence in the government. Further, one might now consider that Ministers also resign because of the Prime Ministers loss of support, a point made by Finer, "The Individual Responsibility of Ministers" (1956) 34 *Public Administration* 377, who stated " ... whether a Minister is forced to resign depends on three factors: on himself, his Prime Minister and his party".

Sir Ivor Jennings, writing in the 20th Century said that the "most elementary qualification demanded of a minister is honesty and incorruptibility." Taking such a statement as the base point, Alder believes that the constitutional requirement to resign exists only when a Minister knowingly misleads Parliament or is personally to blame. For example, Stephen Byers was forced to resign as Secretary of State for Transport after it was revealed that he had lied to Parliament, while Beverley Hughes, a Minister at the Home Office, resigned when it was shown that she had been informed of procedural improprieties concerning the granting of visas to certain categories of workers from Eastern Europe, but had told the House of Commons that if she had been aware of such facts she would have done something about it.

While it is an acknowledged feature of Ministerial responsibility that Ministers will be held to account by Parliament, the nature of the ultimate sanction, resignation, has changed dramatically. Of the 27 Cabinet resignations since 1982, only one has been on a traditional individual ministerial responsibility point, that of Lord Carrington, and even that was subsequently found to be to assist the government in the difficult times ahead rather than out of duty. Ministerial resignations are now characterised by sleaze, with Ministers refusing to resign unless, and until, Prime Ministerial support is withdrawn or public pressure makes their position untenable.

FURTHER READING

Bamforth, N. "Political accountability in play: the Budd inquiry and David Blunkett's **12–036** Resignation" (2005) P.L. 229

Blake, R. *The Office of the Prime Minister* (OUP, 1975)

Brazier, R. "The Monarchy" in Bogdanor, V. (ed.) *The British Constitution in the Twentieth Century* (OUP, 2003)

Hennessy, P. *The Prime Minister: The Job and Its Holders Since 1945* (Penguin, 2001)

Hough, B. "Ministerial responses to parliamentary questions: some recent concerns" (2003) P.L. 211

Scott, R. "Ministerial Accountability" (1996) P.L. 410

Chapter 13

ROYAL PREROGATIVE

INTRODUCTION

In the United Kingdom, power comes largely from statute. However, there remain **13–001** certain common law powers of the Crown, which have the umbrella title the royal prerogative. The word "royal" is slightly misleading, it being a relic of the days when Executive power was exercised by the monarch. Though certain powers remain personal to the monarch, such as the power to appoint the Prime Minister and the power to grant personal honours such as the Order of the Garter, many other powers, though formally vested in the monarch, are exercised on their behalf by Ministers of the Crown. Prerogative powers are exercised either directly by Ministers or by Prerogative Orders in Council. The latter require a formal meeting of the Privy Council in the presence of the monarch.

Prerogative powers represent one of the most fundamentally significant areas of constitutional law, not least because of their definitional difficulties. However, the most controversial aspect remains controlling their use.

DEFINITION

There is little academic and judicial consensus as to the precise definition of prerogative **13–002** powers. Two principal definitions exist, those of Blackstone and Dicey. Blackstone writing in his *Commentaries on the Laws of England* (London: University of Chicago Press, 1979) understood the prerogative as:

> "That special pre-eminence which the king hath, over and above all other persons . . . It must be in its nature singular and eccentrical; that it can only be applied to

those rights and capacities which the King enjoys alone ... and not to those which he enjoys in common with any of his subjects."

Central to Blackstone's definition is its limiting of prerogative power to those powers unique to the Crown. Thus, the power to declare war would be an exercise of the prerogative in the sense advocated by Blackstone. As such, therefore, Blackstone's definition is narrow and does not cover, for example, the creation of an ex gratia compensation scheme such as that recognised in *R. v Criminal Injuries Compensation Scheme Ex p. Lain* [1967] 2 Q.B. 864. For advocates of Blackstone, the Scheme was created by a "third source" of power which arises from the Executive's status as a corporation sole. This "third source" received judicial recognition in *R. (on the application of Hooper) v Secretary of State for Work and Pensions* [2003] EWCA Civ 875 and *R. v Secretary of State for Health Ex p. C* [2000] HRLR 400. In *Ex p. C*, the Court of Appeal upheld the validity of the Department of Health's power to compile a non-statutory list of those suitable to work with children. In doing so, it stated there was no suggestion of any specific prerogative power authorising the action.

In contrast to Blackstone's definition, modern formulations of the prerogative are wider, including all forms of Executive action not derived from statute. Dicey in *An Introduction to the Study of the Law of the Constitution* (10th edn (London: Macmillan, 1959)), for example, described the prerogative as, "the residue of discretionary or arbitrary authority which at any given time is legally left in the hands of the Crown". Under Dicey's definition, the creation of the compensation scheme in *Ex p. Lain* was an exercise of the prerogative. However, Dicey's definition is criticised for being descriptive and overly broad, failing to distinguish between power unique to the Crown and that which is not (see H.W.R. Wade "Procedure and Prerogative in Public Law" (1985) 101 L.Q.R. 180.

Judicial use of these definitions is inconsistent, and although Blackstone's definition has been used by the judiciary, Dicey's has found favour as being broader, thus more inclusive, removing the requirement to identify and define a third source of power.

CATEGORIES OF PREROGATIVE

13–003   The Select Committee on Public Administration, 4th Report (*Taming the Prerogative: Strengthening Ministerial Accountability to Parliament* 4th Report of the Public Administration Select Committee, 2003–04, HC 422, March 2004), identified three broad groups of prerogative power: the monarch's constitutional prerogatives, legal prerogatives of the Crown, and Executive prerogatives.

1. Monarch's constitutional prerogatives

These are the personal powers of the monarch though, as a constitutional monarch, the **13–004** Queen accepts advice over their exercise. These powers include the right to advise, encourage and warn Ministers in private (discussed in Ch.12), the right to appoint the Prime Minister and other Ministers, and the right to assent to legislation and prorogue or dissolve Parliament. They are largely governed by convention and raise few constitutional issues relating to their exercise in practice.

(a)   *Appointment of Prime Minister and other Ministers*

According to constitutional theory the Queen has the right to appoint the Prime **13–005** Minister (see Jennings, *The Law and the Constitution* (5th edn (London: University of London Press, 1959). However, this has been diminished by the Life Peerages Act 1958, the House of Lords Act 1999, by convention and other practical rules. By convention, the Queen must appoint the leader who can command a majority in the House of Commons. Generally this is the Leader of the main political party. Problems can arise where, for example, no party has a majority—a "hung" Parliament—or where the current Prime Minister resigns on grounds of ill health or for other reasons (such was the case for Ramsey Macdonald 1935, Winston Churchill 1955, Anthony Eden, Stanley Baldwin 1937, Harold Wilson 1976 and Margaret Thatcher 1990). In these situations there is uncertainty over the course of action the Queen should take.

In 1974 the Conservative Party lost the general election by a small margin. The then Prime Minister, Edward Heath, did not immediately resign as per convention but entered into negotiations with the Liberal party over forming an alliance. Negotiations were unsuccessful and Heath eventually resigned and the Queen invited the Leader of the Labour Party, Harold Wilson, to become Prime Minister. The situation raised the issue of whether Heath had acted constitutionally in not resigning immediately, and illustrated the ambiguity over the role of the Queen—what should she do in those circumstances?

In cases of resignation, the government may still retain the mandate of the people and a general election is often not immediately called. Instead, the party will choose the new Prime Minister according to their party rules; the Queen has little practical say. On occasions there may not be an obvious choice such as in 1957 following the resignation of Anthony Eden. Following the resignation, the Queen consulted Conservative party elders and appointed Harold Macmillan. Although the situation appeared to have been easily resolved, it raised questions such as whether the Queen might have chosen her own Prime Minister on receipt of impartial advice. Since the 1957 problem, the parties have selection procedures to remove any discretion from the Queen. For example, in 1990 following the resignation of Margaret Thatcher as Prime Minister, the Conservative party elected John Major as their new leader and he was duly appointed as Prime Minister by the Queen under prerogative.

(b)   *Royal Assent*

13–006   The Queen, as part of Parliament, has an important role in assenting to legislation. Today, this is also governed by convention and it is difficult to envisage the Queen refusing her assent. The last time Royal Assent was officially refused was in 1704 by Queen Anne, though George V was encouraged to veto the Ireland Home Rule Bill and believed he had that power. On George V's situation, Jennings in *Law of the Constitution* (1959 at p.400) commentated: "It was assumed by the King throughout that he had not only the legal power but the constitutional right to refuse assent." Jennings recognised, however, the constitutional difficulties if a monarch were to refuse assent stating that, " . . . this exercise of the power would involve the resignation of Ministers, a dissolution of Parliament and a general election in which the main issue would be the prerogatives of the Crown". Despite the inevitable constitutional difficulties, academics have maintained that a situation could be envisaged when it would be an acceptable use of the prerogative (see for example, Blackburn, "Monarchy and the Personal Prerogatives" (2004) P.L. 546).

(c)   *Prorogue or dissolution of Parliament*

13–007   The Queen retains the right to prorogue, i.e. summon or dissolve Parliament. However, by convention this right is exercised on the advice of the Prime Minister. The last time Parliament was dissolved on the monarch's own initiative was in 1835 by William IV where the King misjudged the situation believing there to be strong public opinion against the government. Since that time, it has been suggested that it would be "unconstitutional" for the monarch to act on their own (see for example Jennings). Bagehot in *The English Constitution* (1867, reprinted OUP, 2001) believed the power "had almost, if not quite, dropped out of the reality of our constitution". Dicey, however, disagreed. He believed the Crown retained the right, in extreme circumstances, such as where the opinion of the House was not the opinion of the electors. Credence is given to this view by the fact that Queen Victoria believed she retained the right to dissolve without the advice of her Ministers. In legal theoretical terms, Dicey's view is correct, although it hard to imagine an occasion when this would happen. If such a situation did occur, a severe constitutional crisis would undoubtedly ensue.

Likewise, a constitutional crisis could arise in a situation where the Prime Minister does not request a dissolution of Parliament and the Queen has to make a decision. For example, a party forms an alliance with another to obtain a majority in Parliament. The alliance breaks down and the two opposition parties then form an alliance. The Prime Minister is in the minority yet refuses to step down. The Queen would be faced with two constitutional principles; that dissolution is a matter for the Prime Minister, yet the Prime Minister should be appointed from the majority party.

2.   Legal prerogatives of the Crown

This category contains certain quaint, historical prerogatives such as the monarch's   **13–008**
right to Sturgeon, certain swans and whales. However, others under this heading are
more fundamental.

The administration of justice was traditionally the prerogative of the monarch who as
the "fountain of justice" could do no wrong. Today it is expressed as Crown immunity.
Such immunity has been limited by the Crown Proceedings Act 1947, and though the
monarch's personal immunity is preserved, the courts have been able to impose limitations regarding the scope of immunity on the Executive. In *Re M* [1994] 1 A.C. 377,
the House of Lords held that the Home Secretary could be found in contempt of court
despite the Crown Proceedings Act 1947 s.21(2). This was achieved by splitting the
Crown into two separate personalities: personal and official. The first was immune, but
the second accountable through the courts for their actions.

Another prerogative having modern significance is the principle that the Crown is not
bound by statute except by express words, for example Land Registration Act 2002
s.129, or necessary implication. The test for displacing immunity is strict. In *Lord
Advocate v Dumbarton District Council* [1989] 2 A.C. 580, the Ministry of Defence
wanted to build new security fences along the perimeter of it submarine base. In order
to do this, they needed to place temporary works on a public road. Normally, in order
to do this, permission was required pursuant to the Roads (Scotland) Act 1984.
However, the Ministry claimed they were not bound by the statute. Lord Keith (at
p.604) in the House of Lords agreed with the Ministry stating that, "the Crown is not
bound by any statutory provision unless there can somehow be gathered from the terms
of the relevant Act an intention to that effect."

This decision can be contrasted with the Australian case of *Bropho v State of Western
Australia* [1990] 64 A.I.J.R. 374 in which the High Court of Australia departed from
their previous strict approach and indicated that the principle should be re-evaluated.
Brennan J. suggested the presumption of immunity should be reformulated so the
Crown is bound by statute unless a contrary intention can be discerned from all the
relevant circumstances.

The logic of the High Court's approach can be easily understood and should be
applied in the United Kingdom. It is right that in a country based on the rule of law the
Crown should be legally responsible for it actions. The decision in *Re M* [1994] 1 A.C.
377 perhaps assists in a movement towards greater accountability of the Crown. Whilst
maintaining the immunity of the monarch, the Executive, acting in its official capacity,
should be bound by statute unless Parliament makes it clear otherwise. Despite the *Re
M* decision though the position relating to Crown immunity is by no means clear.

3.   Executive prerogatives

These powers are the most constitutionally controversial, having a significant impact   **13–009**
upon the State and individual citizens.

These include the power to:

(a)   make and ratify treaties;

(b)   conduct diplomacy;

(c)   govern British Overseas territories;

(d)   deploy and use the armed forces overseas, or within the UK to maintain the peace in support of the police, for example, a decision to go to war is not taken by Parliament but by the government of the day;

(e)   appoint and remove Ministers, recommend peerages, honours and powers of patronage. These powers are vested in the Prime Minister;

(f)   recommend honours by the FCO and Defence Secretary;

(g)   organise the civil service;

(h)   grant and revoke passports;

(i)   grant pardons. Within this is the Attorney-General's power to discontinue any criminal proceedings on indictment (*nolle prosequi*). This is a useful power which allows the Crown to grant immunity from criminal prosecution in return for information.

CONTROL OF THE PREROGATIVE

13–010   The United Kingdom's partly codified and partly uncodified constitution (see Ch.1) rests upon the principle of constitutionalism incorporating the rule of law. One difficulty with our constitutional make-up is ensuring this principle is upheld and government is accountable for its actions. This problem is especially acute with prerogative powers relating to the Executive as their ambiguous definitions and scope make the task of regulation and constraint, both by Parliament and the Judiciary, no easier.

1.   Political control

13–011   Political control of the prerogative through Parliament is fairly weak and largely ineffective. Although Parliament does not expressly deliberate upon and confer authority for Executive action taken under the prerogative, it can still scrutinise such actions. This scrutiny takes places in both chambers of the House, and through various Select Committees, such as the Public Administration Select Committee. In recent years concern over Parliament's control over use of the prerogative has heightened. In particular, control over use of the Executive prerogatives and the power to declare war and deploy troops following the deployment of troops to Iraq. In 2006, the House of Lords Select Committee on the Constitution (15th Report of Session 2005–06, *Waging War: Parliament's role and Responsibility*, HL Paper 236–I (2006)) reported on the government's powers under prerogative to declare war and deploy armed forces. In its conclusion they stated:

"the exercise of the Royal Prerogative by the government to deploy armed forces overseas is outdated and should not be allowed to continue as the basis for legitimate war-making in our 21st century democracy. Parliament's ability to challenge the Executive must be protected and strengthened." (at para.103)

Alternative mechanisms of control exist, such as Parliament's traditional means of accountability through a motion of no-confidence and the doctrine of ministerial responsibility. Further safeguards such as conventions and non-legal rules have also been adopted. A good example is the Ponsonby rule requiring that Treaties be laid before Parliament for ratification. Similarly, any Treaty purporting to alter national law requires the express approval of Parliament by the passing of a statute. For example, the Treaty of Rome was given effect in English Law by the European Communities Act 1972. However, in reality, little parliamentary time is given over to the debate and scrutiny of Treaties. An example of a convention possibly developing is in relation to the prerogative to commit troops abroad or declare war. Following the government's decision to commit troops to war in Iraq, the Prime Minister allowed a vote in Parliament on the issue. This has led to discussion as to whether this is the start of a constitutional convention that Parliamentary approval will always be sought. One thing to remember however is that conventions are not legally enforceable; whilst the Prime Minister could have ignored an adverse vote and gone ahead with the deployment, this would have raised issues about the constitutionality of such action.

(a)   *Statute and prerogative*

Parliament's primary control over the prerogative is its power to expressly or impliedly amend or circumscribe it by passing a statute regulating the area. In *De Morgan v Director-General of Social Welfare* [1998] A.C. 275, Lord Browne Wilkinson recognised that express words were not required to limit or abolish the prerogative; it was enough if the statute excluded the prerogative by "necessary intendment". Here the Court found that the right of appeal to the Privy Council was limited by the Judicial Committee Acts 1833 and 1844. Where a statute covers the prerogative, the prerogative falls into abeyance and cannot be used contrary to the statute. If the statute is repealed the prerogative may be revived. A more modern example of statute replacing prerogative is control of the intelligences services. Prior to the Security Services Act 1989, regulation, control and operation of the intelligence services was solely an exercise of prerogative.

13–012

(i)   The De Keyser principle

Where a statute does not expressly restrict or suspend a prerogative, the matter is more complicated. The leading authority on the matter is *De Keyser's Royal Hotel Ltd, Re* [1920] A.C. 508. In this case, the government requisitioned a hotel during the First World War by power conferred by the Defence of the Realm Regulations. In a claim for compensation by the owners, the Army Council argued they had used the prerogative and, as such, there was no right to compensation.

13–013

The House of Lords held that the Regulations took precedence over the prerogative and should have been observed by the Crown. Lord Atkinson gave the leading opinion. He reasoned that if the prerogative did exist, the Crown could not choose whether to act under that power or under the statute. The rationale was that by granting the statutory power, Parliament was presumed to have intended that power to be the one used; the government could not pick and choose as it suited.

The *De Keysers* principle, as it is known, was considered in *Laker Airways v Department of Trade* [1977] Q.B. 643. This case concerned the regulation of transatlantic air routes. In order to operate on the route, an airline had to fulfil two conditions. First, it had to become a designated carrier under the Bermuda Agreement 1946 (created by prerogative) and secondly, obtain a licence from the Civil Aviation Authority, a body created by the Civil Aviation Act 1971. By s.3(1) of the Civil Aviation Act 1971, the CAA was empowered to award licences according to certain criteria. These included whether the carrier promoted low fares, high safety standards and competition on major routes. Section 3(2) provided that the Secretary of State could give guidance to the CAA concerning the operation of its licensing function. Laker Airways received a licence but were awaiting approval from the United States regarding its "designation" under the Treaty. During this time, the Secretary of State announced a new policy granting British Airways a monopoly on the transatlantic route and issued guidance to the CAA to cancel Laker Airways designation and licence.

Though the case largely turned on whether the Secretary of State's guidance to the CAA was ultra vires (beyond the power of the Secretary of State), it was also argued that the Secretary of State had the power under prerogative, insofar as the Treaty was concerned, to withdraw the designation. It was held by the Court of Appeal that although the Secretary of State was entitled to give guidance, this meant the ability to supplement, explain or amplify policy and not to reverse or contradict it. The effect of the Secretary of State's guidance would have been to reduce competition and increase prices which was not the objective of the CAA and was therefore ultra vires the power.

Unlike *De Keysers*, here the prerogative and statute were intertwined. The statute was not intended to replace the prerogative but to work with it. Lord Denning M.R. concluded that as the power to revoke the licence was provided by statute, the Secretary of State could only use the prerogative in accordance with the statute. In doing what they had, the government was using its prerogative powers to frustrate a statutory objective. If the government wanted to pursue objectives which were contrary to the Act, they would have to persuade Parliament to enact new legislation.

(ii) Expansion of the De Keyser principle

13–014 In *R. v Secretary of State for the Home Department Ex p. Fire Brigades Union* [1995] 2 A.C. 513, the House of Lords were asked to consider ss.108–117 of the Criminal Justice Act 1988. Sections 108–117 gave a statutory footing to the Criminal Injuries Compensation Scheme. As is common with a number of statutes, it contained a commencement clause which provided that the Secretary of State could bring those sections into force "on such day as he may appoint". The scheme was never brought into effect. In 1993 the government deemed the scheme too expensive and sought to introduce an alternative scheme using prerogative powers. The decision was challenged on a number of grounds, including whether the statutory scheme, though not in force, limited the prerogative power.

The Court of Appeal, on a similar line of reasoning to the Court in Laker Airways held that the prerogative could not be used to frustrate the intention of Parliament. If the Secretary of State wished to amend the scheme, he would need the approval of Parliament. The House of Lords adopted a more reticent approach. In a 3–2 split, their Lordships concluded that although the scheme did not have statutory force or create enforceable rights, it did represent Parliament's intention. The Secretary of State had the power to delay its commencement (although could not fetter his discretion by never considering commencement), but could not bypass the statute entirely using the prerogative. The decision therefore represents an extension of *De Keysers* to those statutes not in force.

(iii)   Retreat from the De Keyser principle?

A more controversial decision in this area is *R. v Secretary of State for Home Department Ex p. Northumbria Police Authority* [1989] Q.B. 26. As was the case with *De Keysers* and *Laker*, the statute, the Police Act 1964, did not expressly cover the prerogative. The background and facts of *Ex p. Northumbria* are complex, though put simply, s.4 of the 1964 Act granted power to the police authority to maintain equipment for the provision of police purposes in their area. Power was also granted to the Home Secretary to provide and maintain provisions if he considered it necessary or expedient.   **13–015**

The Home Secretary announced he would be issuing plastic baton rounds and CS gas canisters to police forces irrespective of approval by any police authority. Northumbria Police Authority challenged the legality of the Home Secretary's action. The Home Secretary argued that irrespective of the statute, he had the prerogative power to issue batons.

The Court of Appeal, in an obiter statement, concluded that the Home Secretary had authority, under prerogative to keep the peace, and that since the statute did not expressly or unequivocally prohibit use of the prerogative, the Home Secretary could provide batons. The court further reasoned that it could not have been Parliament's intention to put the prerogative into abeyance where it was being exercised for the protection of the public, rather than in *De Keysers* where it was used to deny individuals protection given by statute.

The decision is controversial for two reasons. First, the court found a prerogative which had not previously existed, namely the prerogative to keep the peace. This, it reasoned, was a sister prerogative of defence of the realm. Nourse L.J. (at p.58) summed up stating that, "the scarcity of reference in the books to the prerogative of keeping the peace within the realm does not disprove it exists. Rather it may point to an unspoken assumption that it does". This reasoning seems hard to reconcile with the rule of law and appears contrary to *Entick v Carrington* (1765) 19 St. Tr. 1029 and Lord Camden's view that if a lawful exercise of power existed it would be found in the books. However, there is no doubt that the flexibility and lack of precise definition inherent in prerogative powers assisted the court in *Ex p. Northumbria*. Thus, it might be concluded that there is a fine line between creating a new prerogative and updating an old one.

Secondly, the court assumed that using CS gas and plastic batons was for the benefit of the public, though presumably not for those on the receiving end. The court concluded that s.4 did not expressly grant a monopoly but rather created a situation where they coexisted. Unlike *Laker*, the coexistence appeared to be contradictory.

2.   Prerogative and the courts

(a)   *Existence and extent*

13–016   In relation to the existence and extent of prerogative powers, the courts imposed some limitations. In the *Case of Proclamation* (1611) 12 Co. Rep. 74, the court concluded that even though absolute in one sense, the prerogative was still limited by law; the monarch only had prerogatives which the law of the land allowed. In *BBC v Johns* [1965] Ch. 32, Diplock L.J. (at p.79) made it clear that, "it [was] 350 years and a civil war too late for the Queen's courts to broaden the prerogative". Thus, the courts have demonstrated a willingness to keep the exercise of prerogative power under review to ensure its use is lawful. In *Entick v Carrington* (1765) 19 St. Tr. 1029, the court concluded that the warrant issued by the Home Secretary did not have any legal basis in prerogative and so constituted an unlawful interference with Mr Entick's property.

Although, these decisions seem fairly certain, a lack of clarity over definition means there is considerable flexibility in determining the exact scope of the prerogative. It can allow for the creation of "new" prerogatives (though formally an "ancient" prerogative) such as that found in the *Northumbria* decision.

(b)   *Exercise of the prerogative*

13–017   Despite the robust approach of the court in *Entick*, judicial scrutiny of the exercise and operation of the prerogative was slow and piecemeal. There was some early judicial movement towards extending the power of judicial review to the prerogative, most notably by Lord Devlin in *Chandler v DPP* [1964] A.C. 763. That case suggested courts should be able to intervene to correct excesses or abuse of prerogative power. Further, Lord Denning M.R. in *Laker Airways* (at p.705) also saw no reason, in principle, why the prerogative could not be the subject of judicial review considering it was a discretionary power, "to be exercised for the public good". These views, though obiter and not representing the majority view in the cases where expressed, could be said to have influenced the seminal decision of *Council for Civil Service Unions (CCSU) v Minister for the Civil Service* [1985] A.C. 374, the *GCHQ* case.

The *GCHQ* case represents the starting point for any analysis of the courts' present approach to judicial review of the prerogative. Under art.4 of the Civil Service Order in Council 1982 (made under prerogative), the Minister for the Civil Service had the power to issue instructions relating to the employment terms of the Civil Service. As a result of strike action throughout the United Kingdom, the Minister, using the Civil Service Order power, prohibited members of GCHQ (Government Communication

Headquarters) from membership of any trades union. Where changes to employment conditions were considered previously, consultation was always undertaken. However, on this occasion no such consultation was observed. The Minister, in taking this decision, was fearful strike action would spread, disrupting intelligence work undertaken at GCHQ. The CCSU brought an action seeking a declaration that the instruction was unlawful due to lack of consultation.

In coming to their decision, the House of Lords removed any doubts as to the jurisdiction of the court to scrutinise the exercise of prerogative power. Their Lordships concluded that the power in question was, in principle, subject to judicial review. The past practice of consultation had created a legitimate expectation that employees would be consulted prior to a change in their working practice. However, this expectation could be frustrated by national security concerns. Despite coming to the same conclusion, their Lordships differed in their reasoning.

Lords Fraser and Brightman adopted a slightly more restrictive approach to judicial review of the prerogative. They stated that since the decision was taken under power of Order in Council, which was akin to delegated legislation, the decision could be subject to review. On the other hand, Lords Diplock, Roskill and Scarman dealt specifically with the question of judicial review of the direct prerogative. They concluded that the mere fact that the power being exercised was a prerogative power did not mean it could not be reviewed.

The decision in *GCHQ* signalled a more robust approach by the courts towards judicial review of the exercise of prerogative power. The main focus of the case moved away from the source of prerogative as being determinative of reviewability and instead the House adopted alternative criteria for reviewability. Lords Roskill, Scarman and Diplock emphasised to some degree the suitability of the subject-matter of the decision for judicial review. Lord Roskill, rather than defining any such criteria proceeded by way of exclusion, giving a non-exhaustive list of those he deemed unsuitable for review. These included the prerogative of mercy, defence of the realm, making of Treaties, granting of honours, dissolution of Parliament and appointment of Ministers.

> " ... I do not think that that right of challenge can be unqualified. It must, I think, depend upon the subject matter of the prerogative power which is exercised ... Prerogative powers such as those relating to the making of treaties, the defence of the realm, the prerogative of mercy, the grant of honours, the dissolution of Parliament and the appointment of Ministers as well as others are not, I think, susceptible to judicial review because their nature and subject matter are such as not to be amenable to the judicial process. The courts are not the place wherein to determine whether a Treaty should be concluded or the armed forces disposed in a particular manner or Parliament dissolved on one date rather than another." (at p.418)

Although not immediately apparent from the list, the defining issue seems that they are largely political exercises of power for which Parliamentary scrutiny is more appropriate or questions of policy for which the judicial process is not suitable (questions of separation of powers). The prerogative of mercy perhaps stands out as being the odd one as it involves individual rights and consideration of issues suitable for judicial scrutiny. However, aspects of this prerogative do have a heavy political/policy content and as a result warranted inclusion on Lord Roskill's list.

(c)   *Beyond GCHQ*

13–018   Since *GCHQ*, the courts have developed the scope of judicial review of the exercise of prerogative powers into those supposedly "non-justiciable" areas identified by Lord Roskill. A number of cases will be considered below and what can be seen from is if the subject-matter concerns the rights of individuals or raises a legitimate expectation the matter is more likely to be justiciable. Those cases which concern high policy are likely still to be non-justiciable.

(i)   Mercy

13–019   In *R. v Secretary of State for the Home Department Ex p. Bentley* [1993] 4 All E.R. 442, the Divisional Court considered a judicial review application by the sister of Derek Bentley. Bentley, who had a mental age of 11, was convicted of the murder of a policeman and hanged in 1953. The Secretary of State decided not to exercise the prerogative of mercy on the basis that it was settled policy to grant a full pardon only if the person concerned was "morally and technically innocent" and this had not been established. The Divisional Court held Lord Roskill's "non-justiciable" list to be obiter and stated that the exercise of the prerogative of mercy was open to judicial review. Watkins L.J., giving the judgment of the court, accepted that the criteria whereby someone could be granted a posthumous pardon were entirely a matter of policy and so non-justiciable. However, the circumstances surrounding the nature of the prerogative were held to be justiciable. The court held that the Home Secretary had made an error of law by failing to consider that the prerogative of mercy was capable of being exercised in many forms. The court made no order given the circumstances of the case, but did invite the Home Secretary to reconsider the matter.

The court's approach in *Bentley* in respect of the reviewability of the prerogative of mercy was adopted in *R. (B) v Secretary of State for the Home Department* (2002) EWHC 587 (Admin). The claimant, a serving prisoner, had provided the police with valuable assistance post-sentence. The Secretary of State awarded the claimant three years' remission from his sentence. The claimant sought judicial review of this decision arguing that the Home Secretary had left out a relevant consideration when making his decision. The court held that the exercise of the prerogative of mercy, by granting remission, was not immune from judicial scrutiny as the courts were well qualified to deal with matters relating to sentencing and appropriate reductions in sentence.

(ii) Foreign affairs

In decisions in 1989 and 2003, the courts, far from declining jurisdiction solely on a **13–020**
general principle that the subject-matter was non-justiciable, considered the suitability
of the facts themselves to judicial process.

In the first of these cases, *R. v Secretary of State for Foreign and Commonwealth
Affairs Ex p. Everett* [1989] Q.B. 811, the Court of Appeal held that the grant of a
passport (under prerogative) did not fall under the scope of "high policy". It was an
administrative action affecting the rights of individuals and their freedom to travel and
was, thus, reviewable. The second, *R. (Abbasi) v Secretary of State for Foreign and
Commonwealth Affairs* (2002) EWCA Civ 1598, represents a bold step taken by the
Courts to the question of justiciability in this area. Feroz Abbasi was a British national
captured and detained by the United States in Guantanamo Bay. The claimants
(Abbasi and his mother) sought an order, by way of judicial review, to compel the
Foreign Office to make diplomatic representations to the United States Government.
The government argued that the court did not have jurisdiction in the matter, as
diplomatic representations were matters falling within the foreign affairs prerogative of
the Crown, a non-justiciable area. Although, the court ultimately rejected Mr Abbasi's
claim, they did not do so on the basis that the subject-matter of foreign affairs was non-
justiciable. The Court of Appeal (at para.106) stated: "It is not an answer to a claim for
judicial review to say that the source of the power of the Foreign Office is the prerogative. It is the subject matter that is determinative". The court re-emphasised the
importance of judicial abstention from the conduct of foreign policy itself calling it a
"forbidden area" yet recognised that Abbasi had a legitimate expectation in respect of
diplomatic assistance, a factor which was suitable for judicial review as it did not
impinge on the "forbidden area". In assessing this legitimate expectation, the court
examined the government's policy of offering diplomatic assistance concluding that
Abbasi had a legitimate expectation that the Foreign Office would consider rendering
diplomatic assistance. In summary, they stated that the legitimate expectation was
limited (to consider only) and the Secretary of State enjoyed a wide discretion in
relation to the exercise of his prerogative power of diplomatic assistance. There was
evidence before the court that the Foreign & Commonwealth Office had considered
Abbasi's request for assistance and that British detainees were the subject of discussions
between the UK and US. In the circumstances, the court found there was no evidence
that the Secretary of State had acted unreasonably. Though the court's finding was, in
some respects, limited, the reason given for rejecting Abbasi's claim indicates that, on
different facts, the decision could go the other way.

In *R. (on the application of Al Rawi) v Secretary of State for Foreign and Commonwealth Affairs* [2006] EWCA Civ 1279 a similar question arose. This case concerned
three detainees at Guantanamo Bay who, although British residents, were, unlike
Abbasi, not British nationals. They also sought an order to compel the Foreign Office
to make a formal request for their release. The Court of Appeal concluded that the
appellants had no legitimate expectation as they were not British nationals and refused
to extend their review into the so-called "forbidden areas" of foreign policy.

Litigation relating to the forced exile of inhabitants from the Chagos Islands has also
raised questions about justiciability of the prerogative; in this case the prerogative of
colonial governance. The Chagos Islands in the Indian Ocean were ceded to Britain

from France and now forms part of the British Indian Ocean Territory (BIOT). In the late 1960s and early 1970s, under prerogative, the British government compulsorily removed all the inhabitants to allow construction of an American air-base on the principal island, Diego Garcia. The base is recognised as being of strategic importance for defence and security responsibilities in the Arabian Gulf, the Middle East, South Asia and East Africa, and has been used in many operations in the gulf area.

In the first case in 2000 (*Bancoult (No.1)* [2001] Q.B. 1067), the High Court quashed the 1971 order which authorised the removal of the islanders, on the ground of illegality. The government subsequently accepted the court's decision and indicated the Islanders would be able to return. A feasibility study (completed in June 2002) was commissioned to look at repatriating the islanders to the outer islands (islanders could not be repatriated to Diego Garcia for military and Treaty obligation reasons). It concluded that resettlement would be difficult, precarious and costly, mentioning floods, earthquakes and global warming as possible hazards. As a result, on June 10, 2004 the British Indian Ocean Territory (Constitution) Order 2004 made under prerogative of colonial governance was passed. This declared that no person has the right of abode in BIOT nor the right without authorisation to enter and remain there. In effect, the order overruled the High Court's earlier decision and exiled the islanders again. It became clear that no permit would be granted to allow the exiled Islanders to resume living in any of the islands. In *R. (Bancoult) v Secretary of State for Foreign and Commonwealth Affairs (No.2)* [2007] EWCA Civ 498 a challenge was made to the validity of the order. Counsel for the Foreign Office argued that because of its subject-matter, the prerogative of colonial governance was outside the ambit of judicial review.

The Court of Appeal made some interesting comments regarding the justiciability of the prerogative in this area, and it is worthwhile considering most of the relevant paragraph:

"It can be observed without disrespect, particularly since Lord Roskill (in *GCHQ*) was careful to express himself tentatively, that a number of his examples could today be regarded as questionable: the grant of honours for reward, the waging of a war of manifest aggression, or a refusal to dissolve Parliament at all, might well call in question an immunity based purely on subject matter. By the same token, one can readily accept that the colonial use of the prerogative power is for the most part beyond the reach of judicial review, but not that it is always or necessarily so. As we shall see, considerable latitude is given to the Executive in deciding what makes for the peace, order and good government of a colony ... even if its subject matter is incontestably the peace, order and good government of the colony, it is capable of being rendered invalid by jurisdictional error or malpractice ... In the second place, it must also be open to challenge if its subject matter, on examination, is manifestly not the peace, order and good government of the colony ... For these reasons I would hold that the use of the prerogative power of colonial governance enjoys no generic immunity from judicial review." (at 46–47)

What can be seen from the above is the Court of Appeal following the line it has taken in dealing with the exercise of the prerogative in national security and foreign affairs. The prerogative of colonial governance did not enjoy a general immunity from review.

Whilst use of the prerogative confers significant discretion on the Executive, it was not unfettered and was reviewable for abuse of power. On the facts, the government had created a legitimate expectation that the Islanders would be able to return home (an enforceable promise; see Ch.18) and it was an abuse of power to go back on this promise without the government providing any compelling justification for their change of mind. As a result, the 2004 Orders were quashed by the court.

(iii)   Treaties

In *R. v Secretary of State for Foreign Affairs Ex p. Rees-Mogg* [1994] Q.B. 552 Lord   **13–021**
Rees-Mogg, a member of the House of Lords interested in constitutional issues, sought a declaration that the UK could not lawfully ratify the Maastricht Treaty. He had three arguments, but it is the third that has some relevance for the prerogative. Lord Rees-Mogg argued that Title V on the Treaty of European Union which established a common foreign and security policy amounted to the transfer by the Crown of its prerogative powers in this area. Lord Rees-Mogg contended that the Crown was not authorised at common law to transfer its prerogative powers to other persons or bodies without the authority of Parliament. In a brief consideration of the issue of justiciability, the court was prepared to assume the Treaty-making prerogative would be justiciable if the issue was whether the Treaty contravened any statute or rule of common law (affirming a similar point made in *Ex p. Molyneaux* [1986] 1 W.L.R. 331). However, the court concluded that Title V did not entail an abandonment or transfer of prerogative power but was an exercise of those powers.

   The case provides little support for the contention that the treaty-making prerogative is justiciable aside from an issue involving conflict between the Treaty and domestic law. It is very likely, that a challenge to a Treaty outside of such an issue would fail on grounds of justiciability.

(iv)   Defence of the Realm and national security

Defence of the Realm is one of the most controversial of the prerogative powers. On   **13–022**
questions of defence and national security, the courts have always been quick to defer to Executive judgment and it was not surprising that they were included on Lord Roskill's non-justiciable list. The benefits of the prerogative in this area cannot be underestimated as they offer much needed flexibility to the government, especially in times of emergency. However, it is in such times that arbitrary exercise can become most apparent. In recent years, the courts, as with foreign affairs, have expanded their reach over control of the prerogative in this area. Jurisdiction is not declined solely because the subject-matter is defence, rather the courts consider the suitability of the facts to judicial process. A number of cases illustrate this fact.

   R. v Ministry of Defence Ex p. Smith [1996] Q.B. 517 concerned a challenge to the rationality of a policy which prohibited homosexual's from service in the armed forces. The operation of this rule was an exercise of prerogative power. Simon Brown L.J. in the High Court (*R. v Ministry of Defence Ex p. Smith* [1995] 4 All E.R. 427) had no hesitation in holding the challenge to the policy to be justiciable on the basis that it did not fall into the category of "national security" which would otherwise prohibit review of its exercise. In Brown L.J.'s view, "only the rarest cases" would "be ruled strictly beyond the court's purview ... only cases involving national security properly so called and where in addition the courts really do lack the expertise or material to form a judgment on the point at issue" (at p.539). He further stated that though it touched upon defence of the realm, it did not involve questions about whether the armed forces should be deployed in a particular manner. The Court of Appeal did not take such a robust view, although agreed in principle with the High Court decision. The Court of Appeal concluded the policy was rational under the principles of judicial review, but the mere fact they reviewed the decision at all can be considered a step forward in expanding the scope of justiciability of the prerogative (note: the ban is no longer applied since the decision of the ECtHR in *Smith and Grady v UK* (2000) 29 E.H.R.R. 493, where the court held that the ban violated art.8 of the ECHR).

In two cases concerning the war in Iraq (2003–present), the High Court clearly stated that decisions involving "defence of the realm" in the sense of declaring war or deploying armed forces are exclusively within the ambit of the Executive and non-justiciable. The consequences of the Executive action have to be judged politically rather than legally by the courts. In *R. (on the application of Campaign for Nuclear Disarmament) v Prime Minister of the UK* [2002] EWHC 2712 (Admin), CND sought a declaration that Resolution 1441 did not authorise military action against Iraq. Simon Brown L.J. stated that it was "accept(ed) that the decision to take military action is beyond the court's purview". More recently, in *R. (on the application of Gentle) v Prime Minister* [2006] EWCA Civ 1689, the claimants applied for judicial review of the government's refusal to hold an independent inquiry into the deaths of soldiers. The claimants argued that refusal was in breach of ECHR art.2 (right to life), both substantively and procedurally. Substantively, because by sending members of the armed forces to take part in the invasion of Iraq without taking reasonable steps to satisfy itself the invasion was lawful as a matter of public international law violated art.2, and because of this, a procedural obligation was imposed to investigate the deaths. The Court of Appeal noted that all parties agreed that if the art.2 issue was removed, the question of whether the UK had acted lawfully in sending its armed forces to Iraq was non-justiciable since it would involve consideration of international instruments and decisions of policy made in areas of foreign affairs and defence. However, the principle of non-justiciability cannot prevent the courts from giving effect to a Convention right once such a right is engaged (see Lords Bingham and Hoffman in *R. v Jones* [2007] 1 A.C. 136). The application was rejected by the Court of Appeal as they reached the conclusion that art.2 was not engaged as it did not impose such an obligation on the state (at para.42). (Note, at the time of writing a nine-strong Appellate Committee of the House of Lords handed down its decision affirming the conclusions reached by the Court of Appeal on the art.2 point (*R. (on the application of Gentle) v the Prime Minister* [2008] UKHL 20).)

The war prerogative is perhaps one of the most controversial of the prerogatives and came to prominence with the decision to go to war in Iraq. The cases above show the courts are more willing to declare an issue of foreign affairs or defence justiciable where it raises individual rights or the ECHR. However, they also clearly demonstrate the court's unwillingness, rightly, to become involved in matters of high policy such as a declaration of war. The "war" prerogative is currently under consultation for reform and it may be the case that eventually a constitutional convention requiring parliamentary consent is more firmly established or, alternatively, the prerogative is placed on a statutory footing.

3. Final thoughts and the impact of human rights on prerogative powers

As has been seen, since the landmark decision of *GCHQ* in 1985 the courts have **13–023** increased their justiciability over the exercise of prerogative. Whilst there are still "forbidden", or "no-go" areas, the courts are more prepared to make assessments on a case-by-case basis and very few areas enjoy complete immunity. There are, however, some from Lord Roskill's list which continue to enjoy complete immunity, examples being the prerogative of the dissolution of Parliament, the appointment of Ministers and conferment of honours. It is difficult to envisage the exercise of such prerogative ever finding their way into court. Allowing what are essentially political matters to become justiciable would inevitably lead to cries of judicial usurpation of the political process, and accusations of the judiciary trampling on separation of powers principles.

The impact of human rights in increasing the scope of justiciability needs also to be considered. Orders in Council made under the prerogative are deemed primary legislation under s.21 of the Human Rights Act 1998 (HRA). As a result, the court can declare them incompatible with human rights under HRA s.4. The House of Lords' decision in *R. (A) v Secretary of State for Home Department* [2004] UKHL 56 signifies growing judicial activism in a previously untouchable area. Although the case did not involve the use of prerogative power, it is significant for the fact that under guise of human rights, their Lordships appeared more prepared to tackle issues in this area. A similar observation can be made when considering the *Gentle* case where the existence of the art.2 issue made the issue justiciable.

4. Reform of the prerogative

(a) *Legislative reform*

Reform of the prerogative has often found its way onto the legislative agenda, normally **13–024** through private members' Bills, with the aim of increasing parliamentary control and/or placing aspects of the prerogative onto a statutory footing. In 1988, Tony Benn MP introduced a Private Members' Bill to place prerogative powers under statutory authority. However, the 1988 Crown Prerogatives (House of Commons Control) Bill did not proceed through the legislative process. On March 3, 1999 the Crown Prerogatives (Parliamentary Control) Bill was presented to the House of Commons. The Bill's purpose was also to place the exercise of Crown Prerogatives on a statutory footing. The government did not adopt the Bill and it did not progress. Following Select Committee reports (see below), two further unsuccessful legislative attempts at reform of the prerogative were made in 2005 and 2006. The Armed Forces (Parliamentary Approval for Participation in Armed Conflict) Bill 2005 proposed that parliamentary approval would be required for the armed forces to participate in armed conflict. This Bill never progressed beyond the House of Commons. The second attempt was The Constitutional Reform (Prerogative Powers and Civil Service) Bill 2006 which proposed codification of various prerogatives. This Bill got through its House of Lords readings and was passed to the House of Commons in July 2006, where it stalled.

(b) *Select Committees*

13–025   In March 2004, the Public Administration Select Committee ("Taming the Prerogative: Strengthening Ministerial Accountability to Parliament", fourth Report of the Session 2003–04, HC 422, London, The Stationary Office, March 16, 2004) suggested that the prerogatives to declare war or commit United Kingdom forces to armed conflict, to sign or ratify treaties and to grant passports should be put on a statutory footing. The report was quite critical of the lack of parliamentary control over the prerogative generally, and probably had an impact in legislation being brought forward in 2005.

The House of Lords Select Committee on the Constitution also reported in July 2006, though this Committee kept its remit to the war prerogative: "Waging War Parliament's role and responsibility" (HL Paper 236, London, The Stationary Office, July 27, 2006). The Committee concluded:

> "the exercise of the Royal Prerogative by the government to deploy armed force overseas is outdated and should not be allowed to continue as the basis for legitimate war-making in our 21st century democracy. Parliament's ability to challenge the Executive must be protected and strengthened." (at p.41)

It recommended "there should be a parliamentary convention determining the role Parliament should play in making decisions to deploy force or forces outside the United Kingdom to war, intervention in an existing conflict or to environments where there is a risk that the forces will be engaged in conflict" (at p.42).

Both these Select Committees seem to have had some impact. In July 2007, Gordon Brown issued a Green Paper, *The Governance of Great Britain* (Cm 7170 July 2007) the aim of which is "to forge a new relationship between government and citizen, and begin the journey towards a new constitutional settlement – a settlement that entrusts Parliament and the people with more power". In the Executive Summary, the government indicates it would "seek to surrender or limit powers which it considers should not, in a modern democracy, be exercised exclusively by the Executive (subject to consultation with interested parties and, where necessary, legislation)".

These include powers to:

- deploy troops abroad;
- request the dissolution of Parliament;
- request the recall of Parliament;
- ratify international treaties without decision by Parliament;

- determine the rules governing entitlement to passports and for the granting

- of pardons;

- restrict parliamentary oversight of the intelligence services;

- choose bishops;

- have a say in the appointment of judges;

- direct prosecutors in individual criminal cases; and

- establish the rules governing the Civil Service.

In a consultation paper issued in October 2007, *The Governance of Britain—War Powers and Treaties: Limiting Executive Powers* (Consultation Paper CP26/07, published on October 25, 2007), the government advanced their earlier commitment. The aim of the government's preliminary proposals is to strengthen parliamentary control and scrutiny over Executive prerogative powers. It recognises the current mechanisms in place, such as conventions, accountability and judicial review, but believes that parliamentary accountability should be more explicit. The consultation paper deals with only two of the prerogatives mentioned in the Green Paper: the power to enter into treaties, and the power to engage the country in war. The government asks for consideration of two options regarding the war prerogative. First, whether to take forward a new Parliamentary convention as favoured by the Lords' Select Committee on the Constitution, in its report—*Waging War: Parliament's role and responsibility* (HL paper 236, London, the Stationary Office, July 27, 2006) or secondly, to propose the development of a legislative framework similar to that suggested by the Public Administration Select Committee in its report "Taming the Prerogative: Strengthening Ministerial Accountability to Parliament". In relation to treaties, the government's proposal is to put the Ponsonby Rule (a convention) onto a statutory footing. The consultation exercise closed in January 2008, and the government issued a draft constitutional renewal Bill. Part 4 of the Bill makes provision for the ratification of Treaties by Parliament, in effect codifying the Ponsonby Rule.

FURTHER READING

Blackburn, R. "Monarchy and the Personal Prerogatives" (2004) P.L. 546   **13–026**
Bradley, A. "Police Powers and the Prerogative" (1988) P.L., Aut. 298–303
Bradley, A. and Ewing, K. *Constitutional and Administrative Law*, 14th edn (Essex: Pearson, 2006)
Brazier, R. "The Monarchy" in V. Bogdanor (ed.), *The British Constitution in the Twentieth Century* (OUP 2003)
Harris, B.V. "The 'Third Source' of Authority for Government Action Revisited" (2007) 123 L.Q.R. 225
Leigh, I. "The Prerogative, Legislative Intent and the Democratic Deficit: The Fire Brigades Union Case" (1995) 3 Web J.C.L.I.

Munro, C. *Studies in Constitutional Law* (OUP, 1999)

Squires, D. "Judicial Review of the Prerogative after the Human Rights Act" (2000) L.Q.R. 116, 572-575

Sunkin, S. and Payne, M. (eds) *The Nature of the Crown* (Oxford: OUP, 1999)

Wade, H.W.R. "Procedure and Prerogative in Public Law" (1985) 101 L.Q.R. 180

Chapter 14

NATURE AND PROCEDURE OF AN
APPLICATION FOR JUDICIAL REVIEW

INTRODUCTION

To allow the Executive to discharge its governmental functions it is vested with considerable powers, whether arising from statute, common law and/or prerogative. In a constitutional democracy founded on the rule of law, it is important that the use of this power is controlled and the Executive remains accountable for its actions. Administrative law is that branch of constitutional law which is concerned with law relating to the administration of the state and the laws, rules and principles governing the exercise of governmental power. This branch of law is broad, concerned with legal control of the power through the mechanism of judicial review, and extra judicial means of control such as tribunals and inquiries. The following chapter outlines what judicial review is, and how an application might be made. Subsequent chapters deal with the grounds of judicial review.

14–001

THE NATURE OF JUDICIAL REVIEW

1. What is judicial review?

Judicial review is the principal way of holding the Executive legally accountable. Essentially, judicial review is a high court procedure by which the applicant asks the court to review the legality of decisions of government Ministers, government departments, local authorities or other public bodies. For example, the court may examine a decision to ensure the body which has made the decision has both the power to make it

14–002

and adhered to principles of fairness and reasonableness. The court is not concerned with the merits of the decision itself, but how the decision was reached. In performing this function, the court takes account of legislation and applies principles of administrative law which have developed through case law.

2.   How does judicial review differ from an appeal?

14–003   Judicial review is not an appeal of the original decision, but a look at the legality of the decision, focusing on matters of form, procedure and jurisdiction. The merits of the decision are not in issue. For example, the courts are not concerned with whether the substance of the decision is good or bad, but rather with how that decision was reached, i.e. a consideration of all the relevant issues, or whether an individual was given a right to respond. On finding against a decision-maker, the courts do not substitute the original decision for their own, but refer the matter back to the body to make the decision again in the correct way. In *Chief Constable of the North Wales Police v Evans* [1982] 1 W.L.R. 1155, Lord Brightman made this distinction clear:

> "Judicial review is concerned, not with the decision, but with the decision-making process. Unless that restriction of the power of the court is observed, the court will in my view under the guise of preventing the abuse of power, be itself guilty of usurping power." (at p.1173)

It is in this way that judicial review can be constitutionally justified. The case of *R. v Cambridge Health Authority Ex p. B* [1995] 1 W.L.R. 898 demonstrates the importance of this distinction. In this case, a young girl who was terminally ill with cancer sought judicial review of the decision not to fund life-saving treatment. Cambridge Health Authority had considered that as the treatment had little chance of clinical success and was extremely expensive, it was a better use of resources not to fund it. The High Court had granted a quashing order (certiorari), which was appealed to the Court of Appeal. Sir Thomas Bingham M.R. (as he then was) stated:

> " . . . the courts are not, contrary to what is sometimes believed, arbiters as to the merits of cases of this kind. Were we to express opinions as to the likelihood of the effectiveness of medical treatment, or as to the merits of medical judgement, then we would be straying far from the sphere which, under our constitution, is accorded to us. We have one function which is to rule upon the lawfulness of decisions." (at p.905)

3.   Constitutional justification for judicial review

14–004   The power to undertake judicial review of administrative action was not conferred on the courts by Parliament, but stems instead from the common law. It is often called its "inherent jurisdiction and has developed from the historical power of the courts to keep inferior bodies within their legal power. Hilaire Barnett, *Constitutional and*

Administrative Law (6th edn, (Cavendish, 2006)) traces the growth of judicial review to industrialisation in the mid-nineteenth century and the corresponding expansion of government regulation and interference. A counter balance of this expansion was an increased need for the regulation of governmental activities by the courts. Judicial review, as a procedure, developed significantly in the 1960s and supplemented reforms in parliamentary procedure. The grounds of review as restated by Lord Diplock in *Council of Civil Service Unions v Minister for Civil Service* [1985] A.C. 374 have developed considerably with a period of judicial activism, a point made clearly by the Court of Appeal in *R. (Q) v Secretary of State for Home Department* [2003] EWCA Civ 364. The courts continue to ignore the merits of a decision, but look closely at the process by which facts have been ascertained and at the logic of inferences drawn from them.

The constitutional justification for judicial review has been the subject of considerable academic debate, there being two main constitutional theories; the ultra vires theory, and the common law theory. However, a third, modified, theory has developed to address criticisms levelled at the first. A brief summary of the theories is discussed below. However, for a fuller discussion look at Forsyth (ed.), *Judicial Review and the Constitution* (Hart Publishing, 2000).

(a) *Ultra vires theory*

Advocates of this theory emphasise that the constitutional justification for judicial **14–005**
review arises from the need to ensure that decision-makers act within the powers conferred by Parliament. Courts may therefore intervene where a body acts ultra vires, meaning "beyond the powers", conferred by legislation. Acts within their powers, "intra vires", are, therefore, outside the court's ambit. This justification operates neatly with parliamentary sovereignty, since Parliament has not prohibited judicial review, it is clearly Parliament's intention to have authorised it.

Craig, "Ultra Vires and the Foundations of Judicial Review" [1998] C.L.J. 63, highlights the limitations of this theory when discussing the development of judicial review. He asserts that developments such as proportionality and legitimate expectation cannot be attributed merely to legislative intent. Moreover, he points out that if legislative intent was the justification for judicial review, it would not explain the court's response to attempts by Parliament to oust/exclude judicial review (see below), nor does it explain the application of judicial review principles to those bodies who do not have statutory power but, for example, are exercising common law power under the prerogative.

(b) *Common law theory*

The alternative view is the common law theory, favoured by Craig (above) and Laws **14–006**
"Law and Democracy" (1995) P.L. Spr. 72. It arose out of the perceived deficiencies in the ultra vires theory and emphasises judicial review being a product of common law. It does not dispute the authority of Parliament, but argues the grounds for judicial review

are judge-made, the justification lying in principles of good and fair administration. This theory more easily accommodates the changing nature of judicial review and its application to non-statutory powers.

(c)   Modified ultra vires theory

14–007   In response to criticisms levelled at the original ultra vires theory, a modified version was put forward. Forsyth and Elliott, "The Legitimacy of Judicial Review" (2003) P.L. 286 state that the modified theory holds that Parliament has a general intent in granting discretionary power and this should be exercised in accordance with the rule of law. Judges, in exercising powers of judicial review, are thus acting in accordance with that general intent. This theory holds Parliament sovereign with the judiciary subordinate to its will.

4.   Relationship of judicial review to other constitutional theories

14–008   Whatever theory is preferred, judicial review is a key component of the UK constitution, and inextricably linked to the three constitutional theories dealt with in Chs 5–8.

(a)   Judicial review and parliamentary sovereignty

14–009   As is mentioned above, parliamentary intent is a key feature of judicial review, and ensuring government bodies act in accordance with statutory powers conferred is one of the main grounds of judicial review (illegality). In this sense, judicial review underpins parliamentary sovereignty. However, the growth of judicial review to cover non-statutory bodies, and the extension of some grounds of review raises questions about the proper role of the courts. Of particular interest is whether the judiciary limits the power of the legislature, or the judiciary is limited by the legislature.

(b)   Judicial review and the rule of law

14–010   Elliot (ed.), *Beatson, Matthews & Elliot's Administrative Law* (OUP, 2005) notes that "the principles of administrative justice are rooted in the constitutional bedrock of the rule of law". The rule of law seeks to control and impose limits on government by insisting that government acts in accord with law and operates within the law; the idea of legality. It also imports standards of fairness, rationality, certainty and consistency. Judicial review is concerned with giving practical effect to the idea of legality and the enforcement of these standards and as such Elliot's statement has much credibility.

(c)   *Judicial review and separation of powers*

The doctrine of separation of powers ensures that no body has too much power and **14–011** supposes a system of checks and balances to guard against abuse of power. In the exercise of its judicial review function, the courts are giving expression to the doctrine by checking the exercise of power by the Executive arm and ensuring it does not abuse its power and position. The doctrine also plays an important role not only in justifying court intervention, but also limiting the role of the courts. In judicial review, the courts are limited to reviewing the decision, then leaving the body charged with making the decision to make the decision again correctly. Constitutionally, the courts then avoid impinging on the constitutional role of the Executive to administer the law.

THE SCOPE OF JUDICIAL REVIEW

1.   Bodies subject to judicial review

Judicial review is only available to review a decision made by a public body. Tradi- **14–012** tionally, judicial review was confined to bodies exercising statutory power. Typically, these would be part of government, examples being departments of state and local authorities. Problems however occur where decisions are made by bodies which are not statutory in nature, but whose decisions impact on individuals or form part of gov- ernmental business. As a consequence of this the ambit of judicial review has been increased in a number of ways. First, following the House of Lords decision in *Council of Civil Service Unions v Minister for Civil Service* [1985] A.C. 374, the exercise of prerogative power is considered judicially reviewable subject to issues of justiciability (see Ch.13). Secondly, the expansion of judicial review to cover decisions made by private or non-governmental bodies who are seen to be exercising de facto public law powers. Inferior courts are also subject to judicial review by the higher Administrative Court (see below at para.14–014).

(a)   *Prerogative powers*

In *Council of Civil Service Unions v Minister for Civil Service* [1985] A.C. 374 **14–013** ("*GCHQ*"), the House of Lords found there to be no reason why prerogative powers could not be subject to judicial review and that it was no longer the source of the power that determined justiciability, but the subject matter. Following this decision, whether a particular exercise of prerogative power is subject to review depends on the content of the power in question, and the circumstances in which it is exercised. For example, a declaration of war would be considered non justiciable but an administrative decision involving dismissal from the army would be.

(b) *Inferior courts*

14–014   Decisions made by courts inferior to the Administrative Court can be subject to judicial review, and include the Magistrates' and Coroners' Courts. According to s.29(3) Supreme Court Act 1981, the Crown Court can also be subject to judicial review, except for trials on indictment. The rationale for this exclusion was that judicial review should not be used as a means of delaying trials and clogging up the criminal process. Decisions by tribunals are also subject to judicial review (see Ch.20).

(c) *Private/non-governmental bodies*

14–015   During the 1980s, government in the UK underwent significant institutional reform. Privatisation of state owned enterprises, such as gas and electricity, became common. Additionally, there was an increase in the self-regulation of industry, contracting-out of public services and the transfer of many responsibilities of central government to non-executive agencies (examples of such agencies would include the Driver and Vehicle Licensing Agency and the Equal Opportunities Commission). The effect was that a number of private bodies started exercising de facto governmental power. Originally, exposure to judicial review was determined on the basis of the source of the body's power, whether statutory or prerogative. Retention of the "source of power" test as the sole determinant would have left a significant lacuna in accountability, so an alternative approach was developed by the Court of Appeal in *R. v Panel on Takeovers and Mergers Ex p. Datafin* [1987] Q.B. 815.

The City Panel on Takeovers and Mergers was a body established by the City of London to regulate takeovers and mergers according to their own City Code. The powers of this body did not come either from statute or the prerogative, though it did operate within a statutory framework. Datafin plc sought judicial review of the panel's decision to reject a complaint they had made. The Court of Appeal accepted that if the nature of a function was purely the exercise of a private law right, it would not be amenable to judicial review. However, they thought that the jurisdiction of judicial review could be extended beyond the "source" test to a body which was private, yet performed public functions. Lloyd L.J. stated: "if the body in question is exercising public law functions, or if the exercise of functions have public law consequences, then that may ... be sufficient to bring the body within the reach of judicial review". The Court concluded that the Panel was exercising de facto public powers as it operated wholly within the public domain, its code of conduct applied universally to all bodies within the city, and it operated and was incorporated into a regulated statutory framework. As such, it was an integral part of a system which performed public law duties and could be judicial reviewed. However, permission for judicial review was refused as on the facts there was no ground for challenging the decision.

The key to the "*Datafin*" test is the nature of the body's function and the degree to which that function is public. However, whilst the decision was a welcome expansion of the jurisdiction of judicial review, the Court of Appeal did not lay down a single definitive test as to what would be enough of a public function which could be easily applied to a variety of organisations. Whilst the test has been easily applied to some regulatory bodies, examples being the Professional Conduct Committee of the Bar Council (*R. v Bar Council Ex p. Percival* [1991] 1 Q.B. 212), the Law Society and the Advertising Standards Agency (see *R. v Advertising Standards Authority Ltd Ex p. Direct Line Financial Services* [1998] C.O.D. 20, the courts have struggled with other regulatory bodies, particularly in the fields of sports and religion. Two cases, *R. v Chief Rabbi of the United Hebrew Congregations of Great Britain and the Commonwealth Ex p. Wachmann* [1992] 1 W.L.R. 1036 and *R. v Disciplinary Committee of the Jockey Club Ex p. Aga Khan* [1993] 1 W.L.R. 909, illustrate this well, and show the courts taking a more restrictive view of what is considered a suitable public function for judicial review.

In *R. v Chief Rabbi of the United Hebrew Congregations of Great Britain and the Commonwealth Ex p. Wachmann*, Rabbi Ivan Wachmann had been removed from his position for serious misconduct. He sought judicial review of the decision of the Chief Rabbi, but was refused permission. The court (at p.1042) held that the functions the Chief Rabbi carried out were "essentially intimate, spiritual and religious which the government could not and would not seek to discharge in his place". It added that to come within the jurisdiction of the courts, there must be "not merely a public but potentially a governmental interest" (para.253) such that the government would consider intervening in such an area. In relation to the decision by the Chief Rabbi, the court added that not only was the Chief Rabbi without any statutory support for his decision-making, but the court would be loathe to intervene in such an area and Parliament would never contemplate legislating in the field.

The second case concerned the susceptibility of the Jockey Club to judicial review. The Jockey Club was created under Royal Charter in 1970 and is responsible for the proper organisation, administration and control of all horse racing, race meetings and racehorse training in the UK. In the case, the Jockey Club disqualified a horse belonging to the Aga Khan and judicial review was sought of this decision. Prior to the case, the Jockey Club had been subject to extensive litigation on its susceptibility, all cases concluding it was not amenable to judicial review. The Court of Appeal, while acknowledging the Club regulated an important national activity affecting the public, that it held a monopoly of power and those connected with racing had to consent to its jurisdiction or be excluded from the sport, nevertheless held it was not a public body. The club was not in its origin, constitution, membership or history a public body and the powers it exercised were in no sense governmental. Although, the grant of a royal charter was a mark of official approval, it did not in any way alter its essential nature, functions or standing. The relationship between the Aga Khan and the Jockey Club was a private law relationship based on contract and, as such, the Aga Khan had an enforceable private law remedy (see, especially, the judgments of Sir Thomas Bingham M.R. and Farquharson at in particular).

The Court of Appeal's decision was the subject of challenge in *R. (Williams Mullins) v Jockey Club Appeals Board* [2005] EWHC 2197 (Admin) when the Administrative Court was asked to consider, again, whether the Jockey Club was susceptible to judicial review. In an attempt to distinguish the earlier Court of Appeal decision, a two-pronged argument was attempted. First, since sport occupies a more significant place in society, the public interest was greater and, secondly, that the passing of the Human Rights Act 1998 (HRA) required a different outcome. The Administrative Court dismissed both arguments, considering the HRA one to make no difference. See also *R. v Football*

Association Ex p. Football League [1993] 2 All E.R. 833 where permission for judicial review was refused against the FA's decision to create the Premier League. Like the Jockey Club, the FA is a body whose powers and relationships are contractual.

In relation to contracting-out, the courts' approach is the same. In *R. v Servite Houses Ex p. Goldsmith* (2001) 22 H.L.R. 35, the Administrative Court considered whether a charitable housing association providing accommodation for the elderly was subject to judicial review. The provision of housing had been contracted out by the local authority pursuant to statute, but the court dismissed the relevance of the enabling legislation and felt there was not sufficient "statutory penetration" to bring the association with the ambit of judicial review. Moses J. felt that simply because legislation permits a public authority to enter into arrangements with a private body, the functions of that body are not to be regarded as public function. In a subsequent human rights case *YL v Birmingham City Council* [2007] UKHL 27, the House of Lords (3:2 majority) found a private care home providing residential accommodation for local authority funded elderly residents not to be a public authority under s.6(3)(b) of the Human Rights Act 1998. Although, a human rights case, the ratio could easily be applied to a similar judicial review case. Lord Scott (at para.28) noted however that the "position might be different if the managers of privately owned care homes enjoyed special statutory powers over residents". Such powers might include the right to restrain, discipline or confine residents to their room. This decision whilst restrictive seems in line with Moses J.'s reasoning in Servite Houses.

In the *Percival* and *ASA* cases, had there been no self-regulatory authority in existence, Parliament would almost inevitably have intervened to control the activity. In particular, these bodies had privatised the business of government and were woven into statutory frameworks. Where the relationship is essentially a private one, the courts are more likely to decline jurisdiction, instead leaving disputes to private law. However, while this remains the situation, many commentators have questioned the propriety of such a stance with the expansion of "contracting out" as a means of providing government services (see for example Paul Craig, "Contracting Out, the Human Rights Act and the Scope of Judicial Review" (2000) 111 L.Q.R. 551.

2.　Public law issues

14–016　The mere fact that a decision is made by a public body is not enough to bring the matter within the ambit of judicial review. The issue at stake must also involve a public law issue. So whilst a body may owe the source of its power to statute, not all of its operations will be regarded as raising public law issues. For example, local authorities and other public bodies frequently operate in ordinary commercial capacities by entering into contracts.

WHEN MUST THE JUDICIAL REVIEW PROCEDURE BE USED?

1. Exclusivity

Prior to 1977 there were a number of ways of enforcing public law rights, the appropriate method being dependent on the remedy sought. For example, if the applicant sought a prerogative remedy, the action would commence in the Divisional Court, or if an equitable remedy was sought, then Chancery was the appropriate court. In 1978 however, a new procedure was introduced to standardise the application procedure under Order 53 of the Rules of the Supreme Court, the main elements being given effect by s.31 of the Supreme Court Act 1981 (SCA). The basic aim of Order 53 was to establish judicial review as the main mechanism for challenging public law decisions, regardless of remedy. Whilst certiorari (quashing order), mandamus (mandatory order) and prohibition (propitiatory order) could still only be granted in judicial review applications, declarations and injunctions could now also be granted as a remedy, these having only been previously possible in private law. The judicial review procedure is also characterised by a number of hurdles which the applicant must surmount in order to proceed. These include, the requirement for permission to be obtained and the short time limits (designed to protect public bodies from frivolous actions). As a result of these stringent requirements, applicants seeking a declaration or injunction could want to bring their public law grievance in private law. Neither Order 53, nor SCA s.31 made it absolutely clear whether an applicant had a free choice to bring a private law action for a grievance of a public nature, or whether they had to commence an application for judicial review, particularly if seeking a traditional private law remedy. Initially, there appeared to be some judicial reluctance to regard the new judicial review procedure as the sole method for challenging public law grievances. In *De Falco v Crawley Borough Council* [1980] Q.B. 460, the Court of Appeal allowed a challenge to a local authority's interpretation of its obligations under the Housing (Homeless) Persons Act 1977 by writ (private action), rather than by judicial review. However, judicial review developed as the exclusive procedure for challenging public law matters, finally being settled by the House of Lords in *O'Reilly v Mackman* [1983] 2 A.C. 237.

In the case, four prisoners took part in a riot at Hull Prison and were subsequently charged with offences contrary to the Prison Rules 1964. An inquiry into each case was held by a Board of Visitors who upheld the charges and imposed various penalties, including loss of remission for good behaviour. All four commenced private law actions against the Board seeking declarations that the board's findings and penalties were null and void due to its failure to observe the principles of natural justice, i.e. their hearings were not fair. The Board of Visitors sought to have proceedings struck out as an abuse of process, claiming they should have proceeded by way of judicial review. The House of Lords confirmed the order to strike out, stating that the incorrect procedure had been used. Lord Diplock, who gave the only opinion with which the other Law Lords agreed, stated that since the reforms of 1978 a clear procedure for judicial review had been established. It would be contrary to public policy and an abuse of the process of the court for an individual to seek a redress for a public law grievance by a private law action. He further stated:

14–017

"I have described this as a general rule ... there may be exceptions, particularly where the invalidity of the decision arises as a collateral issue in a claim for infringement of aright of the plaintiff arising under private law, or where none of the parties objects to the adoption of the procedure by writ or originating summons." (at p.285)

Following *O'Reilly*, the general principle that public law grievances should be dealt with by judicial review came into being; the exclusivity rule. Whilst the policy reasoning for the decision related to the procedural protection for public bodies in a judicial review application and the removal of the disadvantages to applicants under the old system (relating to disclosure of documents), the decision in *O'Reilly* was heavily criticised as being unduly restrictive. It generated a wealth of litigation as the courts attempted to draw distinctions between matters of public and private law in order to determine whether the correct procedure has been adopted. This had consequences for litigants left unsure as to the correct procedure in that they might be denied rights should they choose the wrong course, as the four prisoners found in *O'Reilly* (see, further, Wade (1985) 101 L.Q.R. 180 and Forsyth (1985) C.L.J. 415).

2.   Exceptions to the O'Reilly Principle

14–018   In the years since *O'Reilly*, case law has developed (and added to) the exceptions identified by Lord Diplock (above): firstly, where none of the parties object to the use of ordinary proceedings (i.e. they waive the use of judicial review) and, secondly, where public law arises as a collateral issue.

(a)   *Waiver*

14–019   The purpose of exclusivity is to ensure the protections offered to public bodies in judicial review proceedings operate. If a public body does not object to a private law action being commenced and is happy to lose the protections within the judicial review procedure (i.e. they have waived the option for judicial review either impliedly or expressly), then the court will not insist upon the use of the judicial review procedure.

(b)   *Collateral Issues*

(i)   Mixed public and private matters

14–020   Where public law has impacted upon a private law right the courts have held that judicial review is not the exclusive procedure. This was the decision of the House of Lords in *Roy v Kensington and Chelsea Family Practitioner Committee* [1992] 1 A.C. 624. The claimant, Dr Roy, entered into an agreement with the Committee to provide medical services to the NHS. Payment to Dr Roy was provided for by statutory regulation stating that a doctor would be eligible for the full rate of basic practice allowance where devoting a substantial amount of his time to NHS work. The claimant had been absent from his practice during the period 1979–1987 for, on average, between one-third and one-half of each year, so the Committee reduced his basic allowance by 20 per cent. Dr Roy brought a private action against the Committee's withholding of the payment. The Committee sought to have the action struck out as an abuse of process.

Lord Lowry in the House of Lords identified two approaches to collateral issues arising from the *O'Reilly* case; narrow and broad approaches. The narrow approach assumed that the exclusivity rule applied to all proceedings where public law was challenged, subject to exceptions when private law rights were the dominant element of any claim. The broad approach merely required an individual to proceed by judicial review when private law rights were not at stake (i.e. just a public law matter) so where any private rights were at stake an individual could bring a private law action. Whilst Lord Lowry preferred the broad approach as he believed it would rid law of a procedural minefield, he decided the case on the narrow approach. Where a litigant was asserting a private law right which incidentally involved the examination of a public law issue, he could seek to establish that right in a private law action. On the facts, Dr Roy had a bundle of private law rights, including the right to be paid for work done, which entitled him to sue for the alleged breach. The investigation as to the breach *incidentally* involved examining the Committee's decision; the public law matter. It was not an abuse of the process of the court to proceed as the doctor had done.

The decision in *Mercury Communications Ltd v Director-General of Telecommunications* [1996] 1 W.L.R. 48 shows the court taking a more relaxed approach to the exclusivity rule, allowing it to give way not just when private rights are at stake as in Roy, but also where a public law decision is capable of affecting an applicants private law relationship with others. In effect, the case developed the broader approach identified by Lord Lowry. The case concerned BT and Mercury, both of whom were granted licences to operate telecom systems under the Telecommunications Act 1984. In 1986, they entered into contractual relationship allowing Mercury access to BT's telecommunications network. A subsequent disagreement over phrases in BT's telecommunication licence was referred to the Director-General, but Mercury disagreed with the Director-General's interpretation and issued a private law action. Both the Director-General and BT claimed this was an abuse of process as the Director-General's decision was a public law matter. The House of Lords said it was important to retain some flexibility about the precise limits of "public law" and "private law" and that the overriding consideration for the court was whether the proceedings constituted an abuse of process. Even though the office of the Director-General was created by statute, and the decision essentially one of public law, it affected Mercury's private law position as it impacted upon the contractual relationship between Mercury and BT. Therefore, Mercury's decision to bring an action in private law was not an abuse of process and the choice of procedure well-suited and possibly better.

A similar approach was taken by Lord Woolf in *Trustees of the Dennis Rye Pension Fund v Sheffield City Council* [1998] 1 W.L.R. 840, where emphasis was again placed on the need of the court not to get immersed in technical distinctions between public and private law rights, but rather to focus on the practical consequences of pursuing different actions. A court should be slow to strike out a case on the basis of exclusivity if the choice of proceedings brought no significant disadvantages for the parties.

However, Lord Woolf offered valuable advice for the litigant in doubt; proceed by judicial review.

All of the above cases concern the application of the exclusivity rule prior to the Civil Procedure Rules which came into force in 2000. The Order 53 procedure has been made subject to the Civil Procedure Rules (CPR) Pt 54. The following case, *Clark v University of Lincolnshire and Humberside* [2000] 3 All E.R. 752, considered the nature of the changes the CPR would bring about. Clark, a student, was awarded 0 per cent in one of her papers due to an allegation of plagiarism. She commenced a private action alleging breach of the contractual rules under the University's student regulations. Lord Woolf considered the CPR provided a layer of protection to all parties in a private law action as it was under an obligation by the overriding objective in Part 1 to make sure any case was dealt with justly, expeditiously and fairly. The court could therefore strike out a claim if it appeared there was an abuse of process, such as an attempt to flout the protections offered to public bodies in Order 53. Lord Woolf at [38–39] stated:

"Where a student has, as here, a claim in contract, the court will not strike out a claim which could more appropriately be made under Order 53 solely because of the procedure which has been adopted. It may however do so, if it comes to the conclusion that in all the circumstances, including the delay in initiating the proceedings, there has been an abuse of the process of the court under the CPR."

The court concluded that because of the contractual issues Clark was not prevented from pursuing her claim by an action in contract.

Whilst the decision in *Clark* concerned a mixed public and private matter, the fact there was a contract might lead to the argument it adds nothing new to Roy. However, Elliot in *Administrative Law Text and Materials* (p.468) feels that the implications of Lord Woolf's judgment are more far-reaching, stretching beyond mixed public and private law issues. Irrespective of whether a claim concerning a public law matter is brought by judicial review or private law, the court will apply the same test. If judicial review is used, the protections in the judicial review procedure apply. If however private law is used, the court can still look at issues such as time and delay and, if they conclude that had it been brought as a judicial review application permission would have been refused, then summary judgment can be given. Elliot says the upshot is that the procedure by which a claim starts now matters very little. It therefore appears that in certain circumstances the wheel has turned full circle.

So, the decision in *Clark* sees the courts move away from concentrating solely on form (i.e. the procedure) to looking more at substance (i.e. whether the protection offered to public bodies is being undermined). Yet, the categorisation of an issue as public or private is still important for if the matter is exclusively one of public law, the claimant must either use the judicial review procedure or, if they bring under ordinary proceedings, the court must be satisfied that the requirements of permission and time would have been met.

(ii)   Using public law as a defence to a private law matter

In the above cases, the claimant instigated the action. However, in other cases, an **14–021**
individual may be a defendant to an action and wish to raise a public law issue as part
of any defence. In both criminal and civil matters, the courts have concluded this is not
an abuse of process and the validity of a public law issue can be questioned in defence.

   In *Boddington v British Transport Police* [1999] 2 A.C. 143, Boddington was convicted
of breaching a bye law by smoking on a train. The House of Lords held he was not
prevented from raising, in his defence, the contention that the bye-law was ultra vires
the Transport Act 1962. On the facts, it was held that the bye-law was lawful.

   In *Wandsworth London Borough Council v Winder* [1984] 1 A.C. 461, Wandsworth
LBC commenced proceedings in the County Court for rent arrears and possession of a
council house occupied by Winder. Winder, in his defence, relied on the contention that
the rent increases were ultra vires and void. The House of Lords stated that in the
absence of clear words to the contrary, an individual had the right to challenge a local
authority's decision in his defence. In such circumstances, to not allow an individual to
do so would be unfair. Winder had not abused the process of the Court as he did not
select the procedure to be adopted, he was merely seeking to defend the proceedings
brought against him by the Council.

PROCEDURE FOR BRINGING A JUDICIAL REVIEW APPLICATION

Once it has been determined that a judicial review application will be made a specific **14–022**
procedure must be followed which differs in many ways from the procedure for bringing
a private law action. Formerly, the procedure for judicial review was found in Order 53
of the Rules of the Supreme Court and the Supreme Court Act 1981. This has now been
brought within the Civil Procedure Rules Pt 54 which came into force in 2000, though
standing requirements are still found in the Supreme Court Act 1981. The basic outline
of the procedure is as follows.

1.   Pre-action protocol and claim

Before commencing proceedings, the claimant should write to the public body identi- **14–023**
fying the issues at stake, to which the defendant should reply. Whilst not obligatory, the
purpose of the protocol is to avoid litigation and achieve a settlement, so the court will
normally expect all parties to have complied with it. Non-compliance can be taken into
account when giving directions for case management or considering an award of costs.

   Claims for judicial review are made to the Administrative Court and follow two
additional stages: (i) permission and (ii) the substantive hearing. Cases are brought by
the Crown on behalf of the applicant against the defendant public body, e.g. *R. (on the
application of another) v Hertfordshire County Council*.

2. Permission to apply for judicial review

14–024   Judicial review is not available as a right and under r.54.4 the applicant requires the court's permission. This was formerly known as leave to apply. The permission hearing acts as a filter allowing the court to sift the vexatious claims. It protects public bodies and facilitates good administration by ensuring public bodies arc not hampered by unnecessary litigation in discharging their public duties. Permission was formerly sought ex parte, i.e. without the other side, but the application is now inter parties allowing the court to be better informed about both sides of the matter. Permission hearings are largely based on written submissions, though an oral hearing might be convened if necessary on the facts.

(a) *Time limits*

14–025   Under r.54.5, there is a strict time limit completing a claim form. It must be filed "promptly" (r.54.5(1)(a)), and in any event no later than three months after the grounds to make the claim first arose (r.54.5(1)(b)). The stricture of the time limit provides public bodies with a degree of certainty, namely that after three months, a decision may not be reviewed.

(b) *Standing*

14–025A   Permission will not be granted unless the applicant has standing, formerly known as locus standi (considered in more detail below).

3. Substantive hearing

14–026   At the substantive hearing, the court gives detailed consideration of whether the public body has infringed one of more of the grounds of judicial review (see Chs 15–18). At this stage it can also reconsider the issue of standing.

STANDING FOR JUDICIAL REVIEW

14–027   Standing will be granted where the applicant has "sufficient interest in the matter to which the application relates" (SCA 1981 s.31(3)). The wording of s.31(3) suggests that standing is considered at the permission stage, but following the *National Federation* case (see below) standing can also be considered at the substantive hearing.

    The crucial aspect of standing is the meaning of "sufficient interest". Following the reforms in 1978, the House of Lords in *R. v Inland Revenue Commissioners Ex p.*

National Federation of Self Employed and Small Business Ltd [1982] A.C. 617 considered the meaning of the test. The National Federation sought judicial review of a decision by the Commissioners to offer amnesty to casual workers in the newspaper industry on Fleet Street in respect of non-payment of income tax on casual earnings. The deal was an amnesty as long as they registered for tax purposes in the future. The majority of the House of Lords concluded that the National Federation did not have standing as it failed to demonstrate any grounds on the merits.

The general thrust of the decision was there should be a uniform test towards standing which has two elements to it. First, the applicant must show what the matter is and establish an arguable case and, secondly, the applicant must show his or her relationship to that matter. In effect, the test is a mixture of fact and law and it is clear the merits of the case will affect standing. If the applicant fails to show a prima facie case, the court would be in error if it granted permission. Following this approach, the court can consider issues such as the nature of the power involved, the seriousness of the alleged breach, the subject matter of the claim and the likelihood of success. Cane, "Standing, Legality and the Limits of Public Law" (1981) P.L. 322, has criticised the test saying that it requires all the issues to be looked at as a whole, rather than having standing as a filter and that "the 'new' law of standing ... by focusing on the issue of legality, has turned the question of standing very largely into a matter of fact and discretion", as opposed to one of law.

Whilst the House of Lords envisaged standing would generally be dealt with at the permission stage, they recognised that it could be reconsidered at the substantive hearing. This is because the sufficiency of interest as stated above is not considered in the abstract and is taken within the whole legal and factual context, i.e. it depends on the merits of the case which are not fully considered until the main hearing.

Following the *National Federation* decision the following categories have been granted standing:

1.   Individuals

The courts have been very flexible and have granted standing in a variety of situations   **14–028** where the merits of the case appear to justify intervention. Where an individual is directly or indirectly affected by a decision taken by a public body, and can show an arguable case on the merits, the grant of standing is straightforward. The liberal approach of the courts can be well illustrated by the following two cases. In *R. v Secretary of State for Foreign and Commonwealth Affairs Ex p. Rees Mogg* [1994] Q.B. 552, Lord Rees Mogg was granted standing to challenge the decision of the United Kingdom to ratify the Maastricht Treaty because of his "sincere concern for constitutional issues". Similarly, in *R. v HM Treasury Ex p. Smedley* [1985] Q.B. 657, Smedley was granted standing to challenge the validity of an order in Council approving a supplementary budget for the EC because he was a taxpayer.

2.   Representative standing: pressure groups and organisations

14–029   Groups and organisations may be granted standing if they are a recognised group acting in the interests of the wider public. An early decision, *R. v Secretary of State for the Environment Ex p. Rose Theatre Trust* [1990] 1 Q.B. 504 highlights a restrictive approach to the issue of representative standing. The Rose Theatre Trust concerned the discovery during development of the remains of the Rose Theatre in Southwark, a theatre where both Christopher Marlow's and William Shakespeare's plays had been performed. The Secretary of State for the Environment refused to add the remains to a schedule of monuments of national importance, which would have required the land-owner to preserve the remains. A group of interested persons formed the Rose Theatre Trust with the sole purpose of challenging the decision. The High Court, at the sub-stantive hearing, held the trust did not have sufficient interest, concluding that "a group of people, none of whom had standing individually, could confer standing on them-selves by forming a company". The decision was criticised and perceived as a set back for representational standing. Elliot in *Administrative Law* (OUP, 2004) notes that Schiemann J. appears to have assumed that individuals could establish standing only by demonstrating some personal stake in the decision and overlooks the possibility that sufficient interest could be established by considering the importance of the matter and whether it is in the public interest.

The restrictive approach taken in *Rose Theatre* was pointedly not followed in *R. v HM Inspectorate of Pollution Ex p. Greenpeace (No.2)* [1994] 4 All E.R. 329 nor *R. v Secretary of State for Foreign and Commonwealth Affairs Ex p. World Development Movement* [1995] 1 W.L.R. 386. In the first case, Greenpeace sought to challenge a decision allowing British Nuclear Fuels to discharge radioactive waste from its Sella-field plant in Cumbria. As an internationally-renowned environmental campaign group with a large membership amounting to some 400,000 in the UK and, importantly, 2,500 in the Cumbria region, Greenpeace was granted standing. Despite distinguishing the *Rose Theatre* on the 2,500 individual's basis, Otton J. took the law further in the direction of representative standing by pressure groups. He found a number of other factors relevant in finding that Greenpeace had standing, in particular, he later men-tions the fact that Greenpeace represented the wider public interest and the case was in furtherance of Greenpeace's general campaign against the use of radioactive material.

The second case seems to confirm that representative standing can be granted to a pressure group if the issue is sufficiently serious. The World Development Movement sought to challenge a decision by the Secretary of State to grant financial aid to fund the construction of the Perguua dam in Malaysia, arguing that the grant was illegal and contrary to the statutory provisions. WDM was granted standing because it was in the public interest that the matters raised were considered by the court. The facts raised serious issues of illegality and it was important to vindicate the rule of law and allow the possibility of a challenge. The court further considered that no other challenger was likely and WDM itself was a reputable body with expertise. Importantly, in widening the scope of representative standing, no individual member of the movement was affected, in contrast to Greenpeace. The case demonstrates that where the issue is important the court appears to be more flexible in its approach.

3.   Local government

Judicial review can be used by one member of the Executive against another and is not   **14–030**
just restricted to private individuals and organisations. For example in *Nottinghamshire
County Council v Secretary of State for the Environment* [1986] A.C. 240, Nottinghamshire CC was granted standing to challenge a decision relating to local authority
expenditure.

4.   Standing and human rights

Where an application for judicial review is brought alleging a breach of human rights,   **14–031**
the test for standing is that found in s.7 of the HRA. This is a more restrictive test than
the sufficient interest test, requiring the applicant be a victim. The effect of this test
prohibits representative standing such as found in the *World Development Movement*
case above. Unless the members of the pressure group are themselves directly affected
by an actual or potential violation of their human rights then they will not be given
victim status under the HRA (see Ch.21).

EXCLUSION OF JUDICIAL REVIEW

Parliament, as the supreme body, may seek to exclude the jurisdiction of the courts in   **14–032**
relation to the exercise of power. Such attempts are known as ouster clauses and are
typically phrased in the following way: "Shall not be questioned in any legal proceedings whatsoever". Such exclusions by Parliament have the effect of undermining the
rule of law and the separation of powers by weakening the ability of the judiciary to
curb arbitrary rule, protect individual rights and check the Executive's power. As such,
the courts have historically resisted such clauses, despite the fact this brings them into
conflict with the will of the supreme Parliament. In *Anisminic v Foreign Compensation
Commission (FCC) (No.2)* [1969] 2 A.C. 147, the House of Lords interpreted a clause
that "any determination by the FCC shall not be called into question in any court of
law" as meaning only a legal and valid determination. On the facts of the case, the FCC
had made an error of law in interpreting the criteria to be applied when distributing
funds for compensation arising out of acquisition of property in Egypt during the Suez
crisis. Therefore, the House of Lords concluded that the clause did not apply as no
determination had been made due to the illegality.

  The *Anisminic* decision was followed in *R. v Secretary of State for the Home
Department Ex p. Fayed* [1997] 1 All E.R. 228 where Al Fayed was permitted to seek
judicial review of a decision not to grant him British Nationality, despite the British
Nationality Act 1981 including a clause that "the decision of the Secretary of State . . .
shall not be subject to appeal . . . or review in any court of law". The court concluded
that a decision would only be one which the decision making authority had jurisdiction
to make.

The courts are however more willing to accept partial ouster clauses which restrict jurisdiction to a limited time. Such clauses are common in planning and land law where certainty is paramount. Wade and Forsyth in *Administrative Law* (9th edn, (OUP, 2004) at p.719) have noted that in relation to absolute ouster clauses, "[t]he policy of the courts ... becomes one of total disobedience to Parliament, but in relation to limitation clauses the approach is one merely of strict construction". Such an example is *Smith v East Elloe RDC* [1956] A.C. 736. Mrs Smith sought to challenge a compulsory purchase order made under the Acquisition of Land (Authorisation Procedure) Act 1946. The Act contained a clause that an aggrieved person had six weeks to challenge the order. The Court felt itself bound to accept and apply the clause as it was clear and unambiguous in that once the six week period had passed there was no judicial redress.

REMEDIES

14–033   The court may grant one of the following remedies:

(1)   a mandatory order which requires the public body to do carry out its function as required by law (mandamus);

(2)   a prohibiting order which restrains a public body from acting outside its jurisdiction or in an illegal way (prohibition);

(3)   a quashing order which quashes a decision which has been made unlawfully, confirming it is a nullity and having no legal effect. The decision is remitted back to the decision-maker to be made again (certiorari);

(4)   a declaration which is a formal statement by the court of the legal position can be granted under the CPR Pt 54.3;

(5)   an injunction preventing a public body from acting in a certain way;

(6)   damages which can only be awarded only if they would have been in a private law action.

FURTHER READING

14–034   Cane, P. *Administrative Law* (OUP, 2004)
Cane, P. "Standing, Legality and the Limits of Public Law" (1981) P.L. 322
Elliot (ed.) *Beatson, Matthews and Elliott's Administrative Law: Text and Materials*, 3rd edn (OUP, 2005)
Forsyth, C. "Beyond O'Reilly v Mackman: The foundations and Nature of Procedural Exclusivity" (1985) C.L.J. 415
Wade, H.W.R. "Procedure and Prerogative in Public Law" (1985) 101 L.Q.R. 180
Wade, H.W.R. and Forsyth, C. *Administrative Law*, 9th edn (OUP, 2004)

Flowchart on the nature and procedure for bringing an application for judicial review

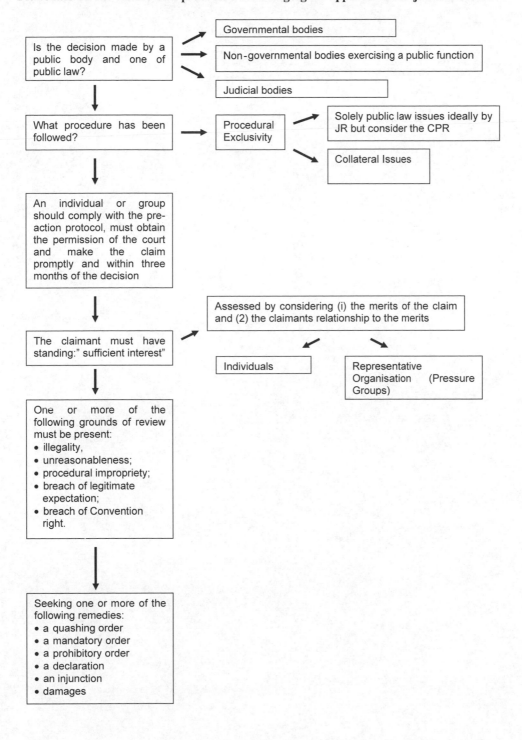

Is the decision made by a public body and one of public law?

Governmental bodies

Non-governmental bodies exercising a public function

Judicial bodies

What procedure has been followed?

Procedural Exclusivity

Solely public law issues ideally by JR but consider the CPR

Collateral Issues

An individual or group should comply with the pre-action protocol, must obtain the permission of the court and make the claim promptly and within three months of the decision

The claimant must have standing:" sufficient interest"

Assessed by considering (i) the merits of the claim and (2) the claimants relationship to the merits

Individuals

Representative Organisation (Pressure Groups)

One or more of the following grounds of review must be present:
• illegality,
• unreasonableness;
• procedural impropriety;
• breach of legitimate expectation;
• breach of Convention right.

Seeking one or more of the following remedies:
• a quashing order
• a mandatory order
• a prohibitory order
• a declaration
• an injunction
• damages

Chapter 15

UNLAWFULNESS: ILLEGALITY AND ULTRA VIRES

INTRODUCTION

An application for judicial review might be made on a number of grounds. In *Council of*   **15–001**
Civil Service Unions v Minister for Civil Service [1985] 1 A.C. 374 (*GCHQ*), Lord
Diplock famously categorised grounds of judicial review:

> "Judicial review has I think developed to a stage today when without reiterating
> any analysis of the steps by which the development has come about, one can
> conveniently classify under three heads the grounds upon which administrative
> action is subject to control by judicial review. The first ground I would call
> 'illegality', the second 'irrationality' and the third 'procedural impropriety'." (at
> p.410)

While noting these three grounds (unlawfulness (illegality), unreasonableness (irrationality) and unfairness (procedural impropriety)), his Lordship noted the grounds
may require expansion at a future date and, further, they are mutually exclusive as
many of the grounds overlap. In particular, Lord Diplock noted that proportionality
may be developed and, with the advent of the Human Rights Act 1998 (HRA), to a
large extent this has happened (see further Ch.16). Further, the HRA, has generated a
sub-ground to illegality namely, acting unlawfully contrary to HRA s.6. To these
grounds, a fourth legitimate expectation might be added. Whilst the concept of legitimate expectation existed in 1985 and was, in fact, the basis of the claim in *GCHQ*, this
ground raises aspects of all the others and is more usefully considered on its own.

DEFINITION AND CLASSIFICATION OF ILLEGALITY

1.   What is illegality?

15–002   In *GCHQ*, Lord Diplock defined illegality in the following way:

> "By 'illegality' as a ground for judicial review I mean that the decision-maker must understand correctly the law that regulates his decision-making power and must give effect to it." (at p.410)

This concept however does not have one element, but can be subdivided into ways a decision-maker may have acted illegally. These are:

(1)   mistakes of jurisdiction, which include acting outside of their power known as simple ultra vires; misinterpreting their power and so making an error of law and making factual mistakes or misinterpreting his jurisdiction known as error of fact;

(2)   abuse of discretion, which includes taking into account irrelevant considerations and ignoring relevant ones and acting for an improper purpose;

(3)   retention of discretion, which includes a failure to exercise discretion by either limiting his decision-making through the making of rigid rules or illegally delegating his discretion to someone else; and

(4)   acting in a way which is incompatible with the rights contained in the European Convention on Human Rights (ECHR) contrary to s.6 of the HRA.

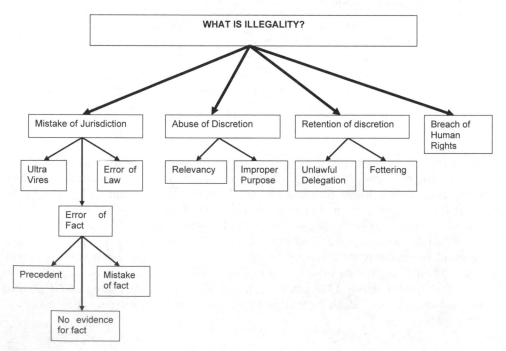

MISTAKES OF JURISDICTION

1. Simple ultra vires

The principle of simple ultra vires is where the decision-maker has acted outside the   **15–003**
powers conferred on them. For example, a statute grants power to do X, but the
decision-maker does Y. In this scenario, the decision-maker is said to be acting ultra
vires. If, however, he does X, the decision-maker acts intra vires as he acts within the
power and, therefore, legally. The decision in *Att-Gen v Fulham Corporation* [1921] 1
Ch. 440 illustrates this principle well. The Baths and Wash-house Acts 1846–78
authorised the provision of washhouses by local authorities for residents to have baths
and launder their clothes. Fulham created a laundry where, for a small fee, customers
could bring their clothes and have them washed by Council employees. The court
concluded this was outside the statutory power granted to them. Another example is *R.
v Lord Chancellor Ex p. Witham* [1998] Q.B. 575. In this case, the Lord Chancellor,
acting under the authority of s.130 of the Supreme Court Act 1981 (SCA), removed the
exemption from payment of court fees for litigants who received income support
(Supreme Court Fees (Amendment) Order 1996 art.33). Mr Witham, who was on
income support, was unable to institute proceedings and sought judicial review arguing
art.3 was ultra vires the SCA. The Divisional Court found that removal of access to
justice, a constitutional right, was not expressly provided for in the SCA so art.3 was
ultra vires.

A body may do something which is not expressly provided for by statute, but is
incidental to it and this will not be ultra vires. In *Att-Gen v Great Eastern Railway Co*
(1879 80) L.R. 5 App. Cas. 473, Lord Selborne said:

> " ... whatever may be fairly regarded as incidental to, or consequential upon,
> those things which the legislative has authorised, ought no ... to be held, by
> judicial construction, to be ultra vires."

2. Errors of Law

Errors of law are the natural continuum of the ultra vires principle and occur where a   **15–004**
public body misinterprets its legal power. Not every interpretation will involve an error
of law. As Lord Reid noted in *Brutus v Cozens* [1973] A.C. 854, the meaning of ordinary
words of the English language is not a question of law, whereas the proper construction
of a statute is a question of law.

The traditional view emphasised a distinction between jurisdictional and non-
jurisdictional errors of law. A jurisdictional error is one where the decision-maker
misinterprets words which go to whether they have the power to act or not. For
example, a statute which provides that A can do X, and X is misinterpreted would be a
jurisdictional error and reviewable. Where a decision-maker had the power to act (X),
but in the course of exercising that power misinterpreted words such as criteria

(Y and Z), this would be a non-jurisdictional error of law and not reviewable. Such mistakes could only be remedied through traditional appeal mechanisms. One problem with the distinction is the lack of clarity over defining the boundary between the two. The House of Lords in *Anisminic Ltd v Foreign Compensation Commission* [1969] 2 A.C. 147, is a seminal case in this area. Following the Suez Crisis in 1956, the United Kingdom received £27.5 million from Egypt to be distributed amongst British nationals and companies whose property had been seized or destroyed. The Foreign Compensation Commission established under the Foreign Compensation Act 1950 was given power under the Foreign Compensation (Egypt) (Determination and Registration of Claims) Order 1951 (SI 1951/625) to assess and distribute the funds. Anisminic was a British Company whose Egyptian property had been sequestrated. They later sold the property to an Egyptian company below its market value. The Commission made a finding that Anisminic was not entitled to compensation as the successor in title of the land was a non-British national and, accordingly, did not comply with art.4(1)(b)(ii). The SI gave no clear guidance as to whether the status of successor in title was relevant to whether the Commission had the power to award compensaton at all (jurisdictional) or whether it was merely one of the factors which might come up in the process of reaching the decision to make compensation (non-jurisdictional). Whilst the Commission could be argued to be acting within jurisdiction in the traditional sense (a view taken by Lord Morris who dissented), the House of Lords gave a wider meaning to the concept of jurisdiction. In exercising their power, the Commission had made an error of law by misinterpreting what they needed to ask themselves. They should have focused on the nationality of the owner at the time the property was sequestered, rather than the current owner of the property. This misinterpretation was a key factor and went to the Commission's jurisdiction to award compensation.

Following *Anisminic*, a number of cases clarified the court's position regarding errors of law and the jurisdiction/non-jurisdiction debate. In *R. v Lord President of the Privy Council Ex p. Page* [1992] 3 W.L.R. 1112, the House of Lords settled the position holding that public bodies must correctly interpret all their power. Further, that all errors of law are reviewable and go to jurisdiction in the wider sense. The rationale for this is that Parliament could not have intended administrative bodies, officials or inferior courts, to have the power to determine conclusively questions of law.

15–005   Another problem posed is where a question of law is capable of more than one reasonable answer. In such cases, what is the role of the reviewing court? In *R v Monopolies and Mergers Commission Ex p. South Yorkshire Transport Ltd* [1993] 1 All E.R. 289, the court concluded that as long as the answer given by the decision-maker was within the range of reasonable responses, the reviewing court will not intervene. The *South Yorkshire* case concerned s.64(1)(a) of the Fair Trading Act 1973, which gave power to the Secretary of State to refer a merger of a company to the Monopolies and Mergers Commission (MMC) where the merger could result in more than 25 per cent of services being supplied by one company "in a substantial part of the UK". Two merged bus companies sought judicial review of an MMC investigation on the basis that the land area did not amount to a substantial part of the UK. The court found that "substantial" could be interpreted in different ways and that a person might reasonably disagree about an interpretation. In such a situation, a decision would only be ruled unlawful if the interpretation given by the body was outside the range of reasonable responses and could be classed as aberrant. On the facts, the MCC had not acted unlawfully.

(a)   Exceptions to the general principle

There are some exceptions to the general principle that all errors of law are reviewable. **15–006** These include the following:

(1)   the error of law must be relevant or material to the decision;

(2)   where the inferior body is interpreting a special system of rules, the courts will be less likely to intervene as they lack expertise. This point was made in *Page* where the claimant was challenging a decision to make him redundant. The claimant sought a declaration from the University Visitor that this was contrary to University Statutes. The House of Lords found that judicial review did not lie against a decision of the University Visitor acting within their jurisdiction. According to Lord Browne-Wilkinson, the inability of the court to intervene was founded on the fact that the applicable law was not the common law of England and Wales, but a peculiar or special type of law;

(3)   mistakes of law by inferior courts are subject to a different test and depend on the construction of the statute as to whether Parliament intended questions of law to be left to an inferior court.

3.   Errors of fact

Whilst review of errors of law is justifiable, review of an error of fact is less so. Public **15–007** bodies are given power and inevitably make factual determinations in relation to the exercise of that power. The public body is invariably armed with all the relevant facts and knowledge to make such decisions. Courts on the other hand lack both the expertise and the knowledge to make such decisions and have been reluctant to intervene in judicial review proceedings on these grounds. To do so would amount to the courts acting as administrators, blurring the separation of powers between the courts and the Executive. However, the courts have been prepared to intervene where a particular fact has to be established in order for the legal power to operate. This is known as a precedent fact or, where a decision has been based on no evidence.

(a)   Precedent fact

A precedent fact, also known as a jurisdictional fact, is a fact which must be decided **15–008** before the public body can use the power conferred on it. For example, if the Secretary of State for the Home Department has the power to sentence child murderers, two precedent facts need to be determined before the Secretary can use the power: (i) is the defendant in fact a child and (ii) a murderer. Use of the power to sentence an adult or a child convicted of criminal damage would be illegal. Review of such facts by the court is justified because, according to Wade and Forsyth in *Administrative Law* ((OUP, 2004), p.253), it has a "bearing on the limits of the power" and so review fulfils the court's constitutional duty of ensuring public bodies act within their power.

The principle can be traced to the case of *White and Collins v Minister of Health* [1939] 2 K.B. 838 which still provides a useful example. Under the Housing Act 1936, a local authority had the power to compulsorily purchase land as long as it did not "form part of any park, garden or pleasure ground" (s.75). Before this power could be used, the local authority had to make a factual decision whether the land in question formed part of any park, garden or pleasure ground. The applicant questioned the validity of a compulsory purchase order and an inquiry was held by the Minister of Health, who confirmed the order. This was then judicially reviewed. At first instance, the court found that as the Minister had made up his mind on proper materials and without mis-directing himself, it was not open to the court to interfere by rehearing the case and evidence. The Court of Appeal overturned this decision, finding that if the decision-maker was able to determine conclusively what parkland was, the statutory restriction would have been meaningless. Luxmoore L.J. stated:

"The first and most important matter to bear in mind is that the jurisdiction to make the order is dependent on a finding of fact; for, unless the land can be held not to be part of a park or not to be required for amenity or convenience, there is no jurisdiction in the borough council to make, or in the Minister to confirm, the order. In such a case it seems almost self-evident that the Court which has to consider whether there is jurisdiction to make or confirm the order must be entitled to review the vital finding on which the existence of the jurisdiction relied upon depends. If this were not so, the right to apply to the Court would be illusory." (at pp.855–856)

Similarly, in the case of *Khawaja v Secretary of State for the Home Department* [1984] A.C. 74, the court reviewed a factual finding that Mr Khawaja was an illegal immigrant. Under the Immigration Act 1971 deportation of an individual could be pursuant to such a factual finding. The House of Lords felt it their duty to inquire whether there had been sufficient evidence to justify the belief that entry was illegal. On the facts, as Mr Khawaja had initially used fraud to gain entrance to the United Kingdom, he was an illegal immigrant.

(b) *No evidence for a finding of fact*

15–009 A further basis for the court's review under error of fact is where there is no or very little evidence for a finding of fact. In *Ashbridge Investments Ltd v Minister of Housing and Local Government* [1965] 1 W.L.R. 1320 a factual decision to designate a property as a house unfit for human habitation, which subsequently led to a lesser award of compensation when the land was compulsorily purchased, was challenged. The claimants tried to argue on the basis of fresh evidence the designation was incorrect. Lord

Denning M.R. (at p.1326) stated the court, "can interfere with [a] decision if [the decision-maker] has acted on no evidence; or if he has come to a conclusion to which on the evidence he could not reasonably come". However, the court concluded that they could only consider the material available before the Minister at the time he made the decision and so the new evidence was not admitted.

A similar conclusion was reached in *Coleen Properties Ltd v Minister of Housing and Local Government* [1971] 1 W.L.R. 433, a case based on similar facts to Ashbridge. Under the Housing Act 1957, a local authority could compulsorily purchase slum property for redevelopment and other property where this was "reasonably necessary for the satisfactory development" of the area. A compulsory purchase order was made against Coleen Properties who appealed the decision. At the subsequent inquiry, the local authority offered no evidence relating to the need to acquire the property and the Inspector recommended it be excluded. However, the Minister confirmed the purchase order. The Court of Appeal held that since there was no evidence the acquisition of the building was "reasonably necessary for the satisfactory development or use of the cleared area" as required by the Act, the Minister's decision reversing the inspector's recommendation was ultra vires.

(c) *Mistake of fact*

Review both for precedent fact and no-evidence for a factual decision are now con-   **15–010**
sidered non-controversial and a logical extension of the court's power of control over decision-making. However, the no evidence rule has been extended to controversially allow review where there has been a mistake of fact. In *Secretary of State for Education and Science v Tameside MBC* [1977] A.C. 1014 a local council submitted, and had approved by the Secretary of State, a policy creating a system of comprehensive education in Tameside. Following an election fought on the issue of selective grammar school education, the new council refused to implement the policy. The Secretary of State, under s.68 of the Education Act 1976, directed the authority give effect to the proposals approved by him and to implement the arrangements previously made for the allocation of pupils to secondary schools for the coming year on a non-selective basis. His letter stated "A change of plan at this stage of the year, designed to come into effect less than three months later, must ... give rise to considerable difficulties ... ". The question for the court was whether there was evidence upon which the Secretary of State could be satisfied that the council was acting unreasonably. In affirming the unanimous decision of the Court of Appeal, the House of Lords found that the Secretary of State's objection that their policy was creating a dilemma for parents was unsupportable in view of the fact that the electorate, including many parents, had voted for a selective basis of secondary education which the authority were providing and so the decision of the Local Authority was not unreasonable. Lord Wilberforce said:

> "If a judgment requires, before it can be made, the existence of some facts, then, although the evaluation of those facts is for the Secretary of State alone, the court must inquire whether those facts exist, and have been taken into account, whether the judgment has been made upon a proper self-direction as to those facts, whether

the judgment has not been made upon other facts which ought not to have been taken into account." (p.1047)

This case prompted Wade and Forsyth in *Administrative Law* (9th edn, OUP, 2004 at p.278) to say that "It now seems clear that it [a 'wrong factual basis' doctrine] has arrived, and that it should consign much of the old law about jurisdictional fact etc. to well-deserved oblivion". While the decision in *Tameside* is not clear as to whether mistake of fact is a ground of review, subsequent developments seem to be moving in this direction. In *R. v Criminal Injuries Compensation Board Ex p. A* [1999] 2 A.C. 330, Lord Slynn, obiter, was prepared to accept mistake of fact as ground for review of the board's decision not to award criminal injuries compensation. The mistake concerned testimony given to the board by a female police officer that the victim had not been raped. In fact, the police doctor's report, which was not before the board, was consistent with the applicant's claims. The Court of Appeal found against the board on a different ground, unfairness. The court found it was not sufficient for the police officer to have given oral evidence without inquiries having been made as to the existence of a doctor's report, such an action was unfair. However, the obiter remains nonetheless important. Lord Slynn (at para.53) made similar comments in *R. (Alconbury Developments Ltd) v Secretary of State for the Environment, Transport and the Regions* [2003] 2 A.C. 295 where he said: "In *Ex p. A* I accepted that the court had jurisdiction to quash for misunderstanding or ignorance of an established fact. I remain of that view".

The final case which suggests mistake of fact may now be a ground of judicial review is *E v Secretary of State for the Home Department* [2004] Q.B. 1044. E and others were asylum seekers who claimed they would be at risk if they were returned to their home country. The Immigration Appeal Tribunal (IAT) refused leave to appeal to the Court of Appeal. The applicant alleged that the IAT had erred by not taking into account new evidence available after the initial hearing which supported their claim. The Court of Appeal ruled that the IAT should reconsider the decision, taking into account the new evidence. Giving the judgment of the court, Carnwath L.J. (at para.66) held that, "the time has come to accept that a mistake of fact giving rise to unfairness is a separate head of challenge in an appeal on a point of law". His Lordship concluded there would normally be four requirements to show the requisite unfairness and hence justify setting aside a decision for mistake of fact. These included:

(1)   mistake as to an existing fact including a mistake as to the availability of evidence on a particular matter;

(2)   fact must have been established in sense it was uncontentious and objectively verifiable;

(3)   the appellant or his advisers must not have been responsible for the mistake;

(4)   the mistake must have played a material though not necessarily decisive part in the decision.

E was not a judicial review case so its strength as authority for mistake of fact as a separate ground depends on how widely it is taken to apply. It is important to note that Carnwath L.J. thought there to be no material distinction that the case had reached the

Court of Appeal on a point of law as opposed to judicial review. This suggests that the principles can easily be applied to judicial review case (see further discussion at paras 40 and 82). Elliott in *Beatson, Matthews and Elliott's Administrative Law* (3rd edn (OUP, 2005), p.73) feels that the requirement the fact in question be "uncontentious and verifiable" suggests the ground of review may operate in fairly limited circumstances. However, Paul Craig in "Judicial review, appeal and factual error" (2004) P.L. 788 has argued "intervention is [now] possible in principle for all species of mistake of fact" and that the narrow misunderstanding or ignorance of an established and relevant fact category has evolved, subsuming the other categories of evidential review and jurisdictional fact to create one large category of "material error of fact" which is the direct equivalent of "relevant error of law". Rebecca Williams in "When is an error not an error? Reform of jurisdictional review of error of law and fact" (2007) P.L. 793 states that if this is the case, *E* is the page of errors of fact and it is now possible to conclude all errors, whether of law or fact, are in principle "jurisdictional", or "reviewable". Such a development is not without controversy as it increases the court's intervention. Indeed, the Court of Appeal has noted in *R. (on the application of Iran) v Secretary of State for the Home Department* [2005] EWCA Civ 982, that to make too great a use of the ground of review in E would be to "reintroduc[e] an appeal based on errors of fact through the backdoor". It remains to be seen how far the decision in *E* will be taken in judicial review cases.

ABUSE OF DISCRETION

Public bodies are invariably given wide discretion to assist them in exercising their public law duties. A body acts illegally where it abuses discretion, such as taking into account factors not relevant to the exercise of the power, or making a decision for a purpose not connected to the power or, not considering factors which are relevant.   **15–011**

1.   Relevant and irrelevant factors

When establishing what are, and are not, relevant considerations, regard must first be had to the statute itself. Simon-Brown L.J., in *R. v Somerset CC Ex p. Fewings* [1995] 1 W.L.R. 1037 (at p.1049) identified three types of factors.   **15–012**

(1)   those factors which must be taken into account when exercising the power (mandatory);

(2)   those factors which must NOT be taken into account when exercising the power (prohibitory);

(3)   discretionary factors to which the decision-maker may have regard if, in his judgment, he thinks it right to do so. Here there is a margin of appreciation in which the decision-maker may decide just what considerations should play a

part in his reasoning process and the court will only interfere if the decision-maker has acted unreasonably.

Not all factors are found in statutory provisions and the court can intervene if it feels that matters clearly pertinent to the decision have not been considered or alternatively those not pertinent have been considered. Assistance may be found in a policy or circular, or might be implied by assessing the purpose of the power as a whole. In *Roberts v Hopwood* [1925] A.C. 578, the House of Lords found that the decision of Poplar Council to increase the minimum wage it paid to employees was influenced by an irrelevant consideration, namely, "to be guided by some eccentric principle of socialistic philanthropy or by a feminist ambition to secure equality of the sexes" (at p.594).

This ground of review gives the courts considerable discretion to involve itself in questions as to the validity of a decision. In a number of cases, allegations have been made that judges' decisions are influenced by political or other values. In *Bromley Borough Council v Greater London Council* [1983] 1 A.C. 768, the decision of the Labour run GLC to provide cheap and subsidised public transport pursuant to an election mandate was held illegal. Their Lordships felt the provision in the London Transport Act 1969 that transport should be run "economically and efficiently" meant that fares should be fixed "in accordance with ordinary business principles". It has been argued that the *Bromley* decision, as was the *Roberts* one before it, were more politically-based than legal, their Lordships in *Bromley* believing that the GLC should have given greater weight to their fiduciary duty to the ratepayers and the control of public spending, and rather less to their political mandate.

R. v Secretary of State for the Home Department Ex p. Venables [1998] A.C. 407 shows the difficulties and differing opinions the judiciary may take in assessing relevancy. The case concerned the decision by the Home Secretary under the Criminal Justice Act 1991 to set a 15–year tariff period before he would consider the release of the child murderers, Robert Thompson and Jon Venables. In coming to his decision, he was informed by the strong public feelings surrounding the case and the petition gathered by newspapers which had been presented to him. In giving their opinions their Lordships, while accepting that the decision was illegal (Lord Lloyd dissenting), took different stances as to why. Lord Goff (p.114), with whom Lord Steyn and Lord Hope agreed, decided that the decision was illegal because the Home Secretary had taken into account an irrelevant consideration, namely the public petition. Their Lordships thought because the Home Secretary was exercising a function which was closely analogous to a judicial sentencing function, he was under a duty to act with the same constraints as a judge. Whilst a judge might take account of general considerations of public confidence in the administration of justice, he would ignore, as irrelevant, public clamour or public opinion as expressed in the media. However, Lord Browne-Wilkinson thought the decision was illegal because the Home Secretary had failed to take account of a relevant factor, namely the welfare of the children and their future progress and development.

A further area of contention is the extent to which taking account of resource allocations is a relevant factor. Whether resources is a relevant factor depends largely on the statutory power and two cases merit consideration. *R. v Gloucestershire CC Ex p. Barry* [1997] A.C. 584, concerned a decision to withdraw Mr Barry's cleaning and laundry services due to the fact that the Council received a reduced sum of money from central government. The court held that the local authority had to balance the severity of the applicant's disability, against the cost of arrangements. The availability of resources was a proper consideration. However, in *R. v East Sussex County Council Ex p. Tandy* [1998] A.C. 714 resources was held to be an irrelevant factor. The House of Lords, in allowing the appeal, held that the meaning of "suitable education" in the Education Act 1998 s.298 suggested a standard determined purely by educational considerations, such as the efficiency and suitability to the child's age, ability, aptitude and needs. There was nothing in the Act to suggest that the availability of financial resources was relevant to the question of what constituted "suitable education".

2. Improper purpose

Statutory powers must be used for the express or implied purposes for which they were given and any action contrary to that purpose amounts to illegality. The case of *Padfield v Minister of Agriculture, Fisheries and Food* [1968] A.C. 997 provides a useful example. Under the Agricultural Marketing Act 1958, the Minister was granted discretion to send complaints regarding the operation of a milk marketing scheme to a committee of investigation. Padfield made a complaint which the Minister refused to refer. The House of Lord granted a mandatory order (mandamus) requiring the Minister to consider the complaint. In concluding that the Minister had acted for an improper purpose, Lord Reid said:

15–013

> "Parliament must have conferred the discretion with the object that it should be used to promote the policy and objects of the Act … if the Minister, by reason of his having misconstrued the Act or for any other reason, so uses his discretion as to thwart or run country to the policy and objects of the Act, then our law would be very defective if persons aggrieved were not entitled to the protection of the court." (at p.1030)

The Minister had argued that under the Act he had absolute discretion whether or not to refer a complaint. The House of Lords held his discretion was not unlimited and that he had to use his discretion to promote the purpose of the Act which was that "relevant and substantial complaints should go to the committee in the absence of good reasons to the contrary". The Minister had also been concerned about the political repercussions of referring the complaint thereby indicating he had an alternative political motive.

As with relevancy, the purpose of a statute may not be express or easily discernable and as such the courts may imply a purpose by interpreting the statute as a whole. In the case of *Congreve v Home Office* [1976] Q.B. 629 the Home Office announced plans to increase the TV licence fee. Congreve, and a number of others, renewed their licences early to avoid paying the increased charge. The Home Office became aware of this and, being conscious of the lost revenue, wrote to all demanding payment of the difference, or their licences would be revoked. The Court of Appeal held that the licences were valid. Whilst the Minister had discretion to revoke licences under the Wireless

Telegraphy Act 1949 s.1(4), the purpose of s.1(4) was to enable revocation where the terms of the licence had been breached. The Minister had used the power to revoke the licences for his own purpose, namely the want of money, which was illegal.

A similar line of reasoning can be found in *Wheeler v Leicester City Council* [1985] 1 A.C. 1054 where Leicester CC passed a resolution banning Leicester Rugby Football Club from using the Council's recreation facilities. The reason for the ban was they felt the club had not done enough to dissuade three of their players from going on an England Rugby tour of South Africa during the Apartheid era. The House of Lords held that whilst the club had power under the Race Relations Act 1976 to consider race relations, the RFC had done nothing illegal or improper and so the Council were using their power for an improper purpose, that of punishing the club for legal conduct.

RETENTION OF DISCRETION

15–014 The final main category of illegality also concerns discretion, but deals with situations where the exercise of power is by someone other than the person to whom it was intended, or where discretion is not used due to the existence of a rigid policy.

1. Unlawful delegation

15–015 It is a fundamental principle of administrative law that discretionary power should not be delegated; where this is done, unlawful delegation occurs. For example, where a statute confers power to body X, yet body Y uses the power instead. It is sometimes expressed as the latin *maxim delegatus non potest delegare*, meaning that the body to whom power has been delegated may not itself delegate the power. The principle of non-delegation is well-illustrated by *Barnard v National Dock Labour Board* [1953] 2 Q.B. 18 which represents a clear case of power being given to another body. Barnard had been suspended by his local port manager and argued this was unlawful delegation. The Labour Board was given power under the Dock Workers (Regulation of Employment) Order 1947 and was authorised to delegate specific disciplinary functions to local dock boards, including the right to suspend workers. The Court of Appeal found this to be a case of unlawful delegation as the power was given to the local dock board composed of equal numbers of workers and employers and not to an individual, in this case, the dock manager.

The rationale for the principle of non-delegation is parliamentary intention; if Parliament has specified that a particular body has power then a simple application of parliamentary sovereignty dictates that that body should exercise the power. There are also practical reasons why a body may have been given specific power. First, Parliament has given the power to a particular body because it has the expertise and knowledge to make decisions in the area, what Elliot in *Beatson, Matthews & Elliot's Administrative Law* calls "institutional reasons". Secondly, the body with the power will be accountable for its use, either legally or politically; "accountability reasons".

The rule against delegation is applied flexibly and takes effect as a presumption. The court, when interpreting a statute, starts from the position that Parliament did not intend delegation, then looks to see whether anything in the legislation, express or implied, rebuts that presumption. Some legislation, for example expressly permits delegation. For example, under the Local Government Act 1972 ss.101 and 102, local authorities are given power to delegate certain functions to committees, sub-committees and officers and under the Deregulation and Contracting Out Act 1994, a Minister may delegate certain functions to others, e.g. a commercial company. Where a statute is silent as to delegation, the courts consider the nature, purpose and context of the power. Where the nature of the power is judicial or quasi-judicial, the courts are reluctant to allow delegation and construe legislation narrowly; see *General Medical Council v UK Dental Board* [1936] Ch. 41.

In the interests of administrative efficiency, where the nature of the power is governmental, the courts are realistic to the idea that delegation may occur. The functions given to Ministers are so varied that no Minister could ever personally attend to them all, so delegation within the department for which the Minister is responsible is allowed. In *Carltona Ltd v Commissioners of Works* [1943] 2 All E.R. 560, under reg.61 of the Defence (General) Regulations 1939, the Commissioners made a decision to take possession of a factory. Carltona argued there had been an unlawful delegation of statutory power because the decision had not been made by the Commissioner, but by his assistant secretary. In rejecting this argument, Lord Greene M.R. said:

> "The duties imposed upon Ministers and the powers given to Ministers are normally exercised under authority of the Ministers by responsible officials of the department. Public business could not be carried on if that were not the case. Constitutionally, the decision of such an official is, of course, the decision of the Minister. The Minister is responsible. It is he who must answer before Parliament for anything that his officials have done under his authority, and, if for an important matter he selected an official of such junior standing that he could not be expected competently to perform the work, the Minister would have to answer for that in Parliament." (at p.562)

In *R. v Secretary of State for the Home Department Ex p. Oladehinde* [1991] 1 A.C. 254, the applicant submitted that in matters of such fundamental importance as deportation, it was not appropriate for the Minister to delegate his function to an Immigration Inspector. In rejecting that submission, Lord Griffiths indicated it would be impracticable to require the Minister to take every deportation decision. However, the House of Lords held the decision must be taken by a person of suitable seniority in the Home Office, which inspectors were.

Without formally doing so, a public body may surrender or abdicate its power or apply a pre-formed view or recommendation without due consideration. Such a situation would be unlawful and is illustrated by *Lavender and Son Ltd v Minister of Housing and Local Government* [1970] 3 All E.R. 871. The Minister for Housing was given power to consider appeals against a refusal of planning permission by a local authority. Lavender appealed against refusal of planning permission for mineral extraction, refusal being on the basis that the Minister of Housing had a policy that permission would only be granted if the Minister of Agriculture, Fisheries and Food agreed. It was held that, in effect, the discretion given to the Minister for Housing was exercised by the Minister of Agriculture. Willis J. said, "by applying and acting on his stated policy I think that the Minister has fettered himself in such a way that in this case it was not he who made the decision for which Parliament made him responsible. It was the decision of the Minister of Agriculture ... ". As a result, the application was allowed and the purported decision quashed.

2.   Fettering of discretion

15–016   Where discretion is conferred that body must not surrender, hamper or bind itself in exercising the discretion. This is known as fettering of discretion. Discretion conferred on a decision-maker is often granted in wide terms, for example, "as the Council thinks fit", and so decision-makers adopt policies to assist them in the exercise of their discretion. Whilst it would appear the adoption of a policy hampers or fetters the exercise of discretion, it is desirable as it guides individuals by providing a coherent and consistent set of guidelines. It is consistent with the rule of law and allows for consistency and certainty. However, whilst the existence of a policy does not bring the decision-maker into conflict with the fettering principle, a rigid application of that policy will. A decision-maker must be prepared to consider each application and make exceptions where it would appear appropriate, in other words, they should keep their minds open. This premise can be traced to the decision in *R. v Port of London Authority Ex p. Kynoch Ltd* [1919] 1 K.B. 176. Kynoch owned land adjoining the Thames, and wished to construct a deep water wharf for which he needed permission from the port authority. Permission was refused on the ground that Parliament had charged the authority with the duty of providing such facilities. Bankes L.J. highlighted the difference between two approaches:

> "There are on the one hand cases where a tribunal in the honest exercise of its discretion has adopted a policy, and, without refusing to hear an applicant, intimates to him what its policy is, and that after hearing him it will in accordance with its policy decide against him, unless there is something exceptional in his case ... no objection could be taken to such a course. On the other hand there are cases where a tribunal has passed a rule, or come to a determination, not to hear any application of a particular character by whomsoever made. There is a wide distinction to be drawn between these two classes." (at p.184)

On the facts, before reaching their decision, the authority had fully considered the case on its merits and in relation to the public interest, so they had not fettered their discretion and the decision was upheld.

This rule was applied in *British Oxygen Ltd v Minister of Technology* [1971] A.C. 610 which also demonstrates a flexible attitude towards consideration of policies by the Court. Section 1(1) of the Industrial Development Act 1966 provided that the Board of Trade could provide grants to businesses towards the cost of purchasing plant equipment. The Board developed a policy of refusing grants for any item of plant equipment costing less than £25. Pursuant to that policy, the Board rejected an application from British Oxygen whose equipment cost £20 each. British Oxygen contended the policy had precluded proper consideration of their application. The House of Lords, and in particular, Lord Reid, articulated the general rule that anyone exercising statutory discretion must not "shut his ears to an application". Even though the policy was so precise it could be called a rule, there was no objection to the existence of this, as "long as the authority is always willing to listen to anyone with something new to say" (p.625). On the facts, the Board had considered all that British Oxygen had to say and so had not closed their mind.

The fact that a decision-maker says it has not shut its ears, but has considered each application on its merits, is not determinative of the matter. The courts will look behind the purported exercise to ensure it has not been fettered. So, in the case of *R. v Warwickshire CC Ex p. Collymore* [1995] E.L.R. 217 a student grants policy was found to be fettering the Council's discretion when no award had ever been made despite 300 appeals. Similarly, in *R. v North West Lancashire Health Authority Ex p. A* [2000] 1 W.L.R. 977 the court stated it was not enough for an authority to assert it was prepared to consider departing from its policy in exceptional circumstances, but that it must show this preparedness is real and not fiction. In this case, a policy of the health authority to deny gender reassignment surgery for three transsexuals was unlawful. The Court of Appeal recognised it was reasonable for an authority to adopt a general policy, e.g. to place transsexualism low in an order of priorities of illness for treatment and to deny treatment, save for exceptional circumstances such as overriding clinical need. However, the operation of their policy was, in effect, meaningless because of the authority's reluctance to recognise gender re-assignment as treatment for transsexualism. The Court concluded that there was no genuine application of the policy.

BREACH OF HUMAN RIGHTS

1.   Acting unlawfully contrary to section 6 of the Human Rights Act 1998

The final broad category of illegality is a breach of human rights. Under s.6 of the   **15–017**
Human Rights Act 1998 (HRA), it is unlawful for a public authority to act incompatibly with Convention rights. Therefore, it is now possible for a claimant to seek judicial review of a public body on grounds of illegality; namely that a public body has violated the rights set out in the European Convention on Human Rights (see further Chs 20–24).

FURTHER READING

Craig, P. "Judicial review, appeal and factual error" (2004) P.L. 788   **15–018**
Craig, P. *Administrative Law*, 5th edn (Oxford: OUP, 2004)
Elliot (ed.) *Beatson, Matthews and Elliott's Administrative Law: Text and Materials*, 3rd edn (Oxford: OUP, 2005)
Fordham, M. *Judicial Review Handbook* 4th edn (Oxford: Hart Publishing, 2004)

Jones, T. "Mistake of Fact in Administrative Law" (1990) P.L. 507

King, J.A. "The justiciability of resource allocation" (2007) M.L.R. 70(2), 197–224

Leyland, P. and Woods, T. *Textbook on Administrative Law*, 5th edn (Oxford: OUP 2004)

Williams, R. "When is an error not an error? Reform of jurisdictional review of error of law and fact" (2007) P.L. Win, 793–808

Chapter 16

UNREASONABLENESS AND PROPORTIONALITY

INTRODUCTION

As has been seen, judicial review is concerned with the legality of a decision and the   **16–001**
process by which the decision is made, not the substance of the decision. This links to
the fact that judicial review is not an appeal, thereby confining the court to the decision-
making process, rather than the merits of the decision. The ground of unreasonableness
is, when set against this context, somewhat controversial in that it requires the court to
quash a decision because the end result, i.e. the substance, is unreasonable. Despite this
controversy, unreasonableness has been one of the areas of administrative law which
has seen considerable judicial activity in recent years. Until 1968, the ground was rarely
invoked. Now, according to Wade and Bradley, *Administrative Law* ((OUP, 2005),
p.353), it appears almost every week and in a substantial number of cases it is invoked
successfully. By these cases and others, the reasonableness doctrine has been refined,
and in some contexts, a more rigorous standard of review applied. Further, the advent
of proportionality as a principle from EU and Human Rights law has charged debate
and uncertainty as to the interplay between the two, and whether unreasonableness
might continue as a ground of review.

DEFINITIONS

1. Concept of unreasonableness

In *Associated Picture Houses Ltd v Wednesbury Corporation* [1948] 1 K.B. 223, Lord   **16–002**
Cooke identified two types of unreasonableness. Under s.1 of the Sunday Entertainment Act 1932, the corporation could grant licences to cinemas to open on Sunday

"subject to such conditions as the authority think fit to impose". They granted a licence to the Associated Picture House with the condition that no children under the age of 15 be admitted to the cinema on Sundays. The claimant argued the condition was ultra vires.

Given the wide discretion in s.1 the Court of Appeal held the condition was not, on its face, illegal. Giving the judgment of the court, Lord Greene M.R. set out two propositions of the term unreasonable. In his first proposition Lord Greene M.R. felt:

> "a person entrusted with a decision must, so to speak, direct himself properly in law. He must call his own attention to the matters which he is bound to consider. He must exclude from his consideration matters which are irrelevant to what he has to consider. If he does not obey these rules, he may truly be said, and often is said, to be acting unreasonably." (at p.229)

This can be considered a general proposition for all types of error dealt with under abuse of discretion (see Ch.15). Lord Greene's second proposition was that the courts can interfere, "if a decision on a competent matter is so unreasonable that no reasonable authority could ever have come to it" (p.230). This formulation can be considered a separate and distinct head of review and is what has properly become known as *Wednesbury* unreasonableness. It would apply to those cases which fall outside illegality and normal cases of abuse of discretion where the decision is so absurd that it can easily be said that no reasonable decision-maker would have come to it. On the facts of the case, the corporation was entitled to take into account the moral welfare of children and the court could not intervene simply because they might have come to a different conclusion. There was nothing unreasonable about what the corporation had done.

Unreasonableness is a high threshold test as indicated by Lord Greene himself who said it would require something "overwhelming" for a decision-maker to be acting unreasonably. Such an example found in the dicta of Warrington J. in *Short v Poole Corporation* [1926] Ch. 66, is the red-haired teacher dismissed because she had red hair. The restrictive vision of the test also reflects the nature of judicial review, that of legality, not the substance of a decision. Unreasonableness, as a ground, imposes a substantive rather than procedural limitation of power. The restrictive vision lends justification for court intervention in this area; they will only intervene if the decision is so flawed. It is important to remember, however, that courts should not substitute their view for that of the decision-maker; the test is not what the courts think is reasonable, but whether a reasonable body would make the same decision. To do otherwise would bring the courts into conflict with separation of powers as they would be seen to be exercising Executive powers.

2.   Irrationality

16–003   In *Council of Civil Service Unions v Minister for Civil Service* [1985] 1 A.C. 374 (*GCHQ*) Lord Diplock reformulated unreasonableness. He preferred to use the term "irrationality".

"By irrationality I mean what can now be succinctly referred to as '*Wednesbury* unreasonableness' … it applies to a decision which is so outrageous in its defiance of logic or accepted moral standards that no sensible person who had applied his mind to the question to be decided could have arrived at it." (at p.410)

There is debate whether "irrationality" is a better word. Lord Donaldson M.R. in *R. v Devonshire County Council Ex p. G* [1989] A.C. 573 disliked it stating (at p.577) "although it is attractive as being shorter than '*Wednesbury* unreasonable' … it is widely misunderstood by politicians, both local and national, and even more by their constituents, as casting doubt on the mental capacity of the decision-maker". Wade and Forsyth, *Administrative Law* (9th edn (OUP, 2004) at p.354) similarly question its benefit, noting that virtually all decisions are rational in the sense they are made up for intelligible reasons. Irrationality naturally means devoid of reasons, whereas unreasonableness means devoid of satisfactory reasons.

3.   Other formulations of unreasonableness

Aside from use of irrationality to replace unreasonableness, the courts are also **16–004** inconsistent in the form of the test chose. Lord Greene M.R. (at p.230) preferred to say an unreasonable decision was one that "is so unreasonable that no reasonable authority could ever have come it". Lord Cooke in *R. v Chief Constable of Sussex Ex p. International Trader's Ferry* [1992] 2 A.C. 418 thought this "tautologous" and preferred to ask, "whether the decision in question was one which a reasonable authority could reach". Lord Scarman in *Nottinghamshire County Council v Secretary of State for the Environment* [1986] A.C. 240 (at p.247) referred to an action as being "so absurd that he has taken leave of his sense" "so unreasonable as to be verging on an absurdity". Other formulations include referring to a decision as "perverse" (see *Reid v Secretary of State for Scotland* [1999] 2 A.C. 512) or "totally unreasonable". Whatever words or phrases are chosen though makes little difference, as conceptually they are the same: has the decision-maker abused their power?

4.   Constitutional problem with unreasonableness

In considering challenges on this ground, courts have consistently pointed out the **16–005** distinction between review of a decision's merits, i.e. its substance and review of its form, i.e. legality. Unreasonableness sits uncomfortably as a ground of review because its nature is concerned with the substance of a decision and whether that decision can be classed as unreasonable. Judicial review on the ground of unreasonableness can only be justified on the basis that Parliament may have intended to grant wide discretion as to how a power should be exercised but it never intended that power to be used unreasonably. However, the courts have to be careful not to overstep their constitutional boundary interfering in decisions which are properly the remit of the Executive. As Wade and Forsyth, *Administrative Law* (9th edn (OUP, 2004) at p.362) point out, "the doctrine that powers must be exercised reasonably has to be reconciled with the no less important doctrine that the courts must not usurp the discretion of the public authority which Parliament has appointed to take that decision". Equally, the courts have to be careful how they make a finding of unreasonableness. They must not quash a decision simply because they would not have come to the same decision themselves. To do this would mean the court has stepped over the boundary of what review is about and substituted their decision for that of the decision-maker, thus turning judicial review into judicial appeal. Despite being mindful of their constitutional boundary, there are cases where a finding of unreasonableness has led to accusations of judicial interference.

As a result of these constitutional difficulties, the courts have set a high threshold for the test of unreasonableness, applying the test with varying intensity depending on the nature of the subject-matter. They apply a less rigorous standard for politically-controversial decisions, such as national security or financial matters (see below), while retaining a more rigorous test for matters involving human rights.

DEFERENCE AND VARYING INTENSITY OF REVIEW

16–006   The concept of unreasonableness is flexible and adapted to different types of decision. Consequently, courts vary the intensity of review looking for evidence of unreasonableness depending on the context and the nature of the power being exercised. Writing extra-judicially, John Laws in Forsyth and Hare (eds), *The Golden Metwand and the Crooked Cord* ((Oxford: Clarendon Press, 1998) at pp.186–187) states that:

> "On the surface at least the test of unreasonableness or irrationality ... is monolithic; its leaves no scope for a variable standard of review according to the subject matter of the case ... But in fact the courts, whiles broadly adhering to the monolithic language of *Wednesbury*, have to considerable extent in recent years adopted variable standards of review [to suit the subject matter of the case before them] ... "

In some situations, the courts will only intervene if the decision crosses a high threshold of unreasonableness, so-called, "super-*Wednesbury*". The courts apply this principle to cases where, constitutionally, they feel it inappropriate for judicial intervention. Typically, such cases involve complex policy decisions, national security or financial issues. In *Nottinghamshire CC v Secretary of State for the Environment*, the Secretary of State issued guidance, approved by the House of Commons, as to the amount of funding local council's would receive. The applicant councils contended the guidance contravened a statute (see Local Government, Planning and Land Act 1980 s.59(11A)), and that it disproportionately disadvantaged a small number of councils and was therefore *Wednesbury* unreasonable. After rejecting the first contention, their Lordships turned to the second. In rejecting the conclusion that the Secretary of State had acted unreasonably, Lord Scarman gave two reasons. First, it was not constitutionally appropriate, except in exceptional circumstances, for the courts to quash guidance issued by a Secretary of State and which had also been approved by the House of Commons, on grounds of unreasonableness. Secondly, the nature of the decision concerned public expenditure which necessitated the courts reviewing the exercise of discretion by the Secretary of State which had required from him a political judgment and, which was approved by the House of Commons. It was not a decision capable of being reviewed by judges in their judicial capacity.

The case raises an important question as to the limits of judicial review and the separation of powers. Whilst the court would be happy to rule on whether the Secretary of State had acted illegality in setting the guidance, it was not constitutionally appropriate for a court either to interfere in political judgments, or to say that guidance approved by Parliament was perverse. However, it is important to note that simply because it was a political decision does not mean it will automatically preclude review on this ground, nor have such decisions always afforded a high level of defence. In *R. (Asif Javed) v Secretary of State for the Home Department* [2001] EWCA Civ 789, Lord Phillips M.R. [49] made this point when he noted it was the subject-matter of the power in the Nottinghamshire case which was important in determining the court's approach. As it concerned economic and political considerations evaluated by a Minister and Parliament, it was at the extreme end of the spectrum and, as such, the decision not to intervene was one of "practical reality". In *Javed*, the inclusion of Pakistan on a list of countries where there was generally no serious risk of persecution was considered unreasonable. Lord Phillips (at p.152) made it clear the decision in Nottinghamshire could not be treated as, "a proposition of law applicable to any order subject to affirmation resolution [by the House of Commons]".

In considering the reasonableness of a policy banning homosexuals from the armed forces, Sir Thomas Bingham M.R. in *R. v Ministry of Defence Ex p. Smith* [1996] Q.B. 517 affirmed the general principle that the nature of the decision decides the level of scrutiny:

> "The greater the policy content of a decision, and the more remote the subject matter of a decision from ordinary judicial experience, the more hesitant the court must necessarily be in holding a decision to be irrational ... Where decisions of a policy-laden, esoteric or security-based nature are in issue even greater caution than normal must be shown in applying the test, but the test itself is sufficiently flexible to cover all situations." (at p.556)

The reverse argument to the above is that in some circumstances courts will be more rigorous in their scrutiny of the reasonableness of a decision, known as heightened-*Wednesbury*. This was particularly prominent in the 1980s and 1990s in human rights cases before the Human Rights Act 1998 came into force. In *Bugdaycay v Secretary of State for the Home Department* [1987] A.C. 514 the applicants, having obtained entry into the United Kingdom, applied for asylum. Most of the applicants' appeals were dismissed, but in relation to one applicant (Mr Muisi) there was concern that removal back to Uganda would put his life in danger. In relation to that prospect, Lord Bridge (at p.531) said that the level of scrutiny must depend on the gravity of the issue, and that since the applicant's right to life was at issue, "the decision must surely call for the most anxious scrutiny". In the end, it was determined that the Home Secretary had failed to give sufficient consideration to the risk and his decision was quashed as being unreasonable.

This more rigorous standard of review was considered in *R. v Ministry of Defence Ex p. Smith*, which also raised issues applicable to the other end of spectrum (national security and policy). Smith had been dismissed from the armed forces pursuant to a policy banning homosexuals. The policy had been debated and supported by both Houses of Parliament and a Select Committee, but was challenged by Smith as being irrational. In discussing the standard of review, Sir Thomas Bingham M.R. (at p.556) recognised the conflict between deferring to the expertise of the Executive on policy matters and the need to "do right to all manner of people". He gave specific recognition to argument put forward by the applicants that the human rights context is important and said, "the more substantial the interference with human rights, the more the court will require by way of justification before it is satisfied that the decision is reasonable" (at p.554). Despite the more rigorous standard of review, the court found the policy to be rational.

Examples of Unreasonableness

16–007   Though *Wednesbury* unreasonableness is often raised as a ground of review, success on this ground is difficult due, in principle, to the high threshold and concerns about appropriate judicial interference. Whether a decision is unreasonable or not depends on the court's assessment of the arguments for and against it, and the nature of the power being exercised. Judicial decisions in this area are difficult to understand, and it is often the case that courts find an abuse of power without recourse to the phrase "*Wednesbury* unreasonable". As a result, it is difficult to set down categories of when a decision may be unreasonable.

An early finding of unreasonableness came in the case of *Hall & Co Ltd v Shoreham-by-Sea UDC* [1964] 1 W.L.R. 240. Hall applied for planning permission to develop land for industrial purposes. The land adjoined a busy road, already overloaded with traffic, and the highways authority had planned to widen it in the future. Hall was granted permission subject to conditions that they build an ancillary road to join the main road, at their own expense, giving the public right of passage over the road without any compensation from the Council. The Court of Appeal recognised that requiring the construction of an ancillary road was consistent with good traffic engineering, but the requirement to give right of passage and not provide any form of compensation was unreasonable.

Further examples of justifications for a finding of unreasonableness include:

- inappropriate balance of relevant considerations;

- lack of logic or flawed reasoning;

- oppression.

1. Inappropriate balance of relevant considerations

A defect in the decision-making process which does not fall under illegality could lead **16–008** to a decision being found to be unreasonable. Such a situation could arise where a decision-maker has taken into account relevant considerations but put too much emphasis on one of them, such that a reasonable decision-maker would not have done. In *West Glamorgan CC v Rafferty* [1987] 1 All E.R. 1005, a number of gypsies occupied, as trespassers, council-owned land which formed part of an industrial redevelopment area. The gypsies caused a nuisance to the local area and the council wished to redevelop the area so sought an order for possession of the land. The Court of Appeal found that the council, in deciding to evict the gypsies, had acted unreasonably in treating the interference with the redevelopment of the site as outweighing the effect the eviction would have on the gypsies and on those to whose area they would be moved. This was especially so when the effect of the eviction was caused by the council's own breach of duty under the Caravan Sites Act 1986 s.6(1) which placed an obligation on the council to provide accommodation for gypsies residing in its area. Gibson L.J. did not feel the court was precluded from finding the decision void for unreasonableness, "merely because there are admissible factors on both sides of the question. If the weight of the factors against eviction must be recognised by a reasonable council, properly aware of its duties and its powers, to be overwhelming, then a decision the other way cannot be upheld if challenged" (at p.1022).

2. Oppressive

A decision can be unreasonable if it imposes excessive hardship on the person to whom **16–009** the decision is directed or, alternatively, if the decision represents an infringement of the applicant's rights. Such a situation was found in *Wheeler v Leicester City Council* [1985] A.C. 1054. In this case, three members of Leicester City Rugby Football club were invited by the Rugby Football Union to join a tour of South Africa during the apartheid period. The local council objected to the tour and wished the rugby football club to put pressure on their members to withdraw. The club declined to condemn the tour or ask its members to reconsider their participation, so the council banned them from using the local recreation centre. The club sought to have the decision quashed. The House of Lords quashed the decision as an abuse of power because the council had used their statutory power for an improper purpose (see Ch.15) and because the decision was unreasonable.

3. Flawed reasoning

R. (on the application of Rogers) v Swindon NHS Primary Care Trust [2006] EWCA Civ **16–010** 392 is a more recent case of irrationality. Ms Rogers made an application to be provided with Herceptin, a non-licensed cancer treatment drug. Ms Rogers had been receiving Herceptin paid for privately, but was unable to continue paying. She requested that Swindon NHS Primary Care Trust ("Swindon") pay, but they refused stating they had a policy not to fund treatment with unlicensed drugs except where a patient had a special healthcare problem that presented an exceptional need for treatment. Ms Rogers contended that the policy was irrational. The Court of Appeal held that a policy of withholding assistance except in unspecified exceptional circumstances would be rational provided it was possible to envisage what such exceptional circumstances might be. If it was not possible to envisage any such circumstances, the policy would be, in practice, a complete refusal of assistance and be so irrational as it was not what it was seeking to be. In deciding whether Swindon's policy was rational, the court considered whether there were any relevant exceptional circumstances that could justify Swindon granting treatment to one Herceptin patient but refusing it to another. It concluded there was no rational basis for distinguishing between patients on the basis of exceptional clinical circumstances. The court said once Swindon had decided it would fund Herceptin for some patients and that cost was irrelevant, the only reasonable approach was to focus on the patient's clinical needs and to fund patients within the eligible group who had been properly prescribed Herceptin by their physicians. They had not done this, and as it was not possible to envisage any such exceptional circumstances for patients within the group; Swindon's policy was irrational.

Proportionality

1.   What is proportionality?

16–011   Proportionality is a concept with origins in European Community and Human Rights laws. In *De Freitas v Permanent Secretary of Ministry of Agriculture, Fisheries, Lands and Housing* [1999] 1 A.C. 69, Lord Clyde advanced a three-part test, later endorsed by the House of Lords in *R. (Daly) v Secretary of State for the Home Department* [2001] UKHL 26 (discussed below):

(1)   whether the legislative objective is sufficiently important to justify limiting a fundamental rights;

(2)   whether the measures designed to meeting the legislative objective are rationally connected to it; and

(3)   whether the means used to impair the right or freedom are no more than is necessary to accomplish the objective.

Proportionality is more concerned with the aims of the decision-maker and whether the decision-maker has achieved the correct balance. As Leyland and Anthony, *Textbook on Administrative Law* (5th edn (OUP, 2005), p.331) state:

"proportionality works on the assumption that administrative action ought not go beyond what is necessary to achieve its desired result (in everyday terms, that you should not use a sledgehammer to crack a nut) and, in contrast to irrationality, is often understood to bring the courts much closer to reviewing the merits of a decision."

2. Wednesbury unreasonableness and proportionality compared

Though courts consider cases with a human rights perspective with more acute scrutiny, **16–012** heightened-*Wednesbury* and proportionality are different legal tests and capable of achieving different outcomes. This is nicely illustrated by the Smith litigation (*R. v Ministry of Defence Ex p. Smith* [1996] Q.B. 517 and *Smith and Grady v UK* (1999) 29 E.H.R.R. 493).

In the first *Smith* case, the domestic courts found the government's policy of banning homosexuals from service in the armed forces rational, despite applying a rigorous scrutiny of the decision and because English courts had no obligation under the Convention, they could not apply its doctrines. The claimant took their case to the ECtHR alleging violation of art.8 (right to private and family life). The ECtHR held the blanket policy which required an automatic discharge regardless of service record was a disproportionate interference with art.8. This clearly shows that the test for unreasonableness, even at its high water mark of anxious scrutiny, is not always capable of protecting human rights to the degree that the European Convention on Human Rights requires. The proportionality test is more rigorous and exacting than the unreasonableness/irrationality test and, as the case shows, it was easier to show the policy was rational, having been debated by Parliament, than it was to demonstrate that a blanket policy was necessary to achieve the aim of protection of national security. It is because of this, however, that the test has often been criticised in the United Kingdom as it insists the courts assess whether the decision-maker has achieved the correct balance and is felt to impinge on the competence of the Executive decision-maker.

In *R. (on the application of Daly) v Secretary of State for the Home Department* [2001] UKHL 26; [2001] 2 A.C. 532, Lord Steyn [at 547] noted that the criteria of proportionality are, "more precise and more sophisticated than the traditional grounds of review" and went on to outline three concrete differences between the two:

(1) proportionality may require the reviewing court to asses the balance the decision-maker has struck, not merely whether it is within the range of rational or reasonable decisions;

(2) proportionality test may go further than the traditional test as it may require attention to be directed to the relative weight accorded to interest and considerations; and,

(3) even the heightened scrutiny test developed in *R. v Ministry of Defence Ex p. Smith* is not necessarily appropriate to the protection of human rights.

Despite this, Lord Steyn also felt most cases would be decided in the same way whatever approach adopted, though conceded for human rights cases proportionality was the appropriate test.

3.   Proportionality in judicial review

16–013   As is seen from the preceding discussion, application of proportionality to a decision is capable of producing different results than application of the traditional test. With this in mind, to what extent is proportionality a ground of judicial review? In *Council of Civil Service Unions v Minister for Civil Service*, Lord Diplock noted proportionality as a potential ground of judicial review. Since then, there have been attempts to incorporate proportionality more directly into judicial review outside of human rights and EU cases. However, this has met with judicial reluctance in some quarters.

   R. v Secretary of State for the Home Department Ex p. Brind [1991] A.C. 696 concerned a challenge to the decision by the Secretary of State to ban broadcasts on any matter consisting of words spoken by terrorist organisations. In particular, it was designed to prevent the IRA from being heard on television. Whilst not preventing broadcasters showing the images of the person speaking their words were dubbed with the voice of an actor. Brind and others, who were journalists, complained the decision was unreasonable and, further, contrary to the European Convention on Human Rights art.10 (the right to freedom of expression) as it was disproportionate and unnecessary in a democratic society. Their Lordships found the decision was not unreasonable on *Wednesbury* grounds, then rejected the idea that they were capable of determining whether the decision was proportionate as that would involve them determining whether the decision was necessary in a democratic society; incorporating the Convention by the backdoor. Lord Lowry (at p.766) stated there is no authority for saying that, "proportionality ... is part of the English common law".

   Following the incorporation of the European Convention of Human Rights, proportionality is applied domestically in human rights cases. In *R. (on the application of Daly) v Secretary of State for the Home Department*, the House of Lords concluded that a policy that prisoners should be absent from their cells when searched and officers permitted to examine, but not read, legal correspondence was unlawful and a breach of art.8 of the ECHR. Lord Bingham reached his conclusion on an orthodox application of common law principles, but applying proportionality as the standard of review. He concluded that the "infringement of a prisoners" rights to maintain the confidentiality of their privilege legal correspondence is greater than is shown to be necessary to serve the legitimate public objectives already identified" (at para.19). The House of Lords stressed that for all cases raising a human rights issue, proportionality was the appropriate standard of review.

4.   The end of Wednesbury unreasonableness?

16–014   Following the *Daly* decision, the position in English administrative law is that there are two tests; proportionality for cases raising human rights, and unreasonableness for everything else. A residuary issue is whether this means the end of unreasonableness or whether the tests continue to co-exist.

   In recent years, unreasonableness has been subjected to criticism on the ground that the test lacks clear formulation and is not transparent (see J. Jowell and A. Lester,

"Beyond *Wednesbury*: Substantive Principles of Administrative Law" (1987) P.L. 368 and G. Wong "Towards the Nutcracker Principle: Reconsidering the Objections to Proportionality" (2000) P.L. Spr. 92–109). As we have seen the *Wednesbury* test as formulated by Lord Greene M.R. is tautologous and there are variations of the test such as irrationality and perversity. In addition, there is often a lack of judicial reasoning as to why a decision is unreasonable, perhaps as M. Elliot (ed.) in *Beatson, Matthews and Elliott's Administrative Law: Text and Materials* (3rd edn (OUP, 2005)) suggests, because of concerns over judicial decision-making by intuition. As a result it makes it hard to determine what makes a decision unreasonable. Proportionality, on the other hand, is more precise and sophisticated than the traditional *Wednesbury* unreasonableness test, which makes its preference by the courts all the more understandable. However, proportionality does have its critics (see in particular the House of Lords in *Brind*), who suggest the main problem in using the more rigorous proportionality test is the concern it requires courts to substitute their view as to the correct balance for achieving a particular objective, for that of the designated decision-maker, leading the courts more into merits-style review. This concern was raised by the House of Lords in *Brind* when they refused to recognise the existence of proportionality in judicial review outside human rights. Lord Lowry (at p.767) in particular felt that proportionality-style review would be an "abuse of the judges' supervisory jurisdiction". He believed judges were not equipped with the training or knowledge to decide answers to questions where the scales were more evenly balanced, and that such style of review would jeopardise stability and relative certainty, leading to an increase in judicial review applications.

> "The decision-makers, very often elected, are those to whom Parliament has entrusted the discretion and to interfere with that discretion beyond the limits hitherto defined would itself be an abuse of the judge's supervisory jurisdiction … The judges are not generally speaking, equipped by training or experience, or furnished with the requisite knowledge and advice, to decide the answer to an administrative problem where the scales are evenly balanced." (pp.766–767)

Such strong views that proportionality was inappropriate for judicial review were echoed by Lord Ackner in the same case (at pp.762–763). Despite the views of the House of Lords in *Brind*, judicial dissatisfaction with unreasonableness as a test has continued to grow and the possibility of proportionality becoming a separate ground for review has at least received judicial recognition, if not support. Lord Slynn in *R. (Alconbury Developments) v Secretary of State for the Environment, Transport and the Regions* [2001] 2 All E.R. 929, a complex planning case, argued for proportionality to become a fourth ground of judicial review:

> " … even without reference to the [HRA] the time has come to recognise that [proportionality] is part of English Administrative law, not only when judges are dealing with [EU law] but also when they are dealing with acts subject to domestic law. Trying to keep *Wednesbury* principle and proportionality in different compartments seems to me to be unnecessary and confusing." (at 976)

Lord Slynn again made the argument that proportionality should be employed outside human rights cases in *Rehman v Secretary of State for the Home Department* [2003] 1 A.C. 153. This case concerned a decision to deport a Pakistani national with alleged links to an Islamist terrorist group on national security grounds. The applicant's appeal against the Secretary of State's successful appeal to the Court of Appeal was dismissed by the House of Lords.

Whether both tests should continue to co-exist was considered by the Court of Appeal in *R. (on the application of Association of British Civilian Internees: Far East Region) v Secretary of State for Defence* [2003] Q.B. 1397. Giving judgment, Dyson L.J. confirmed that unreasonableness lingers on, continuing:

" ... it seems to us that the case for [recognising proportionality as a general principle of review in domestic law] is indeed a strong one ... it is true that sometimes proportionality may required the reviewing court to assess for itself the balance that has been struck by the decision-maker, and that may produce a different result form one that would be arrived at on an application of the *Wednesbury* test ... The *Wednesbury* test is moving closer to proportionality and in some cases it is not possible to see any daylight between the two tests ... But we consider that it is not for this court to perform its burial rites. The continuing existence of the *Wednesbury* test has been acknowledged by the House of Lords on more than one occasion. The obvious starting point is *R. v Secretary of State for the Home Department Ex p. Brind* ... in which all of their Lordships rejected proportionality ... in other words, they closed the door to proportionality in domestic law for the time being." (at paras 33–34)

This conclusion has been accepted in subsequent cases in the Administrative court, *R. (Isle of Anglesey County Council v Secretary of State for Work and Pensions* [2003] EWHC 2518 (Admin) and *R. (Ann Summers Ltd) v Jobcentre Plus* [2003] EWHC 1416 (Admin).

It appears, for the time being, both tests continue to co-exist. Questions over the respective roles of the judges and decision-makers continue to concern some of the judicial and academic communities alike. However, Wade and Forsyth, *Administrative Law* ((OUP, 2004) pp.371, 372) have commented that, "the *Wednesbury* doctrine is now in terminal decline", but the "coup de grace has not yet fallen despite calls for it from very high authority".

FURTHER READING

16–015   Craig, P. *Administrative Law* 5th edn (Oxford: OUP 2004)

Elliott, M. "The Human Rights Act 1998 and the Standards of Substantive Review" (2001) C.L.J. 301

Elliot, M. (ed.) Beatson, *Matthews and Elliott's Administrative Law: Text and Materials* 3rd edn (OUP, 2005)

Jowell, J. "Beyond the Rule of Law; towards constitutional judicial review" (2000) P.L. 671

Jowell, J. and Lester, A. "Beyond *Wednesbury*: Substantive Principles of Administrative Law" (1987) P.L. Aut. 368–382

Laws, J. in Forsyth, C.F. and Hare, I. (eds) *The Golden Metwand and the Crooked Cord* (Oxford: OUP, 1998) at pp.186–187

Leyland, P. and Woods, T. *Textbook on Administrative Law* 5th edn (Oxford: OUP, 2004)

Wade, H.W.R. and Forsyth, C. *Administrative Law* 9th edn (Oxford: OUP, 2004) at p.441

Wong, G. "Towards the Nutcracker Principle: Reconsidering the Objections to Proportionality" (2000) P.L. Spr. 92–109

Chapter 17

Unfairness: Procedural Impropriety

Introduction

1. Definition

A public body may act within its legal powers, or use its discretion reasonably and **17–001** according to law, yet fail to act in accordance with the correct procedure. Lord Diplock in *Council of Civil Service Unions v Minister for Civil Service* [1985] 1 A.C. 374 (*GCHQ*) described this third head of judicial review as "procedural impropriety", a ground which includes:

> "a failure to observe basic rules of natural justice or failure to act with procedural fairness towards the person who will be affected by the decision ... [and] also [a] failure by an administrative tribunal to observe procedural rules that are expressly laid down in the legislative instrument by which its jurisdiction is conferred, even where such failure does not involve any denial of natural justice." (at p.411)

Two different procedural failings come under this ground of review. First, a failure to comply with procedural requirements found in a statute (procedural ultra vires) and secondly, a failure to observe the common law rules of natural justice.

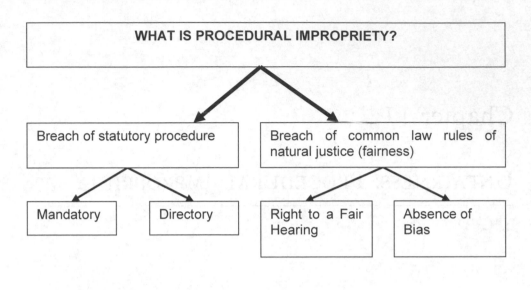

BREACH OF STATUTORY PROCEDURE

17–002   A decision-maker must conform to the procedures set down in statute by Parliament. Such rules may include something as critical as a duty to consult with A and B, or the requirement that a public body reply within 28 days. Historically, the courts have distinguished between two types of statutory requirements: mandatory and directory. A mandatory procedural requirement must be followed, failure to do so generally rendering the decision void. Failure to comply with a directory requirement, on the other hand, would not affect the validity of the decision. A requirement to consult has generally been held to be a mandatory. For example, in *Agricultural, Horticultural and Forestry Industry Training Board v Aylesbury Mushrooms Ltd* [1972] 1 W.L.R. 190, the Industrial Training Act 1964 s.1(4) provided for consultation with "interested organisations" prior to the Minister making a decision. The Minister consulted with the National Farmers Union but not a subsidiary, the Mushroom Growers' Association. The court held that s.1(4) of the Act was mandatory, requiring some consultation with the Association. As a consequence the Association did not have to abide by the decision.

It is a matter of construction as to what terms are mandatory and what are directory. The statute itself might use obligatory words such as "must" though generally, this is not the case and so it falls to the court to determine precisely whether a term is mandatory or directory. In recent years, the significance of the difference between the two requirements has been downplayed. Lord Hailsham in *London and Clydeside Estates Ltd v Aberdeen DC* [1980] 1 W.L.R. 182, when considering whether the requirement under art.3(3) of the Town and Country Planning (General Development) (Scotland) Order 1959 (SI 1959/1361) for written notice of appeal was mandatory, warned against the approach "of fitting a particular case into one or other of mutually exclusive and starkly contrasted compartments" (pp.188–90). Similarly, Lord Woolf

M.R. in *R. v Immigration Appeal Tribunal Ex p. Jeyeanthan* [2000] 1 W.L.R. 354 echoed Lord Hailsham's sentiment stating that attention should be placed on what Parliament intended should be the consequence of the non-compliance. In this case, under r.13(3) of the Asylum Appeals (Procedure) Rules 1993, an application for leave to appeal against an asylum decision by the Secretary of State was to be made in a prescribed form. The Secretary of State applied for leave to appeal by letter rather than using the form. The letter contained all the relevant information required by the prescribed form, except a declaration of truth.

Lord Woolf (at paras 360–362) thought the question of whether a requirement was directory or mandatory was only at most a first step. A more just and intended result could be achieved by considering the following questions:

(1) The substantial compliance question: "Is the statutory requirement fulfilled if there has been substantial compliance with the requirement and, if so, has there been substantial compliance in the case in issue even though there has not been strict compliance?"

(2) The discretionary question: "Is the non-compliance capable of being waived, and, if so, has it, or can it and should it be waived in this particular case?"

(3) The consequences question: "If it is not capable of being waived or is not waived then what is the consequence of non compliance?"

Lord Woolf stated which question arises depends on the facts of the case and the nature of the particular requirement. In this case, the Secretary of State, by omitting the declaration of truth in his application for leave to appeal, had not substantially complied with the requirements of r.13(3) of the Rules of 1993. However, the requirement as to the form of the notice of application for leave to appeal was not to be interpreted restrictively and the Secretary of State's omission was an irregularity which had been waived by the tribunal in the first case and had been impliedly waived by the asylum seeker in the second case. Therefore, the application for leave to appeal were not to be considered null. In *Att-Gen's Reference (No.3 of 1999)* [2001] 2 A.C. 91, the House of Lords expressly endorsed this approach when considering the proper interpretation of s.64(3B) of the Police and Criminal Evidence Act 1984.

THE COMMON LAW RULES OF NATURAL JUSTICE

A breach of the common law rules of natural justice is the second of procedural failing **17–003** outlined by Lord Diplock which forms part of the ground of procedural impropriety. Natural justice and art.6 of the European Convention on Human Rights provide minimum standards of fairness in respect of public decision-making. It is composed of two aspects:

(1) the right to a fair hearing (*audi alteram partem*; literally, to hear the other side); and

(2)   the rule against bias (*nemo judex in causa sua* (or *nemo debet esse judex in propria causa*).

According to Wade and Forsyth, *Administrative Law* (9th edn (OUP, 2004) at p.441), these concepts should be considered "implied mandatory requirements, non-observance of which invalidates the exercise of power". The concepts are not new, in *Bonham's Case* (1610) Coke C.J. commented that a statute which would make a man judge in his own cause, or was against common right or reason, would be void.

Contrary to Coke C.J.'s statement, there is now no right to invalidate a statute for failure to observe natural justice due to the doctrine of parliamentary sovereignty. However, the principles do apply to the exercise of public law power and delegated legislation. In *R. v Chancellor of the University of Cambridge* (1723) 1 Str. 557, Fortescue J. (at p.567) tracked the requirements of fairness back to the very beginnings of the universe, saying that "even God himself did not pass sentence upon Adam, before he was called on to make his defence".

1.   Fairness and the Human Rights Act 1998

17–004   The Human Rights Act 1998 means individuals have the protection of arts 5 and 6 of the European Convention on Human Rights. Since they are not regarded as part of the common law of procedural fairness an individual may choose to rely on these articles as they offer additional protection. These include the right to a hearing within a reasonable time, and the right to legal assistance of one's own choosing. However, whilst an individual might rely on these articles, they do not cover all decisions made by public bodies. For example, art.6 only extends to the determination of criminal charges or civil rights or obligations, and does not extend to all administrative matters. In *R. (Smith & West) v Parole Board* [2005] UKHL 45, the House of Lords found a decision by the Parole Board to revoke a licence was not a determination of a criminal charge. The majority thought it was not necessary to resolve the question whether or not the civil limb of art.6(1) was engaged, as the decision of the Parole Board attracted the common law protection of procedural fairness. Lord Bingham, speaking for the majority, was not persuaded that the civil limb, even if applicable, would afford any greater protection. Lords Slynn and Hope did deal with the question and felt the decision did not fall within the idea of a civil obligation in any event. See Ch.22 for a fuller discussion on the distinction between civil rights and criminal charge.

2.   History and development

17–005   Originally, natural justice applied to decisions which had serious consequences for the legal rights of those affected, *Cooper v The Board of Works for the Wandsworth District* (1848) 14 CB (NS) 180 providing a good early example. In this case, Cooper had started to build a house and was informed by the Board he had not served the proper notice. Consequently, they were entitled to demolish the building. The Board then started to demolish the building without giving Cooper a hearing. Cooper claimed a duty to hear him should be implied into the statute (Metropolis Local Management Act 1855 s.75). One of the District's arguments was that if a duty existed, it only applied to judicial, not administrative decisions. Erle C.J. found a duty to grant Cooper a hearing existed as there were grave consequences for Cooper, i.e. the demolition of his house. The focus of whether natural justice applied concerned the consequences of the decision, and was not restricted to matters which were purely judicial in nature. If the consequences of the exercise of a decision-maker's powers were severe, it was possible for an administrative body to be held to possess quasi-judicial or judicial powers.

However, in the first half of the 19th century, the courts took a regressive step and focused on the function of the decision-making body and whether it was judicial or administrative in the traditional sense. As a result, the right to natural justice was restricted to those bodies with a judicial or quasi-judicial function. A number of cases illustrate this and will be discussed below; *Errington v Minister of Health* [1935] 1 K.B. 249; *Franklin v Minister of Town and Country Planning* [1948] A.C. 87; *Nakkuda Ali v Jayarante* [1951] A.C. 66 and *R. v Commissioner of Police of the Metropolis Ex p. Parker* [1953] 1 W.L.R. 1150.

In *Errington*, the court confirmed that if a Minister who authorised a slum clearance was acting administratively, he would not be bound to comply with the rules of natural justice. However, they decided on the facts the Minister was found to be acting quasi-judicially as he had to ascertain the law and make a decision on that basis (though note that some of the court were reluctant to use this phrase as being something of a "vague character" (see Maugham L.J. at p.269) . In *Franklin*, the Minister proposed to designate Stevenage (draft Stevenage New Town (Designation) Order 1946) as a new town under the New Towns Act 1946. Franklin applied to have the Order quashed on the ground that the Minister was biased, the Minister having made a number of comments at a public meeting which suggested he had pre-judged the issue. In the House of Lords, Lord Thankerton considered that no judicial or quasi-judicial duty was imposed on the Minister as he was acting in a purely administrative capacity. Similar approaches were taken in *Nakkuda Ali* and *Parker* where revocation of licences was held to be administrative, despite the consequences such revocation would have for the individual concerned: loss of livelihood. In *Parker* it was a taxi licence, and in *Nakkuda Ali* the loss of a licence to deal in textiles.

Elliot in *Beatson, Matthews & Elliot's Administrative Law* (3rd edn (OUP, 2001) at p.349) feels that the *Franklin* decision epitomises the judicial approach which "determined the province of procedural fairness by reference to a narrow, formal analysis of power, without any appreciation of the wider implication of its exercise". Wade, "The Twilight of Natural Justice" (1951) L.Q.R. 67, 103 viewed this line of case law as the product of a "distorted understanding of the earlier decisions in which the terms 'judicial' and 'administrative' merely expressed a conclusion as to impact".

The retreat from the older authorities was ended by *Ridge v Baldwin* [1964] A.C. 40, where the House of Lords once more focussed on the consequences of the decision. Ridge, a Chief Constable, had been tried and acquitted of conspiracy to pervert the course of justice. Two other officers charged with him were convicted and, in sentencing, the Judge made adverse comments about the Chief Constable's leadership. Ridge was subsequently dismissed by his local watch committee under s.191(4) of the Municipal Corporations Act 1882 and he complained the requirements of natural justice had not been met. It was accepted by the court this was an administrative act but the consequences of the decision were such that natural justice should apply. Their Lordships revived the eighteenth century authorities and confirmed the emphasis on whether the rules of natural justice applied was the impact of the administrative decision on the individual's rights and interests.

3.   The duty of fairness

17–006   Though *Ridge v Baldwin* restored the orthodox view that natural justice depended not on the nature of the decision but the consequences of the decision, the case did not precisely eliminate the judicial/administrative divide. Little actual guidance can be gleaned from the case as to when natural justice should apply. The idea of a duty to act judicially was perpetuated throughout the decision, though such a duty could be found more easily. In *Re HK (an infant)* [1967] Q.B. 617, a new approach was suggested when the court talked about a duty of fairness. The applicant attempted to gain entry to the UK on the basis he was the son of a resident of the United Kingdom and under 16 years of age. Immigration officials doubted his age and began inquiries. They believed he was over 16 and decided to deport him. The applicant argued that in deciding whether or not the boy was under 16 years of age, the immigration officer was acting in a judicial or quasi-judicial capacity, and the rules of natural justice required the officer to give him an opportunity to put his case. In coming to his conclusion, Lord Parker C.J. doubted whether the immigration officials were acting in a judicial or quasi-judicial capacity and so were not required to act judicially, but found there was at least a minimum requirement to act fairly. In this case, the investigation satisfied that minimum requirement and so the action was dismissed.

(a)   *Natural justice or a duty to act fairly or both?*

17–007   The development of the right to fairness in *Re HK* left open the question as to the meanings of natural justice and procedural fairness and, in particular, the exact demarcation between the two. It appears Lord Parker envisaged a duty to act fairly as a sub-set of the rules of natural justice, imposing a less onerous duty on the decision-maker. Similarly, Megarry V.C. in *McInnes v Onslow Fane* [1978] 1 W.L.R. 1520 seemed to take the view that fairness was a more appropriate term for decisions made at the administrative end:

> "I do not think that much help is to be obtained from discussing whether 'natural justice' or 'fairness' is the more appropriate term. If one accepts that 'natural justice' is a flexible term which imposes different requirements in different cases, it is capable of applying appropriately to the whole range of situations indicated by terms such as 'judicial', 'quasi-judicial' and 'administrative'. Nevertheless, the further the situation is away from anything that resembles a judicial or quasi-judicial situation, and the further the question is removed from what may reasonably be called a justiciable question, the more appropriate it is to reject an

expression which includes the word 'justice' and to use instead terms such as 'fairness', or 'the duty to act fairly." (at p.1530)

It seems the above distinction is purely linguistic, not substantive. Thus, an alternative and more simplistic view is that any attempt to draw a distinction between the two is largely artificial and both concepts might be subsumed within the terminology of procedural fairness. The general trend seems to suggest a movement toward a notion of procedural fairness. As a broad principle, it imports a sliding scale which, according to Elliot in *Beatson, Matthews & Elliot's Administrative Law* (2001), does not require clear distinctions to be drawn between judicial, quasi-judicial and administrative, but means the content of what is procedurally fair will depend on the decision in question. *Mullan* (1975) 25 U.T.L.J. 281 at p.300 believes "that the development of procedural fairness is a most desirable advance ... It is desirable primarily because it allows the courts to ask what kind of procedural protections are necessary for a particular decision-making process unburdened by the traditional classification process".

However, the doctrine's development has not been without its criticism: Loughlin, "Procedural Fairness: A Study of the Crisis in Administrative Law Theory" (1978) 28 U.T.L.J. 215 has criticised the flexibility inherent within the notion of fairness and believes the approach is, "flawed because it requires the court to engage in activities which are inconsistent with its [traditional] role ... it will lead the court into controversial areas of policy which it is required to avoid". The shift to procedural fairness is said to alter fundamentally the basis of procedural intervention and it can no longer be restricted to adjudicative settings. As a result, the courts are required to engage in a difficult balancing exercise, taking into account the nature of the individual's interest against the increased procedural protections upon the administration. See also P. Craig, *Administrative Law* (5th edn (Oxford: OUP, 2004)).

RIGHT TO A FAIR HEARING

1.   General Principles

Fairness is a flexible concept and its exact requirements will vary according to the circumstances of the case, though may include all or a number of the following elements: **17–008**

(1)   the right to be informed of the case against such as the charge or allegation;

(2)   the right to prepare a response in reasonable time and notice;

(3)   the right to make representations;

(4)   the rights to cross examine any witness;

(5)   the right to be legally represented;

(6)   the right to reasons for the decision.

The courts employ many criteria to assist in determining the precise requirements of fairness. In *Lloyd v McMahon* [1987] A.C. 625 (for the facts, see below), Lord Bridge in the House of Lords noted the following:

"My Lords the so-called rules of natural justice are not engraved on tablets of stone. To use the phrase which better expresses the underlying concept, what the requirements of fairness demand when any body, domestic, administrative or judicial, has to make a decision which will affect the rights of individuals depends on the character of the decision-making body, the kind of decision it has to make and the statutory or other framework in which it operates." (at p.702)

The case of *McInnes v Onslow Fane* [1978] 1 W.L.R. 1520 provides a good example of the different levels of fairness decisions can attract. The case concerned an application for a boxing manager's licence. McInnes had previously held a promoter's licence which had expired and two other licences which were revoked on grounds of misconduct. He applied for a licence and was turned down. McInnes sought a declaration the decision was flawed by procedural fairness as he was given no oral hearing or notice of the case against him. Sir Robert Megarry V.C. considered the type of decision important and gave a three-fold categorisation of licensing:

(1)   forfeiture cases where a decision takes away some right or position or where a member of an organisation is expelled or licence revoked;

(2)   application cases where the decision merely refuses to grant the application the right or position that he seeks such as membership of an organisation;

(3)   expectation cases which differ from application cases as the individual has some expectation of receiving the benefit or that the licence will be granted. This category would include existing licence holders applying for a renewal or a person already appointed seeks confirmation from a confirming authority.

Forfeiture cases would attract a higher level of fairness and, according to Megarry V.C., should expect the right to an unbiased tribunal, the right to notice of the charges and the right to be heard in answer to those charges. On the other hand, mere application cases involved nothing being taken away and so no notice of any charges and no requirement of the opportunity to be heard regarding those charges was necessary. Expectation cases lay somewhere in between. On the facts of the case, McInnes was applying for a licence as he had never had a manager's licence, so there was no obligation to provide a hearing. All the Board had to do was "reach an honest conclusion without bias and not in pursuance of any capricious policy".

Although, the case involved licensing and should not be "read as establishing rigid categories" (Elliot in *Beatson, Matthews & Elliot's Administrative Law* (2001), p.365) it is useful as a guide to illustrate the factors the court may consider relevant in determining how and where on the scale a particular decision should be.

There are, of course, situations where a duty of fairness will be minimal or obsolete because of the particular nature of the decision. Such examples can be found in the following:

(1)   National security concerns may impact to limit the duty of fairness owed or defeat it entirely. Thus, in *Council of Civil Service Unions v Minister for Civil Service* [1985] 1 A.C. 374, whilst the House of Lords found an expectation of a hearing based on past conduct, the concerns the Minister had over national security were enough to defeat the procedural fairness owed.

(2)   Where a body has been given power to deal with matters of urgency or emergency, or where it is necessary to avoid public danger, the courts will not require strict procedural fairness. For example, in *R. v Secretary of State for Transport Ex p. Pegasus Holdings (London) Ltd* [1988] 1 W.L.R. 990, the Secretary of State did not act unfairly when he summarily suspended the flying permits of a number of airline pilots registered with the Romanian Civil Aviation Authority because of concerns for safety after they failed flying tests. Schiemann J. considered the rules of fairness to be engaged, but because of the potential magnitude of the risk, the duty was very low and not breached in this case.

(3)   An individual may waive their right to fairness and, in such situations, the court may be slow to re-impose obligations. In *Lloyd v McMahon* [1987] A.C. 625, the district auditor for Liverpool sent a letter to the city council detailing issues relating to rates and financial implications for each councillor personally. On receiving the letter, the council made a collective written statement. The auditor proceeded to write to them informing them that they were jointly and severally liable for £106,103. The applicants complained there had been a breach of fairness as they had not been afforded an oral hearing. The court dismissed their appeal saying they had waived their right to an oral hearing because they had adequate notice of the issues against them and had responded to them in their collective statement.

KEY FEATURES OF THE DUTY OF FAIRNESS

Having considered the nature and impact of the decision, it is necessary to examine the key features the duty of fairness may impose. The case law in this area is voluminous, so only a selection of cases is provided below. For further discussion, see Craig, *Administrative Law* (2004) and Elliot, *Beatson, Matthews & Elliot's Administrative Law: Text and Materials* (2005).   **17–009**

1.   The right to be informed of the case against

The general premise was well expressed by Lord Denning in *Kanda v Government of the Federation of Malaya* [1962] A.C. 322 (at p.337) who stated that, "If the right to be heard is to be a real right which is worth anything, it must carry with it a right in the accused man to know the case which his made against him. He must know what evidence has been given and what statements have been made affecting him". The right   **17–010** was further explained and applied in *R. v Secretary of State for the Home Department Ex p. Fayed* [1998] 1 W.L.R. 763. Fayed applied for, and was refused, British nationality under the British Nationality Act 1981. Pursuant to the statute, the Secretary of State gave no reasons for the decision. The majority of the Court of Appeal concluded that whilst there was no obligation to give reasons, it would be unfair not to give notice of the areas of concern (see para.17–013 below). Lord Woolf M.R. recognised the right of notice is limited:

" ... [the duty to give notice] does not require the Secretary of State to do more than identify the subject of his concern in such terms as to enable the applicant to make such submissions as he can. In some situations even to do this could involve disclosing matters which it is not in the public interest to disclose, for example, for national security or diplomatic reasons)." (at pp.776–77)

However, while there is a duty to know the case against, it does not require the decision-maker to cite "chapter and verse" (i.e. all) public interest arguments for example may hold that being given the general gist is sufficient. For example, fairness does not require disclosure of information which might be injurious to national security and closed material may be withheld from an appellant before the Special Immigration Appeals Commission (see in particular *MB & AF v Secretary of State for Home Department* [2007] UKHL 47 discussed in Ch.22. Details of the case against may also be withheld or limited if prejudicial to the fight against crime or entails release of confidential information. Such was the situation in *R. v Gaming Board Ex p. Benaim and Khaida* [1970] 2 Q.B. 417. Here the applicants who already ran a gambling (gaming) house needed to apply for a licence pursuant to new statutory rules. Prior to an application being made, a certificate of consent from the Gaming Board was required. At an interview with the Board, the applicants were asked, and answered, a wide-range of questions based on information already in the Board's possession, though its source and detailed content were not disclosed to the applicants. The applicants were invited to submit further information and the Board finally denied a certificate. The applicants sought judicial review contending they should have been given details of the case against them. The Court of Appeal found the Board had acted fairly in the circumstances. The Board was not dismissing the applicant from any office as in *Ridge v Baldwin*, or depriving him of his property as in *Cooper v Wandsworth Board of Works*, but were inquiring as to the applicant's fitness to apply for a licence. As the Board was entrusted by statute with the duty of controlling gaming, it was allowed to seek and use all reliable information to enable them to perform their duty. As a result, they were not obliged to disclose their sources or details of the information obtained.

2. The right to prepare a response in reasonable time and advance notice

17–011 In order for an individual to defend themselves, or prepare a response to concerns or allegations, it is necessary they are given reasonable time. In *R. v Magistrates' Court Ex p. Polemis* [1974] 2 All E.R. 1219, Polemis, a ship captain, was given notice at 10.30am to appear in court at 4pm the same day to answer alleged pollution offences. His subsequent conviction was quashed on the basis that it was unfair not to give him adequate opportunity to prepare his case.

3. The right to make representations

The essence of this rule is that an individual should be given the opportunity to make representations to the decision-maker concerning his case. The right to representations can be satisfied by written submission or, more onerously, the provision of an oral hearing. Not giving an individual the right to make representations can often fall foul of procedural fairness. However, written submissions can be sufficient to satisfy the duty of fairness, for example *R. v Secretary of State for the Home Department Ex p. Doody* [1994] 1 A.C. 531. Here the Secretary of State was required to give prisoners serving mandatory life sentences the opportunity to make written submissions concerning the period they should serve before the Secretary of State set the date for their first review. There was no requirement to give an oral hearing to each prisoner.

17–012

(a) *Right to an oral hearing*

Often, where breach of procedural fairness is alleged in this context, it is because the applicant was denied an oral hearing. There is no rule of fairness which requires an oral hearing and it depends on the nature of the case. Oral hearings are more onerous on the decision-maker in terms of cost and time. However, the advantages are that they allow for cross-examination of witnesses in person. In assessing whether fairness requires an oral hearing, the court has to balance the requirements of fairness to the individual against the impact providing a hearing will have on the decision-maker. The court must then assess whether in all the circumstances fairness requires an oral hearing to be given. *R. v Army Board of the Defence Council Ex p. Anderson* [1992] 1 Q.B. 169 gives some indication as to the factors the court should consider. A soldier made a complaint of racial discrimination which was referred to the Army Board. His request for an oral hearing was rejected by the Board as it had a policy of never granting oral hearings. Taylor L.J. in the Court of Appeal stated the issue of whether an oral hearing is necessary:

17–013

> " ... depends upon the subject matter and circumstances of the particular case and upon the nature of the decision to be made. It will also depend upon whether there are substantial issues of fact which cannot be satisfactorily resolved on the available written evidence. This does not mean that, whenever there is a conflict of evidence in the statements taken, an oral hearing must be held to resolve it. Sometimes such a conflict can be resolved merely by the inherent unlikelihood of one version or the other. Sometimes the conflict is not central to the issue for determination and would not justify an oral hearing. Even when such a hearing is necessary, it may only require one or two witnesses to be called and cross-examined." (at p.188)

Taylor L.J. concluded there was no general rule that the Army Board hold an oral hearing, and it was their decision, once it had seen all the statements and transcripts, whether an oral hearing was necessary to resolve the issues. On the facts, the issues were cut-and-dried and an oral hearing would probably not have been necessary. However, the Army Board's policy of never having oral hearings was unlawful as it amounted to a fettering of discretion.

In *R. v Parole Board Ex p. Smith*; *R. v Parole Board Ex p. West (Conjoined Appeals)* [2005] UKHL 1, the House of Lords held that before a parole board revoked a licence, an oral hearing might be necessary. Two prisoners who had been released on licence were recalled to prison due to various licence breaches. In considering what procedural fairness was required in the present context, the House took into account the various interests at stake: on one side, the safety of the public with which the Parole Board could not gamble and, on the other side, the prisoner's freedom which was conditional upon behaviour. Lord Bingham (at paras 30–35) thought the common law duty of procedural fairness did not require an oral hearing in every case where a prisoner's licence was revoked. He noted that whilst oral hearings are generally necessary when facts are in issue, it may even be so where important facts are not in dispute. Such facts may be open to explanation or mitigation, or may lose some of their significance in the light of other new facts. Additionally, the Board may be assisted by exposure to the prisoner or the questioning of those who have dealt with him in assessing the prisoner's character, demeanour and the veracity of his statements. In the circumstances, the Board had breached the prisoner's duty of fairness.

4.   The right to call and cross-examine any witness

17–014   Whether there is a right to cross-examine any witnesses will only arise if there is an oral hearing. A decision-maker is under an obligation to consider all the evidence placed before it and, in appropriate cases, will be required to hear witnesses. For example, in *R. v Board of Visitors of Hull Prison Ex p. St Germain (No.2)* [1979] 1 W.L.R. 1401, a prisoner found guilty of a number of offences against prison rules following a riot complained he had not had an opportunity to call witnesses. Geoffrey Lane L.J. (at p.1406) said "[T]he right to be heard will include, in appropriate cases, the right to call evidence ... mere administrative difficulties ... are not in our view enough. Convenience and justice are often not on speaking terms". Where there is, as there was in this case, hearsay evidence, fairness might demand an opportunity to deal with that evidence by cross examination of witnesses.

In *Bushell v Secretary of State for the Environment Appellant* [1981] A.C. 75, the House of Lords did not feel a public inquiry inspector's decision not to allow cross-examination of expert witnesses as to the reliability and statistical validity of evidence had been a breach of the rules of fairness. The House of Lords was mindful of the need not to "over-judicialise" the inquiry by insisting on observance of the procedures of a court of justice. The House did not feel the only fair way of ascertaining matters of fact and expert opinion was by the oral testimony of witnesses who were then subjected to cross-examination on behalf of parties who disagreed with what they have said. They concluded the procedure had not been unfair.

5.   The right to be legally represented

When appearing before a criminal court a person has the right to be legally represented.   **17–015**
This is guaranteed under art.6 of the European Convention of Human Rights, and is
also part of the requirements of common law procedural fairness. Whether the right to
legal representation is applicable to administrative decisions depends on whether there
is an oral hearing and whether that hearing cannot be conducted fairly without legal
representation. Whilst legal representation brings the skill of advocacy, allowing the
effective presentation of a case, it can overcomplicate and lengthen proceedings. In
Enderby Town Football Club Ltd v Football Association Ltd [1971] Ch. 591, the football
club was denied legal representation at a hearing where it was fined and censured. Lord
Denning M.R. noted (at p.605) there is no absolute right to be legally represented and,
in some cases, it may be a good thing for proceedings to be conducted informally
without legal representation. "Justice can often be done in them better by a good
layman than by a bad lawyer". He felt this was especially so in football and other sports
where no issues of law arises and instead is often a question of the bodies rules and
procedures.

In *R. v Secretary of State for the Home Department Ex p. Tarrant* [1985] Q.B. 251, the
Divisional Court (at p.284) outlined the criteria to consider when exercising discretion
in this area, these included:

(1)   the seriousness of the charge and potential penalty;

(2)   where any points of law were likely to arise;

(3)   the capacity of the prisoner to present his own case;

(4)   the complexity of the procedure;

(5)   the need for reasonable speed in decision-making;

(6)   the need for fairness between prisoners and between prisoners and prison
officers.

Whilst the case concerned prisoners and their right to be represented before a disciplinary hearing, the first five can be considered of general application.

6.   The right to reasons for the decision

According to Craig, *Administrative Law* ((2004) at p.436) there are many advantages to   **17–016**
the giving of reasons, these include:

(1)   assisting the court in the exercise of its supervisory functions as it can show
that factors have been considered or ignored or disproportionately
considered;

(2)   focuses the decision-makers mind by ensuring they think through their decisions;

(3)   demonstrates that other rights such as consultation have not merely been paid lip service; and

(4)   improves public confidence in the administrative process and enhances its legitimacy as the public can see that the decision is not arbitrary.

However, there are equally disadvantages to giving reasons; notably they can stifle the exercise of discretion and place a heavy burden on the administration. However, it is fair to say that the advantages outweigh these few disadvantages. Despite this, the House of Lords in *R. v Home Secretary Ex p. Doody* [1994] 1 A.C. 531 made it clear that at common law there is no general duty to give reasons.

In some circumstances, the law imposes such a duty, be it by statute or common law. Statute may impose an obligation to give reasons. For example, the Tribunals and Inquiries Act 1958 imposes a duty on any tribunal, listed in Sch.1, to give written or oral reasons which are "proper, intelligible and adequate" (see *Re Poyser and Mills Arbitration* [1964] 2 Q.B. 467). The common law has also developed specific situations where such a duty will be imposed; these are where:

(1)   The decision is aberrant. Where a decision appears devoid of reason and potentially irrational, the decision-maker will be under a duty to provide reasons so it can be determined whether the aberration is real or merely apparent. This occurred in *R. v Civil Service Appeal Board Ex p. Cunningham* [1991] 4 All E.R. 310, where the Board decided to give an abnormally low award to a prison officer who had been unfairly dismissed.

(2)   If a fundamental issue is at stake. In *R. v Home Secretary Ex p. Doody* [1994] 1 A.C. 531, a duty to give reasons was found where the Home Secretary decided to depart from the recommended tariff period given by the judge. It was felt it would be unfair to a prisoner given a mandatory life term to be treated less favourably than a prisoner sentenced to a specific term who was given reasons by the trial judge (see also *R. v Secretary of State for the Home Department Ex p. Hindley* [1998] 2 W.L.R. 505). In *R. (Wooder) v Feggerter* [2003] Q.B. 219, reasons had to be given when certifying that medication should be given to a competent but non-consenting patient.

In addition, duties have been found in relation to a decision of the General Medical Council relating to a doctor's fitness to practice (*Stefan v General Medical Council (No.1)* [1999] 1 W.L.R. 1293), and to decisions of a court martial (*R. v Ministry of Defence Ex p. Murray* [1998] C.O.D. 134).

However, while in some circumstances there is a duty to provide reasons, in others, a duty will not be imposed. This is likely where to impose such a duty would be costly or burdensome to the public body or where the issues are particularly complex; two such cases illustrate this. In *R. v Higher Education Funding Council Ex p. Institute of Dental Surgery* [1994] 1 W.L.R. 242, the applicants were aggrieved by the research rating given them by the Council as it was lower than expected and, it was estimated, would result in a loss of research funding in the region of £270,000. No reasons had been given. Sedley J. felt the decision could be distinguished from *Cunningham* and *Doody* as it was neither aberrant nor affected fundamental interests. The court felt it could not intervene simply because the decision had serious consequences for the institute as this would be tantamount to imposing a general duty to give reasons on all administrators ("a point to which the court … cannot go" (at p.260)). A similar point was made in *R. (Asha Foundation) v Millennium Commission* [2003] EWCA Civ 88 where a claimant's application for lottery funding was turned down because his application was less attractive than others. The court felt that imposing a duty to give greater reasons would be unduly onerous as it would require the decision-maker to write down what each thought about all the other applications and why this one was less attractive.

(a)   *If a duty to give reasons is imposed what does it require?*

As with most issues in procedural fairness, the level of detail for reasons depends on the subject-matter. In *South Buckinghamshire District Council v Porter* [2004] UKHL 33, in relation to a planning matter Lord Brown commented:

> "The reasons for a decision must be intelligible and they must be adequate. They must enable the reader to understand why the matter was decided as it was and what conclusions were reached on the "principal important controversial issues", disclosing how any issue of law or fact was resolved. Reasons can be briefly stated, the degree of particularity required depending entirely on the nature of the issues falling for decision." (at para.36)

17–017

It is clear from the cases that a range of criteria are considered when deciding whether to impose a duty to give reasons. Elliot (ed.) *Beatson, Matthews and Elliott's Administrative Law: Text and Materials* (2005) feels that giving reasons for a decision should be treated as a central facet of procedural fairness. He feels heartened from his study of the cases that English law now takes seriously the duty to give reasons and views with increasing scepticism the argument that forcing decision-makers to give reasons imposes an intolerable burden. He believes it is only to be a matter of time before a general duty to give reasons is acknowledged (see also Wade and Forsyth, *Administrative Law* ((2004) at pp.522–527)).

The Rule against Bias

The second limb of natural justice is that decisions should be free from bias. It is a fundamental tenet of administrative law that no man should be a judge in his own cause (*nemo judex in re sua*), in that he should have no interest in the outcome of the case or decision, or have made any pre-judgment. In the memorable words of Lord Hewart C.J. in *R. v Sussex Justices Ex p. Marcarthy* [1924] 1 K.B. 256, it is of "fundamental importance that justice should not be done, but should manifestly be seen to be done"

17–018

(at p.259). Any decision-maker is therefore to be disqualified from making a decision in which there is actual presumed or apparent bias.

1.   Actual bias

17–019   If the decision-maker has been influenced as to the actual outcome of a decision or actively favours one party this would amount to actual bias. Examples of actual bias are rare as they are difficult to prove, though if found a person is automatically disqualified from sitting or making the decision. As Lord Goff noted in *R. v Gough* [1993] A.C. 646, "if actual bias is proved, that is an end of the case; the person concerned must be disqualified" (at p.661).

2.   Presumed bias: automatic disqualification: direct interest

17–020   A decision-maker with a direct interest in a decision or case is presumed to be biased, automatically disqualified, and any decisions made are void. There is no need to show actual bias as the basis of the disqualification is the existence of the interest which is sufficient to provide a motive for bias and so automatically disqualifies the decision-maker. Its potential effect on the decision-maker's mind is irrelevant and he is disqualified without any investigation as whether in fact there was any possibility of bias. Historically, this aspect of bias solely covered financial interests but has since been extended to exceptionally cover non-financial interests.

Where a person has a financial interest, no matter how small, the appropriate course of action is for the decision-maker to stand down. *Dimes v Grand Junction Canal* (1852) 10 E.R. 301 illustrates this approach. The Lord Chancellor, Lord Cottenham, heard an appeal by Dimes and affirmed the decision of the lower court in favour of Grand Junction Canal Company. Unbeknownst to Dimes, the Lord Chancellor had a substantial shareholding in the Grand Junction Canal. Dimes appealed on the basis that the Lord Chancellor should have been disqualified by reason of his financial interest and his decision set aside. In the House of Lords, their Lordships agreed and set the decision of the Lord Chancellor aside. They noted there was no inference the Lord Chancellor was actually biased, but the principle that no man should be a judge in his own cause was not confined to a case in which he was a party, but also where he had an interest. However, if the financial interest is too remote, a person will not have to stand down. In *R. v Rand* (1865–66) L.R. 1 Q.B. 230, two justices who were trustees of institutions holding bonds in the Bradford Corporation, which was a party to the case, were not disqualified from sitting as a result in favour of the Corporation would not have resulted in any tangible benefit for the justices. A similar point was made in *Locabail (UK) Ltd v Bayfield Properties Ltd* [2000] Q.B. 451 at para.10.

This principle was extended in *R. v Bow Street Metropolitan Stipendary Magistrate Ex p. Pinochet Ugarte (No.2)* [2000] 1 A.C. 119, where the House of Lords clarified the position in *Dimes*, stating that any direct interest, whether financial, proprietary or otherwise, would lead to the automatic disqualification of the decision-maker. Senator Pinochet was Chile's Head of State of Chile from 1973–1990. During that time it was alleged various crimes against humanity had taken place. Whilst Pinochet was in the UK receiving medical treatment, Spain issued international arrest warrants to enable his extradition to Spain to face trial for crimes against humanity. Senator Pinochet contended he was immune from suit as a former Head of State. The question for the court was the extent of that immunity. In a 3–2 majority decision, the House of Lords concluded that Senator Pinochet was not entitled to immunity. Of the three in the majority, Lords Nicholls and Steyn delivered speeches, while Lord Hoffmann agreed with them, without giving separate reasons for allowing the appeal. It later transpired that Lord Hoffman was a director and chairperson of Amnesty International Charity Ltd (AICL), a subsidiary of Amnesty International; one of the parties seeking extradition. Senator Pinochet sought to have the decision set aside on the grounds that Lord Hoffman was biased.

Lord Browne-Wilkinson, with whom the other Law Lords agreed, felt that even though there was no financial interest, there was no good reason for limiting automatic disqualification to financial cases only. He noted the rationale for the rule that no man can be a judge in his own cause arose from civil litigation where the matters normally had an economic impact and, therefore, if a judge stands to make a financial gain he is automatically disqualified. The present case, however, concerned the promotion of a cause and the rationale disqualifying a judge applied just as much if the judge's decision would lead to the promotion of that cause. Though Lord Hoffman was a director of AICL and not a member of Amnesty International, Lord Browne-Wilkinson considered them to be "various parts of a movement working in different fields but towards the same goals". Lord Hoffmann had an interest to promote the causes advanced by them and that was sufficient to make him a judge in his own cause.

> "If the absolute impartiality of the judiciary is to be maintained, there must be a rule which automatically disqualifies a judge who is involved, whether personally or as a director of a company, in promoting the same causes in the same organisation as is a party to the suit. There is no room for fine distinctions if Lord Hewart C.J.'s famous dictum is to be observed." (at p.135)

The House of Lords placed emphasis on the unusualness of this case and the decision does not preclude judges from sitting on cases concerning charities which they are involved in but only where the judge is a trustee or director of a charity which is closely allied to and acting with a party to litigation.

3. Apparent bias: non-automatic disqualification: non-direct interests

The second category concerns cases where there is no direct personal interest but instead an appearance of bias arising out of a non-direct interest. Any disqualification under this head is not automatic, but depends on all the circumstances of the case and whether in those circumstances a fair-minded person would conclude there was a real possibility of bias.   **17–021**

(a) History

17-022   The law on this area was confused and two tests for determining bias were given by the courts. The first test arose in the nineteenth century and the court would ask whether there was a real likelihood of bias ("the real likelihood test"). This test was quite restrictive and the court had to assess, on the facts, whether there really was a real likelihood of bias. It was applied in cases such as *R. v Rand* above. In *R. v Sussex Justices Ex p. McCarthy* [1924] 1 K.B. 256, Lord Hewart CJ thought a reasonable suspicion the decision-maker was biased was enough ("the reasonable suspicion test"). However, in the mid-20th century the second, more restrictive, test re-gained favour in *R v Camborne Justices Ex p. Pearce* [1955] 1 Q.B. 41. Lord Denning somewhat confused the issue more in *Metropolitan Properties (FGC) Ltd v Lannon* [1969] 1 QB 577 (at 598–600 and 606) when he resurrected Lord Hewart's test of suspicion, yet in the same case talked about likelihood. The House of Lords in *R. v Gough* [1993] A.C. 646 then took the opportunity to clarify the law.

(b) Pre-Human Rights Act 1998

17-023   The test laid down in *R. v Gough* [1993] A.C. 646 was accepted as the standard test before the Human Rights Act 1998 came into force. Gough was convicted of conspiracy to rob and appealed on the grounds that a member of the jury was his brother's next door neighbour. Lord Goff noted there was a "bewildering" array of authorities and thought there should be one unified test. He stated that "having ascertained the relevant circumstances, the court should ask itself whether, having regard to those circumstances, there was a real danger of bias ... in the sense that he might unfairly regard (or have unfairly regarded) with favour, or disfavour, the case of a party to the issue under consideration by him" (at p.669) ("the real danger test"). Interestingly, Lord Goff thought it was not necessary to formulate the test in terms of the reasonable man. He believed the court personified the reasonable man and moreover the court could better ascertain the relevant circumstances which had a bearing on the issue, thus making it fairer. This part of the test subsequently led to concerns over its compatibility with art.6(1) of the European Convention on Human Rights (see below).

The resulting "real danger" test was applied in *R. v Inner West London Coroner Ex p. Dallaglio* [1994] 4 All E.R. 139. The coroner in the Marchioness disaster was reported as describing relatives of the deceased as "mentally unwell" or "unhinged". The Court of Appeal concluded the use of the words indicated a real danger of unconscious bias. It was also held by the High Court to apply to administrative decisions as well as judicial decisions in *R. v Secretary of State for the Environment Ex p. Kirkstall Valley Campaign Ltd* [1996] 3 All E.R. 304 where the KVC, a community action group, applied for judicial review of decisions of the Leeds Development Corporation (LDC) to grant planning permission for the development of a supermarket on a rugby ground owned by Headingley Football Club. The chairman of the LDC owned land to which the rugby club was considering moving, and other members of LDC had connections with the rugby club. KVC argued there was apparent bias and the decisions were contaminated by such undeclared interests and therefore were vitiated. Whilst such a connection would undoubtedly fall foul of the bias rule, on the facts the plan to move the rugby club to land owned by the chairman was no longer an option at the time the decision was made and so there was no apparent bias.

(c)   Current test

There were concerns the courts emphasis on the facts was not compatible with art.6(1)   **17–024**
of the European Convention of Human Rights as it did not appear to be objective, nor be from the point of view of a reasonable man or fair minded observer. The Court of Appeal in *Locabail (UK) Ltd v Bayfield Properties Ltd* [2000] Q.B. 451 (at p.477) examined the question whether the real danger test would lead to a different result from that which the informed observer would reach and concluded in the majority of cases the application of the two tests would lead to the same outcome. However, slight modification was offered by the Court of Appeal in *Re Medicaments and Related Classes of Goods (No.2)* [2001] 1 W.L.R. 700 and this was confirmed by Lord Hope in House of Lords in *Porter v Magill* [2001] UKHL 67 which set out a two stage test:

(1)   the court must first ascertain all the circumstances which give rise to bias; then

(2)   it must then ask whether in those circumstances a fair-minded and informed observer would conclude that there was a real possibility of bias.

Lord Hope substituted real danger for real possibility believing them to mean the same thing, but real possibility to be more in tune with Strasbourg. The test set down in Porter is the current test and was confirmed by the House of Lords in *Lawal v Northern Spirit* [2003] UKHL 35. (See Ch.22 for further information on the impact of human rights on bias).

The decisions in *Lawal* and of the House of Lords in *Gillies v Secretary of State for Work and Pensions* [2006] UKHL 2 merit consideration. Both cases concern questions of bias over tribunal members and in both cases the House of Lords discussed aspects of the fair-minded and informed observer. *Lawal* concerned the question of whether an Employment Appeal Tribunal was biased because counsel appearing before it was also a part-time judge in the Tribunal. Importantly, counsel had previously sat with one or two of the lay members hearing the case. The House made it clear the fair-minded and informed observer should adopt a "balanced approach" and be "neither complacent nor unduly sensitive nor suspicious" (at para.14) and concluded that on these facts there was a real possibility of such lay members being subconsciously biased in favour of counsel's submissions.

Gillies v Secretary of State for Work and Pensions [2006] UKHL 2 concerned whether there was a real possibility of bias from a member of a disability appeals tribunal who was also Examining Medical Practitioner (EMP) for the Benefits Agency. Gillies contended the tribunal member would be biased in favour of the EMP report given in her case by another EMP. Lord Hope stated that " ... the fair-minded and informed observer can be assumed to have access to all the facts that are capable of being known by members of the public generally, bearing in mind that it is the appearance that these facts give rise to that matters, not what is in the mind of the particular judge or tribunal member who is under scrutiny" (at para.17). Lord Hope concluded there was no issue of bias as the doctor's relationship with the Benefits Agency was as an independent expert adviser. A fair-minded observer would appreciate the doctor was just as capable of exercising professional detachment and the ability to exercise her own judgment when sitting as the medical member of a disability appeal tribunal. As a result, the administration of justice was not "compromised by the use of specialist knowledge or expertise when the judge or tribunal member is examining the evidence" (at para.23). The difference between the two cases lies in the fact that in *Lawal*, counsel was known and had sat with some of the Tribunal members hearing the case, whereas in *Gillies*, though the tribunal member was also an EMP, she had no connection to the EMP in the case and would still be able to evaluate the report objectively and impartially.

FURTHER READING

17–025   Craig, P. *Administrative Law* 5th edn (Oxford: OUP, 2004)

Cross, T. "Predispositions, predeterminations and the test for apparent bias: some reflections post *National Assembly for Wales v Condron*" (2007) *Journal of Planning & Environment Law*

Elliot (ed.) *Beatson, Matthews and Elliott's Administrative Law: Text and Materials*, 3rd edn (Oxford: OUP, 2005)

Fordham, M. *Judicial Review Handbook* 4th edn (Oxford: Hart Publishing, 2004)

Wade and Forsyth, *Administrative Law*, 9th edn (OUP, 2004) at p.441

Chapter 18

LEGITIMATE EXPECTATION

INTRODUCTION

1. Definition

Legitimate expectation is the doctrine that an expectation of a procedure or benefit   **18–001**
arising from a promise or practice may be protected by law. Lord Denning first used the
phrase legitimate expectation in English public law in 1969 in *Schmidt v Home Secretary*
[1969] 2 Ch. 149 (see below). At that time, the doctrine was limited to procedural
legitimate expectations where the court could insist the rules of natural justice were to
be observed. More recently, the doctrine has been recognised as extending to promises
of a substantive nature, i.e. a promise of a benefit and, has been considered under the
grounds of fairness and reasonableness (see para.18–013 below). At the heart of the
developing doctrine is a conflict between the desire to protect an individual's confidence
in promises made by a public body, and the need for the public body to maintain
flexibility in the pursuit of changing policy objectives. The law in this area is complex as
the courts continue to develop the principles. As such it is easier to consider legitimate
expectation as a separate ground of judicial review whilst recognising the overlaps with
fairness and unreasonableness.

2. Rationale for legitimate expectation

At the heart of the motivation for protecting legitimate expectation is the idea of   **18–002**
fairness, good government and upholding the rule of law. Four broad principles for
protecting a legitimate expectation can be established:

(1)   Certainty: At a time when discretionary power is rife, the principle of legal certainty is a key feature of the rationale. In the exercise of discretion, the rule of law dictates that like cases are treated alike. Consequently, there should be a degree of predictability and constancy such that individuals can plan their lives with reference to administrative decisions. Frequent changes may undermine individual rights by creating uncertainty, while departure from a representation may cause disappointment and financial loss.

(2)   Trust in government: If an individual is informed by an official he will receive a particular procedure or benefit and that representation is subsequently denied, or reneged on, trust in government is impaired.

(3)   Reputation: A general tendency for promises to be broken may damage the reputation of the administration as a whole.

(4)   Participation: The willingness of individuals to participate in the decision-making process and comply with decisions may diminish if trust and confidence are damaged.

However, equally there are cogent reasons for allowing decision-makers to go back on promises, the primary reason being administrative autonomy. Public bodies must be free to develop and change their policies in the public interest. The principle of legality states that a public body cannot fetter its discretion, thus allowing a body to fetter its discretion by making a binding promise may contravene that principle (see in particular, Steele, "Substantive legitimate expectations: striking the right balance?" (2005) L.Q.R. 121 (Apr) 300. As a result, there appears to be an inherent conflict between fairness on one hand, and legality on the other. Other reasons for not upholding the doctrine include:

(1)   Where the representation is itself unlawful, i.e. where the body has no power either to make the representation or to fulfil the promise. In such situations the principle of legality is again breached if the promise is nonetheless fulfilled.

(2)   In some cases, public confidence in government may in fact be enhanced by judicious departure from, rather than slavish adherence to, past promises;

(3)   From a more practical perspective, holding bodies to their representations may have a "chilling effect" on the provision of informal advice, denying individuals the opportunity to plan ahead in the first place.

3.   Types of legitimate expectation

18–003   There are two types of legitimate expectation: procedural and substantive. A procedural legitimate expectation is a promise that a particular procedure will be followed. Such an example is found in *Att-Gen of Hong Kong v Ng Yuen Shiu* [1983] 2 A.C. 629. Ng Yeun Shiu entered Hong Kong illegally from China in 1976 and, pursuant to a policy existing at that time, was allowed to stay. Following a change of policy in 1980, the government gave an undertaking those illegal immigrants from China would be interviewed personally and each case assessed on its merits. Ng Yeun Shiu was served with a deportation order without being provided with the opportunity to make full representations. The Privy Council quashed the deportation notice as the undertaking had created a legitimate expectation of a fair hearing which had not been honoured (see also *Council for Civil Service Unions v Minister for Civil Service* [1985] 1 A.C. 374).

The second type of legitimate expectation is substantive. This is where Y is led to believe, by X, that they will get Z, or continue to receive Z (a benefit). The arrival of this type of legitimate expectation has been traced to *R. v Secretary of State for Home Department Ex p. Khan* [1985] 1 All E.R. 40. Khan wished to adopt his brother's child from Pakistan. The government's policy on adopting children from overseas was set out in a Home Office circular and a pro forma letter which outlined four stages an applicant had to follow. Khan complied with these requirements, but the adoption was refused on the ground that the natural parents were capable of caring for the child; a factor not in the original letter. The applicant argued a legitimate expectation that the application would be processed in a particular way (procedural) and therefore, if met, the adoption would follow (substantive benefit). The refusal of entry clearance was quashed as the court held that he had a legitimate expectation.

How Can a Legitimate Expectation Arise?

In *Council for Civil Service Unions v Minister for Civil Service* [1985] 1 A.C. 374, Lord **18–004** Fraser identified two ways a legitimate expectation can arise: "legitimate expectation may arise from either an express promise given on behalf of the public authority of from the existence of a regular practice which the claimant can reasonably expect to continue" (at p.401).

1.   Express promise

The most common way a legitimate expectation might arise is by an express promise or **18–005** specific representation to an individual or group. In *R. v Liverpool Corporation Ex p. Liverpool Taxi Fleet Association* [1972] 2 Q.B. 299, an express promise from the Liverpool Corporation it would not increase the number of taxi licences in the area without consultation with the Association was held to create a legitimate expectation of consultation.

Policies are also capable of creating legitimate expectations as in *Khan* (above). This is more controversial, especially where the expectation is of a substantive benefit, as decision-makers must be allowed to change policies in order to avoid fettering their discretion and acting illegally (see Ch.15). Where a claimant raises legitimate expectation based on policy, typically, they are seeking to argue that in their particular circumstances the change or departure from policy should be prohibited. They are not seeking to argue that the policy should never be changed but that in their particular circumstances to change the policy is unjust or causes unfairness. A good example is *Khan* (above) where the policy was not applied (see also *R. (on the application of*

Rashid) v Secretary of State for the Home Department [2005] EWCA Civ 744). For a policy to create a legitimate expectation it would have to satisfy the requirement of clarity and may require knowledge and reliance (see below). Moreover, the recognition of a substantive legitimate expectation created by a policy does not mean that the applicant will get the benefit (see later discussion on frustration).

2.   Existence of regular practice

18–006   If it has been usual practice to give a person a hearing or provide reasons, this may give an individual a legitimate expectation of like treatment. Such an example can be found in *Council for Civil Service Unions v Minister for Civil Service* where the continuous practice of consultation before changes to conditions of service led to the legitimate expectation there would be consultation before the Minister abolished membership of the trade union. Lord Fraser, at p.400, stated:

> "In the present case the evidence shows that, ever since GCHQ began in 1947, prior consultation has been the invariable rule when conditions of service were to be significantly altered. Accordingly in my opinion if there had been no question of national security involved, the appellants would have had a legitimate expectation that the Minister would consult them before issuing the instruction of 22 December 1983."

In *GCHQ*, the period of practice was about 35 years, which was a significant amount of time over which to establish the existence of regular practice.

3.   Criteria

18–007   A specific representation or past practice may seem to suggest a legitimate expectation has arisen. However, the courts have also held that certain criteria must be satisfied for the promise or practice to gain legal enforceability in public law.

(a)   *The promise must be clear, unambiguous and precise*

18–008   In *R. v Inland Revenue Commissioners Ex p. MFK Underwriting Agents Ltd* [1990] 1 W.L.R. 1545, a case concerning assurances by the Inland Revenue regarding the tax liability of Lloyd's underwriters, the court stated that for a legitimate expectation to arise, the representation made must be "clear, unambiguous and devoid of relevant qualification" and given in response to full disclosure of all material information (p.1569). In applying the criteria, the court concluded the assurance did not give rise to a legitimate expectation.

Short of a clear and unequivocal assurance by the public authority, the individual's interest does not assume special weight so as to impose upon the public authority a duty of particular care (beyond the usual public law duties) in relation to decision-making affecting that individual. In *R. (Association of British Civilian Internees (Far East Region) v Secretary of State for Defence* [2003] EWCA Civ 473, the Court of Appeal observed that:

> "[I]t will be only in an exceptional case that a claim that a legitimate expectation has been defeated will succeed in the absence of a clear and unequivocal representation. That is because it will only be in a rare case where, absent such a representation, it can be said that a decision-maker will have acted with conspicuous unfairness such as to amount to an abuse of power." (at para.71)

The issue of whether the representation is clear and unambiguous will be considered with regard to the context in which the representation was made. For example, the width of the class to whom the representation is directed may be a relevant factor. In the Divisional Court in *R. v DPP Ex p. Kebilene* [1999] EWHC Admin 278, four applicants sought to rely on a legitimate expectation that following the passing of the Human Rights Act 1998 (HRA), the Director of Public Prosecutions would exercise his discretion to prosecute only in accordance with the Convention. This was before the HRA came into effect in 2000. Such expectations was said to derive from three points:

(i)   ratification of the Convention by the United Kingdom;

(ii) enactment of the Human Rights Act; and

(iii) from public statements made by Ministers since the passing of the Act.

The court refused to find a legitimate expectation, Lord Bingham C.J. observing that he would be "very hesitant to hold that a legitimate expectation could be founded on answers given in Parliament to often very general questions" (at para.25). He considered that Ministers will rarely have formulated their responses with specific reference to the facts of particular cases that might arise in the future. Similarly, in *R. v Secretary of State for Education and Employment, Ex p. Begbie* [2000] 1 W.L.R. 1115, which concerned a pre-election promise made by the Labour party that children already benefiting from the assisted-places scheme would continue to receive this until the end of their schooling. This promise was held to be unclear and, consequently, no legitimate expectation arose. The court stated it was clear that a party in opposition would not know all the facts and ramifications of such a promise until it gained office, and that to hold a pre-election promise binding on a new government would not be good government.

The requirement that the representation be clear, unambiguous and devoid of any relevant qualification is an important requirement and, only the clearest assurances will give rise to the creation of a legitimate expectation. The requirement will be very strictly applied when an individual seeks to enforce an expectation or conferment of a substantive benefit. See also *R. (on the application of Begum) v Returning Officer for Tower Hamlets LBC* [2006] EWCA Civ 733. In this case, the Court of Appeal held that Begum did not have a legitimate expectation that a returning officer would check the nomination papers for errors. This was because the returning officer had not clearly and unequivocally stated that she would check every nomination paper but had just offered to help in an informal way.

(b)   *The legitimate expectation must be legal*

18–009   A consistent line of authority shows that an unlawful representation will not give rise to a legitimate expectation. To allow such representations would bring the decision-maker into conflict with principles of legality by allowing it not only to enlarge its powers, but possibly prevent the performance of its public duty, or cause it to interfere with a third party's rights. Sedley J. (as he then was) made this clear in *R. v Ministry of Agriculture, Fisheries and Food Ex p. Hamble (Offshore) Fisheries Ltd* [1995] 2 All E.R. 714 (at p.731) when he stated that to bind public bodies to an unlawful representation would have the "dual effect of unlawfully extending the statutory power and destroying the ultra vires doctrine by permitting public bodies arbitrarily to extend their powers". In *R. (Bibi) v Newham London Borough Council* [2001] EWCA Civ 607 (at para.46), it was stated that in order for an expectation to be legitimate, the party seeking to invoke it must show that it lay within the powers of [the body] both to make the representation and to fulfil it".

Whilst, the justification for not allowing an unlawful representation is strong, the prospect of a public body arguing it had no power to make a representation and therefore should not be bound by it is unattractive. Allowing the body to avoid being bound on this basis is unfair to the individual to whom the representation was made. An individual may have every reason to believe the body was acting within its powers in making the representation, and denial of the benefit could cause unacceptable hardship (see Paul Craig, *Administrative Law* (5th edn (Oxford: OUP, 2004), pp.665–680). Furthermore, it is conceivable the individual's interest in his expectation being upheld may outweigh the public interest in the body not being bound by its representation.

Although, the law seems fairly clear, following the ECtHR decision in *Stretch v UK* (2004) 38 E.H.R.R. 12, there may be some development in this area which mitigates the harshness of the ultra vires rule. In *Stretch*, the applicant entered into a lease with a borough council for a term of 22 years, which included an option to renew for a further 21 years. Near the end of the term, the parties entered into negotiations for a new lease. A draft lease was produced, and a price agreed. The applicant signed his copy of the draft lease, and entered into negotiations with sub-tenants. However, the local authority then informed the applicant his option could not be exercised as it had been ultra vires the Borough Council. The ECtHR held Stretch had a legitimate expectation in obtaining the effective realisation of a property right under the ultra vires lease and the legitimate expectation was itself a "possession" for the purposes of art.1, First Protocol of the European Convention on Human Rights. In frustrating the applicant's legitimate expectation under the lease, the local authority had unlawfully interfered with the applicant's rights under art.1 of the First Protocol.

The implications of *Stretch* were considered in *Rowland v Environment Agency* [2003] EWCA Civ 1885. The Environment Agency had made representations that certain waterways did not have public rights of navigation. Rowland subsequently bought adjoining land and put up signs to that effect that the waterway was private property.

This continued for many years until the Agency realised it was wrong. It then instructed Rowland to remove the signs. Rowland sought to have the decision quashed on the basis that the Agency's conduct had raised a legitimate expectation. The court re-stated the position that "a representation by a public authority, which the public authority has no power to make, is not binding and cannot sustain a legitimate expectation". They then considered the impact of the European Convention of Human Rights on the issue and concluded that following *Stretch*, the creation of a legitimate expectation cannot simply be defeated because of illegality and on the facts of this case a legitimate expectation had arisen which constituted a possession under art.1 of the First Protocol. However, they also concluded that to continue to allow the waterway to be private was illegal and would involve forcing the relevant public body to act beyond the scope of its powers and against the public interest. As the Council had given due consideration to the impact on the Rowlands (for example they gave assurances not to promote public use) they could resile from the expectation (i.e. the interference was not disproportionate or unjustified).

A more problematic area arises where a representation is made which is intra vires the power, but ultra vires the person, i.e. it is within the powers of the public body to give the promise, but the person who made the promise did not have the authority to do so. The court's have held that though a person may not have actual power, they could have what is termed ostensible authority or apparent power. In *South Buckinghamshire DC v Flanagan* [2002] EWCA Civ 690, the court confirmed a legitimate expectation could be created by someone with ostensible authority. In this case, a solicitor's firm acting for the Council was given authority by letter to discontinue prosecutions against Flanagan but not to withdraw enforcement notices relating to a planning dispute. At the prosecution hearing, a solicitor from the firm reached an agreement with the defendants and withdrew the enforcement notices. The question was whether the defendant had a legitimate expectation the enforcement orders were withdrawn and would not be the basis of any further prosecution. On the facts, the court concluded that a solicitor appointed to prosecute for breach of an enforcement notice did not have the authority to agree a withdrawal of the notice itself, hence no legitimate expectation arose on the facts.

Whilst a representation from a person with ostensible authority can form the basis of a legitimate expectation, Elliott, "Unlawful Representations, Legitimate Expectations and Estoppel" (2003) J.R. 71 at p.76, says it will only do where two conditions are met:

(1) delegation to the officer is not forbidden by statute (see Ch.14 on delegation);

(2) the promise must be within the powers of the body as a whole, i.e. it is not ultra vires.

(c) *Knowledge and reliance*

An issue which has caused some difficulty is whether or not the applicant has to know **18–010** about and rely on the representation. It might appear that some knowledge is always required, otherwise how can someone expect a promise to be kept if they do not know of the promise in the first place. This is generally true and would certainly apply where a specific representation is made to an individual. However, it is not a requirement in cases of departure from an existing policy. Even if an individual does not know what the public body's policy is on a particular matter, it is legitimate to expect the public body to apply whatever its policy is to their own case. This exception to the general requirement of subjective knowledge of the promise is based on the overriding principles of equality and consistency of treatment. Steele, "Substantive legitimate expectations: striking the right balance?" (2005) 121 L.Q.R. 300 says to expect knowledge of something like a policy would be tantamount to discrimination if those who knew could rely and those who did not could not rely. This point was made clear in *R. (on the application of Rashid) v Secretary of State for the Home Department* [2005] EWCA Civ 744 where the Court of Appeal found a legitimate expectation that the Secretary of State would apply his policy on asylum to a claim for asylum. Whether or not the claimant knew of the policy was not relevant as it would be grossly unfair if the court's ability to intervene depended at all upon the claimant's knowledge of a policy. The court found that although Rashid had suffered detriment in breach of his legitimate expectation, it was not appropriate for the court to make a declaration that he was entitled to refugee status but they declared that he was entitled to a grant of indefinite leave to remain in the UK as remedy for the unfairness.

Whilst knowledge is generally required for a legitimate expectation, reliance to one's detriment is not. However, as De Smith, Woolf & Jowell, *Judicial Review of Administrative Action* (5th edn (London: Sweet & Maxwell)) have stated it may be relevant in two situations:

> " . . . first, it might provide evidence of the existence or extent of an expectation. In that sense it can be a consideration to be taken into account in deciding whether a person was in fact led to believe that the authority would be bound by the representations. Second, detrimental reliance may be relevant to the decision of the authority to revoke a representation."

In *Begbie* Peter Gibson L.J. (at para.47) accepted the applicant's submission it was not necessary for a person to have changed their position as a result of a representation for a legitimate expectation to exist. However, he further commented it would be wrong to understate the significance of reliance and that the absence of reliance was the exception rather than the rule, citing with authority the passage above. It is important to note that whilst detrimental reliance is not necessary to establish a legitimate expectation, existence of such reliance is important when considering whether the decision-maker can go back on their promise. This point was made clearly in *R. (on the application of Bibi) v Newham LBC (No.1)* [2001] EWCA Civ 607 when the court confirmed where an individual has suffered no hardship, there would generally be no reason to hold the decision-maker to its promise.

FRUSTRATION OF LEGITIMATE EXPECTATIONS

18–011   Once it is established a legitimate expectation exists, the issue becomes whether its existence requires the decision-maker to give the promise, or whether there is a countervailing public interest, such as national security, to defeat the promise. In these situations, the courts have to achieve a balance between the decision-maker not fettering his discretion and fairness to the individual.

1. Procedural legitimate expectations

To require a public body to give a particular procedure is not onerous for the decision-maker and, therefore, the court will require the procedure to be given unless there is an overriding public interest which justifies going back on the promise. In *R. v Liverpool Corporation Ex p. Liverpool Taxi Fleet Association* [1972] 2 Q.B. 299, there was no such interest for a failure to consult the taxi drivers as per their promise. Lord Denning noted the "public interest may [actually] be better served by honouring their undertaking than by breaking it" (at p.308). In contrast, in *GCHQ* the overriding interest of national security defeated the past practice of consultation with the trade unions.   **18–012**

2. Substantive legitimate expectations

Requiring a decision-maker to give the promise of a substantive benefit is more controversial as the imposition of this requirement can be more onerous on the decision-maker and, equally, lead to greater unfairness for the individual. Tension between two sets of views lies at the heart of the developing case law. Initially, the courts struggled over who should decide on whether the decision-maker could choose to frustrate a substantive legitimate expectation. One approach was advocated by Sedley J. in *R. v Ministry of Agriculture, Fisheries and Foods Ex p. Hamble Fisheries (Offshore) Ltd* [1995] 1 All E.R. 714. The Ministry had a policy of permitting the transfer or aggregation of licences from one vessel to another and the applicants relied upon it when investing in the industry. As a result of EU fisheries policy and declining fish stocks, the Ministry refused Hamble's licence. Sedley J. held it was for the court, not the decision-maker, to decide if the change in policy should defeat Hamble's expectation of financial support. On the facts, there was an overriding public interest in the need for the change.   **18–013**

A different approach was advocated by the Court of Appeal in *R. v Secretary of State for the Home Department Ex p. Hargreaves* [1997] 1 W.L.R. 906 which partly overruled Hamble Fisheries. The applicants, Category C Prisoners, were issued with notices on arrival at prison informing them they would be eligible for home leave (a privilege) after they had served one-third of their sentence. At the same time, each applicant signed a "compact" in which they agreed to be of good behaviour and, in return, the prison promised to consider them for home leave when they became eligible. Three years later the policy on home leave was changed and the eligibility period increased to one-half the time served. The aim of the new policy was to improve public safety and increase public confidence in the administration of justice. The applicants applied for judicial review on the grounds that the change of policy was unlawful because it frustrated their legitimate expectation, namely the eligibility of home leave, which had been created when they signed the compact. Their appeal was dismissed. The court stated that the only legitimate expectation the prisoner's might have was that their applications for home leave would be examined individually in light of the policy applying at the date of application (a point made clear by Lord Scarman in *Findlay, Re; sub nom, Findlay v Secretary of State for the Home Department* [1985] A.C. 318). The Court of Appeal concluded that the "balancing" approach taken in Hamble Fisheries should be confined to alleged procedural irregularities, not to substantive legitimate expectations, over-ruling *Hamble Fisheries* on this point.

Further, the court was clear that no substantive legitimate expectation had arisen in the present case, but that if one had arisen, the correct approach to be taken by the court was to consider whether the Home Secretary's decision was *Wednesbury* unreasonable. In strong words, Hirst L.J. agreed with counsel for the Home Secretary (Mr Beloff) that Seldey J.'s approach in *Hamble* amounted to "heresy" (at p.921).

In *R. v North and East Devon Health Authority Ex p. Coughlan* [2001] Q.B. 213, the Court of Appeal considered the competing authorities and settled the approach to be taken. Coughlan, a chronically-ill person, was resident at a nursing home. When she moved into the home she was given oral assurances it would be her "home for life". The court held the assurance bound the Health Authority. The court confirmed different types of protection to be available depending on the category into which the legitimate expectation fell. In particular, Lord Woolf (at para.57) identified three categories:

(1)   A case where the public body is only required to bear in mind its previous policy or other representation, giving it the weight it thinks right, but no more, before deciding whether to change course. Here the Court can intervene only if Wednesbury unreasonable by considering whether the public body has given proper weight to the implications of not fulfilling the promise; this was the situation in *Hargreaves*.

(2)   A case where there was a promise as to a procedure. Here the appropriate test was to give the promise unless there was an overriding public interest.

(3)   Where the court considered a lawful promise or practice has induced a substantive legitimate expectation. Here, too, the court will decide whether to frustrate the expectation is so unfair that to take a new and different course will amount to an abuse of power. Here, once the legitimacy of the expectation is established, the court has the task of weighing the requirements of fairness against any overriding interest relied upon for the change in policy.

In *Coughlin*, the promise was put in the third category because of the importance of what was promised. It was made to a few individuals and the consequences of requiring the health authority to honour its promise was financial only.

The approach established in *Coughlan* was a more subtle and sophisticated approach than previous attempts to articulate a "one-size-fits-all" standard of review. Rather than simply laying down a single standard of rationality or fairness which the decision-maker had to attain in deciding to frustrate an expectation of a particular outcome, *Coughlan* acknowledged a more flexible approach was needed. However, there are two problems with this approach. First, the main problem is determining what category a case falls into. Lord Woolf (at para.59) drew attention to the difficulty of classifying cases by reference to these three categories, particularly what type of cases fit into the more restrictive first category. He recognised the court's role in the third category was still controversial and observed that most cases in this category were likely to be where the expectation was confined to one person or a few people, giving the promise or representation the character of a contract. A second problem relates to the test itself: what does so unfair that it amounts to an abuse of power actually mean, and what exactly is the legal basis for the test?

The later case of *R. v Secretary of State for Education and Employment Ex p. Begbie* [2000] 1 W.L.R. 1115 shows that a single standard of review cannot be articulated. The case was decided just over a month after judgment was given in *Coughlan* and involved a child who was on an Assisted Places Scheme. In opposition, the Labour Party had given assurances the applicant and other children in a like position would not be adversely affected by proposals to abolish the assisted places scheme until their placement ceased. After the general election of May 1, 1997, the new government introduced legislation, the Education (Schools) Act 1997. The consequence of this meant Begbie would retain her assisted place only until the end of her primary education, unless the Secretary of State exercised discretion and extended it. The government announced a policy outlining circumstances in which the Secretary of State was more likely to exercise his discretion; Begbie did not fall into those circumstances. Her parents contended that earlier assurances and some later statements and letters given by government gave rise to a legitimate expectation they would be honoured.

However, the application was dismissed on the basis there was no legitimate expectation. In any event, the court would not give effect to a legitimate expectation if it would require a public authority to act contrary to the terms of a statute. Importantly, Laws L.J. made a number of important comments in relation to the *Coughlan* categories. He recognised (at para.1130) the categories (unreasonableness and fairness) were not "hermetically sealed" and that "each is a spectrum, not a single point" and thus "they shade into one another". In determining where on the scale an expectation rests is dependent on an analysis of the class of person to whom the representation is directed:

> "The more the decision challenged lies in what may inelegantly be called the macro-political field, the less intrusive will be the court's supervision. More than this: in that field, true abuse of power is less likely to be found, since within it changes of policy, fuelled by broad conceptions of the public interest, may more readily be accepted as taking precedence over the interests of groups which enjoyed expectations generated by an earlier policy." (para.1130)

Laws L.J. made clear that where a decision is political, as in prison policy, it is not for the courts to intervene, and review will only be available on *Wednesbury* grounds. At the other end of the scale, cases like *Coughlan*, where the representation is made to a small number of persons and where there is probably detrimental reliance, the promise is more akin to a contract and will fall into the third category. In such situations frustration would be an abuse of power and remedy is likely to be the substantive benefit itself. Upholding such an expectation is likely to have less dramatic consequences for the administration than upholding one generated by a policy where the identical expectations of many others in the same situation as the applicant may also have to be upheld in order to ensure consistency of treatment. As a result of *Begbie* Elliot, "Legitimate Expectation: The Substantive Dimension" (2000) C.L.J. 421 states "we have moved from the rather crude *Coughlan* dichotomy, which would admit of only two different types of review, to a sliding scale of review".

3. Post-Begbie approach and remedies for breach of a legitimate expectation

18–014 In *R. (on the application of Bibi) v Newham LBC (No.1)* [2001] EWCA Civ 607, the Court of Appeal provided additional guidance on how the court should approach legitimate expectation cases:

> "In all legitimate expectation cases, whether substantive or procedural, three practical questions arise. The first question is to what has the public authority, whether by practice or by promise, committed itself; the second is whether the authority has acted or proposes to act unlawfully in relation to its commitment; the third is what the court should do. This formulation of the questions is we think a more helpful way of approaching the problems in this type of case than the fivefold question adopted during argument." (para.19)

Bibi, a refugee, had been accepted by the Council as unintentionally homeless and provided with temporary accommodation. They sought to rely on a promise which the council had made to provide secure accommodation within 18 months. The promise had been given under a misapprehension as to the authority's statutory function as it believed it owed a duty but, in fact, had a discretion. The court found the existence of a legitimate expectation and an abuse of power in failing to fulfil the promise.

The obvious remedy for breach of a legitimate expectation is to require the body to give the applicant what he was promised. Thus, in *Bibi*, the provision of accommodation would have fulfilled the legitimate expectation. However this was not ordered by the court, two factors being conclusive:

(1) the absence of detrimental reliance brought the case down the scale from the *Coughlan* scenario;

(2) to insist on the provision of accommodation would amount to the judiciary taking on an Executive role. In this case, the court concluded it would be better simply to declare the authority is under a duty to consider the applicant's application for suitable housing on the basis they had a legitimate expectation that they will be provided with suitable accommodation (para.67).

As this case shows, where the legitimate expectation is substantive, i.e. requiring the decision-maker to give the benefit, it may produce dramatic effects. A countervailing public interest may not be so compelling as to justify denying any protection to the applicant's expectation, yet may be sufficiently compelling to justify denying full substantive protection. An example would be where requiring full substantive protection would force a public body to spend vast sums of public money over a long period of time. In such situations, the public interest in public bodies making their own decisions as to how best to allocate public funds is likely to be sufficiently compelling to reduce the remedy down from the full benefit. Steele, "Substantive Legitimate Expectations: Striking the Right Balance?" (2005) 121 (Apr) L.Q.R. 300 makes the point that in such situations compensation may be an appropriate remedy.

4.   Proportionality as the standard of review

Following *Coughlan* and *Begbie*, the test for substantive review is a sliding scale of **18–015** intensity depending on the type of decision that was made. Steele (at p.315) feels that this sliding scale will soon be explained entirely using the language of proportionality and the *Coughlan* categories relegated. Proportionality, like the test advocated in *Coughlan* and *Begbie*, can be adjusted to give due weight to the fact that the decision-maker may have greater expertise and/or democratic legitimacy than the court, and a court can apply the test with varying degrees of intensity by scrutinising more or less closely a decision-maker's claims that it was necessary to frustrate the applicant's expectation. The case of *Abdi and Nadarajah v Secretary of State for the Home Department* [2005] EWCA Civ 1363 sheds some light on whether proportionality may eclipse the current approach. *Abdi and Nadarajah* were combined appeals to the Court of Appeal concerning art.8 ECHR, asylum and the application of a Home Office policy. Both tried to argue an enforceable legitimate expectation that a government policy (Family Links Policy) should be applied to their asylum applications. Laws L.J. reviewed the authorities concerning legitimate expectation and made a number of obiter comments which he hoped would move the law's development further down the road (Note, Laws L.J. adjudicated in *Begbie*).

First, Laws L.J. thought the test and principle of abuse of power/fairness was not helpful and that actually the principle underpinning legitimate expectation was not fairness, but good administration; that public bodies ought to deal straightforwardly and consistently with the public. More controversially, he cast doubt on the wording used in the *Coughlan* tests, preferring instead to use the proportionality test in assessing whether it was in the public interest to frustrate a legitimate expectation. Finally, he believed there should be no difference in the tests between procedural and substantive legitimate expectation (see paras 68–69).

In reality, both tests are similar and it may simply be a question of semantics. However, though proportionality may be on its last legs (see Ch.17), as yet it has not established itself as a basis for review outside human rights and European law issues and, on this basis the approach based on fairness, advocated in *Coughlan* and *Begbie* by Laws is the current approach.

CONCLUSION

The development of legitimate expectation has not been without controversy. As **18–016** mentioned at the beginning of this chapter, the courts have had to deal with the competing interests of legal certainty (fairness to the individual) and administrative flexibility (which may require the expectation to be frustrated) in developing their approach. The flexibility of the *Begbie* approach in considering whether a legitimate expectation should be frustrated reflects the courts' recognition of these competing interests. The approach has its merits in that it allows each case to be considered on its facts, rather than by setting down a general rule that one side trumps the other.

This approach is, itself, reflective of developments in administrative law with the courts taking a more active role in controlling the exercise of discretionary power and upholding the rule of law, while recognising that in appropriate situations some deference to the Executive is necessary. The possible development of proportionality with its more structured approach to review in legitimate expectation would somewhat simplify the law; a development that may be seen in the future as these principles continue to develop.

Though there was initial judicial reluctance, the development of substantive legitimate expectation is a welcome advance. However, it is this area that proves the most contentious as the courts struggle with the drawing the line between legitimate judicial intervention and judicial interference. Requiring a public body to confer the benefit of a promise made is always attractive for the individual to whom it has been made, while at the same time developing good practice in making public bodies act responsibly. However, to dictate to that public body that it should act in a particular way in the performance of its public duties risks allegations of judicial interference in areas outside their competence, and violations of separation of powers principle. No doubt as the concept of legitimate expectation continues to develop maintaining a balance will be at the forefront.

FURTHER READING

18–017 Craig, P. *Administrative Law*, 5th edn (Oxford: OUP, 2004)

Elliot (ed.) *Beatson, Matthews and Elliott's Administrative Law: Text and Materials*, 3rd edn (Oxford: OUP, 2005)

Elliot, "Legitimate Expectation: The Substantive Dimension" (2000) C.L.J. 421

Fordham, M. *Judicial Review Handbook*, 4th edn (Oxford: Hart Publishing, 2004)

Sales and Steyn, "Legitimate Expectation in English Public Law: An Analysis" (2004) P.L. 564

Steele, I. "Substantive legitimate expectations: striking the right balance?" (2005) 121 (Apr) L.Q.R. 300

Summary of Legitimate Expectation

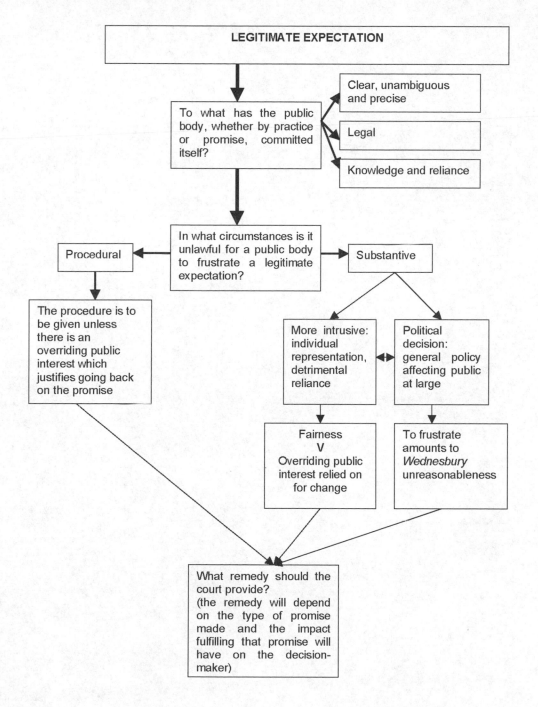

Chapter 19

ALTERNATIVE MEANS OF REDRESS—
OMBUDSMAN AND TRIBUNALS

INTRODUCTION

Recourse to judicial mechanisms for challenging decisions made by the Executive, **19–001** whilst effective in their own right, are not always the most desired nor most effective mechanism for all complaints. As a result, a number of alternative forms of redress arc available to individuals who feel aggrieved by actions of the Executive. Two means of redress will be considered in this chapter: ombudsman, a non-judicial mechanism which allows investigation of maladministration by a government department or agency which has caused injustice to an individual, and tribunals, an informal "legal" mechanism for redress.

OMBUDSMAN

1. Background

The 1960s saw a period of significant growth in the role of government in the every day **19–002** lives of citizens. The response to this growth was a recognition there needed to be some effective and efficient form of redress against government action beyond the developing concept of judicial review which, even at that early stage, was recognised to be expensive and complicated. Tribunals, of course, already existed, but tended to be concerned with more specific "legal" type questions. Something else was needed, and it took a relatively insignificant parcel of unremarkable agricultural land in Dorset to highlight administrative shortcomings at the heart of government.

In 1938, the government compulsorily purchased 725 acres of agricultural land near Crichel Down in Cornwall on behalf of the Air Ministry who wanted it for bombing practice. In 1941, promises had been made that the land would be offered for sale to its former owners after the war. This promise was not honoured and instead the land was given to the Department of Agriculture in 1950 who intended to use it for farming purposes and sub-let to a pre-selected tenant. A public inquiry was eventually held and revealed a catalogue of ineptitude and maladministration. The affair led to the resignation of the Minister for Agriculture and highlighted the lack of an independent means for citizens to raise complaints about public administration in the UK or to secure a remedy for injustice derived from the improper handling of their affairs. It was as a consequence of the "Crichel Down Affair" and the broader growth of government that "Ombudsmania" was born.

The term ombudsman is Scandinavian in origin and broadly means a grievance or complaints officer. In 1961, Justice produced a report (the "Wyatt Report") recommending that the United Kingdom should operate an ombudsman scheme. The Conservative government of the day did not heed these calls out of fear this would lead to the decline of representative parliamentary democracy. However in 1964, the sixties were swinging and the Labour Party, in its election manifesto ("Let's Go with Labour for a New Britain" (1964)) committed itself to introducing an ombudsman for central government. They won the election of that year, and the Parliamentary Commissioner for Administration came into existence. The early ombudsmen were given the title Commissioner, but the term ombudsmen was later adopted and remains today.

Nowadays, there are many ombudsmen in the United Kingdom perhaps deservedly leading to Marshall's label "ombudsmania" (H.W.R. Wade in D.C. Rowat (ed.), *The Ombudsman: Citizen's Defender* (London: George Allen & Unwin, 1965) at p.173). For example, there are ombudsmen for estate agents, legal services, the financial services and so on. However, in this chapter, we are concerned with public sector ombudsman, defined by Collcut and Hourihan (*Review of the Public Sector Ombudsman in England: A report by the Cabinet Office* (London, 2000) at para.1.11) as a body, "created by statute ... independent from the government and ... impartial in their dealings with complainants and those complained about. They exist to consider complaints by citizens that public organisations have caused them injustice by maladministration".

There are two main public sector ombudsmen: (i) the Parliamentary and Health Service Ombudsman (incorporating the former Parliamentary Commissioner for Administration and the Health Service Commissioner) and (ii) the Local Government Ombudsman.

PARLIAMENTARY AND HEALTH SERVICE OMBUDSMAN

1.   Parliamentary Ombudsman

19–003   The first ombudsman in the UK was the Parliamentary Commissioner for Administration, now incorporated into the Parliamentary and Health Service Ombudsman. The Parliamentary Ombudsman owes its existence to the Parliamentary Commissioner Act

1967 (PCA) which came into effect on the April 1, 1967. Initially concerns were raised about the PCA and the introduction of an ombudsman system. It was felt that not only would it conflict with the convention of ministerial responsibility, but that the role of Members of Parliament and Parliament itself would be undermined. As a consequence of these concerns, the PCA created a uniquely British model of the ombudsman which was far from a defender of citizens, as they tend to be in continental jurisdictions, and operated as an "aid" to Parliament in its accountability of the Executive. This model, therefore, had the result that citizens were unable to petition the ombudsman direct but had to make their complaint to their MP, who would act as a rather crude filter.

Not only were there political concerns at the PCA, but there was also a cautious and sceptical reception in the broader world. In an article published in the *Journal of Politics* in 1973, Gwyn famously referred to the Act as an "ombudsmouse" and Marshall in *Annals of the American Academy of Political Science*, published in 1968 referred to the PCA as "a limping and restrictive statute ... undoubtedly botched ... [and which] would not do".

2. Functions of the Parliamentary Ombudsman

The purpose of the Parliamentary Ombudsman is to assist Parliament in its scrutiny of **19–004** the Executive. According to the 2006–2007 Report of the Parliamentary Ombudsman, the ombudsman performs three primary roles:

(1) a source of dispute resolution;

(2) guardian of good public administration; and

(3) systematic check upon department effectiveness.

The Parliamentary Ombudsman is an Officer of the House of Commons appointed by the Crown. The ombudsman's powers and responsibilities are set out in the 1967 Act. By s.5(1)(a) of the PCA 1967, the function of the Parliamentary Ombudsman is "to investigate complaints that an injustice has been caused by maladministration on the part of a government department, its agencies and the NHS in the exercise of administrative functions". As the notions of "maladministration" and "injustice" are not defined by the statute, the quest for a definition must lead to extraneous sources.

(a) Meaning of "Maladministration"

The statute's failure to define the key concept of "maladministration" provides the **19–005** ombudsman considerable definitional discretion. This has the obvious advantage of flexibility, but consequently leads to a lack of certainty. The flexibility in the definition is regarded as a positive by the 1990–1996 ombudsman, Sir William Reid, who expressed the following view in the 1993 Annual Report:

"To define maladministration is to limit it. Such a limitation could work to the disadvantage of individual complainants with justified grievances which did not fit within a given definition."

However, assistance in arriving at a definition comes from the Parliamentary debates on the PCA and the comments of Richard Crossman, the Minister responsible for the Bill, when he observes that it meant, "bias, neglect, inattention, delay, incompetence, inaptitude, perversity, turpitude, arbitrariness and so on". This list, known as the "Crossman Catalogue", is illustrative and certainly not exhaustive, as indicated by the "and so on". The "and so on" allows the ombudsman to consider other things where appropriate and where the circumstances of the individual case might require it.

In looking for maladministration, the ombudsman will typically consider failure in processes, for example, how a policy was made or implemented, as opposed to the merits or substance of a policy. Guidance for complainants on the Parliamentary and Health Service Ombudsman website (*www.ombudsman.org.uk*) seems to bear this out. Complaints which they would typically consider include:

- a failure to provide a service;

- delay that could have been avoided;

- faulty procedures, or a failure to follow correct procedures;

- not informing people about the rights of appeal open to them;

- unfairness, bias or prejudice;

- giving advice which is misleading or inadequate;

- refusing to answer reasonable questions;

- rudeness and not apologising for mistakes;

- mistakes in handling claims; and

- not putting things right when something has gone wrong.

The guidance further states that the ombudsman cannot consider complaints about government policy or the content of legislation (merits). This would also appear to suggest that the substance of any policy or decision is not readily considered. However, it is implicit in s.12(3) of the PCA that the ombudsman can look at the substance as long as there is maladministration. So for example, a policy that is wholly unreasonable could be a clear example of maladministration.

In March 2007, after a period of consultation, the ombudsman published a set of good principles public authorities should strive to achieve. It would seem to follow that departure from these principles would be maladministration. These principles include:

(1)   Getting it right.

(2)   Being customer focused.

(3)   Being open and accountable.

(4)   Acting fairly and proportionately.

(5)   Putting things right.

(6)   Seeking continuous improvement.

(i)   The courts and "maladministration"

In *R. v Local Commissioners for Administration for the North and East Area of England*   **19–006**
Ex p. Bradford Metropolitan City Council [1979] Q.B. 287, the Court of Appeal gave
consideration to the meaning of "maladministration" and accepted the Crossman
Catalogue. It also indicated that maladministration had nothing to do with the intrinsic
merits of the decision (see also *R. v Commissioner for Local Administration Ex p.
Eastleigh Borough Council* [1988] Q.B. 853).

(b)   *Meaning of "injustice"*

The meaning of "injustice" has, as a general rule, tended to cause less controversy than   **19–007**
the meaning of maladministration. In *R. v Parliamentary Commissioner for Administration Ex p. Balchin (No.1)* [1996] EWHC Admin 152, Mr Justice Sedley (as he then
was) approved the definition provided by de Smith, Woolf & Jowell, *Judicial Review of
Administrative Action* (London: Sweet & Maxwell, para.1–102). This is a broad definition
and covers "not merely injury redressible in a court of law, but also the sense of outrage
aroused by unfair or incompetent administration, even where the complainant has suffered no actual loss". The quote utilises the language of Richard Crossman, speaking as
Leader of the House of Commons during the Parliamentary debates on the PCA.

2.   Jurisdiction

(a)   *Who is included?*

Schedule 2 to the PCA lists those bodies subject to the jurisdiction of the ombudsman.   **19–008**
Included are central government departments, and Crown agents such as the Inland
Revenue. They also have jurisdiction over non-departmental bodies which exercise
Executive or administrative functions, e.g. the Child Support Agency.

(b)   *What is excluded from the ombudsman's jurisdiction?*

Some matters are specifically excluded from the ombudsman's jurisdiction (s.5 of and   **19–009**
Sch.3 to the PCA). Section 5(2) of the PCA states that the ombudsman shall not

conduct an investigation into any actions where the aggrieved person has a right of appeal to a tribunal (s.5(2)(a)), or has a remedy in a court of law (s.5(2)(b)). However, these sections do not preclude any investigation if, in the opinion of the ombudsman, it is not reasonable in the circumstances to expect the complainant to resort to a tribunal or court of law. The House of Commons Public Administration Select Committee (PASC), First Report of Session 2005 06 made the following point in the context of the Debt of Honour case (see below).

> "The entire basis of the 1967 Parliamentary Commissioner for Administration Act is that it is possible for a measure to be legal, and yet to be maladministered. The fact that legality has been established through Judicial Review may be irrelevant to maladministration. There may even be circumstances where the Ombudsman feels it is appropriate to conduct an investigation while Judicial Review proceedings are taking place, so that she can subsequently report without delay." (A Debt of Honour, HC 735 (2006) para.20)

The Court of Appeal in *R. v Commissioner for Local Administration Ex p. Croydon London Borough Council* [1989] 1 All E.R. 1033 also considered the scope of the exception. Croydon LBC sought judicial review of the Commissioner's decision there was maladministration in allocating school places. They argued the Commissioner had acted outside his jurisdiction as the parents had a legal remedy. This case concerned s.26(6)(c) of the Local Government Act 1982 (an identical provision is found in s.5 of the PCA). Woolf L.J. adopted a broad approach indicating that in exercising his discretion, the Commissioner did not have to consider whether proceedings in court would succeed. He merely had to be satisfied that a "court of law is an appropriate forum for investigating the subject matter of the complaint" (at p.1044).

Section 5(3) of the PCA excludes investigation by the ombudsman of any matter found in Sch.3 which includes matters affecting international relations, commencement of civil or criminal proceedings, the prerogative of mercy, the conferment of honours and, it also excludes contractual and commercial transactions. The exclusion of contractual and commercial transactions is, however, controversial, especially in view of the growth of such transactions within government. Indeed, the Select Committee on the Parliamentary Commissioner for Administration (the predecessor to the PASC), Fourth Report 1979–80, recommended removal of the restriction, while the Public Administration Select Committee, Review of the Public Sector Ombudsman in England 1999–2000 (HC 612), though not specifically mentioning the commercial contracts exemption, argued all limits on the ombudsman jurisdiction should be removed.

3.   The investigation process

19–010   There are three stages to the investigation process:

(a) *Stage 1: MP Filter*

There is no direct access to the ombudsman for citizens and complaints must in the first **19–011** instance be made to a Member of Parliament who may then pass it on to the ombudsman. This is provided by s.5(1) of the PCA which states that the ombudsman may only investigate matters which have reached him or her via a Member of Parliament. The filter was designed to protect the constitutional position of the MP, one of whose functions is to resolve problems of their constituents and, to prevent a flood of complaints. Drewry and Harlow (1990) 53 M.L.R. 745 noted that empirical research indicated the ombudsman would be inundated if the filter did not exist. However, the argument that the filter, "allows the MP to settle the trivial administrative muddles" (Harlow (1978) 41 M.L.R. 446 at 451) has less weight when considered in the context of the Cabinet Office's review which indicated that some 51 per cent of MPs *automatically* refer complaints to the ombudsman.

In 2004, the Public Administration Select Committee and the Public Administration Ombudsman conducted a joint survey of MPs. Of those who responded, two-thirds favoured removal of the MP filter which would bring this ombudsman into line with others such as the Local Government Ombudsman. Indeed, according to the current Parliamentary Ombudsman, Ann Abraham, this would assist the office in its continuing efforts to become more transparent and open to complainants (Memoranda to PASC 2004–05, The Work of the Ombudsman). Removal of the filter was also recommended by the independent Policy Commission on Public Services, set up by the National Consumer Council, in their recent report on public service reform. Legislation was introduced into the House of Lords in the 2004–05 session to remove the filter and allow direct public access, however the Bill, The Parliamentary Commissioner Amendment Bill, did not progress any further.

(b) *Stage 2: Investigation*

Once a complaint is received from an MP, the ombudsman has discretion under s.5 of **19–012** the PCA whether to investigate and how that investigation should be conducted. The ombudsman has wide powers similar to those of a court, which enable him or her to require government Ministers or members of government departments to provide information, documents, attend meetings and allow examination of witnesses (s.8(2) of the PCA). This includes information which is subject to the Official Secrets Acts or similar legal restriction and so ensures the ombudsman has access to all relevant information. Though s.8 of the PCA does not allow the ombudsman to publish anything in the subsequent report which might damage national security, under s.9 refusal to comply with a request can be referred to the High Court who have power to deal with the matter as if it were contempt of court. Though the ombudsman has similar powers to the court, the approach is more inquisitorial than adversarial.

(c) Stage 3: Report

19–013 Section 10(2) of the PCA states that the findings of the ombudsman will be made clear in a report and the public authority will respond accordingly. In its early years, the ombudsman tended to use tough and formal investigatory techniques, producing lengthy reports which drew criticism from Parliament and led to inevitable delay. Keen to respond to criticism, the ombudsman has adopted a much more informal approach.

The PCA is silent on what redress the ombudsman can offer. The ombudsman can make recommendations as to the specific remedy to be awarded. For example, it can suggest financial payments be made or recommend changes in the way an organisation works so mistakes are not repeated. Broadly, the aim is to return the complainant to the position they would have been in but for the maladministration and in doing so, the ombudsman is able to take account of any outrage or inconvenience the complainant has endured. However, though it may have powers, s.10 of the PCA states that the ombudsman is unable to enforce recommendations. Though this might be regarded as a considerable weakness in the PCA, and one which has attracted criticism, the lack of any enforcement powers, especially where recommendations have policy implications, does appear to a degree justified.

Though lacking enforcement powers, by s.10(3) of the PCA the ombudsman is able to lay a special report before both Houses of Parliament where it appears the injustice done will not be remedied. Of course, a recommendation from the ombudsman has powerful persuasive value and most governments would fear the negative public opinion which would follow a refusal to accept a recommendation. On only four occasions in recent history have recommendations not been followed:

(1) 1977–78 concerning the Department of Transport's refusal to meet late claims for compensation;

(2) 1994–95 concerning the Department of Transport's refusal to accept maladministration in its dealing with hardship caused by blight arising out of the delay in determining the Channel Tunnel Rail Link route;

(3) 2005–06 concerning the Ministry of Defence ex gratia compensation scheme for former civilian internees in the Far East region (Debt of Honour);

(4) 2005–06 Occupational Pensions Scheme (Trusting in the Pensions Promise). The ombudsman found that maladministration had led to as many as 125,000 people suffering the loss of their pension. The government refused to accept the finding of maladministration and any of the recommendations in the report.

The PASC can also add further pressure for compliance by laying its own report on the issue to Parliament, doing this in relation to (3) and (4) outlined above. In the latter, PASC conducted its own investigation, agreeing with the ombudsman's conclusion and produced its own report to add further pressure (6th Report 2006). In the report, the committee stated that the system established under the PCA would only work, "if there [was] a common understanding between the ombudsman, Parliament and government as to what constitutes maladministration, and who has authority in identifying it". The Committee were "increasingly concerned" that the government had been treating ombudsman's reports less seriously than it should and in this case had been too ready to dismiss the ombudsman's findings of maladministration.

The government responded to PASC's report in November 2006 (Government Response to the Public Administration Select Committee's Sixth Report of Session 2005–06 "The Commissioner in Question: the Ombudsman's report on pensions and its constitutional implications", HC 1081) and, as requested by the Committee, looked again at what might be done for those who had suffered injustice but remained of the view that alternatives were not feasible. Further, they persisted with the view that they were not responsible, and therefore there was no maladministration on behalf of the Department of Work and Pensions.

A recent development arising out of the Occupational Pensions Scheme report comes from the decision of the Administrative Court in *R. (on the application of Bradley, Duncan, Parr and Waugh v Secretary of State for Work and Pensions* [2007] EWHC (Admin) 242. Four individuals affected by the loss of their pension applied for judicial review of the Secretary of State's decision to reject two of the findings and one of the recommendations at the heart of the ombudsman report. It was argued by the applicants that the "findings" of the ombudsman were binding unless flawed in law or *Wednesbury* unreasonable. The alternative view forwarded by the government was that they were entitled to reject "*findings*" on the basis of a difference of view unless the rejection itself was flawed in law or *Wednesbury* unreasonable. In partially finding for the applicants, Mr Justice Bean, relying on the Court of Appeal decision of *Ex p. Eastleigh* quashed the decision of the Secretary of State in relation to rejection of the first finding.

There is merit in this decision. As stated in the case itself, the objective of independent scrutiny would be undermined if the government could simply ignore relevant findings and act on its own assertions. At the time of writing, the case awaits a hearing in the Court of Appeal.

Thus, even with the decisions on the occupational Pensions Schemes, the track record of laying reports under s.10(3) suggests that despite any criticisms as to lack of enforceability the ombudsman recommendations are generally followed.

4.   Health Service Ombudsman

The Health Service Ombudsman's powers derive from the Health Service Commis-   **19–014** sioners Act 1993 (HSC). The HSC replaced earlier legislation contained in the Health Service Act 1977 and the Health Service (Scotland) Act 1978. The Act created three ombudsman, one each for England, Wales and Scotland, however, devolution means the Act no longer applies to Scotland and Wales. The Act has been subject to amendments, but remains the main statute governing the role and powers of the ombudsman. Though the Parliamentary Ombudsman and the Health Service Ombudsman are governed by different statutes, the role is held by the same person. Many of the functions and procedures are similar; the major difference being there is direct access (i.e. no MP filter) for complainants of the Health Service (see below).

(a)   *Functions of the Health Service Ombudsman*

19–015   The Health Service Ombudsman (HSO) has a similar remit to the Parliamentary Ombudsman. The HSO's function is to investigate complaints made against one of the bodies over which it exercises jurisdiction. Typically, such bodies would include complaints against all Health Authorities, NHS Trusts, GPs, dentists, opticians and independent providers carrying out services on the NHS' behalf (s.2 of the HSC, as amended).

By s.3(1)(c)), the function of the ombudsman is to investigate complaints that a person has "sustained injustice or hardship in consequence of a failure in service or provision of a service or maladministration connected with any action taken by or on behalf of a body". The meanings of injustice and maladministration are the same as for the parliamentary ombudsman.

The sort of complaints that the ombudsman can deal with include:

- receiving the wrong or poor treatment;

- errors in diagnosis or treatment;

- communication problems within or between services;

- significant mistakes over appointments to see a doctor or go to hospital;

- failure by an organisation to provide or pay for a service;

- delay that could have been avoided;

- faulty procedures, or failing to follow correct procedures;

- unfairness, bias or prejudice;

- giving advice which is misleading or inadequate;

- rudeness and not apologising for mistakes; and

- not putting things right when something has gone wrong.

Ideally, a complainant should have complained to the organisation or practitioner involved first, then the Healthcare Commission, before finally making recourse to the ombudsman. A significant distinction between the Parliamentary Ombudsman and the Health Services Ombudsman is the right of citizens to complain directly to the ombudsman. The Health Care Services Ombudsman has similar jurisdictional limits to the Parliamentary Ombudsman, for example, an exclusion relating to personnel (s.7), and where the complainant can pursue a legal action before a court or tribunal (s.4). As with the PCA, the ombudsman has discretion if satisfied that, in the particular circumstances, it is not reasonable to expect the person to resort to legal action.

The Health Service Ombudsman has the same powers in respect of information and access to witnesses as the Parliamentary Ombudsman. Once an investigation has been completed, the ombudsman reports which is then submitted to the Secretary of State for Health who is required to lay the report before Parliament.

LOCAL GOVERNMENT OMBUDSMAN

The second main public service ombudsman is the Local Government Ombudsman   **19–016**
who has responsibility for complaints regarding local government. The Ombudsman's
powers derive from the Local Government Act 1974 (LGA) for England and Wales and
the Local Government (Scotland) Act 1975 for Scotland.

1. Jurisdiction

By s.26 of the LGA, the Local Government Ombudsmen investigate complaints of   **19–017**
"injustice in consequence of maladministration in connection with action taken by
... an authority in excess of [its] administrative functions". There are three Local
Government Ombudsman for England each dealing with a specific area of the country.
The ombudsman can hear complaints relating to council matters such as housing,
planning, education social services and council tax.

2. Procedure

As with the Health Service Ombudsman, under s.26 of the LGA complaints can be   **19–018**
made direct to the ombudsman. An alternative route is to make a complaint to a local
councillor who can then refer the complaint. The complaint should have been brought
to the attention of the local authority first, preferably using their complaints procedure
and the local authority should be given reasonable time to respond. At the end of the
investigation, the ombudsman reports their findings, copies of which are given to the
complainant, the local authority and to any councillor through whom the complaint
was made. The commissioners have no power to insist on compliance with their reports,
though as a decision not to comply has to be taken by the whole Council, compliance is
usual.

REFORM

The three ombudsman discussed above have recently been granted new power with the   **19–019**
aim of improving the way they work together. The Regulatory Reform (Collaboration
Between Ombudsmen) Order 2007 which came into force in August 2007 allows the
three ombudsman to share information, carry out joint investigations and issue joint
reports on common issues. Prior to this order, a complaint which crossed their
respective jurisdictions had to be dealt with by each ombudsman separately, a notable
example being the *Balchin* case which involved a Department of State and a Local
Authority. These new powers will allow cases such as *Balchin* (see para.19–007) to be
investigated jointly by the relevant ombudsmen, with the result that investigations

should be speedier. The reform has been welcomed by the ombudsman and matches with their aim of increasing efficiency and simplifying matters for the complainant.

TRIBUNALS

1. Definition

19–020   It is difficult to provide a precise definition of a tribunal. Broadly, they are permanent "judicial" bodies which sit periodically to resolve disputes between the citizen and government agencies, or between individuals. Sir Oliver Franks (*Report of the Committee on Administrative Tribunals and Inquiries* Cmnd 218 (1957) at 40)), noted that:

> "Tribunals are not ordinary courts, but neither are they appendages of government departments ... We consider that tribunals should properly be regarded as machinery provided by Parliament for adjudication rather than as part of the machinery of administration."

There are a wide variety of tribunals principally in the social welfare context, ranging from employment to immigration, social security to land. Broadly, there are two main types, those that deal with disputes between individuals and government agencies, such as the Social Security Appeals Tribunal, and those that resolve disputes between individuals, an example being the Employment Tribunal. Some tribunals exercise first instance jurisdiction, though most have appellate jurisdiction.

2. Development of the tribunal system

19–021   Tribunals arose primarily as a result of the increasing role of government, but particularly out of the development of the Welfare State in the post-war period. In November 1955, the government appointed a Committee to consider and make recommendations on administrative tribunals and Inquiries. The Committee, under the chairmanship of Sir Oliver Franks, reported in July 1957 (*Report of the Committee on Administrative Tribunals and Inquiries* Cmnd 218 (1957)), concluding that tribunals were part of the "machinery of adjudication rather than part of the machinery of administration". They identified three characteristics which were to be the "hallmarks" of the tribunal system, namely, openness, fairness and impartiality. Sir Oliver Franks explains them in the following way:

> "Take openness. If these procedures were wholly secret, the basis of confidence and acceptability would be lacking. Next take fairness. If the objector were not allowed to state his case, there would be nothing to stop oppression. Thirdly, there is impartiality. How can a citizen be satisfied unless he feels that those who decide his case come to their decisions with open minds?"

The report led to the Tribunals and Inquiries Act 1958 and the establishment of the Council of Tribunals. The principle functions of the Council of Tribunals was laid down in the Tribunals and Inquiries Act 1992. These included:

- to keep under review the constitution and working of the tribunals specified in Sch.1 to the Act, and, from time to time, to report on their constitution and working;

- to consider and report on matters referred to the Council under the Act with respect to tribunals other than the ordinary courts of law, whether or not specified in Sch.1 to the Act; and

- to consider and report on matters referred to the Council, or matters the Council may consider to be of special importance, with respect to administrative procedures which involve or may involve the holding of a statutory inquiry by or on behalf of a Minister.

The growth of the Welfare State and state regulation led to an increase in the number of tribunals. This growth has been piecemeal, with tribunals developing their own procedures and structures, a point Lord Irvine of Lairg made clear in a speech to the Council of Tribunals in 2000:

"from the 30 or so tribunals of the 1950s [there were now] close on 100 ... [which were] very diverse; the largest tribunal hears over 300,000 cases a year; some rarely sit. Some are based on a presidential structure, some are regional. Some panels are legally qualified. Some are not. Some are very formal, with legal representation common. Many are not." (Lord Chancellor's Department, Press Notice 158/00, May 18, 2000, accessed at *http://www.tribunals-review.org.uk/pn18–05–00.htm*)

As a result of these problems, Lord Irvine appointed Sir Andrew Leggatt, a former Lord Justice of Appeal, to conduct a review of tribunals. The terms of reference were:

"To review the delivery of justice through tribunals other than ordinary courts of law, constituted under an Act of Parliament by a Minister of the Crown or for purposes of a Minister's functions; in resolving disputes, whether between citizens and the state, or between other parties, so as to ensure that:

- There are fair, timely, proportionate and effective arrangements for handling those disputes, within an effective framework for decision-making which encourages the systematic development of the area of law concerned, and which forms a coherent structure, together with the superior courts, for the delivery of administrative justice;
- The administrative and practical arrangements for supporting those decision-making procedures meet the requirements of the European Convention on Human Rights for independence and impartiality;

- There are adequate arrangements for improving people's knowledge and understanding of their rights and responsibilities in relation to such disputes, and that tribunals and other bodies function in a way which makes those rights and responsibilities a reality;
- The arrangements for the funding and management of tribunals and other bodies by government departments are efficient, effective and economical; and pay due regard both to judicial independence, and to ministerial responsibility for the administration of public funds;
- Performance standards for tribunals are coherent, consistent, and public; and effective measures for monitoring and enforcing those standards are established; and
- Tribunals overall constitute a coherent structure for the delivery of administrative justice."

The Leggett Report (*Tribunals for Users: One System, One Service* (The Stationary Office, 2001) was published in 2001 and was critical of many aspects of the tribunal system. Key among the criticisms was the sheer number of tribunals; of the 70 in existence at the time of the report in 2001, only 20 heard more than 500 cases a year, whereas a significant number were defunct. In addition, the standard and quality of these tribunals varied. The government responded to the report in a White Paper (Transforming Public Services: Complaints, Redress and Tribunals CM 6243 (DCA, 2004) in which they stated their intention to reform the tribunal system. Two keys developments have taken place since the White paper: first, the establishment of the Tribunals Service to provide administrative support to tribunals and secondly the Tribunals, Courts and Enforcement Act 2007 which creates a simplified statutory framework. The Act received Royal Assent in July 2007 and some parts have now been brought into force.

3. Independence and organisation

19–022 One of the three characteristics identified by the Franks report was impartiality. There is no general principle that all tribunals be similarly constituted and much depends on the enabling legislation. Usually there will be a legally qualified person with one or two additional members. SIAC for example usually has three panel members: one who has held high judicial office, one who is or has been a senior legally qualified member of Asylum and Immigration Tribunal and a third who is usually someone with experience in national security matters. The advantage of this is the expertise that all can bring to the adjudication.

The Council on Tribunals in its report (*Tribunals: Their Organisation and Independence* Cm 3744 (London, 1997) [at 2.2] said:

" ... [S]ince tribunals are established to offer a form of redress, mostly in disputes between the citizen and the State, the principal hallmark of any tribunal is that it must be independent. Equally importantly, it must be perceived as much. That means that the tribunal should be enables to reach decisions according to law without pressure either from the body or person whose decision is being appealed, for from anyone else."

Whilst independence must be guaranteed it is also important that there is a good relationship between the tribunal and its relevant department for example, the Social Security Tribunals works with the Department for Work and Pensions. However, the way the relationship is constituted is important in ensuring the maintenance of independence. The Leggatt review concluded that by 2001 many tribunals were too inextricably linked to the department they reviewed, he uses the term "sponsored department". For example, financial resources, administrative and IT support were at that stage provided for the tribunal by the sponsored department. Leggatt concluded:

"At best, such arrangements result in tribunals and their departments being, or appearing to be, common enterprises. At worst, they make the member of a tribunal feel that they have become identified with its sponsoring department, and they foster a culture in which the members feel their prospects of more interesting work, of progression in the tribunal, and of appointments elsewhere depend on the departments against which the case that they hear are brought." (at 2.20)

Leggatt suggested there needed to be clearer separation between tribunals and departments. In recognition of the important place that tribunals play in regulating the administrative system he further suggested they be re-organised into "a coherent system to sit alongside the ordinary courts, with administrative support provided by the Lord Chancellors Department" (now the Ministry of Justice).

In addition to the concerns regarding independence, the haphazard growth of the tribunal system meant that there were a variety of different procedures and practices which led to Leggatt pointing out (at para.1.3) that, "the result is a collection of tribunals, mostly administered by departments, with wide variations of practice and approach, and almost no coherence". For those seeking to use the tribunal services, it was difficult and incoherent.

Following the Leggatt report, in May 2003, the government proposed bringing together a majority of the existing tribunals under a single tribunal agency (The Tribunal Service (*www.tribunals.gov.uk*). The Tribunal Service was created in April 2006 and is an agency of the Ministry of Justice. It was created within the Ministry of Justice as this department does not make decisions which are subject to appeals in tribunals and because the department is charged with safeguarding judicial independence. The Tribunal Service provides administrative support for the tribunals under its remit and so removes one of the main criticisms in the Leggett report of the links between a sponsoring department and relevant tribunal. It is also intended to make the tribunal system easier for users to understand and navigate; by bringing the tribunals together under one roof it will promote best practice and ensure greater consistency in processes.

The Tribunal Service has created "divisions" which represent tribunals with similar remits. By 2007, 10 divisions had been created in the Tribunal Service which accounted for 27 tribunals and organisations (some such as the Gender Recognition Panel are not technically tribunals). Local Government Tribunals are at present not included in this structure. The Tribunal Service is presided over by the Senior President of Tribunals, a judge of experience and standing equivalent to a Lord Justice of Appeal. Each division is led by a president who is charged with providing judicial leadership and also provides the necessary quality of independence. Independence is further guaranteed by ss.1 and 2 of the Tribunals, Courts and Enforcement Act 2007, these sections came into force on September 19, 2007 (Tribunals, Courts and Enforcement Act (Commencement No.1) Order 2007 (SI 2007/2709)).

Elliot in *Beatson, Matthews & Elliot's Administrative Law: Text and Materials* (3rd edn (OUP, 2005) at p.708) likens the new structure to a federal style system. Whilst individual tribunals will remain, there is greater integration and commonality amongst them. The intention is for the new system to have a strong overarching identity and which will enable them to provide a higher standard of service and make it easier for those wishing to use the system.

4.   Procedure

19–023   Tribunal proceedings are more informal than court proceedings but still conducted on an adversarial model (as opposed to ombudsman which is more inquisitorial). The rules of fairness apply to tribunal proceedings though the level of fairness will not be as high as a normal court of law. There is no one set of procedural rules that tribunals follow, it depends very much on the tribunal in question. Although there is some attempt to streamline some procedures by the Tribunal Service, by necessity there will be some disparity. For example, Mental Health Review Tribunals and Immigration Appeals Tribunals are conducted more formally than the transport tribunal, principally because of the issues concerned. Normally tribunal hearings are oral and in public, though written submissions can be used for routine cases with the consent of the complainant. Witnesses can be called and cross-examined though this is often not necessary. Likewise, legal representation is also available though importantly legal aid is not for a vast majority; the exceptions being the Lands Tribunal, Employment Appeals Tribunal, Mental Health Tribunals and the Revenue Commissioners. Tribunals are under a statutory duty to provide reasons for their decision (Tribunals and Inquiries Act 1992 s.10). The strict rules of evidence applicable in court cases do not apply to tribunals and tribunal members can rely on their own knowledge and expertise and not just the facts adduced before them.

There is no inherent right of appeal against a tribunal decision and much depends on the enabling legislation. Right of appeal on law only may lie to a higher tribunal, for example Employment Tribunal to Employment Appeals Tribunal. Appeal may also lie to the Court of Appeal, for example, an appeal on a point of law can be made from the Special Immigration Appeals Commission to the Court of Appeal.

5. Advantages of tribunals

Even before the reforms to modernise and streamline the tribunal system, tribunals **19–024**
have a number of advantages over the traditional court route. These can be collated
into four main points:

(1) cost and efficiency;

(2) accessibility and informality;

(3) expertise; and

(4) eases the burden on the court system.

(a) *Cost and efficiency*

Perhaps the most obvious benefit of a dispute going to tribunal as opposed to court is **19–025**
the lower costs involved. First, there is no court fee to pay for lodging the claim and
secondly, because tribunals deal with cases relatively quickly and informally. This
obviates the need for lawyers and attendance of expert witnesses. Though it is important to note that in some tribunals such as the Mental Health Review Tribunal and
Immigration Appeals Tribunal parties do use lawyers.

  Aside from the benefit to the individual bringing the dispute, the administrative
efficiency of government departments is increased when decisions are made quickly and
disputes resolved speedily. It also has the benefit of increasing confidence in the
administrative system as disputes are more easily resolved. The streamlining of processes and procedures under the Tribunals Service and the Tribunals, Courts and
Enforcement Act 2007 will hopefully improve this efficiency.

(b) *Accessibility and informality*

Tribunals are intended to be accessible and follow a more informal process to adju- **19–026**
dication than the court system, for example, they do not tend to follow strict rules of
evidence. This helps individuals to more readily understand the proceedings, to fully
participate and represent themselves effectively. The Leggatt report noted that an
individual is more likely to appear before a tribunal than a court (see para.3.29).
However, as noted above, there is no uniformity amongst tribunals with some taking a
more legalistic approach with lawyers and observing more greatly the rules of evidence.
Whilst others take a more active role to helping unrepresented applicants (Social
Security Tribunals: Baldwin, Wikeley & Young, *Judging Social Security* (Oxford: OUP
1992), Ch.4).

(c)   *Expertise*

19–027   The creation of tribunals with specific jurisdiction enables them to become specialists and at least one member of a tribunal panel is an expert in the particular area. This has the obvious benefit of improving the quality of their adjudication as they can more easily understand the legislative and/or policy rules which are the subject of the hearing. The expertise within the panel also means the tribunal can dispense with expert evidence in many cases; a factor which speeds up the process and also keeps costs down. The new grouping together of tribunals into chambers by the Tribunal Service will also allow for expertise to grow and be easily disseminated amongst the chamber.

(d)   *Easing the burden on the court system*

19–028   There are a vast number of disputes arising out of the administrative system and operation of the welfare state. If all disputes had to proceed through the court system that system would become overburdened and unworkable. This point was made clearly by the Franks Committee in 1957 who stated: " . . . if all decisions arising from new legislation were automatically vested in the ordinary courts, the judiciary would by now have been grossly overburdened". Considering the growth of administrative law since the 1960s, this position would be much worse than the Franks Committee anticipated.

6.   Disadvantages of tribunals

19–029   There are equally a number of disadvantages to the tribunal system, the principal ones being the haphazard natures of the system and questions marks over their independence. Two other points merit consideration: the lack of legal representation and delay.

As has been noted, the tribunal system has developed in a haphazard way with a myriad of procedures and processes. Furthermore, the close links with their sponsoring departments raised question marks over the independence of the tribunal. The establishment of the Tribunals Services has gone a long way to dealing with this problem and will continue to do so over the next five years as the key provisions of the Tribunals, Courts and Enforcement Act 2007 are brought into effect (see para.19–022 above).

One problem which is currently being investigated (by Professor Adler at the University of Edinburgh) is the impact of the lack of legal representation at tribunal hearings. Whilst legal representation is permitted, there is no entitlement to legal aid and as a result many individuals are self-represented. Whilst tribunals are intended to be informal and legal representation should not be required, it may be shown that individuals legally represented are likely to be more successful.

The final disadvantage present in the current system are the delays in processing cases, a point highlighted in the Leggatt report. However, early evidence indicates that in the first year of operation of the tribunal service these delays are reducing. For example, in the Employment Tribunals 79 per cent of cases were heard within 26 weeks; this is with a 25 per cent increase in cases and compared to 78 per cent achieved the year before. In the Asylum and Immigration Tribunal 74 per cent were heard within six months, compared to 67 per cent the previous year (Tribunals Service Annual Report and Accounts 2006–07).

7.   Reform

Not only is the Tribunals Service now operational and providing the administrative service to the main tribunals but streamlining within the tribunals themselves is also slowly happening. The Immigration Appellate Authority, a two-tier system incorporating the Immigration Adjudicator and the Immigration Appeals Tribunal established by the Immigration Act 1971 was replaced by a single-tier Asylum and Immigration Appeal Tribunal created in 2005 by the Asylum and Immigration (Treatment of Claimants, etc) Act 2004. The primary purpose behind this was to speed up immigration and asylum appeals whilst continuing to ensure that they were handled fairly and reduce the number of onward appeals. In a review conducted in 2006, 32 per cent of respondents felt that AIT was better than the old system, whilst 34 per cent felt it was the same (question 49, AIT Review Report 2006). Interestingly, a majority of respondents felt there was an increase in the number of unrepresented applicants, which a number felt increased the length of the hearing and required a more inquisitorial approach by the panel. Moreover, a number felt that this imposed an additional burden on the panel to ensure that all relevant points were raised and there was a visible perception that appellants felt they had not had a fair hearing. **19–030**

In additional to the streamlining currently progressing, the Tribunals, Courts and Enforcement Act 2007 is being brought into force over the next few years. The Act creates a two-tier structure of tribunals: first tier tribunals and second tier tribunals which will principally be appellate, hearing appeals from first-tier tribunals. According to the Act, the tribunals under each tier will be grouped into Chambers, a process already ongoing. Two major tribunals, the Asylum and Immigration Tribunal and Employment Tribunals (Employment Tribunal and Employment Appeal Tribunal) will sit outside the new structure but remain under general oversight of the Senior President. The aim of the two-tier structure is to make the appeals process more streamlined.

The Act creates a Senior President who has general oversight of the system and replaces the Council on Tribunals with the Administrative Justice and Tribunals Council which will have a broader remit than the Council (this came into force on November 18, 2007). The Administrative Justice and Tribunals Council not only oversees the new tribunal system and its arrangement but also has the following additional powers:

- keeping under review the performance of the administrative justice system as a whole, drawing attention to matters of particular importance or concern;

- reviewing the relationships between the various components of the system (in particular ombudsmen, tribunals and the courts) to ensure that these are clear, complementary and flexible;

- identifying priorities for, and encouraging the conduct of, research;

- providing advice and making recommendations to government on changes to legislation, practice and procedure which will improve the workings of the administrative justice system.

Chapter 20

THE EUROPEAN CONVENTION ON HUMAN RIGHTS

INTRODUCTION

The European Convention on Human Rights is now directly enforceable in domestic law   **20–001**
by citizens of the United Kingdom since the enactment of the Human Rights Act 1998.
The study of human rights in the UK requires an understanding of the Convention itself
and so the first chapter in the human rights section of this book focuses on the key
features of the Convention, its principles and approaches. Subsequent chapters will then
provide an overview of how the Human Rights Act 1998 operates (Ch.21) and some of
the key rights found within the Convention that the Act now incorporates (Chs 22–24).

THE EUROPEAN CONVENTION ON HUMAN RIGHTS (ECHR)

1.   Background

After the six years of the Second World War, and the subsequent revelations about   **20–002**
human rights abuses which arose out of it, a desire among European nations that such
things should not happen again grew. Consequently, in May 1949, 10 states (Belgium,
Denmark, France, Ireland, Italy, Luxembourg, the Netherlands, Norway, Sweden and
the UK) signed the Treaty of London, establishing the Council of Europe. The Council
of Europe, a separate organisation from the institution of what is now the European
Union, was established to secure greater understanding and co-operation between
European nations, promoting the ideals of democracy, social and economic development and to advance the cause of the protection of human rights across the continent.

One of the Council's first acts was to draft the European Convention on Human Rights (ECHR). The Convention was signed in Rome on November 4, 1950, coming into force on September 3, 1953, and has been ratified and enacted by 47 nations, the two most recent ratifying nations being Monaco, in November 2005, and Montenegro, who ratified the Convention in March 2004 and enacted it in June 2006 (source *www.conventions.coe.int*).

The principal aim of the ECHR is the promotion of uniform human rights which the framers anticipated would strengthen resistance to fascism and communist dictators. The rights and freedoms in the Convention represent the minimum signatories should adhere to, i.e. the most fundamental and important rights. It was believed, at the time, that the ten original signatories already observed these basic rights, so the ECHR might be seen as not only a desire to preserve, but also to protect from the threat of communism as it spread through Eastern Europe.

INSTITUTIONS OF THE EUROPEAN CONVENTION ON HUMAN RIGHTS

20–003   Prior to 1998, the ECHR was administered by three institutions: the European Commission, the Committee of Ministers and the Court of Human Rights. All three performed some judicial functions. In particular, the European Commission (not to be confused with the Commission of the European Community) was responsible for the admissibility of applications and acted as a general filter before cases went to the court. An increase in the volume of cases and also in the number of contracting states led to considerable delays before cases would be heard. As a consequence, institutional reform was proposed to improve the Commission's decision making process and simplify the system. Protocol 11, which came into effect on November 1, 1998, abolished the Committee of Ministers quasi-judicial role, deleted clauses relating to individual applications, and created a single unified court which would perform the functions of both the Commission and the court. By these reforms, the Commission was abolished, though it remained for a transitional period of one year. The Convention's main institutions now compose the Committee of Ministers and the European Court of Human Rights (ECtHR).

1. Committee of Ministers

20–004   The Committee of Ministers is a political body comprised of the Minister for Foreign Affairs of each contracting state. Its primary responsibility in relation to the ECHR is the supervision and execution of the ECtHR's judgments (art.46).

2.   The European Court of Human Rights (ECtHR)

(a)   *Composition of the court*

Following ratification of Protocol 11, the court is now a full-time permanent body. The   **20–005**
court consists of Committees, Chambers and a Grand Chamber. The provisions governing the structure and procedures of the courts are found in arts 19–51. The number
of judges is equivalent to the number of contracting states. Judges are elected by the
Parliamentary Assembly of the Council of Europe from lists of three nominees proposed by each contracting state. Judges serve a six-year term, though they might be reelected. For their term, judges enjoy secure tenure and cannot be dismissed unless the
other judges agree by a two-thirds majority that the judge in question has failed to fulfil
the conditions required of judicial office. Judges must remain impartial and independent, refusing to engage in any activity which might contradict these conditions.
Importantly, judges of the ECtHR sit in an individual capacity and not as representatives of their contracting state. Each judge is assigned to one of five sections. Each
section's composition is gender and geographically balanced and reflects the different
legal systems of the Contracting states. Membership of each section is varied every three
years.

In addition to the ECtHR, there is a body known as the Plenary Court which has
responsibility for the election of the President and Vice-President of the European
Court, to set up the Chambers and elect their respective Presidents. The Plenary Court
also has responsibility for setting the Rules of the European Court.

(b)   *Committees*

Committees of three judges are set up within each section for a fixed 12–month period.   **20–006**
Their function is to consider the admissibility of applications brought by individuals
under art.34.

(c)   *Chambers*

A majority of decisions are given by Chambers comprising seven judges and constituted   **20–007**
within each section. The Section President and the judge from the state against whom
the case is brought sit in each case along with another judge appointed by the President.
Chambers can decide on the admissibility of applications either jointly with the merits
of an application or separately. They can relinquish their jurisdiction to the Grand
Chamber.

(d)   *The Grand Chamber*

20–008   The Grand Chamber is composed of 17 judges, including the President, Vice-President and Section Presidents. A judge from the Respondent State will sit as an ex officio member of the Grand Chamber. The Grand Chamber deals with cases that raise serious questions of interpretation or application or on a matter of general importance. The Grand Chamber hears cases which have either:

(1)   been referred to it by a Chamber which has relinquished jurisdiction before giving judgment and with both parties consent (See *Goodwin v UK* (2002) 35 E.H.R.R. 18); or

(2)   As an appeal court under art.43 where a referral has been requested from either party following judgment from the Chamber and within three months of the date of judgment; *Hatton v UK* (2003) 37 E.H.R.R. 28 provides such an example. Here the Grand Chamber overruled the decision of a Chamber that night flights violated art.8, right to respect for private and family life. If a request is granted then a full re-hearing is given.

3.   Procedure for taking a case to Strasbourg

20–009   Applications can be made by one of two ways:

(1)   Article 33: One contracting state against another contracting state, known as an inter-state application. In *Ireland v UK* (1978) 2 E.H.R.R. 25, for example, the Irish government brought an inter-state application against the UK in respect of alleged violations of art.3, freedom from tortures over the UK's treatment of terrorist suspects.

(2)   Article 34: An individual against a state. Under this article the court can receive applications from "any person, non-governmental organisation or group of individuals claiming to be a victim of a violation by one of the High Contracting Parties of the rights set forth in the Convention". A person can be both a natural or a legal person (*Sunday Times v UK* (1979–80) 2 E.H.R.R. 245). It includes not only those who have directly suffered, but also family representatives of an alleged victim. This is particularly important in cases of unlawful death as in *McCann v UK* (1995) 21 E.H.R.R. 97. Here the families of four IRA members killed by the SAS in Gibraltar brought actions against the UK alleging a violation of art.2, the right to life. The definition provided under art.34 excludes, by implication, government bodies from the ability to bring an action. For example, a local authority would not be able to bring an action alleging an interference with their freedom of expression by central government.

The final part of the requirement in art.34 requires the person or organisation to be a "victim". In *Klass v Germany* (1978) 2 E.H.R.R. 214, the court defined a victim as someone who is "directly affected" by a violation. Pressure groups or organisations which are representative of victims are excluded under this definition. Such bodies can only bring an action if the organisation itself has been directly affected. Normally the victim will have suffered some personal disadvantage, i.e. suffered a violation. However, in *Dudgeon v UK* (1982) 4 E.H.R.R. 149, the applicant brought a claim concerning the compatibility of the law banning homosexual activity with the rights in the ECHR even though he had not been prosecuted under the law and as such had suffered no direct disadvantage.

Once an application is made it is assigned to one of the five sections where it will then either go to the Committee or to the Chamber for that section. An application must satisfy the admissibility criteria in art.35 in order to proceed. These provide that:

(1) all domestic remedies must have been exhausted. The Convention machinery is seen as subsidiary to national systems and should only be used as a last resort. This is known as the principle of subsidiarity.

(2) the application must be lodged no more than six months from the date on which the final decision was made.

(3) the application must not be anonymous or on a matter which is substantially the same as one which has previously been examined by the court.

(4) the application must not be incompatible with the provisions of the convention.

(5) the application must not be manifestly ill-founded such that there is no prima facie case.

(6) the application must not be an abuse of the right to complain such as bringing a case for a political reason.

Where the court has declared an application admissible, it examines the case and under art.38(1)(b) it must "place itself at the disposal of the parties concerned with a view to securing a friendly settlement". Friendly settlement negotiations are an informal way of resolving the dispute. From the applicant's point of view, a friendly settlement can lower the costs associated with a full hearing, while still affording the applicant the opportunity to obtain compensation or serve a change in the law. Some friendly settlements are agreed with no admission as to liability by the state, but with compensation still paid out. All settlements are confidential and without prejudice to the parties' arguments before the court, should it progress to a full hearing.

An individual application against a state under art.34 will be considered by the Committee who can declare it inadmissible or strike it off. In such an instance a unanimous vote is required. Individual applications where no unanimous decision can be reached and Interstate applications under art.33 are referred to the Chamber. Chambers can deal both with issues of admissibility and merits, though decisions on admissibility are generally taken separately, unless the court decides it is an exceptional case. Chambers decisions are by majority vote and become final three months after judgment is delivered. Within that time, any party can request the case be referred (i.e.

appealed) to the Grand Chamber if it raises a serious question affecting the interpretation of the Convention, or where the resolution may have a result inconsistent
with a previous judgment of the court. Where a violation is found, and the domestic law
of the State allows only partial reparations to be made, the court can under art.41
afford "just satisfaction" to the injured party. This is often in the form of an award of
monetary compensation. Final judgments are binding in international law on the
respondent state. The court also has additional power under art.47 to give an advisory
opinion on legal questions relating to the interpretation of the Convention and its
protocols. Such opinions are usually at the request of the Committee of Ministers.

The court operates an adversarial system of advocacy, hearing cases in public,
though the majority are dealt with by written submission. Oral proceedings are conducted through legal representation, and legal aid is available from the Council of
Europe.

The following flowchart taken from the European Court of Human Rights website
shows the process of a typical application.

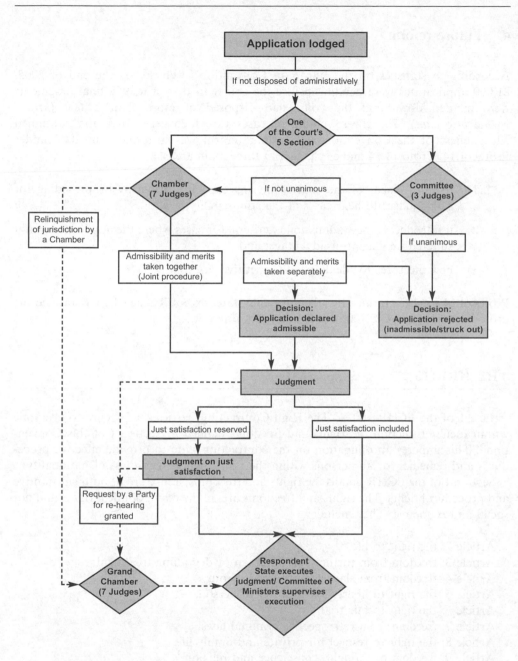

Source: *http://www.echr.coe.int/NR/rdonlyres/BA3F06A3–133C-4699–A25D-35E3C6A 3D6F5/0/PROGRESS_OF_A_CASE.pdf*

4.   Future reform

20–010   According to statistics on the European Convention's website, by the end of 2005, 81,000 applications were pending before the court. In that year, 958 final judgments were handed down and the court had disposed of more than 27,600 (*http://www.echr.coe.int*). The sheer volume of cases raised concerns over the continued effectiveness of the Convention and further reform was introduced in 2004 under Protocol 14. Protocol 14 makes changes in three main areas:

(1)   re-enforcement of the court's filtering capacity, primarily by providing for single judges to hear cases at the admissibility level;

(2)   it introduces a new admissibility criteria for cases where the applicant has not suffered significant disadvantage; and,

(3)   new measures for dealing with repetitive cases.

Protocol 14 has been ratified by all contracting states except Russia (the UK ratified the protocol on January 28, 2005). It is not yet in force.

THE RIGHTS

20–011   Article 1 of the ECHR states "The High Contracting Parties shall secure to everyone within their jurisdiction the rights and freedoms defined in Section I of this Convention". This imposes an obligation on the contracting state to provide effective procedures and remedies for all persons within their jurisdiction regardless of nationality.

Section I of the ECHR details the rights and freedoms; a mixture of both substantive and procedural rights. The rights and freedoms are, in the main, political rights and not social and economic. They include:

Article 2: the right to life;
Article 3: freedom from torture and inhuman or degrading treatment;
Article 4: freedom from slavery and forced labour;
Article 5: the right to liberty and security of person;
Article 6: the right to fair trial;
Article 7: freedom from retrospective criminal laws;
Article 8: the right to respect for private and family life;
Article 9: freedom of thought, conscience and religion;
Article 10: freedom of expression;
Article 11: freedom of assembly and association;
Article 12: the right to marry and found a family;
Article 13: the right to an effective remedy in national law where Convention rights or freedoms have been violated;
Article 14: freedom from discrimination in the enjoyment of Convention rights and freedoms.

In addition to the 14 articles above, six protocols have been added to the Convention. These include:

- Protocol 1 which includes the right to protection of property, right to education and free elections;

- Protocol 6 which abolishes the death penalty except in time of war; and

- Protocol 13 which extends protocol 6 and provides for the abolition of the death penalty in all circumstances.

All of the above have been ratified by the United Kingdom. Other protocols which have not yet been ratified by the UK and so not in force include:

- Protocol 4 which prohibits imprisonment for debt, freedom of movement and expulsion of nationals;

- Protocol 7 which provides procedural safeguards relating to the expulsion of aliens, the right of appeal in criminal matters, compensation for wrongful conviction, right not to be punished twice for the same offence and equality between spouses; and

- Protocol 12 which imposes a general prohibition on discrimination have not yet been ratified by the UK and so are not in force.

1.   Categorisation of the rights

There are three broad categories of rights found within the Convention; absolute,   **20–012** limited and qualified.

Very few of the rights expressed in the Convention are absolute, rather a number of rights are subject to exceptions and might be lawfully restricted in particular circumstances. As Lord Steyn noted In *Brown v Stott* [2003] 1 A.C. 681, such circumstances may include a conflict with one of the other rights: "The fundamental rights of individuals are of supreme importance but those rights are not unlimited: we live in communities of individuals who also have rights". Interference may also include justifications on grounds of public interest and national security. Those which are absolute include arts 3, 4 and 7(1). These rights can never be overridden or interfered with regardless of justification provided by the state or no matter how pressing the social need. In *Millar v Procurator Fiscal* [2002] 1 W.L.R. 1615, the absolute right to an independent and impartial tribunal was upheld despite the prediction that it would plunge the Scottish legal system into chaos (see J. Oldham and A. Jamieson, "Law Lords Rule Against Sheriffs", *The Scotsman*, July 26, 2001.

The second category of rights are limited rights and include arts 2, 5, and much of 6. These rights can be interfered with but only in accordance with the specific and limited circumstances prescribed in the articles themselves. For example, art.5 (1) guarantees the right to liberty and security of the person. This right is subject to six limitations such as conviction by a competent court (art.5(1)(a); reasonable suspicion of having committed an office (art.5(1)(c)) and detention with a view to deportation or extradition (art.5(1)(f)). In *Engel v Netherlands (No.1)* (1976) E.H.R.R. 647 at 57 it was made clear that this is an exhaustive list. Moreover, any interference must be in accordance with a procedure prescribed by law.

The final category of rights is qualified rights. The principal rights in this category are art.8 (right to private and family life), art.9 (religion), art.10 (expression) and art.11 (assembly and association). Exercise of these rights is qualified where the state has a legitimate aim for such interference. These aims/qualifications are necessarily broad and are found in the text of the article itself. Like art.5 above, any restriction must accord with law and be necessary in a democratic society.

Absolute	Limited	Qualified
Article 3: freedom from torture	Article 2: right to life	Article 8: right to private and family life
Article 4(1): freedom from slavery	Article 4(2): freedom from forced labour	Article 9: freedom of thought, conscience and religion
Article 6(1): fair trial	Article 5: right to liberty	Article 10: freedom of expression
Article 7: freedom from retrospective criminal law	Article 6: fair trial (part of it)	Article 11: freedom of assembly and association
Article 12: the right to marry (subject to the qualification according to "national law")		

2.   Interpretation of the rights

20–013   There are many different considerations attached to the interpretation of each convention right. However, there are some concepts which are key to determining incompatibility.

(a)   *In accordance or prescribed by law*

20–014   Any interference with a convention right must comply with the rule of law and the principle of legality and certainty. The principle of "in accordance or prescribed by law" is reflective of this, and its meaning was considered in *Sunday Times v UK* (1979) 2 E.H.R.R. 245. The Sunday Times complained that an injunction to restrain them from publishing an article dealing with thalidomide victims and the settlement of their compensation claims constituted a breach of art.10. The House of Lords had held that publication of the article would lead to The Sunday Times being in contempt of court as the article would "prejudge the issue of negligence" and expose Distillers (the company accused of causing thalidomide) to the pressures and prejudices of pre-judgment, leading to "trial by newspaper". In considering the meaning of "prescribed by law", the court said it must meet the following requirements:

(1)   There must a legal basis for the restriction, i.e. there must a law. This can be either statute or common law.

(2)   The law must be adequately accessible. This means that an individual must be able to have an indication of the legal rules applicable in any given case. This must be what is adequate in the circumstances.

(3)   The law must be formulated with sufficient precision to enable the citizen to regulate his conduct. By this, an individual must be able to foresee, to a degree that is reasonable in the circumstances, the consequences of his action. This does not equate to absolute certainty as excessive rigidity should be avoided. Laws are often couched in vague terms requiring judicial interpretation.

Even if the above three are satisfied, the interference can still be open to criticism on the ground that it was applied in a way which was not proportionate (see *R. (on the application of Rottman) v Commissioner of Police of the Metropolis* [2002] UKHL 20 at 35).

Consideration and application of this principle can be seen in *Malone v UK* (A/82) (1985) 7 E.H.R.R. 14. Mr Malone's telephone had been tapped in the course of a criminal investigation which, he contended, violated art.8, and, further, that tapping was not in accordance with law. The court indicated that the phrase did not merely refer to the existence of the domestic law but also the quality of the law, requiring it to be compatible with the rule of law (para.85). The ECtHR found a violation of art.8 on the basis that it could not say with any certainty what elements of the powers to intercept were incorporated in legal rules and what elements remained within the discretion of the Executive.

"In the opinion of the Court, the law of England and Wales does not indicate with reasonable clarity the scope and manner of exercise of the relevant discretion conferred on the public authorities. To that extent, the minimum degree of legal protection to which citizens are entitled under the rule of law in a democratic society is lacking." (p.45)

The phrase prescribed by law is interpreted and applied identically according to *Silver v UK* (1983) 5 E.H.R.R. 327.

(b)   *Legitimate aims*

20–015   For those rights which are qualified, not only must the interference be in accordance with a law, but it must pursue a legitimate aim. These aims are found in the second paragraph of arts 8–11. For example, in art.10 (freedom of expression):

> "The exercise of these freedoms ... may be subject to such ... restrictions, conditions and formalities as are prescribed by law and necessary in a democratic society, in the interests of national security, territorial integrity, public safety, the prevention of disorder or crime, the protection of heath or morals, the protection of reputation and or right of others, the prevention of the disclosure of information received in confidence and the maintenance of the authority and impartiality of the judiciary."

The court must be satisfied that the aim is being genuinely pursued.

(c)   *Necessary in a democratic society*

20–016   An interference with a right may pursue a legitimate aim and have a basis in a clear and accessible law, but it must also be necessary in a democratic society. The meaning of this term was considered in *Handyside v UK* (A/24) (1979–80) 1 E.H.R.R. 737. Mr Handyside had published a book for children over the age of twelve entitled the "little red schoolbook" which was a reference book dealing with such issues as sex. He was convicted under the Obscene Publications Act 1959 (as amended by the Obscene Publications Act 1964) and took his case to the ECtHR contending that his right to freedom of expression had been unlawfully interfered with. It was accepted by the parties that the interference with Mr Handyside's art.10 right was in accordance with domestic law and pursued the legitimate aim of protection of morals found in para.10(2). However, the issue for the court was whether the interference was necessary in a democratic society for the protection of morals. The court discussed both the scope of the phrase, and the court's role in respect of it. The court (at para.48) noted that the adjective "necessary", was not the same as "indispensable", or "absolutely necessary" nor did it have the flexibility of such expressions as "useful", "reasonable" or "desirable" but that it implied the existence of a "pressing social need". The court recognised that it was for national authorities to make the initial assessment but that the ECtHR was to exercise supervision over this. The ECtHR needed to ensure both the existence of the pressing social need, that the interference corresponded to this social need, that the restriction, condition or penalty was proportionate to the legitimate aim pursued and whether the reasons given by the national authorities to justify it's interference were "relevant and sufficient (paras 49–50).

3. Proportionality

The concept of proportionality is well established in the jurisprudence of the ECtHR. It **20–017** is a specific requirement of "necessary in a democratic society" and is implicit when considering interference with the other rights. Proportionality ensures there is a fair balance between pursuing a legitimate aim and the protection of the Convention right. The court will consider the nature of the right and the extent that it has been interfered with, balancing this against the legitimate aim the state has asserted. Any interference or restriction must be no more than is necessary to achieve the legitimate aim.

In *Bowman v UK* (1998) 26 E.H.R.R. 1, the applicant distributed leaflets in the Halifax parliamentary constituency prior to the 1992 general election. The leaflets purported to inform electors of the opinions on abortion of those candidates standing for election. Bowman was charged under s.75 of the Representation of the People Act 1983 which prohibits the expenditure of more than five pounds by an unauthorised person with a view to promoting or procuring the election of a candidate immediately before an election. Bowman argued this was an interference with art.10 in that the five pounds limit was disproportionate. The government maintained the spending limit in the Act pursued the aim of protecting the rights of others. The government maintained that the limit only imposed only a partial restriction on expenditure which was no more extensive than was necessary to achieve the legitimate aims pursued (para.31). The court found that the 1983 Act operated as a total barrier to Mrs Bowman publishing information with a view to influencing voters. Whilst recognising that the Act pursued a legitimate aim of protecting the rights of others to ensure equality, the court did not feel that the low limit was necessary to achieve this aim, particularly as there were no restrictions on the press to support or oppose a candidate, or upon the political parties themselves. Therefore, the restriction was disproportionate to the aim pursued.

20–018   (a)   *Flowchart for qualified rights*

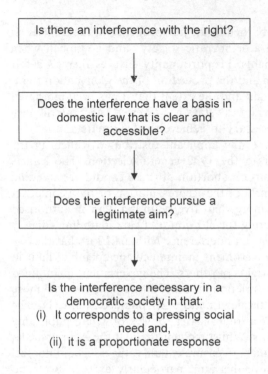

PRINCIPLES OF THE ECHR

1.   Interpretation of the Convention

20–019   The Convention is regarded as a "living instrument". In *R. (on the application of Pretty) v Director of Public Prosecutions* [2001] UKHL 61 it was stated "as an important constitutional instrument the convention is to be seen as a "living tree capable of growth and expansion within its natural limits". If this were not the case, the rights contained within the Convention would become outdated and incapable of developing as social, cultural and political conditions changed. They are open to interpretation and change over time. For example, the right of same sex couples to marry would not have been regarded as part of the right to family life in the 1960s, but later became part of that right (see *Goodwin v UK* (2002) 35 E.H.R.R. 447, *Bellinger v Bellinger*; see further para.21–013). In the UK, domestic courts have made clear there are limits on how far the living instrument approach can be taken. In *Brown v Stott* [2003] 1 A.C. 681, Lord Clyde stated that as the Convention deals with the realities of life, it is not to be applied in ways which are contrary to reason and common sense.

The ECtHR does not have a formal doctrine of precedent. In *Cossey v UK* (1991) 13 E.H.R.R. 622 the applicant contended that a refusal to issue her with a "new" birth following gender re-assignment treatment was contrary to art.8. One issue was whether the court was bound by an earlier decision, *Rees v UK* (1987) 9 E.H.R.R. 56, where no violation was found. The court stated that it was not bound by its previous decisions, but in an attempt to ensure a reasonable degree of certainty and maintain the orderly development of Convention case law, they generally followed their precedents. However, the court indicated this "would not prevent the Court from departing from an earlier decision if it was persuaded that there were cogent reasons for doing so. Such a departure might, for example, be warranted in order to ensure that the interpretation of the Convention reflects societal changes and remains in line with present-day conditions."

2. Margin of appreciation

The doctrine of a margin of appreciation is a principle of interpretation applied by Strasbourg. In deciding whether there has been a violation of one of the Convention rights and in determining whether the State has achieved the correct balance the court allows the states a certain measure of discretion when taking legislative, administrative or judicial measures which restrict ECHR rights. The doctrine is based on the assumption that contracting states have a better knowledge of the political, social and cultural traditions influencing their countries, and this should be respected.

20–020

> "By reason of their direct and continuous contact with the vital forces of their countries, state authorities are in principle in a better position than the international judge to give an opinion on the exact content of those requirements [of morals] as well as on the "necessity" of a "restriction" or "penalty" intended to meet them ... " (*Handyside v UK* (1976) 1 E.H.R.R. 737 at para.48)

Nevertheless, the exercise of state discretion is not unlimited; it is still subject to supervision by the ECtHR. In *Handyside v United Kingdom*, the ECHR explained:

> "the Court ... is responsible for ensuring the observance of those States engagements, is empowered to give the final ruling on whether a "restriction" or "penalty" is reconcilable .... The domestic margin of appreciation thus goes hand in hand with a European supervision." (at para.49).

The doctrine is flexible, the court offering either a wide or narrow margin dependent wholly on the circumstances. Where morals are concerned, it is accepted that a wider margin of appreciation will be offered. In *Handyside v UK* (above) the court recognised it was hard to find a uniform conception of morals within the Member States, particularly as morality varies from time to time and from place to place. The court stated that individual states were in a better position to give an opinion of moral requirements than the international court. In contrast, where an interference impinges on press freedom a narrower margin is offered. In *Sunday Times v UK* (above), the court took the view there was a "fairly substantial measure of common ground" in the area of impartiality of the judiciary. Therefore, it accorded less discretionary power of appreciation and more extensive supervision from the court.

3. Positive obligations

20–021   At first sight, the Convention imposes merely negative obligation on a state, i.e. they must not take action which interferes with Convention rights. There is no requirement that the State take action to ensure action between private individuals does not violate the rights. In recent years the court has developed a concept of "positive state obligation" requiring states to take positive steps to stop violation of rights by providing a system of laws, law enforcement and public administration. This positive obligation is based on the general duty found in art.1 requiring a state "to secure to everyone within that jurisdiction the rights and freedoms defined in the Convention". In an early case involving art.8, *Marckx v Belgium* (1979–80) 2 E.H.R.R. 330, the court stated that the obligation under art.8 did not merely compel a state to abstain from interference with that right but also included positive obligations inherent in an effective "respect" for family life (para.31).

4. Derogation and reservations

20–022   Article 15 of the Convention allows a state to derogate (not comply) from certain Convention articles in limited circumstances. A derogation can only occur "in time of war or other public emergency threatening the life of the nation" and it must only be to the extent strictly required by the situation (i.e. proportionate) and must not be inconsistent with the state's other obligations under international law. If a derogation is considered necessary, a declaration must be lodged with the Secretary General of the Council of Europe. No derogation is allowed against art.2 (right to life), art.3 (freedom from torture), art.4(1) (prohibition of slavery) or art.7 (prohibition of retrospective legislation).

The European Court considered the meaning of the term "public emergency threatening the life of the nation" in *Lawless v Ireland* (1961) 1 E.H.R.R. 15, a case concerned with IRA terrorist activity in Northern Ireland. The Irish government derogated from art.5 in July 1957 in order to permit detention without charge or trial. The court, in finding there was a public emergency, stated that such a state of affairs exists when there is an "exceptional situation of crisis or emergency which affects the whole population and constitutes a threat to the organised life of the community of which the State is composed" (para.28).

In the *Greek Case* (1969) 12 Y.B. 1, Greece failed to persuade the Commission (as it then was) that a public emergency existed. The Commission stated that a public emergency would have the following characteristics:

> "1. It must be actual or imminent;
> 2. Its effects must involve the whole nation;
> 3. The continuance of the organised life of the community must be threatened;
> 4. The crisis or danger must be exceptional, in that the normal measures or restrictions permitted by the Convention for the maintenance of public safety, health and order, are plainly inadequate."

In *Ireland v United Kingdom* (1978) 2 E.H.R.R. 25, the parties agreed that the art.15 test was satisfied in respect of the troubles in Northern Ireland. The court noted that a wide margin of appreciation is given to states under art.15(1).

> "It falls in the first place to each Contracting State, with its responsibility for 'the life of [its] nation', to determine whether that life is threatened by a 'public emergency' and, if so, how far it is necessary to go in attempting to overcome the emergency. By reason of their direct and continuous contact with the pressing needs of the moment, the national authorities are in principle in a better position than the international judge to decide both on the presence of such an emergency and on the nature and scope of derogations necessary to avert it. In this matter, Article 15(1) leaves those authorities a wide margin of appreciation." (para.207)

The qualifying threshold was also reached when the UK lodged a derogation in 1988 in respect of the danger posed by the *IRA (McBride v UK* (1993) 17 E.H.R.R. 25). Another derogation was entered in 2001 in respect of art.5(1) following the terrorist attacks in the USA. This allowed the UK to pass legislation (Anti Terrorism Crime and Security Act 2001 s.23) authorising the indefinite detention without charge or trial of non-UK nationals suspected of terrorist activities. This derogation was successfully challenged in the House of Lords in 2004 in *A v Secretary of State for the Home Department* [2004] UKHL 56. The House of Lords, in considering the validity of the derogation order, recognised there was a public emergency threatening the life of the nation (Lord Hoffman giving a powerful dissent), but concluded that the measures taken were not "strictly required by the exigencies of the situation". The main thrust of this conclusion was that the measures did not apply to UK nationals and that the Act allowed foreign nationals to leave for any country willing to take them, even though such a person's capacity to inflict serious damage to the UK could be unchanged from that country (see Ch.5).

A related and further point was the claim that the measures discriminated against the appellants in their enjoyment of the right to liberty under art.5 on the basis of their nationality. The UK had not derogated from art.14 and therefore the UK had to establish that any difference in treatment was "objective and reasonable". The House of Lords stated that the threat was not confined to non-UK nationals and there are many UK nationals who have been defined as "suspected international terrorists". The House of Lords made a quashing order in respect of the Derogation Order and a declaration under s.4 of the HRA that s.23 of the Act was incompatible with arts 5 and 14 of the Convention. The government subsequently passed the Prevention of Terrorism Act 2005 which provided for the imposition of control order which restricts movement of those suspected of terrorism. A number of those previously detained where made the subject of control orders.

Article 57 of the Convention allows a state to make a reservation against specific provision of the Convention at the time of ratification. A reservation has to be specific, i.e. it cannot be made against a whole right and can only be made in respect of laws in existence in the state at the time of ratification. The UK made a reservation with regard to Protocol 1, art. 2, which guarantees the right to education and respects the right of parents to ensure any education is in conformity with their own religious and philosophical convictions. The UK has accepted art.2 only insofar that it is compatible with the provision of efficient instruction and training and the avoidance of unreasonable public expenditure. This is pursuant to the Education Acts in force at the time.

5.   Relationship between the ECHR and the European Union

20–023   The ECHR is not part of the European Community. Although it has been signed by all Member States, it has signatories who are not members of the European Community. However, there is a close relationship between the EC and the ECHR. The ECJ has often indicated its willingness to be guided by the jurisprudence of the ECtHR. This was given formal recognition in the Treaty of European Union 1992, EC art.6, which provided that the Union "shall respect fundamental rights as guaranteed by the European Convention". This does not, however, amount to a formal incorporation of the ECHR into Community law. Individuals cannot raise a human rights compatibility issue between Member States; it is only relevant where it relates to the meaning of community law, *Kremzow v Austria* [1997] E.C.R. I-2629. The EC has developed its own human rights charter, the Charter of Fundamental Human Rights of the European Union, completed in October 2000. The Charter has not, as yet, been ratified by Member States and no timetable set for its implementation. In terms of its relationship to the ECHR, the Charter is more ambitious and wide-ranging than the ECHR and intended to compliment it. Article 52(3) of the Charter makes it clear that where it contains rights which correspond to those contained in the ECHR, those rights will be given the same interpretation as given by Strasbourg.

6.   The ECHR prior to the Human Rights Act 1998

20–024   Prior to implementation of the HRA in October 2000, the status of the ECHR was like any other international Treaty not incorporated into domestic law, i.e. it did not have direct domestic effect. Whilst it was binding internationally, it could not be directly relied upon in domestic court proceedings; see *Malone v MPC* [1979] Ch. 344, where Megarry VC refused to develop the common law to create right to privacy.

As with other international instruments, there is a presumption that Parliament intended to legislate compatibly with its international obligations and as such the Convention could be used as an aid to interpretation where the words of a statute were ambiguous or unclear; a point made clear by Lord Denning M.R. in *Chief Immigration Officer Heathrow Airport Ex p. Bibi (Salamat)* [1976] 1 W.L.R. 979, 985. In *Re M and H (minors)* [1990] 1 A.C. 686, a case concerning parental rights of access to an illegitimate child, Lord Brandon highlighted the limits of the interpretative obligation stating that, "while English courts will strive when they can to interpret statutes as conforming with the obligations of the UK under the Convention, they are nevertheless bound to give effect to statutes which are free from ambiguity ... even if those statutes may be in conflict with the Convention" (at p.722).

FURTHER READING

Bingham, T. "The European Convention on Human Rights: Time to Incorporate"   **20–025**
  (1993) 109 L.Q.R. 390.
Hoffman, D. and Rowe, J. *Human Rights in the UK: An Introduction to the Human
  Rights Act 1998* 2nd edn (Harlow: Pearson Education, 2006)
Merris, A. *Human Rights Law* (Hart Publishing, 2006)
Woolf in "Droit Public—English Style" (1995) P.L. 57

Chapter 21

THE HUMAN RIGHTS ACT 1998

INTRODUCTION

Prior to the Human Rights Act 1998 (HRA), the UK's Constitution did not contain **21–001** any positive enactment of rights. Instead UK citizens had "residual rights" meaning they had the right to do anything not prohibited by law. The foundation for this approach was the belief that freedom was the natural and residual attribute of the citizen and should only be restricted to the extent necessary for the prevention of crime, in the public interest, or where the defence of the realm and national security were at issue. As a result, there was little call for a positive and express enactment of rights. The task of protecting human rights, therefore, fell dually to Parliament, by its control of the Executive, and to the courts through the common law. Dicey, writing in the *Introduction to the Study of the Law of the Constitution*, recognised this when he articulated his third premise of the rule of law, namely that the civil liberties of individuals would be recognised by the judiciary and protected through the common law. In addition to these residual rights, any individual could take a claim to Strasbourg alleging a violation of the Convention.

The HRA received Royal Assent on November 9, 1998, coming into effect in England and Wales on October 2, 2000. From that date, the rights and freedoms contained within the European Convention on Human Rights (ECHR) became enforceable domestically. Before looking in detail at the main provisions of the HRA, it makes sense to consider what changed that necessitated legislation which positively protects individual citizens rights in the UK.

HUMAN RIGHTS BEFORE 2000

21–002   Changes in the political structure of the UK during the 20th century with the development and growth of popular political parties led to governments with significant majorities. This meant that the government could easily pass through Parliament its legislative programme. A proliferation of statutes led to the piecemeal encroachment on individual liberties. Such statutes included:

- Public Order Act 1986 which restricted public protest;

- Police and Criminal Evidence Act 1984 which gave greater powers to the Police;

- Interception of Communications Act 1985 which allowed the interception of communications;

- numerous anti-terrorist legislation which allowed detention for extended periods and stop and search without reasonable suspicion;

- Criminal Procedure and Investigations Act 1996 which restricted the right of access to material collected by the Prosecution.

Parliament also became much weaker in its ability to check the Executive effectively and control discretion given to it by such statutes.

It became apparent that there was a lack of confidence in the court's ability, through common law, to protect civil liberties. Lord Bridge in *Att-Gen v Guardian Newspapers* [1987]1 W.L.R. 1248 at p.1286 stated that his confidence in the capacity of the common law to safeguard fundamental freedoms essential to a free society was "severely undermined" after the House of Lords decision to uphold an interim injunction prohibiting publishing of Peter Wrights book "Spycatcher". Similarly in *Malone v MPC*, the court held that the government could intercept Mr Malone's telephone calls, rejecting his argument that he had a right to respect for private life in domestic law. In *Malone v UK* (1985) 7 E.H.R.R. 14, the ECtHR found a violation of Mr Malone's art.8 rights as the interference by the government was not in accordance with a procedure prescribed by law. The law relied on by the government, the prerogative to intercept mail, could not logically be extended to cover telephone calls.

The most obvious evidence that rights were not adequately protected by domestic law could be drawn from the number of cases in which the European Commission (this institution no longer exists) and the European Court of Human Rights (ECtHR) found the UK to have violated Convention rights. Of the total 144 cases before the court between 1966 and June 1990, 37 involved the UK government; the closest to this was Belgium with 20 cases. However, the statistics cannot tell the whole story and the reason for the UK's violations is in no way indicative of the government's disregard for human rights. For example, interpretation of the Convention had developed reflecting changes in society and the UK has not always kept up with these changes.

In the period in question, judicial interest in human rights grew and judges, writing extra-judicially, set forth the view that rights needed more direct protection at home. Lord Woolf in "Droit Public – English Style" (1995) P.L. 57 at 70, took the view that a "British Bill of Rights would avoid the difficulty which exists at present in protecting some or our basic rights". See, also, Lord Bingham, "The European Convention on Human Rights: Time to Incorporate" (1993) 109 L.Q.R. 390.

On the international front, positive statements of human rights were the norm in most constitutions. Almost all the signatory states had gradually incorporated the Convention into their domestic law, with the exception of the Republic of Ireland which had its own Bill of Rights in their constitution (under the fundamental rights section).

1.   The incorporation debate

Despite the perceived problems in protecting rights domestically, a Bill of Rights or   **21–003** Human Rights Act seemed unlikely in the 1980s; indeed, Prime Minister Margaret Thatcher took the view that such a change was not needed. In responding to the demands of Charter 88 (a campaign group), she argued that "that [the] present constitutional arrangements continue to serve us well and that the citizen in this country enjoys the greatest degree of liberty that is compatible with the rights of others and the vital interest of the state". There were also constitutional objections. The doctrine of Parliamentary Sovereignty meant that any "Bill of Rights" would have no special status and are consequently subject to express or implied repeal in the same as any other Act. This, in turn, could serve only to undermine the effectiveness of the Act. In addition, there were some concerns about the power given to the judiciary charged with the task of interpreting the principles of any Human Rights Act. Whilst this concern ultimately depended on the nature of the Act itself, such an Act had the potential to empower and embolden the judiciary transferring the power in the State from the elected body to the appointed one. In response to incorporation of the ECHR as a course of action, one particular problem was the age of the Convention; some 40 years old at the point of incorporation. The Convention also does not include nearly enough specific provisions with regard to sexual and religious equality and makes no statement about general economic and social rights at all.

On the other side, one main problem associated with not incorporating the ECHR was that enforcing rights meant going to Strasbourg, with the accompanying delays and expense involved. On average, a claim took five years, costing in the region of £30,000. Incorporating the ECHR, or *bringing rights home*, to use the language of the government literature, would mean British people could argue their rights in domestic courts without the inordinate delay and cost. It also meant rights would become integrated into the jurisprudence of the courts.

There were, however, attempts in the early 1990s to achieve some statutory protection of rights through incorporation of the ECHR. Liberal Democrat Peer, Lord Lester of Herne Hill Q.C. introduced two private members Bills with the aim of incorporation into the House of Lords in 1994 and 1996. However, it was not until the Labour Party adopted the incorporation of the ECHR as a manifesto commitment that a UK Bill of Rights seemed more likely. In 1996, the Labour Party published "Bringing Rights Home" (London, Labour party 1996), setting out, in detail, the benefits of incorporation viewed as a way to "change the relationship between the state and citizen, and redress the dilution of individual rights by an over-centralising government." Following their election in 1997, the "new" Labour government quickly introduced a White Paper

Rights Brought Home (Cm 3782, London: HMSO) which accompanied a draft Bill. The new Bill became the Human Rights Act 1998, which came into force in 2000.

2.   Aims of the Human Rights Act 1998

21–004   The long title of the HRA states that it is "An Act to give further [my emphasis] effect to rights and freedoms guaranteed under the European Convention on Human Rights". The use of the word "further" reflects the view that the rights and freedoms were given effect domestically prior to the HRA, a view clearly articulated by Lord Clyde in *R. v Lambert* [2001] UKHL 37, where his Lordship commented that the Act is "a procedural mechanism which has opened a further means of access to justice for the citizen". The White Paper adds more clarification and states the aim of the Act being "to make more directly accessible the rights which the British people already enjoy under the Convention ... to bring those rights home" (at para.1.19). By bringing rights home, the Act intended to "redress the dilution of individual rights by an over centralising government that has taken place over the past two decades" (White Paper Rights Brought Home (Cm 3782).

In addition to these general aims, it was hoped that the Act would bring about the creation of a human rights culture in the UK (see evidence by the Home Secretary to the Joint Committee on Human Rights, 2000–01 HL 66 HC 332 and before the House of Commons, October 21, 1998 HC Deb, vol.317, col.1358; Lord Chancellor before the House of Lords, November 2, 1997 HL Deb, vol.582, col.1228).

The move in the protection of human rights, from the tradition of residual rights, to one of positive rights, fills the gaps left in the traditional approach to protecting rights. Lord Irvine L.C., Hansard HL, November 3, 1997, col.1228, stated, "the traditional freedom of the individual under a written constitution to do himself that which is not prohibited by law gives no protection from misuse of power by the state, nor any protection from the acts of public bodies ... incompatible with ... human rights under the Convention".

In *Wilson v First Country Trust* [2003] UKHL 40, Lord Hobhouse described the structure of the Act as "unique". The Act maintains the three separate structures of the state recognising that the judiciary apply and enforce Convention rights, the Executive are liable for breaches of the Convention and recognises the supremacy of Parliament by providing that laws may be passed which are incompatible with Convention rights. Otherwise, the Act is merely procedural, the substantive rights being included as appendices to the Act. In s.1, these rights are defined as arts 2–12 and 14, arts 1–3 of Protocol 1, and arts 1–2 of Protocol 6, ECHR. All must be read with arts 16–18 and are subject to derogations or reservations which are in place. Article 13, the right to an effective remedy is specifically excluded as it was thought by the government that an effective remedy was provided by s.8 of the HRA which gives the court the right to grant a remedy for any breach of the ECHR (see in particular Lord Irvine (*Hansard* HL Vol.583, col.475).

The rights included in the Human Rights Act 1998:

Article 2: The Right to Life
Article 3: Freedom from Torture and Inhuman and Degrading Treatment
Article 4: Freedom from Slavery and Forced Labour
Article 5: Liberty and Security of Person
Article 6: Right to a Fair Trial
Article 7: Prohibition on Retrospective Criminal Law and Penalties
Article 8: Right to Private and Family Life, Home and Correspondence
Article 9: Freedom of Religion, Thought and Conscience
Article 10: Freedom of Expression
Article 11: Freedom of Association and Peaceful Assembly
Article 12: The Right to Marry
Article 14: Freedom from discrimination in the enjoyment of Convention rights and freedoms

Article 1 of the First Protocol: The Right to Peaceful Enjoyment of Possessions
Article 2 of the First Protocol: The Right to Education
Article 3 of the First Protocol: The Duty to Hold Free Elections and the Right to Vote

Article 1 of the Sixth Protocol
Article 2 of the Sixth Protocol

3.   Retrospective effect of the Human Rights Act 1998

Section 22(4) of the HRA makes specific reference to the retrospectivity of the Act. It **21–005** states that s.7(1)(b), the shield provision, applies retrospectively to:

(1)   defend proceedings brought by a public authority and,

(2)   defend an appeal by a public authority in respect of a decision

Aside from this provision, there is little guidance in the HRA itself. In its early years, proceedings (often in criminal cases) sought to test the retrospective operation of the Act. In *R. v Lambert* [2001] UKHL 37, the first such case, Lambert had been convicted in 1999 of possession of a controlled drug with intent to supply contrary to the Misuse of Drugs Act 1971. At his appeal, he alleged that art.6(2) had been violated by the requirement that he had to prove that he did not know he had the drugs. The decision is complex, their Lordships giving differing reasons, though the majority concluded that proceedings brought against a public authority did not include an appeal from the decision of a court by an unsuccessful defendant.

   The difficulties with the decision in *Lambert* were highlighted in *R. v Kansal* [2001] UKHL 62, where the majority of the House of Lords concluded that Lambert had been wrongly decided, but nevertheless should be followed. In subsequent cases *Lambert* has continued to be followed (see *R. v Allen* [2001] UKHL 45). Following these early cases, it is clear the HRA does not apply to the acts of courts, tribunals or public authorities which took place prior to October 2, 2000.

A similar approach has been taken in respect of civil cases. In *JA Pye (Oxford) Ltd v Graham* [2002] UKHL 30 the HRA was held not to apply to an appeal of a decision made before October 2, 2000. In *Wilson v First County Trust Ltd (No.2)* [2003] UKHL 40, the House of Lords held that the Court of Appeal had been wrong to grant a declaration of incompatibility in respect of a cause of action arising before the Act came into force. The same principle applies to the court's powers of interpretation. In *R. (Hurst) v HM Coroner for Northern District Council* [2007] UKHL 13, the respondent's son was stabbed to death by a neighbour on May 25, 2000. The House of Lords held that the art.2 obligation to hold an effective investigation did not apply retrospectively to a death that occurred prior to the coming into force of the HRA and that, therefore, the Coroners Act 1988 could not be so interpreted.

RELATIONSHIP BETWEEN THE HRA AND THE ECHR

21–006   When dealing with a potential human rights violation, s.2(1) of the HRA requires domestic courts to "take into account" any relevant decisions of the ECtHR, the Commission on Human Rights or the European Committee of Ministers. There is no strict system of precedent as the obligation is to take into account rather than to follow Strasbourg case law.

In a majority of cases, the obligation to take into account is construed as an obligation to follow. In *R. (on the application of Alconbury Developments Ltd) v Secretary of State for the Environment, Transport and the Regions* [2001] 2 All E.R. 929, Lord Slynn reasoned that, in the absence of special circumstances, the court should follow any clear and consistent jurisprudence of the ECtHR. He reasoned that if the court did not follow Strasbourg case law in this situation then a further avenue of appeal was open to take the case to Strasbourg; the likelihood was that Strasbourg would then follow their precedent. In *R. v Secretary of State for Home Department, Ex p. Anderson* [2002] UKHL 46 (a case concerning the compatibility of the Home Secretary's power to determine life tariffs with art.6) it was argued that the House of Lords should not follow the ECtHR judgment in *Stafford v UK* (2002) 35 E.H.R.R. 32. Lord Bingham held that the House would not, without good reason, depart from the principles laid down in a carefully considered judgment of the court sitting as a Grand Chamber.

The implication of this statement suggests that where a decision is not so "considered", or the reasoning of the ECtHR is inadequate, then the House will more readily consider departing from a decision of Strasbourg. In *Brown v Stott* [2003] 1 A.C. 681, the Privy Council concluded that s.172 of the Road Traffic Act 1988, which required the keeper of a vehicle to identify the person driving at the time of an offence, was not incompatible with art.6, or the privilege against self-incrimination, despite there being Strasbourg decisions suggesting the contrary view in *Saunder v UK*. Lord Hope described the reasoning of the ECtHR in *Saunder v UK* as "unconvincing", noting:

"the general approach which is revealed by the judgment appears to be out of keeping with the mainstream of the jurisprudence which the court itself has developed as to the nature of the application of the rights which it has read into Art 6(1)." (p.721)

In *Kay v Lambeth London Borough Council & Price v Leeds County Council* [2006] UKHL 10, the House of Lords stated that courts had to adhere to the English rules of precedent. If a judge felt a decision was inconsistent with Strasbourg authority, he had to follow the binding precedent from the domestic court, but could give leave to appeal as appropriate.

WHO MAY BRING A CLAIM AND WHO MUST ACT COMPATIBLY?

Not every person may bring a claim under the HRA, and not every person is obliged to act compatibly with its provisions. The HRA lays down some general criteria for each under ss.6 and 7. These provisions have been designed to mirror those requirements in the ECHR, the objective being to ensure those who can bring a claim under the ECHR in Strasbourg, might do so domestically. Likewise, those considered subject to the obligations under the Convention internationally are under similar domestic obligations. It also works the other way around and does not allow application of the HRA to those that would not be able to rely on the rights at Strasbourg.

21–007

1. Human Rights Act 1998 section 7

Section 7(1) of the Human Rights Act provides that persons who are, or would be, a "victim" of an unlawful act of a public authority under s.6(1) have the right to:

21–008

(1) bring legal proceedings against the authority (a "sword"); or

(2) rely on ECHR rights in any legal proceedings for example as a defence to a criminal or civil action (a "shield").

Section 7(7) of the HRA provides that the term "victim" has the same meaning as that under ECHR art.34 (see para.20–009).

Section 7 appears at first glance clear and concise. However, Lord Hope in *Aston Cantlow and Wilmcote with Billesley Parochial Church Council v Wallbank (Billesley)* [2003] UKHL 37 at [36] held that despite this apparent clarity it "leave[s] a great deal of open ground. There is room for doubt and for argument". What is clear, however, is that the "victim" test is narrower than the "sufficient interest" test in judicial review proceedings (see Ch.14 for a discussion of the sufficient interest test).

Aside from those people who have suffered an actual violation of their Convention rights, s.7 applies to the following categories of people:

- Potential victims. Provision is made for this in s.7(1) which applies to "would be" victims of a violation of a convention right.

- Relatives of a victim. In *Re McKerr* [2004] UKHL 12, the House of Lords accepted that a son questioning why his father was killed by agents of the state was a victim.

- Non-nationals and those living outside the UK as long as the violation was committed within the UK's jurisdiction. In *R. (on the application of Al Skeini) v Secretary of State for Defence* [2007] UKHL 26, Iraqi relatives of Iraqi nationals killed by British forces in Iraq were entitled to bring proceedings alleging a violation of art.2. At the time of the alleged violation the Iraq nationals were detained in prison in Basra, Iraq. The House of Lords held that an action could be brought as the prison was under the effective control of the army and so came within the jurisdiction of the United Kingdom (para.29–033 and see also *Bankovic v Belgium* (2001) B.H.R.C. 435). Similarly in *R. (on the application of Farrakhan) v Secretary of State for the Home Department* [2001] EWHC (Admin) 781, the Secretary of State conceded the fact that even though the individual was neither a citizen of a Member State nor within the territory of a Member State did not preclude application of the Convention.

However, it equally excludes the following:

- Governmental organisations. Article 34 applies to non governmental organisations therefore it implicitly excludes governmental organisations. That s.7 excludes core public authorities was recognised in the *Billesley* case. However, it would include hybrid public authorities.

- Representative groups: Section 7 excludes applications from pressure groups or other interest/representative groups unless their members are themselves victims, see s.7(3).

There were initial concerns over the application of s.7 when an applicant was seeking a declaration of incompatibility under s. 4, or an interpretation under s.3. In *R. (on the application of Rusbridger) v Att-Gen* [2003] UKHL 28, the Guardian newspaper brought proceedings for a declaration that s.3 of the Treason Act 1848 did not apply to newspaper reports advocating republicanism. The House of Lords concluded that the Guardian had standing to bring such an action despite the fact that a prosecution was not brought. This is consistent with decisions made by the ECtHR such as *Norris v Ireland* (1989) 13 E.H.R.R. 186. However, the House of Lords was at pains to stress that save in exceptional circumstances, members of the public should not brings proceedings testing the compatibility of legislation and whether proposed conduct is lawful. Lord Walker at [61] stated:

> "Sections 3 and 4 of the HRA are intended to promote and protect human rights in a practical way, not to be an instrument by which the courts can chivvy Parliament into spring cleaning the statute book, perhaps to the detriment of more important legislation. Such a spring-cleaning process might have some symbolic significant but I can see no other practical purpose which this litigation would achieve."

Moreover, it is clear following the Court of Appeal decision in *Lancashire County Council v Taylor* [2005] EWCA Civ 284 that a declaration of incompatibility cannot be obtained in a purely hypothetical case where the applicant would not be affected by a violation of a convention right. In such a case, the applicant is clearly not a victim.

Under s.7(5) actions under the HRA must be commenced within one year of the date of the act complained of. An extension of time may be granted in exceptional cases where the court considers it "equitable" to do so in all the circumstances.

2. Section 6 of the Human Rights Act 1998 and Public Authorities

Section 6(1) of the HRA makes it "unlawful for a public authority to act in a way which is incompatible with [ECHR] rights". However, consistent with parliamentary sovereignty, a public authority will not breach the obligation imposed by s.6(1) if: **21–009**

1. it is required to so act by primary legislation: HRA s.6(2)(a), or

2. it is acting so as to give effect to or enforce incompatible primary or subordinate legislation: HRA s.6(2)(b).

As s.6(1) imposes legal duties only on a "public authority", it is important to know which people or bodies fall into that category. This has caused some difficulty as the concept of "public authority" is not specifically defined in the Act. The White Paper suggested that the definition of public authority would cover the following bodies: " ... central government (including Executive agencies), local government, the police, immigration officers, prison, courts and tribunals themselves; and, to the extent that they are exercising public functions, companies responsible for areas of activity which were previously within the public sector, such as privatised utilities" (para.2.2). Statements from the Home Secretary during the Bill's passage through the House of Commons equally suggested that a wide range of bodies would fall under the obligation including privatised or contracted-out bodies (HC Deb, February 26, 1998 Col 773; HC Deb June 17, 1998, Col 409–10). The HRA itself reflects these intentions as by s.6(3)(a), a public authority includes a court or tribunal and under s.6(3)(b) provision is made for including traditionally private bodies " ... whose functions are of a public nature". The only further clarification of the scope of s.6 comes under s.6(5) which provides that a person is not acting as a public authority by virtue of s.6(3)(b) if the nature of the Act is private. The Act also negatively defines a public authority as not including either House of Parliament, except the House of Lords in its judicial capacity s.6(4), thus preserving parliamentary privilege. From this, three broad categories of public authorities can be identified:

(1) core or pure public authorities;

(2) hybrid or functional public authorities;

(3) courts and tribunals.

The distinction is important as it appears that "core" public authorities are subject to the s.6(1) obligation in respect of all their acts (both public and private), whereas "hybrid" public authorities are only subject to the obligation in respect of their public acts (*Aston Cantlow and Wilmcote with Billesley Parochial Church Council v Wallbank* [2001] 3 All E.R. ("*Billesley*")).

Important in determining the scope of protection afforded by the HRA is the breadth given to the term public authority. There is no definitive test in deciding whether or not a particular body is a public authority under the HRA, or into which category of public authority it might fall. The House of Lords in *Billesley* favoured the jurisprudence of the ECtHR as a starting point in deciding the issue. Lord Hobhouse at [87] stated "the relevant underlying principles are to be found in human rights law, not in community law and not the administrative law of England and Wales".

(a)   Core or Pure Public Authorities

21–010   What constitutes a core or pure public authority has only been discussed in one case to date, *Aston Cantlow and Wilmcote with Billesley Parochial Church Council v Wallbank (Billesley)*. Lord Nicholls at [7] suggested that the phrase "public authority" in s.6 of the HRA is "essentially a reference to a body whose nature is governmental in a broad sense". His Lordship further suggested that the following factors could be considered relevant in determining whether a body is a "core" public authority:

- the possession of special powers;
- democratic accountability;
- public funding in whole or in part;
- an obligation to act only in the public interest;
- a statutory constitution.

Typically, such core public authorities include government departments, local authorities and the police. A further useful indicator is the use of the phrase "non-governmental" organisation in ECHR art.34. The House of Lords considered that a body which would be classified as non-governmental under art.34 should not be classified as a core public body. The effect of a classification as core would be to prevent the body from relying on Convention rights under the HRA. In other words, a core public authority could not be a victim and bring an action under the HRA. Lord Nicholls at [8] said: "it must always be relevant to consider whether Parliament can have intended that the body in question should have no Convention rights".

As mentioned above, classification as a core public authority also requires that body to comply with the Convention when undertaking both their public duties and also when undertaking private duties such as making contracts.

In overturning the decision of the Court of Appeal, the House of Lords held that the Parochial Church Council was not a pure public authority. Whilst it had some statutory basis and could exercise statutory powers (The Parochial Church Councils (Powers) Measure 1956), it was not governmental in nature, being principally concerned with the administration of church affairs.

(b) Functional/Hybrid Public Authorities

The second category of public authorities is the functional or hybrid authority. The **21–011** term "hybrid" was coined by Lord Nicholls in the *Billesley* case. However, the Joint Human Rights Select Committee (2003–04 Report) found the term "hybrid" to be unhelpful as it focuses too much on the intrinsic nature of the body rather than the function in question (at [7]).

The law on the meaning of functional public authorities has proved problematic and, at times, confusing. Section 6(3)(b) provides that the term "public authority" includes "any person certain of whose functions are functions of a public nature" but this does not include acts performed by such bodies that are of a "private nature" s.6(5) of the HRA. Ministerial statements made during the passage of the Human Rights Bill indicated that the purpose of s.6(3)(b) was to make the Act comprehensive rather than restrictive in its application. Lord Chancellor, Lord Irvine of Lairg, noted it was designed to "provide as much protection as possible for the rights of the individual against the misuse of power by the State" (HL Deb, November 24, 1997, col.808).

A number of Court of Appeal cases have considered the scope of s.6(3)(b), the first was *Poplar Housing and Regeneration Community Association Ltd v Donoghue* [2001] EWCA Civ 595. In this case, the question was whether a housing association, which had taken over a local housing authority's housing stock, and was providing rental accommodation on behalf of the authority, fell under s.6(3)(b). The court rejected a functional approach to the application of s.6(3)(b) and set down the general principle that "the fact that a body is performing an activity which otherwise a public body would be under a duty to perform cannot mean that such performance is necessarily a public function. A public body, in order to perform its public duties, can use the services of a private body" (at para.58). The court considered what factors would be relevant in identifying whether a body was performing a public function and mentioned the following:

- statutory authority for what is being done can help to establish the act as being public;

- the extent of control over the function exercised by the state (or a core public body);

- the proximity of relationship between the private body and the delegating authority.

In *Poplar* the last factor was decisive, the court finding that the Housing Association was so "enmeshed" in the activities of the local authority that it was a functional public authority. The approach of the court in *Poplar*, was to confuse the issue. It considered the identity of the body and how close the relationship was between the Local Authority and the private body, rather than deciding whether the act undertaken was indeed public.

The second case to deal with s.6(3)(b) was *R. (Heather) v Leonard Cheshire Foundation* [2002] 2 All E.R. 936. Here, residents of a private care home alleged an art.8 right to private and family life violation over the decision to close the home and house its residents elsewhere. The home was run by a charity and places were funded by the local authority under statutory authority (National Assistance Act 1948). The Court of Appeal concluded that the managers of the care home did not fall under s.6(3)(b). In reliance on *Poplar*, the court noted there was no material distinction between the services provided for residents funded by the local authority, and those provided to privately funded residents. Furthermore, although the foundation was performing a function delegated under statutory authority, it was not itself exercising statutory powers. The foundation was therefore not "enmeshed" in the activities of the local authority in the same way Poplar Homes had been.

Three other cases worthy of consideration are *R. (on the application of A) v Partnerships in Care Ltd* [2002] 1 W.L.R. 2610, *Billesley* and, finally, *R. (on the application of Beer (t/a Hammer Trout Farm)) v Hampshire Farmers Markets Ltd* [2003] EWCA 1056 at this stage.

Partnerships in Care (PIC) was a private provider of mental health care. The claimant in the case was receiving treatment at one of their homes for a severe personality disorder. Her placement was funded by the local health authority. In this case, the Administrative Court emphasised the public nature of the function being undertaken, in particular the fact the hospital was authorised under the Mental Health Act 1983 to receive and detain patients and that treatment was governed by further statutory regimes. Contrary to core considerations in *Poplar* and *Leonard Cheshire*, PIC were neither "enmeshed" with a state body, nor was there direct statutory authority, yet it concluded that PIC fell under the scope of s.6(3)(b).

In *Billesley*, the applicants (Wallbank) were freeholders of a farm which was former church land. This imposed on the owner an obligation to contribute towards the cost of repairing the local parish church. The Parochial Church Council of Aston Cantlow was responsible for supervising the care, maintenance, preservation and insurance of the church and pursuant to s.2 of the Chancel Repairs Act 1932 served repair notices on Wallbank. Wallbank disputed the notices as inconsistent with human rights. The main question for the court was whether the Parochial Church Council was a public authority. The House of Lords stressed that the court's focus should be on the nature of the function being performed, contrary to the approach taken in *Poplar* and *Leonard Cheshire*. However, rather unhelpfully, the decisions in *Poplar* and *Leonard Cheshire* were not overruled. Lord Nicholls suggested that there should be a "generously wide" interpretation of public function so as to further the statutory aim of promoting human rights protection. He suggested looking at the extent to which in carrying out the function the body is (at [12]):

- publicly funded;
- exercising statutory power;
- taking the place of central government or local authorities;
- providing a public service.

In determining whether the Parochial Church Council was performing a public function, the House of Lords concluded that the PCC was trying to enforce an obligation to repair against the lay rectors. This had nothing to do with the responsibilities owed to the public by the state and was in essence a private act.

The final case is *Hampshire Farm Market Ex p. Beer*. Here, the Court of Appeal appeared to restrict the more generous approach taken by the House of Lords. The case concerned a farmers' market which had been initially established by Hampshire County Council who established a private company to run the market. County Council staff provided assistance in establishing and developing the private company, and one of its managers was appointed a Director. A farmer who had been excluded from the Market sought to challenge the decision. The court concluded that the market fell under s.6(3)(b), pointing to two key factors. First, the existence of the market came from the County Council, was given assistance by the council and was performing a function previously performed by the council. Secondly, as the market was a public market, and the organisation had power to control right of access, this constituted a sufficient public element.

As a consequence of these decisions, the tests applied by the courts appear inconsistent and confusing. The Audit Commission Human Rights: Improving Public Service Delivery (September 2003) stated as a result of these decision "most private organisations that contract with public bodies to provide services do not constitute public bodies for the purposes of the HRA, despite the public nature of its work". This left a gap in protection, particularly for more vulnerable people such as the elderly and mentally ill. If the HRA was supposed to be about bringing rights home, making enforceability swifter and more direct, the interpretation given by the courts was not allowing the Act to achieve its objectives. The Joint Select Committee on Human Rights in their 7th report on the Meaning of Public Authority under the HRA (7th report of session 2003–04), felt that in many cases an organisation can "stand in the shoes of the State" yet not have responsibilities under the HRA. This meant that the protection of human rights was "dependent not on the type of power being exercised, nor on its capacity to interfere with human rights, but on the relatively arbitrary criterion of the body's administrative links with institutions of the State". It felt that the application adopted by the court called into question the ability of the HRA to actually bring rights home and it concluded by stating a preference for the approach in *Billesley*.

The House of Lords finally had the opportunity to give specific consideration to the scope of s.6(3)(b) in a case concerning a private care home which provided care to elderly residents, namely, *YL v Birmingham City Council (formerly R. (on the application of Johnson) v Havering Borough Council)* [2007] UKHL 27. In the Court of Appeal, Buxton L.J. affirmed the decision in *Leonard Cheshire*, that a private care home when providing accommodation was not performing the functions of a public authority under s.6(3)(b) of the 1998 Act. He emphasised the fact that the appellants would still remain the responsibility of their local authority which has obligations under the HRA towards them. The appellants could also, if necessary, bring a private action against the private care providers and the courts, as public authorities, would be obliged to consider any relevant Convention rights. The House of Lords, in a 3–2 majority decision, confirmed that the care home was not a functional public authority for the purposes of the HRA 1998. The key to their reasoning seems to be the focus on the contractual relationship between the private body and the local authority. The lack of any special statutory powers over the residents such as the right to restrain or confine the residents to their rooms was also relevant as a distinguishing factor from Partnerships in Care. Lord Scott, in the majority, at [26] summarised as follows:

"Southern Cross is a company carrying on a socially useful business for profit. It is neither a charity nor a philanthropist. It enters into private law contracts with the residents in its care homes and with the local authorities with whom it does business. It receives no public funding, enjoys no special statutory powers, and is at liberty to accept or reject residents as it chooses (subject, of course, to anti-discrimination legislation which affects everyone who offers a service to the public) and to charge whatever fees in its commercial judgment it thinks suitable. It is operating in a commercial market with commercial competitors."

Lord Bingham and Baroness Hale in the minority believed that as the function being performed was pursuant to statutory arrangements (the National Assistance Act 1948), the home was given public funding, and involved a particularly vulnerable section of society, Parliament must have intended that s.6(3)(b) be interpreted to cover such functions.

The minority dissents of Lord Bingham and Baroness Hale serves only to confuse the issue of the appropriate approach as no clear distinction can be discerned between the reasoning of the majority and minority, however following the majority decision in *YL*, it appears that the more restrictive option is in current favour. In a situation where the local authority or some other government body has contracted out its obligations, there needs to be greater statutory underpinning than the mere contracting out statute. The existence of special statutory powers as in the *Partnerships in Care* case increases the likelihood of that body falling under s.6(3)(b).

(c)   *Courts and tribunals and the horizontal effect of the Human Rights Act 1998*

21–012   The final category of public authority under the HRA is in s.6(3)(a), namely courts and tribunals. This states their judgments and orders must be compatible with Convention rights, even in proceedings between private parties. This has the potential to allow Convention rights to affect the substance of private law by virtue of the courts duty, owed to litigants, not to act incompatibly with their Convention rights. This consequence between private parties is referred to as "horizontal effect" (as distinct from "vertical effect" between a private party and a state body). However the HRA makes no express provision for horizontal effect and the idea is controversial (This point is further discussed in relation to art.8 in Ch.12).

The HRA is intended primarily to have vertical effect imposing obligations on the state to protect human rights. However, by virtue of s.6(3)(a), the HRA can have indirect horizontal effect. This section creates the final category of public authority under the HRA, courts and tribunals. The obligation imposed by s.6(1) means that their judgments and orders must be compatible with Convention rights even in cases involving private parties. Moreover, a duty to develop the common law in light of human rights can also be seen. This is most evident in developing the law of confidentiality, so it protects private information between individuals consistent with ECHR art.8. However, it does not mean the creation of a free-standing cause of action based directly upon Convention rights under the HRA between private parties, a point made clear by the House of Lords in *Wainwright v Home Office* [2003] UKHL 53, where their Lordships declined to create a free-standing tort of privacy.

HUMAN RIGHTS ACT 1998 SECTIONS 3 AND 4

1. Human Rights Act 1998 section 3

Once it has been established that the HRA applies to a decision, the court's next step is   **21–013**
to determine whether or not the Act is incompatible with Convention rights. Under the
HRA, courts are given increased powers to interpret legislation in a manner compatible
with the ECHR. Section 3(1) provides that:

> "[s]o far as possible to do so, primary and subordinate legislation must be read and
> given effect in a way which is compatible with Convention rights".

The section applies to legislation existing at the time of enactment of the HRA as well
as to future legislation s.3(2)(a). However, it does not affect the validity or continual
enforcement of any incompatible legislation s.3(2)(b).

The constitutional significance of s.3 depends wholly on how the courts are prepared
to use it. The issue is the word "possible" and the exact scope of its meaning, a fact was
recognised by Lord Nicholls in *Ghaidan v Godin-Mendoza* [2004] UKHL 30 at [27]. The
government's White Paper on *Rights Brought Home* at para.2.7 suggested that the s.3
instructs the courts to go "far beyond the present rule which enables the courts to take
the Convention into account in resolving any ambiguity in legislative provision".
During the Bill's committee stage in the Commons, the Home Secretary appeared to
favour giving s.3 a narrow meaning: "it is not our intention that the courts, in applying
[s.3] should contort the meaning of words to produce implausible or incredible results"
(House of Commons debate, June 3, 1999, col. 421). What is clear, however, is that if
s.3 is read in conjunction with s.4, Parliament must have intended there would be cases
where legislation could not be so interpreted and that a s.4 declaration of incompatibility was more appropriate.

The first major case dealing with the scope of the obligation was *R. v A (Complainant's Sexual History) (No.2)* [2001] UKHL 25. Section 41 of the Youth Justice and
Criminal Evidence Act 1999 (YJCEA) restricted the circumstances in which evidence
and questioning about a complainant's previous sexual history could be permitted in
trials concerning sexual offences. The section replaced s.2 of the Sexual Offences
(Amendment) Act 1976 which allowed unregulated discretion. The defendant, who had
been charged with rape, wished to adduce evidence of a past sexual relationship
between himself and the victim in the weeks prior to the alleged rape. The issue was
whether this evidence was admissible under s.41. The contention being that the provision could prejudice the defendant's right to a fair trial under ECHR art.6.

The House of Lords agreed that if s.41 was interpreted with ordinary methods of
interpretation, such evidence would be inadmissible. They felt s.41 was a disproportionate interference with the defendant's right to a fair trial and was, as Lord Steyn at
[43] called it, "legislative overkill". As a consequence of this finding, their Lordships
went on to consider their obligations under s.3. Lord Steyn advocated a "wide"
approach to interpretation under s.3. He reasoned at [44]:

" ... [T]he interpretative obligation under section 3 of the 1998 Act is a strong one. It applies even if there is no ambiguity in the language in the sense of the language being capable of two different meanings ... Parliament specifically rejected the legislative model of requiring a reasonable interpretation. Section 3 places a duty on the court to strive to find a possible interpretation compatible with Convention rights ... In accordance with the will of Parliament as reflected in section 3 it will sometimes be necessary to adopt an interpretation which linguistically may appear strained."

The House of Lords "read in" an implied provision that evidence which is required to ensure a fair trial under ECHR art.6 could be admitted by the trial judge. Whilst ultimately agreeing with the decision in the case, Lord Hope, at [109], was cautious about the scope of s.3 and felt that the reading in of a provision enabling the court to exercise wider discretion than permitted by s.41 contradicted the plain intention of Parliament.

The decision in *R. v A* was heavily criticised by a number of academics. Danny Nicol in "Statutory interpretation and human rights after *Anderson*" (2004) P.L. 273, in a play on Lord Steyn words, called it "judicial overkill" at [276] and thought the judges had effectively rewritten the legislation, a view shared by Klug, "Judicial Deference under the Human Rights Act 1998" [2003] E.H.R.L.R. 125 at 128–129 and Gearty, "Reconciling Parliamentary Democracy and Human Rights" (2002) 118 L.Q.R. 248 at 267.

Aileen Kavannagh, "Unlocking the Human Rights Act: the "radical" approach to s.3(1) Revisited" (2005) E.H.R.L.R. 259–275, on the other hand, does not believe the House of Lords was being radical in their use of s.3 in *R. v A*. She points to the fact that despite his Lordship's cautious overtones, Lord Hope agreed with the other Law Lords in the decision in *R. v A*. Moreover, Lord Steyn, viewed as being radical, in *R. v A* was well aware of his constitutional role. Whilst recognising the decision in *R. v A* gave more discretion to trial judges, she believed it an exaggeration to say the position under s.2 of the SOA 1976 was reinstated. Moreover, the discretion is not open-ended and must be exercised within the framework of the other subsections of s.41. Declaring s.41 incompatible would itself have been a contentious decision in the early days of the HRA, and failed to protect the defendant's right to a fair trial.

Four other cases illustrate the courts approach to their obligation under s.3. In *Re S (Children) and Re W (Care Orders)* [2002] UKHL 10, the House of Lords found the Court of Appeal had undertaken a very radical re-interpretation of provisions of the Children Act 1989. The Court of Appeal read into the Act a range of new powers and procedures by which the courts could supervise and monitor the implementation of care orders by local authorities through the use of "starred schemes". The House of Lords reversed their decision, Lord Nicholls stressing the importance of being mindful of the limits between interpretation and legislating. He thought a meaning which departs substantially from a fundamental feature of an Act of Parliament was crossing the line. This was especially so where the departure had "important practical repercussions which the court is not equipped to evaluate". He believed the judgment of the Court of Appeal went beyond the scope of possible Convention-compliant interpretations because the starred scheme incorporated into the legislation by the Court of Appeal had "wide practical ramifications" that should properly have been examined by Parliament. The decision in *R. v A* was not questioned.

Following this, it seemed that where the use of s.3 would represent a major change in the law with far-reaching consequences, the courts would be less willing to "radically" interpret. An approach similar to that taken in *Re S* can be seen in *Bellinger v Bellinger* [2003] UKHL 21. Mrs Bellinger was a transsexual female who had undergone gender reassignment surgery and treatment. In 1981 she married a man. Mrs Bellinger, supported by her husband, wanted a declaration the marriage was valid. According to s.11(c) of the Matrimonial Causes Act 1973, a marriage is void unless the parties are "respectively male and female". The question for the court was whether Mrs Bellinger was female at the time of the marriage. At the time of the case, determination of sex was by criteria laid down in *Corbett v Corbett*, being a chromosomal, gonadal and genital test. This test had come in for criticism in the ECtHR *Goodwin v UK* (2002) 35 E.H.R.R. 447, another right to marry case. The ECtHR had, on previous occasions, afforded the UK a margin of appreciation in this area, but by the time of *Goodwin* felt that with increasing surgical and hormonal treatments, reliance on the chromosomal test could be considered outdated. The House of Lords refused to re-interpret s.11(c) under s.3 of the HRA. Lord Nicholls stated that recognition of Mrs Bellinger as female for the purposes of s.11(c) of the Matrimonial Causes Act 1973 would necessitate giving the expressions "male" and "female" in that Act a novel, extended meaning: that a person may be born with one sex but later become, or become regarded as, a person of the opposite sex. This would represent a major change in the law, "having far reaching ramifications" at [37]. He stated that such issues call for extensive research and a balanced approach and are ill-suited for determination by courts and court procedures. Such issues are pre-eminently a matter for Parliament to decide, especially when the government, in unequivocal terms, has already announced its intention to introduce comprehensive primary legislation on this difficult and sensitive subject following the decision in *Goodwin v UK*.

Lord Nicholls cited three broad reasons for his conclusion that re-interpretation was not possible:

(1)   There was no clear cut universal answer as to under which circumstances and from which point gender reassignment should be recognised for the purposes of marriage, or where the line should be drawn and from which particular point in time person should be considered of another gender.

(2)   He stated that recognition of gender is part of a much wider problem that should be considered as whole and cannot be dealt with in a piecemeal fashion. The question of gender reassignment for the purpose of marriage cannot be viewed in isolation and other areas, such as access to education, taxation, immigration, inheritance, etc. should also be considered. Therefore Lord Nicholls expressed a view that coherent policy should be drawn to tackle all of the issues altogether.

(3)   Finally, he mentioned that the institute of marriage was based on the religious and social culture of this country, and meant union between biological male and biological female. A different approach, according to His Lordship, would involve fundamental change of the traditional concept.

In *R. (Anderson) v Secretary of State for the Home Department* [2003] 1 A.C. 837, the House of Lords held that the Home Secretary's power to decide on the tariff to be served by mandatory life sentence prisoners was incompatible with art.6 of the ECHR. The House found a s.3(1) interpretation not possible and made a declaration of incompatibility under s. 4.

Ghaidan v Godin-Mendoza [2004] UKHL 30 concerned the compatibility of Sch.1, para.2(2) to the Rent Act 1977 with art.8 and art.14 of the ECHR. The schedule provided that on the death of a protected tenant, a person living with the original tenant "as his or her wife or husband" was to be treated as the spouse of the original tenant. Mr Godin-Mendoza had lived in a flat with his homosexual partner who had been granted a residential tenancy. On his partner's death, the landlord, Mr Ghaidan, sought possession. Lord Nicholls, at para.30 of his opinion, discussed the obligation imposed by s.3 of the HRA and recognises its "unusual and far-reaching character". He further stated:

> "Section 3 may require the court to depart from this legislative intention, that is, depart from the intention of the Parliament which enacted the legislation. The question of difficulty is how far, and in what circumstances, section 3 requires a court to depart from the intention of the enacting Parliament."

Asserting the principle evident in the decisions in *Re S* and *Bellinger*, Lord Nicholls stated that the court should not adopt a meaning inconsistent with a fundamental feature of legislation. Any interpretation must be "compatible with the underlying thrust of the legislation being construed". In this case, the House examined the social policy underlying the Act and its amendments and found the extension of security of tenure to a couple living together as husband and wife was equally applicable to homosexual couples living together in a close and stable relationship. Their Lordships were able to interpret the words to mean "as if they were living together as if they were his wife or husband" and so protected the tenancy.

It seems that as a general rule the judiciary are unwilling to use s.3 in a manner that involves radical statutory reform. This follows from the proper sphere of power judges should exercise, i.e. they should not make broad changes, but rather leave that to Parliament. However, this begs the question of what constitutes "radical" or "broad-ranging" change rather than legitimate interpretation under s.3? Cases such as *Re S and Bellinger* provide good examples of proposed statutory changes considered to fundamentally alter a crucial part of the relevant statute for s3 not be considered a legitimate course to pursue. The use of s.3 in such cases would not have been restricted to the provision of judicial relief in the individual cases but would have set in motion a whole series of social, political and administrative consequences that a court is not best placed to initiate. In contrast, *R. v A* although prima facie radically altering a fundamental tenet of the statute, did not have the same far-reaching non-judicial consequences.

2.   Human Rights Act 1998 section 4

21–014   When it is not possible to interpret legislation so it is compatible, a court at the level of the High Court or above may make a declaration of incompatibility under s.4 of the HRA. A declaration of incompatibility does not affect the continual validity of the legislation and so affords little remedy to the victim. It merely puts Parliament and the government on notice that the legislation is incompatible with Convention rights and for them to change if they wish. There is no requirement that they must change the legislation, though a failure could result in cases being taken to Strasbourg. Parliament and the government are not bound to act following a declaration of incompatibility.

Where the court considers making a declaration, they should give notice to the Crown so that they may be joined to the proceedings (HRA s.5). This enables the Crown to argue the legislation's compatibility.

Section 10(2) of the HRA provides that, in response to a declaration of incompatibility made under s.4 or to a decision of the ECHR, Ministers of the Crown may take remedial action to amend the relevant legislation as necessary to remove the incompatibility. Schedule 2 to the HRA sets out two procedures:

(1)   Standard. This requires that the draft amending order be laid before Parliament for 60 days before being approved by a resolution of both Houses of Parliament. The draft orders should be accompanied by an explanation of the incompatibility and reasons for the proceeding by way of remedial order rather than primary legislation.

(2)   Urgent. In this situation the order may come into effect before being laid before Parliament for approval. The order will cease to have effect unless approved by a resolution of both Houses within 120 days (HRA Sch.2, para.2).

In a review of the Human Rights Act conducted by the Department for Constitutional Affairs in July 2006, a total of 15 declarations of incompatibility had been made.

REMEDIES

A court or tribunal may, under s.8 of the HRA, "grant such relief or remedy or make   **21–015** such order within its powers as it considers just and appropriate". For a majority of individuals whose rights have been breached, the best remedy is for the breach to end. This can be achieved through one of the traditional remedies available for abuses of public power.

Under s.8(3), damages may be awarded by a court if it is "satisfied that the award is necessary to achieve just satisfaction to the person in whose favour it is made". Compensation may be awarded both for:

- "*pecuniary*" damage for financial loss consequent on a breach of a Convention right that can be quantified, and,

- "*non-pecuniary loss*", where, for example, an applicant has suffered distress or anxiety as a result of the violation of any of the protected rights. See *Aksoy v Turkey* [1997] 23 E.H.H.R. 533, where damages for non-pecuniary losses were awarded for distress to the father of the applicant who continued the case after his son had died.

A review of the implementation of the HRA published by the Department of Constitutional Affairs (July 2006), noted that s.8(3) has been interpreted very strictly by the Courts and it is very difficult to obtain damages. The House of Lords also held in *R. (Greenfield) v Secretary of State for Home Department* [2005] 1 W.L.R. 673 that the finding of a breach is generally sufficient redress. In this case, their Lordships declined to award damages even where the breach had resulted in a prisoner serving an extra 21 days in prison. In considering an award of damages, the Court of Appeal in *Anufrijeva v London Borough of Southwark* [2003] EWCA Civ 1406 at [57] noted that s.8(4) of the HRA requires the court to take into account the principles applied by the ECtHR when deciding whether to award damages and the amount of an award. The court stated that their approach "should be no less liberal than those applied at Strasbourg or one of the purposes of the HRA will be defeated and claimants will still be put to the expense of having to go to Strasbourg to obtain just satisfaction". Awards of damages are equitable and factors considered include the seriousness, scale and manner of the violation. It is recognised that levels of compensation are lower than available for breach of domestic torts.

In the absence of remedial legislation, or administrative action to provide an effective remedy for the individual, the claimant may have recourse to the ECtHR, since all available domestic remedies will have been exhausted.

FURTHER READING

21–016   *General*

Bingham, T. "The European Convention on Human Rights: Time to Incorporate" (1993) 109 L.Q.R. 390

Ewing, K. "The Futility of the Human Rights Act" (2004) P.L. 829

Hoffman, D. and Rowe, J. *Human Rights in the UK: An Introduction to the Human Rights Act 1998*, 2nd edn (Pearson Education, 2006)

Merris, A. *Human Rights Law* (Hart Publishing, 2006)

On the Human Rights Act 1998 ss.3 and 4

Kavanagh, A. "Unlocking the Human Rights Act: the 'radical' approach to section 3(1) revisited" E.H.R.L.R. 259

Nicol, D. "Original Intent and the European Convention on Human Rights" (2005) P.L. 152

Phillipson, G. "(Mis)-Reading Section 3 of the Human Rights Act" (2003) L.Q.R. 119 (Apr), 183–188

On section 6

Joint Committee on Human Rights, *The Meaning of Public Authority under the Human Rights Act*, 7th Report of session 2003–04

Joint Committee on Human Rights, *The Meaning of Public Authority under the Human Rights Act*, 9th Report of session 2006–07

Sunkin Maurice, "Pushing Forward the Frontiers of Human Rights Protection: The Meaning of Public Authority under the Human Rights Act" (2004) P.L. 643

Chapter 22

LIBERTY AND DUE PROCESS

INTRODUCTION

Since Magna Carta (1215) and the development of the writ of habeas corpus allowing **22–001**
the prisoner to challenge their detention, liberty has been a fundamental aspect of the
law of England (and Wales). In the words of Charter itself:

> "No free man shall be taken or imprisoned or dispossessed, or outlawed or exiled,
> or in any way destroyed ... except by the lawful judgment of his peers or by the
> law of the land."

Such noble pronouncements concerning liberty have resonance today where senior
judges have taken the opportunity provided by case law to restate its importance. For
example, Lord Hope in *R. (A) v Secretary of State for Home Department* [2004] UKHL
56 commented that it was impossible to overstate the importance of the right of liberty
in a democracy, while in the same case, Lord Nicholls equally observed that indefinite
detention is an anathema to the rule of law.

    However, as important as the right to liberty may be, it means little if an individual
cannot challenge their detention through an unbiased court system, open to all. To this
degree, the right of due process, as it is often know, is today protected by a mixture of
common law and statute, in particular arts 5(2)–5(5) and 6 of the ECHR.

    This chapter considers how liberty and due process are protected today through the
Human Rights Act 1998 and considers some situations in which interference is considered legitimate.

LIBERTY AND SECURITY OF PERSON

22–002 Magna Carta is given modern expression in art.5(1) of the European Convention on Human Rights (ECHR) where "everyone has the right to liberty and security of person." In *Engel v The Netherlands (No.1)* (1976) 1 E.H.R.R. 647 at [58] the ECtHR said this embodies more than depravation of the freedom to live one's life as one pleases, but it also means being deprived of one's physical liberty.

1. What is a deprivation of liberty?

22–003 Article 5 is concerned with the protection of liberty of the person by ensuring an individual is not deprived of their liberty without good cause, i.e. something which has basis in law. But art.5 is not merely concerned with restriction on movement or of liberty, for these are protected by art.2 of Protocol 4, so this rather begs the question: what distinguishes deprivation from a restriction? Generally, a common sense approach can be taken to most situations, and obvious examples of a deprivation of liberty include being locked up in a gaol or being detained in a secure hospital. However, it is not always simple to distinguish between the two, and consideration inevitably turns to the facts of each individual case. In such cases, account must be taken of the cumulative effect of the various restrictions. For example, in *X v Austria* (1979) 18 D.R. 154, the Commission thought deprivation meant being forced or obliged to be at a particular place where one does not choose to be. However, as Baroness Hale pointed out in *Secretary of State for Home Department v JJ* [2007] UKHL 45 (see below) this is not always enough. Merely being required to live at a particular address or to keep within a particular geographical area does not, without more, amount to a deprivation of liberty. There must be some greater degree of control over one's physical liberty, and *Guzzardi v Italy* (1980) 3 E.H.R.R. 333, represents a leading authority on this area.

Mr Guzzardi was an alleged "mafiosi", described by the Italian authorities as "one of the most dangerous" of individuals. He had been confined to an area of 2½ km² on a small island for 16 months. The area contained a basic village inhabited by others subject to similar orders. His family could live with him and did so for fourteen of the sixteen months. He was able to leave his dwelling between the hours of 7am and 10pm, socialise with others in the area and work, if he so wished. He had to report to the police twice a day and obtain permission from the police before making a phone call or seeing a visitor. This situation was compared by the ECtHR to that of a person in an open prison. In considering whether this amounted to a deprivation or restriction of liberty (at [93]), the court noted that the difference between the two is one of "degree or intensity". The "starting point" of analysis was the "concrete situation" and account must be taken of "a whole range of criteria such as the type, duration, effects and manner of implementation of the measure in question." Taking this approach, the court concluded that the cumulative impact of the restrictions amounted to a deprivation of liberty.

The court then dealt with the argument put forward by the Italian government, that the deprivation was in accordance with any of the limitations contained in art. 5. None were found to apply and specifically in relation to art.5(1)(c), the court noted that while the argument that the measures were taken because they were "reasonably considered necessary to prevent [Mr. Guzzardi] committing an offence" might seem applicable, it could not succeed. Article 5(1)(c) could not be adapted to a policy of general prevention directed against individuals who might have a propensity to commit a crime but is applicable to prevent concrete and specific offences.

Not only must the cumulative effect of the restrictions be considered, but also the purpose for which the restrictions are imposed. The Court of Appeal in *R. (on the application of the Secretary of State for the Home Department) v Mental Health Review Tribunal (PH)* [2002] EWCA Civ 1868 made this clear when distinguishing between those restrictions made for the benefit of the subject and those for some other purpose. In this case, the Mental Health Review Tribunal had directed that PH be discharged subject to a number of conditions such as the requirement to reside at specialist accommodation with security and not to leave without an escort. The court concluded that as the security measures were imposed to protect PH, they did not believe that they were depriving him of his liberty.

(a) *Control orders and deprivation of liberty*

One particular area where this question has arisen for determination is the imposition of control orders on suspected terrorists. Following the House of Lord's decision to quash the derogation order in respect of art.5, and the subsequent declaration of incompatibility relating to s.23 of the Anti-Terrorism Crime and Security Act 2001 (*R. (A & Others) v Secretary of State for the Home Department* [2004] UKHL 56, the government passed the Prevention of Terrorism Act 2005. The 2005 Act's purpose is "to provide for the making against individuals involved in terrorism-related activity of orders imposing obligations on them for purposes connected with preventing or restricting their further involvement in such activity." Section 1(1) defines a control order as meaning, "an order made against an individual that imposes obligations on him for purposes connected with protecting members of the public from a risk of terrorism". Section 1(4) specifies the obligations which a control order "may include". Such obligations can include bans on mobile phones, internet use, travel and movement restrictions, curfews, tagging and such like. The list contains 16 potential obligations running from (a) to (p) and, whilst detailed, it is not exclusive and different obligations may be added.

22–004

The Act draws a distinction between derogating and non-derogating control orders. Derogating control orders are orders which contain obligations which are incompatible with the right to liberty under art.5 (see s.15(1)). A formal derogation under ECHR art.15 from the requirements of Article 5 would have to be made by the Home Secretary before a derogating control order could be issued (see s.4(3)(c)). Non-derogating control orders are defined in s.15(1) to mean orders containing an obligation considered compatible with art.5.

Under s.2(1) of the Act, the Secretary of State has the power to make non-derogating control orders if he:

"(a) has reasonable grounds for suspecting that the individual is or has been involved in terrorism-related activity; and (b) considers that it is necessary, for purposes connected with protecting members of the public from a risk of terrorism, to make a control order imposing obligations on that individual."

Whilst, the Secretary of State has the power to make control orders, the court also has a role. At the preliminary hearing before a non-derogating order is made, or immediately after in case of urgency, the court's function is to consider whether the Secretary of State's decision is "obviously flawed" (s.3(2) and s.3(3)). In relation to derogating control orders, the Court's role is much more significant.

Whilst, the Secretary of State may believe he has made a non-derogating control order, whether such an order is taken to be non-derogating depends on the extent of the obligations imposed and whether the restrictions amount to a deprivation or a restriction and a number of cases have reached the House of Lords on this point, namely *Secretary of State for Home Department v JJ* [2007] UKHL 45; *MB & AF v Secretary of State for Home Department* [2007] UKHL 46 and *Secretary of State for Home Department v E* [2007] UKHL 47.

In *JJ*, similar control orders had been imposed on six people (the controlees). The restrictions included an 18–hour curfew in one-bedroom flats, provided by the state, during which time they were not allowed to enter the common areas of their flats. Visitors to the flats had to be authorised by the Home Office, including giving their name, address and photographic identity. The controlees were forbidden to use or possess communication equipment of any kind, save for one fixed line telephone maintained by a monitoring company. When allowed out of the flats, they were electronically tagged, had to report to a monitoring company every time they first left, and were restricted to urban areas, the largest of which was 72 square kilometres. Except for one controlee (GG), none were in an area they had lived before. In a 3–2 majority decision, the House of Lords upheld the decision of the Court of Appeal that the non-derogating control orders imposed amounted to a deprivation of liberty. Lord Bingham at [26–27] felt the effect of the restrictions meant the controlees, "were in practice in solitary confinement for a lengthy period every day for an indefinite duration, with very little opportunity for contact with the outside world, with means insufficient to permit provision of significant facilities for self-entertainment and with knowledge that their flats were liable to be entered and searched at any time". Whilst the area available to them during their non-curfew hours was much larger than in Guzzardi, Lord Bingham felt it amounted to detention in an open prison, except worse, as the controlled persons did not enjoy the association with others and the access to entertainment facilities which a prisoner in an open prison would enjoy. Taking a contrary view, Lord Hoffman, dissenting, found it impossible to say the controlees were for all practical purposes in a prison. He considered that to describe them in such a way was "an extravagant metaphor" (at [45]). As a consequence of the majority's finding, the House of Lords quashed the control orders on the grounds that the Secretary of State had acted outside his powers in making what was a derogating control order.

In the second case, AF was subject to a 14–hour curfew and restricted to an area of nine square miles outside curfew time. He remained in his own flat and was permitted certain visitors during curfew time but not permitted communication equipment of any kind. The House of Lord found this did not amount to a deprivation of liberty.

In *E*, the obligations imposed on the appellant were similar to those in the *JJ* case, but differed in that the period of curfew was 12 hours (7pm–7am). In addition, E was allowed to remain in residence at his own home with his wife and family, was subjected to no geographical restrictions outside curfew, and could see named friends which, according to the first instance judge, meant he did not lack a social network. The House of Lords unanimously felt that these restrictions did not amount to a deprivation of liberty. In doing so, particular weight was given to the period of curfew.

It appears from these three cases that the main emphasis when considering whether something amounts to a deprivation is the length of any curfew and the associated restriction on social activity during that curfew. Whilst it was held that 14 hours did not deprive one of his liberty, 18 hours did. It could be argued, therefore, the line is somewhere between the two. However, it is worth noting that two of their Lordships disagreed with the decision in *JJ* despite the 18–hour restriction. Restrictions after curfew, such as to a particular geographical area, and as to friends is a relevant factor, but less so.

(b)   *Stop and search*

Whilst an arrest and subsequent detention triggers the protection in art.5(1), powers of **22–005** "stop and search", which fall short of arrest, nevertheless prevent an individual from doing what they like. This has generated something of a grey area in the law. For example, in *R. (on the application of Gillan) v The Commissioner of Police for the Metropolis* [2004] EWCA Civ 1067, a case concerning stop and search under the Terrorism Act 2000, the court did not conclusively decide the matter. However, it noted that because of the existence of art.2, Protocol 4, the ambit of art.5 should be construed narrowly. Therefore, it is likely that a short detainment pursuant to stop and search powers probably does not engage art.5. This is perhaps supported by *Austin v Metropolitan Police Commissioner* [2005] EWHC (QB) 480. In this case, a crowd of May Day protestors had congregated around Oxford Circus, London. By mid-afternoon, approximately 3,000 people were within the Circus itself, with thousands more to the North and West of it. The police cordoned off the Circus and prevented people from leaving, with most being kept for over seven hours. The Divisional Court felt because the police had temporarily detained the protestors for the protestors this was not a deprivation of liberty.

2.   Article 5(1)

Whilst art.5(1) guarantees liberty and security of person, the right is linked to the **22–006** broader aim of protecting individuals against arbitrary arrest and detention. In modern democratic societies, the right to liberty cannot be absolute, and circumstances may exist justifying detention, e.g. following conviction for a crime. To this end, art.5(1) lists a number of conditions (or limitations) under which an individual can be lawfully deprived of their liberty (art.5(1)(a)–(f)):

"(a)   the lawful detention of a person after conviction by a competent court;

(b)   the lawful arrest or detention of a person for non-compliance with the lawful order of a court or in order to secure the fulfilment of any obligation prescribed by law;

(c)   the lawful arrest or detention of a person effected for the purposes of bringing him before the competent legal authority on reasonable suspicion of having committed an offence or when it is reasonable considered necessary to prevent his committing an offence or fleeing after having dome so;

(d)   the detention of a minor by lawful order for the purpose of education supervision or his lawful detention for the purpose of bringing him before the competent legal authority;

(e)   the lawful detention of persons for the prevention of the spreading of infectious disease, of person of unsound mind, alcoholics or drug addicts or vagrants;

(f)   the lawful arrest or detention of a person to prevent his effecting an unauthorised entry into the country or of a person against whom action is being taken with a view to deportation or extradition."

This list, as the ECtHR has repeatedly emphasised, is exhaustive and narrowly interpreted (see, for instance, *Engel v Netherlands (No.1)* (1976) 1 E.H.R.R. 647, para.57 and *Kurt v Turkey* (1998) 27 E.H.R.R. 373, para.122). This reflects the importance attached by the Convention to the right to liberty and security. Thus, an individual may not be deprived of his liberty unless the case falls within one of the listed classes.

However, restricting liberty, even if in accordance with a listed condition, will not be lawful unless it accords with a procedure prescribed by law. As discussed in para.20–014, this means there must be a law which is accessible and formulated with sufficient precision to enable the citizen to regulate his conduct.

(a)   *Detention following conviction by a competent court*

22–007   Article 5(1)(a) provides that detention will be lawful if it follows conviction by a competent court. There must be sufficient connection between a finding of guilt and the detention. In *Stafford v UK* (2002) 35 E.H.R.R. 32, the applicant had been sentenced to life imprisonment for murder and, after release on life licence, committed fraud and sentenced to six-years imprisonment. As a result, his life licence was revoked by the Secretary of State. Three years later, the parole board recommended his release on life licence, which the Home Secretary refused believing there to be a risk of him committing more non-violent imprisonable offences in the future. Stafford argued his detention following the parole board hearing violated art.5(1). The ECtHR held there was insufficient connection between imposing a mandatory life sentence for murder, and the subsequent recall and detention on the basis he would commit crimes of a non-violent nature. Therefore, there was a violation of art.5(1).

According to the House of Lords in *R. v Governor of Brockhill Prison Ex p. Evans (No.2)* [2001] 2 A.C. 19, once the date for release has passed, detention is no longer lawful. Here, the applicant was entitled to a reduction in the actual period to be served due to the time spent in prison prior to trial. The Governor miscalculated the date according to his understanding of the law. The House of Lords concluded detention after this period was unlawful.

(b)   *Non-compliance with a court order imposed by law*

Article 5(1)(b) permits the arrest and detention of an individual who has not complied **22–008** with a court order. Such obligation would include an arrest for failure to pay a fine or detention for contempt of court.

In *Steel v UK* (1998) 28 E.H.R.R. 603, three separate groups of individuals were arrested and charged with breaches of the peace arising from demonstrations. At their trials, a number were bound over to keep the peace which they refused to agree to and were subsequently detained. The ECtHR held that detention following non-compliance with an order by the court to be bound over to keep the peace fell within the scope of art.5(1)(b).

(c)   *Detention on suspicion of commission of a criminal offence*

Article 5(1)(c) is the one where detention is most readily justified. It permits an indi- **22–009** vidual to be deprived of their liberty where they are being lawfully arrested on reasonable suspicion of committing a criminal offence, or where it is necessary to prevent them committing an offence or fleeing after having done so. The important aspect is that any arrest made under this section must be made on "reasonable suspicion". In *K-F v Germany* (1997) 26 E.H.R.R. 390, the ECtHR held that for "reasonable suspicion" there must exist facts or information which would satisfy an objective observer that the person concerned might have committed the offence. This does not require that the facts raising the suspicion be of the same level required for conviction at trial or bringing of a charge.

An example of legislation which falls under art.5(1)(c) is the Police and Criminal Evidence Act 1984 (PACE). Section 24 of PACE (inserted by the Serious Organised Crime and Police Act 2005), provides that an arrest may be made in relation to "any offence". These powers are exercisable where a police officer has "reasonable grounds" to believe that an arrest is necessary for one of the following reasons:

- To enable the name of the person in question to be ascertained.

- To enable the address of the person in question to be ascertained.

- To prevent the person in question from—

    (i)   causing physical injury to himself or any other person;
    (ii) suffering physical injury;
    (iii) causing loss of or damage to property;
    (iv) committing an offence against public decency;
    (v)   causing unlawful obstruction of the highway.

- To protect a child or other vulnerable person from the person in question.

- To allow the prompt and effective investigation of the offence or of the conduct of the person in question.

- To prevent prosecution of an offence from being hindered by the disappearance of the person in question.

An area of difficulty is where an individual is arrested on suspicion of being a terrorist. Terrorist offences pose problems both in relation to information which may be available at the time of the offence and the special risk to loss of life and property such offences create. In *Fox, Campbell and Hartley v UK* (1990) 13 E.H.R.R. 157 the government tried to argue that the "reasonableness" of the suspicion justifying such arrests could not always be judged according to the same standards as are applied in dealing with conventional crime. The applicants in this case were arrested under s.11(1) of the Northern Ireland (Emergency Provision) Act 1978 on suspicion of being a terrorist, detained for approximately 40 hours and released without charge. Under the Act, a constable could arrest, without warrant, any person who he "suspects" of being a terrorist. The court recognised the government does not have to establish the reasonableness of the suspicion by disclosing confidential sources, or even facts which would be susceptible of indicating such sources or their identity. However, the court felt that despite the difficulties in dealing with suspected terrorist crimes, it did not justify stretching the notion of reasonableness to the point where the essence of the safeguard was impaired. However, the lack of reasonable suspicion in the statute did not automatically mean a violation of art.5(1)(c), as long as there is reasonable suspicion on the facts. Consequently, the government have to furnish at least some facts or information capable of satisfying the court that the arrested person was reasonably suspected of having committed the alleged offence. In this case, the government had not provided enough information which would allow an objective observer to conclude there was reasonable suspicion, the fact that Fox and Campbell had previous convictions for acts of terrorism connected with the IRA was not enough to form the sole basis for their arrest some seven years later.

Not only must the suspicion be objectively justified, but an offence must be suspected. It is not enough that suspicion is of some vague conduct. In relation to terrorist offences, the case of *Brogan v UK* (1989) 11 E.H.R.R. 117 provides some assistance. Mr Brogan was arrested under Prevention of Terrorism (Temporary Provisions) Act 1984 which provided for arrest on suspicion of committing a terrorist offence. Section 14(1) of the 1984 Act, defined terrorism as meaning the use of violence for political ends, and included any use of violence for the purpose of putting the public or any section of the public in fear. The applicants maintained their arrest and detention were grounded on suspicion, not of having committed a specific offence, but rather of involvement in unspecified acts of terrorism, something which did not constitute a breach of the criminal law in Northern Ireland and could not be regarded as an "offence" under art.51(c). The ECtHR considered two factors in assessing whether an actual offence was suspected. First, the definition of acts of terrorism was "well in keeping with the idea of an offence (at para.51) and secondly, subsequent questioning the applicants underwent was in regard to specific offences. The ECtHR concluded that the arrests were based on reasonable suspicion.

In some respects, current law is in conformity with art.5(1)(c) as under s.41(1) of the Terrorism Act 2000, power is given to arrest a person without warrant whom the officer "reasonably suspects is a terrorist". Whilst a reading of s.41(1) would appear to satisfy art.5(1)(c), problems may arise when the definition of a terrorist is considered. A terrorist is defined in s.40 of the Act as a person who has either committed an offence under various sections of the Act (s.40(1)(a)), or "is or has been concerned in the commission, preparation or instigation of acts of terrorism" (s.40(1)(b)). The s.41 power read with s.40(1)(b) does not contain a requirement as to reasonable suspicion that an offence has been committed or is about to be committed by the person in question before an arrest can be made. Fenwick (*Text, Case and Material Public Law and Human Rights* (Cavendish, 2003) at p.1030) argues that, in the absence of questioning about specific offences (as in *Brogan*), an arrest under s.40(1)(b) of the Terrorism Act 2000 may not satisfy the art.5(1)(c) "reasonable suspicion" standard. As Fenwick (at p.1017) notes, arrest under s.41 as read with s.40(1)(b) "is not for an offence but in practice for investigation, questioning and general intelligence gathering".

(d)   *Detention of minors*

Article 5(1)(d) permits the detention of minors by lawful order for the purpose of   **22–010**
educational supervision or lawful detention for the purpose of bringing them before a competent legal authority. Educational supervision is given a wide meaning and extends beyond school. In *Re K (a child) (secure accommodation: right to liberty)* [2001] 2 W.L.R. 1141 the court held that the meaning of education supervision was similar to "the general development of the child's physical, intellectual, emotional, social and behavioural abilities." Education need not be the sole purpose of detention, such that detention in secure accommodation as in *K*, above, also falls within art.5(1)(d). K was detained under the Children Act 1989 because of his disruptive behaviour, complex social and educational needs, and mental health problems. The court found that though the primary purpose was to restrict K's liberty and the Children Act 1989 made no mention of education, K's detention was justified under art.5(1)(d). On the facts, K was receiving education which was carefully supervised and from which he was clearly benefiting. Also, it was implicit that education would be provided as, under the Education Act 1996, education is compulsory for all children under 16.

(e)   *Detention to prevent the spread of infectious diseases*

Under art.5(1)(e), detention is lawful if for the prevention of spreading infectious dis-   **22–011**
eases, or detaining persons of unsound mind, alcoholics, drug addicts and vagrants. The area that has generated most litigation concerns mental health detention. The ECtHR will not interfere with domestic definitions as to what amounts to unsound mind, but does require a decision is objectively justified and that a true mental disorder be established. In *Ashingdane v UK* (1985) 7 E.H.R.R. 528, Mr Ashingdane was convicted of various offences and diagnosed with paranoid schizophrenia of such a degree it warranted detention in a psychiatric hospital. The court made a hospital order and he

was detained in a secure special hospital. His condition later improved and a transfer to a local psychiatric hospital was authorised. However, due to staffing problems, the hospital refused to accept him and he remained in the secure special hospital. Two years later, he was eventually transferred. Mr Ashingdane complained that the two additional years he served in the secure special hospital, when he should have been transferred, violated art.5(1). The ECtHR held that to justify Mr Ashingdane's continued detention the existence of a mental disorder of sufficient degree had to be established on the basis of objective medical expertise. The court concluded there was no reason to doubt the medical evidence and Mr Ashingdane would still have been in detention even if transferred, so there was no violation of art.5(1).

In *R. (H) v Mental Health Review Tribunal, North and East London Region* [2001] EWCA Civ 415, the Court of Appeal found a violation of art.5(1). H was detained under the Mental Health Act 1983. Section 73 placed a burden on the detained patient to show he was no longer suffering from a mental disorder. This was found incompatible as art.5 requires discharge of a detained person unless it can be shown he is currently suffering from a mental disorder. As a result of the declaration of incompatibility, the Mental Health Act 1983 (Remedial) Order 2001 (SI 2001/3712) was passed which reversed the burden of proof.

In *R. (H) v Home Secretary* [2003] UKHL 59, s.73 of the Mental Health Act was further challenged. This challenge arose where a Mental Health Review Tribunal (MHRT) had decided that a patient's medical condition could be treated outside hospital and ordered conditional release. In H's case, his release could not be effected because the conditions of treatment could not be met. The House of Lords concluded that at no time had H been unlawfully detained. The MHRT had not decided he was of sound mind simply, that he could be treated outside of the detained hospital environment if certain conditions were met. The decision of the House of Lords seems to have been confirmed by a similar challenge taken to the European Court of Human Rights. In *Kolanis v United Kingdom* (2006) 42 E.H.R.R. 12, the ECtHR found no violation of art.5(1) where a schizophrenic was not released as a result of the conditions of discharge not being met. The MHRT's decision found that K was still suffering from mental illness and continued to require treatment to control her illness. They decided she could be released if appropriate treatment and supervision could be arranged. In the absence of such conditions being met, detention continued to be necessary and in line with the purpose of art.5(1)(e).

(f)   *Detention of an illegal entrant pending deportation or extradition*

22–012   The requirements under art.5(1)(f) allow for detention of an illegal entrant pending deportation. This section has also been the subject of much litigation. In *R. (Saadi) v Secretary of State for the Home Department* [2002] UKHL 41, the House of Lords concluded that the detention of asylum seekers for short periods of time (7 to 10 days) at Oakington Reception Centre was compatible with art.5(1)(f). The asylum seekers were detained to enable a speedy determination of their case by keeping them available and the House of Lords agreed that this was not a violation of art.5(1) nor was it a disproportionate response to the reasonable requirements of immigration control.

Where an individual is being held because action is taken to secure their deportation, then this will not be a violation of art.5(1). However, the deportation has to be pending which means the detention is limited to a period which is reasonably necessary for that purpose. If deportation is not possible, for example, because of the serious risk that the deported person will suffer torture, inhuman or degrading in their home country then, detention will be a violation of art.5(1). This was the situation which necessitated the government lodging a derogation against art.5(1) in respect of s.23 of the Anti- Terrorism, Crime and Security Act 2001, which then allowed for the indefinite detention of foreign nationals suspected of terrorist offences.

DUE PROCESS GUARANTEES UNDER ARTICLE 5

Once a person has been arrested, art.5 imposes additional obligations or due process **22–013** guarantees on a public authority or state which seeks to further protect the individual.

1.   Article 5(2): Prompt reasons for arrest

Once a person has been arrested, they should be informed promptly and clearly of the **22–014** reasons for their arrest and any charge against them. This is an additional safeguard against arbitrary arrest as if a person cannot say why they are arresting someone this suggests the arrest may be arbitrary. In *Fox, Campbell and Hartley v UK* (1990) 13 E.H.R.R. 157, the ECtHR held that simply informing someone at the time of their arrest they were being arrested on suspicion of being a terrorist did not satisfy the article. However, subsequent questioning in relation to specific offences did provide enough detail for the person questioned to understand why they were arrested, so satisfying the requirements of art.5(2).

2.   Article 5(3): Prompt appearance before a court

This is one of the most important due process guarantees under art.5. It ensures that **22–015** everyone arrested or detained within the provision of art.5(1)(c) should be "brought promptly before a judge or other officer authorised by law to exercise judicial power and shall be entitled to trial within a reasonable time or to release pending trial. Release may be conditioned by guarantees to appear for trial".

The aim of this provision is to ensure an individual is not detained indefinitely nor without judicial approval of such a detention. There are three rights within this article:

(1)   judicial review of detention;

(2)   reasonably speedy trial;

(3)   release on bail.

Judicial review of detention ensures a court either authorises continuance of detention or releases the individual either on bail or unconditionally. The requirement is that a person is brought "promptly" before a judge, which has been the subject of litigation. In *Brogan v UK* (1989) 11 E.H.R.R. 117, Brogan, and a number of others, were arrested under s.12 of the Prevention of Terrorism (Temporary Provisions) Act 1984. They were detained for periods ranging from four days six hours to 6 days 16½ hours authorised under the Secretary of State for Northern Ireland under s.12(4). None were brought before a judge. The ECtHR stressed the importance of the provision in upholding the rule of law and whilst recognising the difficulties associated with terrorist-related offences, held that the minimum detention period of four days six hours violated art.5(3) in that the individual was not brought "promptly" before a judge. The court felt that to allow a wider interpretation of "promptly" for terrorist offences would import a "serious weakening of a procedural guarantee to the detriment of the individual and would entail consequences impairing the very essence of the right protected by this provision" (para.62).

The Prevention of Terrorism (Temporary Provisions) Act 1984 was replaced by the Terrorism Act 2000 which seeks consistency with art.5(3) by providing that any detention of a terrorist suspect beyond 48 hours can only continue on judicial approval up to seven days. The Terrorism Act 2006 extended this to 28 days. Fenwick suggests that the 7–28 days detention period may be incompatible with art.5(3) simply because it is relatively long and so may not be prompt. At the time of writing the government had proposed extending the period of maximum detention to 42 days (Counter Terrorism Bill). The Joint Committee on Human Rights (Counter Terrorism Policy and Human Rights: 42 Days, 2nd Report 2007–08, HL 23, HC 156) concluded (p.101) that the government had not made out a case for extending pre-charge detention. The Bill is in Committee (May 2008).

Under normal circumstances, the Police and Criminal Evidence Act 1984 (PACE) provides that once arrested and taken to a police station, an individual can be detained before charge for two reasons: if "the custody officer has reasonable grounds for believing that his detention without being charged is necessary to secure or preserve evidence relating to an offence for which he is under arrest or to obtain such evidence by questioning him" (PACE s.37(2)). The basic length of the detention without charge is 24 hours (s.41(7)), which is timed from the moment the suspect first arrives at the police station (s.41(2)(d)). However, under certain circumstances, detention can be extended up to 36 hours if authorised by a police officer with the rank of superintendent or higher (s.42(1)). Under ss.43(1) and 44(1) detention beyond 36 hours may be authorised, but only by a magistrates' court granting a warrant of further detention on conditions similar to those which apply in the first instance under s.42(1) (s.43(4)). The maximum period of detention is 96 hours (s.44(3)(b)). It would appear that the provisions contained with PACE are consistent with the obligations under art.5(3).

(a)   *Release may be conditioned by guarantees to appear for trial*

22–016   Under art.5(4) release pending trial can be subject to conditions. In the United Kingdom, this is governed by the Bail Act 1976 which provides that a person should be granted bail unless particular circumstances exist. These include a risk that the defendant may fail to surrender or may commit further crimes whilst on bail. Under s.25 of the Criminal Justice and Public Order Act 1994 bail could not be granted if a defendant was charged with homicide or rape or had been previously convicted of a similar offence. This requirement was found to be incompatible with art.5(3) in *Caballero v UK* (2000) 30 E.H.R.R. 643. Mr Caballero had been convicted of manslaughter in 1987, sentenced to imprisonment and released in 1988. In 1996, he was arrested on suspicion of attempted rape. No bail application was made on his behalf because of s.25. Mr Caballero complained that the automatic denial of bail was a violation of art.5(3). Prior to the case being determined by the ECtHR, the UK government concurred and amended s.25 with the Crime and Disorder Act 1998 which provides that bail can be granted if there are exceptional circumstances.

3.   Article 5(4): Right to challenge lawfulness of decision

Article 5(4) provides that everyone deprived of their liberty by arrest or detention shall be entitled to take proceedings by which the lawfulness of their detention shall be decided speedily by a court and his release ordered if the detention is not lawful. This means that where a person is deprived of their liberty by the Executive, they have the right of access to a court or similar body to question the legality of the decision, including any evidence. Effectively, this is the writ of habeas corpus. Article 5(4) requires not only an initial right of access to a court or tribunal to discover whether the detention is lawful, but also a review of lawfulness to be available at reasonable intervals. **22–017**

As with art.5(3) and "promptly", the question of what is meant by "speedily" has arisen. In *MH v Secretary of State for the Health Department* [2005] UKHL 60 a question arose as to the compatibility of ss.2 and 29(4) of the Mental Health Act 1983. MH was severely mentally disabled as a result of Down's Syndrome and formally admitted to hospital for assessment under s.2 of the 1983 Act. Section 2 provided for an initial assessment of up to 28 days. The patient can apply to a Mental Health Review Tribunal within 14 days of admission for discharge. Prior to the end of the 28 day period, an application for guardianship of MH was made. As a result, under s.29(4) of the Act, MH's detention was automatically extended until the application for guardianship had been resolved. This amounted to a further two years' detention. It was argued that the law did not comply with art.5(4) in two respects. First, it did not provide a practical and effective right of access to a court for a patient detained under s.2 who lacked the capacity to apply to a tribunal by themselves. Secondly, the law did not provide a right of review at reasonable intervals for a patient who finds themselves detained by virtue of s.29(4). The Court of Appeal had found both sections to be incompatible with art.5(4), but this was overturned by the House of Lords. Baroness Hale found there were ample mechanisms for review by a tribunal, county court or via a reference from the Secretary of State and that both sections were capable of being used compatibly with art.5(4).

An area which has attracted particular attention under art.5(4) is the review of detention of life prisoners and, in particular, the power of the Home Secretary to determine the tariff period (the period of time the prisoner has to serve before eligible for parole). In *Hirst v UK* (2001) ECHR 477, a discretionary life prisoner eligible for parole argued that delays of 21 months and two years between reviews of his continued detention amounted to a breach of art.5(4). The ECtHR agreed.

In *T and V v UK* (2000) 30 E.H.R.R. 121, the applicants were two ten year old boys convicted of murder and detained at her Majesty's Pleasure with a recommended tariff of 15 years. They contended there had been no review of their detention by a judicial body. The ECtHR held that because the sentence of detention during Her Majesty's Pleasure was indeterminate and the tariff was initially set by the Home Secretary that the supervision required by art.5(4) had not been incorporated into the sentence. They also found that because the decision in setting the tariff had been quashed by the House of Lords and no new tariff substituted, the applicant's entitlement to access to a tribunal for periodic review remained unclear. This was followed by *Stafford v UK* (2002) 35 E.H.R.R. 32 concerning the power of the Home Secretary to set the tariff period for mandatory life adult prisoners. The ECtHR held that art.5(4) had been violated and felt the role of the Home Secretary in setting such tariffs was "increasingly difficult to reconcile with the notion of separation of powers between the Executive and the judiciary".

4.   Article 5(5): Right to compensation for breach of article 5

22–018   Article 5(5) provides that everyone who has been a victim of an art.5 violation can claim compensation. Whilst this is an important right, it is already protected in the UK through the right to claim compensation by way of damages for wrongful arrest and detention.

DUE PROCESS GUARANTEES UNDER ARTICLE 6

22–019   Article 6 is principally a due process right, setting down safeguards as to the conduct of any criminal trial or civil hearing. The core aspect of the right is that of a fair trial and the focus of the article seeks to ensure this is achieved. It contains principles which underlie the rule of law such as an individual not being punished unless they have committed a crime and being presumed innocent until proven guilty.

Like liberty, the idea of fair trial was not introduced by the ECHR, but has been recognised in the United Kingdom since the Magna Carta which guaranteed an impartial and speedy legal process. Other protections in existence pre-Human Rights Act 1998 include public trials and the prosecution's burden of proof in criminal cases. Equally the laws on evidence have regulated the admissibility of hearsay and improperly obtained evidence. As a result, it is fair to say that art.6 has not had a major effect on how trials are conducted but instead serves to enhance the protections already offered. However, re-examination of some of the principles in light of the Convention is inevitable.

1.   Civil and criminal rights

Article 6(1) guarantees the right to a fair and public hearing before an impartial and **22–020** unbiased court or tribunal. It only applies in the "determination of civil rights or obligations or of any criminal charge against him." Due to the extra procedural protections guaranteed in art.6 for criminal matters, there have been a number of cases on the distinction between civil obligations and criminal law. What amounts to a civil right or obligation is not precisely defined, but generally covers the rights and obligations of private persons in their relationships with each other. In *Engels v Netherlands* (1976) 1 E.H.R.R. 647 (at para.82), a case concerning military discipline and whether penalties imposed amounted to criminal or civil, the court noted that whether proceedings constituted a criminal charge depended on three criteria:

(1)   The classification of the proceedings in domestic law. This factor serves only as a starting point and simply because the proceedings are treated as civil in domestic law, does not mean it is civil. See *Benham v UK* below.

(2)   The nature of the proceedings. This carries more weight than the first.

(3)   The severity of the punishments.

Examples of matters which have been found to be criminal include prison disciplinary proceedings where the penalty is sufficiently serious; *Campbell and Fey v UK* (1985) 7 E.H.R.R. 165 and *Ezeh and Connors v UK* (2002) 35 E.H.R.R. 691 and (2004) 39 E.H.R.R. 1, and imprisonment for non-payment of the community charge *Benham v UK* (1996) 22 E.H.R.R. 293. In *Campbell and Fey v UK*, the ECtHR, whilst recognising the need for allowances due to the prison context and reasons of policy in favour of establishing a special prison disciplinary regime, felt that considering the fundamental nature of the fair hearing guarantees in art.6, there was no warrant for depriving prisoners of the safeguards of that article. In *Benham*, the ECtHR found that whilst the proceedings were considered a civil issue in domestic law, it noted that the law concerning liability to pay the community charge and the procedure upon non-payment was of general application. In addition, the proceedings had some punitive elements such as committal to prison. In was finally noted that the punishment was quite severe, with the applicant facing a maximum penalty of three months imprisonment. Having regard to these factors, the court concluded that the applicant was charged with a criminal offence.

Two further cases where the distinction was important concerned the imposition of "orders" controlling behaviour; *R. (McCann) v Manchester Crown Court* [2002] UKHL 39 and *Secretary of State for Home Department v MB* [2007] UKHL 46. *R. (McCann) v Manchester Crown Court* concerned the issue of whether anti-social behaviour orders were criminal or civil. Anti-social behaviour orders under s.1 of the Crime and Disorder Act 1998, were made again three brothers, SM, MM and JM. The brothers appealed against the making of the order to the Crown Court where the judge held that the proceedings for the making of an order were civil rather than criminal and, therefore, hearsay evidence, which would have been considered inadmissible in criminal proceedings. The House of Lords held that under domestic law the proceedings for making of anti-social behaviour order were civil, beginning as a complaint. The Crown

Prosecution Service (CPS) was not involved at all, and there was no requirement to establish mens rea or criminal liability. Furthermore, the making of the order was not a conviction or statement that the person was guilty of a criminal offence and no penalty was imposed. The second case, *MB*, concerned control orders, and similar to the above decision, the House of Lords concluded that they were equally civil obligations.

2.   Is article 6 unqualified?

22–021   On its face, art.6 appears an absolute right save for one express qualification relating to public hearings. The ECtHR has further implied a number of additional protections into art.6 so as to give effect to the right to a fair trial. For example, there is the express requirement of the presumption of innocence under art.6(2), and implied into this is the right not incriminate oneself. Whether the words of art.6 imply additional protections, and whether there are qualifications to the protections in art.6 depends on the circumstances of the case. In *Brown v Stott* [2001] 1 W.L.R. 817, the Privy Council considered the requirement under s.172 of the Road Traffic Act 1988 (RTA) which obliges the keeper of a car to give information as to the identity of the driver at the time of the offence. Mrs Brown was arrested on suspicion of theft from a supermarket and, after admitting that she had come to the supermarket by car, was subsequently required to provide details under s.172 as to whether she was driving. Lord Bingham recognised there was nothing to suggest the overall fairness of a trial can be limited, qualified or compromised in any way. This is regardless of the circumstances and whatever the public interest is in convicting the offender. However, the constituent rights (i.e. art.6(2)), whether express or implied in art.6 are not themselves absolute. Lord Bingham noted that limited qualification of these constituent rights is acceptable if, "directed by national authorities towards a clear and proper public objective and if representing no greater qualification than the situation calls for". In considering s.172 of the RTA, Lord Bingham felt that the high incidence of death and injury on the roads posed a very serious problem and the need to address it in an effective way for the benefit of the public could not be doubted. Whilst s.172 may conflict with art.6(2) and the privilege against self-incrimination, the right to a fair trial was not undermined on the facts of this case. Such an approach was confirmed in July 2007 when the ECtHR ruled that s.172 did not interfere with art.6(2) (see *O'Halloran and Francis v UK* [2007] (Applications Nos. 15809/02 and 25624/02).

3.   Fair and public hearing

22–022   The right to a fair hearing is at the heart of the article and, as mentioned above, the overall fairness of proceedings cannot, generally, be compromised. However, it might be compromised even if none of the constituent rights are themselves interfered with. An example can be seen in the *International Roth* case (*International Roth GmbH v Secretary of State for Home Department* [2002] EWCA Civ 158). Under the Immigration and Asylum Act 1999, lorry drivers and owners were liable to a fixed penalty of £2,000 if a person seeking to enter the country illegally was found concealed in the vehicle. This penalty was regardless of the blameworthiness of the driver or owner. A group of 60 drivers challenged the scheme and penalty as inconsistent with their art.6 rights. The Court of Appeal took into account the aims of the scheme which was to prevent illegal immigration and promote vigilance on the part of cross-channel transporters, and balanced them against the inflexibility of the statutory penalty. Overall they considered the scheme to be unfair and contrary to art.6.

A fair hearing also means that the hearing should be before an impartial and independent court or tribunal and free from the appearance of bias (see Ch.17). Whilst the idea of a hearing free from bias is a requirement of natural justice, so applicable prior to the HRA in traditional judicial review proceedings, incorporation of the ECHR and the HRA has brought closer scrutiny on the notion of independence and had perhaps its greatest impact here. One of the main modifications has come in relation to the actual test for bias. Prior to the HRA, the test for bias was whether a reasonable man, in light of all the relevant circumstances, would consider there was a real danger of bias. However, the court characterised the reasonable man (see *R. v Gough* [1993] A.C. 646). In light of Strasbourg jurisprudence on art.6, the Court of Appeal in *Re Medicaments and Related Classes of Good (No.2) and Director General of Fair Trading v Propriety Association of Great Britain* [2001] 1 W.L.R. 700 approved a modification to the *Gough* approach. This case concerned an application to remove a doctor who was part of the court hearing a restrictive practice case. The application was made on the grounds that during the proceedings she had applied for a job with a firm which provided expert witness services for the other party. The Court of Appeal felt modification was required concerning the role of the court in personifying the reasonable man, particularly where the potential bias concerned the court. It changed this to that of a fair-minded and informed observer and felt that a fair minded and informed observer would be concerned that if the doctor respected the firm enough to apply for a job, she might consciously or unconsciously be inclined to consider it a more reliable source of expert opinion than its rivals. This approach to the bias test was confirmed by the House of Lords in *Porter v McGill* [2001] UKHL 67 and *Lawal v Northern Spirit Ltd* [2003] UKHL 35 (see Ch.17 for more detail).

Another area under particular scrutiny has been the court martial system for crimes committed by members of the armed forces. *Findlay v UK* (1997) 24 E.H.R.R. 221 is a leading case in this area. Findlay, a Lance Sergeant in the Army was tried for a shooting incident which he attributed to post-traumatic stress disorder. The Army court martial consisted of five members of the armed forces all of whom were subordinate to the convening officer who had played a significant role before the hearing, was central to the prosecution, and had power to dismiss the court martial. The ECtHR held that because of the overlapping roles of the convening officer, there was an interference with art.6(1). It is objective impartiality which is seen as important and the ECtHR identified the following as important considerations:

(1)   manner of appointment;

(2)   terms of office;

(3)   existence of guarantees of independence against outside pressures;

(4)   whether the body presents an appearance of independence.

As a result, changes were made to the court martial system and they now have permanent presidents with additional safeguards to ensure independence. Since this decision, the House of Lords in *Boyd v Army Prosecuting Authority* [2002] UKHL 31 has confirmed that the new system is compatible with art.6(1).

The third consideration (above) identified by the ECtHR in *Findlay*, was the relevant issue in *Starrs and Chalmers v Ruxton* [2000] U.K.H.R.R. 78. Prior to the HRA 1998, no thought was given to whether outside pressures might give the appearance of bias. In *Starrs*, the complainant had appeared before a temporary sheriff. A temporary sheriff was the start of a route to higher judicial office, and appointment to the position was dependent on a recommendation of the Lord Advocate. The Lord Advocate also conducted the prosecution in this case. The court held there was an appearance of a lack of objectivity because of potential pressure due to the manner of appointment and the lack of tenure of office.

Freedom from political bias is equally important in the fairness of a hearing. Two cases provide examples and have led to changes in domestic law. In *T and V v UK* (2000) 30 E.H.R.R. 121 the role of the Home Secretary, a political figure, in determining the tariff period to be served by the two boys was held to violate art.6. In setting the period of time to be spent in prison, the Home Secretary, part of the Executive, was clearly not independent. This led to the loss of tariff-setting powers for the Home Secretary, with the consequence that sentencing is governed for juveniles by the Powers of Criminal Courts (Sentencing) Act 2000, and for adults by the Criminal Justice Act 2003. Similarly, in *McGonnell v UK* (2000) 30 E.H.R.R. 289, the role of the Bailiff of Guernsey who had an arm in all hand organs of the state (similar to the old Lord Chancellor) was held to violate art.6. This case led to the Lord Chancellor's decision not to sit on judicial cases and ultimately led to reform of role of the Lord Chancellor in the Constitutional Reform Act 2005.

Article 6 can be violated where there is evidence of bias from a jury. Recently, the House of Lords in *R. v Abdroikof* [2007] UKHL 37 found that the presence of a full-time salaried Crown Prosecution Service (CPS) lawyer on a jury and a police officer led to the appearance of bias. In the first, the prosecution of the case by another member of the CPS and the presence of juror who was also a member of the CPS would naturally lead a fair minded and informed observer to conclude the possibility of bias. In the second, the particular circumstances of the case were paramount. In this case, the victim was a police officer and there was an evidential dispute between the defendant and the victim. The majority of the House of Lords felt that the juror, who was also from a local service background, though a different force, had a natural instinct to prefer the evidence of the *brother* officer over that of the defendant.

Article 6(1) also guarantees an individual receives a fair trial within a *reasonable time*. This applies to the length of the judicial proceedings including appeals. What amounts to reasonable time depends on all the circumstances of the case.

4.   Right of access to a court

22–023   Article 6(1) is not limited to guaranteeing the right to a fair trial in legal proceedings already pending, but secures a right of access to the courts to persons wishing to commence a legal action in order to have his civil rights and obligations determined. In *Golder v UK* (1976) 1 E.H.R.R. 523, the ECtHR held that the right of access to the courts is implicit in art.6. Mr Golder had been convicted of robbery with violence and serving a fifteen-years sentence. Whilst in prison, he was wrongly accused of assaulting a prison officer following a disturbance. Charges were made against him, and entries made on his prison record, though the charges were not pursued. Mr Golder wrote to the Secretary of State asking to see a solicitor with a view to taking civil action for libel. Pursuant to the Prison Rules 1964, which have the status of a statutory instrument, Golder was denied both. He then alleged a violation of art.6(1). The Home Secretary was not formally denying Golder his right to institute proceedings, but in refusing access to a solicitor the Home Secretary was impeding his access to a court. The ECtHR found that such hindrance contravenes the Convention.

Access to the court also includes providing facilities so that individuals can seek legal redress, for example, by providing legal aid, this issue arising in *Benham v UK* (1996) 22 E.H.R.R. 293, where the ECtHR held that failure to provide legal aid to Benham to enable him to defend a civil allegation of non-payment of community charge violated art.6(1).

Domestic law must not place procedural obstacles in the way. In *Osman v UK* (2000) 29 E.H.R.R. 245 the applicants brought civil proceedings against the police for negligence. Domestic courts held no action could lay against the police with respect to the investigation and suppression of crime. The ECtHR held that the blanket application of the rule unjustifiably deprived the applicants of their rights and constituted a disproportionate restriction on the applicants art.6 rights.

5.   Right to effective participation in the trial

Article 6(1) impliedly guarantees the right to put legal arguments before the court in support of one's case. This right is supplemented by the right to legal assistance found in art.6(3)(c). In order to adequately put a case forward, an individual should be aware of the nature of the charge, be able to participate constructively in the hearing, and have access to the case against him. For example, in *T and V v UK* (2000) 30 E.H.R.R. 121, the subjection of 11-year-old defendants to adult trial violated art.6 as they could not participate effectively in the process.   **22–024**

Refusal to order disclosure of evidence may interfere with this basic right. It is not an absolute right, and disclosure may be refused on national security grounds or because of the need to protect witnesses or keep secret, police methods of investigation of crimes. However, as with all rights, any interference must be balanced against the right to a fair trial and be no more than proportionate. *MB & AF v Secretary of State for Home Department* [2007] UKHL 47, a case concerning control orders, shows the difficulties in achieving this balance, particularly where terrorism is concerned. Under the Prevention of Terrorism Act 2005, the Secretary of State for the Home Department may impose a control order if he "has reasonable grounds for suspecting that an individual is or has been involved in terrorism-related activity; and ... considers that it is necessary, for purposes connected with protecting members of the public from a risk of terrorism, to make a control order imposing obligations on that individual". Under s.3(2) of the Act, a court reviewing the decisions of the Secretary of State through which a control order has been issued are limited to determining if those decisions were "flawed".

The two individuals in the case brought a challenge alleging a violation of art.6. In particular, the material which was crucial to demonstrating the reasonable basis of the Secretary of State's suspicions or fears was not disclosed in any way which would enable the controlled person to reply to such allegations. The Act, however, allows for the use of Special Advocates, who are security-cleared lawyers instructed to represent a person's interests in relation to material kept from that person and his ordinary lawyers, but analysed by a court. These had been initially introduced under the Anti-Terrorism, Crime and Security Act 2001. The issue was whether the use of the special advocate system was enough to protect the individual's right to fair trial under art.6. The problem is that whilst the special advocate may know the material, he cannot take instruction on it as the material cannot be disclosed to the controlee. The House of Lords in *MB and AF* felt that the use of the special advocate system could, in some situations, be an appropriate safeguard accommodating both legitimate national security concerns and still accord the individual a substantial measure of procedural justice. However, not all situations would be adequately protected by the use of Special Advocates, particularly in situations where the sole basis for making the control order is on closed evidence, such as in the case of *MB & AF*. If, despite all the efforts of the judge and the special advocates to ensure fairness, the judge feels more material should be disclosed, on the face of the relevant provisions in the PTA, the judge is precluded from ordering disclosure. This is even where he considers that disclosure is essential in order to give the controlled person a fair hearing (note Lord Hoffman dissenting felt the special advocate procedure provided sufficient safeguards to satisfy art.6 (at [54]). This would not itself matter if the judge could quash the order, but he is precluded from quashing the order unless the decision is flawed. The situation is then that the order must stand, but that the hearing has been unfair. The majority of the House of Lords felt this situation was easily remedied by interpreting into the PTA a requirement that it should be read subject to an individual's right to fair trial. In such circumstances, where the judge feels the material should be disclosed, the Secretary of State has the choice to either disclose it or withdraw it. If it is withdrawn and the decision to make a control order based predominantly on this evidence, the decision becomes flawed and can be quashed.

6.   Article 6(2): Presumption of innocence

22–025   In the UK, the prosecution in criminal matters must prove the accused committed the crime beyond all reasonable doubt. This is guaranteed under art.6(2) which states that everyone charged with a criminal offence shall be presumed innocent until proven guilty. In conjunction with art.6(1), art.6(2) also includes the right not to incriminate oneself and thus the right to silence.

(a)   Right to silence

Whilst the right to silence is important, it is not absolute (*Murray v UK* (1996) 22   **22–026**
E.H.R.R. 29). Two issues merit consideration where limitations have been raised. First,
where under statutory legislation an individual is required to give information, and,
secondly, the drawing of adverse inferences if a defendant remains silent during
interview.

(i)   Required to give information

In *Saunders v UK* (1996) 23 E.H.R.R. 313, Mr Saunders had been required to answer   **22–027**
questions put to him by the Department of Trade and Industry in the course of their
investigations and which was subsequently used at trial. The use of coerced evidence at
trial was found to breach art.6. However, in *Brown v Stott* [2001] 1 W.L.R. 817 (see
para.22–021), the Privy Council considered that s.172 of the Road Traffic Act 1988
(RTA) which obliges the keeper of a car to give information as to the identity of the
driver at the time of an alleged driving offence and thus could mean that keeper
incriminate themselves, did not violate art.6(2). The right to silence is not absolute, and
the benefit to the public in trying to address the high incidence of death and injury on
the road outweighed the right. This was confirmed in *O'Halloran and Francis v UK*
[2007] (see above).

(ii)   Adverse inferences

A similar point was made in *Condron v UK* (2001) 31 E.H.R.R. 1. This case concerned   **22–028**
s.34 of the Criminal Justice and Public Order Act which allowed adverse inferences to
be made where a defendant gave a "no comment" interview and later gave an explanation in defence. Here, the applicants were drug addicts who had been advised by their
lawyer not to answer questions as he felt they were unfit to be interviewed. At trial, both
gave explanations and the jury were directed to consider drawing an adverse inference.
The ECtHR affirmed that the right to silence is not absolute and each case should be
assessed on its merits. The court found that the fact that the issue was left to the jury
was not of itself incompatible with art.6. The incompatibility arose from the trial
judge's failure also to direct the jury that adverse inferences should only be drawn
where the jury was satisfied the refusal could only be based on the defendants having no
answer to the case put to them by the police, or one which would not stand up to cross-
examination. Overall, particular caution is required before a domestic court should
invoke a defendant's right to silence against them, and adequate safeguards should
implemented. A conviction cannot not be based solely on adverse inferences drawn
from a defendant's silence. However, where a situation clearly called for an explanation
from a defendant, their silence could be taken into account in assessing the persua-
siveness of the case against them.

7.   Article 6(3)

22–029   Article 6(3) contains a number of express rights that apply to everyone charged with a criminal offence. These include the right to:

(a)   be informed promptly of the nature of the charge against him in language he understands;

(b)   adequate time and facilities to prepare a defence including the right to appoint and communicate with a legal adviser;

(c)   defend the case personally or through legal representation;

(d)   obtain the attendance and examiner witnesses on his behalf;

(e)   be assisted by an interpreter if he cannot understand the language used in court.

The right to be informed of the charge and to be given adequate time to prepare a defence overlap with the implied right to participate fully with the hearing. As with the other constituent rights, they are not absolute and may, for example, be limited in the interest of national security (see *MB & AF v Secretary of State for Home Department*). These safeguards are protected in domestic law principally through the Police and Criminal Evidence Act 1984 and its relevant codes.

Of particular importance is the obligation found in art.6(3)(c) which states that everyone has the right to defend themselves against any criminal charge in person or through legal assistance of one's own choosing. This is guaranteed in domestic law by s.58 of the Police and Criminal Evidence Act 1984 and Code C for most offences, and para.7 of Sch.8 to the Terrorism Act 2000, for terrorist-related offences. An issue which has arisen is whether this right can be delayed in certain circumstances. In *Murray (John) v UK* (1996) 22 E.H.R.R. 29, the ECtHR recognised that in certain circumstances denial of access to legal advice during questioning of a criminal suspect will call into question the fairness of any subsequent trial process. In this case, Murray was denied access to legal advice for the first 48 hours of his detention and questioning in circumstances where adverse inferences could be drawn from his refusal to answer. Consequently, this was found to compromise the overall fairness of his trial.

Following the ECtHR decision, the UK government amended the Criminal Justice and Public Order Act 1994 to prevent adverse inferences being drawn from silence where a suspect "has not been allowed the opportunity to consult a solicitor". Delay of access to legal advice is provided for under s.58(6), Code C and Annex B of PACE which allows for a delay of up to 36 hours where the person is detained for an indictable offence, and an officer ranked superintendent or above authorises it. Likewise, under Sch.8 of the Terrorism Act, where a person has been detained under the Act, an officer of the rank of superintendent or above may delay access to legal advice for up to 48 hours (para.8(1)).

In addition, the obligation extends to the provision of legal aid if the defendant cannot afford legal assistance and where the interests of justice demand it, see *Benham v UK* (1996) 22 E.H.R.R. 293 discussed at para.20–020 above.

Further Reading

Bakalis, C. "ASBOs, 'Preventative orders' and the European Court of Human Rights"   **22–030**
   (2007) *European Human Rights Law Review* 4, 427–440

Chapter 23

RIGHT TO RESPECT FOR PRIVATE LIFE

INTRODUCTION

Prior to the Human Rights Act 1998 (HRA), respect for private life was somewhat **23–001** undeveloped, especially when compared with freedom of expression. There was no enforceable right of privacy in domestic law, and the government could legitimately interfere with an individual's private life if they had lawful authority. This was made clear in *Malone v MPC* [1979] Ch. 344 where Malone's telephone was tapped, yet nevertheless deemed lawful as it was pursuant to Home Office guidelines. Further, the Court demonstrated an unwillingness to develop or recognise a right to privacy in the common law to protect Malone. This latter point was further confirmed by the Court of Appeal in *Kaye v Robertson* [1991] F.S.R. 62. Here, a newspaper obtained an interview and photographs of the actor Gordon Kaye from his hospital bed following an accident. The newspaper did not have Kaye's informed consent to the interview or the photographs, yet this did not interfere with his privacy because, as Lord Justice Glidewell said, "it is well know that in English law there is no right to privacy".

Despite this, the pre-HRA position was not all bad as protection existed for an individual's private rights through a piecemeal arrangement of common law and statute. For instance, reputation was protected by the law of defamation, personal property through the tort of private nuisance, information by the concept of confidence and the Data Protection Act 1984, since replaced by the Data Protection Act 1998, and, finally, the person through the Protection from Harassment Act 1997.

Since the HRA has come into force, private life has been given a positive footing by ECHR art.8. Now, not only must the government refrain from unlawful interference with an individual's private life, but it must, in some circumstances, take positive steps to protect interference by others. This chapter considers how right to respect for private life is protected today in the UK. Brief consideration is also given of the developing law of confidence in actions between private individuals.

ARTICLE 8

1. Aims of article 8

23–002   Under ECHR art.8 "Everyone has the right to respect for his private and family life, his home and his correspondence".

Two aims are evident from the operation of art.8. In *Sheffield and Horsham v UK* (1999) E.H.R.R. 163, the ECtHR considered the meaning of respect. First, it aims to protect the individual from intrusion into their private life by the state unless for good reason. The idea is that individuals should have the freedom to improve their life, conduct their personal affairs, fulfil personal ambitions and develop individuality; so-called moral autonomy. Secondly, the court has also found that the state must take positive steps to ensure that others do not interfere with an individual's private life (discussed further below). A similar point by was made by Lord Bingham in *R. (on the application of Countryside Alliance) v Att-Gen* [2007] UKHL 52 when considering whether the hunting with hounds ban introduced by the Hunting Act 2004 violated the applicant's art.8 rights.

In *Campbell v MGN Ltd* [2004] UKHL 22, Lord Nicholls (at para.12) recognised the importance of art.8, stating that a "proper degree of privacy is essential for the well-being and development of an individual" and that "restraints imposed on government to pry into the lives of citizens go to the essence of a democratic state".

DEFINITION

23–003   Article 8 has been broadly interpreted by the court and a great many cases, both domestic and those from the ECtHR are concerned with the meaning of art.8(1). It is clear that there are four interests which art.8(1) tells us are to be respected:

(1)   private life;

(2)   family life;

(3)   home; and

(4)   correspondence.

Whilst these are distinct ideas, there is a degree of overlap. Each will be considered in detail.

1. Private life

23–004   The idea of private life starts with the person and has been given a wide meaning by the Courts. In *R. (on the application of Razgar) v Secretary of State for the Home*

Department [2004] UKHL 27, Lord Bingham at para.9 pointed out that whilst it a "broad term", the court has "wisely eschewed any attempt to define it comprehensively." So, what does it cover? In *Pretty v UK* (2002) 35 E.H.R.R. 1 at pp.61–62, the ECtHR noted that private life covered the:

"physical and psychological integrity of a person (*X & Y v Netherlands* (1985) 8 EHRR 235 at para [22]), it ... embraces aspects of an individual's physical and social identity. Elements such as, for example, gender identification, name and sexual orientation and sexual life fall within the personal sphere protected by Article 8. Article 8 also protects a right to personal development, and the right to establish and develop relationships with other human beings and the outside world ... the court considers that the notion of personal autonomy is an important principle ... "

At a general level, the right covers all aspects of a person's physical identity and their freedom to live as they might choose. It includes elements such as a person's physical and moral integrity, their identity (including personal information), appearance, gender, sexual orientation and physical searches to the person.

In *Evans v UK* (2006) 43 E.H.R.R. 21, the ECtHR felt that in addition to the above, art.8 also incorporates the right to respect both the decision to become and not to become a parent. In this case, Evans had undergone cancer treatment prior to which she had frozen some of her eggs which had been fertilised by her then boyfriend with his consent pursuant to the Human Fertilisation and Embryology Act 1990. The Act provided that either party could withdraw their consent at any stage up to the point of implantation and this was explained to both parties. Their relationship later failed and the boyfriend withdrew his consent for further use of the embryos. The ECtHR concluded that there was no violation of Evans' art.8 rights. The UK had not upset the fair balance required under the article nor had they exceeded their margin of appreciation in adopting in the Human Fertilisation and Embryology Act 1990.

(a)   *Physical and psychological integrity of a person*

In *Costello-Roberts v UK* (1995) E.H.R.R. 112, the court considered that "private life" **23–005** covered a person's physical and moral integrity. Costello-Roberts, a young boy at boarding school, had received corporal punishment consisting of three "whacks" of a slipper on his clothed bottom. This was in accordance with the school's disciplinary rules. He argued a breach of arts 3 and 8. In a unanimous decision, the court found the punishment did not come within the scope of art.8 as it did not have a sufficiently serious effect of the applicant's moral or physical integrity.

It also extends to things such as medical treatment including the taking of samples without consent. In *Whitefield v General Medical Council* [2002] UKPC 62, their Lordships accepted that any medical treatment including the taking of samples without consent is an interference with art.8(1). On the facts of the case it was held that a doctor with a history of alcoholism who was required to submit to testing to establish whether he had been drinking engaged art.8(1) but was a lawful interference. The interference pursued the legitimate aim of protection of health and the rights and freedoms of others and was necessary in a democratic society (at para.31).

(b) *Physical and social identity*

(i) Personal information and photographs

23–006   Personal information and photographs are capable of attracting the protection of art.8. Information about a person's health (see *Campbell v MGN Ltd* below), private conversations (*Khan v UK*), DNA samples (*Att-Gen's Reference (No.3 of 1999)* [2000] UKHL 63) and documentation clearly fall within the article.

The holding, disclosure and refusal to allow access to such personal information may constitute an interference with the right. In *Baker v Secretary of State for Home Department* [2001] U.K.H.R.R. 1275, the Home Secretary refused to disclose to Baker whether information on him was held by the security services. Baker made an application pursuant to the Data Protection Act 1998, but was informed that the security services were exempted from the Act, pursuant to a certificate issued by the Secretary of State. The court found that the certificate imposed a blanket exemption regardless of whether there was a national security issue. Such a blanket exemption was a breach of art.8.

Protection can also extend to the sale of personal information. In *Robertson v Wakefield Metropolitan District Council* [2001] EWHC (Admin) 915 at para.34, the applicant contended that the sale of the Electoral Register to commercial organisations was a violation of art.8 (Note this was prior to the Representation of the People Act which allowed registrants to indicate consent to the dissemination of details which is compliant with art.8). The court felt that it was not simply the raw data (names and addresses) but also the anticipated use that the information would be put to (i.e. marketing purposes) that engaged art.8.

It is also clear that photographs come under this interest if they are of a private nature. Baroness Hale in *Campbell* at para.154 found that the photograph of Ms Campbell leaving a Narcotics Anonymous meeting came within art.8.

(ii) Appearance

23–007   Private life includes personal dignity and appearance. Therefore, a requirement to wear a particular type of uniform such as a prison uniform may engage art.8. In *McFeely v UK* (1981) 3 E.H.R.R. 161, the Commission found this to be the case, but concluded that such an interference was justified in accordance with art.8(2) in the interests of public safety and prevention of crime.

(iii)   Gender and sexual orientation

Sexual orientation and fulfilment are bound up in respect for private life. Not only does   **23–008**
it cover within a person's home, but it might also cover the workplace. In *Smith &*
Grady v UK (2000) 29 E.H.R.R. 493, the applicants were members of the Armed
Forces. Pursuant to government policy prohibiting homosexuals from serving in the
armed forces, the applicants were interviewed about their sexual orientation and subsequently dismissed. The ECtHR found not only that art.8 was engaged, but that the
policy was an interference with the right.

A number of cases in the UK have concerned a person's right to change their gender
and the lack of legal recognition of such a change. In the UK, a person's sex is
determined by the criteria set down in *Corbett v Corbett* [1970] 2 W.L.R. 1306. A
person's gender is determined by their biology, looking at the gonadal, chromosomal
and genital tests to see whether they are congruent, medical intervention is excluded. In
Goodwin v UK (2002) 35 E.H.R.R. 18, the ECtHR found a violation in the UK's refusal
to recognise a new legal status for transsexuals. Similarly, in *Bellinger v Bellinger* [2003]
UKHL 21, the House of Lords found the Matrimonial Causes Act 1973 to be
incompatible with art.8 because there was no provision for the recognition of gender
reassignment so as to allow a marriage between a gender reassigned person and another
to be legal.

(iv)   Searches of a person

Individuals are often required to submit to a body and belongings search whether by   **23–009**
police officers or by security guards when entering public buildings. This can be effected
by a physical search, or by requiring a person to pass through an x-ray machine. In *R.*
(Gillan) v Commissioner of Police of the Metropolis [2006] UKHL 12, the House of
Lords considered whether stop and search powers in ss.44 to 47 of the Terrorism Act
2000 breached art.8 of the ECHR. Lord Bingham at [28] stated that in order to engage
respect for private life under art.8, intrusions had to reach a certain level of seriousness
and that, accordingly, an ordinary superficial search to the person or perhaps the
opening of bags, akin to that undertaken at airports, could scarcely be said to reach this
level. In *Wainwright v UK* [2007] 44 E.H.R.R. 40 the ECtHR held that a requirement to
submit to a strip-search would generally amount to an interference with the right to
respect for private life under art.8.

(c)   *Personal autonomy*

Whilst art.8(1) protects personal autonomy, it can only be taken so far and does not   **23–010**
include the right to choose to die; see *Pretty v UK*, above. The taking of films and video
without consent can also engage the idea of personal autonomy. In *Douglas v Hello*,
Sedley L.J. felt that the unauthorised photographs of a "celebrity" wedding was an
interference with personal autonomy (at [26]).

(d)   *What does not come with "private life"?*

23–011   Some matters are, however, excluded, the case of *Orejudos v Royal Borough of Kensington and Chelsea* [2003] EWCA Civ 1967 providing a good example. Orejudos was a homeless person and, as such, was provided with temporary accommodation. He had to sign a contract which stated that he was required to stay at the accommodation every night, otherwise his accommodation would be cancelled and, further, that if wished to stay away from the accommodation, he should discuss the reason with the relevant person in advance. The applicant was absent on about ten occasions, and his accommodation cancelled. He contended that the condition he reside there every night interfered with his freedom of action and his right to live as an ordinary citizen. Whilst recognising the width of the article, the court did not feel that art.8 was engaged and in doing so referred to the decision of the ECtHR in *Bensaid v UK* (2001) 33 E.H.R.R. 10 which had stated that "not every act or measure which adversely affects moral or physical integrity will interfere with the right to respect for private life guaranteed by Article 8". The Court of Appeal felt that the conditions imposed were an ordinary and necessary part of providing accommodation and, consequently, did not come with art.8. Thus, it would appear that even though private life is given a broad interpretation, not everything comes its scope.

Equally, in the recent decision *R. (on the application of Countryside Alliance) v Att-Gen* [2007] UKHL 52, the House of Lords in considering whether the ban on fox hunting engaged art.8, affirmed the decision of the Court of Appeal on the point that it did not engage art.8. The applicant's contention that they were using their own land for hunting and a decline in hunting was likely to jeopardise their homes and livelihood was based on an over wide definition of the ambit of art.8.

2.   Family life

23–012   The second interest protected under art.8 is right to respect for family life. The definition of family in Convention terms is broad and given the diversity of family relations it is impossible to set down a precise meaning. There is a presumption that close personal ties exist between parent and child. In *Ahmut v The Netherlands* (1996) 24 E.H.R.R. 60 at [60], the ECtHR stated, "from the moment of the child's birth and by the very fact of it, there exists between him and his parents a bond amounting to 'family life', which subsequent events cannot break save in exceptional circumstances." Equally in *Marckx v Belgium* (1979) 2 E.H.R.R. 330 at [45] the ECtHR recognised that family life also "includes at least the ties between near relatives, for instance, those between grandparents and grandchildren, since such relatives play a considerable part in family life".

It is obvious in the two cases above that the relationships mentioned are close. However, some relationships have proved more problematic. In *Kroon v Netherlands* (1995) 19 E.H.R.R. 263 a child was born to a stable relationship between Mrs Kroon and Mr Zerrouk. At the time Mrs Kroon was still married. Under Dutch law, Mr Zerrouk could not obtain recognition of his paternity unless Mr Kroon denied paternity. Zerrouk claimed violation of art.8. The court stated:

"The notion of family life in Article 8 is not solely confined to marriage-based relationships, and may encompass other de facto 'family ties' where partners are living together outside marriage. As a rule, living together may be a requirement for such a relationship, exceptionally other factors may also serve to demonstrate that a relationship has sufficient constancy to create de facto 'family ties'."

This statement from Kroon suggests the question which the court typically has to consider is whether there is a close personal relationship with sufficient constancy to create de facto family ties. It is therefore largely a question of fact depending on the existence, in practice, of close personal ties. In *X, Y and Z v UK* (1997) 24 E.H.R.R. 143 at [36], the ECtHR pointed to a number of factors which may be relevant when determining the closeness of the relationship. These include, whether the couple have lived together, the length of their relationship, and whether they have demonstrated their commitment to each other by having children. This case concerned a transsexual (X) who had undergone gender reassignment surgery and was in a stable relationship with (Y). Together they had applied for and been granted treatment for assisted conception which resulted in the birth of (Z). The court found that de facto ties linked the three applicants and found that art.8 was applicable.

A further problem area has concerned the issue of adoption. One of the first domestic cases to consider such an issue was *Singh v Entry Clearance Officer New Delhi* [2004] EWCA Civ 1075. In this case, the question for the court was whether family life existed in a relationship between a seven-year-old Indian boy and his adoptive family who were settled and resident in the UK. The boy had been refused entry clearance to join his adoptive parents on the basis that his Indian adoption was not recognised in the UK and, additionally, ties with his natural parents had not been severed. It was argued that such a refusal was a violation of art.8. The boy lived with his natural parents and siblings in India, but regarded his natural parents as his uncle and aunt. His adoptive family communicated weekly with him, financially supported him, and made decisions concerning his welfare. They also met and stayed together a least once or twice a year, often for several weeks. The young boy regarded them as his parents. The Court of Appeal agreed with the decision of the adjudicator who had found the existence of a family life.

3. Home

The third interest protected under art.8 extends to a persons home. As Sir Edward Coke **23–013** (*Coke's Institutes of the laws of England*, 1628) wrote "A man's house is his castle and each man's home is his safest refuge". As with the previous two interests, the ECtHR has given "home" a wide meaning. Whether a place in question comes within the meaning of home requires a pragmatic approach. It is essentially "where a person lives and to which he returns and which forms the centre of his existence", since "home" is not a legal term of art. Article 8 is not directed to the protection of property interests or contractual rights however (see Lord Bingham in *Harrow London Borough Council v Qazi* [2003] UKHL 43 at [8]).

For the purposes of the "home", it is not necessary to establish a proprietary interest.

In *Harrow London Borough Council v Qazi* [2003] UKHL 43, Qazi lived with his wife and child in a property under a secured tenancy, the freehold belonging to the council. Following the departure of his wife and child, Qazi gave the council four weeks' written notice to quit in accordance with the terms of the tenancy. Qazi was informed, first, that the tenancy had come to an end and was invited to make an application for the tenancy in his sole name and secondly, that there was no guarantee he would be granted the tenancy. His subsequent application was unsuccessful on the ground that he was not, as a single person, entitled to family-sized accommodation. Possession proceedings were initiated by the council. The House of Lords held that the property was Qazi's home because even though the tenancy had been brought to an end, his residence had not (at this time he had been resident for eight years). The property continued to be the place where he lived and so was his home.

Obviously, "home" encapsulates home in the widely-accepted sense, but it also covers premises where the owner has been absent for a period of time, so long as there are "sufficient continuing links" with the property. In *Gillow v UK* (1986) 11 E.H.R.R. 335, the applicants had established a home in Guernsey in 1958. In 1960 they left Guernsey but retained ownership of the house. They kept their furniture in it and always intended to return. During this period, the house was rented out. Some 19 years later (1979), they returned but were required to apply for a licence to occupy their home which was refused. The court at [48] concluded that art.8 was engaged as they were satisfied the Gillows had not established any other home elsewhere in the UK. Although the applicants had been absent for 19 years, they had retained sufficient continuing links with the Guernsey property for it to be considered their home. The above test was elaborated upon by the *Commission in Buckley v United Kingdom* (1996) 23 E.H.R.R. 101:

> " 'Home' is an autonomous concept which does not depend on classification under domestic law. Whether or not a particular habitation constitutes a 'home' which attracts the protection of Article 8(1) will depend on the factual circumstances, namely, the existence of sufficient and continuous links."

We have seen above that home covers the place where one is ordinarily resident and can cover property where there are continuing links. It also extends to maintaining a situation to which a person has become accustomed to living in. In *Coughlan v N and E Devon Health Authority* [2000] All E.R. 850 for example, a decision to close a care home which was the primary residence of a disabled women and which had been promised for life, was held both to engage and violate art.8. This decision, though apparently wide, does not preclude closure of a home or eviction. It merely makes clear to the decision maker that when considering such a course of action, due regard is given to the person's art.8 rights.

"Home" may also extend to business premises and a professional person's office. This was the finding of the ECtHR in *Niemietz v Germany* (1992) 16 E.H.R.R. 97, at [29 and 30] and accepted in *R. (on the application of Miller Gardner Solicitors) v Minshull Street Crown Court* [2002] EWHC (Admin) 3077. In both cases a search of offices was found to engage art.8(1).

It is important to note however, that the right to respect for home is an entirely different concept from the right to a home. Requiring that everyone is provided with a home is an economic and social right to which the ECHR does not extend. Therefore, respect for home life does not extend to the right to be provided with a home. A point made clearly by Lord Hope in *Qazi* above at [69]:

> "The emphasis is on the person's home as a place where he is entitled to be free from arbitrary interference. Article 8(1) does not concern itself with the person's right to the peaceful enjoyment of his home as a possession or as a property right."

It is clear from Lord Hope's statement above that the right to peaceful enjoyment of a home is not automatically covered by art.8(1). It is more appropriately dealt with under Protocol 1, art.1 (peaceful enjoyment of property). However there have been cases concerning the quality of home life. In *Powell and Rayner v UK* (1990) 12 E.H.R.R. 355 the applicants complained about disturbance from daytime aircraft noise, the ECtHR held that art.8 was relevant since "the quality of [each] applicant's private life and the scope for enjoying the amenities of his home [had] been adversely affected by the noise generated by aircraft using Heathrow Airport".

Similarly, in *López Ostra v Spain* (1995) 20 E.H.R.R. 277 people in a village near an industrial plant which treated waste water complained of fumes and smells which made their lives intolerable. The court recognised (at [96]) that art.8 could include a right to protection from severe environmental pollution, since such a problem might "affect individuals well-being and prevent them from enjoying their homes in such a way as to affect their private and family life adversely, without, however, seriously endangering their health".

In *Hatton v UK* (2002) 34 E.H.R.R. 1, residents close to Heathrow airport complained that noise from increased night flights disrupted their home life. The European Court found that though neither Heathrow nor the airplanes were owned by the government, they were under an obligation to ensure that reasonable and appropriate steps were taken to uphold the resident's rights. In this case, the government had failed to strike an appropriate balance between the interests of the residents and the economic welfare of the country. This decision was subsequently overturned by the Grand Chamber in *Hatton v UK* (2003) 37 E.H.R.R. 28 who concluded that this was within the state's margin of appreciation and that the government was better placed to conclude that the economic benefits outweighed the rights of those affected.

4.   Correspondence

The final category of interest protected under art.8(1), correspondence, is arguably the **23–014** easiest to define. As well as covering paper letters, it can also cover electronic mail and telephone conversations. In *Halford v UK* (1997) 24 E.H.R.R. 523, telephone calls conducted from business premises was held to engage art.8 as there was a reasonable expectation of privacy as the applicant had not been made aware that her phone calls might be intercepted. In *Copland v UK* (2007) 45 E.H.R.R. 37, the applicant was employed at a public college as a personal assistant to the College Principal. At the instigation of the Deputy Principal, her telephone, e-mail and internet usage were subjected to monitoring. The applicant alleged that the monitoring activity that took place amounted to an interference with her right to respect for private life and correspondence. The government argued that the monitoring took place in order to ascertain whether the applicant was making excessive use of college facilities for personal purposes. The ECtHR noted that telephone calls from business premises are covered by notions of correspondence and believed that it logically followed that e-mails sent from work should be similarly protected. They equally thought that information derived from the monitoring of personal internet usage was likewise protected. The court found that the collection and storage of personal information relating to the applicant's telephone, as well as to her e-mail and internet usage, without her knowledge, amounted to an interference with her right to respect for her private life and correspondence within the meaning of art.8.

The ECtHR has afforded special protection to legal correspondence which often also engages art.6 (access to the courts). *Golder v UK* (1979–80) 1 E.H.R.R. 524 and *Foxley v UK* (2001) 31 E.H.R.R. 25 provide examples of two such cases. In both, mail between the applicants and their solicitors was intercepted and in both cases, a breach of art.8 was found.

5.   Positive obligations

23–015   In a majority of cases, a violation of art.8(1) will be alleged against the state or government directly. However, the ECtHR has also recognised that in some circumstances the state has a positive obligation to ensure that art.8 is respected. In *Bellinger v Bellinger* [2003] UKHL 21, for example, the House of Lords issued a declaration of incompatibility against s.11(c) of the Matrimonial Causes Act 1973 as it made no provision for the recognition of gender reassignment in marriage. This was based on the government's failure to positively act in this area.

In *Evan v UK* (discussed above), the ECtHR felt that whilst the domestic courts had dealt with the issues regarding Ms Evans right to be a parent as a negative obligation, they felt that it was more appropriate to analyse the case as one concerning positive obligations. By the Human Fertilisation and Embryology Act 1990, the state had chosen to establish a detailed legal framework authorising and regulating IVF treatment. The aim of the Act is to facilitate conception where parties would otherwise find it impossible or difficult to conceive by ordinary means. The ECtHR thought that the question was whether there existed a positive obligation on the State to ensure that a woman who had embarked on treatment for the specific purpose of giving birth to a genetically-related child should be permitted to proceed to implantation of the embryo. This was notwithstanding the withdrawal of consent by her former partner, the male gamete provider. However, the court went on to say that is was not of central importance whether the case was examined in the context of positive or negative obligations. They felt that in both situations, regard had to be had to the fair balance that has to be struck between the competing interests of the individual and of the community as a whole.

In *Von Hannover v Germany* (2005) 40 E.H.R.R. 1 the ECtHR considered whether there was a positive obligation on the state to protect a person's private life in the context of press intrusion. The case concerned a number of photographs which had been taken of Princess Caroline of Monaco. The majority of the photos were taken in public places, though some were of the Princess and her children at a private beach club. The German courts allowed publication of many of the photographs, but prohibited publication of the photographs including her children as this was regarded as breaching her right to family protection. Princess Caroline took her case to Strasbourg complaining about the lack of adequate state protection for her private life and image. The ECtHR re-iterated that art.8 extended to aspects relating to personal identity, such as a person's name or a person's picture, and could cover a "zone of interaction of a person with others, even in a public context". The court confirmed that there might be positive obligations on the state to ensure effective respect for private or family life, including the adoption of measures to ensure respect for private life in the sphere or relations of individuals between themselves (i.e. a law of privacy). They recognised that the boundary between the state's positive and negative obligations under the provision did not lend itself to precise definition but that regard must be had to the fair balance that has to be struck between the competing interests of the individual and of the community as a whole; in both contexts the state enjoys a certain margin of appreciation". The court found that art.8 was engaged and, further, that state protection had been inadequate in the present case.

RESTRICTIONS ON PRIVATE LIFE

Article 8 is a qualified right and, therefore, the state might legitimately interfere with it. **23–016**
Article 8(2) lists the situations in which the state is permitted to interfere:

> " ... in the interests of national security, public safety or the economic well being of the country, for the prevention of disorder or crime, for the protection of health or morals, or for the protection of the rights and freedoms of others."

Such interference must not only fit into one of the legitimate aims above but also accord with law and be necessary in a democratic society in that it fulfils a pressing social need and is proportionate to the aim pursued. As with many of the qualified rights, it is reasonably simple for a public authority to argue their interference falls within one of the legitimate aims. In many cases the interference can fit into more than one aim and this should be borne in mind when considering the cases below.

1. National security

National security was the justification pleaded in the *Baker v Secretary of State for*   **23–017**
Home Department [2001] U.K.H.R.R. 1275 discussed above. Baker's application under the Data Protection Act 1998 for information held on himself was refused. The Secretary of State had issued a blanket exclusion for the provision of data to the Security Services on the basis of protecting national security. The court held the blanket exemption to be wider than was necessary to protect national security. Thus, while the

interference was in accordance with a law, the Data Protection Act 1998 and in pursuant of a legitimate aim, it was not necessary as some personal data could be released which would not endanger national security.

2.   Public safety or the economic well being of the country

23–018   Public safety was used as the justification to deny a prisoner the enjoyment of conjugal rights in *X v United Kingdom* (1975) 2 D.R. 105. Here, the Commission concluded that a system prohibiting conjugal visits to persons detained in prison was covered by the provisions of art.8(2) allowing interference with the right to respect for family life on the ground that it was necessary in the interests of public safety. Therefore, interference with X's rights was justified.

In the case of *Hatton v UK*, the government sought to justify the interference with the applicants art.8(1) rights on the basis that night flights were necessary for the economic well being of the country. The government claimed, for example, some flights from the Far East could arrive at Heathrow only by departing very late in the night which would give rise to "serious passenger discomfort" and a possible loss of competitiveness. Also, the Grand Chamber accepted that there was an economic interest in maintaining a full service to London.

3.   Prevention of disorder or crime

23–019   Interference with an individual's art.8 rights can be justified on the grounds of prevention of disorder or crime. Such interference may include: interception with correspondence and other forms of communication; surveillance; body and property searches; and deportation. An example can be found in *R. (on the application of Samaroo) v Secretary of State for Home Department* [2001] EWCA Civ 1139 where the applicant was deported following his conviction for serious drug offences. He was, however, married to a British citizen and had a child by her and, consequently, had been granted indefinite leave to remain as a foreign spouse. It was accepted by the Court of Appeal that a deportation order made in respect of a person convicted of serious criminal offences was a measure taken in pursuance of a legitimate aim, namely, the prevention of crime and disorder.

A number of cases in this area concern the rights of prisoners. In *Golder v UK* (1975) 1 E.H.R.R. 524 the ECtHR accepted that such an interference with correspondence between a prisoner and his solicitor could be in the interests of the prevention of disorder or crime. However, the authorities must have "sufficient reason to believe that it (is) "necessary" to impose restrictions for the purpose of the prevention of disorder or crime" and on the facts of the case no such reason was found. In *P & Q v Secretary of State for the Home Department* [2001] EWCA Civ 1151, two mothers who were serving substantial prison sentences complained that prison policy forbidding their babies from remaining with them after 18 months of age violated their right to respect for family life. The Court of Appeal found the interference to be at the serious end of the scale as it concerned not only the mother's right to respect for family life, but also the child's.

They concluded that the Prison Service was entitled to have a policy that children should cease to reside with mothers in prison once they reached 18 months old, and that such an interference could be justified under art.8(2) in the interests of public safety or for the prevention of disorder or crime, as well as for the protection of health and protection of the rights of the child. However, having regard to the policy's stated objective of promoting the welfare of the child and of the right to respect for family life afforded to the mothers and children, the Prison Service was not entitled to operate the policy rigidly and insist that all children should leave their mothers.

4.   Protection of health or morals

In *Wainwright v UK* (2007) 44 E.H.R.R. 40, two applicants were subjected to a strip   **23–020**
search whilst visiting a relative in prison who was believed to be involved in drug offences. The court held the interference with their private life was in accordance with the law (the Prison Act 1952 and its rules) and, additionally, pursued the legitimate aim of preventing crime and protecting the health of the prisoners. However, the court were not satisfied that the searches were proportionate to the legitimate aim due to the intimate and specific manner in which they were carried out.

5.   Protection of the rights and freedoms of others

This is fairly open-ended and might operate where the art.8 right comes into conflict   **23–021**
with one of the other rights. Three examples of this justification are considered below:

- Article 6—fair trial. Where the necessity of a fair trial is at issue, then this will usually justify interference with art.8;

- Article 8—private life of another. In some circumstances, it may be necessary to balance the private life of one individual against that of another. For example, in *Evans* (above at para.23–015) both the domestic courts and the ECtHR had to balance Ms Evans right to be a parent against her former partner's right not to be a parent;

- Article 10—freedom of expression. Where art.8 is asserted indirectly through breach of confidence (discussed further below) the court will balance both rights. In *Campbell v MGN Ltd*, Lord Hope at [105] said that "the right to privacy which lies at the heart of an action for breach of confidence has to be balanced against the right of the media to impart information to the public. And the right of the media to impart information to the public has to be balanced in its turn against the respect that must be given to private life". The Court of Appeal in *McKennitt v Ash* [2006] EWCA Civ 1714 confirmed a number of principles which should be taken into account when balancing both rights. This case concerned the publication of an unauthorised biography about Loreena McKennitt (a Canadian folk singer) by Niema Ash (a former friend).

McKennitt had sought an injunction restraining further publication. The principles set down by the case are:

(1) neither article has, as such, precedence over the other. This is despite the inclusion of HRA s.12 which appears to afford extended protection to art.10;

(2) where conflict arises between the values under arts 8 and 10, an "intense focus" is necessary upon the comparative importance of the specific rights being claimed in the individual case;

(3) the court must take into account the justifications for interfering with or restricting each right;

(4) so too, the proportionality test must be applied to each.

Protection of the right of another can also be used to justify interference without reference to any specific right contained within the Convention. In *Copland v UK*, a case concerning the interception of Copland's personal data, the government asserted that in doing so the college was pursuing the legitimate aim of protecting the rights and freedoms of others by ensuring that the facilities provided by a publicly funded employer were not abused. The court concluded that the interference had no basis in law so did not go on to consider the validity of the aim.

Intrusion by Surveillance

23–022   One area of interference which arises in relation to all of the interests discussed above is that of government surveillance and the extent to which the state can legitimately intrude on private activities through surveillance. Nowadays, there is a great deal of advanced technology which might be utilised to intercept or intrude on people's private life. Such technology includes, but is not limited to, closed circuit television, telephone-tapping and bugging, video recording, long-range lens photography, and so on. These are used by the government for a number of reasons, all of which are capable of falling within the legitimate aims in art.8(2). Examples include:

- the Security Services and Scotland Yard may use such technology to bug a suspected terrorist's property;

- local authorities rely on CCTV to prevent and detect crime;

- television detectors to catch television licence evaders.

Following the decision in *Malone v UK* (1985) 7 E.H.R.R. 14, where the ECtHR found that telephone tapping of Malone's phone was not in accordance with a law, the UK passed the Interception of Communications Act 1985. Following the passing of the HRA, the Regulation of Investigatory Powers Act 2000 (RIPA) was passed to consolidate the use of investigatory powers and ensure compliance with art.8. The Act sets out the circumstances in which postal and electronic communication may be intercepted lawfully with or without warrant. Circumstances in which an interception without a warrant would be considered lawful include taping a conversation between a kidnapper and a relative of the hostage (s.3); for the management and maintenance of order and discipline in prisons (s.4) and the recording of transactions in a business call centre (s.4). Interception with a warrant is regulated by s.5 and is allowed where the Secretary of State for the Home Department "believes ... it is necessary and that the conduct authorised is proportionate to what is sought to be achieved in the interests of:

- national security;

- preventing or detecting serious crime;

- safeguarding the economic well being of the United Kingdom;

- to facilitate compliance with international agreements for crime prevents in circumstance where the detection or prevention of serious crime might by involved."

Secondary legislation made under powers conferred by this Act have extended the rights to intercept information and provide that employers could record or monitor employees" communications without consent (The Telecommunications (Lawful Business Practice) Regulations 2000 (2000/2699)). (Note in *Copland v UK*, the Telecommunications (Lawful Business Practice) Regulations 2000 was not in force).

The existence of such legislation does not mean that such intrusions go unchallenged, rather, the court will look at the particular circumstances of the intrusion to check it is justified according to law and, particularly, that the intrusion is no more than necessary to achieve the objectives.

HORIZONTAL ACTIONS

1. Horizontal effect of the Human Rights Act 1998

Since the HRA came into force, an obligation is imposed on public authorities to respect private and family life in their actions and decisions which are subject to legitimate interference. The HRA is intended to confer obligations on public authorities and have vertical effect, i.e. from the state to the individual (see Ch.21 for discussion on the meaning of public authority). However, it has been argued that the HRA is not limited to vertical application, but can be utilised indirectly in claims between private entities, thereby introducing the concept of "horizontal effect". This is the idea that a private person or body has a responsibility not to interfere with the Convention rights of another private person or body; the line of responsibility running horizontally. Horizontal effect is achieved by the obligation imposed on the courts to act compatibly with human rights (s.6(1)). This includes their activities in interpreting and developing the common law. It would seem though that if a private party wishes to invoke a Convention right against another private party, there must be a pre-existing cause of action against the other private party upon which to "hang" the Convention right. In

23–023

this area, where a private individual wishes to allege that another private individual has interfered with his private life, the cause of action is breach of confidence. It is in the development of the modified law of confidence that we can see the real effect the HRA has had on domestic law.

2.   Private law action where article 8 plays an important part: modified breach of confidence

23–024   Following the decision of *Von Hannover v Germany* (2006) 43 E.H.R.R. 7, a positive obligation is now imposed on the state to ensure adequate protection within the private sphere. In the UK, the courts have clearly stated there is no right to privacy in domestic law between private parties (see *Secretary of State for the Home Department v Wainwright* [2003] UKHL 53). However, the UK courts have sought to give effect to the positive obligation through developing the law of confidence and "shoehorning" the jurisprudence of arts 8 and 10 into it, a point made clear in *Douglas v Hello (No.3)* [2006] Q.B. 125 and *Campbell v MGN Limited* [2004] UKHL 22.

In considering such actions, a two stage analysis provides assistance. Firstly, the applicant complaining of intrusion must establish they have a reasonable expectation of privacy and secondly, the courts will balance the applicant's expectation of privacy against the other party's right to freedom of expression.

(a)   *Is there a reasonable expectation of privacy in respect of the material?*

23–025   To establish this, the applicant must demonstrate that the information would be protected as one of the four protected interests found within art.8(1). Fenwick and Phillipson make this point in *Media Freedom Under the Human Rights Act* (OUP, 2006), "the test propounded of a reasonable expectation of privacy, of whether the information is obviously private is to be structured by reference to the Article 8 case law" (at p.764).

The first problem that might arise here is where there is no pre-existing relationship of confidence between the parties. An obligation of confidence might arise from the defendant acquiring information by unlawful or surreptitious means, or knowing that the information received was private. In *Douglas v Hello! (No.3)* [2005] EWCA Civ 595, Lord Phillips C.J. thought that, "information [would] be confidential if it is available to one person (or a group of people) and not generally available to others, provided that the person (or group) who possesses the information does not intend that it should be available to others". He further added:

> "What is the nature of 'private information'? It seems to us that it must include information that is personal to the person who possesses it and that he does not intend shall be imparted to the general public. The nature of the information, or the form in which it is kept, may suffice to make it plain that the information satisfies these criteria." (para.83)

In *McKennitt v Ash*, Eady J. considered that disclosure of relationships with others can be protected. This is so even if it occurs in public or if the person seeking publication waives their own privacy and asserts his/her right to free speech. The court also said that it was irrelevant whether the information revealed was true or false.

If the information is already in the public domain, any protection afforded will be lost. However, just because a person has revealed some aspects of their personal life, does not mean that every aspect of their private life is open to scrutiny.

(b)   *Balance of the two articles (articles 8 and 10)*

Once it is established that there is a reasonable expectation of privacy, the court must **23–026** balance this against the other party's right to freedom of expression. The court asks whether there is a sufficient public interest in the disclosure of the information to outweigh the right to privacy so that in all the circumstances the interests of the owner of private information must yield to the right of expression. In *Mckennitt v Ash*, the Court of Appeal made it clear that the two issues (reasonable expectation of privacy and the balancing act) are separate issues and although, there is some overlap they should be dealt with separately.

In *Vonn Hannover* (above), the ECtHR's view was that when considering both arts 8 and 10, the decisive factor in balancing the competing interests was the "contribution that the published articles made to a debate of general interest". The court drew a distinction between reporting facts, even controversial ones, which were capable of contributing to debate of general interest, and those that did not. In the former circumstance, the press had a "watchdog" role to impart information on matters of pubic interest. In the latter instance the press were satisfying the public's need for gossip. In *Vonn Hannover*, the ECtHR felt that the photographs taken of Princess Caroline made no such contribution as she exercised no official function and they related exclusively to details of her private life. The public did not have a legitimate interest in knowing where the applicant was and how she behaved in her private life, even if she appeared in places that could not always be regarded as secluded. Even if there was such a public interest, this would have to yield to the right to effective protection of family life.

The House of Lords applied the ECtHR's reasoning of *Von Hannover v Germany* in *Campbell v MGN Limited* [2004] UKHL 22. Here, their Lordships were required to determine whether the publication of photographs of the model Naomi Campbell leaving a drug rehabilitation session breached her right to confidentiality, or whether this was outweighed by the Newspaper's right to freedom of expression, especially given Campbell's denials of drug problems. Lord Hope, who gave the leading opinion for the majority, set out a number of factors that the court considered in this case:

(1)   Importance of the "privacy" element on the particular facts. Lord Hope attached great weight to the fact that the details published concerned detailed reportage on attendance at Narcotics Anonymous with accompanying pictures.

(2)   Person's right to privacy may be limited by the public's interest in knowing about certain traits of her personality and private life. Lord Hope stated that

the mere fact of celebrity was not enough to deprive somebody of their right to privacy. On the facts he felt that there was no compelling need for the public to know the name of the organisation Campbell was attending and to provide details of the frequency and timings of attendance.

(3)   When determining on which side the balance should be struck a margin of appreciation should be granted to the journalist in their choice of how to present a news story. In doubtful cases the margin of appreciation should incline a court to find for the journalist. However, in the instant case the text giving information about the Narcotics Anonymous meetings was accompanied by pictures taken in secret of Naomi Campbell emerging from the meeting. Lord Hope argued that the photograph was gratuitous and added no credibility to the story.

The court held that the publication of the fact that Campbell had taken drugs and was seeking treatment was necessary to set the record straight. However, the additional information, including the photographs, was an unjustified intrusion into her private life. Taking these factors into account, and balancing the competing interests, Lord Hope concluded that Campbell's right to privacy under art.8 outweighed the Mirror Group's freedom of expression under art.10.

In *McKennitt v Ash*, two main issues were considered in assessing the relative balance. First, whether there was a legitimate public interest because McKennitt was a public figure and, secondly, whether bad behaviour on the part of the applicant pointed towards disclosure. In dealing with the first, the court considered the principle in *Von Hannover* and contrasted the earlier domestic case of *A v B & C* [2002] EWCA Civ 331. The *A v B & C* case concerned a Premiership footballer who had affairs with two women. The women subsequently sold their stories and the footballer sought an injunction. Lord Hoffmann recognised that a public figure was entitled to have their privacy respected in certain circumstances, but that equally such public figures should expect and accept that their actions will be more closely scrutinised by the media, especially where, for example, they are role models, whose conduct could be emulated by others, or where they have courted publicity. Lord Hoffman felt that the degree of privacy that A was entitled to was "very modest", the Court of Appeal were reluctant to protect the relationships and A lost his case. The court in *McKennitt* thought that the "the width of the rights given to the media by *A v B* could not be reconciled with *Von Hannover*". They preferred the approach taken in *Von Hannover* and did not consider themselves bound by the earlier Court of Appeal decision in *A v B & C* where *Von Hannover* had obviously not been considered. However, the court did not overrule *A v B & C*.

In dealing with the second argument, the Court of Appeal referred to the decision of Eady J. in the High Court where he had set a high threshold test. Whilst casting doubt on the test as being too high, the court gave credence to the idea that a high degree of misbehaviour from the celebrity was required beyond the "mere peccadilloes of celebrity life".

This area of law continues to develop and two recent cases have followed the approach taken by *Von Hannover* and *McKennitt*. The case of *HRH Prince of Wales v Associated Newspapers* [2006] EWCA Civ 1776 concerned extracts from Prince Charles journal written during a visit to Hong Kong. Prince Charles contended that the journal set out private/personal thoughts. The Newspaper argued that the information was not confidential as it was of a political nature and related to the Prince Charles' public life which it was in the public interest to reveal. The court concluded that the claimant had a "reasonable expectation of privacy" in respect of the journals, and that in balancing the competing interests there was a strong public interest in preserving the confidentiality of journals within a private office. This justified the interference with the defendant's right to freedom of expression.

By contrast, in *Lord Browne v Associated Newspapers* [2007] EWCA Civ 205, Lord Browne was unable to restrain publication by Associated Newspapers Ltd of allegations about him. The court concluded that statements made by him did not attract a reasonable expectation of privacy. When reported in the media, much was made of the fact that Lord Browne had apparently misled the court as to his personal behaviour. The question was posed as to whether art.8 rights could be "lost" in a situation where an individual had lied in court. Because no expectation of privacy was identified, this remained a rhetorical question.

FURTHER READING

Hoffman, D. and Rowe, J. *Human Rights in the UK: An Introduction to the Human Rights Act 1998* 2nd edn (Pearson Education, 2006)   **23–027**
Merris, A. *Human Rights Law* (Hart Publishing, 2006)

Chapter 24

FREEDOM OF EXPRESSION

INTRODUCTION

Prior to the enactment of the Human Rights Act 1998 (HRA), while individuals had the **24–001** right to do anything not prohibited by law, they did not enjoy the positive right to expression (speech). Since the enactment of the HRA art.10 (expression) of the ECHR has conferred the right on citizens of the United Kingdom to freely express their views. This chapter considers how freedom of expression is protected today in the United Kingdom, with brief consideration of the pre-HRA position under common law.

FREEDOM OF EXPRESSION

1. Constitutional importance of freedom of expression

Freedom of expression constitutes one of the essential foundations of a liberal **24–002** democracy. In *R. v Secretary of State for Home Department Ex p. Simms* [1999] UKHL 33, Lord Steyn made the point definitively when he stated that, "in a democracy it is the primary right: without it an effective rule of law is not possible" (p.125). This notion has been consistently stated by decisions of the European Court of Human Rights where, for example, in the case of *Handyside v UK* (1976) 1 E.H.R.R. 737 the court stated that "freedom of expression constitutes one of the essential foundations of ... a democratic society, one of the basic conditions for its progress and for the development of man" (para.49).

Fenwick, *Civil Liberties and Human Rights in England and Wales* (2002) gives four reasons why freedom of expression has a special position:

(1)   it is a significant instrument of freedom of conscience and self fulfilment in that it advances the growth of an individual. Access to information can stimulate and foster an individual's intellect and moral growth;

(2)   it enables people to contribute to debates about social and moral issues. By allowing the individual the freedom to choose what information he/she receives supports an individual's moral autonomy. The individual can then make informed decisions and contribute to debates on those issues;

(3)   it allows the political discourse which is necessary in any country which aspires to democracy. There is a definite correlation between free speech an the democratic process. The press need to be able to disseminate information concerning governmental affairs so that there can be free and informed debate. In addition, it is through speech that people can influence their government's choice of policy and hold their government accountable. This point is made clearly by Strasbourg who stress the importance of political speech, *Lingens v Austria* (1986) 8 E.H.R.R. 407 and *Castells v Spain* (1992) 14 E.H.R.R. 445;

(4)   it facilitates artistic and scholastic endeavour of all sorts.

The pan-national constitutional significance of freedom of expression ought not to be underestimated, especially where it is enshrined in the constitutional documents of most liberal democracies and famously accounts for the first amendment to the Constitution of the United States of America. Indeed, prior to the incorporation of the ECHR into domestic law, the courts of England and Wales sought to uphold a principle of free expression, particularly where the press was concerned. The mere fact of the HRA has made the protection of the right more acute.

2.   Freedom of expression and free speech

24–003   Freedom of expression, or speech, is a broad freedom covering a number of aspects of a person's right to express their views, whether publicly or privately. However, it is not merely designed to protect the written or spoken word (i.e. speech), but also include things such as artistic expression (see *Wingrove v UK* (1997) 24 E.H.R.R. 1; religious video and *Muller v Switzerland* (1991) 13 E.H.R.R. 212; exhibition of paintings).

3.   Freedom of expression pre-Human Rights Act 1998

24–004   Prior to the HRA individuals were free to express themselves unless prohibited by law; citizens were at liberty to express themselves. Where legislation or other law existed to curb the freedom, for example, the Obscene Publications Act 1959, or the tort of defamation, the courts would take account of freedom of expression in interpreting the legislation. As such, freedom of expression enjoyed some limited protection at common law, Lord Goff stating in *Att-Gen v Guardian Newspapers Ltd (No.2)* [1990] 1 A.C. 109:

"Freedom of speech has existed in this country perhaps as long as, if not longer than, it has existed in any other country in the world. The only difference is that, whereas Article 10 of the Convention ... proceeds to state a fundamental right and then qualify it, we in this country (where everybody is free to do anything, subject only to the provisions of the law) proceed rather upon the assumption of freedom of speech, and turn to our law to discover the established exceptions to it."

This statement was affirmed by Butler-Sloss L.J. in *Derbyshire County Council v Times Newspapers Ltd* [1992] 3 W.L.R. 28 where the Court of Appeal found that a local authority could not sue for libel as it was contrary to the public interest, the decision being later affirmed by the House of Lords in *Derbyshire County Council v Times Newspapers Ltd* [1992] UKHL 5; [1993] 1 A.C. 534.

Indeed, this judicial willingness to protect freedom of expression seemed especially apparent through the 1990s, not only in the case of *Derbyshire County Council* (1992), but also in *Reynolds v Times Newspapers Ltd* [1999] UKHL 45 and *Simms* [2000] 2 A.C. 115. Reynolds, a former Prime Minister of Ireland, brought libel proceedings in respect of publication in The Times newspaper of an article describing the crisis which led to the fall of the coalition government which he had headed. The article gave no account of Reynold's explanation of events and Reynolds sued for defamation. He contended he had been libelled by statements he had lied to the Irish Parliament and his cabinet colleagues. In *Reynolds*, the House of Lords explicitly recognised the media's role in informing the people on matters of public interest and developed the common law defence of qualified privilege to a defamation claim to reflect this. On the facts of the case, the allegations made by the press were not considered to be in the public interest as they had failed to mention Reynold's explanation. Furthers, in *Simms*, the Home Secretary operated a policy that journalists sign an undertaking that interviews with prisoners would not be published. The policy under para.37 of the Prison Service Standing Order pursuant to r.33 of the Prison Rules 1964, was made on the basis that such interviews would tend to undermine the discipline and control essential to the prison environment. The applicants, convicted murderers, had been interviewed by journalists with the aim of proving their innocence. The journalists refused to sign the undertaking and were prohibited further visits. The applicants argued that if the policy was maintained it would be virtually impossible for a journalist to take on an investigative case, especially where such investigations had proved crucial in the 1980s and 1990s in securing the release of prisoners found to be the victims of miscarriages of justice. In a dramatic decision which overturned the earlier decision of the Court of Appeal, the House of Lords declared the policy unlawful. Their Lordships found para.37 to be lawful but the policy made under it to be unlawful. Since allowing access to journalists served the useful purpose of exposing potential miscarriages of justice, a refusal to allow an interview threatened a prisoner's ability to gain access to justice. Lord Steyn thought it to be administratively workable to allow interviews for such a limited purpose consistently with order and discipline and, as such the blanket ban represented an unjustified curtailment of rights.

Notwithstanding these cases, Fenwick has commented that before the Human Rights Act 1998, "the judiciary did not seem to be united around a clear conception of their role" and, "that common practices as regards fundamental freedoms did not emerge"

(H. Fenwick, *Civil Liberties and Human Rights* (3rd edn (Routledge Cavendish, 2002) pp.110–111).

4. Freedom of expression under the Human Rights Act 1998

24–005 After the passing of the HRA, three routes to the protection of freedom of expression were possible. First, through the principle of liberty, i.e. an individual is free to do anything not prohibited by law; secondly, the constitutional right to freedom of expression; and, thirdly, through art.10 (See *Reynolds v Times Newspapers Ltd* [1999] 4 All E.R. 609). Whilst the following discussion focuses on the impact of the HRA, consideration of art.10 is only possible with the retention of the common law protections in mind as they continue to operate alongside the right.

The right to freedom of expression includes, "freedom to hold opinions and to receive and impart information and ideas without interference by public authorities and regardless of frontiers". This definition of expression covers words, pictures, images and actions intended to express an idea or to present information. It even extends to cover web pages as in the case of *R. v Perrin* [2002] EWCA Crim 747, where Mr Perrin appealed against his conviction of publishing an obscene article (a webpage), contrary to s.2(1) of the Obscene Publications Act 1959, alleging that such interference was not in accordance with law because of a lack of precision in the statutory definition of obscene. It was accepted that art.10 was engaged in the circumstances and that his conviction under the Obscene Publication Act 1959, represented an interference with that article. However, Mr Perrin lost his case as the interference was justified and the Obscene Publications Act being sufficiently clear. Expression also covers specific things such as a refusal to disclose journalistic sources; advertising and artistic expression.

The case law from the ECtHR which has engaged the article include *Handyside v UK* (1976). This case concerned the publication of the "little red schoolbook" which sought to provide children with guidance on issues such as contraception and drugs. The ECtHR made it clear that expression covers not only information or ideas, "that are favourably received or regarded as inoffensive or as a matter of indifference" but is equally applicable to information or ideas, "that offend, shock or disturb the state or any sector of the population." For the court, "such are the demands of that pluralism, tolerance and broadmindedness" that without which there is "no democratic society".

Case law has also interpreted art.10 as protecting the right to be provided with information. In *Open Door Counselling and Dublin Well Women v Ireland* (1992) 14 E.H.R.R. 131, the ECtHR ruled that an injunction prohibiting the dissemination of information regarding advice on and the availability of abortion in Ireland represented an unlawful violation of art.10. In the context of England and Wales, the right to receive information was briefly considered by the Court of Appeal in *R. v Secretary of State for Home Department Ex p. Farrakhan* [2002] EWCA Civ 606, a case concerning the exclusion of Louis Farrakhan from the United Kingdom. In considering his exclusion, the court recognised Farrakhan's exclusion could impinge the rights of those wishing to hear his views and receive his information. Further, in *R v Secretary of State for Health Ex p. Wagstaff* [2001] 1 W.L.R. 292, the High Court ruled that the holding of an inquiry in private into the murders committed by Dr Harold Shipman contravened art.10; this constituted interference with the reception of information that others wish or may be willing to impart. In contrast to this, the court in *Persey v Secretary of State for Environment, Food and Rural Affairs* [2002] EWHC (Admin) 371, concluded that art.10 was not engaged by the refusal to hold an open public enquiry. The High Court stated that art.10 did not impose a positive obligation on the government to provide an "open forum" in all cases, nor did it confer the right of access to information.

5. Human Rights Act 1998 section 12

During the passage of the Human Rights Bill, the media raised concerns about the **24–006** potential for conflict between press freedom and art.8 (private and family life). The response was an amendment to the Bill which subsequently became s.12 of the Act and which specifically deals with freedom of expression. Section 12 applies where a court is considering whether to grant an injunction, the effect of which, if granted, might affect the exercise of the Convention right to freedom of expression.

Section 12(3) sets a threshold test which the court must consider when considering granting relief.

"No such relief [which might affect the exercise of the Convention right to freedom of expression] is to be granted so as to restrain publication before trial unless the court is satisfied that the applicant is likely to establish that publication should not be allowed."

In *Cream Holdings Ltd v Banerjee* [2004] UKHL 44, the House of Lords considered the meaning of "likely" in the context of s 12(3). Lord Nicholls, with whom the other four Law Lords agreed, stated that flexibility was essential, and the degree of likelihood must be assessed in light of the circumstances of the case. He felt that a court should not make an interim order under s.12(3) unless the applicant's prospects of success at trial were sufficiently favourable to justify such an order. As to what degree of likelihood made the prospects of success "sufficiently favourable", Lord Nicholls further stated that, "the general approach should be that courts will be exceedingly slow to make interim restraint orders where the applicant has not satisfied the court he will probably ('more likely than not') succeed at the trial".

Despite the inclusion of s.12, case law has demonstrated that it does not take precedence in a clash between articles. For example, in *Campbell v MGN Ltd* [2004] 2 A.C. 457 and *Re S (FC) (A Child)* [2005] 1 A.C. 593 it was stated that where a clash between arts 8 and 10 arises, " … neither article has as such precedence over the other." In *Ashdown v Telegraph Group Ltd* [2001] EWCA Civ 1142 at [27], the Court of Appeal held that section 12 "does no more than underline the need to have regard to contexts in which [Strasbourg] jurisprudence has given particular weight to freedom of expression, while at the same time drawing attention to considerations which may nonetheless justify restricting that right".

RESTRICTIONS ON FREEDOM OF EXPRESSION

24–007 As has been indicated, freedom of expression is not absolute in any jurisdiction, and will be circumscribed where other interests may conflict with it, such as the protection of public morals or the privacy of individuals. In Convention terms, art.10 is a qualified right and may be legitimately limited by the state. Where this is done, the right is balanced against other competing interests known as legitimate aims. These legitimate aims (competing interests) are set out in art.10(2):

> "national security, territorial integrity or public safety, for the prevention of dis-order or crime, for the protection of health or morals, for the protection of the reputation or rights of others, for preventing the disclosure of information received in confidence, or for maintaining the authority and impartiality of the judiciary."

As discussed in Ch.21, interference with a qualified right must be in accordance with a law that satisfy one of the legitimate aims found within the second paragraph of each right and be necessary in a democratic society in that it is directed to a "pressing social need" and "proportionate to the aim pursued" (see Ch.19). It might be argued that there is a certain ease of argument for a public authority in saying interference falls within one of the legitimate aims, since in many instances, interference might fit into more than one aim. However, the state must act in proportion to the threat and this is the crucial discussion in many of the cases on art.10; whether the interference is proportionate.

1. National security

24–008 Generally speaking, criticism of the state or of government will not attract criminal or civil liability, though there are circumstances where freedom of expression must cede to greater national interest, for example, on grounds of national security.

However, cases where this has been claimed as a legitimate interference are few under the HRA. The case of *R. v Shayler* [2002] UKHL 11, concerned the prosecution of a former officer of MI5, charged with offences under the Official Secrets Act 1989. At a preliminary hearing, the court ruled there was no public interest defence available to Shayler and that this was compatible with art.10. Understandably, Shayler appealed the ruling to the House of Lords which found that the Official Secrets Act 1989 fell within the legitimate aims of art.10(2). The Security and Intelligence Services is an essential element of a state's national security and the need to preserve the confidentiality of information relating to intelligence and military operations to counter terrorist, crim-inal and other hostile activity was equally important. Their Lordships felt the real issue was whether interference was greater than was required to meet the legitimate aim which the State was seeking to achieve (at para.26 per Lord Bingham). In reaching their conclusion, that the interference was proportionate, their Lordships were influenced by the fact that it was not an absolute ban on disclosure, merely a ban on disclosure without lawful authority (per Lord Bingham at [27]; see, also, Lord Hope at [70–71]). A former member could, for example, lawfully disclose to a Crown Servant such as the Attorney-General. Moreover, two other factors were considered important. First, if authority to disclose was refused by such a Crown servant, further remedies were available under judicial review and secondly, the consent of the Attorney-General was required for any prosecution under the OSA.

2.   Prevention of disorder or crime

As with national security, few cases have fallen for decision under this legitimate aim. **24–009** One such case concerned the Home Secretary's decision to refuse Louis Farrakhan, spiritual leader of the Nation of Islam, permission to enter the United Kingdom. The matter went before the Court of Appeal (*R. v Secretary of State for Home Department Ex p. Farrakhan* [2002] EWCA Civ 606). It was felt that Farrakhan's presence in the country might provoke disorder contrary to the Public Order Act 1986. Though no conclusive evidence was put forward, the court concluded that interference with Farrakhan's freedom of expression was legitimate in the prevention of disorder and proportionate to the objective to be achieved.

See also the Racial and Religious Hatred Act 2006 which amends the Public Order Act 1986 discussed further at para.24–011 below.

3.   Protection of health or morals

This legitimate aim is largely concerned with laws regulating obscenity. In the United **24–010** Kingdom, the Obscene Publications Acts are the main statutory provisions which permit legitimate interference with freedom of expression. In determining issues relating to an individual State's morals, the ECtHR has often afforded a wide margin of appreciation. In *Handyside v UK* (1976) 1 E.H.R.R. 737, the UK government used the Obscene Publications Acts 1959 and 1964 to seize all copies of "The Little Red Schoolbook", part of which included a "reference" section promoting experimentation in sexual matters such as masturbation, intercourse, venereal disease and pornography. Handyside was convicted on the basis that, whilst the book had some value as an educational tool, it would tend to corrupt and deprave a significant proportion of the children who read it. In considering whether there had been a violation of art.10, the ECtHR held it was reasonable for the British judges to conclude the book had a tendency to undermine the morals of its juvenile readership. British judges had been afforded discretion by the Convention, allowing them to decide whether or not publication should be restricted—whether it was "necessary in a democratic society" or not. The ECtHR judges stressed the difficulty of identifying a pan-European definition of morals, the matter being best left to national judges. An edited version was published successfully and without interference in 1971.

Similarly in the domestic UK setting, courts also appear to allow the legislature, and the police, a wide margin of discretion. For example, in the case of *R. v Perrin* (2002) (discussed above), where Perrin was prosecuted for publishing a webpage which showed people covered in faeces and promoted coprophilia (using faeces for sexual excitement),

the Court of Appeal commented "there was no public interest to be served by permitting a business for profit to supply material which most people would regard as
pornographic obscene".

Other laws which legitimately interfere with article 10 include common law and
statutory indecency. In *R. v Gibson* [1991] 1 All E.R. 439, Gibson and the owner of an
art gallery were convicted of outraging public decency in exhibiting art work which
consisted of human earrings made from freeze-dried human foetuses. The artist and
gallery applied to Strasbourg alleging breach of art.10 (*S and G v UK* App. No.17634/
91), where the Commission refused their claim as manifestly unfounded. The restriction
on expression, which was sufficiently prescribed by law (common law offence of outraging public decency), pursued a legitimate aim (the protection of morals) and was
necessary in a democratic society. Lewis has however argued that, despite this ruling,
the common law of outraging public decency could fall foul of both the prescribed by
law requirement and the legitimate aim. He draws on the Law Commission Report,
Conspiracies Relating to Morals and Decency (1974 Working Paper No.57), which
stated that "the offence ... is so uncertain in its scope that ... it should not survive a
codification of the law in this area". (Lewis, (2002) 1(2) *Entertainment Law* 50–71).

4.   Protection of the reputation or rights of others

(a)   *Reputation*

24–011   Reputation is an integral and important part of the dignity of the individual and
interference with freedom of expression can be justified if it seeks to protect the
reputation of another. Therefore the law of defamation represents a significant interference with freedom of expression, whilst existing to protect the reputation of others.
The law of defamation has existed for some time, pre-dating the HRA, though the
courts have developed the law with art.10 in mind. One case where this has occurred is
Reynolds, discussed above at para.24–004, where the scope of the defence of qualified
privilege was discussed. Common law qualified privilege historically attached to
information passed under a legal, social or moral duty, whether in public or private, to
another individual with a duty to receive (such as the giving of references). In the case,
The Sunday Times argued for the creation of a new category of occasion/situation when
privilege would derive from the subject matter alone, namely, political information. The
House of Lords rejected this argument as they considered that the proposed new
category of qualified privilege would fail to provide adequate protection for reputation,
but made some modifications. In particular it was established that privilege attached to
the publication itself, rather than the occasion of the publication, and that once it
attaches, there is little scope for a subsequent finding of malice. In developing this, the
House of Lords gave much more weight than earlier law had done to the value of
informed public debate and the promotion of a vigorous and free press to keep the
public informed. It was felt that the *Reynolds* defence would substantially widen the
operation of article 10 for newspapers and other publications, and in particular for
investigative forms of journalism. Loveland, "Freedom of political expression: who
needs the HRA" (2001) P.L. 233 seems to share this view and argues that the judgment

undoubtedly provided a substantial degree of legal protection to diligent press coverage of political stories.

(b) *Rights of others*

Under this legitimate aim, there are a number of cases in which interference with art.10 **24–012** has been held to be legitimate.

(i) Articles 2 and 3

In *Venables v News Group Newspapers Ltd* [2001] W.L.R. 1038, a newspaper had dis- **24–013** covered the whereabouts and new identities of the murderers of two-year-old James Bulger which they wished to publish. However, in a ground-breaking decision Dame Elizabeth Butler-Sloss granted a world-wide injunction prohibiting disclosure on the ground there was a serious risk to their lives if the information was made public.

(ii) Article 8

As discussed in Ch.23, art.8, the right to respect for private and family life can often **24–014** come into conflict with freedom of expression. The typical case is media reporting of celebrity behaviour. Both art.8 and art.10 are enshrined in the common law action of breach of confidence (see below at para.24–017).

(iii) Offensive to others

Interference with free expression can be legitimately achieved under the law of blas- **24–015** phemy. Blasphemy is a common law criminal offence which outlaws the publication of material which is considered scurrilous, abusive or offensive to the Christian Church. Prosecutions for blasphemy are rare, the last successful one was in the 20th century which was the private prosecution of Denis Lemon, publisher of Gay News, by Mary Whitehouse (*Whitehouse v Lemon* [1979] A.C. 617). Lemon was convicted under the offence of blasphemous libel for publication of a poem and illustration entitled, "The Love that Dares to Speak its Name", which related to the homosexual love of a centurion for Christ at the latter's crucifixion. The House of Lords upheld the con-viction on the basis that it was not necessary for the prosecution to prove an intention to blaspheme, merely an intention to publish a matter which was blasphemous. Lemon made an unsuccessful application to the European Court of Human Rights (*Gay News Ltd and Lemon v UK* (1983) 5 E.H.R.R. 123) alleging a violation of art.10.

   In *Wingrove v UK* (1996) 24 E.H.R.R. 1, the applicant had made a film which was refused classification for video release on the grounds that it could be found blas-phemous by a jury. In alleging a violation of art.10, Wingrove tried to argue that the law on blasphemy was unclear and so any interference was not in accordance with a law. The ECtHR found there was no "general uncertainty or disagreement ... as to the definition in English law of the offence of blasphemy" (at para.43), and concluded there was no violation of art.10.

In April 2003, a House of Lords Select Committee reported that the present law on blasphemy was unlikely to result in successful prosecution. The Committee found no consensus as to whether a new law against blasphemy was required, but concluded that if there were to be such a law, it should apply to all faiths.

Issues of taste and decency also arose in the case of *Pro-Life Alliance v BBC* [2003] UKHL 23. The Pro-Life Alliance was a political party registered under the Political Parties, Elections and Referendums Act 2000. As its name suggests, it was opposed to abortion and euthanasia. As a participant in the 2001 general election, they were entitled to make a party election broadcast. A major part of their broadcast was about the processes involved in abortion. In reliance on the Broadcasting Act 1990, the BBC refused to air the broadcast on the grounds that it offended good taste, decency and public feeling. There was no challenge by Pro-Life to the compatibility of the legislation itself and the House of Lords found that the BBC actions under that legislation could not be faulted.

Recently, again, the right to freedom of expression and the protection of the rights of others has come into conflict over the BBC's decision to broadcast Jerry Springer: The Opera in January 2005. Over 47,000 complaints were received by offended Christian viewers who objected to the portrayal of Christ dressed as a baby and purporting to be a "bit gay". Christian Voice commenced a private prosecution for blasphemy in January 2007 which was initially rejected by Horseferry Magistrates Court. Green (a member of Christian Voice) sought judicial review of the Magistrates Court's decision, *R. (on the application of Green) v The City of Westminster Magistrates Court* [2007] EWHC (Admin) 2785. Hughes L.J. held the Magistrates Court was correct as the Theatres Act 1968 s.2(4) which applies to plays (Sch.15, para.6 to the Broadcasting Act 1990 applies to broadcasts which is couched in terms identical to those of s.2(4)) provides that that no one shall be prosecuted for a performance that may be obscene, indecent, offensive, disgusting or injurious to morality. In addition, the court concluded that the offence of blasphemous libel was not made out and so any prosecution of the play would interfere with art.10.

Finally, the Racial and Religious Hatred Act 2006 also has the potential to interfere with art.10. The Act creates an offence of using threatening words or behaviour to stir up religious hatred, not racial, despite its title. The justification is that it protects the right of others and prevents crime. Offences can be committed by written or spoken word, or by actions. Therefore, television, radio and internet broadcasts could be caught, as could the published word in whatever form, and even mime. When the Racial and Religious Hatred Bill was published, it was criticised for excessive interference with freedom of expression. Rowan Atkinson, the comedian, was one of a number who noted that films such as the Monty Python's *Life of Brian* would not be made if laws such as this had been in place at the time (*http://news.bbc.co.uk/1/hi/uk_politics/ 3752232.stm*). As a result of such criticism, the House of Lords proposed a number of amendments, the so called "free speech exemptions" which were successfully agreed to (see for example s.29J). The Act came into force in October 2007.

5.   Preventing the disclosure of information received in confidence

Interference with art.10 can be justified so as to prevent the disclosure of material **24–016** received in confidence. The tort of breach of confidence applies in its original form and also in its modified form as a consequence of art.8. There are a number of defences to an action for breach of confidence which aim to protect freedom of expression. One such argument is that the information is already in the public domain, as was demonstrated by the "Spycatcher" case. The litigation concerned the publication of Peter Wright's memoirs of his time as a spy in the book "Spycatcher" and its subsequent serialization in various newspapers. The Attorney-General sought, and obtained, injunctions against three newspapers preventing publication of Wright's book in the United Kingdom on grounds of breach of confidence, despite the book being published in the United States and copies being brought into the UK. The House of Lords in a 3:2 decision maintained the injunctions against the newspapers (*Att-Gen v Guardian Newspapers (No.1)* [1987] 1 W.L.R. 1248), though they were eventually discharged (*Att-Gen v Guardian (No.2)* [1990] 1 A.C. 109). However, The Observer and Guardian newspapers took the case to the ECtHR (*Observer and Guardian v UK* (1991) 14 E.H.R.R. 153) to determine whether there had been a violation of art.10. The court divided the period of the duration of the injunctions into two: (i) the period before the book's publication in the USA; and (ii) the subsequent period ending with the final determination of the English proceedings. As regards the first period, the court found the injunctions "necessary" as the reasons for their imposition were "relevant", "sufficient" and "proportionate to the aim pursued". The injunctions were limited in their scope and duration and publication would potentially prejudice the breach of confidence actions. The second period, following publication in US, was treated differently. The interest in maintaining confidentiality had ceased with publication. Further, in respect of national security, the damage had been done. The only ground for continuing the injunctions was to promote the reputation of the security services, and this was an insufficient reason.

A similar point can be found in *Att-Gen v Times Newspapers* [2001] 1 W.L.R. 885. Here, The Sunday Times wished to serialise a book, "The Big Breach", written by a former MI6 officer about his experiences in the service. There had been a small amount of publication in Russia and the court had to decide whether the newspaper had to demonstrate prior publication. Counsel for The Times argued that such a requirement would constitute an unjustified fetter on the freedom of expression of the newspaper, and the court agreed.

Following these decisions, an injunction prohibiting publication of material is unlikely to be obtained if there has been any prior publication, even if publication is limited.

(a)   Modified breach of confidence

The UK courts have sought to give effect to the positive obligation in *Von Hannover v* **24–017** *Germany* (2006) 43 E.H.R.R. by developing the law of confidence to protect private relationships (modified law of confidence). This development has had a particular impact on restricting media intrusion into private lives and so impinges on the media's art.10 rights. Where breach of confidence is asserted in this area, the court will balance both rights, *Campbell v MGN Ltd* [2004] UKHL 22 and *McKennitt v Ash* [2006] EWCA Civ 1714. See further para.23–024 for a fuller discussion on breach of confidence and horizontal actions.

(b)   *Disclosure of journalistic sources*

24–018   Both s.10 of the Contempt of Court Act 1981 and art.10 generally seek to enhance freedom of the press by protecting journalistic sources. However, according to the principle laid down in *Norwich Pharmacal Co v Customs and Excise Commissioners* [1973] 2 All E.R. 943, it is possible for disclosure of a journalist's source to be ordered. A Norwich Pharmacal order is where a person, albeit innocently, becomes involved in a wrongful act of another, then that person comes under a duty to assist the person injured by the act by giving him any information that discloses the identity of the wrongdoer. In *Goodwin v UK* (1996) 22 E.H.R.R. 123, the ECtHR found that an order for disclosure of journalistic sources against *Goodwin* violated his freedom of expression as the UK courts had failed to give sufficient weight to the public interest in protecting sources in order to facilitate investigative journalism. Additionally, the court recognised in *Ashworth Security Hospital v MGN Ltd* [2002] UKHL 29 (at para.61), that disclosure of a journalist's sources could have a "chilling effect on the freedom of the press". As a result, disclosure is not ordered lightly. Two such cases where disclosure was ordered can be considered here: *Ashworth Security Hospital v MGN Ltd* (2001) and *Financial Times v Interbrew* [2002] EWCA Civ 274.

In *Ashworth Security Hospital v MGN Ltd*, the Mirror newspaper obtained hospital medical records of Ian Brady, a convicted child murderer. The information had been supplied to the newspaper in breach of confidence and contract by an employee of the hospital. The hospital sought an order requiring the Newspaper to identify their source. The newspaper argued that this would contravene art.10, however, in both the Court of Appeal and House of Lords disclosure was ordered. The court felt that unless the source was identified and dismissed there was a significant risk that there would be further selling of confidential information. Such disclosure of medical records amounted to an attack on an area of confidentiality which should be protected in a democratic society.

In the *Interbrew* case, disclosure was ordered against five media companies requiring them to deliver their copies of a leaked and partially forged document concerning a proposed takeover. The Court of Appeal (at paras 42 and 55) focused on the purpose of the leak which was to "wreck" legitimate commercial activity and felt it less deserving of protection.

In both these cases, art.10 was applied with regard to the public interest in freedom of the press and the confidentiality of their sources. The circumstances in both were exceptional and as such the position remains that protection of journalistic sources is often seen as an essential aspect of art.10.

6. Maintaining the authority and impartiality of the judiciary

The law of perjury (Perjury Act 1911), makes it an offence for a person sworn in as a **24–019** witness to make a statement during judicial proceedings which they know to be false or do not believe to be true. The law of perjury can be justified under art.10(2) as a legitimate interference in serving to maintain the authority and impartiality of the judiciary and the system of administering justice.

Under the HRA, this justification has only been invoked in relation to contempt of court, and then, only rarely. A case from the European Court of Human Rights illustrates how such a justification may work. *The Sunday Times v UK* (1979–80) 2 E.H.R.R. 245 concerned the publication of an article discussing the issue of the drug Thalidomide and the legal conflict between the manufacturers of the drug and the parents of the affected children. The UK courts found that the article pre-judged the legal issues and pressured the manufacturer to forgo their legal rights and seek a settlement. They imposed a prohibitory injunction restricting publication of the proposed article. The ECtHR found that the interference was in pursuance of the legitimate aim of maintaining the "authority and impartiality of the judiciary" as the article could have impacted on the impartiality of future legal proceedings. However, the interference was held to not be "necessary in a democratic society".

FURTHER READING

Fenwick, H. *Civil Liberties and Human Rights* 3rd edn (Routledge Cavendish, 2002)   **24–020**
Hoffman, D. and Rowe, J. *Human Rights in the UK: An Introduction to the Human Rights Act 1998* 2nd edn (Pearson Education, 2006)
Loveland, "Freedom of political expression: who needs the HRA" (2001) P.L. 233
Merris, A. *Human Rights Law* (Hart Publishing, 2006)

INDEX

LEGAL TAXONOMY
FROM SWEET & MAXWELL

This index has been prepared using Sweet and Maxwell's Legal Taxonomy. Main index entries conform to keywords provided by the Legal Taxonomy except where references to specific documents or non-standard terms (denoted by quotation marks) have been included. These keywords provide a means of identifying similar concepts in other Sweet & Maxwell publications and online services to which keywords from the Legal Taxonomy have been applied. Readers may find some minor dierences between terms used in the text and those which appear in the index. Suggestions to *sweetandmaxwell. taxonomy@thomson.com.*

(all references are to paragraph number)